T0340016

# Perspectives on Organizational Fit

# The Organizational Frontiers Series

The Organizational Frontiers Series is sponsored by The Society for Industrial and Organizational Psychology (SIOP). Launched in 1983 to make scientific contributions to the field, the series has attempted to publish books on cutting edge theory, research, and theory-driven practice in industrial/organizational psychology and related organizational science disciplines.

Our overall objective is to inform and to stimulate research for SIOP members (students, practitioners, and researchers) and people in related disciplines including the other subdisciplines of psychology, organizational behavior, human resource management, and labor and industrial relations. The volumes in the Organizational Frontiers Series have the following goals:

1.  Focus on research and theory in organizational science, and the implications for practice.
2.  Inform readers of significant advances in theory and research in psychology and related disciplines that are relevant to our research and practice.
3.  Challenge the research and practice community to develop and adapt new ideas and to conduct research on these developments.
4.  Promote the use of scientific knowledge in the solution of public policy issues and increased organizational effectiveness.

The volumes originated in the hope that they would facilitate continuous learning and a continuing research curiosity about organizational phenomena on the part of both scientists and practitioners.

# The Organizational Frontiers Series

# SIOP Organizational Frontier Series

*Series Editor*

Robert D. Pritchard
*University of Central Florida*

Perspectives on Organizational Fit
*C. Ostroff & T. A. Judge, Editors, 2007*

The Psychology of Entrepreneurship
*J. Robert Baum, Michael Frese, & Robert A. Baron, Editors, 2007*

Situational Judgment Tests: Theory, Measurement, and Application
*Jeff A. Weekley & Robert E. Ployhart, Editors, 2006*

Discrimination at Work: The Psychological and Organizational Base
*Robert L. Dipboye & Adrienne J. Colella, Editors, 2005*

The Dark Side of Organizational Behavior
*Ricky W. Griffin & Anne O'Leary-Kelly, Editors, 2004*

Health and Safety in Organizations
*David A. Hofmann & Lois E. Tetrick, Editors, 2003*

Managing Knowledge for Sustained Competitive Advantage
*Susan E. Jackson, Michael A. Hitt, and Angelo S. DeNisi, Editors, 2003*

Personality and Work: Reconsidering
the Role of Personality in Organizations
*Murray R. Barrick and Ann Marie Ryan, Editors, 2003*

Emotions in the Workplace
*Robert G. Lord, Richard J. Klimoski & Ruth Kanfer, Editors, 2002*

Measuring and Analyzing Behavior in Organizations:
Advances in Measurement and Data Analysis
*Fritz Drasgow & Neal Schmitt, Editors, 2002*

# Perspectives on Organizational Fit

EDITED BY

Cheri Ostroff

Timothy A. Judge

Psychology Press
Taylor & Francis Group

New York   Hove

Cover design by Tomai Maridou

This edition published 2012 by Psychology Press
27 Church Road, Hove, East Sussex, BN32FA
Simultaneously published in the USA and Canada by Psychology Press
711 Third Avenue, New York, NY 10017

First issued in paperback 2012

*Psychology Press is an imprint of the Taylor & Francis Group, an informa business*

© 2007 by Taylor & Francis Group, LLC
Lawrence Erlbaum Associates is an imprint of Taylor & Francis Group,
an Informa business

ISBN13: 978-0-415-65082-3 (PBK)

10 9 8 7 6 5 4 3 2 1

International Standard Book Number-13: 978-0-8058-5195-3—0-8058-5195-X (case)
978-1-4106-1778-1—1-4106-1778-5 (e book)

**Visit the Taylor & Francis Web site at**
**http://www.taylorandfrancis.com**

# Contents

# Series Foreword

This is the 25th book in the Organizational Frontiers Series of books initiated by the Society for Industrial and Organizational Psychology (SIOP). The overall purpose of the Series volumes is to promote the scientific status of the field. Ray Katzell first edited the Series. He was followed by Irwin Goldstein, Sheldon Zedeck, and Neal Schmitt. The topics of the volumes and the volume editors are chosen by the editorial board, or individuals propose volumes to the editorial board. The series editor and the editorial board then work with the volume editor(s) in planning the volume.

The success of the series is evident in the high number of sales (now over 50,000). Volumes have also received excellent reviews, and individual chapters as well as volumes have been cited very frequently.

This volume, edited by Cheri Ostroff and Timothy A. Judge, reflects thinking and research on issues concerning the fit between individuals and their organizations. The idea of fit is an important topic receiving greater and greater attention. However, there has been no systematic integration of this material. There have been many different approaches to fit, and this volume identifies them and uses a strong conceptual focus to integrate these different points of view.

There are several other strengths of this volume. Almost by definition, fit reflects a multilevel perspective ranging from micro, individual-level, variables to macro, organizational, variables. This volume comprehensively addresses this multilevel issue. It also integrates theory and research done in different domains such as selection, recruitment, diversity, and leadership. The volume, especially the concluding chapter, specifically addresses issues of methodology in this area and needed research.

The editors and chapter authors deserve our gratitude for clearly communicating the nature, application, and implications of the theory and research described in this book. Production of a volume such as this involves the hard work and cooperative effort of many individuals. The editors, the chapter authors, and the editorial board all played important roles in this endeavor. As all royalties from the Series volumes are used to help support SIOP; none of the editors or authors received any remuneration. The editors and authors deserve our appreciation for engaging a difficult task for the sole purpose of furthering our understanding of organizational science. We also want to express our gratitude to Anne Duffy, our editor at Lawrence Erlbaum Associates, who has been a great help in the planning and production of the volume.

Robert D. Pritchard
University of Central Florida
Series Editor

# *Preface*

This book is about fit in organizations: the relationship between individuals and the environments in which they find themselves. The basic premise of fit theory and research is that when characteristics of people and the work environment are aligned or fit together, positive outcomes result. When we think about work lives, most of us implicitly or explicitly consider how well we fit our jobs, the work setting, other people, and what is important and valued in the organization. We often ask ourselves questions such as: Does this job and work situation match or fulfill my personal and professional needs? Are the values and goals of this organization consistent with my own? Do I fit in with the other people in this organization? How much we fit can have a tremendous impact on our attitudes, satisfaction, and well-being.

Since the early 1900s, the notion of *fit* (also termed *congruence* or *correspondence*) has pervaded theory and research across many organizational domains, including selection, job design, requirement, attitudes, stress, leadership, goals, teams, human resources management (HRM) practices, and organizational design. Fit theory and research have been concerned with characteristics of individuals in conjunction with some characteristics of their work environment in addition to a match or alignment between aspects of the group or organization. As such, fit theory and research inherently reflect a multilevel perspective of organizations in that relationships among constructs include micro, individual-level variables and macro, contextual or organizational, variables. Despite the almost ubiquitous use of fit across content domains in organizational research, fit research and theory have developed almost independently within each domain. There has been almost no overlap or integration in theoretical perspectives across domains. Further, different techniques and methodologies for assessing fit have been developed within domains, with little cross-fertilization across domains.

We conceived and edited this book with the aim of extending and building upon recent advances in the fit area. By offering a comprehensive treatment of fit across both content domains (e.g., selection, recruitment, diversity, leadership, teams, and HRM practices) and across levels of analysis (e.g., implications for individuals, groups, and organizations), we hope to energize and guide further advancements in the area. Our primary goals were to understand how the notion of fit is used in different content domains, explore an integration of different fit perspectives across domains, and clarify the methodological and statistical issues that plague fit research. Ultimately, we wanted to create a volume that (a) elucidates the commonalties in fit across different domains, (b) examines when, where, and why different perspectives of fit are more or less useful in different domains, for different outcomes, and/or different levels of analysis, and (c) addresses the appropriate methodologies for different conceptualizations of fit. Given the burgeoning interest in fit issues as evidenced by the quickly growing number of articles on fit in the top journals, we felt that this book would be timely and important and could lay the foundation for broader thinking in the area. We hope this book provides a useful source of information about fit that will guide future theoretical and empirical study as well as practical applications in organizations.

The chapter authors have done an admirable job in balancing a wide variety of perspectives as they developed cutting-edge ideas and directions for examining issues of fit in organizations. The book is organized into three parts: Part I—Extending Fit Theory; Part II—Linking Theory and Analysis; and Part III—Commentary and Reflections.

The first chapter by Ostroff and Schulte provides a foundation for thinking about fit research and proposes an integrative model of fit concepts across domains and levels of analysis. In each of the next eight chapters, authors addressed the role of fit in understanding a particular content domain. These chapters pose and begin to address some new directions about fit processes. Further, the ordering of these chapters reflects a movement from micro to more macro levels of analysis starting with the micro perspectives of intraindividual and individual-level fit, moving to the team level, and ending with the organizational level.

In chapter 2, Higgins and Frietas discuss fit from an intraindividual perspective, elucidating how self-regulation theories help individuals achieve fit between their goal orientations and how to pursue goals. Next, the chapter by Kammeyer-Mueller examines the role of personality in fit, and in doing so, provides a new perspective in the integration of theories from personality, socialization, and fit. Person–organization fit is addressed in chapter 4 by Kristof-Brown and Jansen, who provide a comprehensive treatment of the various ways of understanding fit between characteristics of individuals and organizational attributes. In chapter 5, issues of fit in recruiting and selection are explored by Cable and Yu who advance our understanding of the importance of various types of fit during these initial phases of individuals' entrance into organizations.

The notion of dyadic fit between subordinates and supervisors and how this type of fit develops as a process over time is considered in chapter 6, by Atwater and Dionne. In chapter 7, Edwards and Shipp explain the tremendous impact fit can have on stress and job attitudes of individuals. The team level of analysis is considered in chapter 8, by DeRue and Hollenbeck, who underscore the importance of fit between individuals within the team as well as fit among structural elements of the team. In chapter 9, Ellis and Tsui integrate theories from conservation biology with theories of fit to explain the implications of homogeneity of demographic characteristics. In chapter 10, Gerhart turns to the organizational level, discussing alignment among various HRM practices as well as between these practices and organizational strategy.

In part II, two chapters focus on the methodological and statistical issues that pertain to conducting fit research. In chapter 11, the different analytic techniques that are used to study fit are summarized by experts in the area. In chapter 12, Harrison provides a comprehensive analysis that elucidates linkages between different theoretical questions and the analytic techniques that can be used to study them. Finally, in part III (chapter 13), Judge reflects on the contributions from the authors of this volume and highlights the continuing challenges we face in fit theory and research.

Our students, colleagues, and friends in the field have been a source of inspiration for our thinking about fit for many years. Fortunately we were able to ask a number of them to contribute to this volume and they graciously agreed to write chapters. We are very grateful to the chapter authors for their creative, innovative, and excellent contributions, not only to this book but also to our understanding of the fit process more generally. We also express our thanks to Neal Schmitt and Bob Pritchard and the members of the Society for Industrial and Organizational Psychology Organizational Frontiers Series Editorial Board for encouraging us to pursue this project, and for all of the help and support along the way. Finally, we thank Anne Duffy at Lawrence Erlbaum Associates for her patience and help in guiding us through the publication process.

Cheri Ostroff
*University of Maryland*

Timothy A. Judge
*University of Florida*

# Contributors

**Leanne Atwater** received her PhD from Claremont Graduate School in California. She taught as an assistant professor at the U.S. Naval Academy and at Binghamton University. She is now a Professor of Management and Chair of the Management Department at Arizona State University West (ASU). She previously served as Interim Dean of the School of Global Management and Leadership at ASU's West campus. She serves as an associate editor for *Group and Organization Management*. Her research interests are in the areas of leadership and feedback. She has published in journals such as the *Journal of Applied Psychology, Personnel Psychology,* and *Journal of Management*. She is the coauthor of a book entitled *The Power of 360 Degree Feedback* with David Waldman.

**Daniel M. Cable** is a Sarah Graham Kenan Distinguished Scholar and Professor of Management in the Kenan-Flagler Business School at the University of North Carolina. Dan's areas of teaching and research interests include corporate culture, performance management, compensation and total rewards, the organizational entry process, and selection systems. Dan received his PhD and Masters degrees from Cornell University and his BA from The Pennsylvania State University. He has published over 30 articles on person–organization fit, selection, recruitment, pay systems, and career success in leading journals, such as *Journal of Applied Psychology, Personnel Psychology, Academy of Management Review, Academy of Management Journal, Organizational Behavior and Human Decision Processes, Human Relations,* and *Organizational Science*. Dan received the McCormick Award for Distinguished Research Contributions from the Society for Industrial and Organizational Psychology. Dan also likes to renovate old houses. He has renovated houses in Atlanta, GA, Boone, NC, Raleigh, NC, and Chapel Hill, NC.

**David Caldwell** is the Stephen and Patricia Schott Professor in the Leavey School of Business at Santa Clara University. His research focuses on individual and group issues in organizations including person–group fit, group norms, and their effects on the organization processes and boundary activities in groups. He received his PhD from the University of California, Los Angeles.

**Jennifer A. Chatman** is the Paul J. Cortese Distinguished Professor of Management at the Haas School of Business, University of California, Berkeley. Her research focuses on how organizational culture, person–culture fit, cooperation, and demography. She received her PhD from the University of California, Berkeley.

**D. Scott DeRue** is a doctoral student in management and organizational behavior at the Eli Broad Graduate School of Management at Michigan State University. He graduated with honors from the University of North Carolina at Chapel Hill. Scott's research interests focus on leadership, team performance and learning, and negotiation. Before pursuing his PhD in management, Scott was a management consultant and project manager for the Monitor Group, a family of global professional service firms. Scott also served in a senior marketing role with the Hinckley Yacht Company.

**Shelley Dionne** is an Associate Professor of Management at Binghamton University. She received her PhD and MBA from Binghamton University–School of Management in 1998 and 1994, respectively. Her research interests include leadership, creativity, team-building, and training and development, and her publications have appeared in *Journal of Applied Psychology, Leadership Quarterly,* and *Human Relations.* She teaches leadership and organizational behavior in the School of Management's undergraduate, graduate, and executive programs.

**Jeffrey R. Edwards** received his PhD from Carnegie Mellon University and is the Belk Distinguished Professor of Organizational Behavior and Strategy at the Kenan-Flagler Business School at the University of North Carolina. He has published over 50 articles and chapters on person–environment fit in organizations, stress, coping, and well-being, work-family issues, and research methods, including difference scores, polynomial regression, and construct validation. He is past editor of *Organizational Behavior and Human Decision Processes,* has served as associate editor of *Journal of Organizational Behavior and Organizational Research Methods,* and has held editorial board positions with *Academy of Management Journal, Journal of Applied Psychology, Personnel Psychology,* and *Journal of Management.* He is a fellow of the Society for Industrial and Organizational Psychology, the American Psychological Association, and the Academy of Management and has been elected to the Society of Organizational Behavior.

**Aimee Ellis** is a doctoral student from the W. P. Carey School of Business at Arizona State University (ASU). She earned an MBA from the University of Oklahoma and a BA from the University of Chicago. Her research interests are gender and diversity in organizations, work–family balance, and organizational culture. She has coauthored a teaching case published in *Strategic Management*, 6th edition, and the *organizational demography* entry in *The Blackwell Encyclopedic Dictionary of Organizational Behavior*. She is the recipient of ASU's Graduate Scholar award. Ms. Ellis is a member of the Academy of Management, the Society for Industrial Organizational Psychology, the American Psychological Association, and Beta Gamma Sigma. She has worked for the University of Chicago Press, the University of Oklahoma Press, and the University of Utah Press.

**Jazmine Espejo** is a doctoral candidate in the industrial and organizational psychology program at the University of Oklahoma. Her research interests include decision making, skill acquisition, and performance in scientific occupations.

**Antonio L. Freitas** received his PhD in Social Psychology from Yale University in 2002 and is currently an assistant professor at the State University of New York, Stony Brook. His research examines how mental representations of decisions and actions impact a broad range of self-regulatory processes, such as action control, activity engagement, affective evaluation.

**Barry Gerhart** is the Bruce R. Ellig Distinguished Chair in Pay and Organizational Effectiveness and Professor of Management and Human Resources, School of Business, University of Wisconsin–Madison. His major fields of interest are human resource management and strategy, compensation, employee attitudes, and business performance. Professor Gerhart received his B.S. in Psychology from Bowling Green State University and his PhD in Industrial Relations from the University of Wisconsin–Madison. Professor Gerhart is coauthor of the recent book, *Compensation: Theory, Evidence, and Strategic Implications*, as well as coeditor of *Compensation in Organizations* and coauthor of *Human Resource Management: Gaining a Competitive Advantage*, now in its 5th edition. He is a Fellow of the American Psychological Association.

**David A. Harrison** is University Distinguished Professor in the Department of Management and Organization at The Pennsylvania State University. He has doctoral and masters degrees in psychology and applied statistics from the University of Illinois at Urbana–Champaign. His widely published research includes theories and investigations of (a) work role adjustment, (b) diversity, (c) time, and (d) measurement in organizations. He is also currently Editor of *Organizational Behavior and Human Decision Processes*, for which he previously served as Associate Editor.

**E. Tory Higgins** is the Stanley Schachter Professor of Psychology, Professor of Business, and Director of the Motivation Science Center at Columbia University (where he also received his PhD in 1973). He has received a MERIT Award from the National Institute of Mental Health, the Thomas M. Ostrom Award in Social Cognition, the Donald T. Campbell Award for Outstanding Contributions to Social Psychology (Society of Personality and Social Psychology), and the Lifetime Contribution Award from the International Society for Self and Identity. He has also received the Distinguished Scientist Award from the Society of Experimental Social Psychology, the William James Fellow Award for Distinguished Achievements in Psychological Science (from the American Psychological Society), and the American Psychological Association Award for Distinguished Scientific Contributions. He is a Fellow of the American Academy of Arts & Sciences. He is also a recipient of Columbia's Presidential Award for Outstanding Teaching.

**John R. Hollenbeck** received his PhD in Management from New York University in 1984, and he is currently the Eli Broad Professor of Management at the Eli Broad Graduate School of Business Administration at Michigan State University. He served as the acting editor at *Organizational Behavior and Human Decision Processes* in 1995, the editor of *Personnel Psychology* from 1996 to 2002, and currently serves as the associate editor of *Decision Sciences*. Before serving as editor, he served on the editorial boards of these journals, as well as the boards of the *Academy of Management Journal, Academy of Management Review, Journal of Applied Psychology,* and *Journal of Management.* He has published over 60 articles and book chapters on the topics of team decision making and work motivation, much of which was funded by the Office of Naval Research and the Air Force Office of Scientific Research. According to the Institute for Scientific Research this body of work has been cited over 1,000 times.

**Karen J. Jansen** is an Assistant Professor of Management in the McIntire School of Commerce at the University of Virginia. Her research broadly explores the process and impact of change on an organization's employees, focused particularly on building and maintaining momentum for long-term change efforts. She is also interested in the changing nature of fit in organizations and how it affects organizational adaptability and performance. Her research appears in journals such as *Organization Science, Journal of Applied Psychology,* and *Organizational Behavior and Human Decision Processes.* She is on the editorial board for *Journal of Applied Behavioral Science,* and is an ad hoc reviewer for *Administrative Science Quarterly, American Management Review,* and *Academy of Management Journal.* She was recently elected to the board of the Organizational Development and Change Division of the Academy of Management. She received her PhD in strategic human resource management and organizational change from Texas A&M University.

**Timothy A. Judge** is the Matherly-McKethan Eminent Scholar in the Department of Management at the University of Florida. He holds a Bachelor of Business Administration degree from the University of Iowa, and masters and doctoral degrees from the University of Illinois. Before entering graduate school, he worked as a manager at Kohl's Department Stores in Wisconsin and Illinois. Previously, he served on the faculties of the University of Iowa and Cornell University. His research interests are in the areas of personality, leadership and influence behaviors, staffing and careers, and job attitudes.

**John D. Kammeyer-Mueller** received his PhD from the University of Minnesota and has subsequently been working at the Warrington College of Business Administration at the University of Florida. His research has mostly focused on topics related to workplace adjustment including the socialization and adaptation of new organizational members, mentoring, work withdrawal, turnover, and career planning. He has also made occasional research diversions into applied research methods, interpersonal relationships, and personality. His empirical research has appeared in *Journal of Applied Psychology, Personnel Psychology, Journal of Vocational Behavior, Industrial Relations,* and *International Journal of Selection and Assessment.*

**Amy L. Kristof-Brown** is the Weissman/Sinicropi Research Fellow and Associate Professor at the Henry B. Tippie College of Business, University of Iowa. Her research interests center around the compatibility or fit between individuals and their work environments. This interest has led her to study how impression management relates to person–job and person–organization fit in job interviews, person–team compatibility on goals, person–country fit for expatriates, and top management team–chief executive officer goal compatibility. She has published and presented numerous papers on these topics. Her meta-analysis on person–environement fit, with coauthors Ryan Zimmerman and Erin Johnson, won the Academy of Management's Human Resources Division Scholarly Achievement Award in 2006. She is currently an Associate Editor for *Journal of Applied Psychology* and serves on the editorial boards of *Academy of Management Journal* and *Personnel Psychology.* She received her PhD in Organizational Behavior and Human Resource Management from the University of Maryland.

**Michael D. Mumford** is a Professor of Psychology and Management at the University of Oklahoma where he is Director of the doctoral program in industrial and organizational psychology. He received his doctoral degree from the University of Georgia in 1983. Before joining the faculty at the University of Oklahoma, he was a senior research fellow at the American Institutes of Research. He has also held faculty positions at the Georgia Institute of Technology and George Mason University. He is a fellow of the Society for Industrial and Organizational Psychology, the American Psychological Association (Divisions 3, 5, and 14), and the American Psychological Society. He serves on the editorial boards of *The Leadership Quarterly, The Creativity Research Journal,* and *The Journal of Creative Behavior.* He has published more than 150 articles on creativity, leadership, planning, and integrity. He has directed more than 50 grants and contracts. In 2002, he received the Society for Industrial and Organizational Psychology's M. Scott Myers award for applied research in the workplace.

**Charles A. O'Reilly** is the Frank E. Buck Professor of Human Resources Management and Organizational Behavior at the Graduate School of Business at Stanford University. His current research interests include human resources, organizational demography, executive compensation, and organizational innovation and change.

**Cheri Ostroff** is a professor in the organizational psychology program at the University of Maryland. She received her PhD in Industrial/Organizational Psychology from Michigan State University in 1987. Her research interests include levels of analysis issues, organizational climate, person–environment fit, socialization, and human resource management systems. She received the McCormick Award for Early Career Contributions from the Society for Industrial-Organizational Psychology (SIOP), the Distinguished Scientific Award for Early Career Contributions in Applied Research from the American Psychological Association's (APA), and the Scholarly Achievement Award from the Human Resources Division of the Academy of Management. She is an elected fellow of both SIOP and APA. She currently serves on the editorial boards of *Journal of Applied Psychology* and *Academy of Management Review.* She has also served on the editorial boards of *Personnel Psychology* and *Journal of Vocational Behavior,* and was associate editor for *International Journal of Selection and Assessment.*

**Mathis Schulte** is a doctoral student in social–organizational psychology at Teachers College, Columbia University, and a visiting scholar and lecturer at the Wharton Business School at the University of Pennsylvania. He earned an MA and a BA in psychology from the University of Hamburg in Germany. His research interests focus on organizational climate, person–environment fit, and team performance and learning. Before pursuing his PhD, he worked as a human resources consultant in Europe, the Middle East, and the United States.

**Abbie J. Shipp** is an Assistant Professor of Management at Texas A&M University. She received her PhD from the University of North Carolina at Chapel Hill. Before beginning her academic career, she completed a BS and an MBA. at Oklahoma State University and worked in human resources for The Boeing Company and TV Guide, Inc. Her research interests focus on the psychological experience of time at work, person–environment fit, and employee retention and turnover.

**Hock-Peng Sin** is an Assistant Professor in Management in the Eli Broad College of Business at Michigan State University. His research interests include the causes and consequences of performance trajectories and interpersonal dynamics in the workplace as well as levels and temporal issues in organizational research. His work appears in outlets such as *Strategic Management Journal, Personnel Psychology*, and *Journal of Organizational Behavior*. He is also the recipient of two Best Student Paper awards at the Academy of Management meeting, one in 2004 from the Human Resources Division and the other in 2005 from the Research Methods Division.

**Anne S. Tsui** is the Motorola Professor of International Management at the W. P. Carey School of Business, Arizona State University, Professor of Management at the Hong Kong University of Science and Technology, and Distinguished Visiting Professor at Peking University. She was the 14th editor of *Academy of Management Journal* and is a Fellow of the Academy of Management. Her research has received a number of awards including *Administrative Science Quarterly* Scholarly Contribution Award, the Best Paper in the *Academy of Management Journal* Award, and the Scholarly Achievement Award from the Human Resource Division of the Academy of Management. Her book *Demographic Differences in Organizations: Current Research and Future Direction* (1999) with Barbara Gutek was a finalist for the 2000 Terry Book Award, Academy of Management. Dr. Tsui is 87th (among 778) most cited researcher in business and economics (1993–2003) and 21st of the top 100 most cited scholars in management (1981–2001).

**Kang Yang Trevor Yu** is a doctoral candidate at the Kenan-Flagler Business School at the University of North Carolina. His research interests include person–environment fit, values congruence, workgroup climates, and vocational identity. He has published in *Journal of Applied Psychology*.

# Perspectives on Organizational Fit

# PART I

# *Extending Fit Theory*

In part I of this volume, the authors challenge and extend fit research in a number of content domains. Starting with the individual level of analysis, then moving to the group and organizational level of analyses, new perspectives of fit are introduced to explain attitudes, behavior, and performance in organizations. Together, the chapters in part I provide a comprehensive treatment of fit across content domains and across levels of analysis.

# CHAPTER 1

# *Multiple Perspectives of Fit in Organizations Across Levels of Analysis*

Cheri Ostroff
*University of Maryland*

Mathis Schulte
*Wharton, University of Pennsylvania*

The notion that a good fit between person and environment leads to positive outcomes has long held intuitive appeal. Even early philosophers, such as Plato, emphasized the importance of assigning people to jobs that are congruent with their temperaments and abilities (Kaplan, 1950). In social science research, the notion of *fit*, also termed *congruence* or *correspondence,* has pervaded theory and research across many organizational domains since the 1900s.

Like much of the research on organizational phenomena in the past 25 years (cf. Kozlowski & Klein, 2000; Staw & Sutton, 1992), the application of the concept of fit to organizational domains has come to be largely characterized along the two extremes in the micro–macro continuum. On the one hand, there has been a micro-level focus on *person–environment (PE) fit* with the term being applied to a class of measures that are used to examine the relationship between individuals and the organizational environments in which they find themselves (Kristof, 1996; Tinsley, 2000). The basic premise of PE fit theory and research is that when characteristics of people and the work environment are similar, aligned or fit together, positive outcomes for individuals such as satisfaction, adjustment, commitment, performance, reduced stress, and lower turnover intentions result. On the other hand, macro-level theorists and researchers have largely focused on organizational-level phenomena, arguing that components of the organizational system, such as structure, strategy, goals, and culture, must fit together or complement one another to foster effectiveness, adaptation, and survival in the larger environment within which the organization operates (Bedeian, 1986; Katz & Kahn, 1978). We refer to this organizational-level focus as system fit, but also note that system fit can apply to lower levels such as divisions, units, or groups.

PE fit has been examined from a number of disciplines (e.g., organizational behavior, education, and vocational, counseling, social, and industrial/organizational psychology) and across a number of different content domains. For example, in vocational psychology, hundreds of studies have indicated that a greater degree of fit between the interests, preferences, and attributes of individuals and those of occupations is related to occupational choice, career success, and satisfaction (Holland, 1997; Spokane, Meir, & Catalano, 2000; Tinsley, 2000). In industrial/organizational psychology and organizational behavior, the underlying premise of selection testing has been on achieving fit between skills and abilities of workers and skill requirements of jobs (Edwards, 1991). The importance of fit between personal characteristics or needs and job demands or job reinforcers has also been emphasized in studies of stress, job satisfaction, and other attitudes (Edwards, 1991; Kristof, 1996). Similarly, the impact of fit between individuals' needs, goals, or values and those of the job, group, or organization has been examined in studies of recruitment and organizational choice among applicants (e.g., Cable & Yu, chap. 5, this volume) and in studies of individual behavior and attitudes among job incumbents (e.g., Chatman, 1991).

The concept of fit has also been implicit in research on relational demography, leadership, and employee–organization relationships. For example, fit is implied in the area of relational demography owing to its focus on similarity between an individual's demographic characteristics and those of his or her workgroup (Riordin, 2000). Recent work on 360-feedback assumes a fit perspective by focusing on correspondence or agreement in perceptions between a manager's self-evaluation of his or her own behavior and the evaluations of the manager made by others (Atwater, Ostroff, Yammarino, & Fleenor, 1998). Research in leadership has also examined congruence between employee perceptions and attributes and those of their superior (e.g., Atwater & Dionne, chap. 6, this volume). In studying employee–organization relationships, fit has been examined between employee expectations and human resources (HR) practices (Tsui, Pearce, Porter, & Tripoli, 1997) and between employees' and employers' believes about the exchange agreement (Dabos & Rousseau, 2004).

The preceding conceptualizations of PE fit are cross-level in nature because they concern characteristics of individuals in conjunction with some characteristic of their work environment (hence the overarching term PE fit), and because outcomes are based on the individual level of analysis. Yet, the notion of fit is also pervasive at higher levels of analysis (e.g., the group or organizational level), in which the primary focus is on the match or alignment among elements of the group or organizational system, and the outcome of interest is at the higher level of analysis. For example, at the group level, issues of fit have been addressed in team relations and team processes, focusing on fit among the different characteristics of team members (Cannon-Bowers, Tannenbaum, Salas, & Volpe, 1995; Maruping & Agarwal, 2004). Fit has also been addressed in team job design, such as alignment between the task environment and reward systems, structure and technology (see DeRue & Hollenbeck, chap. 8, this volume). At the organizational level, numerous theories speak to the importance of alignment among internal organizational features or elements (system fit), such as the structure, strategy, culture, and processes of the organization as they relate to organizational environment (e.g., Barney, 1991; Pfeffer, 1997; Scott, 1995). Similarly, work on human resources management (HRM) systems has emphasized internal fit among the various HR practices and well as vertical fit between the HRM practices and other elements of the organizational system such as organizational strategy (e.g., Gerhart, chap. 10, this volume).

Despite the almost ubiquitous use of the fit concept across content domains and levels of analysis, fit research and theory have developed almost independently in the macro and micro arenas as well as within each of the various content domains. The result has been that a number of different theoretical perspectives have been offered to explain how fit develops and why it is important, leading some researchers to describe the topic as elusive, imprecise, confusing, or unclear (e.g., Judge & Ferris, 1992; Muchinsky & Monahan, 1987; Rynes & Gerhart, 1990). Our goal in this chapter is to synthesize and extend prior work on the development of fit in organizational research to provide a more parsimonious and generalizable perspective that integrates different types of fit and different content domains. We limit our focus to fit as it applies to organizational settings. As such, we do not discuss person–occupation or person–vocation fit; comprehensive reviews of these research areas are available elsewhere (e.g., Holland, 1997; Spokane et al., 2000; Tinsley, 2000; special issue of *Journal of Vocational Behavior*, 2000). Similarly, we do not fully address fit concepts in the organizational theory domain that focus on understanding how organizations operate within their environmental context. We also note that our intention is not to provide a comprehensive review of the fit literature. Rather, our emphasis is on elucidating core concepts and a broad perspective of fit.

In the first section, we provide a brief review of the historical roots and foundation of fit. In the second section, we attempt to clarify and synthesize the many different types of fit across levels of analysis. In the third section, we highlight some implications of the multilevel model with particular attention to the simultaneous consideration of multiple types of fit. Finally, we focus briefly on fit as a dynamic process that occurs over time.

## A BRIEF HISTORICAL PERSPECTIVE OF FIT

The split into two paradigms of fit research, system fit and PE fit, occurred around the late 1960s and early 1970s as the macro–micro separation in organizational research became prominent. Before that time, the emphasis was largely on the micro-level and individual behavior. The emergence of the human relations movement in the 1920s spurred psychologists to understand individual and group behavior and attitudes in organizations, and researchers began to examine how situational factors such as the structural features or culture of the organization influenced individual responses (Üsdiken & Leblebici, 2001). PE fit notions in psychological research also had their early origins during this time. Murray (1938), with his need-press theory whereby individual's needs could be fulfilled or hindered by the environment, and Goldstein (1939), with his emphasis on the relationship between a person's qualities and the nature of the tasks he or she confronts in the environment, have been credited with early considerations of PE fit in psychology (Schneider, Smith, & Goldstein, 2000).

The transition to a macro perspective began in the 1960s and 1970s. Compared with the earlier emphasis on how structure affected individual attitudes and behaviors, the importance of understanding interrelationships among structural features of organizations began to be emphasized (Bedeian, 1986). Further, organizations began to be conceptualized as social systems, based on the open systems paradigm (Katz & Kahn, 1978). The effectiveness of the organization was purported to depend on the alignment among input, transformation, and output processes, taking into account the available environmental resources (Yuchtman & Seashore, 1967).

During this time, the psychological and behaviorist tradition from the human relations movement and PE fit was integrated with systems views of organizations (Üsdiken & Leblebici, 2001). For example, Likert (1961, 1967) placed a strong emphasis on the congruence of internal processes such as communication, influence, decision-making, control, and reward processes to facilitate stability and equilibrium among employees, stating that "All component parts of any system of management must be consistent with each of the other parts and reflect the system's basic philosophy" (Likert, 1961, p. 222). Appropriate and internally consistent structural arrangements were purported to facilitate the development and self-actualization of employees. Emphasis was also placed on the importance of satisfying employees' physical and emotional needs because only then would employees be willing give their services wholeheartedly to the organization and perform up to their potential (Argyris, 1964; Likert, 1961; McGregor, 1960). Both system and PE fit were also evident in sociotechnical systems theories of organizations (e.g., Emery & Trist, 1960) that emphasized fit between the social (interrelationships among people) and technical (technologically based) subsystems in the organization. As noted by Katz and Kahn (1978), the sociotechnical approach "takes as its target a complex emergent variable: goodness of fit between the social and technical aspects of the organization, and by extension between those aspects of organization and the needs and abilities of individuals" (p. 716).

Although early notions of organizational systems took into account both the importance of fit among the structural and process elements of the organization as well as the human component and the fit of individuals to the organization, the 1960s and 1970s brought a split between the micro, organizational behavior, and the macro, organizational theory, strains (Üsdiken & Leblebici, 2001). On the macro side, contingency theories began to proliferate in the 1970s, triggering an emphasis on the organizational-level and organizational effectiveness outcomes. The focus turned largely to internal design, and interorganizational design and environmental relationships. For example, Miles and Snow's (1978) typology focused largely on fit between organizational strategy, structure, and internal processes. Particular emphasis on alignment between the internal structural arrangement of the organization and the relationship to environmental constraints such as uncertainty was evident in Pennings' (1975) structural-contingency model. Later developments in organizational theory moved toward more complex macro conceptualizations of interrelationships between the organization and environment, focusing on how to reduce or alter resource dependencies (e.g., Pfeffer & Salancik, 1978), the location of organizations in institutional environments defined by the social and cultural context (e.g., Scott, 1995), populations of organizations in environmental niches (e.g., Hannan & Freeman, 1989), configural theories to represent the patterns of relevant contextual, structural, and strategic factors and ideal types (e.g., Doty, Glick, & Huber, 1993), and transactions between managers and stockholders, among board members, and between organizations (e.g., Eisenhardt, 1989). Although the "people" aspect was given some attention, for example, through the information-processing demands placed on decision makers about strategic and structural choice or through the enactment of organizational processes and culture, individual differences and direct attention to how people fit in with the organization were not explicitly addressed. Thus, system fit has come to be largely examined from a macro lens, emphasizing alignments between various internal organizational features and various environmental factors.

On the micro side, more specific attention to the notion that behavior of individuals can only be understood as an interaction between people and their context started to gain momentum. The first PE fit models began to emerge in the late 1960s and early 1970s with the discussion of interactionist theories in personality and social psychology. These theories suggested that attitudes, cognitions, and behaviors are the result of the continuous interaction between person and situation factors. Interestingly, a number of researchers and theorists had earlier emphasized the interplay between personality traits and situational factors for understanding behavior (e.g., Kantor, 1926; Lewin, 1935, 1951; Murray, 1938). However, it was not until an open debate led by "situationist" Mischel (1968) and "personologist" Bowers (1973) brought up the old question of what determines behavior and resulted in a rapprochement of their positions that inspired the formulation and empirical testing of interactionist models (Ekkehammar, 1974; Endler & Magnusson, 1976; Mischel, 1973).

## From Interactionism to PE Fit

The interactionist perspective emphasized that neither traits nor situations were the primary determiners of individuals' responses, but rather, the interaction between the two influence responses (e.g., Schneider, 1983; Terborg, 1981). One problem with interactionism was that it did not specify how the person and situational or environmental elements should interact in influencing responses. PE fit and congruence addressed this issue by proposing that it is necessary to match person characteristics with their corresponding environmental characteristics. Hence, PE fit can be understood as a specific type of person–situation interaction that specifies match or congruence as the way the two factors interact— high congruence between corresponding or commensurate person and environment dimensions yields more positive outcomes (Caplan, 1987; Graham, 1976).

The early work in PE fit was inspired largely by Murray's (1938) need-press model and was conducted outside of organizational psychology. According to the need-press model, congruence between an individual's needs and the equivalent characteristics of the environment (press) can produce either need satisfaction or need frustration. In educational psychology, Stern (1970) conceptualized PE fit as the match between students' personalities (needs) and corresponding school climates (press). Similarly, Pervin (1967, 1968; Pervin & Rubin, 1967) showed that poor fit between students' need for structure and the amount of structure in the educational approach of universities was related to academic dissatisfaction and to dropping out of school for nonacademic reasons. PE fit models were also developed in vocational psychology, addressing the match between individual and occupation characteristics (Tinsley, 2000) and emphasizing fit between the needs of the individual and the supplies of the occupational environment (e.g., Holland, 1964).

In organizational psychology and behavior, need-press theories and demands–ability-demand theories began to be used to investigate the dynamics between people and the context, although the term PE fit did not become widely accepted until the 1990s. The preponderance of work focused on fit between characteristics of individuals and characteristics of jobs. For example, fit between individuals' needs and organizational supplies has been central to most theories of person–job fit (Edwards, 1991), particularly those with a focus on job satisfaction (e.g., Dawis & Lofquist, 1984; Locke, 1976). In personnel selection, ability–demand fit has long been assumed, whereby individuals' skills and abilities are matched to the requirements of the job (Edwards, 1991). Similarly, the importance of congruence between the abilities of a person and the demands of the organization, particularly the job, was discussed in research on job stress (French, Caplan, & Harrison, 1982; McGrath, 1976).

The term *person–organization (PO) fit* became common in the late 1980s and 1990s and was defined as the similarity between the characteristics of people and the corresponding characteristics of organizations (Chatman, 1989; Kristof, 1996). Moving beyond the focus on job characteristics, a broader perspective of organizational dimensions was taken in terms of social attributes of the organization. For example, PE fit research included goal congruence (e.g., Vancouver & Schmitt, 1991), value congruence (e.g., Harris & Mossholder, 1996; O'Reilly, Chatman, & Caldwell, 1991), and personality–climate fit (e.g., Christiansen, Villanova, & Mikulay, 1997), and fit was related to outcomes such as work attitudes and intentions to turn over (Verquer, Beehr, & Wagner, 2003). The dynamic processes underlying the notion of similarity-based PO fit were described by Schneider's (1987a) attraction–selection–attrition (ASA) framework, which posits that similar people are attracted to and then selected and retained by the organization.

As the number of different terms, conceptualizations, and models of fit began to grow, the need for conceptual structure led to different categorizations of fit theories. The distinction of different types of fit by the level of the environment, such as job, group, or organization (Kristof-Brown, Zimmerman, & Johnson, 2005) has become largely accepted in the literature. Accordingly, fit notions can be distinguished as fit to another individual or person–individual (PI) fit, such as the supervisor (Glomb & Welsh, 2005; Tsui, Porter, & Egan, 2002), fit to the job or person–job (PJ) fit (e.g., Edwards, 1991; O'Reilly, 1977), fit to the workgroup or person–group (PG) fit (e.g., Ferris, Youngblood, & Yates, 1985; Guzzo & Dickson, 1996; Kristof-Brown & Stevens, 2001), and fit to the overall organization or PO fit (e.g., Chatman, 1989; Verquer et al., 2003). This focus on environmental subsystems has made it easier to conceptualize fit but has also led to greater compartmentalization in the understanding of PE fit (Kristof-Brown, Jansen, & Colbert, 2002). Recently, researchers have called attention to the need to theoretically integrate multiple types of fit (e.g., Cable & Edwards, 2004; Werbel & Gilliland, 1999) and empirically examine the combined impact of different types of fit on individual outcomes in organizations (e.g., Kristof-Brown et al., 2002).

We hope to continue this trend in this chapter by proposing an integrative model of fit.

## Summary

In summary, the focus of PE fit research has broadened from an emphasis on fit between individuals' characteristics and job characteristics, to a fit between individuals' characteristics and group and organizational attributes such as values, goals, and climate. Nevertheless, the preponderance of this work has focused on the influence of fit on individual outcomes, such as individuals' job attitudes and performance, largely ignoring any role of fit in explaining group or organizational outcomes. At the other extreme, the focus of system fit has broadened from an emphasis on simple internal or external alignment to more complex configurations and interplays between organizational and environmental features and their relationship to organizational performance and survival. However, for the past 40 years or so, micro and macro focuses have been viewed largely independently from one another.

In more recent years, we have seen glimpses of a reintegration of the micro and macro traditions of fit. For example, Bowen Ledford, and Nathan (1991) proposed that, above and beyond individuals being capable of performing the job, organizational effectiveness can be enhanced when employees whose values, goals, and personalities fit with culture, values, and goals of the organization are selected. Schneider and his colleagues (Schneider, Goldstein, & Smith1995; Schneider, Kristof-Brown, Goldstein, & Smith, 1997) argued that a strong emphasis on PE fit may jeopardize the long-term viability of the organization because the homogeneity that results from fit can lead to stultification, lack of creativity, and inability to adapt to a changing environment. On the macro side, more attention to the appropriate personal characteristics of employees has been evident in recent work in strategic HRM systems theory. In this view, different organizational strategies require different capabilities of workers and different sets of HR practices (e.g., Miles & Snow, 1984; Schuler & Jackson, 1995). As such, fit is implied between workers' characteristics, the internal practices used to select, develop, and motivate these workers, and the strategic emphasis of the firm.

We argue that system fit and PE fit are naturally related concepts. At the most general level, the components of the organizational system (e.g., strategic goals, culture, structure, work processes, and leadership) are the major elements that define the E in PE fit. That is, the components of the organizational system provide the context within which PE fit can operate. Further, when the organizational elements are not internally consistent or aligned, the environment into which the individual must fit is too disconnected and disparate to allow for individuals to achieve meaningful PE fit. At the same time, the elements of the organizational system emerge from the people within the organization, and hence the fit among employees helps to define the system elements. Levels of analysis issues are inherent in these views of fit, and we delineate these before turning to our model of theoretical concepts of fit in organizations.

## LEVELS ISSUES AND FIT

Like PE fit research, early efforts to conceptualize and study organizations as multilevel systems were based on the interactionist perspective, stressing the need to see behavior as a combined function of both person (P) and environment (E) or situation factors (Kozlowski & Klein, 2000). Yet, even though concepts of fit inherently involve levels of analysis issues because of the interrelationships of person characteristics with group and organizational system elements, the levels and fit literature have developed relatively independently over the years. Recently, researchers have begun to highlight the notion that fit components and outcomes can be viewed at different levels of analysis (e.g., Ployhart & Schneider, 2002; Rousseau, 2000), although a more comprehensive integration with levels theory and concepts has not been undertaken.

The application of recent developments from the levels of analysis literature can be used to help clarify fit theory and research and can stimulate future directions in the area. In this section, we first explore how fit can be viewed from multiple levels of analysis, and we highlight the notion that individuals can fit to different hierarchical levels of analysis (e.g., to their job, group, or organization), producing different subtypes of fit (e.g., PJ, PG, or PO fit). Second, we define the P and E elements, illustrating how different conceptualizations of the environment result in three broad modes of fit (person–person [PP], person–situation [PS], and situation–situation or system fit), and indicate how subtypes of fit can be crossed with the modes of fit. Finally, we integrate traditional views of supplementary and complementary fit with the concepts of composition, functionally commensurate dimensions, and compilation from the levels literature to derive a more comprehensive and overarching conceptualization of fit across levels of analysis.

### Fit to and at Different Levels of Analysis: Subtypes of Fit

Contemporary PE fit theory generally holds that the fit of a P to an E is good for the individual and further that the E components can be subdivided into different hierarchical levels of analysis such as the job, group, or organization. This view of PE fit implicitly assumes that individuals (P) can achieve fit to different hierarchical levels (e.g., to the supervisor, job, group, or organization) of the organizational environment (E). The subdivision of E elements into different hierarchical levels has led to different types or forms of PE fit as the individual's characteristics (P) are fit to the organizational, group, job, or dyadic level of the E construct. To illustrate, an individual's personal values (P) could be compared to the values of his or her supervisor (I), to the values among members in the same job category (J), to the values among members in the workgroup (G), or to values of members in the organization (O). Although we will return to this delineation of different subtypes of fit later, for now we simply highlight that the fit of P characteristics to one of these higher levels of E produces several different subtypes of fit that have often been termed: PI or dyadic fit, PJ, PG, and PO fit. For simplicity's sake, we use *fit to* when referencing the hierarchical level of the E component in PE fit.

In most fit studies, the criteria of interest are typically based on individual-level consequences such as satisfaction, adjustment, stress reduction, turnover, or performance. That is, some index of fit is linked to outcomes that reside at the individual level of analysis. Yet, the degree of fit can also have consequences for outcomes at higher levels of analysis, such as group or organizational effectiveness. For example, system fit, when represented as alignment among elements of the organizational system (e.g., fit between strategy, structure, and processes) is typically linked to organizational level outcomes such as profitability, survival, or success in the marketplace (Doty et al., 1993; Miles & Snow, 1994). Schneider et al. (1995, 1997) discussed the consequences of PE fit among employees within an organization for the effectiveness and long-term survival of the organization. Thus, an important distinction needs to be made between fit to a level (hierarchical level of analysis of the E variable, which can be another individual, the job, the group, or the organization) and *fit at* a level (focal level of analysis for the outcome variables). Considerations of fit to and fit at should be made concurrently. For example, a researcher could study the consequences of individuals' fit to their groups but do so at the individual level of analysis by focusing on individual-level job performance. Alternatively, a researcher could study the consequences of how employees fit their group overall at the group level of analysis, focusing on group effectiveness outcomes.

*Both the P and E components of the fit construct can be represented at different levels of analysis and can be linked to outcomes at different levels of analysis. Fit researchers are urged to explicitly connote the hierarchical level of E variables to which the P variables are linked as well as the level at which the theory or study is conceptualized (level of outcome variable).*

## General Modes of Fit: PP, PS, and System Fit

PE fit assumes that some characteristic(s) of the person is viewed in combination with some characteristic(s) of the environment. Over the years, different conceptualizations and categorizations of the P and E fit constructs have been offered (e.g., Cable & Edwards, 2004; Edwards, 1991; Kristof, 1996; Schneider et al., 1995). One source of confusion in PE fit literature can be traced to these differing conceptualizations, particularly in defining the context or environment. In the following, we first define the P and E factors and then elucidate three different ways in which the P and E factors can be combined to produce different modes of fit. Further, as is typical of most research in the area, fit is between commensurate P and E dimensions.

On the P side, several different types of variables have been considered, including knowledge, skills and abilities, and related attributes such as experience; personality-based and person-centered attributes such as traits, needs, desires, preferences, interests, goals, values, and perceptions; and demographic and background characteristics such as race, gender, and education; (e.g., Kristof, 1996; Ostroff, 1993b). As we delineate here, different categories of fit result, depending on the combination of these different person variables with different conceptualizations of the environment.

On the environment side, there have been differing views of how the E in PE fit should be conceptualized. In some PE fit studies, the E variable has been based on an assessment of a particular feature of the situational context (e.g., organizational values, organizational goals, or job requirements), whereas in other studies, E has been based on some global or aggregate assessment of the personal characteristics among individuals in the job, unit, or organization (e.g., aggregated personality or interests across individuals in the unit). Van Vianen (2000) recently argued for a distinction between classifying the environment based on the personal characteristics of those comprising the environment and classifying the environment based on a separate contextual or situational construct. Other theorists have drawn similar distinctions between the interpersonal environment (e.g., similarity to others in personal characteristics) and the non-interpersonal environment (e.g., task and situational variables) (Pervin, 1968) and between the interpersonal environment (e.g., coworkers) and the sociocultural environment (e.g., rules and cultural contexts) (Wapner & Demick, 2000).

A number of authors support the view that the E in PE fit be based on the collective characteristics of people or the personal attributes of those who inhabit the environment (e.g., Hogan & Roberts, 2000; Holland, 1997; Muchinsky & Monahan, 1987). Schneider (1987a, 1987b) argued that the E in PE fit should be characterized by the aggregate personal characteristics of individuals within the group or organization because the "people make the place." The underlying rationale is that homogeneity in personal characteristics such as values or personality will occur over time within an organization. People will gravitate to, be attracted to, and remain in environments that are composed of people who have interests, values, personalities, and perceptions similar to their own, which eventually may create organizations composed of people with similar attributes.

In contrast, other fit researchers asserted that the E variables should be conceptualized as situational characteristics, distinct from the personal characteristics of individuals behaving within them (e.g., Chatman, 1989; Roberts et al., 1978). Many attributes of the organization, such as structure, technology, and culture are purported to be at least partially determined by the organization's strategic position and relevant external environment (Van Vianen, 2000). Further, characteristics such as organizational norms and values are likely to be fundamental and enduring, independent of the occupants of the organization (Chatman, 1991). The underlying notion in PE fit research with a situation-based view of E is that some contextual element of the environment affords opportunities for individuals to gratify their needs or desires (e.g., Pervin, 1992; Schneider et al., 1997), allows people to utilize their skills and abilities to their fullest potential (e.g., Wilk & Sackett, 1996), or provides employees with a sense of self-esteem or self-efficacy due to their ability to operate effectively in an environment that is conducive to their attributes (Brief & Aldag, 1981).

Both person-based and situation-based views of the environment appear to have merit and should be treated as person–person (PP) and person–situation (PS) fit, respectively. An environment that is defined through the personal characteristics of those within it (e.g., aggregated personality, values, goals, and abilities) is a fundamentally different conceptualization from an environment defined as a contextual or situational attribute (e.g., culture, climate, organizational goals, and job demands).

Consider, for example, fit on goals. An individual's personal goals could be compared to the aggregated, and presumably relatively homogenous, personal goals of others in his or her organization. Here, the environment is defined through the personal goals of others, and the comparison between an individual's goals and the aggregated goals of others results in PP fit. In contrast, an individual's personal goals could be compared to the "actual" goals of the organization in a study of PS fit. These actual goals could be assessed through global measures such as stated goals in company material or through aggregation of members' perceptions of what the organization's goals are. Although we acknowledge that there is likely to be some overlap between collective personal goals (E defined through personal goals of those inhabiting the environment) and espoused collective goals (E defined through stated or aggregated perceptions of the goals for the organization), the two are not necessarily the same nor do they necessarily encompass the same dimensions. Organizations and people differ, and therefore, the same term, adjective, or descriptor (e.g., learning-oriented) may have a very different meaning when applied to an individual than when applied to an organization (Chatman, 1989). The fact that personal goals can be satisfied by or compatible with the espoused goals of the organization (Argyris, 1964) lends credence to the notion of PS fit in which the environment can be viewed as a contextually based or situation-based attribute, whereas the fact that individuals are attracted to others who have goals similar to their own goals (Schneider & Reichers, 1983) supports a PP view of fit for which the environmental attribute is person-based. We return to these modes of fit and further delineate different views of PS fit in a later section.

Fit to the environment based on the characteristics of the people within it (PP fit) and fit to the environment based on the situational elements (PS fit) can be further distinguished from system or situation–situation (SS) fit. System fit is not a term that has been used in the PE fit literature, but this type of fit has been discussed in macro-level organizational theory, as mentioned earlier. The basic premise is that the contextual elements and features of the organization (e.g., environment, strategy, culture, goals, and human capital) should complement one other to aid effective functioning of the organization. Success, survival, and adaptation of an organization depend on forming a strong external fit between the organization's structure and processes and its external market environment as well as a strong internal fit such that the organization's structure, processes, and culture are internally consistent and support the firm's strategy. The various situational elements are viewed as interdependent and must be appropriately aligned for an organization to be effective (Doty et al., 1993; Drazin & Van de Ven, 1986). Essentially, system fit is a case of SS fit whereby two or more situational elements are combined in such a way as to be aligned or compatible with one another.

*The environment can be conceptualized through two distinct means—person-centered and situation-centered, that in combination with P characteristics yield PP, PS, and SS or system conceptualizations of fit. Thus, congruence can manifest as fit among personal characteristics of people (PP), fit between personal characteristics and a feature of the contextual environment (PS), or fit among elements in the environmental context (SS or system fit).*

### Subtypes Within Modes of Fit

Up to this point, we have explained that fit can be conceptualized through three general modes (PP, PS, and SS), and we have noted that fit to different hierarchical levels results in different subtypes of fit (PI, PJ, PG, and PO). The modes and subtypes of fit can be almost completely crossed such that each general mode of fit can be further subdivided into fit to another individual (e.g., supervisor or peer) at the dyadic level, the attributes of the job, the group, or organization. For example, within the mode of PP fit, individuals' values have been compared to their supervisor's personal values (e.g., Meglino, Ravlin, & Adkins, 1992), and newcomers' preferences for organizational culture have been compared to the personal cultural preferences of recruiters (Van Vianen, 2000). Both of these are examples of PP fit because they compare the personal attributes of the focal individual to the personal attributes of another organizational member, and, further, they represent fit to the dyadic level of analysis (PI fit). Examples of PP fit to the group level (PG) include examinations of the degree of congruence or similarity between individuals' values and those of their coworkers (Adkins, Ravlin, & Meglino, 1996) and between a group members' demographic characteristics and those of their work-group (e.g., Harrison, Price, Gavin, & Florey, 2002; Liao, Joshi, & Chuang, 2004; Sacco & Schmitt, 2005). Similarly, in studies in which a PS mode of fit was used, individuals' values have been compared to organizational level cultural values to assess fit to the organizational level of analysis (e.g., Chatman, 1991; O'Reilly et al., 1991). In other examples falling under the rubric of the PS mode of fit, individuals' skills have been com-pared to job requirements to capture PJ fit (Edwards, 1991), to group requirements to capture PG fit (Hollenbeck et al., 2002; Werbel & Johnson, 2001), and to organizational requirements (e.g., Ployhart & Schneider, 2002).

System or SS fit can also be viewed at different hierarchical levels of analysis, such as fit among the contextual elements at the job level (e.g., Ployhart & Schneider, 2002), among elements of the team context such as between team structure and the team task environment (e.g., DeRue & Hollenbeck, chap. 8, this volume), or among organizational contextual features (e.g., Drazin & Van de Ven, 1986; Miles & Snow, 1984). Moreover, systems fit can be viewed from a cross-level perspective such as the alignment between team structure and organizational structure, which would represent group-organization fit.

## Moving From Supplementary and Complementary Fit to Composition and Compilation

In general, modes of fit refer to the way the two P and E constructs com-bine, whereas the subtypes refer to the hierarchical level of E. In addition to these features of the fit paradigm, a great deal of attention has been devoted to notions of supplementary and complementary fit.

The distinction between supplementary and complementary fit was first proposed by Muchinsky and Monahan (1987). In their conceptual-ization, supplementary fit denoted that the "person fits into some envi-ronmental context because he or she supplements, embellishes, or pos-sesses some characteristics which are similar to other individuals in this environment" (p. 269), whereas complementary fit means that the "char-acteristics of the individual serve to 'make whole' or complement the characteristics of an environment" (p. 271). It is important to note, how-ever, that their conceptualizations were narrowly focused. They articu-lated that supplementary fit was a means for explaining vocational fit and vocational guidance, whereas complementary fit was applicable to personal selection and hiring decisions. Further, they posited that in sup-plementary fit, the "environment is defined primarily by the people in it. It is essentially a model of person-person fit" (p. 270), whereas complementary fit should be viewed from the organization's perspective and that "a 'good fit' from the complementary perspective is that which is designed primarily to achieve organizational objectives" (p. 273). That is, they viewed supplementary fit as a process relevant at the individual level (related to individual-level outcomes) and complementary fit as a process operating at the organizational level.

Since that time, these two concepts have been more broadly applied (e.g., Cable & Edwards, 2004; Edwards, 1991; Kristof, 1996). For example, supplementary fit has been viewed as PS fit or as similarity between personal characteristics (e.g., personality and values) and organizational characteristics (e.g., climate and values) (e.g., Kristof, 1996), not just as PP fit as indicated by Muchinsky and Monahan (1987). Complementary fit has been viewed as a match between individual ability and organizational demands consistent with Muchinsky and Monahan, but also as a match between individuals' needs and organizational supplies (need–supply fit) or between organizational supplies and individual values (supply–value fit).

One problem with the notion that needs–supply fit is commensurate with complementary fit, and similarity on attributes is commensurate with supplementary fit, is the fact that it is often difficult to differentiate between these fit perspectives (Kristof, 1996). For example, congruence between an individual's values and organizational values has been viewed from a supplementary fit perspective in that individuals will be attracted to and have more positive responses in organizations with values similar to their own (e.g., Judge & Cable, 1997). At the same time, from a complementary fit and supply-value perspective, an individual's values, defined as desired levels of a certain organizational feature, are compared to the levels of those characteristics in the job (e.g., Van Vianen, 2000). Further, need fulfillment and reinforcement have been used to explain supplementary fit concepts such as greater fit between students' ratings of themselves and their ratings of the college environment on the same dimensions (Pervin, 1967).

Recently, Cable and Edwards (2004) attempted to more clearly distinguish between a supply–value perspective (complementary fit) and a value congruence (supplementary fit) perspective. They argued that an individual's value in a supply–value framework (or an individual's need in a need–supply framework) is founded on psychological need fulfillment, whereby the value or need is defined as the desired amount of the organizational attribute or how much of that attribute the individual wants. In contrast, value congruence, with a supplementary fit notion, assumes that the value is based on the importance of that attribute to the individual and that individuals are more comfortable working in settings where things that are important to them are also important to the organization. The results of their study revealed that both need fulfillment–based fit and value congruence–based fit are independently related to individuals' satisfaction, intentions to stay, and identification with the organization. Cable and Edwards interpreted their results to mean that both complementary and supplementary fit perspectives operate simultaneously in influencing individual's attitudinal outcomes. We believe this conclusion holds if one accepts the notion that need–supply or supply–value fit is commensurate with a complementary fit perspective. An alternate explanation is simply that their findings reveal the importance of two different psychological processes that underlie fit for individuals and support the two broad classes of theories for explaining the mechanisms underlying individual-level fit—both fulfillment of needs and similarity in attributes are important and independent fit mechanisms.

We argue that this strong link between the different types of fit (supplementary and complementary) and between specific theories to explain the psychological processes underlying fit (supply–value and similarity) has produced additional confusion in the fit literature because it is not directly applicable to fit at higher levels of analysis. That is, although it is certainly possible to take an individual-level perspective on complementary fit based on the notion that a situation fulfills an individual's needs, this interchangeability between the complementary fit and need fulfillment could produce additional confusion when one is attempting to develop a more comprehensive and more generalizable framework. We propose that supplementary and complementary fit definitions should be disentangled from the psychological theories (e.g., need fulfillment) that explain how and why fit operates. Thus, additional confusion can be avoided when one is attempting to apply these concepts more broadly to different E domains at different levels of analysis.

To illustrate, consider Fig. 1–1. It consists of identically shaped moths (representing people) of different shades. The shape and shading represent two different attributes of individuals or two different P factors. Both the shape and shade of the individual moths together comprise the unit level (e.g., group or organization) environmental or contextual attribute. There are several ways in which the shape, shade, and relationships among them can combine to represent different types of fit at different levels of analysis. First, consider that an individual moth's shape is similar to the shape of other individual moths. A different shaped entity, such as a butterfly or a gnat, would not fit with the other individuals. This illustrates the traditional notion of supplementary fit as defined by Muchinsky and Monahan (1987).

At the same time, consider that there is a hole in the system—an individual element is missing from the system, which is the first consideration in achieving complementary fit (represented by the black form in Fig. 1–1). In this case, a dark shaded moth is needed to complete the overall pattern as there are already sufficient moths of other shades. Here, the organizational system is deficient in a particular attribute and needs a particular type of person, of a particular shade, to be effective. Adding

FIGURE 1–1.   Depiction of multiple conceptualizations of fit.

Similarity in shape represents similarity in attributes or supplementary fit. Different colors represent different attributes. Different colored small circles on wing represent different attributes, and the circle of colored dots indicates group members (five members per group) with complementary attributes (compilation and complementary fit). Single dark black shape represents a "hole" in the organization that needs to be filled with a member of similar shape (for supplementary fit) and a particular color combination (for complementary fit).

this different individual attribute serves to make the environment whole, thereby producing a traditional definition of complementary fit. However, if one ignored the different shades and simply focused on adding another moth shape, it would also "make the system whole" and fill the need to complete the organizational system. In this case, we are adding one more of the same shape, and hence the complementary notion of making whole is based on supplementary fit. This illustrates one problem alluded to by Muchinsky and Monahan (1987): that, over time, based on job analyses, individuals are hired because they are deemed to have skills similar to those of others who are successful in the job and hence "more of the same type" may be what is needed or mandated, even though the original set of employees were chosen based on their ability to fill the organizations needs.

This illustration serves to highlight several important points. First, fulfilling a need, either from a need–supply perspective or from an ability–demand perspective, does not necessarily converge with a complementary view of fit. Need–supply notions can apply equally to supplementary and complementary fit. Second, the definition of complementary fit rests, in part, on making whole and filling a void. This can be achieved through supplementary or complementary means as noted earlier. These problems of overlapping conceptualizations in recent years and the fact that the original definitions of complementary and supplementary fit were specific to certain levels of analysis (i.e., supplementary for individual- and complementary for organizational-level outcomes) suggest the need for a more contemporary approach that is more broadly applicable across different categories of fit and different levels of analysis. The concepts of composition and compilation are useful in this regard.

## An Integrated Framework of Modes of Fit Across Levels of Analysis

We propose that the concepts of composition and compilation from the levels literature, when combined with different conceptualizations of the environment (person- or situation-based) provide a more coherent means for distinguishing between different modes and types of fit. Further, they provide greater clarity around the idea that fit can be based on similarity of attributes or fit can be based on different but complementary attributes. According to Kozlowski and Klein (2000), composition and compilation processes are two qualitatively distinct processes that pertain to how lower-level characteristics or elements emerge into higher-level constructs or collective phenomena. The dynamics and interactions of lower-level elements unfold over time to yield structure or collective phenomena at higher levels. These notions are particularly relevant for addressing fit because the E in PE fit is often based on a combination of lower-level elements (e.g., aggregated individual characteristics or arrays of personal characteristics across members of the group).

Composition models refer to situations whereby lower-level elements or characteristics converge and coalesce to result in a higher property that is essentially the same as the elements that comprise it (Chan, 1998; Kozlowski & Klein, 2000). A compositional perspective of fit is based largely on the notion that the person characteristic is compared to a higher-level characteristic that is functionally similar and has the same content or same meaning as the lower-level construct (e.g., individual values compared to organizational values).

Compilation is based on the notion that a particular configuration or profile of lower-level elements or characteristics yields the higher-level construct (Kozlowski & Klein, 2000). Here, the assumption is that different amounts or types of lower-level element properties combine to reveal the higher-level property. The lower-level characteristics vary within a unit, but the pattern or configuration of these lower-level characteristics produces a higher-level attribute and characterizes the unit as a whole. The lower- and higher-level constructs are functionally similar in that they occupy essentially the same role in models at different levels of analysis, but they are not the same or completely isomorphic. A compilation perspective of fit is based on the notion that elements or characteristics vary, but nevertheless they combine in such a way to complement and fit with one another (e.g., different personality characteristics across individuals combine to form a team composed of complementary personality types).

Supplementary and complementary fits refer to different types of fit relationships between the P and E elements. Similarly, composition and compilation concepts can be used to characterize the relationship between P and E by describing different ways that the higher-level E element can be combined from lower-level elements. Supplementary fit is related to the notion of composition in that the environment is composed of people with an identical or very similar characteristic. Fit is achieved when the characteristic of a focal person is identical or very similar to them. Complementary fit and compilation have in common the fact that the environment is defined as a system or configuration based on heterogeneous characteristics. Fit is achieved when the characteristic of a focal person makes the system whole so that a higher-order gestalt can emerge or when elements of E fit together to create a coherent whole. As we develop in the following, supplementary and complementary fit can ultimately be viewed as a continuum.

The integration of composition and compilation processes with different modes of fit across levels of analysis produces various combinations of the P and E elements at different levels of analysis and provides a comprehensive view of fit that is generalizable across different content domains. When viewed this way, the different theories such as need–supply, ability–demand, and similarity–attraction can be used to explain the psychological processes underlying these forms of fit, rather than being viewed as distinct forms of fit per se. In what follows, we gradually develop a model that shows how different combinations of P and E elements represent fit at the individual level and then indicate how individual level conceptualizations of fit emerge into P and E constructs at higher levels of analysis. We also refer readers to Edwards and Shipp (chap. 7, this volume), who developed an integrative model linking different domains of the environment, different conceptualizations of fit, and fit to different levels of analysis in explaining relationships between fit and outcomes. The framework we develop is similar in nature but delves more deeply into understanding how and why fit emerges across different levels of analysis.

## Modes of Fit at the Individual Level

At the individual level of analysis (when the P factor and outcomes are at the individual level), an integration of the concepts of composition and compilation with person-based and situation-based notions of conceptualizing E results in four different modes: PP compositional (identical), social PS compositional (referent shift), technical PS compositional (corresponding functionality), and PP compilation. These four types of fit are summarized in Table 1–1 and are represented in Fig 1–2. The boxes in Fig. 1–2 represent the P and E factors. The P factor box refers to individuals' personal attributes and characteristics (e.g., personality, values, goals, and skills). The E is represented in different ways, based on: similarity in the personal attributes across individuals within the environment (P homogenous), a particular profile of different personal attributes among individuals within the environment (P profile), and the situational context. Solid lines in Fig. 1–2 indicate which combinations of P and E characteristics are used to produce a particular mode of fit (e.g., P factors and the social aspect of the situational factor E combine to form social PS fit at the individual level of analysis). The derivation of each is described in the following.

### PP (Person–Person) Compositional Fit

One mechanism underlying fit rests on the notion of similarity between the person and environmental variables. This notion is implicitly based on composition processes that include homology (corresponding in relative position, structure, and function) such that the phenomena of interest are functionally similar and are essentially the same as they emerge upward across levels.

In PP compositional fit, identical elements are considered for both the P and E components. For example, the personality of the focal individual is assessed in the same form as is the personality of others who comprise the relevant comparison group for the E construct. The personal attributes of the focal individual could be compared to a single assessment of another individual (e.g., a supervisor) and the fit between their personal characteristics represents PP fit. Alternatively, the personality attributes from members of the unit (e.g., job, group, or organization) can be aggregated, and, when they are shared or similar, the aggregated personality represents a collective P attribute. In this conceptualization, the E variable is based on

**TABLE 1–1.**

**PE Fit Conceptualizations at the Individual Level of Analysis**

| Mode by Subtype of Fit | General Description | Levels of Analysis Type | E Factor |
|---|---|---|---|
| PP Compositional | Degree of similarity between the personal attributes of focal individual and the personal attributes of: | Composition and identical: identical P and E elements | Shared or similar collective personal attributes of others (e.g., personal goals, skills, personality, and attitudes) |
| PI fit<br>PJ fit<br>PG fit<br>PO fit | A peer, supervisor, recruiter<br>Individuals within a job category<br>Individuals within a group, unit<br>Individuals within the organization | | |
| Social PS | Degree of fit between the personal attributes of focal individual and the sociopsychological context defined through converging cognitions, perceptions, affects, or behaviors of: | Composition and referent shift: homologous P and E elements but referent for factor shifts from individual to situation | Attribute of the social-psychological context (e.g., culture, climate, espoused values, and espoused goals) that has its theoretical foundation in the cognitions, perceptions, affects, attitudes, or behaviors of people in the context |
| PI fit<br>PJ fit<br>PG fit<br>PO fit | A peer, supervisor, recruiter<br>Individuals within a job category<br>Individuals within a group, unit<br>Individuals within the organization | | |

(continued)

**TABLE 1-1.**
*(Continued)*

| Mode by Subtype of Fit | General Description | Levels of Analysis Type | E Factor |
|---|---|---|---|
| PP Compilation | Degree to which personal attributes of focal individual complements the array of personal attributes of others, where the array is derived from: | Compilation | Profile, pattern, or configuration of personal attributes of others (e.g., configuration of different skills, personalities, and goals) |
| PI fit | A peer, supervisor, recruiter | | |
| PJ fit | Individuals within a job category | | |
| PG fit | Individuals within a group, unit | | |
| PO fit | Individuals within the organization | | |
| Structural PS | Degree of fit or alignment between personal attributes of focal individual and structural-technical environment defined as: | Mostly compositional with corresponding functions: P and E have same functions but different underlying origins (person) | Attribute of the structural-technical context (e.g., job demands, work structure, practices, and reward systems) that has its theoretical foundation in the design and structure of the work context, independent of the personal characteristics of those in the environment |
| PJ fit | A job category | | |
| PG fit | A group, unit | | |
| PO fit | An organization | | |

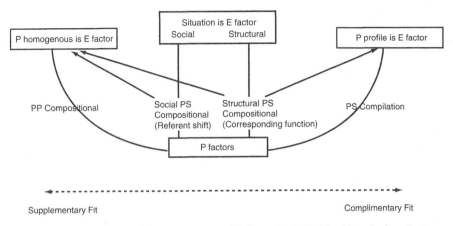

FIGURE 1–2.    Person (P)–environment (E) fit at the individual level of analysis.

the notion of a collective P such that there is some degree of homogeneity in people's attributes within a unit, which reflects what Chan (1998) referred to as a direct consensus composition model. In this mode of PP fit, the focal individual has a personal characteristic (be it a skill, need, value, goal, personality type, attitude, or demographic characteristic) similar to others in the unit (see Table 1–1 and the far left side of Fig. 1–2). Further, this mode of fit reflects a pure form of supplementary fit as defined by Muchinsky and Monahan (1987).

The degree to which the attribute of a particular individual is similar to the same attribute of another individual (e.g., the manager or supervisor or a mentor) or is similar to that of other individuals in the unit (in some aggregate form) has been linked to individual outcomes and behaviors. For example, on the basis of a PP mode of fit and a PI (dyadic) subtype of fit, similarity in demographic characteristics (e.g., Vecchio & Bullis, 2001), similarity in personal values and personality (e.g., Glomb & Welsh, 2005; Meglino, Ravlin, & Adkins, 1989), and similarity in personal preferences (e.g., Van Vianen, 2000) between an individual and the supervisor have been related to individuals' satisfaction, commitment, and performance. In addition, greater similarity in the personal values of a job applicant and a recruiter has been found to be positively related to initial judgments of employability (Adkins, Russell, & Werbel, 1994). In a study reflecting PP similarity in reference to the group (PG type of fit), greater dissimilarity in work status between an individual and others in the group was found to be related to lower organizational-based self-esteem and attitudes toward the group members (Chattopadhyay & George, 2001), whereas the degree of similarity between an individual's demographic characteristics and those of other group members has been positively related to individual attitudes (Riordin, 2000), but the effect of similarity has also been found to differ by sex (Chatman & O'Reilly, 2004).

The psychological mechanisms underlying compositional PP fit are supported by a number of different theories. According to the similarity-attraction paradigm, individuals are attracted to and prefer to associate with others similar to themselves, while tending to avoid dissimilar others (Byrne & Nelson, 1965). Similarity is generally related to attraction because similarity results in reinforcement and a reciprocally rewarding interaction (Pervin, 1968). A related notion is derived from social categorization and identification theories (e.g., Tajfel & Turner, 1985). A greater degree of similarity in social categories, such as background, attitudes, and lifestyles, leads to a feeling of common identity with the referent. More recently, self-verification theory has been proposed to explain more specifically how this attraction and identification work. In this view, individuals proactively seek out areas of similarity with others to verify their own identity and their personal attitudes are strongly related to their perceptions of similarity to others (Swann, Polzer, Seyle, & Ko, 2004). Further, when individuals possess similar attributes or values, they tend to share common aspects of cognitive processing and common methods of interpreting events that can help them reduce uncertainty, cognitive dissonance, stimulus overload, ambiguity, conflict, and other negative features of work interaction (Kalliath, Bluedorn, & Strube, 1999; Schein, 1992). Atwater and Dionne (chap. 6, this volume) provide additional justification specific to dyadic (PI) fit with a supervisor.

*At the individual level of analysis, PP compositional fit references the level or amount of the individual's personal attribute compared to the level or amount of the identical attribute in others in the environment.*

### PS (Person–Situation) Fit

In PS fit at the individual level, the P and S components are compositional in nature in that they are functionally similar and have the same general meaning at the P and S levels of analysis; however, they are not identical nor are they completely isomorphic. There are two ways that the P and S elements combine to form PS fit. The first is based on the type of domain of the situational context: social–psychological or structural–technical. In general, social domains of the environment are based on the notion that people create higher-level social structures in organizations through social–psychological mechanisms such as shared values and norms, whereas the structural domain focuses on the structural and technical elements necessary for task accomplishment (Katz & Kahn, 1978). The second means of conceptualizing PS fit modes is based on different forms of compositional models, namely referent shift and corresponding functions. In PS referent shift models, the referent for the items shifts from the individual in conceptualizing P to the higher level in assessing E. In PS corresponding function models, the P and S factors are not isomorphic but correspond in some elements and function. When P is compared to social domains of S, compositional referent shift models are relevant, and when P is compared to structural aspects of the S, corresponding function models are appropriate (see Table 1–1 and the middle of Fig. 1–2). Social PS fit and structural PS fit are described more fully in the following.

*Social PS Fit.* In social PS fit at the individual level, the P and S components are compositional in nature and have the same general meaning at the P and S levels of analysis. Many conceptualizations of PS fit are based on describing the environment from a social–psychological basis (cf. Dawis & Lofquist, 1984; Kristof, 1996; Schneider & Reichers, 1983). Organizations have long been described as social systems in which people create the social structure by enacting complex patterns of behavior. Roles, norms, and values have been viewed as key social–psychological bases that comprise social systems (Katz & Kahn, 1978). More recently, these notions have fallen under the rubric of *social context theory* (Ferris, Arthur, & Berkson, 1998). In this view, sociopsychological constructs are defined as higher-order socially interactive constructs or social structures that cannot be reduced to an aggregation of the characteristics or perceptions of the individuals currently comprising the organization. Examples of such sociopsychological constructs are organizational culture and climate. Culture has been conceptualized as organizationally embedded assumptions, ideologies, and values that are influenced by symbolic interpretations of events and artifacts (Dennison, 1990; Ostroff, Kinicki, & Tamkins, 2003; Schein, 2000). Because culture is a collectively held construct, it represents the cumulative and inclusive influence of individuals. Another example, highlighted by Kozlowski and Klein (2000), is organizational climate, which is based on shared perceptions among employees about what the organization is like in terms of its practices, policies, routines, and procedures. Climate exists apart from any one current organizational member, and it serves to convey information to employees about expected patterns of activity.

The distinguishing feature of these social components of the environment is that their theoretical foundation resides in the cognitions, affect, behaviors, or attributes of individuals. Through interaction and exchange processes, these individual-level foundations manifest into a higher-level construct. These are distinct from formal unit or organizational characteristics because they are often driven by informal processes such as social interactions, sense-making, and communications among employees (Kozlowski & Klein, 2000).

When social phenomena among individuals create the basis for the emergence of a higher-level construct, referent shift compositional models are often appropriate. Referent shift is a specific form of a composition model that occurs when the same construct is assessed with reference to different levels of analysis (Chan, 1998; Klein, Conn, Smith, & Sorra, 1991). In this case, the referent shifts as one moves from the self or individual (when construing P) to the unit characteristic as a whole (when construing S). For example, the assessment of personal values represents the P side of PS fit and the assessment of the values of the group or organization is used to represent the S side. The referent for the element or the items shifts from the self (e.g., personal values) to the group (e.g., values espoused by the group).

Social PS fit with referent shift has been investigated in several different content areas. A large number of studies have focused on value fit under the rubric of PO fit (see Kristof-Brown & Jansen, chap. 4, this volume). For example, individuals' preferences or desires for cultural values in an organization are compared to the cultural values deemed to be present in the group or organization (e.g., Chatman, 1991; Erdogan, Kraimer, & Liden, 2004; Judge & Cable, 1997; O'Reilly et al., 1991; Van Vianen, 2000). Social PS fit has also been studied in terms of congruence between individuals' goals and those of the team (e.g., Kristof-Brown, 2001) or organization (e.g., Vancouver & Schmitt, 1991) and the degree of goal congruence has been related to individual attitudes and behaviors. As an example of social PS fit to the PI or dyadic level, congruence between an individual scientist's view of the obligation to a research director and the director's beliefs regarding his or her own corresponding obligation to the scientist was related to performance and attitudinal outcomes of the scientist (Dabos & Rousseau, 2004).

Both similarity-based and need fulfillment theories are relevant for explaining the psychological processes underlying social PS fit. From a similarity perspective, individuals are purported to be more attracted to and satisfied when the cognitions, beliefs, attitudes, goals, and values of others in the environment are similar to their own (Schneider & Reichers, 1983). Related theories include the notions that misfit creates emotional distress and cognitive ruminations thereby increasing psychological and physiological stress and strain (Shaw & Gupta, 2004), cognitive demands of learning about and understanding the situation are lessened due to the similarity with the environment (Kalliath et al., 1999), fit guides the stability of behavior in the environment (Holland, 1997), and the environment is seen as reinforcing and satisfying when it resembles the individual (Dawis & Lofquist, 1984).

When the focus of the social context variable is framed in terms of "amount supplied" in the environment and compared to individuals' needs, a need fulfillment perspective is relevant for explaining how fit operates. The underlying premise is that preferences, desires, needs, or other personal characteristics are fulfilled by being in a context that is similar in nature to that personal characteristic or that affords opportunities for personal needs, desires, and/or preferences to be met. In essence, the environment is seen as affording individuals the chance to gratify their needs (Schneider et al., 1997). Cable and Edwards' (2004) study elucidated how the amounts of some social–psychological context variables (e.g., the amount of altruism or the amount of positive relationships with coworkers present in the work context) were related to more positive attitudes of employees when consistent with individuals' desired amount of that variable.

A related issue is one of perceptual fit. Perceptual fit reflects the idea that more positive outcomes occur when an individual's perceptions of the work environment are similar to the perceptions of others. For example, in the climate area, it has been proposed that more positive outcomes are realized when individuals perceive the climate of the group or organization more similarly, regardless of the type of climate (e.g., Lindell & Brandt, 2000; Schneider, Salvaggio, & Subirats, 2002). Perceptual fit is based on the notion that perceptions of the work environment are critical determinants of behavior and attitudes (e.g., Cable & DeRue, 2002; Endler & Magnusson, 1976). Convergence of perceptions can arise because individuals are exposed to common group or organizational features and process; they communicate, interact, and share interpretations with one another; and, through the attraction–selection–attrition process, they have similar viewpoints and cognitive processing mechanisms that facilitate common interpretations (Kozlowksi & Klein, 2000; Ostroff et al., 2003). Perceptual fit can be viewed as a special type of social PS fit. In perceptual fit, the P is based on a perception or cognition of the work environment, as opposed to a personal characteristic such as personality, skills, or goals, and the E is defined through the perceptions of the supervisor or the shared perceptions of others in the job, group, or organization about the social context (Ostroff, Shin, & Kinicki, 2005).

In sum, in social PS models, an individual-level attribute is compared to a homologous situational characteristic, and, further, the situational characteristic is emergent and based on convergence of the perceptions, attitudes, values, behaviors, or goals of individuals within the unit. Referent shift compositional models, whereby the referent for the contextual variable shifts to the higher level, are particularly appropriate when defining the situational construct.

*Compositional PS models will most likely focus on the social–psychological domain of the environmental situation. Social PS fit at the individual level of analysis pertains to fit between a personal attribute of an individual and an emergent social–psychological attribute of the organizational context.*

***Structural PS Fit.*** Structural-PS fit represents another form of a compositional model in which personal characteristics are compared to attributes from the structural–technical environment. Composition models specify the functional relationship between variables at different levels that are presumed to be functionally similar to one another, yet not all compositional models postulate isomorphism (Rousseau, 1985). In isomorphism, the constructs can come from different origins (e.g., from different levels of analysis) but should have the same function. In some cases, however, the constructs at different levels may come from different origins and exhibit only partial functionality. For example, the two constructs may have a similar or corresponding structure but differ slightly in their functional relationship with other variables. When some, but not all, elements are equivalent at the two levels, the result is what has been referred to as partial functionality (Rousseau, 1985) or pooled convergence (Kozlowski & Klein, 2000). An example of a functionally similar pair is individual and group performance. Group performance may not be the simple sum of the performance of individuals within the group because the sum will not reflect complex interactions among people that affect the totality of group performance. Different antecedents and causal factors may give rise to individual versus group performance (e.g., Kozlowksi, Gully, Nason, & Smith, 1999) even though they are functionally similar constructs. Further, aggregation from the individual-level elements may or may not be appropriate in operationalizing the higher-level construct. In many cases, a single global measure of the situational or higher-level variable may be more appropriate (Roberts et al., 1978; Rousseau, 1985). Thus, composition can also be based on two corresponding constructs across levels that are derived through different means.

The importance of assessing both the P and E components with the same or commensurate dimensions has long been touted (e.g., Caplan, 1987; Edwards, 1991; Kristof, 1996). However, the corresponding P and S factors can also take on slightly different forms. That is, the two constructs can be measured along the same dimensions (e.g., autonomy) and with the same underlying meaning yet the two corresponding P and S constructs differ in their underlying origins. To illustrate, the need for autonomy as a P factor is based on an individual's personal needs, whereas the amount of autonomy provided by the job is based on a characteristic inherent in the job structure that is defined independently from the people who inhabit the job. In this view, the P and S factors are not the identical form of the construct at two different levels of analysis, but are two different forms of the same construct assessed at different levels of analysis. In the autonomy example, the antecedents that lead to P, such as an individual's needs (Murray, 1938), are likely to differ from the antecedents that lead to S, such as the technological and work process demands that influence how tasks and work are to be structured.

In structural PS fit, the E domain is not an emergent construct that is theoretically based on convergence among individual's attributes, cognitions, affect, or behaviors, as in social PS fit. The E elements in structural PS fit derive from structural and technical domains of the context. The structural–technical component of the environment is based largely on the notion of the technical or production subsystem (Katz & Kahn, 1978) with an emphasis on task requirements and task accomplishments. Task accomplishment focuses on developing skill standards and methods for accomplishing the tasks in the organization. Related to this are mainte-nance structures, which are essentially mediating mechanisms between task demands and human needs. Many maintenance structures are organi-zational-level procedures or processes that are geared toward formalizing and institutionalizing aspects of human behavior in the interest of enhanc-ing task accomplishment (Katz & Kahn, 1978), such as training employees, developing skills for task accomplishment, or establishing reward systems to motivate employees' behavior in the desired ways. Situational elements falling under the rubric of the structural domain of the environment include task activities, skill and job requirements, job allocation across units, degree of specialization, division of labor, work structure, team structure, work pro-cess, reward systems, and job characteristics.

Much of the research based on this definition of the structural PS fit mode has been conducted at the job level, comparing individuals' skills to job requirements or comparing individuals' preferences for work attributes to the opportunities afforded by the design of the work charac-teristics. A greater degree of structural PS fit has been related to higher performance, satisfaction, and job attitudes and to lower stress, strain, and turnover (e.g., Edwards, 1991; Edwards & Van Harrison, 1993; Shaw & Gupta, 2004). This mode of fit can also be applied to the group or orga-nizational level, for example, comparing individuals' skills and work preferences to the skill requirements and work structure of a team.

Several different theories have been used to explain the psychological mechanisms that underlie this type of fit. In reference to fit between skills of individuals and task requirements, individuals purportedly use their skills to handle specific tasks and to adapt to their environment (Pervin, 1989). Similarly, the ability–demand perspective deals with the extent to which the individual has abilities and skills that fit the demands of the task or work role. The match between a personal competence and an environmental demand should result in more positive behavioral and affective outcomes whereas when environmental demands are too high or low, maladaptive behavior, stress, boredom, and negative affect are likely to result (Walsh, Craik, & Price, 2000).

Moreover, a needs perspective has been applied to understand this type of fit. The extent to which the structural aspects of the situation sup-plies or allows for meeting a need should result in more positive out-comes. For example, the extent to which the task activities (type of work required), reward systems (e.g., incentive-based or seniority-based), train-ing systems, work structure (e.g., team or independent), and job charac-teristics (e.g., autonomy, variety, and complexity) fit an individuals' needs should enhance employees' attitudes, well-being, and performance. One process underlying need fulfillment is based on a cognitive compar-ison of the desired and perceived job conditions (Edwards, 1996). When the environment is deficient in supplying what the individual needs or when the environment supplies more than what the individual needs, emotional distress is likely because too much cognitive rumination about the discrepancy is elicited (Shaw & Gupta, 2004). A related perspective, based on goals and reinforcement, was proposed by Pervin (1987, 1989). He posited that a person searches for opportunities in the environment to satisfy his or her multiple goals. At the same time, the rewards offered in the environment influence the individuals' hierarchy of goals such that some goals or needs become more prominent when they are rewarded by the environment. In general, the match between individuals' needs and environmental supplies is viewed as rewarding, satisfying, and instrumental in obtaining highly valued outcomes (Schneider et al., 2000).

In sum, functionally similar constructs form the basis of structural PS fit models. The P and E (situational) factors have corresponding functions but do not necessarily have identical antecedents. Further, the situational characteristics are independent from the personal characteristics, affect, cognitions, and perceptions of those comprising the situation.

*Structural PS fit at the individual level of analysis pertains to fit between a personal attribute of an individual and a structural, task-related, or technical attribute of the organizational context.*

### PP (Person–Person) Compilation

PP fit is based on a comparison of a focal individual's attributes to the personal attributes of others in the relevant context. As discussed earlier, one form of PP fit is PP composition, in which homogeneity and similarity to others (as opposed to heterogeneity) are the basis for fit. In contrast, another form of PP fit can be based on being different from others, but the different attributes among people complement one another. We refer to this type of fit as PP compilation (see Table 1–1 and right side of Fig. 1–2).

According to Kozlowski and Klein (2000), compilation is another type of emergent property in organizational systems. Compilation is based on the notion that distinctly different phenomena within the same domain combine to form a "whole." That is, the combination of related but distinct elements or characteristics at the lower level yields a higher-level property that is functionally equivalent to the elements that comprise it. In composition models, the type and amount of the element that each individual contributes are the same (e.g., all have the same type and amount of a particular personality). In contrast, in compilation models, discontinuity occurs in that either the type or the amount (or both) of the elemental content is different. Individuals make different contributions, not the same contribution, to form the system. Further, although variance or heterogeneity across individuals in the attribute is needed, this variability is not randomly dispersed. There must be a specific pattern or configuration of the characteristics that results in the emergence of a coherent whole. Thus, it is not simply the degree of heterogeneity but rather the heterogeneity among individuals' characteristics that forms a specific pattern.

Little attention has been directed to a compilation or configural view of fit at the individual level of analysis, but the notion is implicit in several content areas. For example, in the selection area, Werbel and Johnson (2001) argued that the degree to which an individual's skills and attributes complement the skills and attributes of others in the group should be positively related to individual performance. In discussions of diversity, the degree of variability across individuals within a unit on the same attribute (e.g., personality, demographic characteristics, or perceptions) has been viewed as a form of potential complementary fit in teams that is important for individual outcomes (e.g., Jackson, May, & Whitney, 1995). In understanding team processes, different but compatible knowledge across individuals in the team has been purported to compile into a specific configuration of team mental knowledge that forms a congruent whole, which can, in turn, impact individual outcomes (Kozlowski, Brown, Weissbein, Cannon-Bowers, & Salas, 2000; Kozlowski et al., 1999). In these examples, when the attributes of a focal individual are different from the attributes of many others in the group but complement the attributes of others in the unit, compilation PP fit is achieved.

We also note that a compilation form of fit has been addressed at the intraindividual level in terms of complementing attributes within a person, such as fit between an individual's orientation to an activity and the means the individual uses to pursue that activity (see Higgins & Freitas, chap. 2, this volume). Fit or convergence between the interest and knowledge profiles of individuals is another example of a compilation notion of fit at the intraindividual level of analysis (Reeve & Hakel, 2000).

In some ways, a paradox exists between PP composition and PP compilation modes of fit. On the one hand, with PP composition, similarity-attraction and social identity theories suggest that a greater degree of dissimilarity to others results in more negative individual outcomes (e.g., Jackson et al., 1995). On the other hand, PP compilation notions suggest that an individual may be attracted to others who are complementary (Pervin, 1968). Individuals value the prestige they receive from their colleagues when they contribute to the group (Ferris & Mitchell, 1987), and, hence, complementary (not identical) fit to others in the group is likely to motivate individuals to work harder and develop good interpersonal relationships with others (Werbel & Johnson, 2001). In essence, contributing uniquely to the group or organization can enhance feelings of self-worth (Brief & Aldag, 1981). We suggest that some of the conflicting predictions in terms of individual outcomes made by PP compositional and PP compilation modes of fit may be resolved by greater attention to the pattern of variability. For example, dissimilarity may indeed produce negative affective or behavioral outcomes for individuals if there is no coherent pattern to the dissimilarity, whereas dissimilarity may produce positive affective or behavioral outcomes when the differences allow individuals to complement one another and hence produce feelings of contributing in some unique way to the group.

*Compilation PP fit at the individual level reflects the extent to which an individual's attributes complement the profile of attributes across others in the unit.*

## Modes of Fit at Higher Levels of Analysis

The four modes of fit described in the preceding section represent fit at the individual level of analysis whereby some conceptualization of PE fit is linked to individuals' responses. Studies at the individual level of analysis can take one of two forms: (a) a purely individual level with assessment of both P and E variables from the individual's perspective, either as a single global index of fit or as separate assessments of the P and E factors from the individual, or (b) cross-level with assessment of P components from the individual and E components derived from a higher level such as an aggregate score. As we alluded to in our previous discussion of composition and compilation, individual attributes or elements emerge into higher level phenomena through interactions and social exchanges. This bottom-up process explains the person-based and social situation–based domains of the E. We now take this idea one step further by showing how the different modes of fit at the individual level form the P and E components at a higher level and how different modes of PE fit at the higher level can be linked to outcomes at the higher level.

When higher levels of analysis are considered (e.g., group or organization), such as in an examination of the impact of PE fit on organizational effectiveness, both the P and E components of fit need to be considered at the organizational level of analysis. For example, some global or aggregate measure of P (e.g., personality) could be compared to a situationally based organizational level E attribute (e.g., climate) and then related to an organizational effectiveness index (Ostroff, 1993a). Or, some overall assessment across individuals that reflects the degree to which individuals fit the job, group, or organization overall (a type of aggregated PE fit score) could be obtained and related to group or organizational level outcomes. Further, we note that the level of analysis for the outcome variable can be at the same level as or at a lower level than the P and E components.

Our model of different types of fit across levels of analysis is depicted in Fig. 1–3. For the sake of simplicity, we delineate the individual level (with outcomes at the individual level) and a higher level (with outcomes at a higher level of analysis such as the group or organizational level) rather than treating the group and organizational levels separately. The bottom portion of Fig. 1–3 includes the four types of fit at the individual-level analysis that were described in the preceding section: PP compositional; social PS compositional based on referent shift, structural

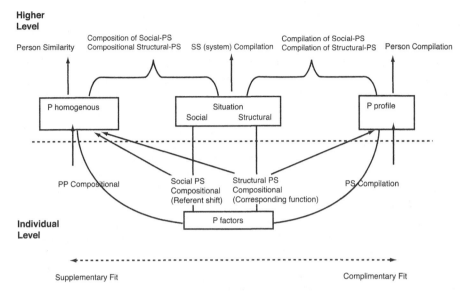

FIG. 1–3. A multilevel model of fit.

PS compositional based on corresponding functionality, and PP compilation. For individual-level fit, the boxes in Fig. 1–3 represent the P and E factors, and the solid lines indicate which combinations of P and E characteristics are used to produce a particular mode of fit. The dashed arrows in the figure depict how a particular mode of fit at the individual level provides the basis for the emergence of a P construct at a higher level of analysis. That is, fit concepts from the individual level emerge into constructs that are then used to examine fit at the higher level of analysis. We first explain the emergent phenomena before moving to fit conceptualizations at higher levels.

### Emergence of Person-Based E Constructs at Higher Levels

As was seen in Fig. 1–2, when one considers fit at the individual level of analysis, individuals' P factors can be compared to E factors that are either situation-based or person-based. The person-based E factors reflect the notion that the work environment is composed of people whose personal characteristics are homogeneous or is composed of people with different characteristics that form a particular profile or configuration. When one moves to examinations of fit at the higher level of analysis, these person-based environment factors (that are construed as the E in PE fit at the individual level) turn into higher-level P factors that can then be compared to higher-level situation-based E factors to form fit constructs at higher levels (see Fig. 1–3).

Homogeneous P characteristics in an environment can emerge through three of the individual-level fit perspectives—PP compositional, social PS or structural PS fit. PP compositional fit rests largely on the assumption of the ASA process—people will gravitate to, be attracted to, and remain in environments that are composed of people who have interests and values similar to their own (Schneider et al., 2000). In support of this notion, the personalities of managers were found to be more similar within organizations than across organizations and industries (Schneider, Smith, Taylor, & Fleenor, 1998). Moreover, through social comparison processes, when discrepancies between the self and others exist with respect to ideas, opinions, attitudes, or abilities, individuals tend to change their own position to be closer to others in the group (Festinger, 1954). Over time, through ASA, attraction-similarity, and social comparison processes, homogeneity in the personal characteristics of individuals within the unit should result. The dashed arrow from PP compositional to P homogeneous in Fig. 1–3 reflects how similarity in personal attributes can produce a higher-level P construct. In examining PE fit at the individual level of analysis, the E factor is conceptualized as the aggregated characteristics of other individuals (listed as E factor: P homogeneous in Fig. 1–2). At the higher level of analysis, this same factor becomes a P factor, representing an aggregated and collective P attribute across individuals at the higher level of analysis that can then be compared to other situational attributes (e.g., social or technical situational factors).

A similar process explains how homogeneity in personal characteristics of unit members can emerge from social PS and structural PS fit at the individual level. Individuals seek out and remain in contexts or environments that are compatible with or similar in nature to their own attributes as in social PS fit or that afford opportunities for their personal needs, desires, and preferences to be met as in structural PS fit. As such, certain types of people will be attracted to and prefer certain types of features in the organizational environment, the result of which is that homogeneity is produced over time because those who fit the context best remain in the context (Schneider et al., 2000). Further, socialization processes, mentoring, or leaders' influences can also change employees' personal attributes, goals, and values in the direction of those of the organization (Chatman, 1991; Fisher, 1986; O'Reilly & Chatman, 1986). At the same time, organizations may specifically select individuals whose personal attributes fit the attributes of the social–psychological context (Bowen et al., 1991), thereby increasing homogeneity. In terms of skills and abilities, the traditional means of defining job requirements typically leads to a set of skills and abilities required to perform the job, and selection systems are then designed to hire people with that set of attributes. This process often results in people within a group, job category, or job cluster who have the same set of knowledge, skills, and abilities (Ployhart & Schneider, 2002). Taken together, these processes suggest that, over time, individuals in the unit are likely to be relatively homogenous in their personalities, needs, desires, abilities, and other personal attributes. Thus, achieving social and structural PS fit at the individual level can produce a higher-level homogenous P factor (as depicted by the dashed arrows from PS fit to P homogenous).

Moreover, the structural PS and PP compilation perspectives of individual-level fit can also foster the emergence of P profiles at the higher level (a particular profile or configuration of different attributes). On the basis of the traditional notion of complementary fit offered by Muchinsky and Monahan (1987), the environment is seen as either deficient or in need of a certain type of person to be effective, which can be offset by the various strengths and weaknesses of the individual. With this type of ability–demand emphasis on structural PS fit, group and organizational outcomes can be maximized when individuals with different attributes complement one another (Werbel & Gilliland, 1999). Similar ideas were proposed by Ployhart and Schneider (2002) in that the practices, tasks, skills, personalities, and other attributes necessary for effectiveness should be derived for different levels of analysis. In doing so, the analysis of the attributes of employees that are needed for effectiveness at the group or organizational level may signal that variability in different attributes would contribute to effectiveness, thereby producing a P profile of different attributes. This notion is depicted in Fig. 1–3 by the dashed arrow from structural PS fit to P profile at the higher level.

### Fit at Higher Levels

The fit process at the individual level of analysis results in the emergence of P attributes at a higher level that are either homogeneous or display a particular profile. These higher-level P attributes can then be compared to the situation-based E characteristics to create different modes of PS fit at the higher level or can produce person-based fit at the higher level. That is, at the higher level of analysis, these two categories of P attributes (P homogenous and P profile) can be crossed with the two situational domains of E attributes (social and structural) to produce seven different modes of fit at the higher level of analysis (see Fig. 1–3). Two of these modes of fit are based solely on person characteristics (Person Similarity PP and Person Compilation PP) and one is based solely on situational characteristics [SS (System) compilation]. The remaining four are based on various combinations of the higher-level collective P and situational-based E attributes.

The degree to which individuals are similar to one another represents a higher-level form of compositional PP fit and is depicted at the top left of Fig. 1–3 as Person Similarity fit. Person Similarity fit can be related to higher-level outcomes. A study of this nature requires an examination across multiple units and assumes that the degree of similarity (or its converse, the degree of dissimilarity) among individuals within the unit varies across units. Essentially, the index of fit here is simply the degree of similarity (variability) across individuals within the unit, and the extent of similarity can be related to outcomes of interest at the unit level. For example, the extent of similarity (variability) among team members on a particular personality construct has been related to team process variables (e.g., cohesion, conflict, and communication) and team performance (e.g., Barrick, Stewart, Neubert, & Mount, 1998; Ellis et al., 2003; Neuman et al. 1999). The degree of similarity in demographic characteristics among team members has been related to unit-level turnover rates (e.g., Jackson, 1991) and group norms and effectiveness (e.g., Chatman & Flynn, 2001). We also note that it would be possible to examine fit between group level P characteristics and organizational level P characteristics.

In Person Compilation fit at a higher level of analysis (top right of Fig. 1–3), variance in personal attributes across members is assumed, but the focus is on the particular configuration of these attributes. For example, individuals may have different personalities, but they combine together in such a way that they form a coherent and meaningful whole higher-level attribute when viewed together. Further, some individuals may contribute more to the collective than others (a difference in amount); yet, collectively the amounts that each person contributes allow for a cohesive whole (Kozlowski & Klein, 2000).

Only very recently have compilation models started gaining momentum in the literature (Kozlowski & Klein, 2000). For example, in understanding team processes, Kozlowski et al. (1999) argued that different types and amounts of knowledge across individuals in the team compiles into a specific configuration of team mental knowledge that contributes to team performance. In studies on the relationship between team personality, cognitive ability, and team outcomes, some evidence of a compilation notion can be seen when a maximum/minimum (e.g., the highest or lowest score for the group) has been examined, implying that it is not just variability alone but some form of a pattern of variability in attributes that is important (cf. Barrick et al., 1998; Neuman et al., 1999; Taggar & Neubert, 2004). At the organizational level of analysis, higher productivity was observed with a moderate level of gender heterogeneity among managers than with very homogeneous or very heterogeneous management groups (Richard, Barnett, Dwyer, & Chadwick, 2004).

To summarize, the theoretical assumption underlying Person Similarity fit at the higher level is that the degree of similarity or convergence in the characteristic represents fit at a higher level of analysis. Person Compilation fit at a higher level of analysis rests upon the notion that people vary in the amount and type of attributes they contribute to the unit but vary in such a way that the attributes complement one another. *Higher-*

*level Person Similarity fit pertains to the degree of convergence or similarity on the attribute among people, regardless of whether individuals within the unit are high or low on some continuum of the attribute. A particular configuration or pattern across the attributes of unit members defines Person Compilation fit at a higher level.*

In SS (System) Compilation fit at the higher level of analysis (middle of top row in Fig. 1–3), elements of the situational context complement or align with one another. For example, the sociotechnical approach to organizational design (e.g., Emery & Trist, 1960) focuses in part on the goodness of fit between the social and technical aspects of the organization. An example is the study by Ostroff and Schmitt (1993), in which different configurations of goals, climate, rules and regulations, and resource inputs were differentially related to effectiveness and efficiency in organizations. System fit can be more generally applied to connote the fact that different features or dimensions at some level in the system (e.g., organization or group) must be aligned in a way that results in a complement or a whole. System fit at the group level is alluded to in discussions of linkages among constructs such as group level task characteristics, work structure, team norms, communication structure, and team competencies (Cannon-Bowers et al., 1995; Hollenbeck et al., 2002; Marks, Mathieu, & Zaccaro, 2001). Team performance has been described as a result of an adaptive network of linkages among tasks, roles, and goals (Kozlowski et al., 1999). System fit can also focus on subelements within a particular environmental or contextual domain. The notion that various HR practices must be aligned with another to create a meaningful HRM system is an example of this (see Gerhart, chap. 10, this volume; Ostroff & Bowen, 2000). Further, system fit can be viewed from a cross-level perspective such as in the alignment between the structure of the organization and the structure of groups. *Thus, SS (System) Compilation fit represents alignment among various situational and contextual elements at a higher level of analysis.*

Different combinations of higher-level P and S factors produce compositionally based or compilation-based PS fit at higher levels of analysis. Compositional Social PS and Compositional Structural PS fit rest on the assumption that individuals within the unit are similar and that their collective and homogeneous P attribute fits or is congruent with either the social or structural situational environment (S). Here, the issue becomes one of assessing the degree to which individuals' attributes in some aggregate form fit with the analogous unit level situational variable. For example, Ostroff (1993a) compared aggregated personality dimensions to commensurate dimensions of organization climate and related the degree of aggregate level fit to organizational level outcomes. This represents Compositional Social PS fit at the organizational level of analysis. Similar ideas are inherent in Compositional Structural PS fit at the higher level. The general notion is that the collective personal attributes are appropriate for or fit with contextual characteristics of the system. For example, in a sample of college students, Stern (1970) matched aggregated need dimensions of students with aggregated and commensurate dimensions of environmental press. Muchinsky and Monahan (1987) provided an example whereby a fit between leaders' styles and the structure of the leadership system in their group would result in more positive group-level outcomes such as satisfaction. Likewise, the notion of shared cognitions and shared mental models of tasks has been gaining momentum, suggesting that the degree to which members of a team share similar models of the work process that are appropriate for the team structure, more positive team outcomes will result (e.g., Ellis et al., 2003). *Compositional models of social PS and structural PS at higher levels of analysis depict fit between a collective, homogeneous P attribute and a commensurate attribute of the social or structural situational environment.*

An alternative view is that individuals' attributes, needs, or abilities within the group, job category, or organization are heterogeneous and form a specific configuration or profile. That is, the P factor at the higher level is based on the notion of compilation. Compilation Structural PS fit is achieved when the different attributes of individuals fit together in such a way that the requirements of the unit are met. In other words, the particular profile of the P characteristics among members of the unit fits the structural environment. For example, the various personalities and skills of group members complement one another in a way that is appropriate for the group's task (Werbel & Gilliland, 1999). In Compilation Social PS fit at higher level of analysis, a similar notion applies. The particular profile of individuals' attributes is aligned with the social aspects of the environment. For example, Schneider et al. (2000) have argued that whereas congruence between individuals' characteristics (e.g., personality, values, or goals) and the climate, culture, and goals of the organization may result in more positive attitudinal responses at the individual level of analysis, the similarity in personal characteristics (what we refer to as P similarity fit at higher levels) that results from this type of fit can lead to stultification, lack of innovation, and a narrowing of perspectives that can ultimately be detrimental to organizational effectiveness and survival. They proposed that for some dimensions, some degree of variability in personalities and values of employees may be important for the long-term success of the organization. This view implies that a particular profile of personality types across individuals may fit a particular type of organizational culture or climate. A similar idea was implied in Keller's (2001) study of functional diversity. Teams comprising individuals from different functional areas were found to deliver higher quality and faster performance, but only in the presence of other team components such as external communication mechanisms. *Overall, compilation-based models of PS fit at the higher level of analysis refer to fit between a particular profile or configuration of P charac-*

*teristics among members of the unit that are aligned with the social or structural situational environment.*

## Summary

Compositional models rest on some degree of similarity between P and E, whereas compilation models rest on particular configurations or profiles of elements that complement one another. As can be seen in Fig. 1–3, a number of different composition and compilation models are produced by various combinations of P and E factors across different levels of analysis. Taken together, however, we argue that there is essentially a continuum of fit ranging from pure supplementary to pure complementary views of fit. Pure supplementary fit (based on Muchinsky & Monahan, 1987) is evidenced in compositional PP fit at the individual level, whereas pure complementary fit is evidenced in PP compilation and PS compilation at higher levels of analysis. As one moves from left to right in Fig. 1–3, the modes of fit produce a continuum ranging from supplementary to complementary notions of fit.

One issue that we have not yet addressed is the functional form of fit. By functional form, we are referring to the joint relationship between the P and E factors and how they operate together in their relationship to outcomes (Edwards, 1991; Kristof-Brown & Stevens, 2001). Early conceptualizations of fit tended to make the assumption that agreement results in higher outcomes than a lack of agreement. In supplementary and compositional modes of fit, the assumption was often that that when both the person and environment variables match, regardless of whether they match at a high or a low level (e.g., when both P and E are high or when both P and E are low) outcomes will be higher than when P and E do not match. Yet, there is no reason to expect that attitudes such as job satisfaction would be just as high when both individual and organizational values are high compared to when they are both low. Because intraindividual differences in values exist and the importance of different values varies, depending on the situation (Stackman, Pindar, & Conner, 2000), congruence should have stronger relationships to work attitudes for values that are deemed important than for values that are not viewed as very important. Thus, one component of the functional form that fit researchers need to consider in their theories (in supplementary and compositional fit) is the slope on the line of agreement (e.g., Is the same level of outcome expected when both P and E factors are high as when both P and E factors are low?).

A second component in considering the functional form of fit deals with incongruence. When people are incongruent with the environment, a symmetric relationship may exist such that outcomes will be equally low when P is greater than E compared to when E is greater than P. Alternatively, an asymmetric relationship may exist depending on whether the individual's characteristic is greater than the organization's characteristic or vice versa. A variety of potential functional forms of congruence that are relevant for compositional modes of fit have been delineated, and we have highlighted only a few of the possible alternatives. For a more complete review, we refer readers to Edwards (1991, 1994; Edwards & Shipp, chap. 7, this volume) and Kulka (1979). Note, however, that when a single, subjective measure of fit is used (i.e., individuals report a global, single assessment of the degree to which they fit), the full range of functional forms cannot be theorized because the P and E factors are not assessed separately (Edwards, Cable, Williamson, Lambert, & Shipp, 2006). In this case, the assumption is that individuals implicitly weigh the factors that are important to them to form an overall perception of fit, and in turn, a greater degree of fit will be related to more positive outcomes.

The above notions about the functional form of fit apply primarily to supplemental modes of fit and compositional modes of PS fit. Researchers also need to theorize about the appropriate form of functional fit in compilation models of fit. A number of data-combination techniques can be used to represent compilation notions, such as the minimum or maximum, indices of variation, profiles, and cluster analysis (see chaps. 11 and 12, this volume). Different techniques imply different theoretical relationships. For example, assessing the maximum or minimum (e.g., the highest- or lowest-scoring person in the group) assumes that a single member can drive or substantially influence the group outcome, and the theoretical rationales for why this is likely must be delineated. A cluster analysis technique assumes that there is a profile or set of profiles that maximize outcomes, and theorizing about what the "ideal" profiles might look like is important. Similarly, testing for nonlinearlity (e.g., a U-shaped curve in the amount of racial diversity in the group) in relationship to outcomes assumes that the best compilation of some attribute might be at some more moderate level. In recent years, researchers have been paying more attention to the theoretical form of the relationship between fit and outcomes for both compositional and compilation modes of fit (e.g., Dabos & Rousseau, 2004; Richard et al., 2004; Van Vianen, 2000; Kristof-Brown & Stevens, 2001), and we hope this trend will continue.

## IMPLICATIONS OF A MULTILEVEL FIT PERSPECTIVE

Thus far, we have argued that fit encompasses different modes that reflect comparisons between the characteristics of people (i.e., PP composition and PP compilation), comparisons between characteristics of individuals and characteristics of the situation (i.e., social PS and structural PS), and comparisons among the characteristics of situations (i.e., SS or system fit). Further, these fit modes can be examined with respect to a particular level of analysis, resulting in different subtypes of fit, such as fit to the supervisor (PI), job (PJ), group (PG), and organization (PO) as well as fit at a different level of analysis (e.g., outcomes investigated at the individual, group, or organizational level). To this point, we have treated these different modes and subtypes of fit independently. We believe that simultaneous consideration of multiple modes and types of fit will further advance fit theory and research.

## Top-Down Processes in Fit

Lower levels are successively embedded in higher levels of an organizational system (Roberts et al., 1978). For example, individuals comprise groups or units, which in turn comprise organizations. Top-down processes involve the influence of higher-level constructs and contextual factors on lower-level constructs (Kozlowski & Klein, 2000). There are a number of ways that the principle of top-down processes can be applied to understanding fit in organizations.

First, SS (system) fit can influence lower-level outcomes. Numerous authors have addressed the importance of alignment among various elements of the organizational systems, for example, between organizational culture and actual organizational practices (Dennison, 1990), among strategy, structure, HR systems, climate and collective attributes of employees (Ostroff et al., 2003), or among the various HR practices that encompass the HRM system (e.g., Wright & McMahan, 1992). SS fit can be viewed as a higher-level contextual variable of the group or organizational system that, in and of itself, has a direct effect on the behavior of individual employees.

Individuals desire consistency in their environment and organizational life (e.g., Kelley, 1973; Siehl, 1985). Inconsistencies in the signals and messages sent to employees about what is expected and valued in the organization are likely when the elements of the system are not in alignment (Bowen & Ostroff, 2004). For example, inconsistencies in espoused values and inferred values (Martin & Siehl, 1983) occur when what senior management says are the organization's goals and values differs from what employees conclude are actually the organization's goals and values. This lack of consistency can lead to intense cognitive dissonance (Siehl, 1985) and other negative perceptions and attitudes for individuals.

Furthermore, the degree to which stimuli in different situations are similar allows for a greater degree of consistency in individuals' responses across these situations (Mischel, 1968). If each employee encounter with an element of the organizational system (e.g., culture, hiring practices, work design, and structure) is conceptualized as a separate situation, then the functional similarity of these situational stimuli will influence the generalizability of individual responses across situations. For example, if team-oriented and customer-service behaviors are desired in the organization, then the extent to which each element of the organizational system signals that these are the desired and rewarded behaviors will influence an individual's behavior to be more stable and consistent. Rousseau (2000) notes that "the term congruence means that the capacities of various components match in a way that promotes effective higher-level processing and sustained lower-level performance . . . producing a whole whose capacities are more than the sum of the parts" (p. 578). This statement implies that higher-level system fit is necessary for organizational functioning, and it influences individual-level outcomes.

Second, other modes of fit at higher levels of analysis are likely to influence individual responses. For example, at higher levels of analysis, when individuals within a group or organization are similar to one another (person similarity), or when individuals converge in their attitudes, cognitions, and attributes, and these person factors fit the social or technical environment (composition social or structural PS fit), a strong situation is likely to have been formed (Ostroff et al., 2003). Strong situations induce individuals to construe the context and events the same way and induce uniform expectancies among individuals about the appropriate ways to behave and respond (Mischel, 1973). Thus, when fit at the group or organization level has been achieved, individuals are likely to view the context similarly and behave and respond in similar ways such that this higher-level fit has a direct impact on individuals' attitudes and responses. As an example, Hollenbeck et al. (2002) found that effects of fit on individual outcomes at a lower level (fit between the group context and the individuals' ability and personality) was influenced by the degree of system fit (fit between team structure and the task environment). These illustrations focus on how fit at a higher level of analysis can influence fit and outcomes at the individual level.

Third, we suggest that fit to different levels—the PI, PJ, PG, and PO subtypes of fit—hierarchically influence one another. Recall that fit to a level refers to fit between individuals' characteristics and the characteristics of another individual (dyadic fit), job, group, or organization. In recent years, a series of studies have supported the notion that people can differentiate between various types and modes of fit. For example, both employees and recruiters were able to distinguish between PJ and PO fit (Kristof-Brown, 2000; Lauver & Kristof-Brown, 2001). Cable and DeRue (2002) found that employees differentiate between PO fit (congruence or similarity between personal values and cultural values in organizations, a form of social PS fit in our model), needs–supply fit (needs are met by organizational rewards, a form of structural PS fit in our model), and ability–demand fit (employees skills meet the requirements and demands of the job, a form of Structural-PS fit in our model). Despite these promising findings, the nesting of hierarchical levels within organizations is not taken into account in these models.

The notion of bond strength indicates that levels closest to one another in the hierarchy are more strongly related to one another (Rousseau, 1985).

Units that are more proximal to one another or that exhibit greater inclusion (have a greater proportion of lower-level unit activities that are devoted to the higher level) should exhibit more meaningful relationships to one another than units that are further apart in the hierarchy or are only loosely coupled (Kozlowski & Klein, 2000). Supervisors, jobs, and groups are nested within organizations. For many of the attributes studied in fit, the extent to which that attribute is present in the organization as a whole is likely to constrain or impact the lower levels of analysis. For example, the values in the organization are likely to constrain or overlap with the values of the supervisor or the group because of the ASA process, cognitive processes, and interactions among employees. Hence, any type of fit to a lower level is likely to have some overlap or some components from fit to the higher level (e.g., fit with supervisor will be constrained to some degree by PG fit, which will be constrained to some degree by PO fit).

## Relative Importance of Modes and Types of Fit

Whereas fit constructs at higher levels of analysis are purported to influence fit constructs and outcomes at lower levels of analysis, simultaneous consideration of different modes and types of fit within a particular level is also important. In the following we briefly highlight the relative importance of different modes and types of fit.

### Multiple Fits at the Individual Level

A recent trend in fit research has been the simultaneous investigation of multiple types of fit at the individual level of analysis (e.g., Cable & DeRue, 2002; Cable & Edwards, 2004; Kristof-Brown et al., 2002; Lauver & Kristof-Brown, 2001). These studies are not only important for examining the relative and unique impact of different types of fit on particular outcomes but also for highlighting the notion that different types of fit are differentially related to outcomes. For example, independent of other types of fit (e.g., PJ fit), PO fit in terms of value congruence (social PS fit mode) was significantly related to job satisfaction, organizational identification, citizenship behaviors, and turnover. In contrast, PJ fit from an ability-demand perspective was not related to attitudinal variables or to task performance, whereas fit to the job in terms of a need–supply perspective was related to job and career satisfaction (cf. Cable & DeRue, 2002; Lauver & Kristof-Brown, 2001).

More complex relationships among the types of fit have also been investigated, suggesting that fit effects may be additive or interactive. That is, different types of fit may not necessarily be strongly related, but they may accumulate and their combination is likely to be important for work adjustment and other work responses (Dawis & Lofquist, 1984;

Meir & Melamed, 1986). To illustrate, an individual who experiences strong fit to both the organization and to his or her workgroup but poor fit to the job may be prompted to attempt a job change within the organization or obtain additional training or skills to enhance PJ fit. In contrast, an individual who experiences strong PO and PJ fit but poor PG fit may be motivated to seek transfers or relocations within the company, whereas an individual who experiences poor PO fit will be likely to attempt to change organizations (Ostroff, Shin, & Feinberg, 2002).

Kristof-Brown et al. (2002) examined the influence of different types of work experience on the relationship between different types of fit and satisfaction. Using a policy-capturing methodology, they found that the relationship between PO fit and satisfaction was stronger when individuals worked in a greater number of companies, whereas the relationships between PJ fit and satisfaction was stronger when individuals spent more time working in a single company. Further, a three-way interaction between PJ, PG, and PO fit indicated that higher fit across all domains was related to higher satisfaction for individuals with more organizational experience. Greater experience may lead to a more complex way of processing fit cues. These latter findings begin to suggest that different types and modes of fit may be more or less important to different individuals, depending on their background and personal attributes. For example, for individuals with strong relatedness needs, fit to the social–psychological domain of their immediate workgroup may be of utmost importance, whereas fit to the structural domain of the job may be less important. For another individual with strong self-actualization needs, fit to the job may predominate, whereas fit to the social aspects of the workgroup may be of lesser importance. This line of thinking suggests that not only do multiple types and modes of fit need to be considered simultaneously but also that more idiographic analyses that take into account the configuration across types of fit and that consider the differences in the importance of the mode or type of fit generally are needed.

### Multiple Fits at the Organizational Level

At higher levels of analysis, the relative importance of different types of fit to different outcomes has received little attention. In terms of SS (system) fit, the focus has largely been on determining combinations of system variables that are related to various effectiveness outcomes rather than in teasing out which configurations are more or less important for which outcomes or which types of fit at higher levels of analysis (e.g., SS, Person Compilation, PS) are relatively more important. Moreover, PE fit at higher levels of analysis (e.g., group or organizational outcomes) has been examined in very few studies, and most of those have focused on the degree of heterogeneity among individuals within the group in terms of personality or demographic variables, which we term *Person Similarity* fit in our model (e.g., Ellis et al., 2003; Harrison et al., 2002; Liao et al., 2004) as opposed to congruence or PS fit (Ostroff, 1993a; Vancouver, Millsap, & Peters, 1994, are exceptions). Yet, in different organizations, different modes of fit may be more or less important for achieving organizational outcomes. Considering the costs that are associated with achieving fit through HR policies and practices, decisions about which modes of PE fit should be established in an organization are an important issue. Thus, not fit in general, but an optimal combination of modes of fit becomes central for achieving high organizational outcomes. That is, among the seven modes of fit at higher levels of analysis, what is the optimal combination across them?

We propose that two factors largely determine this optimal combination. First, the importance of different modes of fit is contingent on organizational characteristics such as work design, culture, strategy, and size. For example, in an organization that structures work in a way that requires minimal levels of cooperation, congruence among coworkers (PP fit) may not be crucial for organizational outcomes. Similarly, an organization with a "weak" culture may not capitalize on the congruence of personal and organizational values (PS fit). Second, the effectiveness of multiple modes of fit is likely to be influenced by how they are interrelated and complement each other. From this second-order configural perspective, the combination of different modes of fit may create synergies that cannot be explained by the sum of their single effects. For example, an organization with teams that require an array of dissimilar abilities and skills (PP Compilation fit) may benefit from high levels of congruence in personalities and values (PP Compositional fit) because the combination of both types of fit may offset potential conflicts among coworkers resulting from their dissimilarities. More research is needed to better understand the relative importance of different types of fit for organizational outcomes and the interaction of multiple types of fit that may result in synergistic effects.

## Multiple Fits Across Levels of Analysis

Schneider et al. (1995, 1997, 2000) articulated a potential paradox of fit across levels of analysis. Specifically, fit in terms of homogeneity and similarity (PP composition and social PS fit) promotes individual satisfaction and adjustment. However, this type of fit also produces homogeneity in the characteristics of employees (Person Similarity in Fig. 1–3) and may be bad for the organization in terms of its long-term survivability and ability to adapt to changes in the external environment (Schneider, 1983). Homogeneity in organizational members is likely to lead to conformity in outlook and an inability to approach key issues from a diversity of perspectives that ultimately lessens the ability of the organization to solve problems, adapt, and change (Schneider et al., 1995).

The means for resolving this paradox focuses attention on good fit for whom and on what (Schneider et al., 1997, 2000). In terms of good fit for whom, similarity-based fit may be more important for lower-level employees than for top managers. Because top managers are largely responsible for strategic decision making and problem solving, they should possess a diverse set of values, competencies, and attributes. At the same time, employee fit on all factors or across all dimensions is not desirable because too much homogeneity in person characteristics will emerge, which in turn will narrow perspectives. Thus, Schneider et al. (2000) proposed a dual model of achieving both supplementary fit (Person Similarity fit in Fig. 1–3) and complementary fit (Person Compilation in Fig. 1–3) simultaneously. Essentially, they argued that supplementary fit on core values and goals is desirable. At the same time, complementary fit or differences in abilities such as problem solving and decision making is desirable such that each person has attributes that fit the organizational needs but individuals do not share these attributes.

The arrangement of moths in Fig 1–1 helps to illustrate how compositional fit (supplementary fit) and compilation fit (complementary fit) can be achieved simultaneously. The whole formation represents an organizational system that is comprised of moths (individuals), and each single moth has two characteristics that make it fit into the whole. The first is shape, and the entire system is composed of identically shaped individuals. Assuming that the shapes of the moths stand for core values among individuals in an organization, the organizational system is built on similarity in values across members, which may result in positive outcomes, especially at the individual level. Individuals with similar core values harmoniously fit to each other, and the process of adjustment to one another takes place more quickly. A moth (or individual) with a different shape (or set of core values) would not fit well, and the result could be less positive outcomes, such as a broken wing (or dissatisfaction).

The second characteristic of the moths is their shading. In this case, moths have different shades, and fit is not determined by similarity but rather by the pattern they form as a whole. For example, the right wings of all moths form circles of six moths each, representing a team. The dots on their right wings have different shades so that in each circle all five shades are present (with one shade being repeated). Each moth needs to have a differently shaded dot than those of its neighboring fellows, but the shade needs to complement the shades of the other wing dots in the circle. The different shades of the wing dots could stand for different skill sets or personalities within the team. Different skills or personalities need to complement one another to produce a whole from the parts and to allow individuals to work effectively with one another. In this case, the compilation of different attributes (shades) leads to positive outcomes at the higher (team) level.

Thus, different characteristics of the same individual can fit differently to the larger system such that both compositional fit (supplementary fit) and compilation fit (complementary fit) exist simultaneously. To yield overall positive results of fit, it is important that similarities and differences among the individuals be balanced, which should be based on their importance to the individual (e.g., similar core values and beliefs) and to the organization (e.g., various skills and personalities). Balancing supplementary fit that produces similarity relevant to individual outcomes with complementary fit that produces enough diversity in attributes that is necessary for organizational effectiveness may produce optimal combinations.

### Summary

Different types and modes of fit are relatively independent and differentially related to outcomes. At the same time, researchers are urged to consider how different combinations of types and modes of fit are differentially related to outcomes across levels of analysis. Whereas initial research suggests that fit effects may cumulate, this assumes a compensatory view such that strong fit in one area may compensate for weaker fit in others. Advances in systems fit have indicated the importance of equifinality whereby multiple configurations of attributes may be equally related to outcomes (e.g., Doty et al., 1993). This notion may be applicable to other types of fit as well. We propose that a more refined analysis, examining various combinations of fit, will produce equifinality in their relationship to outcomes.

### DYNAMIC PROCESSES AND CHANGES OVER TIME

Up to this point, we have treated fit as a static process. However, theories in vocational psychology have highlighted the fact that fit is a dynamic process that unfolds over time. For example, the fluid nature of fit is evident in Holland's (1997) theory, in which he emphasized the fact that individuals can change to suit the environment and the environment can change by changing its demands on those operating within it. According to the Theory of Work Adjustment, "both individuals and work environments are constantly changing. The continuous and dynamic process by which the individual seeks to achieve and maintain correspondence with the work environment is called work adjustment" (Dawis & Lofquist, 1984, p. 55).

In organizational psychology, Cable and Yu (chap. 5, this volume) highlight the role that recruitment and selection plays in the development of individuals' subjective assessments of fit. Kammeyer-Mueller (chap. 3, this volume) develops a process model to explain individual-level fit as a dynamic interplay between characteristics of the context, newcomers, and incumbents. Little attention has been devoted to explicating the dynamic process of fit at higher levels of analysis, with the exception of Schneider's ASA framework (e.g., Schneider, 1983, 1987a, 1987b; Schneider et al., 2000). In this framework, the founder makes decisions on the basis of his or her personality that ultimately shape the goals, management philosophy, strategy, structure, and culture that evolves. Potential employees are attracted to the founder and the organization he or she has created, and selection of employees by the founder is based on similarity to the founder. Over time, these hiring procedures ultimately become more formalized in the organization. Individuals choose organizations that fit their characteristics, and the organization tends to choose individuals who match the collective characteristics of current members and who fit the culture of the organization. However, some errors in terms of fit are made. Hence, individuals who do not fit well leave the organization. The result is that the people who remain constitute a more homogeneous group than those who were initially attracted to the organization.

The potential problem, however, is that although the consequences of good fit for individuals is positive, the consequences for the organization may be negative because too much homogeneity stifles flexibility and adaptability to environmental changes. Whereas Schneider's work clearly highlights how and why homogeneity is likely to result which may ultimately comprise the organization's ability to survive, other theories of PE fit (e.g., Dawis & Lofquist, 1984; Holland, 1997) indicate that both P and E are likely to change over time through an evolving process of adjustment. Theories from evolutionary biology and ecology are relevant for helping to understand both homogeneity and change or adaptation in the fit process.

We begin to extend some of the theorizing about the dynamic process of fit by incorporating concepts from evolutionary biology. Our primary purpose in this section is to stimulate thinking and provide some possible directions for future research and theory about how fit unfolds over time, rather than to fully develop a new theoretical model. Further, we note that some of the terms we use in this section, such as *evolving* and *developing* are based on the definitions and perspectives from evolutionary theory and often have different meaning when used to describe sociopsychological processes. As such, the theories and concepts from evolutionary biology are primarily used as metaphors to explain some of the possible dynamics of fit in organizations over time.

## Variability and Changes in Systems

Organizational processes have long been likened to biological systems, largely through open systems theory (Von Bertalanffy, 1972), which posits that biological organisms and social organizations are critically dependent on their external environments (Katz & Kahn, 1978). Basically, the organization inputs resources (e.g., people and equipment), transforms this input in the creation of a product or service, exports the product into the environment, and receives feedback that is used as the basis for determining new inputs. The ability to survive or at least to persist for long periods of time varies, depending on the organization's ability to change and adapt as the environment changes and adapts. Incorporation of notions from evolutionary biology can be used to further explain how homogeneity (similarity) or heterogeneity (diversity) among characteristics of employees within an organization emerges and influences organizational survival over time.

In biology, survival depends on the ability to adapt to environmental changes and contingencies. The concept of adaptation reflects the notion that species respond to the changing environment by evolving in form, function, or behavior in a way that is better suited to the new circumstance (Gould, 1980). Drawing on Darwin's theory of evolution, Gould (1980, 2002) explained that the adaptation function occurs through two complementary processes, with different forces being responsible for variation and direction. First, there is an intrinsic source of variability in living organisms through alleles (a form of gene responsible for hereditary variation). Direct impacts upon DNA (e.g., radiation or chemicals) in the biophysical environment, random mutations, and other changes at the DNA level that can occur during reproduction are transmitted to offspring, resulting in some degree of variation within a species (Gould, 2002; Lévêque & Mounolou, 2003). The variability that is produced is not directly oriented toward adaptations that may be necessary for environmental conditions. The process of selection provides direction. Resource limitations and changing conditions in the environment operate as mechanisms of selection. Selection works upon these unoriented random variations and changes a population by conferring greater reproductive success to more adaptive variants. The frequency of the variant grows over successive generations. Selection changes allele frequencies and through these changes phenotypes (the observable appearance of an organism resulting from the interaction of the genotype and the environment). The result of these two complementary processes is that variation is always present, but only some of the variants survive over time (Gould, 1980; Solé & Goodwin, 2000).

Evolution or changes in response to the environment can occur through two major modes: phyletic transformation and speciation (Gould, 2002). The core process of phyletic transformation rests upon the entire population changing from one state to another. This type of evolutionary process produces a transformation of one form into another but yields no increase in variability within the species. Individuals comprising the original state of the entity are fairly homogenous as are the individuals comprising the new form of the entity. Phyletic transformation should be rare (Gould, 1980). Large, stable central populations exert a homogenizing influence on individual organisms. New and favorable mutations are diluted by the sheer bulk of the population through which they must spread. Because of this, the variants build slowly and the changing environment usually cancels out the selective value of these the variants long before they can spread and reach fixation. As such, the current population remains largely homogenous and large-scale change from one homogenous state to another is unlikely to occur because there is little mechanism in the system for increasing diversity. That is, the homogenizing influence of the large population reduces the allele frequency or variability in genes that is required for the selection process to operate in effecting change. Without mechanisms for increasing diversity, the species would soon become extinct (Gould, 2002). The probability that the species possesses and is able to reproduce favorable genes is reduced. In such a case, when the environment changes, only by luck will some individuals possess the biological trait favorable for their survival (Lévêque & Mounolou, 2003).

There are several implications of the concept of phyletic transformation for examining fit and change in organizations. First, it supports Schneider's notion that too much homogeneity can be detrimental to the long-term survival of the organization. Second, it suggests that wholesale, concurrent change will not necessarily enhance long-term survival and adaptation. Current theory about large-scale transformational change can be likened to a phyletic type of transformation. That is, a transformational change is revolutionary whereby the core of the organization changes, all systems and elements change, and the involvement of all organizational members is required (Burke, 2002; Weick & Quinn, 1999). The change essentially occurs through a process similar to Lewin's (1958) notion of "unfreeze–movement–refreeze" (Burke, 2002). The end result is a new form of the organization in which members have adopted new ways of working, formed new interpersonal relationships, followed new policies and procedures, and developed new competencies (Bridges, 1996). Although this strategy may prove successful for a period of time, theories from evolutionary biology and biodiversity (Gould, 2002; Lévêque & Mounolou, 2003) suggest that this transformation from one state to another state may still be detrimental to long-term survival because there will still be insufficient variability and diversity within the organization that is necessary for responding to environmental forces and constraints. Hence, if the result of the transformational change process in the organization is a new form, but one that still comprises homogeneous individuals who fit this new form, long-term survival may be compromised. Groupthink, particularly among the top management team, is an example of the detrimental consequences of having a cohesive, homogenous group. Such a group will develop a singular mindset and will be unlikely to either recognize change forces in the environment or develop appropriate strategies for dealing with changes in the external environment (Schneider et al., 2000). That said, we should note that whereas phyletic transformation should be rare in the evolution of species (Gould, 2002), whole-scale change in form is often attempted in organizations. It may be that such transformation is less detrimental for long-term survival when the organizational environment is stable for long periods. In such a case, a continuous process of whole-scale change, without increasing the extent of variability or diversity among characteristics of employees within the organization, may be appropriate.

Speciation is the second major mode of evolution and essentially refers to replenishing and developing multiple new forms that branch from existing stock, some of which eventually die out (Gould, 2002). At its core, speciation implies that variability is present and is then subject to environmental selection forces. Before delving into the process of speciation and change, we first explain in more detail the two competing pressures of homogeneity and variability that exist simultaneously during the evolutionary process.

First, there are pressures for stasis and homogenization. As indicated earlier, a large and fairly stable population can exert a homogenizing influence (Gould, 1980). Similar or redundant forms that are adapted to the current environment are favored and become more frequent over time. Thus, selection can have a stabilizing rather than a diversifying influence (Gould, 2002). This stabilization and homogeneity can be necessary in a group of interacting entities to effectively deal with the current environment and reach a state of equilibrium and can be particularly important in social organizations in which individuals need to cooperate and interact with one another as they function in their current environment. If variability was very high, not only would discordance among individuals be high, limiting their ability to cooperate with each other, but there would also be an insufficient number of individuals with key attributes that are needed to enhance the ability to operate within the current context.

Further, through an evolutionary process known as adaptive radiation, different environmental niches in the same general system become populated by different subgroups who are descended from a common ancestor. In essence, *species flocks* (groups that are morphologically very close) are descended from a common ancestral species whose subpopulations have become progressively differentiated because of their specialization in the use of different resources provided by the environment. These flocks are better adapted to using the different local resources than the single ancestral species (Lévêque & Mounolou, 2003). The adaptations to the local environments allow the species to survive in the longer term. Such flocking is evident in social organizations whereby similar individuals group together to be more effective in their local environment or external market niche.

These notions suggest that there are forces to preserve some degree of homogeneity and that this homogeneity allows the species to effectively operate within the current local environment. However, as argued earlier (Gould, 1980), within-species variability is a necessary prerequisite for long-term survival of a group of interacting individuals, yet too much variability does not allow for a sufficient core of similarity to deal with the current environmental conditions. The implication is that an optimal level of variance must be maintained.

### Optimal Variance

The notion of maintaining optimal variability over time has been demonstrated in biological ecology models in theories of dynamic equilibrium (Lévêque & Mounolou, 2003). The basic tenets of the theory suggest that, in an ecosystem with a particular size and set of resources, there is a balance between the rate of immigration of new types or species and the rate of extinction of types or species over time. Similar theories are proposed among species belonging to a functional group, such that a relatively stable amount of variability in the species exists over time. A constant level of variability or biological diversity for a certain combination of environmental factors is not predicted, but rather, a pattern of fluctuations within a limited range is established that persists over time.

It appears that there is an optimal amount of variability that is necessary to strike a balance between having enough similarity to deal with the current environment and enough variability to adapt to changes in the environment when they occur. As such, we suggest that there is an optimal level of variance that must be maintained in organizations; too little or too much person similarity type of PE fit (resulting from homogeneous P) will produce long-term negative consequences for the organization. Moreover, a corollary of dynamic equilibrium and the notion of optimal variance is that the complexity of the environment is related to increased species richness (Lévêque & Mounolou, 2003). The size and resources in the environment have implications for the amount of diversity that can exist and that is necessary to maintain equilibrium. Thus, the optimal amount of variance among individuals in organizations that operate in more stable and less complex environments should be lower than that for organizations operating in complex, uncertain, and rapidly changing environments. Some indication of this notion is evident in studies of variability and diversity in top management teams. In a study of organizations operating in more volatile environments, a greater degree of variability in goals among the top management team was related to better organizational performance (Bourgeois, 1985). In firms with a strong risk-taking orientation (presumably operating in more uncertain environments), a moderate amount of gender diversity in the team was related to higher organizational productivity than in firms with either very homogeneous or heterogeneous teams. In firms with low risk taking (and presumably operating in more certain external environments), the amount of gender diversity in the team showed little relationship to productivity (Richard et al., 2004).

## Progressive and Sudden Changes

How does this variability operate over time to effect an adaptive change to the environment, and what are the implications for PE fit over time? Two different theories of speciation and the pace of change have been advanced. Evolutionary change can occur gradually and progressively or through sudden bursts followed by stasis. It is important to point out here that, from an evolutionary biology perspective, individuals do not evolve. Rather, genes mutate, individuals are selected, and species evolve such that evolutionary change occurs in a group of interacting individuals or organisms (Gould, 2002), hence, the requirement for variability within a group of interacting individuals.

A progressive and gradual perspective of change stems from Darwin's theory of natural selection as a historic process of successive accumulation of changes. Not only does the selection process gradually eliminate the unfit, but it also creates the fit by building adaptations in a series of steps. When conditions change, the gene combinations producing phenotypes that are best suited for responding to the new conditions in the environment are preserved and are selected in the course of successive generations (Gould, 2002). The conditions that produce variants can arise through the traditional means of random mutation or through the immigration of genetically different individuals into the environment that enriches the genetic diversity of population (Lévêque & Mounolou, 2003). More advanced models have demonstrated that species evolve by means of adaptive walks (Kauffman & Levin, 1987). Here, for any given mutation, if the resulting form produced by the configuration of genes produces a better fit to the environment than the last one, an adaptive walk occurs, and the species moves in the fitness landscape. Species continue this adaptive walk until they reach a local peak in the landscape. The movement of one species toward its local peak changes the landscape for other species in the system, which, in turn, can later impact the landscape for the focal species. Thus, species tune their own landscapes by readjusting their parameters (Solé & Goodwin, 2000).

In essence, the above notions suggest changes in both organisms and in environments that are reciprocally dependent (Lévêque & Mounolou, 2003). Theories from vocational psychology address the dynamic and reciprocal interactions between individuals and their occupations over time, the fundamentals of which are equally relevant to explaining a more gradual process of fit in organizations over time. Both Holland's (1997) theory of vocational choice and the theory or work adjustment (Dawis & Lofquist, 1984) propose that incongruent interactions between people and their environment are likely to stimulate different types of reactions. One response is analogous to the selection and adaptation process of evolution. Here, an incongruent individual changes or adapts to become more like the dominant people or attributes in the environment (which is more likely when the initial degree of fit is higher). Processes such as socialization and mentoring can also enhance adaptation of the individual to the organization (Chatman, 1991). Likewise, an organization can seek out new and more congruent individuals. A second type of response is similar to processes that occur in adaptive walks in changing landscapes and to biological ecology in which humans adapt the environment to suit themselves. Here, individuals can attempt to remake the environment to be more congruent with their attributes. Similarly, when a number of individuals are incongruent with the organizational E, a situation that can occur as new members enter the system, changes can occur in what is demanded of the individuals (which is more likely when the degree of initial congruence is higher). A final type of response is analogous to extinction—individuals leave the organizational environment when they do not fit, or incongruent individuals are rejected (or asked to leave) the organization (Holland, 1997). The flexibility of the individual in terms of individual differences in tolerance for incongruence as well as the degree of flexibility in the environment impacts the types of responses that are more or less likely as well as how quickly they will occur (Dawis & Lofquist, 1984). Nevertheless, the end result is a continual and gradual process of reciprocal changes in both P and organizational E to enhance fit and adjustment.

Another way that gradual change can occur is through the notion of hidden genetic diversity. According to Lévêque and Mounolou (2003), each organism is equipped with different ways of responding to an environment, but not all ways of responding manifest themselves systematically at the level of the individual. To an observer, two individuals may have the same phenotype or observable appearance and may appear identical despite their being genetically different (having a different string of alleles). Thus, there is a hidden reserve of genetic diversity that allows for the selection process to operate in response to an external change. For example, farmers, through selective breeding techniques, have progressively been able to extract new breeds of cows that were previously considered homogeneous.

The implication of this type of change for the study of fit in organizations is that some individuals are likely to have some hidden or suppressed attributes that are not immediately obvious but could be cultivated in times of needed change. Organizations use reinforcements to shape individuals' behavior and promote the stability of behavior in ways that are consistent with what is valued in an organization (Bretz & Judge, 1994; Holland, 1997). These different reinforcements can facilitate or inhibit the expression of different personalities, values, skills, and other attributes of the individual (Bretz & Judge, 1994). A change in the organizational E, such as a change in the reward system, could produce the emergence of previously inhibited attributes that are now necessary for adaptation to a change in the external environment of the organization. In fact, organizational E factors (e.g., organizational climate and reward systems) may be more important than person factors in fit because the supplies in E may change more frequently than personal needs (Cable & Edwards, 2004). Hence, as the organizational E changes, such as a change in a reward system, the previously suppressed attribute of P may be expressed, producing a new fit between P and E that is appropriate for the new external environment of the organization.

These notions also help explain how supplementary and complementary fit can exist simultaneously. Individuals possess a large number of genes, the large majority of which are identical across individuals at any given point of time. The number of alleles (forms of genes responsible for hereditary variation) within an individual is relatively small. The combination of genes results in a phenotype or the observable appearance of an organism resulting from the interaction of the genotype and the environment. The environment also intervenes over the course of an individual's life span by regulating the expression of genes and influencing behavior as well as trait plasticity (the capability of being shaped by the environment). Hence, individuals with different genetic make-ups (variability) can exhibit very similar phenotypes (Lévêque & Mounolou, 2003) or supplementary fit. They function as a unit and maintain stability over time (Gould, 2002). Later, when the environment changes, these previously unobserved differences may be expressed (Lévêque & Mounolou, 2003). At the same time, differences in behaviors and traits among individuals within a species exist because of their different combinations of genes and the way they interact with the environment. That is, within a species, there can be classes with "essential properties of appearance" or groups of organisms that exist side by side (Gould, 2002). An individual with different attributes can be concordant with others because they share a number of similar attributes, and the differences between them are not so fundamental as to cause serious discord (Gould, 1980). Hence, complementary fit, with variability among individuals, can be coupled with supplementary fit so that both factors for stability in the current state and forces for potential change in future states are present.

The types of more gradual change described earlier in achieving new fit between P and E are likely to be more relevant to transactional change processes in organizations. In transactional change, the change consists of incremental steps toward improvement in one specific area of the organization. In contrast to gradual change, evolutionary (and organizational) change can be more sudden and revolutionary (Lévêque & Mounolou, 2003; Solé & Goodwin, 2000)

Gould and Eldredge (1977; Gould, 2002) proposed that a smooth gradual progression is less likely than a process of sudden appearance and stasis. They developed and supported a theory of punctuated equilibrium to explain these cycles of sudden change followed by stasis. In essence, they argued that during most of their history, species change very little. Species remain static for periods of time because of the large central population and its homogenizing influence. However, certain events cause rapid speciation and punctuate this equilibrium. Change is resisted by the system until it reaches the breaking point that occurs after a slow accumulation of stressors. At this point, a large leap can occur in the system through either allopatric or sympatric speciation. Both allopatric and sympatric mechanisms indicate that new forms arise rapidly in very small populations. For the change to be manifested, small periphery groups must be isolated from the larger "parental stock." These small, concentrated groups that possess the variant coupled with rapid change are necessary because the individuals who are different are in potential contact with their forbearers and must move quickly toward reproductive isolation lest their variants be diluted by breeding with their parental forms. Extensions of this basic idea notion of contingencies and sudden revolution change have been applied to explain traffic patterns, economic and stock market performance, and the growth of urban populations, using chaos theory (Solé & Goodwin, 2000).

Two components of punctuated equilibrium theory are particularly intriguing in their application to transformational change and to resulting changes in PE fit in organizations. The first is that smaller, periphery groups that possess the variant must exist; otherwise, the new and more favorable variants will be diluted by the larger and more central population. The second is that the favorable variation must spread quickly. The first of these ideas implies that small, cohesive cores of "different" individuals must exist in an organization. Essentially, the implication is that "pockets of variability" are needed as opposed to evenly spread variability in personalities, values, attributes, and other characteristics across the organization. The pockets of variability within the larger organizational system could be naturally formed (e.g., similar individuals tend to cluster together) or individuals with the new needed P factor could potentially be brought together by management when the need for change is recognized.

In response to an environment change and a resulting need for change in the organization, the small group that possess the most appropriate P attributes for the new context should come to the forefront. The spread of these new attributes to others can take place through several mechanisms. For some biologists, the expression of a new phenotype manifests itself in a change in behavior. Imitation and learning facilitate the spread of and assimilation of the new form within the population involved (Gould, 2002; Lévêque & Mounolou, 2003). Emergent processes in organizations that create homogeneity can also explain how the new P factors can spread. For example, the creation of a coherent, strong, visible, and consistently administered set of practices can foster similarity (Bowen & Ostroff, 2004). Social communications and interaction patterns among individuals over time can result in jointly produced responses that form the basis for the emergence of a collective construct (Morgeson & Hofmann, 1999). Leaders can induce individuals to adjust their behaviors and responses to create a more homogenous group over time (Danesereau, Yammarino, & Kohles, 1999). And finally, the traditional ASA process can operate.

In the process of change, both the P and E components in the organization change. During a change or shift in the organization, the P and E components are likely to become decoupled. Constructs that exist at a particular level of analysis may shift in level over time (Dansereau et al., 1999). Entrainment (Ancona & Chong, 1997) implies that the linkages or the strength of linkages between variables changes over time through cycles. When two things are tightly linked, they are said to be entrained— that is, they "move" together or are correlated. When they are not entrained, the two processes are independent. Further, through pacing of processes over time, entrainment can tightly couple phenomena that are ordinarily loosely linked across levels or could decouple phenomena that had been tightly linked (Kozlowksi & Klein, 2000). From this perspective, we can assume that during periods of change and adaptation, P and E variables that were once closely coupled in an organization become decoupled. Some employees will possess or express the old P's that fit the E, whereas others will possess or express the new P's. Similarly, the E component, particularly the social–psychological domain (e.g., climate) that emerges from similarity in individuals' perceptions, cognitions, and attributes, will be in flux. Until the new policies, procedures, goals, and vision are established in the E, a period of disorientation and uncertainly among employees is likely (Burke, 2002). With the stability of the new E and spread of new P from the concentrated periphery groups, P and E will then become entrained once again. Ellis and Tsui (chap. 9, this volume) also use a biological perspective to highlight some additional processes and mechanisms pertaining to the advantages of heterogeneity and responses to homogeneity that can facilitate survival and fit.

## CONCLUSION

The concept of fit was introduced in psychology about a century ago. However, only in the past 15 years or so have we witnessed a rigorous and consistent exploration of the fit process in organizational domains. As fit research gains additional momentum in upcoming years, the development of a theoretical foundation that is broadly applicable across content domains and levels of analysis is necessary for expanding research and developing more powerful analytic tools.

In this chapter, we summarized concepts and processes pertaining to fit theories and levels of analysis. Our purposes were to review some of the conceptual foundations of fit perspectives in organizations, to integrate them with levels of analysis literature, and to elaborate a more comprehensive model of different types and modes of fit across levels of analysis. We hope the framework presented here will encourage researchers to consider a broad range of phenomena that occur in organizations as people and situations attempt to realize alignment or fit with one another.

In the remaining chapters in this book, authors have applied various theories and concepts of fit to different content domains (e.g., recruitment, leadership, and attitudes) and to different levels of analysis (e.g., teams and organizations). Further, two chapters address the complex methodological and statistical issues involved in the study of fit. Taken together, the set of chapters pushes the boundaries of previous explorations of fit and provides numerous implications of fit in understanding organizational phenomena. Our hope is that these works will stimulate a great deal of future theory and empirical investigations of fit from a broad range of perspectives.

## REFERENCES

Adkins, C. L., Ravlin, E. C., & Meglino, B. M. (1996). Value congruence between coworkers and its relationship to work outcomes. *Group and Organization Management, 21,* 439–460.

Adkins, C. L., Russell, C. R., & Werbel, J. D. (1994). Judgements of fit in the selection process: The role of work value congruence. *Personnel Psychology, 47,* 605–623.

Ancona, D., & Chong, C. (1997). Entrainment: Pace, cycle, and rhythm in organizational behavior. *Research in Organizational Behavior, 18,* 251–284.

Argyris, C. (1964*). Integrating the individual and the organization.* New York: Wiley.

Atwater, L., Ostroff, C., Yammarino, F., & Fleenor, J. (1998). Self-other agreement: Does it really matter? *Personnel Psychology, 51,* 577–598.

Barney, J. (1991). Firm resources and sustained competitive advantage. *Journal of Management, 17,* 99–120.

Barrick, M. R., Stewart, G. L. Neubert, M. J., & Mount, M. K. (1998). Relating member ability and personality to work-team processes and team effectiveness. *Journal of Applied Psychology, 83,* 377–391.

Bedeian, A. G. (1986). Contemporary challenges in the study of organizations. *Journal of Management, 12,* 185–201–.

Bowers, K. S. (1973). Situationism in psychology: An analysis and critique. *Psychological Bulletin, 80,* 307–336.

Bourgeois, L. J., III (1985). Strategic goals, perceived uncertainty, and economic performance in volatile environments. *Academy of Management Journal, 28,* 548–573.

Bowen, D. E., Ledford, G. E., & Nathan, B. R. (1991). Hiring for the organization, not the job. *Academy of Management Executive, 5,* 35–51–.

Bowen, D. E., & Ostroff, C. (2004). Understanding HRM-firm performance linkages: The role of the "strength" of the HRM system. *Academy of Management Review, 29*, 203–221.

Bretz, R. D., & Judge, T. A. (1994). Person-organization fit and the theory of work adjustment: Implications for satisfaction, tenure, and career success. *Journal of Vocational Behavior, 44*, 32–54.

Brief, A. P., & Aldag, R. J. (1981). The "self" in work organizations: A conceptual review. *Academy of Management Review, 6*, 75–88.

Bridges, W. (1986). Managing organizational transitions. *Organizational Dynamics, 15*, 24–33.

Burke, W. W. (2002). *Organization change: Theory and practice.* Thousand Oaks, CA: Sage Publications.

Byrne, D., & Nelson, D. (1965). Attraction as a linear function of proportion of reinforcements. *Journal of Personality and Social Psychology, 2*, 884–889.

Cable, D. M., & DeRue, D. S. (2002). The convergent and discriminant validity of subjective fit perceptions. *Journal of Applied Psychology, 87*, 875–884.

Cable, D. M., & Edwards, J. R. (2004). Complementary and supplementary fit: A theoretical and empirical investigation. *Journal of Applied Psychology, 89*, 822–834.

Cannon-Bowers, J. A., Tannenbaum, S. I., Salas, E., & Volpe, C. E. (1995). Defining competencies and establishing team training requirements. In R. A. Guzzo & E. Salas (Eds.), *Team effectiveness and decision making in organizations* (pp. 333–380). San Francisco: Jossey-Bass.

Caplan, R. D. (1987). Person-environment fit theory: Commensurate dimensions, time perspectives, and mechanisms. *Journal of Vocational Behavior, 31*, 248–267.

Chan, D. (1998). Functional relations among constructs in the same content domain at different levels of analysis: A typology of composition models. *Journal of Applied Psychology, 83*, 234–246.

Chatman, J. (1989). Improving interactional organizational research: A model of person-organization fit. *Academy of Management Review, 14*, 333–349.

Chatman, J. (1991). Matching people and organizations: Selection and socialization in public accounting firms. *Administrative Science Quarterly, 36*, 459–484.

Chatman, J. A., & Flynn, F. J. (2001). The influence of demographic heterogeneity on the emergence and consequences of cooperative norms in work teams. *Academy of Management Journal, 44*, 965–974.

Chatman, J. A., & O'Reilly, C. A. (2004). Asymmetric reactions to work group sex diversity among men and women. *Academy of Management Journal, 47*, 193–208.

Chattopadhyay, P., & George, E. (2001). Examining the effects of work externalization through the lens of social identity theory. *Journal of Applied Psychology, 86*, 781–788.

Christiansen, N., Villanova, P., & Mikulay, S. (1997). Political influence compatibility: Fitting the person to the climate. *Journal of Organizational Behavior, 18*, 709–730.

Dabos, B. E., & Rousseau, D. M. (2004). Mutuality and reciprocity in the psychological contracts of employees and employers. *Journal of Applied Psychology, 89*, 52–72.

Dansereau, F., Yammarino, F. J., & Kohles, J. C. (1999). Multiple levels of analysis from a longitudinal perspective: Some implications for theory building. *Academy of Management Review, 24*, 346–357.

Dawis, R. V., & Lofquist, L. H. (1984). *A theory of work adjustment.* Minneapolis, MN: University of Minnesota Press.

Dennison, D. R. (1990). *Corporate culture and organizational effectiveness.* New York: Wiley.

Doty, D. H., Glick, W. H., & Huber, G. P. (1993). Fit, equifinality, and organizational effectiveness: A test of two configurational theories. *Academy of Management Journal, 36,* 1196–1250.

Drazin, R., & Van de Ven, A. H. (1986). Alternative forms of fit in contingency theory. *Administrative Science Quarterly, 30,* 514–539.

Edwards, J. R. (1991). Person-job fit: A conceptual integration, literature review and methodological critique. *International Review of Industrial/Organizational Psychology, 6,* 283–357.

Edwards, J. R. (1994). The study of congruence in organizational behavior research: Critique and a proposed alternative. *Organizational Behavior and Human Decision Processes, 58,* 51–100.

Edwards, J. R. (1996). An examination of competing versions of the person–environment fit approach to stress. *Academy of Management Journal, 39,* 292–339.

Edwards, J. R., Cable, D. M., Williamson, I. O., Lambert, L. S., & Shipp, A. J. (2006). The phenomenology of fit: Linking the person and the environment to the subjective experience of person–environment fit. *Journal of Applied Psychology, 91,* 802–827.

Edwards, J. R., & Van Harrison, R. (1993). Job demands and worker health: Three-dimensional reexamination of the relationships between person–environment fit and strain. *Journal of Applied Psychology, 78,* 628–648.

Eisenhardt, K. (1989). Agency theory: An assessment and review. *Academy of Management Review, 14,* 57–74.

Ekkehammar, B. (1974). Interactionism in personality from a historical perspective. *Psychological Bulletin, 81,* 1026–1048.

Ellis, A. P. J., Hollenbeck, J. R., Ilgen, D. R., Porter, C. O. L. H., West, B. J., & Moon, H. (2003). Team learning: Collectively connecting the dots. *Journal of Applied Psychology, 88,* 821–835.

Emery, F. E., & Trist, E. L. (1960). Socio-technical systems. In C. W. Churchman & M. Verhulst (Eds.), *Management science models and techniques* (vol. 2, pp. 83–97). London: Pergamon.

Endler, N. S., & Magnusson, D. (1976). *Interactional psychology and personality.* New York: Hemisphere.

Erdogan, B., Kraimer, M. L., & Liden, R. C. (2004). Work value congruence and intrinsic career success: The compensatory roles of leader–member exchange and perceived organizational support. *Personnel Psychology, 57,* 305–332.

Ferris, G. R., Arthur, M. M., & Berkson, H. M. (1998). Toward a social context theory of the human resource management–organization effectiveness relationship. *Human Resource Management Review, 8,* 235–264.

Ferris, G. R., & Mitchell, T. R. (1987). The components of social influence and their importance for human resources research. *Research in Personnel and Human Resource Management, 5,* 103–128.

Ferris, G. R., Youngblood, S. A., & Yates, V. L. (1985). Personality, training performance, and withdrawal: A test of the person–group fit hypothesis for organizational newcomers. *Journal of Vocational Behavior, 27,* 377–388.

Festinger, L. (1994). A theory of social comparison processes. *Human Relations, 7,* 117–140.

Fisher, C. D. (1986). Organizational socialization: An integrative review. *Research in Personnel and Human Resource Management, 4*, 101–145.

French, J. P. R., Caplan, R. D., & Harrison, R. V. (1982). *The mechanisms of job stress and strain.* New York: Wiley.

Glomb, T. M., & Welsh, E. T. (2005). Can opposites attract? Personality heterogeneity in supervisor–subordinate dyads as a predictor of subordinate outcomes. *Journal of Applied Psychology, 90*, 749–757.

Goldstein, K. (1939). *The organism.* New York: American Book.

Gould, S. J. (1980). *The panda's thumb.* New York: W. W. Norton.

Gould, S. J. (2002). *The structure of evolutionary theory.* Cambridge, MA: Harvard University Press.

Gould, S. J., & Eldredge, N. (1977). Punctuated equilibria: The tempo and mode of evolution reconsidered. *Paleobiology, 3*, 115–151.

Graham, W. K. (1976). Commensurate characteristics of persons, groups, and organizations: Development of the trait ascription questionnaire. *Human Relations, 29*, 607–622.

Guzzo, R. A., & Dickson, M. W. (1996). Teams in organizations: Recent research on performance and effectiveness. *Annual Review of Psychology, 47*, 307–338.

Hannan, M. T., & Freeman, J. (1989). *Organizational ecology.* Cambridge, MA: Harvard University Press.

Harris, S. G., & Mossholder, K. W. (1996). The affective implications of perceived congruence with culture dimensions during organizational transformation. *Journal of Management, 22*, 527–547.

Harrison, D. A., Price, K. H., Gavin, J. H., & Florey, A. T. (2002). Time, teams, and task performance: Changing effects of surface- and deep-level diversity on group functioning. *Academy of Management Journal, 45*, 1029–1045.

Hogan, R., & Roberts, B. W. (2000). A socioanalytic perspective on person-environment interaction. In B. Walsh, K. H. Craik, & R. H. Price (Eds.), *Person–environment psychology: New directions and perspectives* (pp. 1–24). Mahwah, NJ: Lawrence Erlbaum Associates.

Holland, J. L. (1964). *Explorations of a theory of vocational choice.* Moravia, NY: Chronicle Guidance Professional Services.

Holland, J. L. (1997). *Making vocational choices: A theory of vocational personalities and work environments.* Odessa, FL: Psychological Assessment Resources.

Hollenbeck, J. R., Moon, H., Ellis, A. P. J., West, B. J., Ilgen, R. R., Sheppard, L., Porter, C. O. L. H., & Wagner, J. A., III. (2002). Structural contingency theory and individual differences: Examination of external and internal person-team fit. *Journal of Applied Psychology, 87*, 599–606.

Jackson, S., Brett, S., Sessa, V., Cooper, D., Julin, J., & Peyronnin, K. (1991). Some differences make a difference: Individual dissimilarity and group heterogeneity as correlates of recruitment, promotions, and turnover. *Journal of Applied Psychology, 76*, 675–689.

Judge, T. A., & Cable, D. M. (1997). Applicant personality, organizational culture, and organization attraction. *Personnel Psychology, 50*, 359–394.

Judge, T. A., & Ferris, G. R. (1992). The elusive criterion of fit in human resource staffing decisions. *Human Resource Planning, 15*, 47–67.

Kalliath, T. J., Bluedorn, A. C., & Strube, M. J. (1999). A test of value congruence effects. *Journal of Organizational Behavior, 20*, 1175–1198.

Kantor, J. R. (1926). *Principles of psychology* (Vol. 2). Bloomington, IN: Principia Press.

Kaplan, J. D. (1950). *Dialogues of Plato*. New York: Washington Square Press.

Katz, D., & Kahn, R. L. (1978). *The social psychology of organizations*. New York: Wiley.

Kauffman, S. A., & Levin, S. (1987). Towards a general theory of adaptive walks on rugged landscapes. *Journal of Theoretical Biology, 128,* 11–44.

Keller, R. T. (2001). Cross-functional project groups in research and new product development: Diversity, communications, job stress, and outcomes. *Academy of Management Journal, 44,* 547–555.

Kelley, H. H. (1973). The processes of causal attribution. *American Psychologist, 28,* 107–128.

Klein, K. J., Conn, A. B., Smith, D. B., & Sorra, J. S. (2001). Is everyone in agreement? An exploration of within-group agreement in employee perceptions of the work environment. *Journal of Applied Psychology, 86,* 3–16.

Kozlowski, S. W. J., Brown, K. G., Weissbein, D. A., Cannon-Bowers, J. A., & Salas, E. (2000). A multilevel approach to training effectiveness: Enhancing horizontal and vertical transfer. In K. J. Klein & S. W.J. Kozlowski (Eds.), *Multilevel theory, research and methods in organizations* (pp. 157–210). San Francisco: Jossey-Bass.

Kozlowski, S. W. J., Gully, S. M., Nason, E. R., & Smith, E. M. (1999). Developing adaptive teams: A theory of compilation and performance across levels and time. In D. R. Ilgen & E. D. Pulakos (Eds.), *The changing nature of work performance* (pp. 240–292). San Francisco: Jossey-Bass.

Kozlowski, S. W. J., & Klein, K. J. (2000). A multilevel approach to theory and research in organizations: Contextual, temporal and emergent processes. In K. J. Klein & S. W. J. Kozlowski (Eds.), *Multilevel theory, research and methods in organizations* (pp. 3–90). San Francisco: Jossey-Bass.

Kristof, A. L. (1996). Person–organization fit: An integrative review of its conceptualizations, measurement, and implications. *Personnel Psychology, 49,* 1–49.

Kristof-Brown, A. L. (2000). Perceived applicant fit: Distinguishing between recruiters' perceptions of person–job and person–organization fit. *Personnel Psychology, 53,* 643–671.

Kristof-Brown, A. L., & Stevens, C. K. (2001). Goal congruence in project teams: Does the fit between members' personal mastery and performance goals matter? *Journal of Applied Psychology, 86,* 1083–1095.

Kristof-Brown, A. L., Jansen, K., & Colbert, A. E. (2002). A policy-capturing study of the simultaneous effects of fit with jobs, groups and organizations. *Journal of Applied Psychology, 87,* 985–993.

Kristof-Brown, A. L., Zimmerman, R. D., & Johnson, E. C. (2005). Consequences of individuals' fit at work: A meta-analysis of person–job, person–organization, person–group, and person–supervisor fit. *Personnel Psychology, 58,* 281–342.

Kulka, R. A. (1979). Interaction as person-environment fit. In R. A. Kahle (Ed.), *New directions for methodology of behavioral science* (pp. 55–71). San Francisco: Jossey-Bass.

Lauver, K. L., & Kristof-Brown, A. (2001). Distinguishing between employees' perceptions of person–job and person–organization fit. *Journal of Vocational Behavior, 59,* 454–470.

Lévêque, C., & Mounolou, J. C. (2003). *Biodiversity*. Chichester, England. Wiley.

Lewin, K. A. (1935). *A dynamic theory of personality: Selected papers*. New York: McGraw-Hill.

Lewin, K. A. (1951). *Field theory in social science: Selected theoretical papers.* New York: Harper.

Lewin, K. A. (1958). Group decision and social change. In E. E. Maccoby, T. M. Newcomb, & E. L. Hartlery (Eds.), *Readings in social psychology* (pp. 197–211). New York: Holt, Rinehart & Winston.

Liao, H., Joshi, A., & Chuang, A. (2004). Sticking out like a sore thumb: Employee dissimilarity and deviance at work. *Personnel Psychology, 57,* 969–1000.

Lindell, M. K., & Brandt, C. J. (2000). Climate quality and climate consensus as mediators of the relationship between organizational antecedents and outcomes. *Journal of Applied Psychology, 85,* 331–348.

Likert, R. (1961). *New patterns of management.* New York: McGraw-Hill.

Likert, R. (1967). *The human organization.* New York: McGraw-Hill.

Locke, E. A. (1976). The nature and causes of job satisfaction. In M. D. Dunnette (Ed.), *Handbook of industrial and organizational psychology* (pp, 1297–1349). Chicago: Rand McNally.

Maruping, L. M., & Agarwal, R. (2004). Managing team interpersonal processes through technology: A task-technology fit perspective. *Journal of Applied Psychology, 89,* 975–990.

Marks, M. E., Mathieu, J. E., & Zaccaro, S. J. (2001). A temporally based framework and taxonomy of team processes. *Academy of Management Review, 26,* 356–376.

Martin, J., & Siehl, C. J. (1983). Organizational customer and counterculture: An uneasy symbiosis. *Organizational Dynamics, 12,* 52–64.

McGrath, J. E. (1976). Stress and behavior in organizations. In M. Dunnette (Ed.), *Handbook of industrial and organizational psychology* (pp. 1351–1395). Chicago: Rand McNally.

McGregor, D. (1960). *The human side of enterprise.* New York: McGraw-Hill.

Meglino, B. M., Ravlin, E. C., & Adkins, C. L. (1989). A work value approach to corporate culture: A field test of the value congruence process and its relationship to individual outcomes. *Journal of Applied Psychology, 74,* 424–432.

Meglino, B. M., Ravlin, E. C., & Adkins, C. L. (1992). The measurement of work value congruence: A field study comparison. *Journal of Management, 18,* 33–43.

Meir, E. I., & Melamed, S. (1986). The accumulation of person–environment congruence and well-being. *Journal of Occupational Behavior, 7,* 315–323.

Miles, R. E., & Snow, C. C. (1978). *Organization strategy, structure, and process.* New York: McGraw-Hill.

Miles, R. E., & Snow, C. C. (1984). Designing strategic human resource management systems. *Organizational Dynamics, 13,* 36–52.

Miles, R. E., & Snow, C. C. (1994). Fit, failure, and the hall of fame: How companies succeed or fail. New York: The Free Press.

Mischel, W. (1968). *Personality and assessment.* New York: Wiley.

Mischel, W. (1973). Toward a cognitive social learning conceptualization of personality. *Psychological Review, 80,* 252–283.

Morgeson, F. P., & Hofmann, D. A. (1999). The structure and function of collective constructs: Implications for multilevel research and application. *Academy of Management Review, 8,* 547–558.

Muchinsky, P. M., & Monahan, C. J. (1987). What is person–environment congruence? Supplementary versus complementary models of fit. *Journal of Vocational Behavior, 31,* 268–277.

Murray, H. A. (1938). *Explorations in personality*. New York: Oxford University Press.

Neuman, G. A., Wagner, S. H., & Christiansen, N. D. (1999). The relationship between work-team personality composition and the job performance of teams. *Group & Organizational Management, 24*, 28–45.

O'Reilly, C. A. (1977). Personality–job fit: Implications for individual attitudes and performance. *Organizational Behavior & Human Decision Processes, 18*, 36–46.

O'Reilly, C. A., & Chatman, J. A. (1986). Organization commitment and psychological attachment: The effects of compliance, identification and internalization on prosocial behavior. *Journal of Applied Psychology, 71*, 492–499.

O'Reilly, C. A., Chatman, J. A., & Caldwell, D. F. (1991). People and organizational culture: A profile comparison approach to assessing person–organization fit. *Academy of Management Journal, 34*, 487–516.

Ostroff, C. (1993a). Relationships between person–environment congruence and organizational effectiveness. *Group & Organization Management, 18*, 103–122.

Ostroff, C. (1993b). Climate and personal influences on individual behavior and attitudes in organizations. *Organizational Behavior and Human Decision Processes, 56*, 56–90.

Ostroff, C., & Bowen, D. E. (2000). Moving HR to a higher level: Human resource practices and organizational effectiveness. In K. J. Klein & S. W. J. Kozlowski (Eds.), *Multilevel theory, research, and methods in organizations* (pp. 211–266). San Francisco: Jossey-Bass.

Ostroff, C., Kinicki, A. J., & Tamkins, M. M. (2003). Organizational culture and climate. In W. C. Borman, D. R. Ilgen, & R. J. Klimoski (Eds.), *Handbook of Psychology* (Vol. 12, pp. 565–593). New York: Wiley.

Ostroff, C., & Schmitt, N. (1993). Configurations of organizational effectiveness and efficiency. *Academy of Management Journal, 36*, 1345–1361.

Ostroff, C., Shin, Y., & Feinberg, B. (2002). Skill acquisition and person–environment fit. In D. C. Feldman (Ed.), *Work careers: A developmental perspective* (pp. 63–90). San Francisco: Jossey-Bass.

Ostroff, C., Shin, Y., & Kinicki, A. J. (2005). Multiple perspectives of congruence: Relationships between value congruence and employee attitudes. *Journal of Organizational Behavior, 26*, 591–623.

Pennings, J. M. (1975). The relevance of the structural-contingency model of organizational effectiveness. *Administrative Science Quarterly, 20*, 393–410.

Pervin, L. A. (1967). A twenty college study of student × college interaction using TAPE. *Journal of Educational Psychology, 58*, 290–302.

Pervin, L. A. (1968). Performance and satisfaction as a function of individual–environment fit. *Psychological Bulletin, 69*, 56–68.

Pervin, L. A. (1987). Person–environment congruence in the light of person–situation controversy. *Journal of Vocational Behavior, 31*, 222–230.

Pervin, L. A. (1989). Persons, situations, interactions: The history of a controversy and a discussion of theoretical models. *Academy of Management Review, 14*, 350–360.

Pervin, L. A. (1992). Transversing the individual–environment landscape: A personal odyssey. In. W. B. Walsh, K. H. Craik, & R. H. Price (Eds.), *Person–environment psychology: Models and perspectives* (pp. 71–87). Mahwah, NJ: Lawrence Erlbaum Associates.

Pervin, L. A., & Rubin, D. B. (1967). Student dissatisfaction with college and the college dropout: A transactional approach. *Journal of Social Psychology, 72*, 285–295.

Pfeffer, J. (1997). *New directions for organization theory.* Oxford, England: Oxford University Press.

Pfeffer, J., & Salancik, G. R. (1978). *The external control of organizations.* New York: Harper & Row.

Ployhart, R. E., & Schnieder, B. (2002). A multi-level perspective on personnel selection: When will practice catch up? *Research in Multi-Level Issues, 1,* 165–178.

Reeve, C. L., & Hakel, M. D. (2000). Toward an understanding of adult intellectual development: Investigating within-individual convergence of interest and knowledge profiles. *Journal of Applied Psychology, 85,* 897–908.

Richard, O. C., Barnett, T., Dwyer, S., & Chadwick, K. (2004). Cultural diversity in management, firm performance, and the moderating role of entrepreneurial orientation dimensions. *Academy of Management Journal, 47,* 255–266.

Riordin, C. M. (2000). Relational demography with groups: Past developments, contradictions, and new directions. *Research in Personnel and Human Resource Management, 19,* 131–173.

Roberts, K. H., Hulin, C. L., & Rousseau, D. M. (1978). *Developing an interdisciplinary science of organizations.* San Francisco: Jossey-Bass.

Rousseau, D. M. (1985). Issues of level in organizational research: Multi-level and cross-level perspectives. *Research in Organizational Behavior, 7,* 1–37.

Rousseau, D. M. (2000). Multilevel competencies and missing linkages. In K. J. Klein & S. W. J. Kozlowski (Eds.), *Multilevel theory, research and methods in organizations* (pp. 572–582). San Francisco: Jossey-Bass.

Rynes, S. L., & Gerhart, B. (1990). Interviewer assessments of applicant "fit": An exploratory investigation. *Personnel Psychology, 43,* 13–35.

Sacco, J. M., & Schmitt, N. (2005). A dynamic multilevel model of demographic diversity and misfit effects. *Journal of Applied Psychology, 90,* 203–231

Schein, E. H. (1992). *Organizational culture and leadership: A dynamic view.* San Francisco: Jossey-Bass.

Schein, E. H. (2000). Sense and nonsense about culture and climate. In N. M. Ashkanasy, C. P. M. Wilderom, & M. F. Peterson (Eds.), *Handbook of organizational culture and climate* (pp. xxiii–xxx). Thousand Oaks, CA: Sage

Schneider, B. (1983). Interactional psychology and organizational behavior. *Research in Organizational Behavior, 5,* 1–31.

Schneider, B. (1987a). The people make the place. *Personnel Psychology, 40,* 437–454.

Schneider, B. (1987b). Environment = f(P,B): The road to a radical approach to the person-environment fit. *Journal of Vocational Behavior, 31,* 353–361.

Schneider, B., Goldstein, H. W., & Smith, D. B. (1995). The ASA framework: An update. *Personnel Psychology, 48,* 747–773.

Schneider, B., Kristof-Brown, A. L., Goldstein, H. W., & Smith, D. B. (1997). What is this thing called fit? In N. R. Anderson, & P. Herriott (Eds.), *International handbook of selection and appraisal* (pp. 393–412). London: Wiley.

Schneider, B., & Reichers, A. (1983). On the etiology of climates. *Personnel Psychology, 36,* 19–40.

Schneider, B., Salvaggio, A. N., & Subirats, M. (2002). Climate strength: A new direction for climate research. *Journal of Applied Psychology, 87,* 220–229.

Schneider, B., Smith, D. B., & Goldstein, H. W. (2000). Attraction-selection-attrition: Toward a person-environment psychology of organizations. In W. B. Walsh, K. H. Craik, & R. H. Price (Eds.), *Person–environment psychology* (pp. 61–86). Mahwah, NJ: Lawrence Erlbaum Associates.

Schneider, B., Smith, D. B., Taylor, S., & Fleenor, J. (1998). Personality and organizations: A test of the homogeneity of personality hypothesis. *Journal of Applied Psychology, 83,* 462–470.

Schuler, R. S., & Jackson, S. E. (1995). Understanding human resource management in the context of organizations and their environment. *Annual Review of Psychology, 46,* 237–264.

Scott, W. R. (1995). *Institutions and organizations.* London: Sage.

Shaw, J. D., & Gupta, N. (2004). Job complexity, performance and well-being: When does supplies–values fit matter? *Personnel Psychology, 57,* 847–879.

Siehl, C. J. (1985). After the founder: An opportunity to manage culture. In P. Frost, L. Moore, M. Louis, C. Lundberg, & J. Martin (Eds.), *Organizational culture.* Beverly Hills, CA: Sage.

Solé, R., & Goodwin, B. (2000). *Signs of life: How complexity pervades biology.* New York: Basic Books.

Spokane, A. R., Meir, E. I., & Catalano, M. (2000). Person–environment congruence and Holland's theory: A review and reconsideration. *Journal of Vocational Behavior, 57,* 137–187.

Stackman, R. W., Pinder, C. C., & Conner, P. E. (2000). Values lost: Redirecting research on values in the workplace. In N. M. Ashkanasy, C. P. M. Wilderom, & M. F. Peterson (Eds.), *Handbook of Organizational Culture & Climate* (pp. 37–55). Thousand Oaks, CA: Sage.

Staw, B. M., & Sutton, R. I. (1992). Macro organizational psychology. In J. K. Murnighan (Ed.), *Social psychology in organizations: Advances in theory and research.* Englewood Cliffs, NJ: Prentice-Hall.

Stern, G. G. (1970). *People in context: Measuring person–environment congruence in education and industry.* New York: Wiley.

Swann, W. B. Jr., Polzer, J. T., Seyle, D. C., & Ko, S. J. (2004). Finding value in diversity: Verification of personal and social self-views in diverse groups. *Academy of Management Review, 29,* 9–27.

Taggar, S., & Neubert, M. (2004). The impact of poor performers on team outcomes: An empirical examination of attribution theory. *Personnel Psychology, 57,* 935–968.

Tajfel, H., & Turner, J. C. (1985). The social identity theory of intergroup behavior. In S. Worchel & W. G. Austin (Eds.), *The social psychology of intergroup relations* (pp. 7–24). Chicago: Nelson-Hall.

Terborg, J. R. (1981). Interactional psychology and research on human behavior in organizations. *Academy of Management Review, 6,* 569–576.

Tinsley, H. E. A. (2000). The congruence myth: An analysis of the efficacy of the person-environment fit model. *Journal of Vocational Behavior, 56,* 147–179.

Tsui, A. S., Pearce, J. L., Porter, L. W., & Tripoli, A. M. (1997). Alternative approaches to employee–organization relationship: Does investment in employees pay off? *Academy of Management Journal, 40,* 1089–1121–

Tsui, A. S., Porter, L. W., & Egan, T. D. (2002). When both similarities and dissimilarities matter: Extending the concept of relational demography. *Human Relations, 55,* 899–929.

Üsdiken, B., & Leblebici, H. (2001). Organization theory. In N. Anderson, D. S. Ones, H. K. Sinangil, & C. Viswesvaran (Eds)., *Handbook of industrial, work & organizational psychology* (Vol. 2, pp. 377–397). London: Sage.

Vancouver, J. B., Millsap, R. E., & Peters, P. A. (1994). Multilevel analysis of organizational goal congruence. *Journal of Applied Psychology, 79*, 666–679.

Vancouver, J. B., & Schmitt, N. W. (1991). An exploratory examination of person-organization fit: Organizational goal congruence. *Personnel Psychology, 44*, 333–352.

Van Vianen, A. E. M. (2000). Person–organization fit: The match between newcomers' and recruiters' preferences for organizational cultures. *Personnel Psychology, 53*, 113–149.

Vecchio, R. P., & Bullis, R. C. (2001). Moderators of the influence of supervisor-subordinate similarity on subordinate outcomes. *Journal of Applied Psychology, 86*, 884–896.

Verquer, M. L., Beehr, T. A., & Wagner, S. H. (2003). A meta-analysis of relations between person–organization fit and work attitudes. *Journal of Vocational Behavior, 63*, 473–489.

Von Bertalanffy, L. (1972). The history and status of general systems theory. In G. J. Klir (Ed.), *Trends in general systems theory* (pp. 21–41). NY: Wiley.

Walsh, W. B., Craik, K. H., & Price, R. H. (2000). Person-environment psychology: A summary and commentary. In W. B. Walsh, K. H. Craik, & R. H. Price (Eds.), *Person–environment psychology: New directions and perspectives* (pp. 297–326). Mahwah, NJ: Lawrence Erlbaum Associates.

Wapner, S., & Demick, J. (2000). Person-in-environment psychology: A holistic, developmental, systems-oriented perspective. In B. Walsh, K. H. Craik, & R. H. Price (Eds), *Person–environment psychology: New directions and perspectives* (pp. 25–60). Mahwah, NJ: Lawrence Erlbaum Associates.

Weick, K. E., & Quinn, R. E. (1999). Organizational change and development, *Annual Review of Psychology, 50*, 361–386.

Werbel, J. D., & Johnson, D. J. (2001). The use of person–group fit for employment selection: A missing link in person–environment fit. *Human Resource Management, 40*, 227–240.

Werbel, J. D., & Gilliland, S. W. (1999). Person–environment fit in the selection process. *Research in Personnel and Human Resources Management, 17*, 209–243.

Wilk, S. L., & Sackett, P. R. (1996). Longitudinal analysis of ability–job complexity fit and job change. *Personnel Psychology, 49*, 937–967

Wright, P. M., & McMahan, G. C. (1992). Theoretical perspectives for strategic human resource management. *Journal of Management, 18*, 295–320.

Yuchtman, E., & Seashore, S. (1967). A system resource approach to organizational effectiveness. *American Journal of Sociology, 68*, 335–345.

# CHAPTER 2

# *Regulatory Fit:*
# *Its Nature and Consequences*

### E. Tory Higgins
*Columbia University*

### Antonio L. Freitas
*SUNY Stony Brook*

When two things fit with one another, they suit or agree with each other; they are in harmony. This captures the sense of "fit" as an adaptive regulatory process. When something is experienced as fitting, it feels correct, proper, or even just. This captures the sense of "fit" as an experience of feeling right about what is happening. Both of these senses of fit are critical to the conceptualization of fit proposed in *regulatory fit theory* (Higgins, 2000). In this chapter we review what is known currently about the nature and consequences of the kind of fit described in that theory.

## THE NATURE OF REGULATORY FIT

When people pursue a goal, they begin with some motivational orientation, they pursue the goal in some manner, and they experience or anticipate some desired outcomes from goal attainment. In traditional models, the manner of goal pursuit can matter because it is either a socially prescribed way to attain desired outcomes (e.g., value from procedural justice) or an effective way to do so (instrumental value). What matters is the relation between manner and outcomes. The relation between orientation and outcomes can also matter. For example, the outcome of a goal pursuit can vary in value depending on the relevance of the goal to fulfilling an individual's general orientation (see Higgins, 2002). In contrast to the relation between manner and outcomes and between orientation and outcomes, the relation between orientation and manner has received relatively little attention. But this relation also matters. In an earlier article (Higgins, 2000), one of us proposed that people experience regulatory fit when their goal orientation is sustained (vs. disrupted) by the manner in which they pursue the goal. Regulatory fit makes them "feel right" about and engage more strongly in what they are doing.

Individuals can pursue the same goal with different orientations and in different ways. Consider, for example, students in the same course who are working to attain an "A." With respect to their orientation toward attaining an A, some students can have a promotion focus, whereas others can have a prevention focus. A goal such as attaining an A is represented as a hope, an aspiration, or an accomplishment (an ideal) for individuals with a promotion focus but is represented as a duty, an obligation, or security (an ought) for individuals with a prevention focus (Higgins, 1997). With respect to their strategy for attaining an A, some students might read material beyond the assigned readings, which is an eager strategy, whereas others might be careful to fulfill all course requirements, which is a vigilant strategy. An eager strategy fits a promotion focus better than a prevention focus, whereas the reverse is true for a vigilant strategy (see Higgins, 1997, 2000).

Regulatory fit occurs when the manner of goal pursuit sustains (vs. disrupts) the orientation of the goal pursuer. It is notable that the term *sustains* has two separate meanings in the dictionary (e.g., Webster's Ninth New Collegiate Dictionary, 1989, p. 1189). One definition of sustain is "to hold up or prolong, to give support, sustenance, or nourishment." This first definition relates to the sense of fit as something that is adaptive by supplying what is needed to carry on. A second definition of sustain is "to allow or admit as valid, to confirm, to support as true, legal or just." This second definition relates to the sense of fit as feeling right about something.

To return to our example, for all students, receiving an A in the course has certain outcome benefits regardless of their orientation and strategies. Independent of this outcome value, however, there is additional value from regulatory fit. Pursuing an A in an eager manner sustains a promotion orientation (it "feels right"), but it disrupts a prevention orientation (it "feels wrong"). In contrast, pursuing an A in a vigilant manner sustains a prevention orientation (it "feels right"), but it disrupts a promotion orientation (it "feels wrong"). As we shall see, such fit (compared with nonfit) increases the intensity of motivational engagement, which in turn can enhance performance. This effect is clearly adaptive. In addition, when people engage in goal pursuit with strategies that sustain their orientation (e.g., promotion/eager vs. prevention/vigilant), they feel right about what they are doing. As we will see, feeling right from fit influences how people evaluate or commit to something. Fit (compared with nonfit) can increase the value of a chosen object, and it can transfer to moral judgments so that actions and decisions can be evaluated as more morally "right."

In this section, we will discuss in more detail the psychological nature of regulatory fit. Regulatory fit will be distinguished from other concepts and variables in three ways. First, regulatory fit will be distinguished from other fit concepts having to do with compatibility, concordance, relevance, and matching. Second, the value experience from regulatory fit will be distinguished from other kinds of value experiences, such as hedonic outcome experiences (pleasure or pain) and moral process experiences. Third, regulatory fit will be distinguished as a unique source of good–bad evaluations. Evidence will be presented that the fit experience contributes to good–bad evaluations independently of hedonic outcome experiences and mood.

## Regulatory Fit as a Distinct Type of Fit

The importance of hierarchical relations between actions and goals, whereby specific actions are valued to the extent that they support attaining more abstract goals, has been documented in a long history of research (e.g., Carver & Scheier, 1981; Miller, Galanter, & Pribram, 1960; Powers, 1973; Shah & Kruglanski, 2000; Vallacher & Wegner, 1987). In that research, *compatibility* refers to an action's instrumentality toward attaining a goal outcome. In distinguishing between (more concrete) *process* goals and (more abstract) *purpose* goals, for instance, people more highly value those process goals (e.g., making conversation) that are compatible with the attainment of their broader purpose goals (e.g., achieving interpersonal closeness; Harackiewicz & Sansone, 1991; Sansone & Harackiewicz, 1996; Tauer & Harackiewicz, 1999).

Attitudes research on "message-matching" similarly has shown that persuasive appeals couched in terms highly relevant to one's current needs and goals are most effective. Individuals particularly concerned with career advancement, for example, are particularly responsive to volunteerism appeals promising career-relevant opportunities (Clary, Snyder, Ridge, Miene, & Haugen, 1994). Moreover, recent message-matching work shows that matching the emotional implications of persuasive messages to participants' current moods increases agreement with the messages: importantly, this effect is mediated by the degree to which participants expect that the actions the messages describe will be instrumental in impacting the outcomes toward which the messages are focused (DeSteno, Petty, Rucker, Wegener, & Braverman, 2004). Although covering a wide array of phenomena and yielding important conceptual divergences, then, research on action–goal compatibility and research on message-matching converge in an important way. Both specifically identify relations between actions and outcomes as important sources of action value.

Quite consistent with the preceding findings on action–goal compatibility and message-matching, recent work on self-concordance demonstrates that the relevance of one's day-to-day actions to one's abstract aims increases action value (e.g., Sheldon & Elliot, 1999). Unique to the concordance research, however, is an emphasis on the contents of one's abstract aims. In an application of Deci and Ryan's (1985) theory of intrinsic motivation, self-concordance research categorizes people's abstract goals in terms of their degree of self-determination, whereby presumably self-determined goals of gaining autonomy and competence are hypothesized to promote value experiences to a higher degree than presumably other-determined goals such has making money. Again, however, and most relevant to the current discussion, the relation of one's current actions to more abstract aims and outcomes is hypothesized to impact action value.

Regulatory fit theory, in contrast, concerns the manner in which a goal is pursued. Importantly, and as shown in empirical studies described later, the manner of goal pursuit can vary independently of instrumentality (i.e., effectiveness in yielding the desired outcomes). We believe that, beyond an action's instrumental relation to a valued outcome, the fit of its strategic manner with one's motivational orientation serves as an additional source of value.

## Regulatory Fit as a Distinct Type of Value Experience

What kind of value do people experience when they pursue goals? Consistent with the preceding discussions of outcome relevance and instrumentality, the classic answer has been in terms of outcomes or utility. People are motivated to pursue goals that produce positive outcomes. When making choices, for example, they want the alternative for which the mix of pleasant or painful outcomes is the most positive. The same outcome can have different subjective value to different people or to the same person at different times. Historically, the critical insight to account for such variability is that the psychological value of an outcome is not simply its objective value (for reviews, see Abelson & Levi, 1985; Ajzen, 1996; Dawes, 1998). One of the great contributions of decision science in the last quarter century has been to identify cognitive operations and representations that influence people's experience of outcome value (e.g., Kahneman & Tversky, 1979; for a review, see Thaler, 1999).

Goal pursuit, such as making a decision, has both outcome benefits and outcome costs. The means used to pursue goals can contribute to outcome benefits by, for instance, being enjoyable in themselves ("getting there is half the fun"). The means used can also contribute to outcome costs. For example, decision means can have high emotional costs (e.g., Janis & Mann, 1977) or high costs in cognitive effort or time (see, for example, Payne, Bettman, & Johnson, 1993; Simon, 1955, 1967). The benefits or costs of the means used to pursue a goal are outcomes of the goal pursuit process itself and are weighed along with the positive and negative consequences of goal attainment in some kind of costs-benefits analysis.

People's experiences of outcome benefits and outcome costs have received the most attention in the literature. This emphasis on outcomes is natural because they concern whether a decision is experienced as "worthwhile" or "worth it." It makes intuitive sense that the value of a decision is related to its worth because the decision science literature typically equates value with utility, and one sense of *utility* is "worth to some end" (Webster's Ninth Collegiate Dictionary, 1989, p. 1300). However, utility has another sense—"fitness for some purpose" (Webster's Ninth Collegiate Dictionary, 1989, p. 1300). The notion of value from regulatory fit concerns this additional sense of utility having to do with how a goal is pursued. In particular, we suggest that the central phenomenology underlying experiences of regulatory fit is, rather than a diffuse, global hedonic feeling of pleasure versus pain, a more particular sense of feeling right about what one is doing. Empirically supporting this prediction requires showing that fit effects on feeling right obtain even when controlling for global hedonic feelings of pleasure versus pain.

It is important to note, however, that value from regulatory fit is not the only value experience from the manner of goal pursuit that is independent of instrumentality. There is another such value experience from which regulatory fit must be distinguished—value from the use of proper means. It has been recognized for centuries that there is value from how a goal is pursued that is independent of the outcomes or consequences of the goal pursuit. This kind of value is captured in cultural maxims such as, "It is not enough to do good; one must do it the right way," "The ends do not justify the means," and "Never good through evil." These maxims distinguish between value from the outcomes of goal pursuit and value from pursuing goals with proper means (see Merton, 1957). The literature has shown that people value the fairness of decision procedures independent of their instrumentality (e.g., Thibaut & Walker, 1975; Tyler & Lind, 1992), and they value means that provide a justification for their decision (e.g., Pennington & Hastie, 1988; Tetlock, 1991; Tversky & Shafir, 1992).

Value from proper means occurs when the manner of goal pursuit agrees with established rules and normative principles. The value derives from the manner of pursuit being the right or proper way to attain outcomes according to established normative rules. In contrast, value from regulatory fit derives from the relation between the manner of goal pursuit and the current self-regulatory orientation of the person pursuing the goal. What matters for value from fit is not whether individuals pursue goal outcomes in a manner that agrees with established rules (value from proper means). Instead, what matters for value from fit is whether individuals' pursue a goal in a manner that sustains or fits their own current self-regulatory orientation (see Higgins, 2000, 2002).

## Regulatory Fit as a Distinct Source of Good–Bad Evaluations

The psychological literature and dictionary definitions provide two predominant answers to the question, "Where does value come from?"—value as shared beliefs about what means and end-states are desirable, and value as need satisfaction. What is remarkable about these answers is their neglect of value as experience (for a more detailed discussion of both what value is and where it comes from, see Higgins, 2006; in press). This is particularly curious given the general emphasis historically on the hedonic principle of motivation—the notion that people are motivated to approach pleasure and avoid pain. From the ancient Greeks, through 17th and 18th century British philosophers, to 20th century psychologists, this principle has dominated our understanding of people's motivation. But what is pleasure and pain if not subjective experiences? Moreover, success and failure to satisfy socialized standards or personal needs produce pleasure and pain experiences. It is reasonable to begin with the (noncontroversial) assumption that the value of activities, objects, and choices must include the pleasures and pains that people experience from them. However, these pleasure and pain feelings are not the only experiences that impart value to objects and activities. Specifically, regulatory fit theory assumes that there is more than one type of value experience.

When considering the value of an object, activity, or choice in terms of experience, the experience that has received the most attention historically has been the pleasures and pains of the outcomes associated with the object, activity, or choice. Perhaps the best known and highly developed model of pleasure and pain outcome experiences is Prospect Theory (Kahneman & Tversky, 1973), which describes differences in the intensity and form of pleasure experiences (in the domain of gains) and pain experiences (in the domain of losses). In decision making, people imagine the pleasures and pains they will experience from the outcomes of different choices. It has been argued that the ability to imagine one's experiences from future events is unique to humans (Taylor, Pham, Rivkin, & Armor, 1998). When deciding which of several actions to take, people are capable of envisioning not only the action outcomes but also the experiences associated with these outcomes (Kahneman & Snell, 1990; Schwarz, 2000; Taylor et al., 1998). How do people imagine what they would feel about making a particular choice? This was the central question asked in a recent article by Idson, Liberman, and Higgins (2004).

The most obvious answer to this question is that people anticipate the pleasure or pain of the outcomes that a particular choice will produce (e.g., Kahneman, Diener, & Schwarz, 1999). People should imagine feeling good about a choice if they expect its outcome will be pleasant, and they should imagine feeling bad about a choice if they expect its outcome to be painful. In addition to this hedonic nature of the outcome, Idson et al. (2004) proposed that people's feelings can also be affected by regulatory fit (Higgins, 2000), specifically, by whether or not the imagined prospective outcome sustains their current regulatory state. They proposed that when an anticipated future outcome sustains or fits a person's current regulatory state, the motivation to engage in the approach or avoidance process that would make that outcome happen (if desirable) or not happen (if undesirable) increases in intensity.

Idson et al. (2004) tested their proposal within the framework of regulatory focus theory (Higgins, 1997, 1998). Regulatory focus theory assumes that self-regulation operates differently when serving fundamentally different needs, such as the distinct survival needs of nurturance (e.g., nourishment) and security (e.g., protection). Differences in socialization can produce chronic individual differences in regulatory focus (see Higgins & Silberman, 1998). Nurturant parenting engenders a *promotion focus,* in which self-regulation is concerned with accomplishments, hopes, and aspirations (i.e., ideals). It involves the presence of positive outcomes (e.g., bolstering) and the absence of positive outcomes (e.g., love withdrawal). Security parenting engenders a *prevention focus,* in which self-regulation is concerned with safety, duties, and obligations (oughts). It involves the absence of negative outcomes (e.g., safeguarding) and the presence of negative outcomes (e.g., criticism).

Momentary situations are also capable of temporarily inducing either a promotion focus or a prevention focus. Just as the responses of caretakers to their children's actions communicate to the children about how to attain desired end-states, feedback from a boss to an employee or from a teacher to a student is a situation that can communicate gain/non-gain information (promotion-related outcomes) or non-loss/loss information (prevention-related outcomes). Task instructions that present task contingency or if-then rules concerning which actions produce which consequences can also communicate either gain/non-gain (promotion) or non-loss/loss (prevention) information. Thus, the concept of regulatory focus is broader than just socialization of strong promotion focus ideals or prevention focus oughts. Regulatory focus can also be induced temporarily in momentary situations.

Regulatory focus theory also distinguishes between different strategic means of goal attainment. It distinguishes between an *eager strategy* and a *vigilant strategy* (see Crowe & Higgins, 1997; Higgins, 1997, 1998). Because an eager strategy ensures the presence of positive outcomes (searching for means of advancement) and ensures against the absence of positive outcomes (do not close off possibilities), it fits promotion focus concerns with the presence and absence of positive outcomes (gains and non-gains). Similarly, because a vigilant strategy ensures the absence of negative outcomes (being careful) and ensures against the presence of negative outcomes (avoiding mistakes), it fits prevention focus concerns with the absence and presence of negative outcomes (non-losses and losses) (see Crowe & Higgins, 1997; Higgins, 1997).

Idson et al. (2004) suggested that, because of its effect on motivational intensity, regulatory fit makes anticipated positive feelings about a prospective positive outcome even more positive and anticipated negative feelings about a prospective negative outcome even more negative. They proposed that imagining making a desirable choice has higher regulatory fit for people in a promotion focus (because it maintains the eagerness that sustains their focus) than for people in a prevention focus (because it reduces the vigilance that sustains their focus). Therefore, people in a promotion focus, more than people in a prevention focus, should have a stronger motivation to approach, and thus should feel more intensely positive when anticipating a prospective desirable choice. In contrast, imagining making an undesirable choice has higher regulatory fit for people in a prevention focus (because it maintains the vigilance that sustains their focus) than for people in a promotion focus (because it reduces the eagerness that sustains their focus). Therefore, people in a prevention focus, more than people in a promotion focus, should have a stronger motivation to avoid, and thus should feel more intensely negative when anticipating a prospective undesirable choice.

To test these predictions, Idson et al. (2004) modified a well-known example from Thaler (1980). All participants were instructed to imagine that they were in a bookstore buying a book for their classes. There were different framing conditions. Participants in the promotion/discount framing conditions were then told: "The book's price is $65. As you wait in line to pay for it, you realize that the store offers a $5 discount for paying in cash. Of course you would like to pay $60 for the book. You have both cash and a credit card and have to choose between them." After reading the scenario, half of the participants answered a gain question (i.e., "How would it feel paying in cash and getting the $5 discount?"), and the other half answered a non-gain question (i.e., "How would it feel using your credit card and giving up the $5 discount?"). Participants in the prevention/penalty framing conditions were told instead: "The book's price is $60. As you wait in line to pay for it, you realize that the store charges a $5 penalty for paying in credit." Half of these participants answered a non-loss question (i.e., "How would it feel paying in cash and avoiding the $5 penalty?"), and half answered a loss question (i.e., "How would it feel using your credit card and paying the $5 penalty?"). All participants answered these questions on a scale that went from *feeling very bad* to *feeling very good*.

As one would expect, the participants felt good when they imagined the positive outcome of paying just $60 for the book, and they felt bad when they imagined the negative outcome of paying $65 for the book. This is the classic outcome valence effect. As predicted, however, there were also within-outcome valence effects. For the positive outcome, promotion focus participants felt better than did prevention focus participants. For the negative outcome, prevention focus participants felt worse than did promotion focus participants.

In a subsequent study, rather than inducing regulatory focus by framing the bookstore scenario as a discount (promotion) or penalty (prevention), regulatory focus was experimentally primed separately from the scenario itself. An unrelated-studies paradigm was used in which participants began the session by writing about either their personal hopes and aspirations (promotion priming) or their personal sense of duty and obligation (prevention priming). Then, in a scenario of planning to buy a book for a course, half of the participants in each priming condition were given either a positive outcome scenario (i.e., "Imagine that you go to the bookstore in a few days, and when you arrive, you find out that there are still copies of the book for sale. You won't have to go to other bookstores to look for it.") or a negative outcome scenario (i.e., "Imagine that you go there in a few days, but when you arrive, you find out that all the copies of the book are gone. You will have to go to other bookstores to look for it."). In addition to an outcome valence effect on feeling good or bad, this study also showed that participants felt better imagining a positive outcome in the promotion than the prevention priming condition and felt worse imagining a negative outcome in the prevention than the promotion priming condition.

These studies support the regulatory fit prediction that the same positive outcome will be experienced more intensely in a promotion focus (gain) than in a prevention focus (non-loss) and that the same negative outcome will be felt more intensely in a prevention focus (loss) than a promotion focus (non-gain) (see also Idson, Liberman, & Higgins, 2000). Idson et al. (2004) included additional measures to examine which value experiences underlay these good–bad feeling effects.

Both imagined pleasure–pain intensity and motivational intensity were measured, and the framing study and priming study used slightly different measures to provide convergent validity. The framing study used the following measure of pleasure–pain intensity: (a) positive outcome—How pleasant would it be get the discount (avoid the penalty)?; or (b) negative outcome—How painful would it be to give up the discount (pay the penalty)? The priming study used a slightly different measure of pleasure–pain intensity: (a) positive outcome—How pleasant would it be to find the book at the local bookstore; or (b) negative outcome—How painful would it be to not find the book at the local bookstore. The framing study used the following measure of motivational intensity: (a) positive outcome—Imagine paying in cash and getting the discount (avoiding the penalty). How motivated would you be to pay in cash?; or (b) negative outcome—Imagine using your credit card and not getting the discount (paying the penalty). How motivated would you be to pay in cash (*not* use your credit card)? Once again, the priming study used a slightly different measure of motivational intensity: (a) positive outcome—How motivated would you be to make this happen."; or (b) negative outcome—How motivated would you be to make this not happen."

Both the framing study and the priming study showed that the imagined pleasure–pain intensity experiences and the motivational intensity experiences accounted for different effects on feeling good or bad. Participants' ratings of their imagined pleasure–pain intensity experiences predicted the basic between-valence outcome effect of feeling better for a positive outcome than a negative outcome, whereas participants' ratings of their imagined motivational intensity did not predict the outcome valence effect (controlling for the pleasure–pain intensity measure). In contrast, participants' ratings of their imagined motivational intensity did predict the regulatory fit within-valence effect of feeling better about a positive outcome in promotion than prevention (feeling better about gain than about non-loss) and feeling worse about a negative outcome in prevention than promotion (feeling worse about loss than about non-gain), whereas imagined pleasure–pain intensity did not predict these effects (controlling for the motivational intensity measure). In sum, these results show that pleasure–pain intensity and strength of motivational force each made significant independent contributions to the perceived value of the imagined outcome (i.e., its goodness/badness).

The results of the Idson et al. (2004) studies clearly indicated that good–bad evaluations are not based on just pleasure–pain experiences. The experience of regulatory fit has an independent effect. There is other evidence for this conclusion that goes beyond the prospective evaluations of these studies. For example, in one set of studies by Higgins, Idson, Freitas, Spiegel, and Molden (2003), participants' chronic promotion and prevention orientations were measured, and then they were told that, over and above their usual payment for participating, they could choose between a coffee mug and a pen as a gift. (Pretesting had indicated that the mug was clearly preferred.) The means of making the decision was manipulated through framing. Half of the participants were told to think about what they would gain by choosing the mug or the pen (an *eager manner* of making the decision), and the other half were told to think about what they would lose by not choosing the mug or the pen (a *vigilant manner* of making the decision). Note that both eager and vigilant participants are directed to consider the positive qualities of the mug and the pen. As expected, almost all participants chose the coffee mug. These participants were then asked either to assess the price of the chosen mug or were given the opportunity to actually buy the mug. Participants in the fit conditions (promotion/eager vs. prevention/vigilant) gave a much higher price for the mug than participants in the non-fit conditions (40–60% higher).

In one of the studies of Higgins, Idson, et al. (2003), the participants' pleasure–pain mood was also measured around the same time as the price measure was collected. The mood items prompted participants to indicate how they felt currently with respect to each of several emotions, including happy, dejected (reverse scored), relaxed, tense (reverse scored), and content. These items were summed to form an index of positive mood. As predicted, Higgins, Idson, et al. (2003) found that the fit effect on price of the mug was independent of the participants' pleasure–pain mood.

Other studies using different paradigms and different dependent measures have also shown that fit effects are independent of pleasure–pain mood (e.g., Camacho, Higgins, & Lugar, 2003; Cesario, Grant, & Higgins, 2004). For example, in an attitude change study by Cesario et al. (2004), discussed more fully later, fit was induced before participants received a persuasive message by having them, ostensibly for a separate study, list either strategies for goal attainment that fit their personal goals (eager strategies/promotion goals vs. vigilant strategies/prevention goals) or did not fit (eager strategies/prevention goals vs. vigilant strategies/promotion goals). After reading the persuasive message, the participants were asked to rate how "happy," "pleased," "overjoyed," and "cheerful" they felt while reading the essay. The scores for these four items were combined to form an index of positive mood. Cesario et al. (2004) found that higher positive mood predicted both higher perceived message persuasiveness and greater message effectiveness in changing opinions in the advocated direction. At the same time, fit had an independent effect of increasing both perceived message persuasiveness and message effectiveness. Thus, regulatory fit and hedonic pleasure–pain mood each had independent effects on persuasion. This is further support for the conclusion that good–bad evaluations are not based solely on pleasure–pain experiences; regulatory fit experiences also play a role.

## THE CONSEQUENCES OF REGULATORY FIT

In the previous section we discussed the distinctive nature of regulatory fit. In this section we describe research on the consequences of this distinct kind of self-regulatory experience. Consequences for task performance, for judgments and decision making, and for attitude and behavior changes will be reviewed.

### Task Performance

The effects of regulatory fit on performance and value creation derive from fit increasing strength of engagement (see Higgins, 2005, 2006). The fit effects on performance reviewed in the following provide indirect evidence of fit increasing engagement strength, but there is also more direct evidence that I will briefly mention. In one set of studies, for example, Förster, Higgins, and Idson (1998) examined both chronic and situational instantiations of regulatory focus orientation. The participants performed an anagram task in either an eager or vigilant manner. Performance of the task in an eager versus vigilant manner was manipulated by using an arm pressure technique (Cacioppo, Priester, & Berntson, 1993). While performing the anagram task, the participants either pressed downward on the plate of a supposed skin conductance machine that was attached to the top of the table (a vigilance/avoidance-related movement of pushing away from oneself) or pressed upward on the plate attached to the bottom of the table (an eagerness/approach-related movement of pulling toward oneself). Participants' arm pressures while pressing downward or upward on the plate was recorded and served as the measure of engagement strength. On a measure of overall on-line arm pressure during task performance, strength of engagement was stronger when there was regulatory fit (i.e., promotion/eager vs. prevention/vigilant) than non-fit (i.e., promotion/vigilant vs prevention/eager). In another study Förster et al. (1998) used persistence as the measure of strength of engagement and found that persistence was greater when there was fit than when there was non-fit.

Using a paradigm similar to the Förster et al. (1998) arm pressure studies that also experimentally controlled for participants' outcome expectancies during task performance, Förster, Grant, Idson, and Higgins (2001) replicated another Förster et al. (1998) finding: On a measure of the steepness of the arm pressure gradients (calculated over the recorded arm pressure values from the beginning to the end of the set of anagrams), the approach gradient (the recorded upward pressure values when the plate was attached to the bottom of the table) was steeper for participants in a promotion than a prevention focus. In contrast, the avoidance gradient (the recorded downward pressure values when the plate was attached to the top of the table) was steeper for participants in a prevention than in a promotion focus. Förster et al. (2001) also replicated the fit effect on persistence found by Förster et al. (1998). Importantly, the fit effects found by Förster et al. (2001) and by Förster et al. (1998) were independent of participants' positive or negative feelings during the task performance. Additional evidence that regulatory fit increases strength of engagement is provided by the Idson et al. (2004) finding described earlier: that participants in the regulatory fit conditions reported higher motivational intensity than participants in the non-fit conditions.

Task performance can be enhanced in different ways through regulatory fit. One way is for fit to increase the strength of the motivational engagement in an activity or task. In studies on anagram performance by Shah, Higgins, and Friedman (1998), for example, participants' regulatory focus varied either chronically or through experimental induction and either an eager or vigilant manner was manipulated by designating particular anagrams in vigilance terms (avoid losing payment by solving) or eagerness terms (gain payment by solving). As predicted, anagram performance was better when there was regulatory fit (i.e., promotion focus/eager strategy vs. prevention focus/vigilant strategy) than non-fit. Förster et al. (1998) also found that anagram performance was better when there was regulatory fit (i.e., promotion focus/eager strategy vs. prevention focus/vigilant strategy) than non-fit. Finally, Freitas, Liberman, and Higgins (2002) found that prevention focus participants did better than promotion focus participants on a task that required vigilance against a tempting distractor.

Investigating another way in which regulatory fit can enhance performance, Bianco, Higgins, and Klem (2003) examined how performance is affected by the fit between people's implicit theories of a given task being either fun or important and task instructions to engage that task in either a fun or important way. On tasks of predictive learning, paired-associate learning, and free recall of movie scenes, they found that performance was enhanced when there was a fit (vs. a non-fit) between participants' implicit theories and task instructions regarding the fun and importance of the task. Interestingly, in one study in which participants' implicit theory of the academic activity was that it was important but not fun, instructing participants that doing the task would be high in both importance and fun (a non-fit) actually undermined performance compared with high importance/low fun instructions (a fit).

There is yet another way that regulatory fit can influence performance. Previous researchers have suggested that the mental simulation of steps needed to implement goal completion facilitates goal achievement (e.g., Gollwitzer, 1996). Given promotion-focused people's tactical preference for eagerly approaching matches to desired end-states, rather than vigilantly avoiding mismatches to desired end-states, Spiegel, Grant-Pillow, and Higgins (2004) predicted that promotion-focused people would perform better at a task if they prepared by eagerly simulating and developing approach-oriented plans rather than avoidance-oriented plans, and the reverse would be true for prevention-focused people. In one study, participants were asked to write a report on how they would spend their upcoming Saturday and to turn it in by a certain deadline to receive a cash payment. Before they left the laboratory, all participants were asked to imagine certain implementation steps that they might take in writing the report (i.e., simulations related to when, where, and how to do the report), and the steps were framed to represent either eager approach means or vigilant avoidance means. Spiegel et al. (2004) found that participants in the fit conditions were almost 50% more likely to turn in their reports than participants in the non-fit conditions.

### Judgment and Decision Making

The mug studies by Higgins, Idson, et al. (2003) described earlier demonstrate that regulatory fit can influence the monetary value of a chosen object. In these studies, it was the fit between promotion and prevention orientations and eager versus vigilant strategies that yielded the fit effect. This fit effect on decision value is not restricted to regulatory focus variables, however. Avnet and Higgins (2003), for example, experimentally induced either a locomotion orientation, which constitutes the aspect of self-regulation that is concerned with movement from state to state, or an assessment orientation, which constitutes the aspect of self-regulation that is concerned with making comparisons (Higgins, Kruglanski, & Pierro, 2003). The participants chose a book-light from among a set of different book-lights using either a progressive elimination strategy (i.e., eliminate the worst alternative at each phase until only one alternative remains) or a full evaluation strategy (i.e., make comparisons among all of the alternatives for all of the attributes and then choose the one with the best attributes overall). The study showed that the participants offered more of their own money to buy the same chosen book-light in the fit conditions than in the non-fit conditions (locomotion/full evaluation; assessment/progressive elimination). In addition, once again, this fit effect was independent of the participants' pleasant or painful mood at the time that they offered to buy the book-light.

Let us now consider other evidence for the impact of regulatory fit on judgments and decision making.

The studies of Higgins, Idson, et al. (2003) and Avnet and Higgins (2003) described earlier illustrate how regulatory fit can influence evaluative judgments and decisions, including how much people are willing to offer to buy a chosen object. When deciding upon the price of a desirable object chosen through a regulatory fit process (compared to a non-fit process), the chosen object will be given a higher monetary price, and this fit effect is independent of the hedonic mood of the decision maker. Higgins, Idson, et al. (2003) proposed that this fit effect is due to participants in the fit conditions feeling right about what they are doing during the decision-making activity, which intensifies their attraction to the chosen object. This fit effect depends on people failing to distinguish between the experience created by regulatory fit and the value experience associated with the desirable consequences of owning the chosen object (outcome value). If so, then the fit effect on pricing should be eliminated if participants' attention is explicitly directed to their feel right experience from the manner in which they made their decision.

In one mug study by Higgins, Idson, et al. (2003), the participants were told that sometimes using certain strategies to pursue goals (and they were reminded of the strategy they used) can make people "feel right" about their goal pursuit. After answering on a scale, "How much do you 'feel right' about your goal pursuit?", they gave their price for the mug. As predicted, the fit effect was eliminated. Cesario et al. (2004) also found that the fit effect on persuasion was eliminated when participants' attention was directed to their feel right experience.

As described earlier, there is considerable evidence that the fit effect on evaluation is independent of people's positive mood when making their evaluations. Thus, the fit effect is not due to fit increasing positive mood, which then enhances evaluations. Another possible factor underlying the fit effect is that fit increases people's perception of the efficiency (ease) or effectiveness (instrumentality) of the goal pursuit process, thereby enhancing the perceived value of the process. This possibility has been addressed in different studies. Higgins, Idson, et al. (2003) and Freitas and Higgins (2002), for example, both found that regulatory fit effects remained significant when perceived efficiency and effectiveness were included as covariates.

If the fit effect occurs from the feeling right experience later influencing the value experience for some object, then it could occur even when the subsequent object evaluation is totally separate from the regulatory fit activity itself. In another study by Higgins, Idson, et al. (2003), participants were asked to list either two promotion goals (i.e., listed two of their personal hopes or aspirations) or two prevention goals (i.e., listed two of their duties or obligations). Then they listed for each of their goals either eager means of pursuit (i.e., strategies they could use to make sure everything goes right) or vigilant means (strategies they could use to avoid anything that could go wrong). Promotion goals/eager means and prevention goals/vigilant means were the regulatory fit conditions. Using the "unrelated studies" paradigm, the participants were later asked to rate photographs of three dogs on "good-naturedness," supposedly as part of a general project to establish average ratings of various stimuli. As expected, the participants in the fit conditions rated the dogs as more "good-natured" overall than did participants in the non-fit conditions.

There is also evidence that regulatory fit can influence the judged importance of something. In another study by Higgins, Idson, et al. (2003), participants were given the task of thinking about things that might improve the transition from elementary school to middle school (i.e., junior high school). The participants could list as many or as few suggestions as they wished. To manipulate regulatory fit, the strategic nature of the improvements that participants were asked to generate was varied. Half of the participants were given an eager strategy of making improvements by instructing them to think about what should be added to middle school to ensure that students gain as many positive experiences as possible during this transition. The other half were given a vigilant strategy by instructing them to think about what should be eliminated from middle school to ensure that students avoid as many negative experiences as possible during this transition. Once participants finished listing their suggested improvements, they were asked to judge the importance of middle school experiences. Consistent with the findings reported earlier on effects of regulatory fit on motivational intensity, participants generated more strategies in the fit than non-fit conditions. Moreover, participants judged middle school experiences themselves to be more important in the fit than non-fit conditions.

The studies reviewed thus far demonstrate that fit can influence evaluative judgments and decisions, including deciding how much money to offer to buy something. To examine how regulatory fit affects value judgments independent of the outcomes of a decision, many of these studies controlled for outcome value by ensuring that all participants made the same choice (e.g., chose the same mug or the same book-light). A remaining question, however, is whether regulatory fit also influences the actual choices people make. There is evidence that it does. One important kind of choice is freely choosing to engage again in an activity when there are now alternative activities in which one could engage instead. This issue has been addressed from a wide variety of perspectives, including learning theory (e.g., Skinner, 1938; Thorndike, 1935), self-determination theory (e.g., Deci, 1971; Deci & Ryan, 1985), dissonance theory (e.g., Festinger, 1957; Wicklund & Brehm, 1976), and self-perception theory (e.g., Bem, 1965; Kruglanski, Alon, & Lewis, 1972; Lepper, Greene, & Nisbett, 1973).

A classic paradigm for studying this issue was introduced by Lepper et al. (1973). In their key "expected reward" condition, individuals perform a fun activity (e.g., children drawing pictures) in an initial situation that makes the manner of engagement serious by adding an award contingent on drawing the pictures. From a regulatory fit perspective, this critical experimental condition relates a fun activity orientation to a serious situation (a non-fit). In the classic unexpected reward comparison condition, the activity is initially performed with no award contingency. The lesser motivation to re-engage the activity in the expected reward condition than in the unexpected reward condition is consistent with there being a non-fit only in the former condition.

A recent study by Higgins, Pittman, and Spiegel (2006) extended the basic Lepper et al. (1973) paradigm to examine directly whether regulatory fit does, indeed, influence choice to re-engage an activity. Undergraduate participants engaged in an activity for which they had either an inherently *fun* orientation (playing the "Shoot the Moon" game; see Pittman, Cooper, & Smith, 1977) or an inherently *important* orientation ("Financial Duties"; see Bianco et al., 2003). For each of these activities, both the initial reward situation surrounding the activity and the subsequent free choice situation were independently manipulated to be either *enjoyable* or *serious*. For the initial reward situation, participants were offered the chance to win an attractive ballpoint pen contingent on their performance. In the enjoyable reward condition, participants were told that the reward had been added to make the game more enjoyable and that they should think of the game as being like something they would play at a carnival where the game is even more fun because they can win a prize at the end. In the serious reward condition, the participants were told that the reward had been added to make the task more serious and that they should think of the task as being like a real-life work situation, which is serious, because you are paid a salary at the end.

For the subsequent free choice situation, all of the participants could choose how much to engage in several different activities during a 5-minute period while the experimenter was away (with the target activity being one choice). In the enjoyable choice condition, participants were told that this was the "free time" portion of the experiment so they should feel free to do anything at all they want. In the serious choice condition, the participants were told that this was the "time management" portion of the experiment so that it was important that they use the time wisely and manage it in an appropriate and prudent manner. As predicted, the study showed that participants chose to spend much more time doing the target activity again in the fit conditions (fun activity/enjoyable reward and choice situations; important activity/serious reward and choice situations) than in the non-fit conditions (fun activity/serious reward and choice situations; important activity/enjoyable reward and choice situations)—over 5 times as much!

In the studies just reviewed, the judgment and decisions are about something in the present (a chosen book-light or mug, photographed dogs and re-engaging in a task). Judgments and decisions can also be about something in the past (retrospective) or future (prospective). We discussed earlier the research by Idson et al. (2004) on how fit affects the intensity of good–bad judgments when one imagines prospective choices. There is evidence that regulatory fit influences retrospective judgments as well. Camacho et al. (2003), for example, had participants in one study think back to a time in their lives when they had a conflict with an authority figure who determined how to resolve the conflict. Different participants were asked to recall different kinds of resolution. For example, some participant recalled a resolution in which the other person encouraged them or set up opportunities for them to succeed (the pleasant/eager condition), and other participants remembered a resolution in which the other person safeguarded them against anything that might cause trouble or made them alert to potential dangers (the pleasant/vigilant condition). Some participants had a predominant promotion focus, and others had a predominant prevention focus (as determined by the Regulatory Focus Questionnaire; see Higgins et al., 2000). Participants judged the resolution to be more "right" if they were predominant promotion and the conflict was resolved in an eager manner or they were predominant prevention and the conflict was resolved in a vigilant manner. Once again, this fit effect was independent of their pleasant or painful mood while making their judgments. Equally important, this fit effect was also independent of whether the manner of resolution was itself pleasant or painful.

There is also evidence that an activity is retrospectively evaluated more favorably if people experienced regulatory fit while doing it. Freitas and Higgins (2002) had participants begin the experimental session by first describing either their hopes and aspirations in life or their beliefs about their duties and obligations in life to induce experimentally either a promotion state or a prevention state, respectively. The participants then began the "next study" in which they acted as scientists working with organic material whose goal was to find as many four-sided objects as possible among dozens of multiply-shaped objects on a sheet of paper. Half of the participants were instructed that "the way to do well on the task was to be *eager* and to try to maximize the helpful four-sided objects." The other half were instructed that "the way to do well on the task was to be *vigilant* and to try to eliminate the harmful four-sided objects." Thus, all participants had the same goal of searching for and noting as many four-sided objects as possible, but they were induced to pursue this goal using either an eager strategy or a vigilant strategy. The study showed that the participants with a promotion orientation evaluated the task more positively when they were given the eager than the vigilant instructions, whereas the reverse was true for the participants with a prevention orientation.

In another set of studies, Freitas et al. (2002) examined participants' evaluation of a task that involved resisting tempting diversions from task completion. Because avoiding obstacles to goal attainment is a favored means of prevention-focused self-regulation, they predicted that this kind of task would better fit a prevention focus than a promotion focus. They indeed found that, whether deciphering encrypted messages or solving math problems, prevention-focused participants later reported greater enjoyment when the task required vigilantly ignoring attractive distracting video clips, whereas promotion-focused participants later reported higher enjoyment when the distracting clips were not presented.

## Attitude and Behavior Change

To change people's attitudes and behavior, one needs to convince them of the value of the advocated change. A standard method is to provide information about the positive outcomes or benefits of such a change. Regulatory fit permits another method for change. To the extent that people have a basically positive response to what is being advocated, then creating a regulatory fit should make that response feel right and increase its effectiveness. That is, the value of change should be enhanced. The results of several studies support this idea. In a recent study by Spiegel et al. (2004), for example, participants read either a promotion-framed health message (health as accomplishment) or a prevention-framed message (health as safety) that contained the same basic information urging them to eat more fruits and vegetables and framed the consequences in terms of either the benefits of complying or the costs of not complying. Over the next 7 days the participants recorded how many servings of fruits and vegetables they ate in a daily nutrition log. As discussed earlier, feeling right from fit should be higher for promotion than prevention when (eager) benefits are emphasized and should be higher for prevention than promotion when (vigilant) costs are emphasized. The results supported these predictions, with promotion/benefits and prevention/costs participants eating about 20% more fruits and vegetables over the following week than promotion/costs and prevention/benefits participants.

Cesario et al. (2004) examined fit effects on persuasion in more detail. In one of their studies, participants who varied chronically in the strength of their promotion or prevention focus read an article eliciting support for a new city tax to create an after-school program that would help elementary- and high-school students in their personal and academic lives. The structure, content, and primary goal of the article were identical for both versions. The only difference was the strategic framing used to advocate the policy. For example, the eager-framed article said that "the primary reason for supporting this program is because it will advance children's education and support more children to succeed, whereas the vigilant-framed article said that "the primary reason for supporting this program is because it will secure children's education and prevent more children from failing." The study found that the message was perceived as more persuasive and was more effective in changing attitudes when there was a fit between its manner of presentation and participants' chronic focus orientation (eager/promotion vs. vigilant/prevention) than when there was a non-fit (eager/prevention vs. vigilant/promotion). As predicted, this fit effect was independent of participants' positive or negative mood.

Because regulatory fit in this study involved the relation between participants' orientation and message framing, other kinds of compatibility between participants' needs and message fulfillment of those needs might have contributed to the results. For example, one could regard the fit effect found as being a special case of message-matching, in which the match is between the regulatory concerns of a message recipient and the persuasive framing of a message. Although this specific type of relation had not been examined previously, there is substantial evidence that matching the topic of a persuasive message to some aspect of the message recipient's cognitive, motivational, or affective system can influence persuasion (e.g., Clary, Snyder, Ridge, Miene, & Haugen, 1994; Evans & Petty, 2003; Fabrigar & Petty, 1999; Petty, Wheeler, & Bizer, 2000). The best way to clearly distinguish a message-matching effect on persuasion from a regulatory fit effect is to experimentally induce regulatory fit before and independent of the persuasion context. In a few additional studies, Cesario et al. (2004) tested whether participants would be more persuaded by an identical message if they had versus had not experienced regulatory fit before even receiving the message.

Using the same fit manipulation as the dog study of Higgins, Idson, et al. (2003), Cesario et al. (2004) asked participants to list either promotion goals or prevention goals and then list for each of their goals either eager or vigilant mens of pursuit. Promotion goals/eager means and prevention goals/vigilant means were the regulatory fit conditions. After the participants had completed this supposed first study on personal goals, they began the supposed second study in which they all received the same persuasive message on the new after-school program. Once again, participants in the fit conditions were more persuaded by the message than participants in the non-fit conditions, despite regulatory fit being induced before the message even was received. The participants in the fit conditions also indicated a greater willingness to volunteer several hours per week for the program at a nearby school.

Given the importance of attitude confidence and certainty for persuasion (e.g., Tormala & Petty, 2002), Cesario et al. (2004) also asked participants how confident they were in their attitude toward the after-school proposal. In the standard condition in which participants' attention was not drawn to their feeling right experience, participants in the fit conditions were more confident in their attitudes than participants in the non-fit conditions. Interestingly, when participants' attention was drawn to their feeling right experience, participants in the fit conditions were less confident in their attitudes than participants in the non-fit conditions. This suggests that the regulatory fit "feeling right" experience contributes to people's confidence in their subsequent evaluations, and if the appropriateness of using this experience is brought into question, as by drawing attention to its source, then its effect is suppressed and even reversed, perhaps through overcorrection (cf. Petty & Wegener, 1998).

Cesario et al. (2004) extended previous research on regulatory fit in yet another way. When regulatory fit influences evaluation of an object, such as the pricing of a mug, does it make people feel right about the object itself or feel right about their reaction to the object? If it is the latter, then it would be critical to know what reactions people were having to the object in the first place. This is not a problem in the mug and book-light studies because these objects were selected to be very positive for the participants. It is well known in persuasion studies, however, that individuals can vary in their positive or negative thought reactions to a message (e.g., Greenwald, 1968). If participants are generating positive thoughts, their experience of feeling right about and strongly engaging in those positive thoughts would make the message more positive and thus more persuasive. In contrast, if participants are generating negative thoughts, their experience of feeling right about and strongly engaging in those negative thoughts would make the message more negative and thus less persuasive (cf. Petty, Briñol, & Tormala, 2002).

Cesario et al. (2004) conducted another study and used the standard thought listing technique to obtain participants' positive and negative thoughts about the message. They found that the fit effect on increasing attitude change occurred only for participants who had positive thoughts about the message. For participants who had negative thoughts about the message, fit had the opposite effect—it decreased attitude change. Thus, it is not that fit makes people feel right about an object or event per se. Rather, fit makes people feel right about their response to an object or event, which intensifies positivity when the response is positive and intensifies negativity when the response is negative.

Lee and Aaker's (2004) recent studies on fit and persuasion not only provide additional evidence supporting the conclusion that persuasive messages can be more effective when their manner fits the recipients' orientation, but also support the notion that stronger engagement while processing the message contributes to this effect. Similar to the findings of Spiegel et al.'s (2004) study on getting people to eat more fruit and vegetables, Lee and Aaker (2004) found that advertising appeals to drink Welch's Grape Juice or use a new sun treatment lotion were more effective when promotion advertising appeals (e.g., energy creation or enjoy life) emphasized the benefits of compliance (eager gain framing) rather than the costs of noncompliance (vigilant loss framing), whereas the reverse was true for prevention advertising appeals (e.g., cancer and heart disease prevention or be safe from sunburns). In subsequent studies, Lee and Aaker (2004) examined the relation between regulatory fit, message engagement, and message effectiveness. As discussed earlier, regulatory fit increases strength of engagement. Indeed, one can think of feeling right from fit as a mild kind of "flow" experience (see Csikszentmihalyi, 1975). Lee and Aaker (2004) found that subjective reports of ease of processing and comprehensibility of the message, accessibility of focus-related words in the message (measured by a perceptual identification task), and number of supportive reasons generated when individuals were asked to write down reasons to use the product were higher in the fit conditions than in the non-fit conditions. Fluency and flow are fit experiences because when there is fluency or flow the orientation of a person toward what they are doing is being sustained. This is independent of how much actual effort is expended (see Higgins, 2006).

## CONCLUSION

In this chapter we describe a source of value experience that is apparently quite influential in everyday life. Complementing the classic concern with relations between decisions, actions or objects and goal outcomes, as when a decision, action or object is instrumental in realizing a goal, the findings reviewed here suggest that the fit between one's motivational orientation and manner of goal pursuit can strongly influence one's engagement in, and one's feeling right about, what one is doing. These regulatory fit effects have emerged across a wide array of value-related variables, including monetary and subjective valuations of the worth of anticipated, experienced, and recalled events, actions, decisions, and objects. Regulatory fit has been shown to impact phenomena such as motivational intensity, performance efficiency and perseverance, attitude change, and moral judgment. Regarding the familiar axiom, "It is not enough to do good; one must do it in *the right way*," these findings suggest that behaving in the right way is determined not only by cultural, moral, and justice-related standards but also by how the manner of one's behavior fits with one's motivational orientation. More specifically, regulatory fit theory (Higgins, 2000) proposes that people experience regulatory fit when their goal orientation is sustained (vs. disrupted) by the manner in which they pursue the goal. Regulatory fit makes them feel right about and engage more strongly in what they are doing, independent of instrumental and moral concerns.

Although the findings reviewed earlier convergently support these claims, important unanswered questions remain. Perhaps primary among these is understanding the more specific psychological mechanisms underlying the findings. Statistical analysis of the mug-value effects (Higgins, Idson, et al., 2003), for example, revealed independent, unique effects of good fit and poor fit, whereby high fit (i.e., prevention/vigilant or promotion/eager) had a positive impact on perceived mug value, and poor fit (i.e., prevention/eager or promotion/vigilant) had a negative impact on perceived mug value. This suggests that feeling right and stronger engagement from a goal means sustaining one's orientation and feeling wrong and weaker engagement from a goal means disrupting one's orientation can both affect subsequent evaluations. However, there is also the possibility that more than one psychological process underlie these independent effects. Future work needs to be done to explore this possibility.

Regarding underlying mechanisms, moreover, the nagging possibility always exists that regulatory fit, rather than being a newly discovered source of value, actually reflects some already understood regulatory process. Might it be, for example, that behaviors sustaining one's motivational orientation are simply more familiar in those particular motivational contexts, with mere familiarity itself driving the value effects, as shown in classic work by Zajonc (1968)? Arguing against that particular possibility, one recent study showed that mere familiarity appears to be a source of value only when one is in a prevention focus rather than a promotion focus, because the safety connotations of familiarity better fit a prevention-focused motivational orientation than a promotion-oriented one (Travers & Freitas, 2004). Accordingly, because we have found equally large fit effects for people in prevention and promotion focuses, it appears unlikely that mere familiarity, which appears especially valued in a prevention focus, underlies fit effects. In addition, if familiarity leads to liking as a main effect, it could not account for the interaction reported by Cesario et al. (2004), in which fit increased message effectiveness for those with positive thoughts about the message but decreased message effectiveness for those with negative thoughts.

Nonetheless, the surest way of demonstrating that regulatory fit is a distinct source of value is to identify the unique mechanism underlying it.

Currently, the single most promising mechanism proposed as underlying fit effects is strength of engagement, in which fit increases engagement strength and non-fit decreases engagement strength (Higgins, 2006). An intriguing question is whether feeling right (or feeling wrong) and engagement strength can each contribute separately to fit effects. Further work is needed to identify just what it is about motivation-sustaining behaviors that increases strength of engagement and makes them feel right. With respect to feeling right, one possibility with interesting implications is that the regulatory fit experience arises from a feeling of behaving naturally, rather than in a constrained manner. For example, much physiological research suggests that frontal brain areas are recruited to inhibit over-learned responses that otherwise would be natural to carry out in particular situations (e.g., Jodo & Kayama, 1992). Responding to a cue in a non-natural way, such as moving a joystick to the right when one respondes to a left arrow, appears to recruit similar frontal structures (e.g., Freitas, Azizian, Berry, Squires, & Paritskaya, 2004).

It is possible that activation of those self-control processes produces an experience of holding back or constraining oneself. Thinking or behaving in a manner that disrupts one's motivational orientation might also require activation of such self-control processes disproportionately, which would produce a similar constraining experience that feels unnatural—it would make one feel wrong about what one was doing. If regulatory fit makes such disproportionate self-control processes unnecessary, the activity would feel more natural and unconstrained—it would make one feel right about what one was doing. This possibility could be explored in future psychophysiological studies that assess recruitment of frontal self-control brain areas under fit and non-fit conditions and relate those physiological indicators to participants' subjective self-reports. Implications of feeling natural and unconstrained ("feeling right") versus feeling unnatural and constrained ("feeling wrong") could also be pursued independent of specific psychophysiological underpinnings.

Finally, we hope that this research program will eventually shed new light on other important interpersonal phenomena, such as how people relate to close others and fellow members of organizations. In relationships research, for example, it has long been recognized that interpersonal attraction is driven by the potential for positive relationship outcomes (e.g., Homans, 1961; Thibaut & Kelly, 1959). Relationship commitment, however, may depend also on the manner in which the relationship unfolds, and regulatory fit may play an important role in this process. For example, if one's romantic partner behaved in a manner supporting one's own motivational orientation, one might experience increased engagement that would intensify one's attraction to one's partner and to the relationship itself, thereby positively impacting relationship commitment. Similar effects could transpire with respect to work colleagues, supervisors, and assistants, thus having an impact on disparate phenomena such as work-related motivation, employee commitment, and group decision making. People may feel right about and strongly engage in group decisions, for example, to the extent that they are reached in a manner supporting their own motivational orientations. Such effects could prove to be either adaptive or maladaptive, in that high regulatory fit in a group context could facilitate harmony and mutual decision satisfaction, on the one hand, but also over-acquiescence on the other (i.e., "groupthink"; Janis, 1972). We look forward to future research examining these and other possibilities.

## REFERENCES

Abelson, R. P., & Levi, A. (1985). Decision making and decision theory. In G. Lindzey & E. Aronson (Eds.), *The handbook of social psychology* (Vol. 1, pp. 231–309). New York: Random House.

Ajzen, I. (1996). The social psychology of decision making. In E. T. Higgins & A. W. Kruglanski (Eds.), *Social psychology: Handbook of basic principles* (pp. 297–325). New York: Guilford.

Avnet, T., & Higgins, E. T. (2003). Locomotion, assessment, and regulatory fit: Value transfer from "how" to "what." *Journal of Experimental Social Psychology, 39*, 525–530.

Bem, D. J. (1965). An experimental analysis of self-persuasion. *Journal of Experimental Social Psychology, 1*, 199–218.

Bianco, A. T., Higgins, E. T., & Klem, A. (2003). How "fun/importance" fit impacts performance: Relating implicit theories to instructions. *Personality and Social Psychology Bulletin, 29*, 1091–1103.

Brunstein, J. C., Schultheiss, O. C., & Graessman, R. (1998). Personal goals and emotional well-being: The moderating role of motive dispositions. *Journal of Personality and Social Psychology, 75*, 494–508.

Cacioppo, J. T., Priester, J. R., & Berntson, G. G. (1993). Rudimentary determinants of attitudes. II: Arm flexion and extension have differential effects on attitudes. *Journal of Personality and Social Psychology, 65*, 5–17.

Camacho, C. J., Higgins, E. T., & Luger, L. (2003). Moral value transfer from regulatory fit: "What feels right *is* right" and "what feels wrong *is* wrong." *Journal of Personality and Social Psychology, 84*, 498–510.

Carver, C. S., & Scheier, M. F. (1981). *Attention and self-regulation: A control-theory approach to human behavior.* New York: Springer-Verlag.

Cesario, J., Grant, H., & Higgins, E. T. (2004). Regulatory fit and persuasion: Transfer from "feeling right." *Journal of Personality and Social Psychology, 86*, 388–404.

Clary, E. G., Snyder, M., Ridge, R. D., Miene, P. K., & Haugen, J. A. (1994). Matching messages to motives in persuasion: A functional approach to promoting volunteerism. *Journal of Applied Social Psychology, 24*, 1129–1149.

Crowe, E., & Higgins, E. T. (1997). Regulatory focus and strategic inclinations: Promotion and prevention in decision-making. *Organizational Behavior and Human Decision Processes, 69*, 117–132.

Csikszentmihalyi, M. (1975). *Beyond boredom and anxiety.* San Francisco: Jossey-Bass.

Dawes, R. M. (1998). Behavioral decision making and judgment. In D. T. Gilbert, S. T. Fiske, & G. Lindzey (Eds.), *The handbook of social psychology* (Vol. 1, pp. 497–548). New York: McGraw-Hill.

Deci, E. L. (1971). Effects of externally mediated rewards on intrinsic motivation. *Journal of Personality and Social Psychology, 18*, 105–115.

Deci, E. L., & Ryan, R. M. (1985). *Intrinsic motivation and self-determination in human behavior*. New York: Plenum Press.

DeSteno, D., Petty, R. E., Rucker, D., Wegener, D. T., & Braverman, J. (2004). Discrete emotions and persuasion: The role of emotion-induced expectancies. *Journal of Personality and Social Psychology, 86*, 43–56.

Evans, L. M., & Petty, R. E. (2003). Self-guide framing and persuasion: Responsibly increasing message processing to ideal levels. *Personality and Social Psychology Bulletin, 29*, 313–324.

Fabrigar, L. R., & Petty, R. E. (1999). The role of affective and cognitive bases of attitudes in susceptibility to affectively and cognitively based persuasion. *Personality and Social Psychology Bulletin, 25*, 363–381.

Festinger, L. (1957). *A theory of cognitive dissonance*. Evanston, IL: Row, Peterson.

Förster, J., Grant, H., Idson, L. C., & Higgins, E. T. (2001). Success/failure feedback, expectancies, and approach/avoidance motivation: How regulatory focus moderates classic relations. *Journal of Experimental Social Psychology, 37*, 253–260.

Förster, J., Higgins, E. T., & Idson, C. L. (1998). Approach and avoidance strength as a function of regulatory focus: Revisiting the "goal looms larger" effect. *Journal of Personality and Social Psychology, 75*, 1115–1131.

Freitas, A. L., Azizian, A., Berry, S., Squires, N., & Paritskaya, Y. (2004, October). *Mapping actions onto perceptions: Psychophysiological implications of conflicting action representations*. Paper presented at the 44th Annual Conference of the Society for Psychophysiological Research, Santa Fe, NM.

Freitas, A. L., & Higgins, E. T. (2002). Enjoying goal-directed action: The role of regulatory fit. *Psychological Science, 13*, 1–6.

Freitas, A. L., Liberman, N., & Higgins, E. T. (2002). Regulatory fit and resisting temptation during goal pursuit. *Journal of Experimental Social Psychology, 38*, 291–298.

Gollwitzer, P. M. (1996). The volitional benefits of planning. In P. M. Gollwitzer & J. A. Bargh (Eds.), *The psychology of action: Linking cognition and motivation to behavior* (pp. 287–312). New York: Guilford.

Greenwald, A. G. (1968). Cognitive learning, cognitive response to persuasion, and attitude change. In A. G. Greenwald, T. C. Brock, & T. M. Ostrom (Eds.), *Psychological foundations of attitudes* (pp. 147–170). San Diego, CA: Academic Press.

Harackiewicz, J. M., & Sansone, C. (1991). Goals and intrinsic motivation: You can get there from here. In M. L. Maehr & P. R. Pintrich (Eds.), *Advances in motivation and achievement* (Vol. 7, pp. 21–49). Greenwich, CT: JAI Press.

Higgins, E. T. (1997). Beyond pleasure and pain. *American Psychologist, 52*, 1280–1300.

Higgins, E. T. (1998). Promotion and prevention: Regulatory focus as a motivational principle. In M. P. Zanna (Ed.), *Advances in experimental social psychology* (Vol. 30, pp. 1–46). New York: Academic Press.

Higgins, E. T. (2000). Making a good decision: Value from fit. *American Psychologist, 55*, 1217–1230.

Higgins, E. T. (2002). How self-regulation creates distinct values: The case of promotion and prevention decision making. *Journal of Consumer Psychology, 12,* 177–191.

Higgins, E. T. (2005). Value from regulatory fit. *Current Directions in Psychological Science, 14,* 208–213.

Higgins, E. T. (2006). Value from hedonic experience *and* engagement. *Psychological Review, 113,* 439–460.

Higgins, E. T. (in press). Value. In A. W. Kruglanski & E. T. Higgins (Eds.), *Social psychology: Handbook of basic principles,* (2nd ed.). New York: Guilford.

Higgins, E. T., Idson, L. C., Freitas, A. L., Spiegel, S., & Molden, D. C. (2003). Transfer of value from fit. *Journal of Personality and Social Psychology, 84,* 1140–1153.

Higgins, E. T., Kruglanski, A. W., & Pierro, A. (2003). Regulatory mode: Locomotion and assessment as distinct orientations. In M. P. Zanna (Ed.), *Advances in experimental social psychology* (Vol. 35, pp. 293–344). New York: Academic Press.

Higgins, E. T., Pittman, T., & Spiegel, S. (2004). *Regulatory fit and choosing how much to re-engage an activity.* Unpublished manuscript, Columbia University.

Higgins, E. T., Pittman, T., & Spiegel, S. (2006). *Regulatory fit effects on the attractiveness of re-doing an activity.* Unpublished manuscript, Columbia University.

Higgins, E. T., & Silberman, I. (1998). Development of regulatory focus: Promotion and prevention as ways of living. In J. Heckhausen & C. S. Dweck (Eds.), *Motivation and self-regulation across the life span* (pp. 78–113). New York: Cambridge University Press.

Homans, G. C. (1961). *Social behavior.* New York: Harcourt, Brace & World.

Idson, L. C., Liberman, N., & Higgins, E. T. (2000). Distinguishing gains from non-losses and losses from non-gains: A regulatory focus perspective on hedonic intensity. *Journal of Experimental Social Psychology, 36,* 252–274.

Idson, L. C., Liberman, N., & Higgins, E. T. (2004). Imagining how you'd feel: The role of motivational experiences from regulatory fit. *Personality and Social Psychology Bulletin, 30,* 926–937.

Janis, I. (1972). *Victims of groupthink: A psychological study of foreign-policy decisions and fiascoes.* Boston: Houghton Mifflin.

Janis, I. L., & Mann, L. (1977). *Decision making: A psychological analysis of conflict, choice, and commitment.* New York: Free Press.

Jodo, E., & Kayama, Y. (1992). Relation of a negative ERP component to response inhibition in a Go/No-go task. *Electroencephalography and Clinical Neurophysiology, 82,* 477–482.

Kahneman, D., & Snell, J. (1990). Predicting utility. In R. M. Hogarth (Ed.), *Insights in decision making* (pp. 295–310). Chicago: University of Chicago Press.

Kahneman, D., & Tversky, A. (1973). On the psychology of prediction. *Psychological Review, 80,* 237–251.

Kahneman, D., & Tversky, A. (1979). Prospect theory: An analysis of decision under risk. *Econometrica, 47,* 263–291.

Kahneman, D., Diener, E., & Schwarz, N. (1999). *Well-being: The foundations of hedonic psychology.* New York: Russell Sage.

Kruglanski, A. W., Alon, S., & Lewis, T. (1972). Retrospective misattribution and task enjoyment. *Journal of Experimental Social Psychology, 8,* 493–501.

Lee, A. Y., & Aaker, J. L. (2004). Bringing the frame into focus: The influence of regulatory fit on processing fluency and persuasion. *Journal of Personality and Social Psychology, 86,* 205–218.

Lepper, M. R., Greene, D., & Nisbett, R. E. (1973). Undermining children's intrinsic interest with extrinsic reward: a test of the overjustification hypothesis. *Journal of Personality and Social Psychology, 28,* 129–137.

Merton, R. K. (1957). *Social theory and social structure.* Glencoe, IL: Free Press.

Miller, G. A., Galanter, E., & Pribram, K. H. (1960). *Plans and the structure of behavior.* New York: Holt, Rinehart, & Winston.

Payne, J. W., Bettman, J. R., & Johnson, E. J. (1993). *The adaptive decision maker.* Cambridge, MA: Cambridge University Press.

Pennington, N., & Hastie, R. (1988). Explanation-based decision making: Effects of memory structure on judgment. *Journal of Experiment Psychology: Learning, Memory, and Cognition, 14,* 521–533.

Petty, R. E., Briñol, P., & Tormala, A. L. (2002). Thought confidence as a determinant of persuasion: The self-validation hypothesis. *Journal of Personality and Social Psychology, 82,* 722–741.

Petty, R. E., & Wegener, D. T. (1998). Attitude change: Multiple roles for persuasion variables. In D. T. Gilbert, S. T. Fiske, & G. Lindzey (Eds.), *The handbook of social psychology* (4th ed., pp. 323–390). New York: McGraw Hill.

Petty, R. E., Wheeler, S. C., & Bizer, G. Y. (2000). Attitude functions and persuasion: An elaboration likelihood approach to matched versus mismatched messages. In G. R. Maio & J. M. Olson (Eds.),*Why we evaluate: Functions of attitudes* (pp. 133–162). Mahwah, NJ: Lawrence Erlbaum Associates.

Pittman, T. S., Copper, E. E., & Smith, T. W. (1977). Attribution of causality and the overjustification effect. *Personality and Social Psychology Bulletin, 3,* 280–283.

Powers, W. T. (1973) *Behavior: The control of perception.* Chicago: Aldine.

Sansone, C., & Harackiewicz, J. (1996). "I don't feel like it": The function of interest in self-regulation. In L. L. Martin & A. Tesser (Eds.), *Striving and feeling: Interactions among goals, affect, and self-regulation* (pp. 203–228). Mahwah, NJ: Lawrence Erlbaum Associates.

Schwarz, N. (2000). Emotion, cognition, and decision making. *Cognition and Emotion, 14,* 433–440.

Shah, J., Higgins, E. T., & Friedman, R. (1998). Performance incentives and means: How regulatory focus influences goal attainment. *Journal of Personality and Social Psychology, 74,* 285–293.

Shah, J. Y., & Kruglanski, A. W. (2000). Aspects of goal networks: Implications for self-regulation. In M. Boekaerts & P. R. Pintrich (Eds.), *Handbook of self-regulation* (pp. 85–110). San Diego, CA: Academic Press.

Sheldon, K. M., & Elliot, A. J. (1999). Goal striving, need satisfaction, and longitudinal well-being: The self-concordance model. *Journal of Personality and Social Psychology, 76,* 482–497.

Simon, H. A. (1955). A behavioral model of rational choice. *Quarterly Journal of Economics, 69,* 99–118.

Simon, H. A. (1967). Motivational and emotional controls of cognition. *Psychological Review, 74,* 29–39.

Skinner, B. F. (1938). *The behavior of organisms: An experimental analysis.* New York: Appleton-Century-Crofts.

Spiegel, S., Grant-Pillow, H., & Higgins, E. T. (2004). How regulatory fit enhances motivational strength during goal pursuit. *European Journal of Social Psychology, 34*, 39–54.

Tauer, J., & Harackiewicz, J. (1999). Winning isn't everything: Competition, achievement orientation, and intrinsic motivation. *Journal of Experimental Social Psychology, 35*, 209–238.

Taylor, S. E., Pham, L. B., Rivkin, I. D., & Armor, D. A. (1998). Harnessing the imagination: Mental simulation, self-regulation, and coping. *American Psychologist, 53*, 429–439.

Tetlock, P. E. (1991). An alternative metaphor in the study of judgment and choice: People as politicians. *Theory and Psychology, 1*, 451–475.

Thaler, R. H. (1980). Toward a positive theory of consumer choice. *Journal of Economic Behavior and Organization, 1*, 39–60.

Thaler, R. H. (1999). Mental accounting matters. *Journal of Behavioral Decision Making, 12*, 183–206.

Thibaut, J., & Kelley, H. H. (1959). *The social psychology of groups*. New York: Wiley.

Thibaut, J. W., & Walker, L. (1975). *Procedural justice: A psychological analysis*. Hillsdale, NJ: Lawrence Erlbaum Associates.

Thorndike, E. L. (1935). *The psychology of wants, interests, and attitudes*. New York: Appleton-Century-Crofts.

Tormala, Z. L., & Petty, R. E. (2002). What doesn't kill me makes me stronger: The effects of resisting persuasion on attitude certainty. *Journal of Personality and Social Psychology, 83*, 1298–1313.

Travers, S., & Freitas, A. L. (2004, February). *Perceptual fluency and liking: A motivational explanation*. Paper presented at the Fifth Annual Meeting of the Society for Personality and Social Psychology, Austin, TX.

Tversky, A., & Shafir, E. (1992). The disjunction effect in choice under uncertainty. *Psychological Science, 3*, 305–309.

Tyler, T. R., & Lind, E. A. (1992). A relational model of authority in groups. In M. P. Zanna (Ed.), *Advances in experimental social psychology* (Vol. 25, pp. 115–192). New York: Academic Press.

Vallacher, R. R., & Wegner, D. M. (1987). What do people think they are doing?: Action identification and human behavior. *Psychological Review, 94*, 3–15.

*Webster's Ninth New Collegiate Dictionary* (1989). Springfield, MA: Merriam-Webster.

Wicklund, R. A., & Brehm, J. W. (1976). *Perspectives on cognitive dissonance*. Hillsdale, NJ: Lawrence Erlbaum Associates.

Zajonc, R. B. (1968). Attitudinal effects of mere exposure. *Journal of Personality and Social Psychology, 9*, 1–27.

# CHAPTER 3

# *The Dynamics of Newcomer Adjustment: Dispositions, Context, Interaction, and Fit*

John D. Kammeyer-Mueller
*University of Florida*

> *Upon those who are stepping into the same rivers*
> *Different and again different waters flow.*
> —Heraclitus

Those who study the process of newcomer adjustment to organizations have been grappling with one major theme for decades: Do people learn to accept an organization's culture, norms, and values as part of the process of fitting in, or are elements of the organization changed in some way to facilitate fit? This parochial question is an instantiation of a deeper psychological dilemma: Are we the products of the social environments we encounter, or are the environments we encounter the products of our interpretations and actions? As the quote from Heraclitus at the beginning of the chapter illustrates, this is a difficult question to answer, because although there are important underlying elements in people and situations that remain the same over time ("stepping into the same rivers"), people and situations are also in a state of constant flux ("different waters flow"). Thus, fit between a person and situation can be a matter of some change in both the person and the situation, but there remains the ground of the person and situation's more stable characteristics.

Whereas person–environment fit research typically questions how static dispositions and static work contexts interface with one another (e.g., Schneider, Goldstein, & Smith, 1995; Ryan & Kristof-Brown, 2003), a body of work that has remained relatively independent of the mainstream fit literature addresses the manner in which individuals and organizational settings engage in a process of mutual adjustment. Unlike most other areas of research in this volume, this dynamic fit perspective takes the malleability of individuals and situations as a fundamental fact, with the goal being the understanding of how people adapt in response to their environments (Ashford & Taylor, 1990; Chan, 2000). Although they are often portrayed as mutually exclusive alternatives, static and dynamic perspectives need not be opposed to one another. Concepts from the fit, adjustment, socialization, and personality literatures can inform one another, helping us to better understand how people interact with their environments over time to create fit.

This chapter is divided into three major sections. In the first section the principles of interactionism and how they apply to fit are described. Second, a review of three established conceptions of dispositions and social context is provided, emphasizing the manner in which newcomers to an organization and workgroup achieve fit. Figure 3–1 is a summary description of these three views of adjustment centered on the ways that fit can develop over time. A critique of the current paradigms will show the promise of research in which the dynamic relationship between individuals and social environments is investigated. Third, modeling implications of these perspectives are provided as a tool for researchers inter-

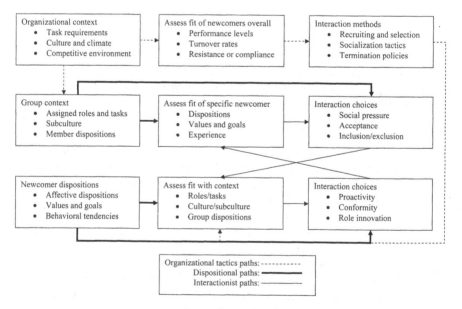

FIGURE 3–1.   Conceptual model.

ested in empirically examining dynamic fit processes. Throughout the chapter special attention is directed toward organizational newcomers and their initial adjustment to an organizational role. The early adjustment period is highlighted because it is easiest to see dynamic shifts in perceived fit and interaction styles when perceptions of fit are in the process of forming.

Before going further, it is worth developing a few operational definitions. Although there are a wide number of constructs that could be invoked under the auspices of dynamic fit processes, for this chapter attention is limited to dispositions, context, interaction, and fit. The *dispositions* of the newcomers and the members of the organization with whom the newcomer will regularly interact are stable individual differences in affect, values, and behavioral tendencies that are observed across situations (Mischel & Shoda, 1998). The second concept is *context*. Contextual variables are a broader class of constructs than dispositions, with examples of relevant contextual variables including socialization methods (Van Maanen & Schein, 1979), workgroup cohesion (Mullen & Copper, 1994), job characteristics (Hackman & Oldham, 1980), reward structures, and role definitions (King & King, 1990). When a newcomer enters the organization, his or her dispositional tendencies come into contact with the context, leading to *interactions*. Interactions are behavioral and cognitive responses designed to improve fit. These interactions can lead to the newcomer adapting himself or herself to fit the context, the context adapting to fit the newcomer, or mutual adaptation. Examples of interactive strategies include role negotiation, information seeking, relationship building, and social information processing (Ashford & Cummings, 1983; Ashford & Taylor, 1990; Miller & Jablin, 1991; Salancik & Pfeffer, 1978).

As newcomers and incumbents interact, there will be continual changes in both the actual and perceived *fit* between the newcomer and the context. Fit occurs when newcomers and contexts are appropriate for one another, either because they are similar in ways that supplement one another's strengths or different in ways that complement one another (Muchinsky & Monahan, 1987). A distinction is drawn between objective fit, as measured by the relationship between a newcomer's values, goals, or other related constructs and an independent measure of the organization's values, goals, or other related constructs, and subjective fit, as measured by directly asking participants how well they believe fit has been achieved (Cable & DeRue, 2002; Cable & Judge, 1996, 1997). Whereas objective fit is likely to be an important predictor of perceived fit, individuals make decisions to adapt their behavior based on perceived fit, so perceived fit will be the focus of this review. Measures of organizational commitment, identification, and role constructs can also indicate subjective fit (Wanous, 1992). Acceptance of the newcomer into the context is an example of a parallel subjective measure of fit taken from the point of view of incumbents.

## A CLASSIC DEBATE: FITTING IN VERSUS MAKING PEOPLE FIT

At the outset, I proposed that there are models of fit that concentrate on time-invariant properties and situations as well as models of fit that concentrate on the continually evolving nature of individuals and situations. However, turning again to Heraclitis' river, pitting static dispositional and contextual predictors of fit against a dynamic conception of fit is not necessarily informative. There is no logical contradiction in proposing that there can be a static entity of a river that is continually changing with the water that flows through it. For human beings, dispositions are the "river" or the general track along which our thoughts, feelings, and behavior flow, whereas the myriad situations we encounter and to which we respond are the "water." Organizations and groups similarly not only have stable core memberships, task characteristics, and situational pressures that direct their actions but also have a constant flow of new members, environmental challenges, and adaptive responses. In behavioral terms, dispositions are enacted in social situations such as organizations, and situations prompt reactions that are affected by dispositions (Eysenck & Eysenck, 1985).

It is worth considering how these components of stability and change are in constant interaction with one another. On the one hand, stable characteristics are manifested by their display across a range of changing situations. For example, dispositions toward helping, competition, and dominance are necessarily observed in the presence of some other individual who can either send or receive social information (Baron & Boudreau, 1987). Absent context, there can be no behavior. As such, the "proportion of variance in behavior explained by adaptive responses to the environment" is 100%. On the other hand, the people and organizations do have considerable continuity from day to day, as shown by the high rank-order correlations of individual traits over time (e.g., McCrae et al., 2000; Roberts, O'Donnell, & Robins, 2004) and consensus among members on organizational culture (Ostroff, Kinicki, & Tamkins, 2003).These stable individuals and organizations mediate the influence of situations on behavior, because "situations" cannot act of their own accord. As such, the "proportion of variance in behavior explained by time-invariant individuals and organizations" is 100%. Further highlighting the interplay of stability and change, a new organization and workgroup represent a change in the environment, prompting newcomers to engage in a process of fitting in; newcomers are simultaneously a change in the environment prompting organizations and groups to engage in a process of making people fit.

Recognizing the interdependence of static and dynamic elements, many personality researchers have adopted an interactionist point of view. According to interactionists, dispositions have their effects on behavior through multiple interactions between people and their social environments (Magnusson, 1999; Mischel & Shoda, 1998; Pervin, 1989).

Interactionism suggests that behavior is cued by each individual's perception of the situation. In other words, because subjective situations are the ones to which people respond, there is room for personality to affect the perceived situation quite strongly (Shoda, Mischel, & Wright, 1994). In addition, individuals interact with situations by selecting environments that fit with their dispositional tendencies. Perceptions of fit are informed by the dispositionally influenced reading the newcomer takes of the situation, and these perceptions in turn lead newcomers to act. Incumbents make dispositionally influenced observations of newcomers' fit and then act based on these observations as well. Although theorized at the individual level, interactionism is an equally valid concept for explaining how organizational culture and systems respond to situational pressures.

Because of the dependence of static and dynamic variables on one another, it is an empirically important proposition to distinguish between variables in terms of their relative stability. To distinguish what dimensions of the newcomer and context are likely to be adapted over time and which might be more usefully treated as dispositional or static, a taxonomy from the development literature that emphasizes how individual behavioral tendencies are more or less amenable to change based on their complexity is useful (Hellervik, Hazucha, & Schneider, 1992). This perspective proposes that tendencies exhibited across a wide variety of contexts have very elaborated schema that will not be easily changed; on the other hand, more specific tendencies are more readily transformed. Whereas research suggests that broad personality traits and values are very stable (e.g., McCrae et al., 2000; Roberts et al., 2004), affective attitudinal variables can fluctuate considerably over time (e.g., Vaidya, Gray, Haig, & Watson, 2002). Simple behaviors, such as discussing tasks with coworkers in a specific context or adopting a friendly demeanor when interacting with customers, may be changed through the course of adjustment; actually producing profound changes in newcomers' well-articulated schemas and values is less likely to happen. Extant organizational members may adjust certain social interactions or modify peripheral parts of their roles, but they will probably not be willing or able to change long-held cultural beliefs or core task requirements (Schein, 1980).

The attraction–selection–attrition (ASA) perspective provides another window on dispositions and fit by noting that in an organizational context, people are the context (i.e., the people make the place; Schneider, 1987; Schneider, Goldstein, & Smith, 1995). Schneider's theoretical work has emphasized the idea that newcomers and environments simultaneously evaluate one another based on the correspondence between newcomer dispositions and the organizational context already in place. These evaluations will in turn lead to behavioral spirals, either increasing acceptance of the other party because of complementary goals, culminating in commitment, or increasing rejection as part of a progression of withdrawal (Hulin, 1991;

Moreland & Levine, 1982). Again, we can see how the interface between two relatively stable entities can set off a dynamic process related to fit.

Social identity theory suggests another mechanism by which individual dispositions might influence fit within a dynamic context. According to social identity theory, the self-concept is a patchwork of numerous identities, such as the demography, occupation, organization, department, and workgroup (Ashforth & Johnson, 2001; Hogg & Terry, 2000), which provide proscriptions for behavior. Depending on contextual pressures, the identity a person adopts will differ. This does not change the fact that the person still has, within himself or herself, the same core set of identities. In other words, the manifestation of stable facets of the self-identity is conditioned on the environmental pressures that are encountered. Whereas context can shape individual identification, dispositional characteristics, such as values, preferences, and affective tendencies, can also lead individuals to find some identities more chronically accessible (Sherman, Hamilton, & Lewis, 1999). Whether a recently hired extrovert "fits" with a workgroup made up exclusively of introverts will depend in part on how strongly the extrovert dispositionally identifies with his or her personality, as well as the strength of counterparts' dispositional identification with their personalities.

To summarize, an interactional model can ground research investigating how individual dispositions and organizational context come into relation with one another in the process of developing fit. Highly elaborated schemas are unlikely to change in newcomers, but more specific behaviors will be adapted to the context; higher order structures and roles are unlikely to change in the context, but more peripheral role constructs will change to meet the newcomers' needs. Perceived fit between the dispositions of the newcomer and the situation will lead to increases in both behavioral and psychological commitment over time, whereas misfit leads to a progression of withdrawal. The importance of any specific domain of fit for this process will be moderated by the dispositional tendency for newcomers and incumbents to find any particular stable aspect of their identity important.

## THREE VIEWS OF ADJUSTMENT: ORGANIZATIONAL TACTICS, INDIVIDUAL DISPOSITIONS, AND SOCIAL INTERACTIONS

Although researchers have proposed numerous stage models of adjustment (see Wanous, 1992, for a review), the importance of dynamic conceptions of perceived fit in this process has seldom been studied. Figure 3–1 provides a conceptual model that can serve as a basis for investigating the ways that fit develops over time. The core components of this model are a set of initial contextual conditions and dispositions, assessments of fit, and a menu of interactive strategies for improving fit. As implied by Fig. 3–1, dynamic fit can be conceptualized on multiple levels, including person–organization fit, person–group fit, and person–job fit (Kristof-Brown, Jansen, & Colbert, 2002).

The literature on dynamic fit is deeply influenced by the debate on whether behavior is a function of persons or situations. In part, this is a reflection of a field that is unusually interdisciplinary. Newcomer adjustment and socialization have been studied extensively in the core literatures of sociology and psychology during time periods in which these perspectives were largely opposed to one another. From this division came distinct literature on organizational socialization tactics that describes how newcomers change themselves to fit on the one hand and the literature on newcomer dispositions as direct effects on fit on the other hand. A third stream of research emerged over time, conducted by both sociologists and psychologists who believed that the real nexus of fit between people and situations can be found only by studying social interactions. These three views of fit will be reviewed in turn, with a particular emphasis on how each school of thought conceptualizes the interaction between the newcomer and the organization, as well as their unique (and often unstated) assumptions about what it means to fit.

## Organizational Tactics

The literature on organizational tactics designed to socialize newcomers is derived from role theory and research on social conformity. According to role theory, newcomers are induced to accept a certain pattern of behavior to help the group meet its goals of constancy and harmonious interaction (Parsons, 1951). Conformity researchers note that individuals are motivated to avoid sanctions for failure to meet role expectations (Cialdini & Trost, 1998). For researchers interested in organizational tactics, dynamic fit is a matter of the newcomer's behavior being brought into synchronization with the demands of the organizational context. The focus is almost exclusively on person–organization fit.

Figure 3–1 depicts the organizational tactics model as dashed lines. The task requirements, culture and climate, and competitive environment of the organization combine to produce expectations for what is required of newcomers (Van Maanen & Schein, 1979). Observation of newcomers occurs in the aggregate; no one individual's fit or lack of fit will produce changes in organizational tactics. The behavior of multiple newcomers over time can be assessed on the basis of aggregate job performance, turnover rates, and resistance or compliance with organizational directives. Based on the overall assessment of the body of employees and their ability to match organizational demands, organizations enact interactive ASA strategies to improve fit by recruiting the right people, selecting these people to be hired, and then establishing termination policies to eliminate those who do not fit (Schneider, 1987).

Whereas ASA strategies all concentrate on newcomers as driven largely by dispositions, institutional and impersonal agents of socialization are also put into place to transform the newcomers so they are more adequate fits (Stryker & Statham, 1985; Van Maanen & Schein, 1979). The "interaction" between individual and organization is largely one way (i.e., it is unlikely that a single newcomer will change the whole organization), with organizations providing training, task structure, guidelines, and reward structures. Organizational factors also dictate the context of the workgroup by assigning specific tasks and providing guidelines on culturally appropriate behavior. The newcomer's role is to accept or reject what is presented over time by assessing fit after organizational tactics are enacted. Structured socialization tactics are hypothesized to induce a unified, coherent vision of the organization and the role in the newcomer, while simultaneously discouraging individual innovation or role modification (Van Maanen & Schein, 1979). Empirical support for these contentions comes from studies showing that formal organizational socialization systems are associated with higher levels of role clarity (Ashforth & Saks, 1996; Jones, 1986; Kammeyer-Mueller & Wanberg, 2003), as well as research showing that participation in organizationally sponsored social activities is positively related to congruence with organizational values (Chatman, 1991). Longitudinal studies have shown that fit between individual and ascribed organizational values can be facilitated through socialization tactics as well (Cable & Parsons, 2001).

Although organizational tactics do explain some adaptive behaviors newcomers engage in to improve their fit, there are significant problems that make this theory incomplete. Researchers must invoke individual motivation and interests as a reason for the acceptance of organizational socialization attempts but seldom describe these individual differences as important. This is a major omission, given the importance of dispositions in motivation (Judge & Ilies, 2002). There are also few, if any, contexts in which the pressures applied by socialization are so powerful that variations in behavior are eliminated. These omissions are acknowledged by institutional socialization researchers, but they consider factors such as values or dispositions "outside an organizational analysis" (Van Maanen & Schein, 1979, p. 230). By excluding individual dispositions and interactions, these theories provide little guidance on why role rejection and deviance happen at all. As an example of a shortcoming in this approach, research has shown that although realistic job preview efforts are not especially effective (Phillips, 1998), individuals who report adequate information about their jobs before their hiring are more likely to be adjusted in terms of commitment and work withdrawal (Griffeth, Hom, Fink, & Cohen, 1997; Kammeyer-Mueller & Wanberg, 2003; Saks, 1994). In other words, although organizational efforts to improve fit may not be successful, individual knowledge and initiative may produce differences in adjustment within a given social setting.

## Individual Dispositions

The dispositional perspective on newcomer adjustment stands in direct contrast to the organizational tactics perspective by de-emphasizing change in the individual due to contextual pressures. Instead, the dispositional perspective focuses on how characteristics of individuals and the contexts they encounter either match or lead to conflict. Fit, for a strict dispositionalist, means that a newcomer has found a work context that is amenable to his or her preexisting individual characteristics. More dynamic dispositional models address how dispositions function to facilitate or inhibit adaptation; some individuals are consistently more adaptable because of higher openness, intelligence, and other adaptive traits (Ashford & Taylor, 1990; Chan, 2000; LePine, Colquitt, & Erez, 2000).

The dispositional paths in Fig. 3–1 are in bold. Newcomers enter a job with their stable dispositions. They assess their fit with the new context by seeking information about roles and job tasks, organizational culture and the subculture of their workgroups, and the dispositional characteristics of individual members of the new workgroup (Morrison, 1993). Based on this assessment, newcomers can proactively engage the situation, conform to or resist established norms, and engage in a process of role modification (Nicholson, 1984). These interaction strategies will partially be determined by the assessment process but will also be directly determined by the dispositions of the newcomer.

One contribution of the dispositional perspective is to show that there is considerable consistency in work attitudes across jobs, demonstrating that even as the context changes, part of the individual's adjustment is consistent and internal (e.g., Staw, Bell, & Clausen, 1986; Gerhart, 1987). Further evidence for a dispositional component to fit comes from the field of behavior genetics, which has demonstrated that genetic factors explain consistency in work attitudes across jobs (Arvey, Bouchard, Segal, & Abraham, 1989) and tendencies to turnover (McCall, Cavanaugh, Arvey, & Taubman, 1997). Dispositional perspectives can take a more processual approach as well, by examining the trajectory from individual dispositions to work attitudes as mediated by factors such as job characteristics (e.g., Judge, Locke, Durham, & Kluger, 1998). Overall, this disposition-focused research suggests that some individuals are more likely to fit into situations in general.

Much of the research incorporating dispositions in the newcomer fit process examines the proactive interactions newcomers use to understand the work context (e.g., Ashford & Taylor, 1990; Miller & Jablin, 1991). Interactions between the newcomer and the environment occur when newcomers seek information (Miller & Jablin, 1991), seek feedback (Ashford & Cummings, 1983), and develop social relationships (Ashford & Taylor, 1990) to increase their own adjustment. Dispositional variables, such as extroversion, openness to experience, and proactive personality, have empirically demonstrated effects on the behaviors newcomers enact to fit into their work environments (Chan & Schmitt, 2000; Kammeyer-Mueller & Wanberg, 2003; Wanberg & Kammeyer-Mueller, 2000). Jones (1986) found that whereas organizational pressures to conform are effective on the whole in encouraging newcomers to accept the job role as it is presented, those who are higher in self-efficacy and have a strong sense of what they want from a job are less likely to succumb to these pressures. Evidence that applicants try to find organizations that match their dispositions in the recruiting process further supports this point of view (Judge & Cable, 1997). These interactions demonstrate how individual dispositions can lead to behaviors that stimulate fit.

The dispositional perspective does provide a useful tonic against the excessively pliable newcomers described by socialization tactics researchers, but it is equally clear that dispositions do not explain all the variance in attitudes and behavior. Although traits are typically stable over time, test–retest correlation between personality questionnaires in adulthood decreases considerably as the lag between testing administration grows longer (Roberts & DelVecchio, 2000). There is also evidence that early career experiences change personality traits (Roberts, Caspi, & Moffitt, 2003). A related shortcoming of most dispositional research on newcomer adjustment is that it seldom addresses the dispositions of those who are already in the social situation and the ways that these dispositions influence the dynamic process of fit. Although this path is depicted in the current model, empirical studies of how the dispositions of established organizational members influence interactions toward newcomers are rare and are primarily from mentoring research rather than newcomer adjustment (Allen, 2003; Bozionelos, 2004). Finally, the interactive processes that might be set into motion by dispositions over the course of a dynamic fit interaction are seldom specified or assessed.

## Social Interactions

Neither the strongly regimented society described by role theory nor the atomized individualism described by the dispositional perspective is typical of most social groups. Alternative models for social structure have been developed that involve interpersonal processes and idiosyncratic role definitions as a means of finding a more comprehensive perspective on newcomer adjustment. Theories rooted in the development of meaning and self-identity through social interactions were developed by symbolic interactionists and advocates of social information processing (Reichers, 1987; Salancik & Pfeffer, 1978; Stryker & Statham, 1985; Zalesny & Ford, 1990). Because established employees have resource control over the flow and interpretation of information between the organization and the newcomer, the most critical socialization may occur within workgroups (Feldman, 1989; Moreland & Levine, 1982, 2001).

Because the social context involves personal interactions, it is likely to be responsive to newcomers and may even change over time in response to newcomer actions. Fit, therefore, is an emergent property of the ongoing and idiosyncratic definitions of the newcomers' role that emerge through the efforts of both the newcomer and the members of the social context. These theories therefore are most directly concerned with endogenous (i.e., interactionist) paths in Fig. 3–1 that link the interaction tactics of newcomers and social groups with one another over time to produce fit.

Several studies have shown that the immediate social environment is related to employee adjustment. There is evidence that individual interactions with coworkers can be an important element of developing adjustment (e.g., Buchanan, 1974; Fullagar, Gallagher, Gordon, & Clark, 1995; Kammeyer-Mueller & Wanberg, 2003; Morrison, 1993). Individuals in mentoring relationships are more knowledgeable about organizational issues and practices (Ostroff & Kozlowski, 1993) and have more knowledge in goals/values, politics, and people domains of socialization (Chao, Walz, & Gardner, 1992) than unmentored individuals. Supervisor support is associated with adjustment outcomes including job satisfaction, organizational commitment, and reduced intention to leave the employing organization (Anakwe & Greenhaus, 1999; Bauer & Green, 1998; Feij, Whitely, Peiró, & Taris, 1995; Fisher, 1985; Ostroff & Kozlowski, 1992). In sum, research suggests that there are important social interactions that develop in the work context that are potent predictors of newcomer adjustment. Strangely, there is an almost complete penumbra over the issue of how newcomers change the attitudes of incumbents.

It may seem that the interactional perspective on organizational behavior is a uniquely well-suited counterpart to the dynamical concept of fit introduced at the outset of this chapter. The greatest strength of the interactional perspective is the way it actively questions the assumptions about static contextual or dispositional models of fit. Because the interactional perspective often goes so far in emphasizing the dynamics of the relationship between newcomers and the social context, the static properties of both the context and dispositions of the newcomer are often dispensed with. There must be some stable organizational and personal attributes that form the initial basis for cycles of subjective interactions (Hulin, 1991). Although it is certainly the case that social information can lead individuals to construe situations more positively or negatively, the role of the initial perceptions that lead to social information in the first place must be remembered. If dispositions shape individual perceptions (Shoda, Mischel, & Wright, 1994), and dispositions have significant effects on both actual and perceived job characteristics (Judge, Bono, & Locke, 2000), then it is clear that dynamically shaped social information is constantly being modified by stable dispositions and contexts.

## Summary

The preceding review of the literature on newcomer adjustment hopefully provides some suggestion of how distinct perspectives on dynamic fit and dispositions can be complementary. Each perspective has something to offer to fit researchers. The overall model suggested by Figure 3–1 can help to identify some of the underlying processes that inform fit. However, a thorough presentation of research on dynamic fit should also provide some suggestions for how empirical research might proceed. This topic is the subject of the next section.

## EMPIRICAL MODELS FOR DYNAMIC RESEARCH

The conceptual model shown in Fig. 3–1 is admittedly so complicated that it is unrealistic to expect that any one study could possibly address all of its propositions. In this section, the model is broken down into discrete, estimable components to better conceptualize the ways researchers can observe how individuals and the organizational contexts produce fit. It is hoped that the increasing availability of statistical techniques for gathering and analyzing longitudinal data during the fit process will move this literature from primarily theoretical propositions toward empirical evidence to either support or refute these propositions.

### Recursive Mediated Models

The simplest method for investigating the development of fit is to eliminate the nonrecursive process of reciprocal interactionism altogether and focus on those elements of the fit process that can be assessed through simple structural models such as those shown in Fig. 3–2. Although the recursive model has some surface similarities to the overall conceptual model, it is distinct in that it has no feedback loops, interaction choices are typically assessed as being determined by dispositional factors, and final assessments of fit are either affective measures of constructs such as commitment or the match between job characteristics and desired characteristics or discrete measures of performance relative to some organizational standard. The use of fit (or fit-like measures) as an outcome means that this research does not provide much information about how individuals use their assessments of fit to shape their behavior. The chief advantage of these recursive models is that they can show how static factors can lead to processes that produce fit without the practical and statistical difficulties of repeated measures designs.

Exploring mediators of the relationship between broad person-level factors, attitudes, and behavioral outcomes has become a dominant method for studying the effects of individual dispositions on work outcomes in a number of fields (e.g., Barrick, Stewart, & Piotrowski, 2002;

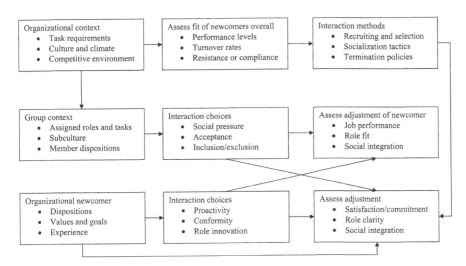

FIGURE 3–2.   Recursive model.

Judge et al., 1998; Wanberg, Watt, & Rumsey, 1996). In newcomer adjustment research, individual dispositions are measured at the point of organizational entry, followed by measures of the behaviors engaged in by the newcomers, and a terminal measure of newcomer adjustment at some point in the future. This is an extremely common method for the study of socialization and newcomer adjustment (e.g., Bauer & Green, 1998; Fisher, 1985; Fullagar et al., 1995; Kammeyer-Mueller & Wanberg, 2003; Ostroff & Kozlowski, 1992; Saks, 1995; Wanberg & Kammeyer-Mueller, 2000). As reviewed earlier, these studies suggest that organizations, groups, and newcomer characteristics do produce fit through the paths shown in Fig. 3–1.

There is certainly a large quantity of research in the recursive tradition, but there is still much to learn. Starting from the organizational level, there is essentially no research examining how organizations structure their decisions about how to help newcomers fit. Anthropological evidence suggests that highly regimented organizations with centralized authority structures may engage in more rigorous screening and socialization efforts (Van Maanen, 1975), but this finding has not been replicated using more comprehensive samples of organizations. For workgroups, as noted earlier, there is essentially no research on how members of extant workgroups perceive organizational newcomers and how the traits of existing organizational members might lead them to engage in different behavioral strategies to convince newcomers to behave differently. For individuals, the role of motivation and goal striving as critical concepts bridging the gap between broad individual dispositions and individual behavior (Kanfer, 1991) has not been addressed. One of the most significant shortcomings of the socialization literature is the failure to measure the motives of newcomers in a systematic manner.

The recursive models on fit may not directly address dynamics, per se, because most constructs are measured only at a single point in time, and no feedback loops are considered. These models can help in the understanding of how dispositions and static contextual features directly lead individuals to interactions and fit. However, if one truly wishes to understand how fit is shaped through dynamic interactions, repeated measures approaches are required.

## Growth Curves

The growth curve approach is designed to examine individual differences in overall and initial levels of adjustment and long-term trajectories of adjustment (Chan, 1998). Figure 3–3 provides an overview of a typical growth curve model. In the growth curve approach, boxes depict the specific measurements of fit and interaction across multiple time waves, with the level being the average or initial value of these constructs, and slope being the trajectory of these values over time. The effect of dispositions on an individual's assessment of fit within a given context can be clearly measured, as well as the effect of dispositions on the use of interactive strategies. The model portrayed here further shows how assessments of fit can lead newcomers to enact strategies to improve

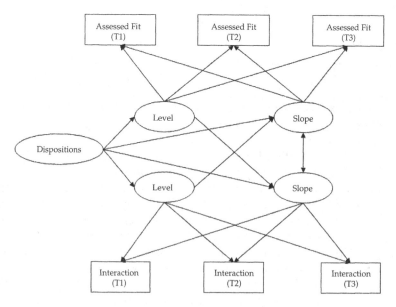

FIGURE 3–3.   Individual growth model.

their fit, and how these strategies for interaction can improve fit. This is clearly a complex system of equations, and researchers interested in pursuing this strategy may find that, for simple computational tractability, it is preferable to separate the dispositional and interactive components of the model (see Chan & Schmitt, 2000, for an example).

Although there have been relatively few studies to implement growth curve modeling with groups of organizational newcomers, insights gained from these initial efforts have demonstrated several dynamic processes. In a study of new doctoral students, proactive personality was related to consistent use of relationship-building strategies, whereas previous transition experience was associated with increasing information seeking from supervisors over time (Chan & Schmitt, 2000). This same study showed that proactive personality was associated with consistently higher levels of task mastery, role clarity, and social integration, but that these relationships did not become stronger over time. Regarding the timing of adjustment, Lance, Vandenberg, and Self (2000) demonstrated a substantial change in work attitudes from the point of initial hire to the third month of employment but relatively minor changes from the third to sixth month of employment. This finding suggests that newcomers become increasingly stable in their attitudes over time. Finally, individuals who are more likely to turnover have more negative perceptions of their new organizations soon after hire, and over time these initial negative interactions become more pronounced as the "leavers" engage in disengagement strategies such as a job search (Kammeyer-Mueller, Wanberg, Glomb, & Ahlburg, 2005).

There are several other theoretical propositions in the dynamic fit domain that could be investigated using a growth curve approach. Jones (1983) proposed that newcomers' preexistent repertoire of responses will affect how much they will be influenced as they enter the organization. The greatest changes will occur for those with the least preentry information or confidence in their knowledge. Empirical studies do show a positive relationship between self-efficacy and an active orientation toward one's role (Jones, 1986), coping resources (Saks, 1995), organizational commitment (Laker & Steffy, 1995), and use of problem-focused coping strategies (Ashforth & Saks, 2000). A logical extension of this research is an examination of dispositional variables on the trajectory of active versus passive interactions over time.

In a related vein, Nicholson's (1984) work–role transitions model proposes that those with a higher desire for feedback are more likely to modify themselves to match the situation than those with a low desire for feedback, whereas those with a higher desire for control are more likely to modify the situation to match their preferences than those with a low desire for control. Studies have shown that desire for feedback is related to perceived personal changes (Ashforth & Saks, 1995), that desire for control is associated with attempts to change the situation (Ashford &

Black, 1996; but see Ashforth & Saks, 1995), and that those with a high desire for both control and feedback report greater role and personal change (West & Nicholson, 1989). However, these studies have relied on single-occasion self-report data to demonstrate changes. Studies to examine how dispositions such as desires for feedback and control affect these interactions with the environment over time would be an ideal application of the growth curve approach.

## Interactive Growth Model

Although all of the aforementioned models do show promise for investigating dynamic fit process, the interactive growth model shown in Fig. 3–4 is the only model that explicitly takes interactive dynamics into account. This model is derived from research in the relationships literature examining how social interactions are shaped by personality (Branje, van Lieshout, & van Aken, 2004). Like the growth curve approach, level and slope parameters are estimated by multiple measurements across multiple time waves. These boxes have been omitted to aid in interpretation of the figure. Unlike the growth curve approach, data are collected from the perspective of the newcomer as well as the extant members of the social situation. Over time, the interaction style of the newcomer is adapted on the basis of the interaction style of the extant members of the

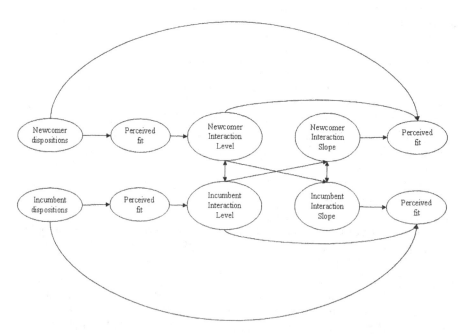

FIGURE 3–4.   Interactive growth model.

context and vice versa. Ideally, repeated measurements of fit would be tractable for modeling purposes, but in reality, it is probably far easier to use more conventionally estimated values of perceived fit at the point of entry and at some subsequent point in time.

The interactive growth model is a very recent development, and, as such, there are few results directly related to its use. However, there are several instances of research related to reciprocal interactionism that can be taken from the relationships literature and applied to questions of longitudinal fit. Research on social support in family contexts combining repeated measures of personality characteristics and social support perceptions showed that social relationship patterns are established relatively early, with few significant shifts in interactions over time (Branje et al., 2004). These studies support the idea that norms for interpersonal relationships are established early and then tend to persist despite changes in the environment (Huston, Niehuis, & Smith, 2001). In a related vein, research suggests that whereas extraversion, neuroticism, self-esteem, and agreeableness are related to changes in relationship quality over time, social relationships exert very little influence on personality over time (Neyer & Asendorpf, 2001).

Organizational behavior researchers have an excellent opportunity to provide new detail to these propositions about the role of dispositions in interactions, because not only do they have a distinct context in which to operate, but also they study relationships that have a much more discrete starting point than do the reciprocal interactions between children and parents or members of friendship groups. Studies examining the ways that newcomers and incumbents interact with one another and change over time in an organizational context would be another interesting area for future research.

## CONCLUSION

This chapter has provided an alternative conceptualization of person–environment fit that takes as a fundamental premise the fact that both individuals and organizations engage in a process of mutual adjustment to produce fit. Although there are examples of research in which this perspective was used, it is clear that dynamic fit remains a largely undiscovered subject area for organizational researchers. New conceptual and statistical models that have been developed in recent years will allow an increase in research related to adjustment. Although examples of ideas for how to model fit over time have been reviewed, it is likely that most readers have recognized dozens of other questions that might be examined from a dynamic, interactive perspective that are not addressed here. Although I highlighted several possible areas for future research that relate to fit in the preceding text, it was in a very broad, conceptually driven manner. Here I offer a few more specific ideas for how future researchers can explore fit in a dynamic framework. These ideas, like most of the chapter, are only the tip of the iceberg in terms of dynamic fit possibilities.

One promising approach to the dynamic interplay between persons and situations is found in the research on affective events (Weiss & Cropanzano, 1996). Research in this area demonstrates how workplace events are significantly related to affective and behavioral reactions (e.g., Ilies & Judge, 2004). To date, an event-based perspective has not been used in the adjustment literature despite the clear possibility for relationships. The most critical stage during socialization is likely to be the initial weeks on the job. Because of the constant new stimuli being provided at this time, it is likely that individuals will be in a state of heightened arousal and attention. As such, this time period may constitute what is referred to as an "emotion episode" (Frijda, 1993). Researchers in the area of affect have suggested that researchers should be especially attentive to these highly charged emotional episodes (Weiss & Kurek, 2003). The measurement of perceived interactive events during the period of organizational entry is a rich area for future development.

Learning how agreement with organizational values is shaped through socialization processes should receive greater attention, given the evidence that the correspondence between newcomer values and newcomer perceptions of organizational values increases over time (Cable & Parsons, 2001). Research generally suggests that the values of adults are well established, and it is not likely that a brief orientation session or training experience will fundamentally change newcomer positions on what is valued (Mortimer & Simmons, 1978). Thus, it seems that organizations may succeed in obtaining values congruence by convincing newcomers that the organization does represent values held in common by newcomers. In other words, orientation sessions may improve newcomer perceptions of values congruence by persuading the newcomers that the organization represents values the newcomers already believe in, rather than persuading newcomers to accept values they do not currently accept. Further research examining how commitment is shaped will help to resolve this issue.

One concluding point is a form of caveat emptor for researchers interested in examining dynamic fit. The interactive processes proposed in this chapter may help researchers better understand the complete picture of dynamic fit, but testing them also requires considerable theoretical discipline. The idea of interactionism is hardly new for organizational behavior researchers, and several previous reviews have suggested that empirical studies begin to take interactionism seriously (e.g., Jones, 1986; Reichers, 1987). However, there are relatively few studies in which dynamic fit was examined. This may partially be due to the lack of empirical models that could adequately address dynamic fit before latent growth or hierarchical linear modeling was available, but a careful reading of the literature also suggests that the sheer complexity of interactive process has resulted in many studies that are too theoretically diaphanous to provide much insight. Although it is clear that studying the dynamics of fit over time is not an easy task, the potential rewards in terms of our understanding of how people relate to one another in the process of mutual adjustment are enormous.

## REFERENCES

Allen, T. D. (2003). Mentoring others: A dispositional and motivational approach. *Journal of Vocational Behavior, 62,* 134–154.

Anakwe, U. P., & Greenhaus, J. H. (1999). Effective socialization of employees: Socialization content perspective. *Journal of Managerial Issues, 11,* 315–329.

Arvey, R. D., Bouchard, T. J., Segal, N. L., & Abraham, L. M. (1989). Job satisfaction: Environmental and genetic components. *Journal of Applied Psychology, 74,* 187–192.

Ashford, S. J., & Black, J. S. (1996). Proactivity during organizational entry: The role of desire for control. *Journal of Applied Psychology, 81,* 199–214.

Ashford, S. J., & Cummings, L. L. (1983). Feedback as an individual resource: The instrumental use of the information environment. *Journal of Organizational Psychology, 58,* 370–398.

Ashford, S. J., & Taylor, S. M. (1990). Adaptation to work transitions: An integrative approach. In K. M. Rowland & G. R. Ferris (Eds.), *Research in personnel and human resources management* (Vol. 8, pp. 1–39). Greenwich, CT: JAI Press.

Ashforth, B. E., & Johnson, S. A. (2001). Which hat to wear? The relative salient of multiple identities in organizational contexts. In M. A. Hogg & D. J. Terry (Eds.), *Social identity processes in organizational contexts* (pp. 31–49). Philadelphia: Psychology Press.

Ashforth, B. E., & Saks, A. M. (1995). Work-role transitions: A longitudinal examination of the Nicholson model. *Journal of Occupational and Organizational Psychology, 68,* 157–175.

Ashforth, B. E., & Saks, A. M. (1996). Socialization tactics: Longitudinal effects on newcomer adjustment. *Academy of Management Journal, 39,* 149–178.

Ashforth, B. E., & Saks, A. M. (2000). Personal control in organizations: A longitudinal investigation with newcomers. *Human Relations, 53,* 311–339.

Baron, R. M., & Boudreau, L. A. (1987). An ecological perspective on integrating personality and social psychology. *Journal of Personality and Social Psychology, 53,* 1222–1228.

Barrick, M. R., Stewart, G. L., & Piotrowski, M. (2002). Personality and job performance: Test of the meditating effects of motivation among sales representatives. *Journal of Applied Psychology, 87,* 43–51.

Bauer, T. N., & Green, S. G. (1998). Testing the combined effects of newcomer information seeking and manager behavior on socialization. *Journal of Applied Psychology, 83,* 72–83.

Bozionelos, N. (2004). Mentoring provided: Relation to mentor's career success, personality, and mentoring received. *Journal of Vocational Behavior, 64,* 24–46.

Branje, S. J. T., van Lieshout, C. F. M., & van Aken, M. A. G. (2004). Relations between Big Five personality characteristics and perceived support in adolescents' families. *Journal of Personality and Social Psychology, 86,* 615–628.

Buchanan, B. (1974). Building organizational commitment: The socialization of managers in work organizations. *Administrative Science Quarterly, 19*, 533–546.

Cable, D. M., & DeRue, D. S. (2002). The convergent and discriminant validity of subjective fit perceptions. *Journal of Applied Psychology, 87*, 875–884.

Cable, D. M., & Judge, T. A. (1996). Person–organization fit, job choice decisions, and organizational entry. *Organizational Behavior and Human Decision Processes, 67*, 294–311.

Cable, D. M., & Judge, T. A. (1997). Interviewers' perceptions of person–organization fit and organizational selection decisions. *Journal of Applied Psychology, 82*, 546–561.

Cable, D. M., & Parsons, C. K. (2001). Socialization tactics and person-organization fit. *Personnel Psychology, 54*, 1–23.

Chan, D. (1998). The conceptualization and analysis of change over time: An integrative approach incorporating longitudinal means and covariance structures analysis (LMACS) and multiple indicator latent growth modeling (MLGM). *Organizational Research Methods, 1*, 421–483.

Chan, D. (2000). Understanding adaptation to changes in the work environment: Integrating individual difference and learning perspectives. In J. R. Ferris (Ed.), *Research in personnel and human resources management* (Vol. 18, pp. 1–42). Greenwich, CT: JAI Press.

Chan, D., & Schmitt, N. (2000). Interindividual differences in intraindividual changes in proactivity during organizational entry: A latent growth modeling approach to understanding newcomer adaptation. *Journal of Applied Psychology, 85*, 190–210.

Chao, G. T., Walz, P. M., & Gardner, P. D. (1992). Formal and informal mentorships: A comparison on mentoring functions and contrast with nonmentored counterparts. *Personnel Psychology, 45*, 619–636.

Chatman, J. A. (1991). Matching people and organizations: Selection and socialization in public accounting firms. *Administrative Science Quarterly, 36*, 459–484.

Cialdini, R. B., & Trost, M. R. (1998). Social influence: Social norms, conformity, and compliance. In D. Gilbert, S. Fiske, & G. Lindzey (Eds.), *Handbook of social psychology* (4th ed., Vol. 2, pp. 151–192). New York: McGraw-Hill.

Eysenck, H. J., & Eysenck, M. W. (1985). *Personality and individual differences: A natural science approach.* New York: Plenum.

Feij, J. A., Whitely, W. T., Peiró, J. M., & Taris, T. W. (1995). The development of career-enhancing strategies and content innovation: A longitudinal study of new workers. *Journal of Vocational Behavior, 46*, 231–256.

Feldman, D. C. (1989). Socialization, resocialization, and training: Reframing the research agenda. In I. L. Goldstein (Ed.), *Training and development in organizations* (pp. 376–416). San Francisco: Jossey-Bass.

Fisher, C. D. (1985). Social support and adjustment to work: A longitudinal study. *Journal of Management, 11*, 39–53.

Frijda, N. H. (1993). Moods, emotion episodes, and emotions. In M. Lewis & J. M. Haviland-Jones (Eds.), *Handbook of emotions* (pp. 381–404). New York: Guilford Press.

Fullagar, C. J. A., Gallagher, D. G., Gordon, M. E., & Clark, P. F. (1995). Impact of early socialization on union commitment and participation: A longitudinal study. *Journal of Applied Psychology, 80*, 147–157.

Gerhart, B. (1987). How important are dispositional factors as determinants of job satisfaction? *Journal of Applied Psychology, 72,* 366–373.

Griffeth, R. W., Hom, P. W., Fink, L. S., & Cohen, D. J. (1997). Comparative tests of multivariate models of recruiting sources effects. *Journal of Management, 23,* 19–36.

Hackman, J., & Oldham, G. (1980). *Work redesign.* Reading, MA: Addison-Wesley.

Hellervik, L. W., Hazucha, J. F., & Schneider, R. J. (1992). Behavior change: Models, methods, and a review of evidence. In M. D. Dunnette & L. M. Hough (Eds.), *Handbook of industrial and organizational psychology* (2nd ed., pp. 823–895). Palo Alto, CA: Consulting Psychologists Press.

Hogg, M. A., & Terry, D. (2000). Social identity and self-categorization processes in organizational contexts. *Academy of Management Review, 25,* 121–141.

Hulin, C. L. (1991). Adaptation, persistence, and commitment in organizations. In M. D. Dunnette & L. M. Hough (Eds.), *Handbook of industrial organizational psychology* (2nd ed., Vol. 2, pp. 435–505). New York: Wiley.

Huston, T. L., Niehuis, S., & Smith, S. E. (2001). The early marital roots of conjugal distress and divorce. *Current Directions in Psychological Science, 10,* 116–119.

Ilies, R., & Judge, T. A. (2002). Understanding the dynamic relationships among personality, mood and job satisfaction: A field experience sampling study. *Organizational Behavior & Human Decision Processes, 89,* 1119–1139.

Jones, G. R. (1983). Psychological orientation and the process of organizational socialization: An interactionist perspective. *Academy of Management Review, 8,* 464–474.

Jones, G. R. (1986). Socialization tactics, self-efficacy, and newcomers' adjustments to organizations. *Academy of Management Journal, 29,* 262–279.

Judge, T. A., Bono, J. E., & Locke, E. A. (2000). Personality and job satisfaction: The mediating role of job characteristics. *Journal of Applied Psychology, 85,* 237–249.

Judge, T. A., & Cable, D. M. (1997). Applicant personality, organizational culture, and organization attraction. *Personnel Psychology, 50,* 359–394.

Judge, T. A., & Ilies, R. (2002). Relationship of personality to performance motivation: A meta-analytic review. *Journal of Applied Psychology, 87,* 797–807.

Judge, T. A., Locke, E. A., Durham, C. C., & Kluger, A. N. (1998). Dispositional effects on job and life satisfaction: The role of core evaluations. *Journal of Applied Psychology, 83,* 17–34.

Kammeyer-Mueller, J. D., & Wanberg, C. R. (2003). Unwrapping the organizational entry process: Disentangling multiple antecedents and their pathways to adjustment. *Journal of Applied Psychology, 88,* 779–794.

Kammeyer-Mueller, J. D., Wanberg, C. R., Glomb, T. M., & Ahlburg, D. A. (2005). Turnover processes in a temporal context: It's about time. *Journal of Applied Psychology, 90,* 644–658.

Kanfer, R. (1991). Motivation theory and industrial and organizational psychology. In M. D. Dunnette & L. M. Hough (Eds.), *Handbook of industrial and organizational psychology* (pp. 75–170). Palo Alto, CA: Consulting Psychologists Press.

King, L. A., & King, D. W. (1990). Role conflict and role ambiguity: A critical assessment of construct validity. *Psychological Bulletin, 107,* 48–64.

Kristof-Brown, A. L., Jansen, K. J., & Colbert, A. E. (2002). A policy-capturing study of the simultaneous effects of fit with jobs, groups, and organizations. *Journal of Applied Psychology, 87,* 985–993.

Laker, D. R., & Steffy, B. D. (1995). The impact of alternative socialization tactics on self-managing behavior and organizational commitment. *Journal of Social Behavior & Personality, 10,* 645–660.

Lance, C. E., Vandenberg, R. J., & Self, R. M. (2000). Latent growth models of individual change: The case of newcomer adjustment. *Organizational Behavior & Human Decision Processes, 83,* 107–140.

LePine, J. A., Colquitt, J. A., & Erez, A. (2000). Adaptability to changing task contexts: Effects of general cognitive ability, conscientiousness, and openness to experience. *Personnel Psychology, 53,* 563–594.

Magnusson, D. (1999). Holistic interactionism: A perspective for research on personality development. In L. A. Pervin & O. P. John (Eds.), *Handbook of personality: theory and research* (2nd ed., pp. 219–247). New York: Guilford Press.

McCall, B. P., Cavanaugh, M. A., Arvey, R. D., & Taubman, P. (1997). Genetic influences on job and occupational switching. *Journal of Vocational Behavior, 50,* 60–77.

McCrae, R. R., Costa, P. T., Jr., Ostendorf, F., Angleitner, A., Hrebickova, M., Avia, M. D., Sanz, J., Sánchez-Bernardos, M. L., Kusdil, M. E., Woodfield, R., Saunders, P. R., & Smith, P. B. (2000). Nature over nurture: Temperament, personality, and life span development. *Journal of Personality & Social Psychology, 78,* 173–186.

Miller, V. D., & Jablin, F. M. (1991). Information seeking during organizational entry: Influences, tactics, and a model of the process. *Academy of Management Review, 16,* 92–120.

Mischel, W., & Shoda, Y. (1998). Reconciling processing dynamics and personality dispositions. *Annual Review of Psychology, 49,* 229–258.

Moreland, R. L., & Levine, J. M. (1982). Socialization in small groups: Temporal changes in individual-group relations. In L. Berkowitz (Ed.), *Advances in experimental social psychology* (Vol. 15, pp. 137–192). New York: Academic Press.

Moreland, R. L., & Levine, J. M. (2001). Socialization in organizations and work groups. In M. E. Turner (Ed.), *Groups at work: Theory and research* (pp. 69–112). Mahwah, NJ: Lawrence Erlbaum Associates.

Morrison, E. W. (1993). Longitudinal study of the effects of information seeking on newcomer socialization. *Journal of Applied Psychology, 78,* 173–183.

Mortimer, J. T., & Simmons, R. G. (1978). Adult socialization. *Annual Review of Sociology, 4,* 421–454.

Muchinsky, P. M., & Monahan, C. J. (1987). What is person-environment congruence? Supplementary versus complementary models of fit. *Journal of Vocational Behavior, 31,* 268–277.

Mullen, B., & Copper, C. (1994). The relation between group cohesiveness and performance: An integration. *Psychological Bulletin, 115,* 210–227.

Neyer, F. J., & Asendorpf, J. B. (2001). Personality—Relationship transaction in young adulthood. *Journal of Personality and Social Psychology, 81,* 1190–1204.

Nicholson, N. (1984). A theory of work role transitions. *Administrative Science Quarterly, 29,* 172–191.

Ostroff, C., Kinicki, A. J., & Tamkins, M. M. (2003). Organizational culture and climate. In W. C. Borman, D. R. Ilgen, & R. J. Klimoski (Eds.), *Handbook of psychology: Vol. 12. Industrial and organizational psychology* (pp. 565–593). Hoboken, NJ: Wiley.

Ostroff, C., & Kozlowski, S. W. (1992). Organizational socialization as a learning process: The role of information acquisition. *Personnel Psychology, 45,* 849–874.

Ostroff, C., & Kozlowski, S. W. (1993). The role of mentoring in the information gathering processes of newcomers during early organizational socialization. *Journal of Vocational Behavior, 42,* 170–183.

Parsons, T. (1951). *The social system.* Glencoe, IL: Free Press.

Pervin, L. A. (1989). Persons, situations, interactions: The history of a controversy and a discussion of theoretical models. *Academy of Management Review, 14,* 350–360.

Phillips, J. M. (1998). Effects of realistic job previews on multiple organizational outcomes: A meta-analysis. *Academy of Management Journal, 41,* 673–690.

Reichers, A. E. (1987). An interactionist perspective on newcomer socialization rates. *Academy of Management Review, 12,* 278–287.

Roberts, B. W., Caspi, A., & Moffitt, T. E. (2003). Work experiences and personality development in young adulthood. *Journal of Personality & Social Psychology, 84,* 582–593.

Roberts, B. W., & DelVecchio, W. F. (2000). The rank-order consistency of personality traits from childhood to old age: A quantitative review of longitudinal studies. *Psychological Bulletin, 126,* 3–25.

Roberts, B. W., O'Donnell, M., & Robins, R. W. (2004). Goal and personality trait development in emerging adulthood. *Journal of Personality & Social Psychology, 87,* 541–550.

Ryan, A. M., & Kristof-Brown, A. (2003). Focusing on personality in person-organization fit research: Unaddressed issues. In M. R. Barrick & A. M. Ryan (Eds.), *Personality and work: Reconsidering the role of personality in organizations* (pp. 262–288). San Francisco: Jossey Bass.

Saks, A. M. (1994). A psychological process investigation for the effects of recruitment source and organization information on job survival. *Journal of Organizational Behavior, 15,* 225–244.

Saks, A. M. (1995). Longitudinal field investigation of the moderating and mediating effects of self-efficacy on the relationship between training and newcomer adjustment. *Journal of Applied Psychology, 80,* 211–225.

Salancik, G. R., & Pfeffer, J. (1978). A social information processing approach to job attitudes and task design. *Administrative Science Quarterly, 23,* 224–253.

Schein, E. H. (1980). *Organizational psychology* (3rd ed.). Englewood Cliffs, NJ: Prentice Hall.

Schneider, B. (1987). The people make the place. *Personnel Psychology, 40,* 437–454.

Schneider, B., Goldstein, H. W., & Smith, D. B. (1995). The ASA framework: An update. *Personnel Psychology, 48,* 747–773.

Sherman, S. J., Hamilton, D. L., & Lewis, A. C. (1999). Perceived entativity and the social identity value of group memberships. In D. Abrams & M. A. Hogg (Eds.), *Social identity and social cognition* (pp. 80–110). Oxford, England: Blackwell.

Shoda, Y., Mischel, W., & Wright, J. C. (1994). Intraindividual stability in the organization and patterning of behavior: Incorporating psychological situations into the idiographic analysis of personality. *Journal of Personality & Social Psychology, 67,* 674–687.

Staw, B. M., Bell, N. E., & Clausen, J. A. (1986). The dispositional approach to job attitudes: A lifelong longitudinal test. *Administrative Science Quarterly, 31,* 56–77.

Stryker, S., & Statham, A. (1985). Symbolic interactionism and role theory. In G. Lindsey & E. Aronson (Eds.), *The handbook of social psychology* (Vol. 1, pp. 311–378). New York: Random House.

Vaidya, J. G., Gray, E. K., Haig, J., & Watson, D. (2002). On the temporal stability of personality: Evidence for differential stability and the role of life experiences. *Journal of Personality & Social Psychology, 83*, 1469–1484.

Van Maanen, J. (1975). Police organization: A longitudinal examination of job attitudes in an urban police department. *Administrative Science Quarterly, 20*, 207–228.

Van Maanen, J., & Schein, E. H. (1979). Towards a theory of socialization. In B. M. Staw (Ed.), *Research in organizational behavior* (Vol. 1, pp. 209–264). Greenwich, CT: JAI Press.

Wanberg, C. R., & Kammeyer-Mueller, J. D. (2000). Predictors and outcomes of proactivity in the socialization process. *Journal of Applied Psychology, 85*, 373–385.

Wanberg, C. R., Watt, J. D., & Rumsey, D. J. (1996). Individuals without jobs: An empirical study of job-seeking behavior and reemployment. *Journal of Applied Psychology, 81*, 76–87.

Wanous, J. P. (1992). *Organizational entry: Recruitment, selection, orientation, and socialization of newcomers*. Reading, MA: Addison-Wesley.

Weiss, H. M., & Cropanzano, R. (1996). Affective events theory: A theoretical discussion of the structure, causes, and consequences of affective experiences at work. In B. M. Staw & L. L. Cummings (Eds.), *Research in organizational behavior* (Vol. 18, pp. 1–74). Greenwich, CT: JAI Press.

Weiss, H. M., & Kurek, K. E. (2003). Dispositional influences on affective experiences at work. In M. R. Barrick & A. M. Ryan (Eds.), *Personality and work: Reconsidering the role of personality in organizations* (pp. 121–149). San Francisco: Jossey Bass.

West, M. A., & Nicholson, N. (1989). The outcomes of job change. *Journal of Vocational Behavior, 34*, 335–349.

Zalesny, M. D., & Ford, J. K. (1990). Extending the social information processing perspective: New links to attitudes, behaviors, and perceptions. *Organizational Behavior & Human Decision Processes, 47*, 205–246.

# CHAPTER 4

# *Issues of*
# *Person–Organization Fit*

## Amy L. Kristof-Brown
*University of Iowa*

## Karen J. Jansen
*University of Virginia*

In 1957 Chris Argyris proposed that organizations were characterized by particular types of climates and that these climates played an important role in the attraction and selection of organizational members. His view, that companies hire people who are the "right types," reflects the notion of differential compatibility between organizations and individuals. In 1987 Benjamin Schneider elaborated on these ideas, in what has become one of the most popular theories of interactional psychology—the attraction–selection–attrition (ASA) framework. At its core, the ASA framework proposes that the three aforementioned processes result in organizations characterized by homogeneity and structures, systems, and processes that reflect the characteristics of the people who "make the place." Although principally concerned with predicting organizational-level outcomes and characteristics, the ASA framework has become the theoretical cornerstone for research on the concept of person–organization (PO) fit.

Understood most broadly as individual-organization compatibility, the notion of PO fit quickly became a topic of interest to academics and practitioners alike. Well over 150 studies and doctoral dissertations have been conducted and written on the topic. Yet despite the increasing interest, there is still little consensus on a number of important issues regarding PO fit. The authors of this chapter have often been approached, at conferences and via e-mail, by students and colleagues who have a deep-rooted interest in fit but are struggling with how to study it. Unlike other topics on person and organization interactions that have emerged in the last 20 years, such as procedural justice or perceived organization support, there appears to be no generally agreed upon way to define, measure, or account for the impact of PO fit. In 1995, when the first author was writing a review of the PO fit literature for a doctoral seminar with Ben Schneider, the level of ambiguity over what fit was and how to best assess it was overwhelming. What started out as a class paper on fit turned into an attempt to explain (to self and others) the various issues involved in studying this complex construct. The resulting article, published in 1996 in *Personnel Psychology* (Kristof, 1996), raised several of the important considerations but did not provide answers as to how future researchers should proceed with studying the topic. Now with 10 additional years of research, our aim in this chapter is to better inform some of those questions.

For the first portion of this chapter, we address two pivotal questions confronted by every scholar embarking on a study of PO fit. First, is PO fit likely to be relevant to my criteria? Second, if I think PO fit does matter, how should I assess it? Embedded in these two straightforward questions are a variety of complex issues that, if not considered thoroughly, can sink even the best-conceived study. To provide answers, or at least guidance, for these questions, we refer to recent meta-analyses (Arthur, Bell, Villado, & Doverspike, 2006; Hoffman & Woehr, 2006; Kristof-Brown, Zimmerman, & Johnson, 2005; Verquer, Beehr, & Wagner, 2003) as well as recent studies dedicated to a better understanding of the concept of fit (Cable & Edwards, 2004; Edwards, Cable, Williamson, Lambert, & Shipp; 2006; Shipp, 2006). Thus, we review the current existing knowledge base regarding outcomes of PO fit and explore the suggestions this provides for how to study fit in the future.

Specifically, when one determines whether PO fit is likely to be a relevant predictor, there are a number of issues to consider, including the criteria that are of interest, other types of fit that may be relevant, and possible moderators that may increase or decrease the impact of PO fit in a given situation. Once a person has determined that PO fit is likely to be an important consideration in his or her setting, issues of measurement and analysis emerge. These include determining the content dimensions along which PO fit should be assessed (e.g., values, personality, and goals), the type of fit (similarity or complementarity), the measurement approach (e.g., direct or indirect or subjective or objective), and the levels-of-analysis issues that are involved. Following these decisions, further questions of the appropriate analytic strategy—difference scores or polynomial regression—must be resolved. By reviewing what is known about these issues, our goal is to help others make these decisions in an informed manner, so that future researchers can be confident in their approach to study design.

The second half of the chapter focuses on an issue that is generating a lot of recent attention—the temporal nature of fit (Jansen & Kristof-Brown, 2006; Shipp, 2006; Shipp & Edwards, 2005). PO fit is at its core an interactional phenomenon, which implies that it should evolve over time as the person and organization influence each other (Chatman, 1989). Although we know conceptually that fit is not a static concept, and our theories accommodate changes in fit over time, rarely does the empirical research reflect this dynamic view. We briefly review what is currently known about temporal fit and introduce some new ideas about how it may evolve and how it might be studied. Our hope is that by the conclusion of this article, researchers interested in fit will have a better sense of what alternatives exist for studying the construct and the implications of these alternatives.

## UNDERSTANDING PO FIT

In an *Academy of Management Executive* article, Bowen, Ledford, and Nathan (1991) articulated the advantages of using PO fit as a selection criterion, in addition to the more traditional person–job match based on skills. Their argument was that if jobs are becoming increasingly fluid and companies are requiring employees to be able to move easily between roles, hiring for fit with the organization's culture may be just as important as hiring someone who is qualified. Since that time, a number of empirical studies examining other benefits of PO fit have been conducted. Recent meta-analyses have substantiated the benefits of PO fit for employee attitudes (Kristof-Brown et al., 2005; Verquer et al., 2003), as well as applicant reactions, strain, various types of performance, and turnover (Arthur et al., 2006; Hoffman & Woehr, 2006; Kristof-Brown et al., 2005). These themes have been echoed often in practitioner-oriented articles, geared to convincing managers about what is already common knowledge in the recruiting world: cultural fit matters (Montgomery, 1996; Siegel, 1998).

### When Does PO Fit Matter?

#### Distinguishing PO Fit

As PO fit became more widely accepted as a construct, researchers took great care to distinguish it from other forms of person–environment (PE) fit, such as person–job, person–group, and person–vocation fit. In some of the earliest studies of PO fit, Chatman (1991; O'Reilly, Chatman, & Caldwell, 1991) differentiated fit with the organization from *person–job* (PJ) fit, defined more narrowly as the relationship between a person's abilities and the demands of a specific job. In a series of studies used to validate the Organizational Culture Profile (OCP), the most commonly used measure of objective PO fit, Chatman and colleagues reported correlations between value-based PO and skill-based PJ fit in the range of .12 to .16. However, when the definition of PJ fit is expanded to include the matching of personal preferences or needs with the attributes of a specific job (Edwards, 1991) and when people are asked directly about their levels of both PO and PJ fit, this correlation becomes much stronger ($r = .58$, uncorrected correlation; Kristof-Brown et al. 2005).

Distinctions have also been drawn between PO fit and *person–group* (PG) or *person–team* (PT) fit, which emphasize the interpersonal and skill-based compatibility between individuals and members of, or the entirety of, their workgroups (Jansen & Kristof-Brown, 2005; Judge & Ferris, 1992; Kristof, 1996; Werbel & Gilliland, 1999). Kristof-Brown et al. (2005) reported an uncorrected correlation of .43 between these two types of fit, and a different pattern of outcomes predicted by each. PG fit was most predictive of team-oriented outcomes, including satisfaction with coworkers, cohesion, and contextual performance. Finally, research on *person-vocation* (PV) fit includes vocational choice theories that propose matching people with careers that meet their interests (e.g., Holland, 1985; Super, 1953), and the Theory of Work Adjustment (Lofquist & Dawis, 1969; Dawis & Lofquist, 1984), which emphasizes that adjustment and satisfaction are the result of employees' needs being met by their occupational environment. Few published studies have addressed the relationship between these types of fit.

### Outcomes of PO Fit

If PO fit is at least marginally related to these other types of fit, the question becomes "For what outcomes is PO fit the primary, or at least a relevant, predictor?" One way to answer this question is to examine the average effect sizes that PO fit has with particular outcomes. This question has recently been examined in several meta-analyses (Arthur et al., 2006; Hoffman & Woehr, 2006; Kristof-Brown et al., 2005; Verquer et al., 2003). Consistent with the notion that people are able to segment their attitudes about various elements of their work environment, Kristof-Brown et al. predicted that PO fit would be most strongly associated with attitudes specifically focused on the organization. In line with this prediction, meta-analytic results show that organizational commitment is the attitude most strongly predicted by PO fit, with values that are consistently higher than those for job satisfaction and intent to quit ($\rho = .51$ for organizational commitment, $\rho = .44$ for job satisfaction, $\rho = -.35$ for intent to quit, Kristof-Brown et al.; $\rho = .31$, $\rho = .28$, and $\rho = -.21$, respectively, Verquer et al.). Alternatively, Kristof-Brown et al. reported that the strongest effect of PJ fit was on job satisfaction ($\rho = .56$) followed by organizational commitment ($\rho = .47$) and intent to quit ($\rho = -.46$).

With regard to behaviors, Kristof-Brown et al. (2005) found PO fit to be a stronger predictor of actual turnover than was PJ fit ($\rho = -.14$ for PO fit; $\rho = -.08$ for PJ fit). Estimates from other meta-analyses show a moderate relationship between PO fit and turnover ($\rho = -.24$, Arthur et al., 2006; $\rho = -.26$, Hoffman & Woehr, 2006). When performance outcomes are examined, the relationship of overall performance with PO fit is generally low ($\rho = .15$, Arthur et al., 2006; $\rho = .07$, Kristof-Brown et al., 2005). However, this effect is substantially higher when the performance domain is limited to contextual or citizenship behaviors ($\rho = .22$, Arthur et al.; $\rho = .21$, Hoffman & Woehr; $\rho = .27$, Kristof-Brown et al.). In the pre-entry context, PO fit was found to have strong effects on organizational attraction ($\rho = .46$) and intent to hire ($\rho = .61$, Kristof-Brown et al.), with values only slightly lower than for PJ fit($\rho = .48$ and $\rho = .67$, respectively). These comparisons demonstrate the relevance of PO fit for pre- and postentry attitudes, turnover, and contextual performance and to a lesser extent for overall performance.

### Relative Impact of PO Fit

A second, somewhat more conservative test, of the relevance of PO is to examine its relative impact on outcomes when multiple types of fit are assessed simultaneously. This approach establishes whether PO fit contributes above and beyond these other types of fit. For example, Cable and DeRue (2002) reported that when PO fit, demands–abilities PJ fit, and needs–supplies PJ fit are assessed simultaneously, PO fit has the greatest influence on organizational identification, perceived organizational support, peer-rated citizenship behaviors, turnover, and peer-rated job performance. Lauver and Kristof-Brown (2001) reported stronger effects for perceived PO fit than for PJ fit for intent to quit and peer-rated contextual performance, but for job satisfaction and task performance the effects were similar for both types of fit. Results by Saks and Ashforth (1997, 2002) demonstrated stronger effects for PO fit than for PJ fit on turnover and organization-focused attitudes, whereas PJ fit was the better predictor of job satisfaction and intention to quit. Taken as a whole, these studies suggest that PO fit has independent effects, often strong ones, on postentry attitudes and behaviors.

Few published investigations have addressed both PJ and PO fit simultaneously in the pre-entry context, although recent dissertations and conference presentations have used this approach. From the recruiter's perspective, Kristof-Brown (2000) reported that although their judgments of applicants' PJ and PO fit were highly correlated ($r = .72$), both types of fit explained unique variance in hiring recommendations. In that study, PJ fit had a stronger influence on recruiters' decisions, which is consistent with results reported by Higgins (2000). Alternatively, two studies conducted from the applicants' perspective showed that perceptions of PO fit were a stronger predictor of job choice intentions (Cable & Judge, 1996) and application decisions (Dineen, 2003) than were PJ fit perceptions. These results generally confirm the unique impact of PO fit in the pre-entry context, particularly for job applicants, although both types of fit appear to play an important role in selection/job choice decisions.

### Moderators of PO Fit Effects

In her original theory of PO fit, Chatman (1989) discussed the potential of individual and environmental characteristics to influence people's responses to PO fit. Specifically, she discussed self-efficacy, personal control, and openness to influence as individual differences that would change people's responses to PO fit or misfit. Although these specific characteristics have not been tested as moderators, several researchers have endorsed the notion that certain people will be more or less influenced by PO fit. Kristof-Brown, Jansen, and Colbert (2002) proposed that individuals' past work experience would determine the emphasis they placed on various types of fit. Evidence from this policy-capturing study showed that individuals who had worked in more companies placed the greatest emphasis on PO fit, whereas overall years of experience (controlling for number of companies) increased only the importance of PJ fit. A dissertation by Shantz (2003) reported that applicant conscientiousness moderated the relationship between PO fit and attraction in a pre-entry setting, but years of work experience did not. She demonstrated a stronger relationship between PO fit and intention to accept and actual acceptance of a job offer for applicants high in conscientiousness. A recent study by Ravlin and Ritchie (2003) showed that PO fit had a greater impact on organizational commitment for individuals with longer tenure in the organization, and Lovelace and Rosen (1996) found weaker effects for PO fit on satisfaction and stress for African-American managers (who also reported lower overall levels of PO fit than their White counterparts). Yet, other studies conducted by Posner (1992) and Sheffey (1994) showed little support for the theory that individual differences moderate PO fit relationships. Currently, it is clear only that additional research is needed on individual differences that may serve as moderators of PO fit.

Chatman (1989) also discussed environmental characteristics that may influence people's responses to PO fit. In particular, she emphasized the fact that people will be more likely to change their personal values when confronted with organizations that have strong cultures (i.e., those with an identifiable set of norms, values, and beliefs; Schein, 1992). The more clearly organizational values and culture can be identified and the more explicitly they are hired for, measured, and rewarded, the more important PO fit should be. There is some preliminary evidence that situation or environmental factors can strengthen or mitigate the impact of PO fit. In a two-sample study of salespeople, Barnes, Jackson, Hutt, and Kumar (2006) reported that stronger cultures lead to higher levels of value congruence in sales organizations. In a study of Turkish teachers, Erdogan, Kraimer, and Liden (2004) demonstrated that the relationship between PO fit and job satisfaction and career satisfaction only existed in conditions under which perceived organizational support and leader–member exchange were low. When these other factors were high, the relationship between PO fit and attitudes was significantly diminished. These studies provide preliminary evidence that situational characteristics can strengthen or reduce the influence of PO fit on attitudes.

Although these findings are preliminary, we believe strongly in the potential for moderators of PO fit. What is missing at this point is a strong, theory-based rationale for what individual, environmental, and other factors are likely to influence the impact of PO fit on individual outcomes. In a recent article, we have begun to address this question by considering the characteristics that are likely to influence the salience of particular types of fit (Jansen & Kristof-Brown, 2006). Issues that are more salient receive greater attention, and because people have limited attentional resources (Kanfer & Ackerman, 1989), those issues receiving the most attention will exert a greater influence on subsequent judgments and behaviors. Thus, individual, environmental, and temporal factors that increase the salience of PO fit to individuals should magnify the effects of PO fit, particularly relative to other types of fit.

## How Should PO Fit Be Studied?

Given the compelling empirical evidence showing that fit makes a difference on attitudinal and behavioral outcomes, the next logical question is, How should we measure it? The answer to this question requires the consideration of several critical issues, any of which can dramatically influence the magnitude and even direction of results. First, the researcher must consider the content dimensions on which to assess PO fit. Values, personality, goals, needs, and knowledge, skills, and abilities have all been examined as components of PO fit. A closely related issue is what conceptualization of fit (similarity or complementarity) should be assessed. Does fit exist when a person is similar to others in the organization, or when his or her personal needs are met by the organization? A third question involves whether the researcher is interested in fit as it actually exists or as it is perceived to exist. Various approaches of direct and indirect measurement can be used, depending on the answers to these questions.

Once these questions have been answered, issues of levels of analysis should be considered explicitly by the researcher. Although PO fit appears on the surface to be a cross-level phenomenon, fit can actually be assessed at the individual level, cross level, and aggregate levels of analysis, each with different conceptual and empirical challenges. Finally, if indirect measures of fit are to be used, there is the question of whether a difference score or polynomial regression approach is more appropriate. We address each of these questions in the following, by reviewing what past research has demonstrated and offering advice for future endeavors.

### Content Dimensions and Conceptualizations

The specific term *person–organization fit* was first used by Chatman (1989), who proposed an interactional model in which individual's values and organizational value systems influenced each other over time to affect both organizational and individual-level outcomes. Her definition of PO fit as "the congruence between the norms and values of organizations and the values of persons" (Chatman, 1989, p. 339) established value similarity as the dominant operationalization of PO fit. The vast majority of studies conducted on PO fit since that time have used value congruence as the exclusive operationalization of the concept (e.g., Adkins, Russell, & Werbel, 1994; Cable & Judge, 1996, 1997; Chatman, 1991; Dineen, Ash, & Noe, 2002; Goodman & Svyantek, 1999; Harris & Mossholder, 1996; Judge & Bretz, 1992; Lauver & Kristof-Brown, 2001; Meglino, Ravlin, & Adkins, 1989, 1991; O'Reilly et al., 1991; Ostroff, 1993; Van Vianen, 2000).

The most well established value congruence measures are the OCP, developed by O'Reilly et al. (1991), and the Comparative Emphasis Scale (CES), developed by Meglino et al. (1989). However, numerous value typologies have been used to assess value–PO fit, including Schwartz's Competing Values (1992) used by Van Vianen (2000) and modified by Cable and Edwards (2004) into the Work Values Survey (Cable & Edwards, 2002). Others include Quinn and Spreitzer's (1991) Organizational Culture Assessment Instrument used by Kalliath, Bluedorn, and Strube (1999) and Rokeach's (1973) Value Survey used by Krishnan (2002). Additional studies have used measures of fit with ethical climate to assess PO fit (e.g., Schwepker, Ferrell, & Ingram, 1997; Sims & Keon, 1997).

Despite the prevalence of the value congruence approach, the concept of individual–organizational compatibility has extended well beyond the realm of values. One of the earliest studies was conducted by Tom (1971), who demonstrated that college students preferred organizations possessing personality traits similar to their own. Following this pattern are studies by Christiansen, Villanova, and Mikulay (1997), Day and Bedeian (1995), Hambleton, Kalliath, and Taylor (2000), Lievens, Decaesteker, and Coetsier (2001), Ryan and Schmitt (1996), and Tischler (1996), which all emphasize the fit of individuals to organizational personalities or climates. In most of these studies new instruments for assessing personality-based fit were developed (e.g., the Organizational Fit Instrument by Ryan & Schmitt, 1996) or existing versions of scales for the Big Five traits (extraversion, conscientiousness, agreeableness, emotional stability, and openness) or the Myers–Briggs personality types were used.

Additional studies by Vancouver and colleagues (Vancouver, Millsap, & Peters, 1994; Vancouver & Schmitt, 1991) and Witt (1998) emphasized the individual-level benefits that result from congruence between individual and organizational perceptions of goal importance. More recent work by Colbert and Bradley (2005) has demonstrated that the fit between goals of top management team members and their chief executive officers is positively related to both individual performance of the top management team members and organizational profitability. However, we note that in goal congruence studies individuals are typically asked to rank the organization's goals rather than to report their own personal goals. Therefore, these studies may be capturing agreement with others on organizational goals rather than fit with one's personal objectives.

If we keep in mind this last caveat, the congruence approach described earlier generally emphasizes the matching or similarity of commensurate individual and organizational characteristics. The process underlying a congruence approach to fit is based on the similarity-attraction paradigm (Byrne, 1971), which suggests that people sharing similar characteristics are attracted to each other and generally have better affective consequences than people who are different. This similarity-attraction mechanism is the basis for what Muchinsky and Monahan (1987) labeled a *supplementary* approach to fit (i.e., birds of a feather flock together).

An alternative conceptualization is the *complementary* approach to fit, which implies that fit can be obtained when one party fulfills a gap or a need in the other (i.e., opposites attract to complete and offset each other). This conceptualization is invoked in studies of how organizational structures or pay systems meet employee needs or complement personality traits to predict individual-level outcomes (i.e., Ivancevich & Matteson, 1984; Koberg & Chusmir, 1987). Demonstrating that individual differences moderate the effects of organizational characteristics or vice versa is a common method used to demonstrate complementary fit. Complementary fit has also been operationalized using direct measures of perceived need-fulfillment (Tziner, 1987) or indirect measures that separately assess commensurate needs and supplies (e.g., Cable & Edwards, 2004; Koberg & Chusmir, 1987; Westerman & Cyr, 2004). In each of these cases, the mechanism of personal need-fulfillment underlies PO fit. Cable and Edwards (2004) demonstrated convincingly that the need-fulfillment process and the similarity-attraction paradigm may function simultaneously but are distinct mechanisms underlying PO fit.

Conceptually, therefore, PO fit can exist on the basis of almost type of similarity or need fulfillment. Empirically, however, results differ widely, depending on what content dimensions of PO fit are assessed. Meta-analytic results consistently show that value-based PO fit has stronger effects on job satisfaction than other types of supplementary PO fit ($\rho$ = .51 values-based; $\rho$ = .08 personality-based, Kristof-Brown et al., 2005; $\rho$ = .35 values-based; $\rho$ = .27 other-based, Verquer et al., 2003). Results by

Arthur et al. (2006) also showed stronger effects of value congruence across all attitudinal criteria when compared to other types of congruence measures ($\rho = .48$ values-based; $\rho = .27$ other forms of congruence). Interestingly though, Kristof-Brown et al. (2005) reported a corrected correlation of needs-based fit (complementary) with job satisfaction of .46, only slightly less than the relationship reported for value-based fit (supplementary). One possible explanation for this similarity is that in many studies in which values are used as the content dimension on which to assess fit, it is done in such a way that the value is framed as a need (i.e., "I prefer to work for an organization that values competition"), rather than a personal value (i.e., "I value competition"). Thus, many common measures of PO fit, including the OCP (O'Reilly et al., 1991) may be assessing value need fulfillment rather than simply value congruence.

Several authors have attempted to capture the totality of PO fit by using multidimensional or combined measures (i.e., those assessing PO fit on multiple dimensions such as values and personality). The combined measure developed by Bretz and Judge (1994), which includes fit on values, personality, needs, and knowledge, skills, and abilities has been utilized in several other studies (i.e., Vigoda, 2000; Vigoda & Cohen, 2002), as has Cable and Judge's (1996) measure of fit on personality and values. Meta-analytic results are reasonably comparable for values-only and combined measures. For job satisfaction the corrected correlation is slightly higher for combined measures ($\rho = .55$) than for values-based measures ($\rho = .51$), but for organizational commitment the magnitude of relationships is reversed ($\rho = .59$ combined measures, $\rho = .68$ values-based measures, Kristof-Brown et al., 2005). Arthur et al. (2006) showed stronger results for the combined measures ($\rho = .48$ values congruence, $\rho = .57$ "value + other based").

The greatest promise, however, may reside in measures that assess both complementary and supplementary fit. Cable and Edwards (2004, p. 830) found support for a simultaneous effects model, in which need fulfillment (complementary fit) and value congruence (supplementary fit) are interrelated but "both contribute independently to outcomes." Thus, the marginal benefits of assessing PO fit in multiple ways may be maximized when the combined measure includes both complementary and supplementary fit conceptualizations. This approach is also consistent with the definition of PO fit articulated by Kristof (1996), "P-O fit is defined as the compatibility between people and organizations which occurs when: (a) at least one entity provides what the other needs, or (b) they share similar fundamental characteristics, or (c) both" (pp. 4–5).

### Perceived, Subjective, and Objective Fit

How an individual experiences fit can be determined in a number of different ways. Seminal research on PJ fit and strain differentiated between subjective fit as it is perceived by an individual and fit as it objectively exists in the environment (French, Rogers, & Cobb, 1974). Researchers in this area concluded with some certainty that actual fit only has an impact on someone if that person perceives that the fit exists. Therefore, the tradition in the stress and strain literature has been to focus on subjective rather than objective fit (Edwards, Caplan, & Harrison, 1998).

Subjective fit can be measured in two primary ways, but it is always individual-level measurement, because a single person evaluates both $P$ and $E$. The first type of measurement was labeled by French et al. (1974) as direct measures of perceived fit, or an overall impression of fit. Recently, Edwards et al. (2006) relabeled this approach as *molar* because it asks respondents to report an overall assessment of the fit between themselves and their organization. An example is the measure developed by Cable and DeRue (2002), in which employees responded to questions such as, "The things I value in life are very similar to the things my organization values." In the organizational entry context, measures developed by Cable and Judge (1996, 1997), consisting of items such as "To what degree do your values, goals, and personality 'match' or fit this organization and the current employees in this organization?" and "To what degree did this applicant match or fit your organization and the current employees in your organization?" are commonly used. A measure developed by Saks and Ashforth (2002) includes similar content dimensions, but uses a complementary conceptualization of PO fit. Items include, "To what extent does the organization fulfill your needs?" and "To what extent is the organization a good match for you?" These direct measures of perceived fit have been used extensively, and meta-analyses demonstrate that they generally have the strongest relationships with outcomes, particularly attitudinal outcomes (Arthur et al., 2006; Kristof-Brown et al., 2005; Verquer et al., 2003—who labeled this category subjective fit). Despite their strong results, direct measures of perceived fit have also been heavily criticized because they are subject to strong halo and consistency biases and invoke the highest potential for common method, single-source bias when used to predict other self-reported variables such as attitudes.

An alternative way to assess subjective fit is using indirect measures (i.e., separate assessments of self and environment) collected from the same person. This involves the person reporting his or her own characteristics and then (generally at a different point in time) reporting the characteristics of his or her organization. Edwards et al. (2006) labeled this approach *atomistic*, highlighting the separate assessment of $P$ and $E$. Fundamentally this approach captures the person's fit with the perceived environment, rather than their overall level of experienced fit. Indirect measures of subjective fit are still subject to halo and consistency biases but tend to focus on more specific dimensions (i.e., value for honesty or value for achievement) rather than on an overall assessment of fit on values. The potential for common method bias is also reduced if the measures are collected at different points in time and at a minimum require separate assessment of self and organizational characteristics. However, single-source bias remains with this approach. Meta-analytic results suggest that indirect measures have the second highest correlations with nearly all outcome measures, but these can be as much as .20–.30 lower than the correlations of direct measures of perceived fit with attitudinal outcomes (Kristof-Brown et al., 2005).

Recently Edwards et al. (2006) delved into the question of whether these approaches to measuring subjective fit are fundamentally assessing the same construct. In a study of 373 job seekers, they examined how people combine beliefs about themselves and their environment into perceptions of PE fit. Specifically, they demonstrated that there is a large amount of unexplained variance between people's indirect assessments of subjective fit (the atomistic approach), direct assessments of PE discrepancies (what they label the molecular approach), and overall direct assessments of fit (the molar approach). In particular, only a small (<.20%), albeit statistically significant portion, of the variance in molar approaches to fit was predicted by the molecular comparison process between P and E components. In almost every case, the molecular fit assessment was disproportionately determined by the person's assessment of the environment. Perhaps their most challenging result, however, was the considerable overlap between direct assessments of fit and satisfaction measures. Their findings led them to conclude, "These results suggest that perceived fit and satisfaction may reflect affective responses such that when people indicate that they fit the environment, they are not reporting the result of a comparison process but instead are effectively saying they are satisfied with the environment" (p. 822). Their results have several implications, most importantly the need to recognize that these approaches to fit are distinct, not just methodologically, but conceptually.

Despite the strong tradition of measuring subjective fit, the earliest advocates of PO fit took an entirely different approach. Chatman (1991) and colleagues (O'Reilly et al., 1991) developed the OCP as an instrument to assess objective fit, that is, the fit between individuals and the organizational environment as it "actually" existed, rather than as it is perceived to exist by the individual. The actual environment can be measured in a number of ways, including using objective organizational characteristics (i.e., pay system or structure), aggregated ratings of the organization (i.e., employees aggregated view of organizational culture), or a single other's view of the firm (i.e., a recruiter or supervisor's report of the organization's values). For example, we recently demonstrated that individuals who are "out of pace" with the hurriedness of the rest of their workgroups (as determined by the aggregate of coworkers' hurriedness scores) experience lower satisfaction and helping behavior toward their coworkers (Jansen & Kristof-Brown, 2005). Some may argue that this approach is still not "objective," but it does avoid the single-source bias concerns that plague subjective measures of fit.

Meta-analyses show that objective fit measures typically have lower correlations with outcomes than subjective measures (i.e., for job satisfaction Kristof-Brown et al., 2005 reported $\rho = .29$ for objective fit, $\rho = .46$ for indirect subjective fit, and $\rho = .56$ for direct perceived fit; for job performance Arthur et al., 2006, reported $\rho = .12$ for objective fit, $\rho = .16$ for indirect subjective fit, and $\rho = .21$ for direct perceived fit). However, it is well documented that objective fit can influence individuals' attitudes and behaviors at work. The strongest evidence for objective fit has been found using measures of value congruence, including the OCP and the CES. Kristof (1996) suggested that objective fit should be a better predictor of nonattitudinal outcomes than perceived or subjective fit. Yet, results from Kristof-Brown et al. (2005) demonstrated that this prediction only holds true for length of tenure ($\rho = .03$ for direct, $\rho = .01$ for subjective, and $\rho = .06$ for objective).

One feature that should be noted for all of the aforementioned operationalizations is that each involves some degree of commensurate measurement. That is, similar individual and organizational characteristics are being assessed or at least considered when PO fit is evaluated. Some scholars argue that commensurate measures are requisite to studies of fit (Edwards et al., 1998; Kristof-Brown et al., 2005). However, in a number of studies a variant of this approach was used to determine the impact of PO fit. In these studies, the interaction of an organizational characteristic (i.e., an objective characteristic or an aggregated climate/culture perception) with a different, but related, individual characteristic is assessed. For example, Turban, Lau, Ngo, Chow, and Si (2001) demonstrated that individuals who were risk averse and had a lower need for pay were more attracted to state-owned versus foreign-owned firms in the People's Republic of China. This is an example of a study assessing the impact of objective PO fit, using noncommensurate measurement, which showed support for the PO fit perspective. Other researchers have examined the interaction between individuals' need for achievement and the company's compensation structure (e.g., performance versus seniority-based pay; Bretz, Ash, & Dreher, 1989) or how the attractiveness of particular pay policies may be heightened by particular individual personality traits (e.g., Cable & Judge, 1994). Although PO fit per se was not assessed in these studies, they are based solidly on the logic of complementary fit, such that an organizational characteristic meets a related individual-level need.

### Levels of Analysis in PO Fit Research

Although PO fit initially appears to be a cross-level concept (person: individual level; organization: organization level), in reality this is frequently not the case. In particular, measures of subjective fit are always conducted at the individual level of analysis. That is, each individual reports, either directly or indirectly, his or her unique level of fit with the organization. That level of fit is used to predict attitudinal or behavioral outcomes for that individual. Alternatively, objective fit is more typically assessed using cross-level measurement. For example, the OCP assesses the congruence between individuals' values or need for a value, and the organization's values as they are reported by an aggregate of others. What differs in these cases is that the environmental characteristics exist at the higher level of analysis—the organizational level. A similar situation occurs for noncommensurate measurement as described earlier. For the Turban et al. (2001) study, the organizational characteristic was an objective characteristic of the organization, not an aggregation of others' perceptions, but existing at that higher level of analysis. Despite this use of cross-level measurement, in most cases outcomes are generally predicted at the individual-level. That is, an individual's fit with his or her organization, characterized by an aggregate of others' characteristics, their perceptions of the organization, or an objective organizational characteristic, influences his or her personal attitudes and behavior in that company.

Thus, for PO fit to become useful for predicting organizational-level consequences (as the ASA model would imply) it may be viewed more accurately as the homogeneity or aggregate level of fit across individuals in an organization. The emphasis on these "aggregate level" fit studies is on determining whether people in organizations are more similar than are people across organizations. Unlike typical fit research, which can be conducted within single organizations, studies of organizational homogeneity require multiple organization samples. Work by Schneider and colleagues (Schneider, Smith, Taylor, & Fleenor, 1998; Schaubroeck, Ganster, & Jones, 1998) has demonstrated that in fact there is a tendency toward homogeneity on personality traits within organizations. This is not to say that organizations hire personality clones but simply that there is generally more diversity in personality across organizations than within. An important next step for this type of organizational-level fit research is to determine whether homogeneous composition is in fact as detrimental to organizational health as its assumed to be.

Rather than resulting in strategic myopia and organizational decline, some evidence suggests that the individual-level benefits of PO fit may be mirrored at the organizational level. For example, Ostroff (1993) examined the relationship between aggregate levels of personality-based fit within schools, and the performance of those schools on multiple performance indicators. Results demonstrated that congruence between the aggregate personality of teachers and the climate of the school was positively related to three major categories of effectiveness criteria for the schools and weakly related to two others. Ostroff (1993) goes on to say that incongruence may be beneficial in limited areas and also for the long-term responsiveness of the schools. However, her results showed a posi-tive effect of high levels of fit within schools. In a second study using gen-erally the same sample, Ostroff and Rothausen (1997) reported that effects of PO fit on tenure were stronger at the aggregate level than at the individ-ual-level, even after correcting for attenuation due to measurement error at the individual level. Thus, they concluded that different processes may be at work at the aggregate level, including the development of organiza-tional norms through selection and socialization practices.

Additional work using multilevel data analysis such as hierarchical lin-ear modeling is also shedding new light on established relationships. For example, Vancouver et al. (1994) reanalyzed a subset of Vancouver and Schmitt's (1991) goal-based PO fit data to determine whether aggregate levels of fit within schools had additional influence on individual-level outcomes. They found that the level of between-constituency goal con-gruence, or the degree to which all teachers in a school agreed with the principal, was related to job satisfaction, organizational commitment, and intentions to quit, even after controlling for individual-level congruence. The level of within-constituency congruence, or the average congruence between individual teachers and other teachers in the school, also pre-dicted individual-level outcomes beyond individual-level congruence. Interestingly, the direction of these relationships was opposite for the between (negative relationship) and within-constituency results (positive relationship) at the aggregate level. These results provide a first glimpse into the complex multilevel interactions that may occur for PO fit.

### Analytic Approaches for Demonstrating PO Fit

The final question, and, from our interactions with other scholars, the one that causes the most angst during stages of study design, is how to best analyze the fit relationship. If a direct measure of perceived fit is used, the answer is simple: fit is entered as a single predictor variable into a regression equation or analysis of variance. However, if the meas-urement approach is indirect, that is, if the P and O variables are reported separately, a fundamental question is whether to use a difference score approach (more appropriately labeled a profile similarity approach) or a polynomial regression. Researchers who have approached PO fit from a values orientation, namely those who developed and use the OCP and CES measures, have strongly advocated for the use of difference scores between individual and organizational value profiles. Their arguments are based on literature demonstrating the hierarchical nature of values; however, this implies ipsative measurement, which has garnered signifi-cant criticism for its failure to address absolute level effects.

In addition to the concerns with ipsative measurement, Edwards (1993, 1994) launched a campaign to reeducate the fit community to the problems inherent in all forms of difference score approaches. Namely, these include conceptual ambiguity, discarded information, insensitivity to the source of differences, and overly restrictive statistical constraints. His criticism did not come without a solution, and the work of Edwards and colleagues (Edwards, 1993, 1994, 1996; Edwards & Harrison, 1993; Edwards & Parry, 1993) ushered in the era of polynomial regression in PO fit research. Fundamentally, this approach avoids collapsing person and environment measures into a single score that captures "fit." Instead, both $P$ and $E$, and associated higher order terms ($P^2$, $P \times E$, and $E^2$) are included as predictors. Because the $P$ and $E$ and the dependent variables are all unique, fit relationships are depicted in three-dimensional surface plots. No unique regression weight is attached to fit using this approach; rather a more precise depiction of the holistic relationships between $P$, $E$, and outcomes is generated.

Kristof-Brown et al. (2005) compared the corrected correlation coefficients of PO fit measures with the average effect sizes of studies using polynomial regression to assess PO fit (e.g., Cable & Edwards, 2004; Finegan, 2000; Fletcher, Major, & Davis, 2004; Gill & Finegan, 2000; Kalliath et al., 1999; Nyambegera, Daniels, & Sparrow, 2001; Taris & Feij, 2001; Van Vianen, 2000). These comparisons demonstrated that the polynomial regression technique consistently produced larger effect sizes. Yet, despite the increase in effect size, examination of the surface graphs in the polynomial regression PO fit studies suggested that the relationships generally diverged from traditional notions of symmetrical fit. These traditional notions of PO fit make two assumptions: first, that fit at all levels ($P$ and O being both high or $P$ and O being both low) will result in better outcomes than misfit; and, second, that misfit in either direction ($P < O$ or $P > O$) is equally undesirable. However, results from the polynomial regression studies generally demonstrated that fit at high levels of $P$ and $E$ is usually better than fit at low levels and the relationship is often asymptotic, such that excess $E$ conditions produce less of a decline in outcomes than do deficiencies in $E$ (e.g., Kalliath et al., 1999; Taris & Feij, 2001). Taken together, results of these studies and those of Edwards et al. (2006) implied that past research may have taken a narrow view of what fit means to individuals.

What are the implications of these results? Clearly, how a researcher decides to assess PO fit will in large part determine the strength of his or her results. It is easier to obtain results using direct measures of perceived fit, particularly for attitudinal outcomes, given that Edwards et al. (2006) found direct/molar assessments of fit to be heavily affect-laden. However, it is the researchers' responsibility to demonstrate that these results represent the true impact of fit, rather than simply reflecting same-source bias. Fit researchers should attend to the popular wisdom for how to reduce the potential for such bias (i.e., Podsakoff, MacKenzie, Lee, & Podsakoff, 2003). This may include collecting predictor and criterion measures at different points in time or using alternative sources for criterion data. Alternatively, researchers could collect separate assessments of $P$ and $O$ characteristics (indirect measures). This can minimize the likelihood of bias (for subjective fit measures) or remove it entirely (for objective measures). We personally advocate collecting as many types of fit assessments as possible and using these data to address questions of what mediates the relationships between objective, subjective, and perceived fit. For example, Cable, Aimen-Smith, Mulvey, and Edwards' (2000) study of the sources of accurate applicant beliefs about organizational culture provides some information on what might cause objective and subjective fit to be more or less related.

We also generally advocate collecting measures of person and organization that are commensurate and normative. This method of collection affords the greatest possible flexibility in analytic approach. Profile similarity indices could be used with these types of data to determine whether, on average, across multiple characteristics, similarity with the organization is beneficial. This is particularly useful if PO fit is going to be tested as a moderator or mediator of other relationships. However, more extensive polynomial regression analyses can then be conducted to verify whether a traditional fit relationship is supported for specific $P$ and $O$ characteristics. Our experience is that perfect symmetrical fit relationships are rarely found but that, in general, similarity or excess need fulfillment is more advantageous than dissimilarity or deficiencies. Unfortunately, there are no easy answers to how best to study PO fit. But as additional empirical studies are conducted, we will continue to learn more about the implications of our study design decisions. We encourage researchers not to become discouraged by the proliferation of approaches that are out there but to consider which approach is best for their particular set of research questions.

These issues are relevant to all PO fit research; however, the conclusions are almost exclusively based on cross-sectional studies of PO fit. Despite Chatman's (1989) exhortation that fit is a dynamic process, rather than an end result, most researchers continue to investigate it at some point in time. Recent research has begun to address this limitation.

## A TEMPORAL APPROACH TO PO FIT

That fit is temporal in nature is not a new notion. Caplan, French, and colleagues introduced the dynamic components of fit in describing coping, adaptation, and defense. Caplan (1983) posited that stress results not just from current fit, but also retrospected and anticipated fit. The very notion of interactional psychology implies that people select into and are selected by particular environments (Emmons & Diener, 1986) and that reciprocal influence occurs once in the situation (Terborg, 1981). Schneider's (1987) ASA framework provides a mechanism for us to understand how people, over time, come to form the very environment against which fit is assessed. Similarly, Chatman (1989) encouraged us to view PO fit as an evolving concept, such that individuals sometimes change to fit an organization and other times change the organization itself.

Despite these supplications to address the temporal side of fit, few researchers actually do so. This is in part due to the difficulty of collecting data over long periods of time. However, there is some evidence to support the notion that people and organizations evolve to attain higher levels of fit. Studies of socialization provide evidence that individuals adopt organizational values through their experiences during organizational entry (Ostroff & Rothausen, 1997). Cable and Parsons (2001) demonstrated that organizations using sequential and fixed content, as well as serial and investiture tactics, raised perceptions of PO fit and actual value congruence. We also know that people experience changes in their values and priorities over time (Howard & Bray, 1988; Schaie & Schooler, 1998), just as organizational culture and values can shift with new leadership, structure, or strategy (Schein, 1992). Thus, even though PO fit may be good at one point in time, it may improve or worsen as either the individual or the organization changes.

We have begun to further extend the temporal aspect of fit theory in our recent work. First, Jansen and Kristof-Brown (2006) proposed a salience-weighted model of fit with multiple dimensions of the work environment. Even without actual change in the individual or organization, we noted that the salience of various aspects of fit is likely to change over time, acknowledging the temporality of fit. In addition, we proposed that fit or misfit with various aspects of the environment may actually interact, such that fit with one dimension of the environment actually changes fit with other dimensions over time. We posit two different models by which this can occur: spillover and spirals.

## Spillover

Drawing from research in the work-life literature (Rice, Near, & Hunt, 1980), we propose that one aspect of fit may influence another in much the same way that halo–horn rater bias influences performance judgments. *Spillover*, which can be either positive or negative, suggests that highly salient aspects of fit are likely to influence or change less important, discrepant fit assessments over time. For example, if an individual experiences strong fit with his or her workgroup, but his or her values differ from those of the organization, over time the individual is likely to be motivated to reduce dissonance by downplaying the importance of PO-value fit, modifying his or her perception of values-based fit, or working to change the organization's values.

## Spirals

Another relationship between fit dimensions that may also manifest itself over time is *mutual reinforcement*, which occurs when high correspondence among fit assessments results in deviation-amplifying spiraling effects (e.g., Fredrickson, 2003; Lindsley, Brass, & Thomas, 1995; Weick, 1979) such that good fit gets better and poor fit gets worse. For example, the better the correspondence is among fit assessments across the environment (i.e., consistently good fit on all dimensions), the more embedded that person is in the work environment, resulting in less stress and greater productivity, which then reinforces the overall perception of good fit. Conversely, an employee who experiences consistently poor fit on all dimensions (assuming the employee has not chosen to leave already) is less embedded in the overall work environment, experiences more stress, and is likely to be less productive, which further exacerbates poor perceptions of fit. It should be noted that neither positive or negative spirals are necessarily good from a temporal perspective because the more embedded the individual is, the less resilient that person is for enduring or weathering a change on one or more of those dimensions, whereas the poor-fitting individual is likely to continue to spiral down until turnover is highly likely. However, these spirals may help to explain long-term tenure in an organization, the series of steps leading to turnover, and Schneider's (1987) ASA model.

A second paper, which we presented at the Annual Academy of Management Meeting in Denver, CO, in 2002, was an effort to expand fit research by considering the temporal element in theory and research. The paper was titled "Beyond 'Fit Happens': A Temporal Theory of Fitting at Work" (Jansen & Kristof-Brown, 2002). In the following, we review the ideas that we presented in that paper to stimulate additional thoughts about how and why fit changes over time.

## Fit versus Fitting

The vast majority of fit research has been conducted using cross-sectional designs, affording researchers only snapshots of fit at particular points in time. Two recent exceptions to this trend are research on surface- and deep-level diversity (Harrison, Price, & Bell, 1998; Jackson, May, & Whitney, 1995) and ASA theory (Schneider, 1987). Drawing on a distinction proposed by Jackson et al. (1995) and Milliken and Martins (1996), Harrison et al. (1998) empirically found that surface-level demographic characteristics were more influential in early stages of group development, but that psychological characteristics (e.g., goals and values) became more influential the longer the group had interacted. If one characterizes surface-level attributes as demographic fit and deep-level attributes as PG fit, this research directly acknowledges a shift in importance from one type of fit to another over time.

As discussed earlier, Schneider's (1987) ASA theory asserted that organizations become more homogeneous over time through a mutual-selection process whereby individuals are attracted to, selected by, and choose to remain in organizations with similar others. Thus, this theory is distinctly temporal in nature. Figure 4–1 graphically illustrates how ASA processes might operate within an organization. The individuals labeled $P_1$ and $P_j$ represent employees who did not fit with other employees and the dominant environment and chose to leave. Individuals $P_2$, $P_i$, and $P_k$ enter the organization, are successfully socialized, and remain. Thus, ASA theory predicts that over time, an organization will begin to resemble the cross-sectional snapshot at $T_4$.

There are two substantial problems with this perspective. First, left- and right-censoring occurs within any one window of time. For example, at $T_2$, we will just miss the fact that $P_1$ is about to exit the organization and that $P_j$, who appears to be a misfit, will eventually leave. At any given point in time, there will be individuals who fit and individuals who do not who are also at various points along a stay–leave continuum. Thus, the $T_4$ snapshot represents an unattainable ideal. With more frequent measures, however, we can begin to identify trends over time to help support the existence of ASA processes at work.

The second concern is that, to some extent, ASA theory has the same problem that traditional fit research does: It ignores the potential for individual or environmental change. In Fig. 4–2, persons $P_2$, $P_i$, and $P_k$ do

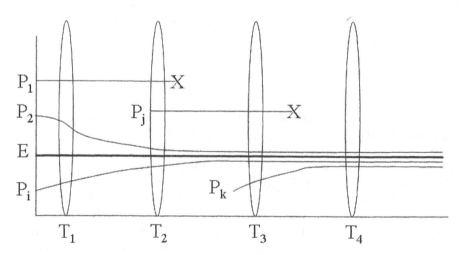

FIGURE 4–1. A temporal representation of ASA theory with snapshots of traditional cross-sectional fit comparisons.

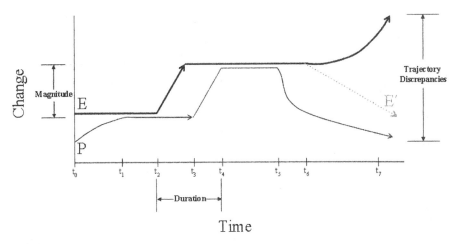

FIGURE 4–2. Temporal periods of fit and misfit between an individual and the work environment.

not significantly change once socialized. Similarly, the work environment remains stable. The presumption is that similarity will continue and that individuals will adapt to changes in the work environment. This presumption does not seem to reflect the reality in organizations today. Strategic directions change, corporate values change, individuals gain and lose skills, and, more importantly, some individuals who do not fit do not always leave.

Thus, there is a clear need for a temporal theory that addresses the following question: Why is it that some people who do not fit stay? Treating either the person or the environment as static is problematic for organizational fit research, yet this is inherently what we do. We believe that the process of socialization has effectively minimized differences between the employee and the work environment. We rarely, if ever, consider resocializing workers 5 years later. However, it is short-sighted to think that once socialized, the individual does not continue to grow and change or that the organization to which an individual was socialized is the same as it was 5 years ago. In fact, Pratt and Ashforth (2003) alluded to fit and alignment in describing the dynamic and ongoing meaning that individuals construct about their work over time. One of our continuing goals is to better understand the dynamism associated with fit assessments, the triggering events that cause a shift between fit and misfit, and how the magnitude, duration, and trajectory of these shifts predict relevant outcomes such as turnover and commitment.

Many years ago, Lewin set forth the proposition that behavior is a function of the person and the environment $[B = f (P, E)]$. Recognizing the dynamic nature of the $P$-$E$ interaction, Furnham (2001, p. 8) concluded that "people as well as environments change over a life span." Adding a temporal dimension to this well-known equation, then, is comparable to taking the first derivative of the equation. In other words, behavior over time is a function of change in the person over time ($\Delta P/t$) and the change in the environment over time ($\Delta E/t$). We examine each of these elements in the following sections and then consider the reciprocal influence they have on each other over time.

### Individual Change ($\Delta P$)

Perhaps the most observable change a person experiences over time is across stages of the individual's career. For example, research suggests that aspirations and goals change over the course of a person's tenure (e.g., Howard & Bray, 1988; Schaie & Schooler, 1998), suggesting that age or career stage may influence not only the importance of fit, but also the congruence between an individual's and an organizations goals and values. In addition, Kohn and Schooler (1983a, 1983b) found that prolonged experience with a job may actually influence an individual's characteristics over time (e.g., dispositions), thus changing the overall fit with the work environment. Finally, Furnham (1994) acknowledged that people adapt to their jobs and can exhibit substantial changes in attitudes and beliefs as a result. Individual change, then can take many forms, including change in interests, aspirations, skills, and values.

### Environment Change ($\Delta E$)

Changes in the work environment are more familiar and more frequently incorporated into research than person change. In the task environment, new technology and work processes may necessitate increased skill demands. Other skills may become obsolete in the face of environmental change. An organization may also change its core values, goals, and culture over time as it pursues new strategies or markets. At a more micro level, there are often frequent changes in reporting structure, supervisors, and workgroup assignments. In the social domain, friends and colleagues may leave the organization, mentors may come and go, and new team members are introduced, changing the dynamics of the group. Finally, Caplan (1983) pointed out that some environment change may be due to economic conditions, illness, or even chance.

### When Forces Collide: $B = f(\Delta P, \Delta E)$

In Fig. 4–2, we present a hypothetical map depicting the course of one individual's process of change superimposed on the change experienced in the individual's work environment to illustrate periods of fit and periods of misfit. We use this figure to then introduce some guiding principles for temporal fit research: magnitude, duration, and trajectory. Beginning with the person, between $t_0$ and $t_1$, the individual is being socialized into the organization. Between $t_1$ and $t_2$ a period of good fit between the individual and environment exists. However, at $t_2$, there is a dramatic change in job requirements, creating misfit between the needs of the job and the current skills of the employee. At $t_3$, the individual begins to receive education and training to work in the changed environment, and by $t_4$, good fit is reestablished. At $t_5$, the hypothetical person receives news that a family member has a life-threatening disease. The person undergoes a series of changes regarding career ambitions, goals, and values, ultimately deciding to place a higher priority on family. During this process ($t_6$), the organization decides to embark on a new strategic direction, placing more demands on the individual to adapt and change to stay competitive. By $t_7$, the individual and organization have moved in very different directions.

Ignoring the $E'$ dotted line for the moment, we can identify several useful measures from the diagram. First, the *magnitude of misfit* reflects the amplitude or amount of misfit between the $P$ and the $E$. It is a measure of degree of change. Second, *duration of misfit* represents the length of time the person has endured misfit (a measure of time).[1] Finally, *trajectory* is a directional vector describing where the $P$ and $E$ have been (or will be) heading. It is a temporal measure of the slope of the path each is pursuing. The amount of discrepancy between the two trajectories can help predict the potential magnitude and duration of differences. Thus, at $t_7$, there is a large trajectory discrepancy between the direction the work environment is going and the path the individual is taking. Assuming the trajectories continue in this way, it is more likely the individual will experience strain, be dissatisfied, and eventually leave the organization. This trajectory comparison is not only a future-facing comparison: The individual may have made the same comparison at $t_2$, but the misfit was of such short duration (and potentially low magnitude) that it was not as probable that the individual would leave.

Returning now to the dotted line beginning at $t_6$, assume for the sake of argument that instead of pursuing a new strategic direction at this point, the organization had instead implemented a new human resources policy permitting temporary leaves of absence to comply with the Family and Medical Leave Act. Both objectively and subjectively, the organization's values would then be more in line with the individual's values, improving fit and reducing the likelihood of an undesirable outcome (turnover).

---

[1]Caplan (1983, p. 61) combined the magnitude and duration components in what he terms *toleration*, which he defines as "the amount of misfit a person will withstand before attempting to reduce the misfit multiplied by the amount of time the person will spend in a misfit situation before attempting to alter the perceived misfit."

In a similar vein, Shipp and Edwards (2005) and Shipp (2006) have proposed a moving window of fit based upon individuals' experience with past, present, and anticipated future fit. Specifically, they reported that past and future fit influence the relationship between current fit and well-being. They also explored temporal focus, temporal distance, and importance as moderators of these relationships. Taken together, a very new and exciting stream of research is developing on temporal aspects of fit.

## CONCLUSION

In the 10 years since Kristof (1996) established a roadmap for the field of PO fit research, much progress has been made. We are beginning to understand what outcomes are affected by PO fit, the conceptual and empirical differences that accompany different measurement strategies, and the variables that determine the strength of PO fit—outcome relationships. Yet, there is much left to be done to better understand the boundary conditions associated with fit and what cognitive and affective processes are involved when people are asked about how they fit in their organization. Research on the temporal nature of fit is still in its infancy. As methodological and measurement advances continue to be made, we expect research on this topic to proliferate with researchers seeking to understand how P-O fit changes over time and interacts with other forms of fit. Our conclusion after 10 years of study is that there are still many unanswered questions. We hope that this chapter has provided a few guideposts for how to begin the next stage of exploration.

## REFERENCES

Adkins, C. L., Russell, C. J., & Werbel, J. D. (1994). Judgments of fit in the selection process: The role of work value congruence. *Personnel Psychology, 47,* 605–623.

Argyris, C. (1957). *Personality and organizations.* New York: HarperCollins

Arthur, W., Jr., Bell, S. T., Villado, A. J., & Doverspike, D. (2006). The use of person-organization fit in employment decision making: An assessment of its criterion-related validity. *Journal of Applied Psychology, 91,* 786–801.

Barnes, J. W., Jackson, D. W., Jr., Hutt, M. D., & Kumar, A. (2006). The role of culture strength in shaping sales force outcomes. *The Journal of Personal Selling & Sales Management, 26,* 255–262.

Bowen, D. E., Ledford G. E., Jr., & Nathan, B. R. (1991). Hiring for the organization, not the job. *Academy of Management Executive, 5,* 35–52.

Bretz, R. D., Jr., Ash, R. A., & Dreher, G. F. (1989). Do people make the place? An examination of the attraction-selection-attrition hypothesis. *Personnel Psychology, 42,* 561–581.

Bretz, R. D., & Judge, T. A. (1994). Person-organization fit and the Theory of Work Adjustment: Implications for satisfaction, tenure, and career success. *Journal of Vocational Behavior, 44,* 32–54.

Byrne, D. (1971). *The attraction paradigm.* New York: Academic Press.

Cable, D. M., Aiman-Smith, L., Mulvey, P. W., & Edwards, J. R. (2000). The sources and accuracy of job applicants' beliefs about organizational culture. *Academy of Management Journal, 43,* 1076–1085.

Cable, D. M., & DeRue, D. S. (2002). The convergent and discriminant validity of subjective fit perceptions. *Journal of Applied Psychology, 87,* 875–884.

Cable, D. M., & Edwards, J. R. (2002, August). *Person-environment fit in organizational behavior research: Toward a theory-testing approach.* Paper presented at the Annual Meeting of the Academy of Management, Denver, CO.

Cable, D. M., & Edwards, J. R. (2004). Complementary and supplementary fit: A theoretical and empirical integration. *Journal of Applied Psychology, 89,* 822–834.

Cable, D. M., & Judge, T. A. (1994). Pay preferences and job search decisions: A person-organization fit perspective. *Personnel Psychology, 47,* 317–348.

Cable, D. M., & Judge, T. A. (1996). Person-organization fit, job choice decisions, and organizational entry. *Organizational Behavior & Human Decision Processes, 67,* 294–311.

Cable, D. M., & Judge, T. A. (1997). Interviewers' perceptions of person-organization fit and organizational selection decisions. *Journal of Applied Psychology, 82,* 546–561.

Cable, D. M., & Parsons, C. K. (2001). Socialization tactics and person-organization fit. *Personnel Psychology, 54,* 1–23.

Caplan, R. D. (1983). Person-environment fit: Past, present, and future. In C. L. Cooper (Ed.), *Stress research* (pp. 35–78). New York: Wiley.

Chatman, J. A. (1989). Improving interactional organizational research: A model of person-organization fit. *Academy of Management Review, 14,* 333–349.

Chatman, J. A. (1991). Matching people and organizations: Selection and socialization in public accounting firms. *Administrative Science Quarterly, 36,* 459–484.

Christiansen, N., Villanova, P., & Mikulay, S. (1997). Political influence compatibility: Fitting the person to the climate. *Journal of Organizational Behavior, 18,* 709–730.

Colbert, A. E., & Bradley, B. H. (2005, August). *Goal agreement in top management teams: The role of CEO transformational leadership.* Paper presented at the Academy of Management National Meeting, Honolulu, HI.

Dawis, R. V., & Lofquist, L. H. (1984). *A psychological theory of work adjustment.* Minneapolis, MN: University of Minnesota Press.

Day, D. V., & Bedeian, A. G. (1995). Personality similarity and work-related outcomes among African-American nursing personnel: A test of the supplementary model of person-environment congruence. *Journal of Vocational Behavior, 46,* 55–70.

Dineen, B. R. (2003, August). *The effects of customizing person–environment fit information to job seekers in a web-based recruitment context.* Paper presented at the Academy of Management Meeting, Seattle, WA.

Dineen, B. R., Ash, S. R., & Noe, R. A. (2002). A web of applicant attraction: Person–organization fit in the context of Web-based recruitment. *Journal of Applied Psychology, 87,* 723–734.

Edwards, J. R. (1991). Person-job fit: A conceptual integration, literature review, and methodological critique. In C. L. Cooper & I. T. Robertson (Eds.), *Inter-*

*national review of industrial and organizational psychology* (Vol. 6, pp. 283–357). Chichester, England: Wiley.

Edwards, J. R. (1993). Problems with the use of profile similarity indices in the study of congruence in organizational research. *Personnel Psychology, 46,* 641–665.

Edwards, J. R. (1994). Alternatives to difference scores as dependent variables in the study of congruence in organizational research. *Organizational Behavior and Human Decision Processes, 64,* 307–324.

Edwards, J. R. (1996). An examination of competing versions of the person–environment fit approach to stress. *Academy of Management Journal, 39,* 292–339.

Edwards, J. R., Cable, D. M., Williamson, I. O., Lambert, L. S., & Shipp, A. J. (2006). The phenomenology of fit: Linking the person and environment to the subjective experience of person–environment fit. *Journal of Applied Psychology, 91,* 802–827.

Edwards, J. R., Caplan, R. D., & Harrison, R. V. (1998). Person–environment fit theory: Conceptual foundations, empirical evidence, and directions for future research. In C. L. Cooper (Ed.), *Theories of organizational stress* (pp. 28–67). Oxford, England: Oxford University Press.

Edwards, J. R., & Harrison, R. V. (1993). Job demands and worker health: Three-dimensional reexamination of the relationship between person–environment fit and strain. *Journal of Applied Psychology, 78,* 628–648.

Edwards, J. R., & Parry, M. E. (1993). On the use of polynomial regression equations as an alternative to difference scores in organizational research. *Academy of Management Journal, 36,* 1577–1613.

Emmons, R. A., & Diener, E. (1986). A goal–affect analysis of everyday situational choices. *Journal of Research in Personality, 20,* 309–326.

Erdogan, B., Kraimer, M. L., & Liden, R. C. (2004). Person–organization fit and work attitudes: The moderating role of leader-member exchange. *Personnel Psychology, 57,* 305–332.

Finegan, J. E. (2000). The impact of person and organizational values on organizational commitment. *Journal of Occupational and Organizational Psychology, 73,* 149–169.

Fletcher, T. D., Major, D. A., & Davis, D. D. (2004, August). *Congruence in personality and perceptions of climate competitiveness in the workplace: A three-dimensional look at the effects on job initiative and perceived stress.* Paper presented at the Academy of Management Annual Meeting, New Orleans, LA.

Fredrickson, B. L. (2003). Positive emotions and upward spirals in organizations. In K. S. Cameron, J. E. Dutton, & R. E. Quinn (Eds.), *Positive organizational scholarship: Foundations of a new discipline* (pp. 316–333). San Francisco: Berrett-Koehler.

French, J. R. P., Jr., Rogers, W., & Cobb, S. (1974). Adjustment as person–environment fit. In G. V. Coelho, D. A. Hamburg, & J. E. Adams (Eds.), *Coping and adaptation.* New York: Basic Books.

Furnham, A. (1994). *Personality at Work.* London: Routledge.

Furnham, A. (2001). Vocational preference and P–O fit: Reflections on Holland's theory of vocational choice. *Applied Psychology: An International Review, 50,* 5–29.

Gill, H., & Finegan, J. E. (2000, April). *The relation between person–organization fit and organizational commitment.* Paper presented at the 15th Annual Conference of the Society for Industrial and Organizational Psychology, New Orleans, LA.

Goodman, S. A., & Svyantek, D. J. (1999). Person–organization fit and contextual performance: Do shared values matter? *Journal of Vocational Behavior, 55,* 254–275.

Hambleton, A. J., Kalliath, T., & Taylor, P. (2000). Criterion-related validity of a measure of person–job and person–organization fit. *New Zealand Journal of Psychology, 29,* 80–85.

Harris, S. G., & Mossholder, K. W. (1996). The affective implications of perceived congruence with culture dimensions during organizational transformation. *Journal of Management, 22,* 527–547.

Harrison, D. A., Price, K. H., & Bell, M. P. (1998). Beyond relational demography: Time and the effects of surface- and deep-level diversity on work group cohesion. *Academy of Management Journal, 41,* 96–107

Higgins, C. A. (2000). *The effect of applicant influence tactics on recruiter perceptions of fit.* Unpublished doctoral dissertation, University of Iowa.

Hoffman, B. J., & Woehr, D. J. (2006). A quantitative review of the relationship between person-organization fit and behavioral outcomes. *Journal of Vocational Behavior, 68,* 389–399.

Holland, J. L. (1985). *Making vocational choices: A theory of careers* (2nd ed.). Englewood Cliffs, NJ: Prentice-Hall.

Howard, A., & Bray, D. W. (1988). *Managerial lives in transition: Advancing age and changing times.* New York: Guilford Press.

Ivancevich, J. M., & Matteson, M. T. A. (1984). Type A–B person–work environment interaction model for examining occupational stress and consequences. *Human Relations. 37,* 491–513.

Jackson, S. E., May, K. E., & Whitney, K. (1995). Understanding the dynamics of diversity in decision-making teams. In R. A. Guzzo & E. Salas (Eds.), *Team decision-making effectiveness in organizations* (pp. 204–261). San Francisco: Jossey-Bass.

Jansen, K., & Kristof-Brown, A. (2002, August). *Beyond "fit happens": A temporal theory of fitting at work.* Symposium presented at the Academy of Management Annual Meeting, Denver, CO.

Jansen, K. J., & Kristof-Brown, A. L. (2005). Marching to the beat of a different drummer: Examining the impact of pacing ,congruence. *Organizational Behavior and Human Decision Processes, 96,* 93–105.

Jansen, K. J., & Kristof-Brown, A. L. (2006). Putting it all together: Toward a multidimensional theory of person-environment fit. *Journal of Managerial Issues, 18,* 193–212.

Judge, T. A., & Bretz, R. D. (1992). Effects of work values on job choice decisions. *Journal of Applied Psychology, 77,* 261–271.

Judge, T. A., & Ferris, G. R. (1992). The elusive criterion of fit in human resource staffing decisions. *Human Resource Planning, 15,* 47–67.

Kalliath, T. J., Bluedorn, A. C., & Strube, M. J. (1999). A test of value congruence effects. *Journal of Organizational Behavior, 20,* 1175–1198.

Kanfer, R., & Ackerman, P. L. (1989). Motivation and cognitive abilities: An integrative/aptitude-treatment interaction approach to skill acquisition. *Journal of Applied Psychology, 74,* 657–690.

Koberg, C. S., & Chusmir, L. H. (1987). Organizational culture relationships with creativity and other job-related variables. *Journal of Business Research, 15,* 397–410.

Kohn, M. L., & Schooler, C. (1983a). Job conditions and personality: A longitudinal assessment of their reciprocal effect. In M. L. Kohn & C. Schooler (Eds.), *Work and personality: An inquiry into the impact of social stratification* (pp. 123–153). Norwood, NJ: Ablex.

Kohn, M. L., & Schooler, C. (1983b). The reciprocal effects of the substantive complexity of work and intellectual flexibility: A longitudinal assessment. In M. L. Kohn, M. L., & Schooler, C. (Eds.), *Work and personality: An inquiry into the impact of social stratification* (pp. 103–124). Norwood, NJ: Ablex.

Krishnan, V. R. (2002). Transformational leadership and value system congruence. *International Journal of Value-Based Management, 15,* 19–33.

Kristof, A. L. (1996). Person–organization fit: An integrative review of its conceptualizations, measurement, and implications. *Personnel Psychology, 49,* 1–49.

Kristof-Brown, A. L. (2000). Perceived applicant fit: Distinguishing between recruiters' perceptions of person–job and person–organization fit. *Personnel Psychology, 53,* 643–671.

Kristof-Brown, A. L., Jansen, K. J., & Colbert, A. E. (2002). A policy-capturing study of the simultaneous effects of fit with jobs, groups, and organizations. *Journal of Applied Psychology, 87,* 985–993.

Kristof-Brown, A. L., Zimmerman, R. D., & Johnson, E. C. (2005). Consequences of individuals' fit at work: A meta-analysis of person–job, person–organization, person–group, and person–supervisor fit. *Personnel Psychology, 58,* 281–342.

Lauver, K. J., & Kristof-Brown, A. (2001). Distinguishing between employees' perceptions of person-job and person-organization fit. *Journal of Vocational Behavior, 59,* 454–470.

Lievens, F., Decaesteker, C., & Coetsier, P. (2001). Organizational attractiveness for prospective applicants: A person-organization fit perceptive. *Applied Psychology, 50,* 30–51.

Lindsley, D. H., Brass, D. J., & Thomas, J. B. (1995). Efficacy-performance spirals: A multilevel perspective. *Academy of Management Review, 20,* 645–678.

Lofquist, L. H., & Dawis, R. V. (1969). *Adjustments to work.* New York: Appleton-Century-Crofts.

Lovelace, K., & Rosen, B. (1996). Differences in achieving person–organization fit among diverse groups of managers. *Journal of Management, 22,* 703–722.

Meglino, B. M., Ravlin, E. C., & Adkins, C. L. (1989). A work values approach to corporate culture: A field test of the value congruence process and its relationship to individual outcomes. *Journal of Applied Psychology, 74,* 424–432.

Meglino, B. M., Ravlin, E. C., & Adkins, C. L. (1991). Value congruence and satisfaction with a leader: An examination of the role of interaction. *Human Relations, 44,* 481–495.

Milliken, F. J., & Martins, L. L. (1996). Searching for common threads: Understanding the multiple effects of diversity in organizational groups. *Academy of Management Journal, 25,* 402–433.

Montgomery, C. E. (1996, January). Organizational fit is key to job success. *HR Magazine, 41,* 94–96.

Muchinsky, P. M., & Monahan, C. J. (1987). What is person-environment congruence? Supplementary versus complementary models of fit. *Journal of Vocational Behavior, 31,* 268–277.

Nyambegera, S. M., Daniels, K., & Sparrow, P. (2001). Why fit doesn't always matter: The impact of HRM and cultural fit on job involvement of Kenyan employees. *Applied Psychology: An International Review, 50*, 109–140.

O'Reilly, C. A., Chatman, J., & Caldwell, D. F. (1991). People and organizational culture: A profile comparison approach to assessing person-organization fit. *Academy of Management Journal, 34*, 487–516.

Ostroff, C. (1993). Relationships between person-environment congruence and organizational effectiveness. *Group & Organization Management, 18*, 103–122.

Ostroff, C., & Rothausen, T. J. (1997). The moderating effect of tenure in person–environment fit: A field study in educational organizations. *Journal of Occupational and Organizational Psychology, 70*, 173–188.

Podsakoff, P. M., MacKenzie, S. B, Lee, J., & Podsakoff, N. P. (2003). Common method biases in behavioral research: A critical review of the literature and recommended remedies. *Journal of Applied Psychology, 88*, 879–903.

Posner, B. Z. (1992). Person-organization values congruence: No support for individual differences as a moderating influence. *Human Relations, 45*, 351–361.

Pratt, M. G., & Ashforth, B. E. (2003). Fostering meaningfulness in working and at work. In K. S. Cameron, J. E. Dutton, & R. E. Quinn (Eds.), *Positive organizational scholarship: Foundations of a new discipline* (309–327). San Francisco: Berrett-Koehler.

Quinn, R. E., & Spreitzer, M. G. (1991). The psychometrics of the competing values culture instrument and an analysis of the impact of organizational culture on quality of life. *Research in Organizational Change and Development, 5*, 115–142.

Ravlin, E. C., & Ritchie, C. M. (2003, August). *Sharing in-use and espoused values: Attitudinal and behavioral outcomes.* Paper presented at the Academy of Management Annual Meeting, Seattle, WA.

Rice, R. W., Near, J. P., & Hunt, R. G. (1980). The job satisfaction/life satisfaction relationship: A review of empirical research. *Basic and Applied Social Psychology, 1*, 37–64.

Rokeach, M. (1973). *The nature of human values.* New York: Free Press.

Ryan, A. M., & Schmitt, M. J. (1996). An assessment of organizational climate and P-E fit: A tool for organizational change. *The International Journal of Organizational Analysis, 4*, 75–95.

Saks, A. M., & Ashforth, B. E. (1997). A longitudinal investigation of the relationships between job information sources, applicant perceptions of fit, and work outcomes. *Personnel Psychology, 50*, 395–426.

Saks, A. M., & Ashforth, B. E. (2002). Is job search related to employment quality? It all depends on the fit. *Journal of Applied Psychology, 87*, 646–654.

Schaie, K. W., & Schooler, C. (Eds.). (1998). *Impact of work on older adults.* New York: Springer.

Schaubroeck, J., Ganster, D. C., & Jones, J. R. (1998). Organization and occupation influences in the attraction-selection-attrition process. *Journal of Applied Psychology, 83*, 869–891.

Schein, E. H. (1992). *Organizational culture and leadership* (2nd ed.). San Francisco: Jossey-Bass.

Schneider, B. (1987). The people make the place. *Personnel Psychology, 40*, 437–453.

Schneider, B., Smith, D. B., Taylor, S., & Fleenor, J. (1998). Personality and organizations: A test of the homogeneity of personality hypothesis. *Journal of Applied Psychology, 83*, 462–470.

Schwartz, S. H. (1992). Universals in the content and structure of values: Theoretical advances and empirical tests in 20 countries. In M. P. Zanna (Ed.), *Advances in experimental social psychology* (pp. 1–65). San Diego, CA: Academic Press.

Schwepker, C. J. J., Ferrell, O. C., & Ingram, T. N. (1997). The influence of ethical climate and ethical conflict on role stress in the sales force. *Journal of the Academy of Marketing Science, 25*, 99–108.

Shantz, C. A. (2003). *Person–organization fit: Individual differences, socialization, and outcomes.* Unpublished doctoral dissertation, Wayne State University.

Sheffey, S. C. (1994). *Person–organization fit: A quantitative assessment of the match between actual and ideal culture.* Unpublished doctoral dissertation, Loyola University of Chicago.

Shipp, A. J. (2006). *The moving window of fit: Extending person-environment fit research with time.* Unpublished doctoral dissertation. University of North Carolina.

Shipp, A. J., & Edwards, J. R. (2005, August). *Recollected, current, and anticipated person–environment fit within the present moment.* Symposium presented at the annual Academy of Management Conference, Honolulu, HI.

Siegel, M. (1998, November 9). The perils of culture conflict. *Fortune, 138,* 257–262.

Sims, R. L., & Keon, T. L. (1997). Ethical work climate as a factor in the development of person-organization fit. *Journal of Business Ethics, 16,* 1095–1105.

Super, D. E. (1953). A theory of vocational development. *American Psychologist, 8,* 185–190.

Taris, R., & Feij, J. A. (2001). Longitudinal examination of the relationship between supplies-values fit and work outcomes. *Applied Psychology: An International Review, 50,* 52–80.

Terborg, J. R. (1981). Interactional psychology and research on human behavior in organizations. *Academy of Management Review, 6,* 569–576.

Tischler, L. (1996). Comparing person-organization personality fit to work success. *Journal of Psychological Type, 38,* 34–43.

Tom, V. R. (1971). The role of personality and organizational images in the recruiting process. *Organizational Behavior and Human Performance, 6,* 573–592.

Turban, D. B., Lau, C., Ngo, H., Chow, I. H. S., & Si, S. X. (2001). Organizational attractiveness of firms in the People's Republic of China: A person-organization fit perspective. *Journal of Applied Psychology, 86,* 194–206.

Tziner, A. (1987). Congruency issue retested using Fineman's achievement climate notion. *Journal of Social Behavior and Personality, 2,* 63–78

Van Vianen, A. E. M. (2000). Person–organization fit: The match between newcomers' and recruiters' preferences for organizational cultures. *Personnel Psychology, 53,* 113–149.

Vancouver, J. B., Millsap, R. E., & Peters, P. A. (1994). Multilevel analysis of organizational goal congruence. *Journal of Applied Psychology, 79,* 666–679.

Vancouver, J. B., & Schmitt, N. W. (1991). An exploratory examination of person–organization fit: Organizational goal congruence. *Personnel Psychology, 44,* 333–352.

Verquer, M. L., Beehr, T. A., & Wagner, S. H. (2003). A meta-analysis of relations between person-organization fit and work attitudes. *Journal of Vocational Behavior, 63,* 473–489.

Vigoda, E. (2000). Internal politics in public administration systems: An empirical examination of its relationship with job congruence, organizational citizenship behavior, and in-role performance. *Public Personnel Management, 29,* 185–210.

Vigoda, E., & Cohen, A. (2002). Influence tactics and perceptions of organizational politics: A longitudinal study. *Journal of Business Research, 55,* 311–324.

Weick, K. E. (1979). *Causal loops and control* (2nd ed.). New York: Addison-Wesley.

Werbel, J. D., & Gilliland, S. W. (1999). Person-environment fit in the selection process. In G. R. Ferris (Ed.), *Research in personnel and human resource management* (Vol. 17, pp. 209–243). Stamford, CT: JAI Press.

Westerman, J. W., & Cyr, L. A. (2004). An integrative analysis of person–organization fit theories. *International Journal of Selection and Assessment, 12,* 252–261.

Witt, L. A. (1998). Enhancing goal congruence: A solution to organizational politics. *Journal of Applied Psychology, 83,* 666–674.

# CHAPTER 5

# *How Selection and Recruitment Practices Develop the Beliefs Used to Assess Fit*

Daniel M. Cable and Kang Yang Trevor Yu
*University of North Carolina*

Individuals and organizations develop employment relationships, in large part, based on fit. Sometimes fit is complementary: Organizations have resources that certain individuals want, and individuals have skills that certain organizations want. Sometimes supplementary fit brings people and organizations together. For example, both organizations and individuals have values about the right ways of doing things, and both parties seem to be more satisfied entering an employment relationship when values are shared. So both organizations and individuals form employment relationships based on perceptions of fit.

What is a fit perception based on? In the context of employment relationships, a fit perception is a comparison between a person and an environment (Cable & DeRue, 2002). For example, a job seeker compares his or her personal values and skills to an organization's culture (Cable, Aiman-Smith, Mulvey, & Edwards, 2000), job roles (Wanous & Colella, 1989), and personalities of future coworkers (Rynes, 1991). On the other side of the employment relationship, an organizational interviewer compares his or her organization's needs and values against a job seeker's values (Cable & Judge, 1997), skills and abilities (Bretz, Rynes, & Gerhart, 1993; Kristof-Brown, 2000), and personality characteristics (Jackson, Peacock, & Holden, 1982). Thus, to form a fit perception, it is necessary to have beliefs about a person and beliefs about an environment (e.g., a job or an organization). Where do these beliefs about people and organizations emerge?

Recruitment and selection practices allow job seekers and organizations to learn about each other and develop fit perceptions. Recruitment refers to organizational activities that are focused on communicating company information and attracting new employees (Barber, 1998; Breaugh & Starke, 2000), whereas selection processes refer to activities that permit evaluation and hiring of job candidates (Heneman & Judge, 2003). Recruitment and selection processes thus create the initial interactions between job seekers and organizations. As such, recruitment and selection processes create a venue for information transfer about people and environments and make perceptions of fit possible.

We know that recruiters develop fit perceptions about job seekers during selection processes (Adkins, Russell, & Werbel, 1994; Bretz, Rynes, & Gerhart, 1993; Cable & Judge, 1997) and that job seekers develop fit perceptions about employers during recruitment (Cable & Judge, 1996; Judge & Bretz, 1992; Judge & Cable, 1997). The topic that has received less attention is how the characteristics of recruitment and selection practices affect beliefs about organizations and job seekers, respectively. This chapter focuses on the beliefs about people and organizations that are created by recruitment and selection practices, and that culminate in fit perceptions. We address this gap in the literature by presenting a model of how beliefs are developed during recruitment and selection, leading to subjective fit perceptions.

## THEORETICAL MODEL

Figure 5–1 presents a model of the formation process of fit perceptions as it occurs during the preorganizational entry stages of recruitment and selection. In general, the model proposes that recruitment and selection processes permit job seekers and organizations to gather information about each other through different sources such as career fairs, Web sites, and interviews. From this perspective, each entity becomes a target about which the other party must form beliefs. The impact—or effect—of information on the beliefs that job seekers and organizational representatives develop about each other is determined by characteristics if the information sources (e.g., the richness and credibility of the media sources). Thus, although Fig. 5–1 shows that people and organizations ultimately use their beliefs to develop subjective fit perceptions, the focus of this chapter is on the process of developing beliefs about the target in the first place.

Next, we discuss the target belief formation process, focusing on how the media richness and credibility of various recruitment and selection

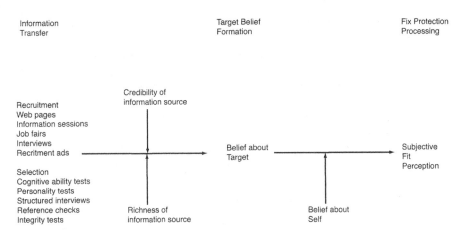

FIGURE 5–1.   Model of the formation process of fit perceptions.

sources may influence the types of beliefs that job seekers and organizations develop about each other. This is followed by a discussion of the media richness and credibility of several widely used recruitment and selection methods. We conclude the chapter with a discussion of the possible implications of our model for the existing literature and for future research.

## Belief Formation, Media Richness, and Media Credibility

Beliefs consist of any stored thoughts that people have about particular entities, and beliefs have been conceptualized as a network of associations that people construct between an entity and various attributes (Eagly & Chaiken, 1993). From an associative model of memory perspective, beliefs comprise nodes (stored information) and links (connections between nodes that vary in strength). A node becomes a source of activation for other nodes when new information is being encoded or when stored information is being retrieved from long-term memory (Anderson, 1983; Wyer & Srull, 1989). For example, a job seeker might develop the belief that a particular organization has a conservative culture that is relatively rule oriented. The nodes—the organization's name, the concept of "conservative"—are linked with some degree of strength in the job seeker's memory such that when he or she hears or thinks of the organization, the linked concept of conservative is recalled. Likewise, an organizational interviewer might generate a set of linkages between a certain job candidate and the concepts "very social person," "solid analytic skills," and "needs some experience with clients."

Many of the beliefs that job seekers hold about potential employers are based on information about these organizations that is gathered during the recruitment process; likewise, many of the beliefs that organizational representatives form about job seekers are based on information gathered during the selection process. We propose that the impact of information collected during recruitment and selection depends on attributes of the sources from which the information is obtained. In associative memory terms, we propose that whether a job seeker or a hiring manager codes information about a target into mental nodes, and the strength of the links between the nodes depends in an important way on the source of the information. We next focus on two attributes of information sources that should be particularly influential in the belief formation process: media richness and media credibility.

### Media Richness

Media richness refers to the ability of an information source to communicate information that is complex, ambiguous, susceptible to multiple interpretations, or unfamiliar to receivers (Daft, Lengel, & Trevino, 1987; Huber & Daft, 1987). In general, Media Richness Theory predicts that richer media (e.g., face-to-face interactions) will be more effective than leaner media (e.g., memos) at transferring information, particularly when a message is ambiguous. The richness of an information source comprises four attributes: feedback, multiple cues, language variety, and personal focus (e.g., Daft et al., 1987; Huber & Daft, 1987; Schmitz & Fulk, 1991).

*Feedback.*   First, information sources vary in their ability to offer timely feedback. Two-way communication and real-time interactions facilitate timely feedback between an information source and the intended recipient and thus contribute to the richness of a particular information source. For example, mailing a letter offers relatively low and slow feedback compared with a phone conversation.

*Multiple cues.*   Information sources may offer an array of communication cues including physical presence, voice inflection, and body language, or they may only offer one cue (e.g., text). Richer information sources are those that allow multiple cues and physical presence. Thus, a face-to-face interaction offers more cues than a phone call, which in turn offers more cues than an e-mail message.

*Language variety.* Information sources can vary in the forms of language that they communicate. The term *language* is used to describe "systems of spoken or written symbols that can communicate ideas, emotions, and experiences" (Daft & Wiginton, 1979, pp. 180–181). Various forms of languages exist, each varying in their ability to transmit information and ideas. Some sources permit language only in the form of the written word (e.g., e-mails) whereas other sources permit a variety of languages including verbal communication, charts and graphs, and numbers and statistics (e.g., business presentations). Thus, business presentations offer high language variety compared with interoffice memos.

*Personal focus.* Information sources can also differ in their ability to provide messages with a personal focus on intended recipients. To have a personal focus, messages and information must be tailored to meet the needs and current context of intended recipients. Thus, a billboard is static and is only personalized by broad region. A television ad may be targeted to the audience according to specific times and shows, whereas a business presentation can be tailored to the unique needs of the audience.

Thus, there are four attributes of information sources that affect media richness. In general, media richness theory suggests that richer media lead to more effective communication (Daft & Lengel, 1984; Daft et al., 1987). However, a media source may be rich but may not affect the recipients' belief structure because it is not credible. For example, an applicant may view a career fair as a rich communication channel because it allows face-to-face questions and answers but may not view the channel as credible because it represents the company's public relations message (e.g., Cable & Turban, 2002; Fisher et al., 1979). Thus, credibility is also an important media attribute to consider when one is predicting changes in audience beliefs (e.g., Austin & Dong, 1994; Gaziano & McGrath, 1986; Johnson & Kaye, 1998; Meyer, 1988), and we next discuss the topic of media credibility.

## Media Credibility

Credibility refers to the perceived accuracy and believability of a particular source of information (Allen et al., 2004). The credibility of a source appears to be a function of two very different facets: expertise and trustworthiness (Fisher et al., 1979; Hovland, Janis, & Kelly, 1953; Petty & Cacioppo, 1981; Tuppen, 1974).

*Expertise.* Expertise deals with the amount of information that a source possesses on a topic of interest. For example, in a recruitment context, expertise refers to the extent to which job seekers perceive an information source as having the ability to provide information that would be useful for their job search. Thus, a source that possesses information about what it is like to be an employee in an organization (e.g., company information sessions) has greater expertise than an information source that cannot provide information about employment at the organization (e.g., product advertisements).

We suggest that the concept of expertise requires a slightly different interpretation in the selection context. For selection activities, we propose that source expertise refers to perceived validity or the extent to which a hiring manager perceives an information source as having the ability to provide data on a relevant job candidate attribute. Thus, selection methods (e.g., cognitive ability tests and drug tests) are processes that do not "possess" information about an applicant but instead are methods used to acquire information about applicants. For these tests, then, perceived expertise refers to whether a manager believes a test offers valid information about the attribute that it is intended to measure. For example, the perceived expertise of a personality test depends on whether an organizational decision maker believes the test offers accurate insight into an applicant's personality traits.

*Trustworthiness.* Trustworthiness refers to the extent to which an information source is seen to provide information that is truthful, or unbiased. Thus, a hiring manager may view the information he or she gathered from a reference check to be low in trustworthiness, because the applicant supplied the references and has clear incentives to provide only positive references. Likewise, job applicants may consider company recruiters to be less trustworthy than other sources of information, because many job applicants believe that recruiters only provide the most positive information about their organizations (Allen et al., 2004; Cable, Aiman-Smith, Mulvey, & Edwards, 2000; Fisher et al., 1979).

## Belief Formation

The basic tenet of Media Richness Theory is that richer media (e.g., face-to-face interactions) will be more effective than leaner media (e.g., memos) for transferring information (Daft & Lengel, 1984; Daft et al., 1987; Dennis & Kinney, 1998). Likewise, credible information sources have a greater influence on people's beliefs than information sources that lack credibility (Allen et al., 2004; Fisher et al., 1979). Despite the intuitive appeal of the links between richness, credibility, and belief formation, the rationale of why richer and more credible media lead to effective communication has been left unaddressed by previous research. Our explanation for these links is based on the depth of information processing and its impact on beliefs. In the following, we describe the Elaboration Likelihood Model (ELM) of information processing and attitude change (e.g., Petty & Cacioppo, 1986) and its implications for media richness and credibility.

The ELM suggests that individuals can process information either through a central route or a peripheral route. Information processing via the central route involves expending cognitive resources to pursue and carefully consider the merits of information, whereas processing via the peripheral route is accomplished using simple informational cues and with little scrutiny placed on the information at hand (e.g., MacInnis & Jaworski, 1989). The distinction between central and peripheral processing is important for our logic because the ELM proposes that when people use central processing, the communicated information is more likely to have an influence on their beliefs (Petty & Cacioppo, 1986). Thus, in the context of the associative model of memory, central processing is more likely to deposit information into nodes and is more likely to strengthen the links between nodes, making future recall of the information more likely.

We propose that job seekers and hiring managers should be more likely to process information centrally when they perceive the information source to be rich and credible. When information sources are rich, they are synchronous, tailored to an individual's interests, and demand reactions and feedback (e.g., Daft et al., 1987), hence setting the stage for more effortful processing of information via the central route. This, in turn, should increase the future accessibility of the communicated information in the receiver's memory (Ajzen, 2000). Some evidence for this contention is available from marketing research, which suggests that information has stronger effects on people's attitudes when it is presented vividly using colorful graphics, pictures, personal anecdotes, or emotionally stimulating information (Keller & Block, 1996, 1997). In a similar fashion, when information sources are credible, they are viewed as more personally relevant and more useful by message recipients (Austin & Dong, 1994; Cable & Turban, 2002; Gaziana & McGrath, 1986; Johnson & Kaye, 1998; Meyer, 1988). This, in turn, should result in more effortful processing of information via the central route.

Thus, job seekers and organizational recruiters should be more motivated to invest the necessary cognitive resources to centrally process information when they perceive its source to be highly rich and credible. Past research suggests that stronger associations are made between concepts when more meaning and personal relevance are attached to information during cognitive processing (Craik & Tulving, 1975; Petty & Cacioppo, 1986). Therefore, we propose that the richness and credibility of recruitment communications should influence job seekers' organizational and job beliefs because they determine the depth at which recruitment information is processed. Similarly, the richness and credibility of information sources used for selection should influence managers' beliefs about particular job candidates because they determine whether the information is centrally or peripherally processed.

## COMMUNICATION PROPERTIES OF SELECTED
## RECRUITMENT AND SELECTION METHODS

Next, we consider the media richness and credibility of several widely used recruitment and selection methods. Specifically, in the recruitment context we consider web pages, interviews, career fairs, word of mouth, and employment agencies. In terms of selection sources we consider interviews, phone screens, work samples, cognitive ability tests, and personality tests. This discussion is reflected and summarized in Table 5–1, which shows the proposed ratings for the recruitment and selection sources in terms of media richness and credibility.

### Recruitment Sources

Recruitment sources serve to communicate information about organizational attributes (e.g., work values and strategic goals) and job requirements to potential job hires. Thus, recruitment information can act as the basis for job seekers' beliefs about organizations. As stated in the Introduction, these beliefs play a crucial role in the job search process because job seekers compare them to their own values, preferences, and skills to

TABLE 5–1.
Hypothesized Perceived Media Richness and Credibility
of Recruitment and Selection Practices

|  | Media Richness | | | | Media Credibility | |
|---|---|---|---|---|---|---|
|  | Timely Feedback | Multiple Cues | Language Variety | Message Tailoring | Source Expertise | Source Trustworthiness |
| Recruitment methods |  |  |  |  |  |  |
| Web site | 1 | 1 | 2 | 1 | 3 | 1 |
| Interview | 3 | 3 | 3 | V | V | V |
| Career fairs | 3 | 3 | 2 | 2 | V | V |
| Social network/ word of mouth | 3 | 3 | 2 | 3 | V | 3 |
| Employment agencies | 3 | 3 | 3 | 3 | 1 | 1 |
| Selection methods |  |  |  |  |  |  |
| Interview | 3 | 3 | 3 | 3 | V | V |
| Phone screens | 3 | 2 | 2 | 3 | V | V |
| Performance tests/ work samples | 3 | 3 | 2 | 3 | 3 | 3 |
| Cognitive ability testing | 1 | 1 | 1 | 1 | 2 | 3 |
| Personality testing | 1 | 1 | 1 | 1 | 2 | 1 |

Key: 1 = low; 2 = medium; 3 = high; V = variable.

generate judgments of how well they fit the prospective job and organization (Cable & Judge, 1996; Cable & Turban, 2002; Judge & Bretz, 1992; Schwab, Rynes, & Aldag, 1987; Turban & Keon, 1993).

*Web Pages*

A company Web page refers to an organization's home page on the Internet, and all links that the company associates with its home page (e.g., information about company history, products, partners, or careers). Company Web sites are very important in the recruitment context and have become the most frequently used resource by job seekers (Heneman & Judge, 2003; "Impact of Internet," 2000). In fact, most, if not all, Fortune 500 firms feature recruitment information on their Web pages (Lievens & Harris, 2003).

Despite their pervasiveness, the richness of Web pages appears to be fairly low. First, notwithstanding advances in Internet technology which have paved the way for real-time interaction over the Internet, such facilities are seldom used by organizations in a recruitment context. Hence, use of the Web site to provide timely feedback to job seekers is still rather limited. Furthermore, much of the information presented on Web sites is either in the form of text or graphics, which hinders the ability to convey multiple informational cues such as physical presence, voice inflection, and body language. Likewise, Web sites generally are restricted in terms of language variety—organizations usually present information in the form of ordinary text-based language and graphics. Thus, most Web sites present relatively precise and exact information with a narrow range of meaning, although some organizations present photographs and personal information about employees and the workforce. Finally, in terms of personal focus, Web sites score low because they typically cater to a wide audience (e.g., all people who have access to the Internet). This generally means that information on Web sites is worded and presented in a relatively formal fashion as it represents messages that are officially endorsed by the organization, thereby restricting the amount of personal focus that Web sites offer job seekers. Overall, these attributes suggest that job seekers will perceive Web sites to be relatively low in terms of media richness (i.e., less rich than other media that allow face-to-face interactions).

It is less clear how company Web sites will be viewed in terms of credibility. On the one hand, Web sites should generally be seen as a relatively expert source of information. Although each company's Web site is set up differently, most sites offer information about the company that would be useful for an individual's job search. Expertise should be viewed as especially high for company Web sites that have specific sections devoted to careers and recruitment because they are focused on presenting information that is directly relevant to working in a particular organization.

On the other hand, company Web sites are not expected to score high in terms of trustworthiness. It is widely recognized among job seekers that companies tend to engage in image management during recruitment, leading them to present overly positive information on their Web sites (e.g., Cable et al., 2000). Moreover, Web sites are entirely under organizations' control and can be manipulated to say whatever a company wishes to say. Therefore, the expertise that Web sites possess may be offset by low trustworthiness, such that Web sites are predicted to be viewed as average in overall credibility by job seekers.

### Interviews

Interviews between companies and applicants are used to perform both a recruitment function (discussed here) and a selection function (discussed later in the chapter). The recruitment interview essentially consists of an organizational representative interacting on a one-on-one basis with the job seeker, providing information about the organization and the job (Stevens, 1998). In many ways, a recruitment interview is a "textbook example" of high media richness. This face-to-face interaction between the two parties facilitates timely and immediate feedback. Thus, organizational recruiters are able to field questions and offer instant replies to job seekers about the organization or job. The interview also enables the transmission of multiple informational cues in the form of verbal (e.g., tone of voice) and nonverbal (e.g., body language) cues. Face-to-face interaction makes it possible for recruiters to use language variety to communicate information about their organizations, such as showing tables of company growth and market share, creating drawings of organizational charts or career paths, and using eye contact and body posture (Daft et al., 1987; Daft & Wiginton, 1979). Furthermore, interviews allow recruiters to tailor their messages to meet the individual needs of job seekers. For instance, recruiters can respond to an applicant's interest in knowing more about the organization's career progression policies. Clearly, then, recruitment interviews should be perceived by job seekers as a rich information source for organizational and job information. However, it also is important to note that for interviewers who stress the selection function of the interview, the interview will offer less time for feedback on applicants' questions and comments, reducing the perceived richness of the source.

The credibility of the recruitment interview appears to depend on the particular interviewers with whom job seekers meet. For example, the perceived expertise of the recruiter is dependent on his or her role in the company. Due to the fact that job incumbents already occupy a particular role in the organization, they naturally are in a better position to provide job-related information. Thus, it is expected that job incumbents are seen as greater experts because they provide more reliable and fact-based information about a job compared with professional recruiters in the human resources department (Schwab et al., 1987; Wanous, 1980).

Likewise, previous research has demonstrated that professional organizational recruiters are typically viewed as less trustworthy than other sources of job information such as a job incumbent, friend, or professor (Fisher et al., 1979). Presumably, this reaction reflects the fact that recruiters—or even hiring managers—have a vested interest in persuading the job seeker to join their organization and fill the opening, even though realistic previews may promote better long-term employment relationships. It is likely that job incumbents offer more even-handed information to applicants, and are therefore viewed as more trustworthy. Thus, the credibility of recruitment interviews is expected to be highly contingent on the role of the interviewer. In general, it is conceivable that a majority of recruitment interviews are conducted by professional recruiters, such that job seekers do not generally perceive the recruitment interview to be a very credible source of organizational and job information.

### Career Fairs

The term *career fair* refers to events whereby recruiters from different companies gather at a large facility in a common, central location (e.g., a school or university), set up booths, and interact with job seekers who are interested in learning more about employment opportunities (Heneman & Judge, 2003). Often, they disseminate company information and artifacts (e.g., brochures, pens, and product samples) and collect resumes from job seekers. Company representatives at career fairs do not make formal presentations, which allows job seekers and employers to exchange information interpersonally.

In general, we expect the richness of career fairs to be high. By virtue of the fact that much of the interaction between the hiring organizations and job seekers occurs face-to-face, career fairs offer immediate feedback so that job seekers can obtain timely answers to their questions. Like the interview, career fairs enable multiple information cues because they permit both verbal (e.g., tone of voice) and nonverbal (e.g., body language) messages. The interpersonal nature of career fairs also should allow recruiters to use different forms of language (e.g., making drawings, showing tables, and nonverbal expression), although the interactions are usually brief, and there is not much time for detailed coverage of issues. Lastly, as recruiters have autonomy over the messages that they present during career fairs, they are able to tailor this information to accommodate the individual needs of job seekers who attend these fairs. At a more global level, recruiters can customize career fairs by stressing information that is most relevant to a given university or a given group, such as a rotational training program for engineers. Thus, based on these attributes, we expect career fairs to be perceived by job seekers as a relatively rich source of organizational and job information.

Like the interview, the credibility of career fairs depends on the perceived expertise and trustworthiness of the particular representatives present at these events. As such, the perceived expertise of the recruiter is likely to depend on his or her role in the company (i.e., high expertise if the company representative is currently performing a job role that closely resembles the position that the organization is hiring for). Trustworthiness also is likely to depend on position, such that organizational recruiters are less trusted by job seekers than job incumbents. Therefore, we propose that career fairs should be perceived by job seekers as somewhat credible if the representative is an incumbent and noncredible if the representative is a professional recruiter.

### Social Networks/Word of Mouth

Firms do not have much direct control over the recruitment information that job seekers obtain from social networks (e.g., friends and family). However, social networks can play an influential role in shaping the job search process (e.g., Barber, Daly, Giannantonio, & Phillips, 1994; Heneman & Judge, 2003). For instance, Kilduff (1990) found that MBA students were more likely to interview with the same companies as those students whom they perceived to be similar to themselves or who were viewed as personal friends. Recruitment via social networks also appears to be effective: One of the most widely reported findings in recruitment studies is that employees recruited through informal sources such as referrals appear to demonstrate higher rates of job survival (Rynes & Cable, 2003).

Whereas research has shown the effects of social networks on job seekers' decisions to join and stay with organizations, little research has been focused on how social networks affect job seekers' beliefs about organizations. This is an interesting distinction because it is possible that social networks lead to job choices and job survival because they create a path of least resistance for job seekers or create indebtedness to friends, without actually changing what job seekers believe about a firm.

We propose that social networks should be perceived by job seekers as rich sources of information. First, information gathered through social networks usually is based on face-to-face or telephone interactions, thereby permitting timely responses to job seekers' questions. This interpersonal form of communication also facilitates the use the multiple informational cues (e.g., voice inflection and body gestures). Although social networks may not provide access to organizational charts or data, there is ample opportunity to engage in both verbal exchange and body language. Finally, the friends and family who comprise social networks can tailor the information they provide to the individual needs and questions of job seekers. For example, a friend within a company will probably take the time to describe in detail the work life and social environment of the organization. Thus, job seekers are likely to perceive social networks as relatively rich sources of information.

Whether job seekers perceive social networks as expert sources of information depends on the position of the person delivering the information. People who are current employees—particularly if they are performing a job function similar to the open position—are likely to be viewed as possessing high expertise. People who have had some first-hand experiences with the company in question—either as a former employee or as a customer or supplier—are likely to be perceived as possessing some expertise as information sources. Regardless of expertise, however, social networks are likely to be seen as trustworthy because these sources typically share a close relationship with job seekers. Thus, word of mouth from social networks should be perceived as possessing medium to high credibility.

### Employment Agencies/Executive Search Firms

Employment agencies and executive search firms—acting as intermediaries in the job market—contact, screen, and present job candidates to employers (Heneman & Judge, 2003). Employment agency representatives communicate organizational and job attribute information to job seekers as positions become available that meet job seekers' needs, preference, and abilities. Communication between agency representatives and job seekers typically begins with several initial face-to-face meetings followed by telephone conversations. If there is adequate interest on both the side of the hiring organization and the side of the job seeker, the employment agency makes the introduction and allows the relationship to develop.

As such, employment agencies should be perceived as rich forms of information. They provide relatively quick feedback to accommodate job seeker queries. Even if communications are often e-mails, either party can resort to phone conversations or even face-to-face meetings if necessary. Accordingly, employment agencies can use multiple cues to communicate recruitment information and also are able to use a high variety of languages, including statistics, charts, and facts about the companies. Finally, given their role as intermediaries, employment agencies tailor information to the individual needs of each of their job seeker clients. For instance, agents may be able to furnish job seekers with additional information about a particular company's selection practices or provide benchmark comparisons for salary and benefits. Therefore, employment agencies should be perceived as relatively rich sources of recruitment information by job seekers.

The perceived credibility of employment and executive search agencies is less positive. With regard to expertise, employment agencies and their agents are by definition a "third party" in the relationship between job seekers and hiring organizations. Because agents represent organizations in which they are not employed, it is unlikely that job seekers perceive them to be in a position to provide deep information about potential employers. This becomes particularly problematic when it comes to specific information about company culture and social environment. With regard to trustworthiness, employment agencies and executive search firms clearly have a vested interest in successfully matching job seekers with hiring organizations, as most of these companies are compensated when organizations hire identified candidates (Heneman & Judge, 2003). Because of this incentive structure, job seekers may view agents with some degree of mistrust since agents might be motivated to stress positive information about potential employers. Therefore, employment and executive search agencies should be perceived by job seekers as relatively low in credibility.

## Selection Sources

In the preceding section, we focused on sources of recruitment information and discussed job seekers' perspectives on the richness and credibility of information from those sources. In this section, focus shifts from the job seeker to the hiring organization, and we analyze the media richness and credibility of several commonly used selection methods. Thus, the goal of selection practices is to transfer information about the job seeker to a hiring organization and more specifically to the decision makers in its employee selection process. This applicant information is compared to the specific needs of the organization and of the particular job opening, and hiring decisions are made on the basis of applicant fit (Cable & Judge, 1997; Rynes & Gerhart, 1990).

### Interviews

The selection interview is the most commonly used method for hiring (Arvey & Campion, 1982; McDaniel, Whetzel, Schmidt, & Maurer, 1994). Interviews vary with regard to their level of structure (Campion, Palmer, & Campion, 1997) and the extent to which they emphasize selection versus recruitment (Stevens, 1998). As noted in the recruitment interview section, however, the interview is the classic example of a rich media because it involves face-to-face, one-on-one interaction between an organizational interviewer and a job candidate. Therefore, interviews allow immediate feedback to interviewers by permitting them to clarify statements or probe into various facets of the candidate (e.g., values, goals, and knowledge) in the hopes of facilitating a more accurate fit assessment. Interviewers can glean information from multiple informational cues that are transmitted from the job candidate (e.g., tone of voice and body language), and language variety is high because in addition to non-verbal communication, job seekers are free to show documents from their portfolio or make sketches to illuminate a point. Furthermore, job seekers clearly tailor their responses and discussion to address interviewers' questions and interests. Consequently, the selection interview should be perceived by organizational decision makers as a rich source of information about job candidates.

It is difficult to predict the perceived credibility of the interview. Although it is clear that the applicant is an expert about himself or herself, the ability of the interviewer to elicit useful information about the applicant is notoriously poor (e.g., Heneman & Judge, 2003). Recall that for selection methods, perceived expertise can be equated to perceived validity or the extent to which a manager believes a test offers valid information about the applicant attribute that it is intended to measure. Accordingly, it is likely that the expertise imparted by the interview depends on the structure of the interview and the training of the interviewer. The validity of interviews increases substantially when they are structured. Thus, interviewers who are trained to use structured interviews may rate the interview's expertise as high. Interestingly, managers who have not received any interview training may not be aware of the benefits of structured interviews and, in fact, may not even be aware of the historically poor validity of the interview. Thus, the highest ratings of expertise for the interview should come either from highly trained professionals who use structured interviews or from completely untrained managers who are unaware of the infamously low validity of the interview!

It also is difficult to form predictions about the trustworthiness of information from an interview. On one hand, job applicants want a job, and it is a well-acknowledged fact that job candidates actively manage the impressions that hiring organizations form of them (e.g., Judge & Ferris, 1992). On the other hand, interviewers who employ structured, behavioral interviews force candidates to describe detailed experiences that they have had, removing much of the opportunity to manage impressions. Moreover, the "consensus at zero acquaintance" research paradigm demonstrates above-chance agreement between self-reported personality traits and ratings by observers who have had minimal exposure with the targets (Albright, Kenny, & Malloy, 1988; Funder & Sneed, 1993; Gangestad, Simpson, DiGeronimo, & Biek, 1992), suggesting that job applicants' basic behavioral tendencies offer some trustworthy information about their personalities, even if they manage impressions to some degree.

### Phone Screens

Phone screens refer to interviews conducted over the telephone. They are often conducted early in the selection process to winnow a large list of applicants to a small list of finalists and are often much shorter than traditional interviews (Blackman, 2002). Phone screens may be gaining in prominence as a result of the recent focus on cost-cutting measures because phone screens reduce travel costs (Fletcher, 1997).

As a telephone conversation between job candidates and organizational interviewers, phone screens facilitate timely feedback because interviewers can obtain immediate answers to questions and concerns. Communication is limited to spoken language and verbal cues, because physical gestures are lost. In addition, a high variety of languages is not possible, because applicants cannot easily show reports or graphics from their portfolios. Phone screens clearly permit a relatively high capacity for personal focus because the applicant can tailor his or her responses to the interviewers' line of questioning. Thus, it appears that phone screens should possess average to high media richness.

For the same reasons presented earlier with regard to the interview, the credibility of phone screens is difficult to judge. Thus, the perceived expertise resulting from a phone screen depends on (a) how much training the interviewer has received and (b) the degree of structure designed into the phone screen. However, we propose that the trustworthiness of information from phone screens will be lower than that for the traditional interview for two reasons. First, phone screens generally are shorter than an interview, leaving less time to drill down into a high level of detail concerning job seekers' responses and therefore allowing more opportunity for impression management. Second, phone conversations do not permit eye contact or the ability to see facial expressions, physical twitches and sweating, and other elements that are valid indicators of deceit or lying (Bond, Omar, Mahmoud, & Bonser, 1990; Ekman, 1985).

### Performance Tests and Work Samples

Performance tests and work samples are used in an attempt to assess the actual behavioral performance of a job candidate on a particular job activity as opposed to trying to assess his or her underlying ability or disposition. These methods thus focus on obtaining samples—as opposed to predictors—of work performance (Heneman & Judge, 2003). An example of this practice would be asking an applicant to a computer programmer position to write a program in Visual Basic to sort and run reports on a dataset.

The perceived media richness of performance tests should be high, although richness will vary according to the degree to which the tests approximate the actual job. For instance, high-fidelity tests that use very realistic equipment, tools and scenarios closely simulate actual job tasks. Examples of high-fidelity tests are having a candidate for a pilot's position undergo tests in a flight simulator and having a candidate for a customer service representative deal with an angry customer on the phone. These activities permit nearly-immediate feedback about performance to the organizational representative who is recording their actions and scoring their performance. Next, regarding multiple cues, perhaps the greatest strength of performance tests is that they capture many different cues at once, ranging from language to body posture to motor and communication skills. Language variety is restricted by the nature of the particular test and the skills that are assessed. Finally, performance tests also score high with regard to message tailoring, because the tests are created specifically to gather information about specific job tasks, and therefore applicant's behaviors are assessed along the dimensions decided by the organizational representative. In general, then, performance tests and work samples should be viewed as moderate to very rich sources of job candidate information by hiring managers. However, it should be noted that if low-fidelity tests and relatively unrealistic versions of such tests are used (e.g., administering a written test for a machinery technician's position), the four dimensions of media richness would all be restricted.

In general, performance tests should be viewed as fairly expert sources of information about job applicants' abilities. First, assuming that the tests are close simulations of actual job tasks, organizational representatives gain a first-hand, behavioral look at how well various applicants can perform the task. Moreover, performance tests offer some of the highest validity coefficients in terms of predicting future performance, so that decision makers who are aware of this research should perceive them to be relatively expert sources of job candidate attributes. Naturally, to the extent that performance tests do not closely approximate actual job tasks, then they will be perceived as lower in expertise. The trustworthiness of performance tests also should be quite high. In fact, the structure of performance tests curtails job candidates' ability to engage in deceit or impression management tactics because one cannot easily fake required job behaviors. Thus, performance tests and work samples should be perceived as high in credibility.

### Cognitive Ability Testing

Cognitive ability tests assess thinking abilities such as perception, memory, reasoning, expression, verbal skills, and mathematical skills (Heneman & Judge, 2003). Because they are typically administered as paper-and-pencil or computer tests, interaction between organizational representatives and job candidates is limited. This limitation undoubtedly restricts the amount of feedback that selection decision makers are able to obtain from job candidates, and it is not generally possible to follow up on a question or learn more about why an applicant answered a certain way. Because minimal communication is taking pace, the only informational cues that are sent by job candidates would be in the form of their responses on these tests. These written responses are of low language variety, as they communicate messages that are unambiguous and specific in nature (i.e., a test score), which is interpreted by organizational representatives in a relatively straightforward manner. Finally, because the tests are not customized around the particular job or company and job candidates only can respond to the demands placed upon them by these tests, there is little opportunity to tailor the information. Thus, cognitive ability tests should be perceived by organizational decision makers as low in media richness.

Cognitive ability tests fare better when it comes to perceived credibility. If one assumes that employers use tests that have been properly developed and validated, cognitive ability tests offer high validity in terms of predicting future performance across job types (Gottfredson, 1986; Hunter, 1986; Ree & Earles, 1991). It is likely that employers using cognitive ability tests are aware of this literature, and therefore should perceive them to be a relatively expert source of job candidates' mental ability. It is likely that cognitive ability tests score lower on expertise than work samples; however, because they only capture one domain of applicants' ability and generally do not approximate actual job tasks. Cognitive ability tests also should be seen as highly trustworthy because the structured format of cognitive ability tests permits direct comparisons between applicants and restricts candidates' impression management tactics because one cannot easily fake the correct answers to mental ability problems. It is therefore proposed that organizational decision makers perceive cognitive ability tests as possessing average-to-high credibility.

### Personality Testing

Personality tests, particularly those based on the Big Five taxonomy of personality, have been increasingly used as a selection method for new employees (Barrick & Mount, 1991; Heneman & Judge, 2003). Because they are administered in the form of a survey, personality tests severely limit the interaction between job candidates and organizational decision makers. Thus, consistent with cognitive ability tests, little opportunity exists for timely feedback if decision makers want to follow up with candidates. The only informational cues are job candidates' responses on the tests, which convey specific information about candidate personality but represent a narrow set of cues. Lastly, because the items on the test are set in advance, candidates are restricted in their ability to tailor information to the decision makers' interests. Therefore, we propose that personality testing should be perceived by decision makers as low in media richness.

The credibility of personality tests may be historically low, but this may be changing. In terms of expertise, decision makers may consider personality tests to be "pop psychology" without predictive validity, and it is true that many personality tests are not valid predictors (Guion & Gottier, 1965; Hough, 1992). However, recent personality research supports the validity of some personality tests, especially the facets of conscientiousness, extraversion, and emotional stability (Barrick & Mount, 1991; Heneman & Judge, 2003; Hurtz & Donovan, 2000; Judge & Bono, 2001). Thus, the perceived expertise of personality tests may be on the rise, although they still can only classify applicants along very specific dimensions that do not reflect the actual job. In terms of trustworthiness, personality tests may not be held in high regard by many managers because the responses are self-reported by applicants who have incentives to positively distort their responses, and there is no way to verify their answers (Barrick & Mount, 1996; Hough, Eaton, Dunnette, Kamp, & McCloy, 1990; Ones, Viswesvaran, & Reiss, 1996). Thus, we predict that personality tests are viewed as possessing low trustworthiness.

## DISCUSSION

In this chapter we started with the assumption that to understand peoples' fit judgments about a target, we must focus on (a) the beliefs that they hold about the target and (b) how they develop those beliefs. We proposed that each party to an employment relationship—job seekers and employers—use a variety of channels to gather information and develop beliefs about the other party. We also proposed that the impact of various information sources on people's beliefs depends on the perceived credibility and richness of the information sources. In other words, regardless of the specific information a decision maker learns about a target, we propose that when information comes from rich and credible sources, it will tend to be encoded deep in memory and be resistant to change. Information from sources low in richness and credibility will tend to be ignored or encoded in a shallow manner that is easily overwritten or forgotten, is not available for future recall, and therefore should not be incorporated into fit judgments. Thus, perhaps the most important general implication of the information-processing perspective proposed in this chapter is that fit perceptions and subsequent employment decisions will not be affected by information from sources with low richness and low credibility.

Note that the model presented in this chapter offers two interesting complements to the "applicant fairness" literature (Gilliland, 1993; Ployhart & Ryan, 1998), which focuses on applicants' perceptions of the validity of firms' selection systems. First, in this chapter the focus is turned from applicant perceptions to organizational decision makers' perceptions of selection test validity. Thus, we propose that both applicants and hiring managers go through the process of evaluating the merits of selection tests used by the organization. For hiring managers, if a selection test is perceived to be low in richness and credibility, they essentially ignore the information or code it in such a way that it does not affect their fit judgments about the applicants they evaluate. The second way that our model complements the applicant fairness literature is that in addition to evaluating firms' selection systems, we propose that applicants likewise evaluate firms' recruitment systems and the information they obtain from different recruitment sources. To the extent that recruitment information is low in richness or credibility, it is discounted or coded such that it does not affect their fit judgments about organizations.

Organizations may be able to use the model presented in this chapter to improve the effectiveness of their recruitment and selection investments. In the context of recruitment, for example, it may be possible to firms to increase the impact of recruitment tactics that typically are low in credibility or richness and therefore have limited effects on applicants' beliefs. For example, although our model suggests that organizational Web sites may have limited impact because of low richness and credibility, firms may find it possible to use Web sites as gateways to interactive chat rooms with organizational incumbents. Thus, job seekers could exchange messages with people who hold jobs similar to those that they are considering, which would be expected to increase both the richness and the credibility of the information. In the hiring context, firms may be investing considerable resources in selection methods that have little effect on decision makers' fit assessments because they are not aware of the validity of the methods. Thus, a hiring manager may not understand that extraversion is a valid predictor of sales performance or that cognitive ability is particularly predictive for managerial jobs. Informing managers about the validity of these tests would be likely to improve perceived expertise regarding the tests, causing the tests to play a greater role in fit judgments about various applicants. Likewise, firms may find that conducting within-organization validation studies, which hiring managers help conduct, improves the perceived expertise of selection tests, thereby increasing the effect of the test on managers' beliefs about job seekers and subsequent fit judgments.

## Belief Change and Communication Effectiveness

The basic tenet of this chapter is that people's beliefs about a target will be affected more by rich, credible sources of information. This tenet can be examined by studying how individuals' beliefs change after encountering communications that vary in richness and credibility and by testing whether the beliefs are retained across time. We believe that this information-processing model is an important contribution to the fit literature, as well as to the recruitment and selection literature, because it shines a light on the genesis of fit perceptions and subsequent organizational entry decisions, and it offers a new approach and methodology for judging recruitment and selection methods.

Although not explicit in the conceptual model, our discussion implies that rich, credible media are more effective forms of communication. In fact, Media Richness Theory is based on the premise that richer media lead to more effective communication (Daft & Lengel, 1986; Daft et al., 1987). Unfortunately, most Media Richness Theory researchers have not actually examined the effectiveness of different communication media and have instead focused on managers' choices between communication media for a given message (e.g., face-to-face meeting vs. memo) (e.g., Daft et al., 1987; Rice & Shook, 1990; Russ, Daft, & Lengel, 1990; Trevino, Daft, & Lengel, 1987; Trevino, Lengel, Bodensteiner, Gerloff, & Muir, 1990). Thus, we have surprisingly little evidence that information actually is communicated more effectively using rich media (Dennis & Kinney, 1998).

To examine the premise that richer and more credible media lead to greater communication in the recruitment and selection areas, future researchers must first conceptualize and then operationalize the concept of communication effectiveness. One approach to understanding the concept of effective communication is that, to be effective, a message must lead to a common perspective and understanding among intended recipients (e.g., Daft et al., 1987). From this perspective, effective communication would be demonstrated in a recruitment context when a particular recruitment message creates a particular shared belief among job seekers. For example, after attending a career fair, a targeted group of applicants has a greater level of agreement that a particular organization offers a team-oriented work environment. In a selection context, this perspective means that effective communication is demonstrated when, after conducting a phone screen, four hiring managers agree significantly more about the accounting skills of an applicant.

However, it is possible that a message leads to greater agreement among a group of people, but that the group did not receive the message that was intended. For example, it is possible that applicants agree with each other about a company's culture but their perceptions are not consistent with the message that the hiring organization intended to communicate. Thus, although the data would be harder to obtain, it seems valuable to complement the concept of recipient agreement with the concept of sender–recipient correspondence. In the recruitment arena, operationalizing sender–recipient correspondence implies comparing an organization's attributes (either as reported by insiders or gathered archivally) to a job seeker's beliefs about those attributes after experiencing a recruitment communication. In a selection context, operationalizing sender–recipient correspondence means comparing a job seeker's self views with the beliefs developed in the minds of organizational decision makers about that job seeker.

## Future Research

On the basis of the conceptual model and the concepts discussed in this chapter, there appear to be a number of fruitful areas for future research. First, it would be interesting and important to examine the predictions derived in this chapter about the perceived richness and credibility of the various recruitment and selection methods. Next, it would be useful to examine whether the effects of perceived richness and credibility on beliefs are additive or interactive. It is possible that credibility fully moderates richness, such that an information source has no effect on a judge's beliefs when credibility is low, regardless of the media richness level. This could occur, for example, in a recruitment interview conducted by a professional recruiter from the organization. Our model would predict that the face-to-face, one-on-one aspect of the interview would lead to the highest level of richness, but credibility would be low because the applicant may not believe the recruiter knows much about the actual position or location where the job is open and also may not trust the recruiter to give a realistic preview about the organization. Thus, despite the rich nature of the information, it may not be coded in the applicant's memory and may be unavailable for future recall. On the other hand, it is possible that the effects of richness and credibility are additive and operate independently, such that information from rich sources gets coded and stored even if the sources are not particularly credible, at least until the applicant encounters more credible sources. This additive perspective would seem to occur in marketing, where brand images are developed in consumers' memories even when information comes from a noncredible source such as a humorous TV advertisement.

It also may be useful to examine the effects of recruitment systems on applicants' beliefs about organizations relative to the effects of selection systems on hiring managers' beliefs about applicants. It is likely that managers' beliefs about applicants typically are based solely on the selection process, because otherwise they would have no idea that a given applicant exists. Job seekers, on the other hand, usually have heard about organizations before the recruitment process. That is, a job seeker knows the company "Intel" and has beliefs coded in his or her memory about Intel before he or she even becomes an applicant. Thus, for applicants, many organizational belief nodes and associations are already "set" in job seekers' minds, which must then be strengthened or modified by organizations (rather than simply developed from scratch). Although additional research is needed on the topic, this detail implies that each piece of information from a selection process has greater leverage on organizational decision makers' beliefs than each piece of information from the recruitment process has on job seekers' beliefs.

Our model also may offer some new insight and testable ideas in the context of realistic job previews. This literature suggests that lower turnover results when firms include both negative and positive job aspects, either because it reduces job seekers' expectations or because it increases their ability to self-select out based on lack of fit (Wanous & Colella, 1989). Despite these plausible explanations for the positive outcomes of realistic previews, we still know little about how job seekers' expectations and beliefs get created in the first place. Our proposed model might help account for this process by calling attention to recruitment source credibility and depth of information processing. Thus, we proposed that job seekers form stronger beliefs about organizations when they perceive information to come from sources that are credible because they process such information with more effort via the central processing route. Because communicating realistic information should cause job seekers to perceive greater expertise and trustworthiness of the source, we would expect greater elaboration and processing and subsequently stronger beliefs. Therefore, understanding the effects of credibility on job seeker beliefs may provide a possible explanation for why the beliefs are coded and acted upon, leading to the positive outcomes observed from realistic previews.

## CONCLUSION

People and organizations enter into employment relationships based primarily on fit, and the topic of fit perceptions has received considerable attention in the selection and recruitment domains over the last decade. We propose that a valuable next step in fit research is documenting the sources and the accuracy of people's fit perceptions and the process through which fit perceptions are created. Toward this end, our proposed model places the focus on the beliefs that job seekers and hiring managers each form about the other party, because the beliefs formed during this period become the fit judgments upon which their employment decisions are based.

## REFERENCES

Adkins, C. L., Russell, C. R., & Werbel, J. D. (1994). Judgments of fit in the selection process: The role of work value congruence. *Personnel Psychology, 47,* 605–623.

Ajzen, I. (2000). Nature and operation of attitudes. *Annual Review of Psychology, 52,* 27–58.

Albright, L., Kenny, D. A., & Malloy, T. E. (1988). Consensus in personality judgments at zero acquaintance. *Journal of Personality and Social Psychology, 55,* 387–395.

Allen, D. G., Scotter, J. R. V., & Otondo, R. F. (2004). Recruitment communication media: Impact on prehire outcomes. *Personnel Psychology, 57*(1), 143–171.

Anderson, J. R. (1983). *The architecture of cognition.* Cambridge, MA: Harvard University Press.

Arvey, R. D., & Campion, J. E. (1982). The employment interview: A summary and review of recent research. *Personnel Psychology, 35*(2), 281–322.

Austin, E. W., & Dong, Q. (1994). Source v. content effects on judgments of news believability. *Journalism Quarterly, 71*(4), 973–983.

Barber, A. E. (1998). *Recruitment employees.* Thousand Oaks, CA: Sage.

Barber, A. E., Daly, C. L., Giannantonio, C. M., & Phillips, J. M. (1994). Job search activities: An examination of changes over time. *Personnel Psychology, 47*(4), 739–766.

Barrick, M. R., & Mount, M. K. (1991). The big five personality dimensions and job performance: A meta-analysis. *Personnel Psychology, 44*(1), 1–26.

Barrick, M. R., & Mount, M. K. (1996). Effects of impression management and self-deception on the predictive validity of personality constructs. *Journal of Applied Psychology, 81*, 261–272.

Blackman, M. C. (2002). The employment interview via the telephone: Are we sacrificing accurate personality judgments for cost efficiency? *Journal of Research in Personality, 36*, 208–223.

Bond, C. F., Omar, A., Mahmoud, A., & Bonser, R. N. (1990). Lie detection across cultures. *Journal of Nonverbal Behavior, 14*, 189–204.

Breaugh, J. A., & Starke, M. (2000). Research on employee recruitment: So many studies, so many remaining questions. *Journal of Management, 26*, 405–434.

Bretz, R. D., Rynes, S. L., & Gerhart, B. (1993). Recruiter perceptions of applicant fit: Implications for individual career preparation and job search behavior. *Journal of Vocational Behavior, 43*, 310–327.

Cable, D. M., Aiman-Smith, L., Mulvey, P. W., & Edwards, J. R. (2000). The sources and accuracy of job applicants' beliefs about organizational culture. *Academy of Management Journal, 43*, 1076–1085.

Cable, D. M., & DeRue, D. S. (2002). The convergent and discriminant validity of subjective fit perceptions. *Journal of Applied Psychology, 87*, 875–884.

Cable, D. M., & Judge, T. A. (1996). Person–organization fit, job choice decisions, and organizational entry. *Organizational Behavior and Human Behavior Processes, 67*, 294–311.

Cable, D. M., & Judge, T. A. (1997). Interviewers' perceptions of person–organization fit and organizational selection decisions. *Journal of Applied Psychology, 82*, 546–561.

Cable, D. M., & Turban, D. (2002). Recruitment image equity: Establishing the dimensions, sources and value of job seekers' organizational beliefs. In G. R. Ferris (Ed.), *Research in Personnel/Human Resource Management* (Vol. 20, pp. 115–163). Greenwich, CT: JAI Press.

Campion, M. A., Palmer, D. K., & Campion, J. E. (1997). A review of structure in the selection interview. *Personnel Psychology, 50*(3), 655–702.

Craik, F. I., & Tulving, E. (1975). Depth of processing and the retention of words in episodic memory. *Journal of Experimental Psychology, 104*, 268–294.

Daft, R. L., & Lengel, R. H. (1984). Information richness: A new approach to managerial behavior and organizational design. *Research in Organizational Behavior, 6*, 191–233.

Daft, R. L., & Lengel, R. H. (1986). Organizational information requirements, media richness and structural design. *Management Science, 32*(5), 554–571.

Daft, R. L., Lengel, R. H., & Trevino, L. K. (1987). Message equivocality, media selection, and manager performance: Implications for information systems. *MIS Quarterly, 11*(3), 355–366.

Daft, R. L., & Wiginton, J. C. (1979). Language and organization. *Academy of Management Review, 4*(2), 179–191.

Dennis, A. R., & Kinney, S. T. (1998). Testing media richness theory in the new media: The effects of cues, feedback, and task equivocality. *Information Systems Research, 9*(3), 256–274.

Eagly, A. H., & Chaiken, S. (1993). *The psychology of attitudes.* Orlando, FL: Harcourt Brace Janovich.

Ekman, P. (1985). *Telling lies.* New York: W. W. Norton.

Fisher, C. D., Ilgen, D. R., & Hoyer, W. D. (1979). Source credibility, information favorability, and job offer acceptance. *Academy of Management Journal, 22*(1), 94–103.

Fletcher, C. (1997). Just how effective is a telephone interview? *People Management, 3,* 2–3.

Funder, D. C., & Sneed, C. D. (1993). Behavioral manifestations of personality: Anecological approach to judgmental accuracy. *Journal of Personality and Social Psychology, 64,* 479–490.

Gangestad, S. W., Simpson, J. A., DiGeronimo, K., & Biek, M. (1992). Differential accuracy in person perception across traits: Examination of a functional hypothesis. *Journal of Personality and Social Psychology, 62,* 688–698.

Gaziano, C., & McGrath, K. (1986, Fall). Measuring the concept of credibility. *Journalism and Mass Communication Quarterly,* 451–462.

Gilliland, S. W. (1993). The perceived fairness of selection systems: An organizational perspective. *Academy of Management Review, 18,* 694–734.

Gottfredson, L. S. (1986). Societal consequences of the g factor in employment. *Journal of Vocational Behavior, 29,* 379–410.

Guion, R. M., & Gottier, R. F. (1965). Validity of personality measures in personnel selection. *Personnel Psychology, 18,* 135–164.

Heneman, H. G., & Judge, T. A. (2003). *Staffing organizations.* New York: McGraw-Hill Irwin.

Hough, L. M. (1992). The "Big Five" personality variables—construct confusion: Description versus prediction. *Human Performance, 5,* 139–155.

Hough, L. M., Eaton, N. K., Dunnette, M. D., Kamp, J. D., & McCloy, R. A. (1990). Criterion-related validities of personality constructs and the effect of response distortion on those validities. *Journal of Applied Psychology, 75,* 581–595.

Hovland, C. I., Janis, I. L., & Kelley, H. H. (1953). *Communication and persuasion.* New Haven, CT: Yale University Press.

Huber, G. P., & Daft, R. L. (1987). The information environments of organizations. In F. M. Jablin, L. L. Putnam, K. H. Roberts, & L. W. Porter (Eds.), *Handbook of organizational communication: An interdisciplinary perspective* (pp. 130–164). Newbury Park, CA: Sage Publications.

Hunter, J. E. (1986). Cognitive ability, cognitive aptitude, job knowledge, and job performance. *Journal of Vocational Behavior, 29,* 340–362.

Hurtz, G. M., & Donovan, J. J. (2000). Personality and job performance: The big five revisited. *Journal of Applied Psychology, 85,* 869–879.

*Impact of Internet in job search growing.* (2000). Retrieved July 6, 2004, from Wet-Feet.com.

Jackson, D. N., Peacock, A. C., & Holden, R. R. (1982). Professional interviewers' trait inferential structures for diverse occupational groups. *Organizational Behavior and Human Performance, 29*(1), 1.

Johnson, T. J., & Kaye, B. K. (1998). Cruising is believing?: Comparing internet and traditional sources on media credibility measures. *Journalism and Mass Communication Quarterly, 75*(2), 325–340.

Judge, T. A., & Bono, J. E. (2001). Relationship of core self-evaluation traits—self-esteem, generalized self-efficacy, locus of control, and emotional stability—

with job satisfaction and job performance: A meta-analysis. *Journal of Applied Psychology, 86,* 80–92.

Judge, T. A., & Bretz, R. D., Jr. (1992). Effects of work values on job choice decisions. *Journal of Applied Psychology, 77,* 261–271.

Judge, T. A., & Cable, D. M. (1997). Applicant personality, organizational culture, and organization attraction. *Personnel Psychology, 50,* 359–394.

Judge, T. A., & Ferris, G. R. (1992). The elusive criterion of fit in human resources staffing decisions. *Human Resource Planning, 15*(4), 47–67.

Keller, P. A., & Block, L. G. (1996). Increasing the persuasiveness of fear appeals: The effect of arousal and elaboration. *Journal of Consumer Research, 22*(4), 448–459.

Keller, P. A., & Block, L. G. (1997). Vividness effects: A resource-matching perspective. *Journal of Consumer Research, 24,* 295.

Kilduff, M. (1990). The interpersonal structure of decision making: A social comparison approach to organizational choice. *Organizational Behavior and Human Decision Processes, 47*(2), 270–288.

Kristof-Brown, A. L. (2000). Perceived applicant fit: Distinguishing between recruiters' perceptions of person–job and person–organization fit. *Personnel Psychology, 53,* 643–671.

Lievens, F., & Harris, M. M. (2003). Research on Internet recruitment and testing: Current status and future directions. In C. L. Cooper & I. T. Robertson (Eds.), *International Review of Industrial and Organizational Psychology* (vol. 16, pp. 131–165). Chichester, England: Wiley.

MacInnis, D. J., & Jaworski, B. J. (1989). Information processing from advertisements: Toward an integrative framework. *Journal of Marketing, 53,* 1.

McDaniel, M. A., Whetzel, D. L., Schmidt, F. L., & Maurer, S. D. (1994). The validity of employment interviews: A comprehensive review and meta-analysis. *Journal of Applied Psychology, 79,* 599–615.

Meyer, P. (1988). Defining and measuring credibility of newspapers: Developing an index. *Journalism and Mass Communication Quarterly, 65,* 567–574.

Ones, D. S., Reiss, A. D., & Viswesvaran, C. (1996). Role of social desirability in personality testing for personnel selection: The red herring. *Journal of Applied Psychology, 81,* 660–679.

Petty, R. E., & Cacioppo, J. T. (1981). *Attitudes and persuasion: Classic and contemporary approaches.* Dubuque, IA: W. C. Brown.

Petty, R. E., & Cacioppo, J. T. (1986). The elaboration likelihood model of persuasion. In L. Berkowitz (Ed.), *Advances in experimental social psychology* (pp. 123–205). New York: Academic Press.

Ployhart, R. E., & Ryan, A. M. (1998). Applicants' reactions to the fairness of selection procedures: the effects of positive rule violations and time of measurement. *Journal of Applied Psychology, 83,* 3–16.

Ree, M. J., & Earles, J. A. (1991). Predicting training success: Not much more than g. *Personnel Psychology, 44*(2), 321–332.

Rice, R. E., & Shook, D. E. (1990). Relationships of job categories and organizational levels to use of communication channels, including electronic mail: A meta-analysis and extension. *Journal of Management Studies, 27*(2), 195–229.

Russ, G., Daft, R. L., & Lengel, R. H. (1990). Media selection and managerial characteristics in organizational communications. *Management Communication Quarterly, 4,* 151–175.

Rynes, S. L. (1991). Recruitment, job choice, and post-hire consequences: A call for new research directions. In M. D. Dunnette & L. M. Hough (Eds.), *Handbook of industrial and organizational psychology* (2nd ed., Vol. 2, pp. 399–444). Palo Alto, CA: Consulting Psychologists Press.

Rynes, S. L., & Cable, D. M. (2003). Recruitment research in the twenty-first century. In W. C. Borman & D. R. Ilgen (Eds.), *Handbook of psychology: Industrial and organizational psychology* (Vol. 12, pp. 55–76). New York: Wiley.

Rynes, S., & Gerhart, B. (1990). Interviewer assessments of applicant 'fit': An exploratory investigation. *Personnel Psychology, 43*, 13–35.

Schmitz, J., & Fulk, J. (1991). Organizational colleagues, media richness, and electronic mail. *Communication Research, 18*(4), 487–523.

Schwab, D. P., Rynes, S. L., & Aldag, R. J. (1987). Theories and research on job search and choice. In K. M. Rowland & G. R. Ferris (Eds.), *Research in personnel and human resources management* (Vol. 5, pp. 126–166). Greenwich, CT: JAI Press.

Stevens, C. K. (1998). Antecedents of interview interactions, interviewers' ratings, and applicants' reactions. *Personnel Psychology, 51*, 55–85.

Trevino, L. K., Daft, R. L., & Lengel, R. H. (1987). Media symbolism, media richness, and media choice in organizations. *Communication Research, 15*, 553–574.

Trevino, L. K., Lengel, R. H., Bodensteiner, W., Gerloff, E. A., & Muir, N. K. (1990). The richness imperativ and cognitive style: The role of individual differences in media choice behavior. *Management Communication Quarterly, 4*, 176–197.

Tuppen, C. J. (1974). Dimensions of communicator credibility: An oblique solution. *Speech Monographs, 41*, 253–260.

Turban, D. B., & Keon, T. L. (1993). Organizational attractiveness: An interactionist perspective. *Journal of Applied Psychology, 78*, 184–193.

Wanous, J. P. (1980). *Organizational entry*. Reading, MA: Addison-Wesley.

Wanous, J. P., & Colella, A. (1989). Organizational entry research: Current status and future directions. In G. R. Ferris & K. M. Rowland (Eds.), *Research in personnel and human resources management* (Vol. 7, pp. 59–120). Greenwich, CT: JAI Press.

Wyer, R. S., & Srull, T. K. (1989). Person memory and judgment. *Psychological Review, 96*, 58–83.

# CHAPTER 6

# *A Process Model of Leader–Follower Fit*

Leanne Atwater
*Arizona State University West*

Shelley Dionne
*Binghamton University*

Fit has been examined largely from three perspectives: person–organization fit, person–vocation fit, and person–group fit (Kristof, 1996). In this chapter we extend the thinking on these conceptualizations of fit to the concept of fit between the leader and followers within the group. Person-organization fit occurs when the organization satisfies employee needs, desires, or preferences. Person–group fit occurs when individuals feel a sense of compatibility with the other members of their workgroup. Person–vocation fit occurs when the individual's skills and competencies fit the requirements for his or her job. Whereas fit research has consistently demonstrated that a greater degree of fit or compatibility results in more positive responses for individuals (Schneider, 1987; O'Reilly, Chatman, & Caldwell, 1991; Schneider, Goldstein, & Smith, 1995), very little work in the fit literature has explicitly focused on fit as it relates to fit between leaders and followers. Leadership theory has implied that leader–follower fit is important (e.g., in discussions of leader–member exchange), but these notions have not been developed from a fit perspective. We contend that in addition to the fit individuals feel with other workgroup members, it also is important for leaders and followers to feel a sense of compatibility or fit with one another. The relationship between superiors and subordinates is an important determinant of how effectively and efficiently organizational members get their jobs done (Tjosvold, 1985). As such, we believe that a look into leader–follower fit will provide another, relevant perspective on the concept of fit in organizations.

Leader–follower fit is potentially relevant from a number of vantage points. For example, a leader may be a representative of the organization's values, and, thus, if the follower's values "fit" with those of the leader, the follower is likely to experience greater person–organization fit. Alternatively, leaders may play an important role in socializing members into the workgroup, thus having an impact on the follower's person–group fit. Leaders also can serve as the gatekeepers, allowing or promoting opportunities for followers to acquire necessary job skills or placing individuals into jobs for which they possess the requisite skills, thereby having an impact on the follower's person–job fit. We use individualized leadership theory as the backdrop for our exploration into leader–follower fit. This theory focuses on one-to-one relationships between leaders and followers and how these relationships impact leaders' and followers' successes in work organizations.

However, before linking leader–follower fit to individualized leadership theory, we discuss the history of leadership research as it relates to fit. We then develop what we believe are new ideas about leadership and fit and suggest their implications for practice and future research.

## BACKGROUND

Leadership has been considered the focus of group process since the early 1900s (see Bass, 1990). For example, Chapin (1924, as cited in Bass, 1990) described leadership as the polarization point for group cooperation. In 1942, Redl described the leader as the focal person who integrates the group (Bass, 1990, p. 11). These early conceptualizations have been built upon over the years, strengthening the notion that the leader and his or her interactions with group members impact the group's cohesiveness, performance, and other significant group outcomes (cf. Baumgartel, 1956, 1957).

The mechanisms by which leaders impact group outcomes have evolved from conceptualizations that focused on the leader's traits to those that focused on behaviors. The trait approaches emphasized the personality, abilities, skills, and values of individuals. The conclusion from much of the research on leader traits (which took place before 1950) was that although there were some traits that seemed to characterize many leaders (e.g., capacity, achievement, and responsibility), "leadership is not a matter of . . . the mere possession of some combination of traits. Rather leadership appears to be a working relationship among members of a group in which the leader acquires status through active participation and demonstration of his or her capacity to carry cooperative tasks to completion" (Bass, 1990, p. 77). Clearly, even at this early juncture in leadership research, the leader's fit with the group was somewhat relevant to the cooperative aspects of leadership.

From the trait approach, we move into the thesis that to understand leadership we must focus not so much on the characteristics of the leader but upon his or her behavior. The primary dimensions of behavior that were discussed were task and relationship behaviors or initiation of structure and consideration (Fleishman, 1973; Halpin & Winer, 1957). However, in later developments attempts were made to identify not just what leaders do but what they do as relevant to group performance. As such, Bowers and Seashore (1966) identified four types of behaviors: leader support, interaction facilitation, goal emphasis, and work facilitation. Interaction facilitation included behaviors leaders needed to use to deal with conflicts and create a positive group atmosphere. Again, fit is being alluded to, although the leader's role is more in line with how to help group members fit with one another.

Because the behavior approaches led to the conclusion that "the degree to which leaders need to exhibit task or people-oriented behaviors depends on the situation" (Hughes, Ginnett, & Curphy, 1996), leadership theorizing evolved into the contingency movement. In the late 1960s, two models that suggested the best leadership style or behavior to use was dependent on characteristics of the situation were proposed. In terms of fit, we can conceptualize this as the leader's style needing to fit followers' levels of maturity (situational leadership theory) (Hersey & Blanchard, 1969) or the characteristics of the job context (contingency theory) (Fiedler, 1967). Whereas situational leadership theory suggests that the fit comes when the leader adjusts his or her style to that of each subordinate, contingency theory suggests that fit results when the leader adjusts the situation to his or her style or selects a situation that fits his or her style.

The normative decision model (Vroom & Jago, 1988; Vroom & Yetton, 1973) also focuses on matching the leader and situation. This model highlights the decision-making method a leader should use and bases that decision on characteristics of the need for a high-quality decision and the degree to which follower acceptance or buy-in to the decision is necessary. Like situational leadership theory, this model presumes that the leader can change his or her decision style to match or fit the decision needs.

Dyadic relationships between leaders and followers became the focus when leader–member exchange (LMX) was first put forward in the works of Dansereau, Graen, and Haga (1975), Graen (1976), and Graen and Cashman (1975). The central premise behind LMX is that within workgroups, different types of relationships develop between leaders and followers. Some LMX relationships are positive, resulting from positive work and emotional exchanges, whereas others are less positive or negative. LMX challenged the belief that leaders behaved in a collective way toward all followers. "Research has shown that approximately 90% of all work units are differentiated in terms of the LMX relationships represented. Only about 10% of the time do leaders form the same type of LMX relationship with all subordinates" (Liden, Sparrowe, & Wayne, 1997,

p. 48). This quote suggests that leader–follower fit is most often dyadic rather than fit between the leader and the group as a whole.

The first studies of LMX focused on the vertical linkages between a leader and each follower (referred to as vertical dyad linkage theory [VDL]). VDL theory was the first to propose that fit between the leader and each follower was critical and that there were no leadership styles per se. It also proposed that leaders interacted differently with each follower, and each follower interacted differently with the leader. The leader's relationship with the workgroup is considered as a set of vertical dyad linkages between the leader and each follower.

LMX proposes that the leader needs to develop a good fit with each follower. The leader cannot presume that all followers need or desire the same from the leader.

The leader, rather than the follower, has more control over the quality of the LMX relationship. To some extent, whether the leader chooses to develop a high-quality relationship with a follower will depend upon the compatibility the leader believes he or she has with a particular group member. Compatibility can be defined as actual similarity (e.g., in age, race, tenure, or beliefs), perceived similarity, or liking (Liden et al., 1997).

Studies have shown that actual similarity on variables such as competence (Snyder & Bruning, 1985) and the need for power (McClane, 1991a, 1991b) was positively associated with LMX. Perceived similarity also has been shown to be positively related to LMX, depending on the variables measured. For example, if the leader perceives that the follower has a similar outlook and approach, the LMX relationship is more likely to develop into a positive one (Bauer & Green, 1996). In addition, the degree of mutual liking also has been positively related to the LMX relationship (Liden, Wayne, & Stilwell, 1993).

The LMX/VDL results taken together suggest that actual similarity, perceived similarity, and liking all represent better dyadic fit between the leader and follower. This "better fit" results in higher LMX, which in turn results in better individual and organizational outcomes (Pulakos & Wexley, 1983; Turban & Jones, 1988). The challenge for the leader is to create high LMX relationships with followers who do not have high degrees of similarity (actual or perceived).

**Individualized Leadership**

Derived from traditional leadership approaches such as average leadership style (ALS) and VDL, individualized leadership (IL) also focuses on the one-to-one relationships between the leader and each follower (Yammarino & Dansereau, 2002). Both the leader and followers need to make investments and realize returns. Generally, the leader needs to provide support for subordinates' feelings of self-worth and the subordinate needs to provide satisfying performance in return. This dyadic theory involves empowerment, in which the focus is on developing individual competencies rather than the more traditional focus of getting people to work together or a newer genre focus of establishing a vision (Yammarino & Dansereau, 2002).

Because IL concerns the notion of reciprocal interdependence between superiors and subordinates developing over time (Yammarino & Dansereau, 2002), dyadic similarity may play a pivotal role in the leadership experience. Similarities on factors such as beliefs, needs, values, the need for achievement, autonomy, and recognition of another have been noted as antecedents of IL (Yammarino & Dansereau, 2002). Similarities between leader and follower on variables considered antecedents of IL are likely to affect the interdependence established in the dyadic relationship, which, in turn, could affect leader–follower fit.

As evidenced in the preceding descriptions of the evolving nature of leadership theory, the notion of leader–follower fit has been a part of the conceptualizations, although the exact nature of fit and its relevance has changed over time. Moreover, fit is generally theoretically implied and/or assumed, and, as such, has not been a primary explicit mechanism for understanding leader–follower relations.

In the remainder of this chapter we use this evolving theoretical base to attempt to understand and continue the theoretical development in the area of leader–follower fit, specifically focusing on the more recent IL theory delineated in Yammarino and Dansereau (2002) and discussed previously in Dansereau and Yammarino (1998) and Dansereau, Yammarino, and colleagues (1995, 1998). Because the primary focus of IL theory concerns developing individual competencies, we assert that IL theory is better primed to promote leader–follower fit, as the leader operates via affecting/impacting the follower's self-worth. Developing the follower's self-worth is likely to result in effective performance (Yammarino & Dansereau, 2002), which then fosters or reinforces the reciprocal interdependent leader–follower relationship. That is, follower self-worth leads to higher performance, which leads to greater leader investment in the follower's development, and so on. This interdependence may better promote feelings of leader–follower fit.

Further, because IL theory asserts that the leader–follower relationship changes over time, a temporal view of fit emerges as well, allowing for fit factors that may be more salient in more mature relationships which emerge at a later time. For example, Jackson, May, and Whitney (1995) discussed "readily detectable" attributes of diversity, which can be quickly and consensually determined with only brief exposure. "Underlying attributes" such as knowledge, skills, attitudes, and personality take longer to discover. As such, we will frame fit within the context of the changing leader–follower relationship over time in IL theory, first focusing on early attraction–similarity among demographic factors such as race, age, and gender, as well as role congruence issues within the dyad. Next we con-

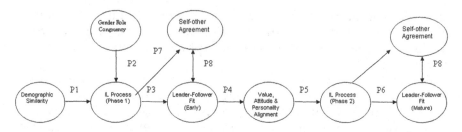

FIGURE 6-1.    Temporal leader–follower fit within individualized leadership process.

sider how, after initial leader–follower relations have formed, personality, values, and attitude alignment may bolster the IL process, which may be used to promote the development of a more mature fit between leaders and followers. These propositions are modeled in Fig. 6–1 and form the basis for the propositions put forth in this chapter.

Lastly, we consider the importance of leader–follower fit from an evaluative perspective of both subordinates and leaders. We discuss the potential impact of fit on evaluative processes such as self–other agreement assessments. Moreover, we assert that the interdependent focus of IL theory builds a case for a broader understanding and conceptualization of self–other agreement and the importance of fit. Traditionally, leader outcomes have been the focus of the self–other agreement literature. However, with the reciprocal, interdependent nature of IL theory leader–follower relations, additional strength for self–other agreement research may be found by examining the contribution of leader–follower agreement to subordinate outcomes.

## DEMOGRAPHIC SIMILARITY

As noted in the preceding section, IL (Yammarino & Dansereau, 2002) takes into account the changing nature of a leader–follower relationship over time. Demography may be a plausible means of viewing leader–follower fit in the earlier phases of the IL process, especially as demographic similarity relates to attraction. Early research on similarity and attraction indicated that individuals are more attracted to those more similar to themselves (Byrne, 1971). Polzer, Milton, and Swann (2002) also demonstrated the importance of interpersonal congruence. Their longitudinal study revealed that groups with high interpersonal congruence had better group outcomes, such as reduced conflict and improved task performance. For some groups, enough interpersonal congruence emerged in their first 10 minutes of interaction to impact outcomes positively. In this short time, congruence was likely based largely on observed demographic similarity.

Because some demographic characteristics such as gender, age, and race are evident upon initial interactions, these demographic factors may serve as key antecedents of IL. Harrison, Price, Gavin, and Florey (2002) demonstrated that demographic similarity is more important to group outcomes in the early stages of team development. If we generalize this finding to leader–follower relationships, we can predict that demographics would be important in the early stages of these relationships as well. The link between demographic similarity and leader–follower fit most likely lies within the attraction factor associated with the similarity, triggering an initial investment by the leader that may include attention, support, and/or assurance.

The attraction between demographically similar individuals may drive and/or forge an interdependent relationship with increased communication and positive affect. Prior research in demography has shown similar findings. For example, Judge and Ferris (1993) found that demographic similarity influenced a supervisor's affect toward subordinates and indirectly influenced performance ratings. Likewise, Tsui and O'Reilly (1989) found that subordinates in dissimilar demographic dyads engaged in less communication and were rated by managers as performing more poorly than those in demographically similar dyads. Although not mentioned by Yammarino and Dansereau (2002) as an antecedent of IL, demographic similarity may be another critical antecedent in establishing the interdependence of the leader–follower dyad.

This notion of demographic similarity initially influencing IL could be illustrated using the demographic characteristic of gender. Consider a new female leader in a large organization with several subordinates, including men and women. Similarity–attraction theory would indicate that the female leader may be more inclined to establish relationships with female subordinates (Byrne, 1971) in that she relates to the experiences they may have shared while establishing their careers and managing work–life balance issues, which are experienced more predominantly by women (Greenglass, Pantony, & Burke, 1989). Female supervisors also may be more inclined to communicate with female rather than male subordinates (Tsui & O'Reilly, 1989).

Owing, in part, to this demographic similarity, the female leader is attracted to the female follower. This attraction may encourage the leader to invest in supporting the subordinate's self-worth, and, in realizing this support, the subordinate provides satisfying performance to reciprocate and thus reinforces the interdependence. This interdependence may serve as a fit factor within the newly established leader–follower relationship. Similar dynamics may operate with other demographic characteristics such as age or race. The individualized leader can use demographic similarities to activate an attraction that can assist him or her in supporting followers' feelings of self-worth and subsequent performance.

Because demographic similarity often is evident upon initial interaction, we view demography as promoting and/or encouraging leader–follower fit early in the IL process. Because of the dyadic nature of IL, the female leader in the earlier case is forming one-to-one bonds with members of her group, but demographic similarity, on a number of characteristics, may be a driving force behind her initial comfort level in forging bonds with subordinates. Her initial willingness to be supportive of followers' self-worth may depend on her attraction to each follower, which may be influenced, in part, by demographic similarity. Moreover, as noted by Yammarino and Dansereau (2002), within IL theory the leader is more likely to make the initial investment, and, therefore, we assert that the leader is more likely to initiate the first investment based on demographic similarities that he or she shares with followers. As such, we offer the following proposition:

Proposition 1. Demographic similarity (on a number of demographic characteristics such as age, race, and gender) will encourage the leader to make an initial investment in the follower's feelings of self-worth.

## GENDER ROLE CONGRUITY AND INDIVIDUALIZED LEADERSHIP

Heilman (1983) proposed a lack of fit model that referred not only to leadership jobs but also to jobs in general. Essentially the lack of fit model suggests that expectations about how successful an individual will be in a job are influenced by the fit between the perceptions of the individual's attributes and the perceptions of the job requirements. Most traits associated with management are generally considered to be masculine (Brenner, Tomkiewicz, & Schein, 1989). According to the lack of fit model, the "skills and abilities perceived to be required to effectively handle masculinely sex-typed jobs, such as managerial ones, do not correspond to the attributes believed to characterize women as a group. Taking a leadership role, making hard-nosed decisions and competing for resources simply are not activities that are consistent with a view of women as the gentle and/or helpless sex" (Heilman, 1983, pp. 279–280).

Eagly and Karau (2002) extended this conceptualization in their presentation of the role incongruity theory of prejudice toward female leaders. Essentially this theory contends that women suffer prejudice when they assume leadership roles because the roles of women and the roles of leaders conflict in many cases. Women are expected to be communal, that is, kind, nurturing, sensitive, and helpful. Leaders are supposed to be assertive, confident, ambitious, and dominant. Clearly the expectations of leaders are more closely aligned with stereotypical male traits than female traits. That is, women experience a lack of fit between their leadership roles and their female roles. As such, when women must enact many of the leadership roles they are required to enact, they must balance the expectations others have of women with expectations they have of leaders. Male leaders have no such balancing act to manage.

The fit between male and female leaders and followers becomes particularly problematic when women are in leadership positions and men are their followers. Men see management as more traditionally male, and men are more likely to react unfavorably toward female bosses than women (cf. Atwater, Carey, & Waldman, 2001; Stevens & DeNisi, 1980). This tendency for difficulties to arise when women supervise men stems in part from what Gutek and Cohen (1987) termed *sex-role spillover*. Essentially, sex-role spillover contends that expected roles for men and women in their social interactions spill over into the workplace. That is, because women are expected to be more submissive and men more dominant socially, these roles will also be expected in the workplace. As such, when men must report to women, the reporting relationship has additional strains because it violates expected male–female interaction patterns.

Although role congruity issues can impact fit early in a leader–follower relationship, we assert that this role congruity fit issue may be more likely to surface after the initial "sizing up" of the new leader. Unlike demographic characteristics that may be visibly evident from the first leader–follower interaction, the degree of role congruity (or incongruity) the leader demonstrates may not be as obviously evident within the first few interactions. In the first few interactions, the leader would be unlikely to feel the need to behave assertively. However, over time, as the leader obtains more information about the follower, he or she may realize that an increased emphasis on improving performance is necessary. At this point, assertiveness or dominance on behalf of the leader may come into play. These typically male behaviors or traits may be viewed by the follower as role incongruent for the female leader and cause problems between the female leader and a follower.

The dynamic nature of IL allows for a changing leader–follower relationship, and one would probably suspect that fit may be dynamic as well. For example, consider a female leader and her new male follower. Initially, the leader takes some time to examine her follower's work habits and performance. She may even initiate supportive, self-worth affirming behaviors toward this subordinate, in an effort to maintain current levels of follower performance. In turn, the follower may have reciprocated the new leader's support by continuing to provide the same level of performance.

However, at some later point if the female leader wants to increase this follower's competencies and the follower resists, the female leader may respond with more assertive actions. Prior research on sex-role spillover (Gutek & Cohen, 1987) indicated that assertiveness by the female leader may strain the leader–follower relationship, and, in turn, could impact the IL process and decrease leader–follower fit. At this point, the IL relationship could change from the previously *rich* dyadic relationship to either a *poor* dyadic relationship (both the leader and the follower think poorly of each other) or become unbalanced, so that either the leader or the follower thinks poorly of the other person in the dyad.

The leader practicing IL needs to reestablish interdependency and fit by reaffirming the self-worth of the follower and offering supportive, yet firm, assistance in developing follower competencies, if there is any hope of moving the dyad back onto the rich path (i.e., lots of giving and receiving by both partners). Although Yammarino and Dansereau (2002) asserted that a poor dyadic relationship (i.e., little giving and receiving by both partners) could continue, they believe the unbalanced relationships will not endure. As such, only one of four possible leader–follower relationships has the greatest potential for success—high investment by both parties. Therefore, the leader needs to invest supportive action to promote continued movement toward mature (i.e., good) leader–follower fit through rich, interdependent dyadic relations.

Although not researched as widely, a role-incongruent situation may occur if a leader views a follower as acting in a role-incongruent fashion. Given the dyadic nature of IL theory, examining a leader's perceptions of a follower acting in a role-incongruent fashion may be pertinent as well. Consider a male leader managing an assertive, dominant female. The follower's role incongruence may strain the leader–follower relationship as well, which may affect the willingness of the leader to offer an investment of support for the follower's self-worth.

Therefore, given the potential of gender role incongruence from either the leader's or follower's perspective to derail the early IL process (we refer to this period as Phase 1), we offer the following propositions:

> *Proposition 2.* Gender role congruity will enhance the formation of "rich" dyads within the IL process.
>
> *Proposition 3.* Rich dyadic IL relationships (in Phase 1) will experience early leader–follower fit.

However, as IL theory is dynamic in nature, the likelihood that less evident antecedent factors will emerge that could influence the IL process is high. Harrison et al. (2002) and Harrison, Price, and Bell (1998) showed that as time passes, demographic diversity within teams becomes less important and diversity in psychological characteristics (including personality, values, and attitudes) becomes more important. We could expect a similar pattern within leader–follower dyads. Specifically, issues such as value and attitude similarities may begin to impact the dyadic leader–follower interdependence evident within IL theory, and, in fact, may come to supersede demographic similarity or even gender role congruence in importance.

> *Proposition 4.* Early leader–follower fit will lead to an attempt to align values, attitudes, and personality similarities between the dyad.

Therefore, similarity-based demographic antecedents may have temporal relevance within the reciprocated interdependency process, in which similarities or alignment regarding personality, values, and attitudes may trigger continued interdependence, but promote deeper, more mature leader–

follower fit. Therefore, we examine psychological factors and their potential relationship with IL theory in more detail in the following.

## ATTITUDE, VALUE, AND PERSONALITY ALIGNMENT

Whereas many researchers have addressed the notion of fit in terms of demographic variables, others have addressed more subtle or less objectively apparent aspects of similarity such as the congruence in values, attitudes, and personality. Meglino, Ravlin, and Adkins (1989) found that value congruence between workers and their supervisors was positively related to satisfaction and commitment on the part of subordinates. Thus, an employee who perceives that his or her supervisor shares similar values has more positive attitudes toward the organization as a whole. Turban and Jones (1988) found that the degree of trust and confidence subordinates had in their leader was related to both the subordinates' and the supervisors' reports of how much alike they believed they were in how they see things.

Other studies have shown positive relationships between personality congruence among leaders and followers and follower performance (Bauer & Green, 1996) as well as relationships between leader and follower value and attitude congruence and positive outcomes (Miles, 1964; Senger, 1971; Zalesny & Kirsch, 1989). Senger (1971) found that when managers' and subordinates' values were compared, managers gave subordinates with more dissimilar values lower performance ratings. This result was not based on the leader's knowing the subordinates' responses to the value survey. The value survey results were not shared among managers and subordinates. It does, however, suggest that perceived similarity may influence supervisors' ratings of subordinates.

Additionally, this research suggests that as leaders and followers begin to learn about each others' values, attitudes, and personality similarity, continuation of the investments and returns within the IL relationship can be enhanced if there is similarity or negatively impacted if dissimilarity is severe. For example, even if an early leader–follower fit was established, as the leader–follower relationship progresses over time, a leader may find that a follower has a weak work ethic. Understanding that personality and values are somewhat stable over time and therefore difficult to change, an individualized leader valuing a strong work ethic may reduce the investments in the follower at this point, because of the hopeless dissimilarity on primary work-related values. Thus, we expect leader–follower fit to decrease, especially as the investments from the leader decrease.

Similarly, if the follower receives reduced returns from the leader, without leader support for follower feelings of self-worth, the follower may reduce the investments and become less likely to provide satisfying performance. This reduction in investments and returns is what Dansereau and Yammarino (2002) referred to as a poor dyadic relationship. Likewise, any unbalanced alignment from either a leader's or a follower's perspective is likely to have a negative impact on the dyadic relationship as well, as the unbalanced relationship is unlikely to continue (Dansereau & Yammarino, 2002). He or she who is not receiving will stop giving.

> *Proposition 5.* Alignment between attitudes, values, and personality of the leader and the follower will lead to rich, dyadic IL relationships. Misalignment between leaders and followers on attitudes, values, and personality will lead to poor or unbalanced dyadic IL relationships.

As before, we expect rich dyadic IL relationships to lead to leader–follower fit; however, we assert this fit is more mature and meaningful and likely to enhance the types of investments made by leaders and followers. This later phase (we refer to this period as Phase 2) is likely to be focused on development of follower competencies in such a way as to increase the reciprocal interdependencies. Dansereau and Yammarino (2002) asserted that interdependence is established in the more mature leader–follower dyadic relationships and will enhance the relatedness of leader and follower perceptions.

When considering leader–follower fit, the compatibility experienced by the dyad may evolve over time. Relationship development theory, especially that for relationships focused on trust, may provide insight into the differences between early and mature fit. Lewicki and Bunker (1996) noted that relationships develop in three stages, for which Stage 1 characterizes a relationship where there is a surge of positive feelings and idealization of the partner, with the hope of a prospering relationship overshadowing differentiation regarding trust or other emotions. This stage may characterize what we refer to as early fit, in which a new dyadic partnership is in an initial "getting to know you phase" characterized by excitement and anticipation.

However, as the relationship progresses, development of trust and other emotions takes a more significant role (Lewicki & Bunker, 1996), and we suggest these phases of relationship development encompass the development of mature fit. Mature fit aligns more closely with Lewicki and Bunker's (1996) second and third stages of relationship development. In these two stages partners are operating within an evaluative (Stage 2) and accommodative (Stage 3) relationship, characterized by trust taking root through a process of reciprocal self-disclosure and response, as well as negotiation of conflicting needs, expectations, and perceived incompatibilities. Thus, mature fit characterizes a leader–follower relationship in which both individuals have solidified their trust in each other and are committed to continuation of the working relationship through the process of accommodation.

*Proposition 6.* Rich dyadic IL relationships (in Phase 2) will experience mature leader–follower fit.

## LEADER–FOLLOWER SELF–OTHER AGREEMENT AND FIT

Wexley, Alexander, Greenawalt, and Couch (1980) created three similarity measures: the difference between the subordinate's description of the manager and the manager's self description, referred to as *subordinate* perceptual similarity (in other words, how similarly does the subordinate see the manager compared to how the manager views himself or herself); the difference between the manager's description of the subordinate and the subordinate's self description referred to as *manager* perceptual similarity (in other words, how similarly does the manager see the subordinate compared to how the subordinate sees himself or herself); and actual similarity or the difference between the manager's and subordinate's self-ratings. Whereas both perceptual measures were related to performance ratings (subordinate perceptual similarity was related to subordinate ratings of the manager, and manager perceptual similarity was related to manager ratings of the subordinate), actual similarity was unrelated to performance ratings. These results suggest that the *agreement in perceptions* between manager and subordinate is more important than actual similarity in views. If the manager believes the subordinate is similar to him, their degree of actual similarity is less important.

A relatively new way of thinking about supervisor subordinate fit has to do with the extent to which the supervisor has self-perceptions of his or her leadership that agree with the perceptions subordinates have of the leader. The implication is that agreement suggests that the leader is more self-aware or better aware of how others see him or her. However, self–other agreement also could be conceptualized as an aspect of fit because it suggests a degree of compatibility or similarity in terms of how supervisors and subordinates see things (in this case the supervisor's behavior).

A significant amount of research has been done in the area of self-other agreement between leaders and followers and its relationship to outcomes for the leader. Most of this work has been done as part of the multisource feedback process wherein leaders provide self-ratings of their behavior and subordinates provide ratings of the leader on the same dimensions. The degree of agreement between the leader's self-ratings and the aggregated ratings from his or her followers are compared, and the leader is categorized in accordance with the type and degree of agreement or disagreement. The four agreement categories most frequently used are (cf. Atwater, Ostroff, Yammarino, & Fleenor, 1998) *agree/good* (i.e., leader and followers agree that the leader's behavior is good or positive); *agree/poor* (i.e., leader and followers agree that the leader's behavior is poor or negative); *Over-rater* (the leader provides higher self-ratings than he or she receives from followers); and *under-rater* (the leader provides lower self-ratings than he or she receives from followers). Essentially, the theoretical underpinnings suggest that agreement between leader and follower is preferable to disagreement and agreement that the leader is doing well results in the best outcomes (Atwater et al., 1998).

The dyadic wholes nature of IL theory (i.e., balanced) probably contributes to agreement, regardless of whether leader and follower experience a rich or poor relationship. A rich IL relationship is likely to result in an agree/good response set because of the supportive, attentive nature of the leader–follower exchange. A poor IL relationship is likely to result in an agree/bad response set because of the decreased investments on behalf of both leader and follower. The unbalanced dyadic IL relationships may result in either the over- or under-rated response sets, depending on the specific situation. Again, because of the unbalanced, weak IL relationship, leader–follower perceptions are probably mismatched as well.

The theoretical rationale underlying self-other agreement and its relationship to performance and other outcomes (e.g., promotions) stems from control theory. Control theory (Carver & Scheier, 1981) proposes that individuals are continuously matching their behavior to goals or standards. One possible standard could be the perceptions others have of the individual. For example, a leader may want to be seen by his or her subordinates as decisive. If the leader recognizes, given feedback from subordinates, that subordinates do not perceive him or her as decisive, the leader may make behavioral changes in an attempt to modify their perceptions.

According to control theory, individuals must do three things to bring their behavior in line with standards. First, they must have a standard they are trying to achieve (e.g., positive perception by one's subordinates that they are decisive). Second, they must recognize that their behavior or the individual's perception is not in line with that goal. Third, they need to enact behavior in an attempt to change perceptions and meet the goal. In this case, if the leader is self-aware and realizes that his or her goal to be viewed as decisive by subordinates has not been achieved, he or she may decide to make quicker decisions or communicate those decisions more assertively. If the leader has a goal to be seen as decisive, recognizes that this goal has not been achieved, and enacts behavior to achieve this goal, the three steps to bring behavior in line with goals have been achieved.

The relevance of self–other agreement in this process is that the individual who does not recognize the discrepancy between his or her and others' perceptions will not see the need to alter behavior to change others' perceptions. The relationship between fit and self–other agreement occurs because we can anticipate that the aforementioned similarities in attitudes, beliefs, values, demographics, and so on will be related to the degree of agreement between self and other ratings. For example, in terms of actual similarity or fit, if the leader and subordinate share beliefs in the importance of particular work values and are similar in terms of demographics such as age, we could anticipate that the leader's self-ratings may be more similar to the subordinates' ratings of that leader. The Gen Xer, who cannot possibly appreciate the values of the manager in his or her 60s, is less likely to rate the manager similarly to the way the manager rates himself or herself than a subordinate of similar age with similar work values.

Ashford (1989) pointed out the relevance of self–other agreement because it is important for individuals to develop skills in observing and evaluating their behavior in a manner that is consistent with how others perceive and evaluate it. Accurate (or in-agreement) self-assessments should be associated with more positive outcomes because they help leaders correct mistakes or inaccurate perceptions and help them tailor their behavior to the work setting. Smircich and Chesser (1981) suggested that self-ratings and other ratings or perceptions that are in-agreement, are preferable because they indicate a degree of mutual understanding.

Traditionally, the way in which fit contributes to self–other agreement may stem in part from greater communication that occurs when individuals perceive fit (Tsui & O'Reilly, 1989). Fit also may contribute to greater self–other agreement because both groups of raters will share a mindset or frame of reference for rating the behavior. Additionally, it is likely that subordinates who perceive fit will be part of the "in-group" and will share experiences with the supervisor both within and outside of work that will allow subordinates to have a better understanding of the leader's self-perception and the leader to have a better understanding of how he or she is viewed by followers. Self-awareness also has been noted as an important element of emotional intelligence that, in turn, has been associated with effective leadership (Megerian & Sosik, 1999).

In sum, we see rich IL relationships resulting in better leader–follower fit, which in turn, contributes to greater self–other agreement. Greater agreement is an indicator that the leader is self-aware and that followers perceive the leader accurately. Greater self–other agreement also should serve as an indicator of fit and promote healthier leader–follower relationships.

*Proposition 7.* Rich IL will result in greater self–other agreement between the leader and follower.

*Proposition 8.* Self–other agreement between leader and follower and leader–follower fit will be positively related at both early and mature stages of fit.

## GOOD AND BAD LEADER–FOLLOWER FIT

Generally, we have discussed fit as though it were advantageous to individual and organizational outcomes. That is, we expect fit between supervisors and subordinates to result in better communication because of greater similarities, better interdependent leader–follower relationships, higher LMX relationships, followers that are in the in-group, and high self–other agreement, all of which should impact outcomes positively. However, it is worth exploring situations in which leader–follower fit may be disadvantageous. For example, do we really want leaders and followers to share beliefs and attitudes if the leader is unethical or Machiavellian? When and under what circumstances might we expect leader–subordinate fit to be disadvantageous to individuals or organizations?

We can certainly think of cases in the news recently in which not just one leader but a leader and a number of followers were behaving unethically, illegally, and in self-serving ways. Had the leaders and followers not shared these values and beliefs, significant problems may have been averted. We also can think of examples in which a low-performing leader surrounds himself or herself with low-performing subordinates so the subordinates do not outperform the leader and make him or her look bad. Many of us in academia can recount incidents in which top-performing faculty were being recruited, only to be denied a position by senior faculty who felt threatened by the recruit's fine performance record. This type of fit is clearly not in the best interest of the organization. The point to be made here is that it is not only similarity or fit per se but also the content of the similarity that is important.

Likewise, a third case may be when the subordinate is in a dead-end job with no potential for advancement, yet he or she does not want to leave the job because he or she fits with the supervisor. Alternatively, the supervisor may not deal with a poor-performing subordinate because the supervisor and subordinate like each other and have many similarities. Clearly, whereas leader follower fit is generally positive, if not managed properly, fit can have some undesired effects.

As a fourth example of bad fit, we propose the "similarity breeds stagnation" concept in terms of organizational change. Most of us have experienced situations in which we choose to bring in a person ("new blood") from outside the organization when hiring. This person is supposed to suggest new ideas that those who have been in the organization for some time may not think about, which is the argument made for diversity. In fact, Polzer et al. (2002) found that diversity tended to improve creative task performance. That is, differences in perspective are conducive to innovation and inhibit groupthink.

The question becomes how do we have fit without groupthink or stagnation? Perhaps we can conceptualize a situation in which the leader has sufficient similarity with followers to allow good dyadic IL relationships to develop and yet has sufficient difference to minimize stagnation. Leaders and followers could be similar on different things. For example, some followers may fit with the leader in terms of demographics whereas others fit in terms of personality or values. Regardless, we need to be cautions about too much fit and the potential for like-mindedness that may not be conducive to optimal decision making.

## HOW CAN A LEADER IMPACT FIT?

As early as 1939, Lewin, Lippitt, and White observed that differences in leadership styles affected employees' climate perceptions. Kozlowski and Doherty (1989) found that subordinates who had higher-quality relationships with their supervisors had better perceptions of organizational climate and had perceptions that were in more agreement with their supervisors than those subordinates with lower-quality relationships. IL theory is in alignment with these findings in that rich dyadic relationships represent higher-quality relationships. As such, we would expect IL theory to result in followers with better perceptions of organizational climate and perceptual agreement with leaders.

Additionally, this hypothesis tentatively suggests that if leaders develop higher-quality relationships with followers then their degree of fit also will be greater. The fact that they share perceptions that the organization's climate is more positive also suggests that the person–organization fit of these followers may be greater because of the more favorable interdependent, dyadic relationship they have with their leader.

Within IL theory, one way leaders can develop more favorable relationships with followers is by acting as a filter. A study by Waldman and Atwater (1994) showed that a significant role adopted by the most effective supervisors was to "protect" employees from bureaucratic red tape and unnecessary information, which allowed employees to put greater concentration on the job at hand. Many of us can appreciate a leader who filters and translates information in a way that is sensitive to followers' needs.

Other mechanisms for improving fit are selection, socialization, and communication. These are mechanisms that also have been touted as valuable for improving person–organization and person–job fit. In the case of selection, supervisors seldom want to give up the opportunity to interview prospective job candidates who will be working for them. Rarely are supervisors able to discern much about the prospective employee's potential performance, but they often can get an idea about interpersonal fit: "Is this someone I can work with?" Presuming we have supervisors with desirable values and attitudes, it makes sense to allow them to have a say in the selection process, in that they may select individuals with a higher probability of fit and positive leader–follower relationships.

This notion aligns with the previous discussion on similarity in values and attitudes triggering the reciprocal investments and returns with IL theory. Within the selection process, leaders have the opportunity to assess similarity in values, attitudes, and personality. This discovery of similarity during the selection process may encourage the leader to trigger investments in follower self-worth more quickly, effectively reducing a sizing-up period that may involve more basic, observable similarities such as demographic characteristics. Selection of a follower with attitudes, values, and personality similar to those of the leader may encourage the development of follower competencies more quickly within the IL process and result in better person–job fit.

Socialization is another mechanism that may improve leader–follower fit. As stated by Ostroff and Kozlowski (1992):

> Organizations should focus efforts on training supervisors to be more aware of their importance to new members. This training might follow from VDL theory or leader–member exchange by emphasizing the development of dyadic relationships between supervisors and new members . . . supervisors are not only key models but they also mediate information from the broader organizational context and are critical for integrating newcomers into the group. (p. 872)

Similarly, IL training may be an important means of socializing new members, especially because the IL leader is particularly attuned to promoting follower self-worth. Socialization of the new subordinate enables the subordinate to feel like a valuable member of the dyad, and, in turn, this attraction may promote fit from the perspective of the subordinate.

Supervisors also could be trained to look for and emphasize similarities between themselves and followers. For example, the leader and follower do not necessarily have to be the same age or gender, but they may discover that they have other work or nonwork interests or values that allow them to perceive greater fit. For example, a male supervisor and a female subordinate may have children the same age who attend the same school. An older supervisor and a younger subordinate may discover that they both prefer to get to the office early and have their coffee and read the newspaper before the day starts. Even simple similarities can allow leaders and followers to perceive fit, and within the support-based IL theory framework, the likelihood of a leader tapping these similarities to promote interdependency and fit is probably high. Additionally, within the IL theory framework, supervisors can increase leader–follower fit by emphasizing competency development. Whereas the leader and follower may not share much demographic or perceptual similarity, if they both see the pursuit of competency or professional development as a worthwhile, common goal and each can see the other's contribution toward its accomplishment, the interdependent nature of this pursuit will probably improve perceptions of fit.

## CONCLUSIONS AND IMPLICATIONS

Leader–follower fit is a ripe area for exploration. Linking IL theory to traditional perceptions of leader–follower fit has provided a means for examining temporal progression of fit as well as suggestions for assessing gender role congruence, self-other agreement, and their relationships to fit. In the following, we explicate some of the implications of the relationships between leaders, followers, and fit.

## Implications of Gender Role Congruency Between Leader and Follower

Gender role congruency, IL theory, and the subsequent fit between female leaders and male followers have a number of potential implications. First, and foremost, female managers need to recognize the potential for lack of fit between their gender and leadership roles. Female leaders should realize the need to balance their gender roles and leadership roles. There are a number of ways they might do this. For example, female managers may need to provide feedback assertively, yet in a more nurturing, or sensitive way than male managers. That is, they integrate some of the expected characteristics of both roles in a given situation.

IL theory may be better suited to address this incongruity between gender role and leadership characteristics. Again, because the IL leader focuses on developing follower competencies and establishing interdependence, supporting a follower's feelings of self-worth is paramount to the successful development of the leader–follower relationship. As such, this supportiveness is a necessary component of successful leadership regardless of the gender of the leader. However, the ability for a female leader to develop a male follower's self-worth may be challenged if the male follower does not see the female leader as behaving "in role."

Female managers may need to size up a situation and decide if a characteristically male approach is needed. In other words, the female manager can balance her female and leadership roles by enacting predominantly female roles in some situations and male roles in others. She can be assertive when making tough decisions but sensitive and empathetic to a follower experiencing a personal crisis. IL theory allows for the leader to balance gender-characteristic and gender-uncharacteristic approaches to leadership, provided these approaches promote the self-worth of the follower and are used for the purpose of further developing follower competencies.

Reciprocating the IL leader's actions to develop self-worth and competencies, followers too can play a role in enhancing leader–follower fit. For example, male and female followers should recognize the tendency they may have to apply inaccurate or distorted perceptions of a female leader's abilities, merely based on their gender expectations and without consideration of the female leader's true abilities. Additionally, it would be helpful if followers could recognize the difficult balancing act that female managers face and give them a little slack.

Future researchers need to address the ways in which female leaders can optimize their effectiveness when carrying out male leadership roles; however, there is some evidence that a dyadic leadership approach, such as IL, for example, may be more effective for female leaders to use to encourage satisfying follower performance. For example, Brett, Atwater, and Waldman (2005) found that when delivering corrective feedback, positive outcomes were more likely to result for female managers when they allowed the recipient to express their views and provided the feedback in a considerate way. These behaviors did not impact the effectiveness of the feedback when delivered by male managers.

Because IL theory is relatively new and empirical investigation has been limited (Yammarino & Dansereau, 2002), it is unclear what other managerial issues may test the interdependent leader–follower relationship. For example, other managerial roles are considered primarily masculine such as problem-solving, strategic decision-making, and allocating resources (Atwater, Brett, Waldman, DiMare, & Hayden, 2003). How might women perform these roles in a manner that is consistent with their gender role?

Additional questions we might ask about gender, leadership, and fit are the following: Is role congruity more important in some organizational contexts than others? Does the leader's level in the organizational hierarchy require a different set of in-role behaviors for female managers? Role congruity theory may apply not only to individuals reacting to leaders but also to the leaders themselves. How does the self-fulfilling prophecy among female managers affect their ability and confidence in managing others?

## Implications of Leader–Follower Attitude, Value, and Personality Alignment

Harrison et al. (2002) concluded that among team members, outward, demographic differences are perceived quickly and used to make judgments about one another. However, as team members collaborate to work on tasks more, the impact of demographic differences are reduced. We could expect a similar outcome between leaders and followers. That is, with more frequent interaction demographic differences will be less relevant. However, if demographic differences make collaboration less likely or less frequent, we could anticipate that the time it takes for the importance of demographic differences to diminish could put those who differ from the leader at a disadvantage.

Over time, with more frequent interaction, internal psychological differences may emerge as being more important than demographic similarity. Future researchers should address the relevance of surface-level, demographic similarity and deep-level, psychological similarity between leaders and followers at different phases of their relationship. The outcomes of the differing types of diversity (e.g., leader/follower relationships, conflict, and work outcomes) may change over time.

Clearly, fit among followers and leaders is more complicated than mere perceptions of surface-level, demographic similarity. Assessments of attitudes, values, and beliefs and whether leaders and followers believe they share similarities on these dimensions is relevant to fit and to outcomes. Research by Jackson, Brett, Sessa, Cooper, Julin, and Peyronnin (1991) noted that attitudes are more similar when demographic characteristics are similar. Both types of similarity reinforce the attraction between individuals, which can impact interdependency within individualized leadership as well and ultimately influence leader–follower fit.

Thus, it would be of interest to continue to pursue questions about the importance of value–attitude similarity and outcomes. For example, are there particular values that are most important to share? Are work values more important than personal values? Do leaders' and followers' values and attitudes become more similar over time? If so, how does this impact optimal decision making? Are we creating like minds?

Again, because values and attitudes may be less evident upon initial interactions, we assert that within the IL theory framework, fit issues surrounding values and attitudes are likely to occur sometime after the initial demographic similarity fit has been established (or not established because of demographic dissimilarity). As was the case with gender congruity issues impacting leader–follower interdependency, and ultimately fit, in a dynamic way, IL theory allows for values and attitudes to potentially alter the leader–follower fit previously experienced within the dyadic relationship.

Additionally, rather than view similarity as a trigger for the initial investment on behalf of the leader, a more substantive question may be asked: If similarity increases does it result in improved IL, or does improved IL result in more perceived similarities? It also is possible that over time leaders and followers may perceive more differences rather than more similarities. How does this impact the IL relationship that has been established? Does increased similarity among attitudes and values improve the IL relationship over time, or does it result from it?

## Implications of Leader–Follower Self–Other Agreement and Fit

One of the problems with traditional self–other agreement research to date is that it is almost always operationalized as agreement between a leader's self-rating and aggregated ratings from followers. If predictions from VDL that 90% of managers use a dyadic approach to each follower are correct, what exactly does agreement between the leader's self-rating and the aggregated follower rating represent? If the leader rates himself or herself 3 on some aspect of behavior and his three followers rate him or her 1, 3, and 5 respectively, they will be in perfect agreement if the followers' ratings are averaged. However, either the leader really agrees with only one follower, or the leader has done some cognitive averaging, recognizing that the followers perceive him differently.

Yet, from the self–other data, we cannot know which of these scenarios is the case. A dyadic test of leader–follower agreement, in which the leader rates his or her behavior in relation to each follower and each follower rates his or her behavior in relation to the leader, would be advantageous. These dyadic agreement scores could serve as the basis for a better sense of true self–other agreement. We would anticipate that the leader who can differentiate among the selves he or she projects to different followers would be more effective. That is, the leader who has matching self–other scores because of cognitive averaging would be more effective than the leader who really only has self-ratings that agree with a few followers. The optimal case would be when the leader and all followers agree that the leader is doing well, that is, all followers are in the in-group. Much research is needed to explore dyadic self–other agreement and its outcomes for leaders, followers, and the organization.

An additional new direction that self-other agreement fit could take is to explore the relationship between leader–follower agreement and follower outcomes. To date, the leader's performance or effectiveness has been studied with respect to self–other agreement but others' performance or effectiveness has not. Using the IL theory framework, one could hypothesize that if the leader and follower agree about the leader's behavior, they may have better communication and a more compatible relationship, which could be expected to result in better subordinate performance. Again, we would expect agreement that the leader was doing well to result in the best follower outcomes.

Additionally, it might be relevant to investigate how leader–follower agreement about the follower's performance is related to outcomes. Although reactions to feedback from bosses has been explored to some extent in the 360-degree feedback literature (cf. Brett & Atwater, 2001) follower outcomes as a result of agreement between follower and leader ratings have not been studied. Again, given the dyadic, interdependent nature of leader–follower relations within the IL theory framework, expanding the concept of self-other agreement to include follower performance could promote further follower competency development. Clearly much more research is needed in relation to self–other agreement and fit with particular dyadic relationships as the referent.

## Implications of IL Theory, Fit, and Levels of Analysis

Although we take a predominantly dyadic approach to leader–follower fit through the use of the IL theory framework, future researchers may want to examine higher levels of analyses as they relate to fit. For example, as long as a follower feels like a valued member of the leader–follower dyad, the follower may be less sensitive to outside pressure to view leader actions in a negative light and continue in a good fit relationship. However, if a subordinate does not feel valued by the leader, person–group fit may become more salient. Therefore, the appropriate level of analysis under which to view fit may shift. Future researchers may want to examine this potential phenomenon.

Additionally, future researchers may want to examine how a leader can promote fit at other levels of analysis as well, such as the group level. With an increased emphasis on teams, is IL theory sophisticated enough to be rolled out to the next higher level, or are other leadership theories more appropriate? For example, is there a concept such as group self-worth (similar perhaps to group self-efficacy) (cf. Jung & Sosik, 2003; Gibson, Randel, & Earley, 2000) that would enable a leader to support the construct by emphasizing/creating team norms and a strong team culture? Could this be viewed as team-level competency development? Variations in IL theory may enable adaptation to the group level of analysis; however, more research is needed within the IL theory framework to assess its appropriateness.

In sum, although there are a large number of questions surrounding leader–follower fit, there also exist promising new areas of research to investigate, which may significantly expand our understanding of leader–follower relations and performance.

## REFERENCES

Ashford, S. (1989). Self-assessments in organizations: A literature review and integrative model. In L. L. Cummings & B. M. Staw (Eds.), *Research in organizational behavior* (Vol. 11, pp. 133–174). Greenwich: JAI Press.

Atwater, L., Brett, J., Waldman, D., DiMare, L., & Hayden, M. (2003). Male and female perceptions of the gender-typing of management sub-roles. *Sex Roles, 50*, 191–199.

Atwater, L., Carey, J., & Waldman, D. (2001). Gender and discipline in the workplace: Wait until your father gets home. *Journal of Management, 27*, 537–561.

Atwater, L., Ostroff, C., Yammarino, F., & Fleenor, J. (1998). Self-other agreement: Does it really matter? *Personnel Psychology, 51*, 577–598.

Bass, B. (1990). *Bass and Stogdill's handbook of leadership: Theory, research, and managerial applications* (3rd ed.). New York: Free Press.

Bauer, T. N., & Green, S. G. (1996). The development of leader–member exchange: A longitudinal test. *Academy of Management Journal, 39*, 1538–1567.

Baumgartel, H. (1956). Leadership, motivation, and attitudes in research laboratories. *Journal of Social Issues, 12*, 23–31.

Baumgartel, H. (1957). Leadership style as a variable in research administration. *Administrative Science Quarterly, 2*, 344–360.

Bowers, D. G., & Seashore, S. E. (1966). Predicting organizational effectiveness with a four factor theory of leadership. *Administrative Science Quarterly, 11*, 238–263.

Brenner, O. C., Tomkiewicz, J., & Schein, V. A. (1989). The relationship between sex role stereotypes and requisite. *Academy of Management Journal, 32*, 662–670.

Brett, J., & Atwater, L. (2001). 360 degree feedback: Accuracy, reactions and perceptions of usefulness. *Journal of Applied Psychology, 86*, 930–942.

Brett, J. F., Atwater, L. E., & Waldman, D. A. (2005). Effective delivery of workplace discipline: Do women have to be more participatory than men? *Group and Organization Management, 30*(5), 487–513 .

Byrne, D. E. (1971). *The attraction paradigm.* New York: Academic Press.

Carver, C. S., & Scheier, M. F. (1981). *Attention and self-regulation: A control-theory approach to human behavior.* New York: Springer-Verlag.

Dansereau, F., Graen, G., & Haga, W. J. (1975). A vertical dyad linkage approach to leadership within formal organizations: A longitudinal investigation of the role making process. *Organizational Behavior and Human Performance, 13*, 46–78.

Dansereau, F., & Yammarino, F. J. (1998). The multiple-level approaches to leadership: Introduction and overview. In F. Dansereau & F. J. Yammarino (Eds.), *Leadership: The multiple-level approaches* (Pt. A, pp. xxv–xliii; Pt. B, pp. xxv–xliii). Stamford, CT: JAI Press.

Dansereau, F., Yammarino, F. J., Markham, S. E., Alutto, J. A., Newman, J., Dumas, M., Nachman, S. A., Naughton, T. J., Kim, K., Al-Kelabi, S. A., Lee, S., & Keller, T. (1995). Individualized leadership: A new multiple-level approach. *Leadership Quarterly, 6*, 413–450.

Dansereau, F., Yammarino, F. J., Markham, S. E., Alutto, J. A., Newman, J., Dumas, M., Nachman, S. A., Naughton, T. J., Kim, K., Al-Kelabi, S. A., Lee, S., & Keller, T. (1998). Extensions to the individualized leadership approach: Placing the approach in context. In F. Dansereau & F. J. Yammarino (Eds.), *Leadership: The multiple-level approaches* (Pt. A, pp. 429–441). Stamford, CT: JAI Press.

Eagly, A., & Karau, S. (2002). Role congruity theory of prejudice toward female leaders. *Psychological Review, 109*, 573–598.

Fiedler, F. E. (1967). *A theory of leadership effectiveness.* New York: McGraw-Hill.

Fleishman, E. A. (1973). Twenty years of consideration and structure. In E. A. Fleishman & J. G. Hunt (Eds.), *Current developments in the study of leadership* (pp. 1–37). Carbondale, IL: Southern Illinois University Press.

Gibson, C., Randel, A., & Earley, C. (2000). Understanding group efficacy: An empirical test of multiple assessment methods. *Group and Organization Management, 25*, 67–98.

Graen, G. (1976). Role-making processes within complex organizations. In M. D. Dunnette (Ed.), *Handbook of industrial and organizational psychology* (pp. 1200–1245). Chicago: Rand McNally.

Graen, G., & Cashman, J. (1975). A role making model of leadership in formal organizations: A developmental approach. In J. G. Hunt & L. L. Larson (Eds.), *Leadership frontiers* (pp. 143–165). Kent, OH: Kent State University Press.

Greenglass, E. R., Pantony, K., & Burke, R. J. (1989). A gender-role perspective on role conflict, work stress and social support. In E. B. Goldsmith (Ed.), *Work and family* (pp. 23–44). Newbury Park, CA: Sage.

Gutek, B., & Cohen, A. (1987). Sex ratios, sex role spillover and sex at work: A comparison of men's and women's experiences. *Human Relations, 40*, 97–115.

Halpin, A. W., & Winer, B. J. (1957). A factorial study of the leader behavior descriptions. In R. M. Stogdill & A. E. Coons (Eds.), *Leader behavior: Its description and measurement* (pp. 39–51). Columbus, OH: Ohio State University, Bureau of Business Research.

Harrison, D., Price, K., & Bell J. (1998). Beyond relational demography: Time and the effects of surface- and deep-level diversity on work group cohesion. *Academy of Management Journal, 41*, 96–107.

Harrison, D., Price, K., Gavin, J., & Florey, A. (2002). Time, teams and task performance: Changing effects and surface- and deep-level diversity on group functioning. *Academy of Management Journal, 45,* 1029–1045.

Heilman, M. (1983). Sex bias in work settings: The lack of fit model. *Research in Organizational Behavior, 5,* 269–298.

Hersey, P., & Blanchard, K. H. (1969). Life cycle theory of leadership. *Training and Development Journal, 23,* 26–34.

Hughes, R., Ginnett, R., & Curphy, G. (1996). *Leadership: Enhancing the lessons of experience* (2nd ed.). Chicago: Irwin.

Jackson, S. E., Brett, J. F., Sessa, V. I., Cooper, D. M., Julin, J. A., & Peyronnin, K. (1991). Some differences make a difference: Individual dissimilarity and group heterogeneity as correlates of recruitment, promotions, and turnover. *Journal of Applied Psychology, 76,* 675–690.

Jackson, S. E., May, K. E., & Whitney, K. (1995). Understanding the dynamics of diversity in decision making teams. In R. A. Guzzo & E. Salas (Eds.), *Team effectiveness and decision making in organizations* (pp. 204–261). San Francisco: Jossey-Bass.

Judge, T. A., & Ferris, G. R. (1993). Social context of performance evaluation decisions. *Academy of Management Journal, 36,* 80–105.

Jung, D., & Sosik, J. (2003). Group potency and collective efficacy: Examining their predictive validity, level of analysis, and effects of performance feedback on future group performance. *Group and Organization Management, 28,* 366–390.

Kozlowski, W. J., & Doherty, M. L. (1989). Integration of climate and leadership: Examination of a neglected issue. *Journal of Applied Psychology, 74,* 546–553.

Kristof, A. (1996). Person-organization fit: An integrative review of its conceptualizations, measurement and implications. *Personnel Psychology, 49,* 1–49.

Lewicki, R., & Bunker, B. (1996). Developing and maintaining trust in work relationships. In R. M. Kramer & T. Tyler (Eds.), *Trust in organizations: Frontiers of theory and research* (pp. 114–139). Thousand Oaks, CA: Sage.

Lewin, K., Lippitt, R., & White, R. K. (1939). Patterns of aggressive behavior in experimentally created social climates. *Journal of Social Psychology, 10,* 271–301.

Liden, R. C., Sparrowe, R. T., & Wayne, S. J. (1997). Leader-member exchange theory: The past and potential for the future. *Research in Personnel and Human Resources Management, 15,* 47–119.

Liden, R. C., Wayne, S. J., & Stilwell, D. (1993). A longitudinal study on the early development of leader-member exchanges. *Journal of Applied Psychology, 78,* 662–674.

McClane, W. E. (1991a). The interaction of leader and member characteristics in the leader–member exchange (LMX) model of leadership. *Small Group Research, 22,* 283–300.

McClane, W. E. (1991b). Implications of member role differentiation. *Group and Organization Studies, 16,* 102–113.

Megerian, L. E., & Sosik, J. J. (1999). Understanding leader emotional intelligence and performance: The role of self-other agreement on transformational leadership perceptions. *Group & Organization Management, 24,* 367–391.

Meglino, B. M., Ravlin, E. C., & Adkins, C. L. (1989). A work values approach to corporate culture: A field test of the value congruence process and its relationship to individual outcomes. *Journal of Applied Psychology, 74,* 424–432.

Miles, R. (1964). Attitudes toward management theory as a factor in managers' relationship with their superiors. *Academy of Management Journal, 7,* 308–314.

O'Reilly, C. A., Chatman, J., & Caldwell, D. F. (1991). People and organizational culture: A profile comparison approach to assessing person-organization fit. *Academy of Management Journal, 34,* 487–516.

Ostroff, C., & Kozlowski, S. (1992). Organizational socialization as a learning process: The role of information acquisition. *Personnel Psychology, 45,* 849–874.

Polzer, J. T., Milton, L. P., & Swann, W. B., Jr. (2002). Capitalizing on diversity: Interpersonal congruence in small work groups. *Administrative Science Quarterly, 47,* 296–324.

Pulakos, E. D., & Wexley, K. N. (1983). The relationship among perceptual similarity, sex, and performance ratings in manager subordinate dyads. *Academy of Management Journal, 26,* 129–139.

Redl, R. (1942). Group emotion and leadership. *Psychiatry, 5,* 573–596.

Schneider, B. (1987). The people make the place. *Personnel Psychology, 40,* 437–453.

Schneider, B., Goldstein, H., & Smith, D. (1995). The ASA framework: An update. *Personnel Psychology, 48,* 747–773.

Senger, J. (1971). Managers' perceptions of subordinates' competence as a function of personal value orientations. *Academy of Management Journal, 14,* 415–423.

Smircich, L., & Chesser, R. (1981). Superiors' and subordinates' perceptions of performance: Beyond disagreement. *Academy of Management Journal, 24,* 198–205.

Snyder, R. A., & Bruning, N. S. (1985). Quality of vertical dyad linkages: Congruence of supervisor and subordinate competence and role stress as explanatory variables. *Group and Organization Studies, 10,* 81–94.

Stevens, G. E., & DeNisi, A. S. (1980). Women as managers: Attitudes and attributions for performance by men and women. *Academy of Management Journal, 23,* 355–360.

Tjosvold, D. (1985). Power and social context in superior-subordinate interactions. *Organizational Behavior and Human Decision Processes, 35,* 281–293.

Tsui, A. S., & O'Reilly, C. A. (1989). Beyond simple demographic effects: The importance of relational demography in superior-subordinate dyads. *Academy of Management Journal, 32,* 402–423.

Turban, D. B., & Jones, A. P. (1988). Supervisor-subordinate similarity: Types, effects and mechanisms. *Journal of Applied Psychology, 73,* 228–234.

Vroom, V. H., & Jago, A. G. (1988). Managing participation: A critical dimension of leadership. *The Journal of Management Development, 7,* 32–43.

Vroom, V. H., & Yetton, P. W. (1973). *Leadership and decision making.* Pittsburgh, PA: University of Pittsburgh Press.

Waldman, D., & Atwater, L. (1994). The nature of effective leadership and championing processes at different levels in a R&D hierarchy. *The Journal of High Technology Management Research, 5,* 233–245.

Wexley, K. N., Alexander, R. A., Greenawalt, J. P., & Couch, M. A. (1980). Attitudinal congruence and similarity as related to interpersonal evaluations in manager-subordinate dyads. *Academy of Management Journal, 23,* 320–331.

Yammarino, F. J., & Dansereau, F. (2002). Individualized leadership. *Journal of Leadership and Organizational Studies, 9,* 90–99.

Zalesny, M. D., & Kirsch, M. P. (1989). The effect of similarity on performance ratings and inter-rater agreement. *Human Relations, 42,* 81–96.

# CHAPTER 7

# *The Relationship Between Person–Environment Fit and Outcomes: An Integrative Theoretical Framework*

Jeffrey R. Edwards and Abbie J. Shipp
*University of North Carolina*

A considerable amount of research has investigated the relationship between person–environment (PE) fit and outcomes. This research has examined various types of PE fit, such as the fit between the needs of the person and the supplies available in the environment (Edwards & Harrison, 1993; Locke, 1976; Porter & Lawler, 1968), the fit between the demands of the environment and the abilities of the person (Edwards, 1996; McGrath, 1976), and the fit between the values of the person and those of the organization and its members (Cable & Judge, 1996; Chatman, 1989; Judge & Bretz, 1992; Meglino, Ravlin, & Adkins, 1989). Outcomes of PE fit have included occupational choice, job satisfaction, job performance, organization commitment, turnover, and psychological and physical well-being (Edwards, 1991; Kristof, 1996; Spokane, Meir, & Catalano, 2000; Verquer, Beehr, & Wagner, 2003).

Research on the effects of PE fit reflects three overriding assumptions. First, it is generally assumed that PE fit leads to positive outcomes. This assumption is evident in theoretical discussions of PE fit (Chatman, 1989; Dawis & Lofquist, 1984; Holland, 1997; Wanous, 1992; Werbel & Gilliland, 1999) and underlies most empirical studies of PE fit (Edwards, 1991; Kristof, 1996; Spokane et al., 2000; Verquer et al., 2003). Second, it is often assumed that the effects of PE fit are the same across different person and environment constructs. This assumption is demonstrated by studies using measures that collapse different types of PE fit (Bretz & Judge, 1994; Mitchell, Holtom, Lee, Sablynski, & Erez, 2001; Saks & Ashforth, 1997; Spokane et al., 2000) or combine substantively different person and environment dimensions (Caldwell & O'Reilly, 1990; Meglino et al., 1989; O'Reilly, Chatman, & Caldwell, 1991). Third, it is widely assumed that the effects of PE fit are the same regardless of the absolute levels of the person and environment or the direction of their difference. This assumption is manifested by research that operationalizes PE fit as the similarity between person and environment profiles (Cable & Judge, 1996; Caldwell & O'Reilly, 1990; Meglino et al., 1989; O'Reilly et al., 1991; Rounds, Dawis, & Lofquist, 1987; Vancouver & Schmitt, 1991) or asks respondents to directly report their fit with the environment (Cable & DeRue, 2002; Judge & Cable, 1997; Lauver & Kristof-Brown, 2001; Saks & Ashforth, 1997). Although these assumptions have been occasionally questioned (French, Caplan, & Harrison, 1982; Edwards, 1996; Rice, McFarlin, Hunt, & Near, 1985; Schneider, Kristof, Goldstein, & Smith, 1997), they remain widespread in theoretical and empirical PE fit research.

In this chapter, we outline an approach to conceptualizing the effects of PE fit that probes the assumptions summarized above. As with any area of science, the assumptions that underlie PE fit research merit scrutiny, as they represent boundaries that constrain inquiry and leave fundamental questions unanswered. One way to gauge the advancement of a science is by whether its key assumptions are evaluated and either affirmed or set aside as too limiting or simplistic (Kuhn, 1996). The conceptual approach we describe is intended to encourage PE fit researchers to critically examine assumptions that characterize the investigation of the effects of PE fit on outcomes, with the ultimate goal of advancing our collective understanding of PE fit.

The approach we set forth addresses three key issues concerning the effects of PE fit on outcomes. The first issue involves the concept of PE fit itself, reflecting the premise that any discussion of the effects of PE fit should begin by stating what is meant by PE fit. As noted earlier, different types of PE fit have been investigated, yet the boundaries between these types of fit are sometimes obscured or confound multiple distinctions. We present a framework for describing PE fit that integrates, clarifies, and extends existing typologies. The second issue concerns the conceptual mechanisms that explain the effects of PE fit on the outcome. We suggest that these mechanisms should be drawn from theories of the outcome, such that PE fit operates through causes identified with research on the outcome itself. Most outcomes of interest in PE fit research, such as satisfaction, commitment, well-being, and performance, have generated enormous amounts of research intended to explain their causes. This research provides an appropriate starting point for conceptualizing the effects of PE fit. The third issue involves the functional form relating

PE fit to the outcome. The assumptions underlying PE fit research translate into a function relating the person and environment to the outcome that is simplistic and represents one of many possibilities. Rather than accepting this function as the default, we show how alternative functional forms can result from developing conceptual arguments that describe the joint effects of the person and environment on the outcome.

Before we proceed, we should clarify the nature of the theoretical contribution we intend to offer. We do not presume to develop a grand theory relating PE fit to outcomes. Such a task is impractical, given the numerous ways in which different types of PE fit and outcomes can be combined. Rather, our goal is to demonstrate a general approach to theorizing the effects of PE fit (Weick, 1995) that can be applied and extended in various specific streams of PE fit research. Although some aspects of our presentation suggest hypotheses to be tested, our chief objective is to provide some initial conceptual spadework that delves into assumptions that underlie PE fit research, with the hope that these assumptions will be further probed in future PE fit research.

## THE CONCEPT OF PE FIT

PE fit has been conceptualized in various ways. In its most general sense, *PE fit* can be defined as *the congruence, match, similarity, or correspondence between the person and the environment*. Within this general definition, different types of PE fit have been distinguished (Dawis & Lofquist, 1984; Edwards, 1991; French et al., 1982; Kristof, 1996; Muchinsky & Monahan, 1987). In this section, we integrate and extend different ways of distinguishing PE fit, resulting in a framework that resolves ambiguities in the PE fit literature and highlights distinctions that have received little attention. This framework clarifies the meaning of PE fit and provides a useful basis for conceptualizing the effects of PE fit on outcomes.

### Supplementary and Complementary Fit

One key distinction in the PE fit literature is between supplementary and complementary fit (Kristof, 1996; Muchinsky & Monahan, 1987). *Supplementary fit* occurs when the person "supplements, embellishes, or possesses characteristics which are similar to other individuals" in the environment (Muchinsky & Monahan, 1987, p. 269). Thus, supplementary fit concerns the comparison between the person and his or her social environment, such that the environment is defined by the people in it. Although the terms *supplement* and *embellish* imply that the person brings something unique to the social environment, further discussions of supplementary fit have equated it with interpersonal similarity (Cable & DeRue, 2002; Day & Bedeian, 1995; Kristof, 1996; Muchinsky & Monahan, 1987).

*Complementary fit* exists when a "weakness or need of the environment is offset by the strength of the individual, and vice versa" (Muchinsky & Monahan, 1987, p. 271). In other words, complementary fit involves the extent to which the person and environment each provide what the other requires. Complementary fit can be further distinguished in terms of whether requirements are imposed by the environment or the person (Dawis & Lofquist, 1984; Edwards, 1991; French, Rodgers, & Cobb, 1974; Kristof, 1996; Wanous, 1992). Requirements of the environment refer to demands placed on the person and may emanate from the task, work role, or broader social context. The degree to which these demands are fulfilled by the knowledge, skills, abilities, and resources (e.g., time and energy) of the person signifies *demands–abilities fit* (French et al., 1982; Kristof, 1996; McGrath, 1976). Requirements of the person reflect his or her needs, which include biological requisites for survival and psychological desires, motives, and goals (French et al., 1974). The degree to which the person's needs are fulfilled by supplies in the environment represents *needs–supplies fit* (French et al., 1982; Kristof, 1996).[1] Although Muchinsky and Monahan (1987) discussed complementary fit in terms of demands and abilities, other researchers have expanded this concept to include needs–supplies fit (Cable & DeRue, 2002; Kristof, 1996). We adopt this expanded perspective in the present discussion.

Although the distinctions between supplementary fit, demands–abilities fit, and needs–supplies fit are fundamental to PE fit research, they are sometimes overlooked or obscured. For instance, in some studies respondents have been asked how well a person fits a job (Feldman, 1976) or organization (Adkins, Russell, & Werbel, 1994; Kristof-Brown, 2000) without specifying whether fit should be interpreted as supplementary or complementary. In other studies different types of fit have been combined into a summary index (Bretz & Judge, 1994; Mitchell et al., 2001; Saks & Ashforth, 1997). A prominent example of this approach is vocational fit research in which the person is assessed using the Self-Directed Search (Holland, 1979), which combines abilities (i.e., activity competencies) and desires (i.e., activity preferences and occupational interests) into a single score (Assouline & Meir, 1987; Spokane et al., 2000; Tranberg, Slane, & Ekeberg, 1993). When used to gauge person–vocation fit, this score effectively confounds demands–abilities fit with needs–supplies fit. These types of fit should be distinguished because they are conceptually dis-

---

[1]Some studies of the fit between psychological needs and environmental supplies have used the term *supplies–values fit* (Choi, 2004; Edwards, 1996; Edwards & Rothbard, 1999; Livingstone, Nelson, & Barr, 1997; Taris & Feij, 2001) to reflect the distinction between values as conscious desires and biological needs that may operate outside of awareness (Locke, 1969). Here, we refer to needs–supplies fit to encompass both psychological and biological needs and to avoid confusion with value congruence, which is a form of supplementary fit (Chatman, 1989; Meglino et al., 1989; Kristof, 1996).

tinct and have different effects on outcomes (Dawis & Lofquist, 1984; French et al., 1982).

## Levels of the Environment

Another approach to distinguishing PE fit involves the level at which the environment is conceptualized (Kristof, 1996). Although PE fit research treats the person at the individual level, it frames the environment at different levels. For supplementary fit, the environment refers to the people in it (Muchinsky & Monahan, 1987), so environmental levels refer to varying degrees of aggregation of people in the environment. Thus, research on supplementary fit has included examinations of similarity between the person and other individuals, such as supervisors (Barrett, 1995; Tsui, Porter, & Egan, 2002), subordinates (Engle & Lord, 1997; Murphy & Ensher, 1999; Yukl & Fu, 1999), and coworkers (Antonioni & Park, 2001; Schaubroeck & Lam, 2002; Strauss, Barrick, & Connerley, 2001), and between the person and social collectives, such as incumbents of a particular job (Chatman, Caldwell, & O'Reilly, 1999; Costa, McCrae, & Kay, 1995) and members of workgroups (Ferris, Youngblood, & Yates, 1985; Hollenbeck, 2000; Kristof-Brown, Jansen, & Colbert, 2002; Kristof-Brown & Stevens, 2001), departments (Enz, 1988; McCain, O'Reilly, & Pfeffer, 1983), organizations (Chatman, 1989; Kristof, 1996; Verquer et al., 2003), and vocations (Hildebrand & Walsh, 1988; Hoeglund & Hansen, 1999; Upperman & Church, 1995).

Different levels of the environment can also be distinguished for complementary fit. In the case of demands–abilities fit, demands can be unique to the experiences of an individual or shared by all incumbents of a job or members of a workgroup, department, organization, or vocation. Research on demands–abilities fit often frames demands as unique to the individual, as illustrated by studies in which respondents describe the demands they personally face (Cable & DeRue, 2002; Edwards, 1996; French et al., 1982; Lauver & Kristof-Brown, 2001). Although the demands faced by an individual might be shared by others in the same job, this research does not attempt to generalize demands beyond the indiviadual level. Other studies examine demands at the job level, as when job seekers rate the fit between their abilities and the demands of jobs for which they interviewed (Cable & Judge, 1996) or raters assess the demands of a position or job (Caldwell & O'Reilly, 1990; Higgins & Judge, 2004; Kristof-Brown, 2000; Kristof-Brown, Barrick, & Franke, 2002). This research reflects the premise that the same demands are encountered by all incumbents of the position or job. Studies also frame demands at higher levels, such as teams (Hollenbeck et al., 2002), functions (Chan, 1996), and vocations (Greenberg, 2002; Holland, 1997; Spokane et al., 2000).

For needs–supplies fit, supplies can be framed at levels analogous to those of demands. Typically, supplies are conceived at the individual level, such that needs–supplies fit concerns the supplies available to a particular person irrespective of whether those supplies are available to other people (Cable & DeRue, 2002; Edwards, 1996; French et al., 1982). A few researchers have treated supplies at the group level (Burch & Anderson, 2002; Shaw, Duffy, & Stark, 2000), and numerous researchers examined supplies at the organizational level (Bretz & Judge, 1994; Chatman, 1991; Christiansen, Villanova, & Mikulay, 1997; O'Reilly et al., 1991; Tziner & Falbe, 1990; van Vianen, 2000; Vigoda & Cohen, 2002) and vocational level (Assouline & Meir, 1987; Spokane et al., 2000; Tranberg et al., 1993). In principle, supplies could also be conceived at the job level, reflecting the assumption that all incumbents of a job have access to the same supplies, but studies that adopt this approach are rare.

In PE fit research, differences in environmental levels are sometimes confounded with the distinction between supplementary and complementary fit. For instance, person–organization fit often refers to supplementary fit in which people in the environment are at the organizational level (Adkins et al., 1994; Cable & Judge, 1996; Chatman, 1991), and person–job fit has been used as a label for demands–abilities fit in which demands are at the individual level (Kristof-Brown, 2000; Kristof-Brown, Barrick et al., 2002) or job level (Cable & Judge, 1996; Higgins & Judge, 2004). When conceptualized in this manner, person–organization fit and person–job fit confound differences between the individual, job and organization levels of the environment with the distinction between supplementary fit and demands–abilities fit. This problem is avoided when person–organization fit is defined by its treatment of the environment at the organizational level without restricting the environment to members of the organization (Kristof, 1996) and person–job fit is defined by its characterization of the environment at the job level, at which the job can refer to demands, supplies, or other people who hold the same job. This perspective isolates the distinction between person–organization fit and person–job fit to the level of the environment and treats supplementary versus complementary fit as a separate but equally important distinction.

## Content of Person and Environment Dimensions

A third approach to distinguishing conceptualizations of PE fit involves the content of the dimensions on which the person and environment are compared. These dimensions can be placed on a continuum ranging from general to specific. Here, we consider three points on this continuum that represent global, domain, and facet levels of person and environment dimensions. For supplementary fit, the global level refers to similarity in a general sense, without reference to any dimensions of comparison. This level is exemplified by studies examining perceived overall similarity between the person and other people or combining broad areas of comparison, such as beliefs, attitudes, and values (Pulakos

& Wexley, 1983; Turban, Dougherty, & Lee, 2002; Turban & Jones, 1988; Wayne & Liden, 1995; Zalesny & Highhouse, 1992). The domain level isolates broad areas of comparison but does not distinguish dimensions within each area. Such areas of comparison include values (Adkins, Ravlin, & Meglino, 1996; Cable & Judge, 1996; Meglino et al., 1989; Saks & Ashforth, 1997), goals (Kristof-Brown & Stevens, 2001; Vancouver, Millsap, & Peters, 1994; Vancouver & Schmitt, 1991), personality (Chatman et al., 1999; Schaubroeck & Lam, 2002), and demographic characteristics (Chatman, Polzer, Barsade, & Neale, 1998; Tsui, Egan, & O'Reilly, 1992). Research at the facet level includes examination of similarity on specific dimensions within broader areas, as when studies of personality similarity distinguish the dimensions of the Big Five (Antonioni & Park, 2001; Day & Bedeian, 1995) or studies of demographic similarity separately examine similarity according to age, gender, race, and education (Chattopadhyay, 1999; Tsui & O'Reilly, 1989; Vecchio & Bullis, 2001).

Dimensions of comparison for demands–abilities fit can also be arranged hierarchically. The global level concerns the overall fit between demands and abilities without regard to any dimensions of comparison. Studies of demands–abilities fit at the global level either collapse across specific demand and ability dimensions (Caldwell & O'Reilly, 1990; Rosman & Burke, 1980) or assess perceptions of overall demands–abilities fit (Cable & DeRue, 2002; Cable & Judge, 1996; Kristof-Brown, 2000; Saks & Ashforth, 1997). The domain level captures broad distinctions among demand and ability dimensions, such as training (Chisholm, Kasl, & Eskenazl, 1983), education (Coburn, 1975; French et al., 1982), experience (Johnson & Johnson, 1996), and work load (Beehr, Walsh, & Taber, 1976; Jamal, 1984; Schaubroeck, Cotton, & Jennings, 1989). The facet level examines demands–abilities fit for specific tasks or activities, such as generating new ideas (Choi, 2004; Livingstone et al., 1997), motivating and rewarding subordinates (Edwards, 1996), and playing a musical instrument in an orchestra (Parasuraman & Purohit, 2000).

For needs–supplies fit, the global level is illustrated by studies of the overall fit between needs and supplies that assess general perceptions of need fulfillment (Cable & DeRue, 2002; Riordan, Weatherly, Vandenberg, & Self, 2001; Saks & Ashforth, 1997) or aggregate needs–supplies fit across a broad set of dimensions (Hollenbeck, 1989; Rounds et al., 1987). The domain level concerns fit on general need and supply dimensions, such as job complexity (Edwards & Harrison, 1993; French et al., 1982), job enrichment (Cherrington & England, 1980; Greenhaus, Seidel, & Marinis, 1983), and social relationships (Cook & Wall, 1980; Edwards & Rothbard, 1999; O'Brien & Dowling, 1980; Porter & Lawler, 1968). The facet level involves needs–supplies fit regarding specific aspects of work, as when job scope is separated into autonomy, variety, task identity, and participation in decision making (Alutto & Acito, 1974; Conway, Vickers, & French, 1992; Cook & Wall, 1980; O'Brien & Dowling, 1980; Wanous &

Lawler, 1972) or social relationships refer to different people, such as supervisors, coworkers, and clients (Rice, McFarlin, & Bennett, 1989).

An important issue regarding the content of person and environment dimensions is that the dimensions must be commensurate (Dawis & Lofquist, 1984; French et al., 1974; Murray, 1938). Commensurate dimensions have two features. The first is *nominal equivalence,* meaning the person and environment are described in the same terms. For instance, when supplementary fit involves personality similarity, the person and members of his or her social environment must be compared on the same traits, such as dimensions of the Big Five (Antonioni & Park, 2001) or the Jungian typology (Schaubroeck & Lam, 2002). Likewise, for demands–abilities fit, demands and abilities must refer to the same dimension, such as required and attained education (Coburn, 1975; French et al., 1982). Similarity, needs–supplies fit must frame needs and supplies in the same terms, such as desired and actual autonomy (Conway et al., 1992; Edwards & Rothbard, 1999; Elsass &Veiga, 1997). Nominal equivalence can be achieved by translating taxonomies that describe people into environmental terms, such as the use of Maslow's need hierarchy to frame both needs and supplies (Hall, Schneider, & Nygren, 1970; Lawler & Hall, 1970; Porter & Lawler, 1968). Nominal equivalence can also be obtained when taxonomies that describe the environment are adapted to the person, as when job activity frameworks are used to describe the job and the person (Edwards, 1996). Nominal equivalence also results when the person and environment are described on the same dimensions without drawing from preexisting person or environment frameworks, a practice that is common in PE fit research (Caldwell & O'Reilly, 1990; French et al., 1982; O'Reilly et al., 1991; Wanous & Lawler, 1972).

The second feature of commensurate dimensions is *scale equivalence,* meaning the person and environment are assessed on the same metric (French et al., 1974). For example, supplementary fit for supervisor–subordinate goal congruence requires supervisors and subordinates to rate goals on the same metric, such as importance (Jauch, Osborn, & Terpening, 1980; Vancouver & Schmitt, 1991). Similarly, demands–abilities fit for education requires a common scale for required and actual education, such as years (French et al., 1982), and needs–supplies fit for autonomy requires the same scale for supplies and needs, such as perceived and desired amounts (Conway et al., 1992; Elsass & Veiga, 1997). Metric equivalence is achieved by using the same response scale for the person and environment and different item stems to distinguish between the person and environment. This approach is illustrated by the Porter Need Satisfaction Questionnaire (Porter & Lawler, 1968), which uses the same 7-point response scale to assess supplies and needs with stems that ask "How much is there now" and "How much should there be," respectively.

In some cases, research framed in terms of PE fit involves person and environment dimensions that are not commensurate. For instance, the job characteristics model has been cast in terms of needs–supplies fit, in which needs refer to growth need strength and supplies refer to the five-core job dimensions (Blau, 1987; Kulik, Oldham, & Hackman, 1987). Although growth needs and the core job dimensions are conceptually related, they are not nominally equivalent, given that growth needs refer to the overall desire for an enriched job, whereas the core job dimensions describe specific aspects of an enriched job. Nominal equivalence is achieved when needs and supplies both refer to overall job enrichment (Cherrington & England, 1980) or individual core job dimensions (Cook & Wall, 1980; O'Brien & Dowling, 1980; Wanous & Lawler, 1972).

Other research exhibits nominal equivalence but not scale equivalence. For example, in studies of needs–supplies fit based on the theory of work adjustment (Dawis & Lofquist, 1984) supply amount is compared to need importance (Betz, 1969; Rounds et al., 1987; Scarpello & Campbell, 1983). Although these studies describe needs and supplies are on the same dimensions, such as variety, security, and recognition, these dimensions are assessed on different metrics. Unless supplies and needs are both assessed on the same metric, such as amount, it is impossible to determine whether supplies exceed or fall short of needs and, hence, the degree of needs–supplies fit. Scale equivalence is also undermined by studies of value congruence comparing the characteristicness of organizational values to the importance or desirability of personal values (Chatman, 1989; O'Reilly et al., 1991) and studies of demands–abilities fit comparing the importance of job competencies to the degree to which competencies characterize employees (Caldwell & O'Reilly, 1990; Chatman, 1991).

## An Integrative Framework

Figure 7–1 presents a framework that integrates the foregoing approaches to distinguishing PE fit. This framework shows how distinctions within each approach can be combined to yield different conceptualizations of PE fit. For example, research on personal and organizational value congruence that collapses across value dimensions (Cable & Judge, 1996; Chatman, 1991; Lovelace & Rosen, 1996) would be classified as supplementary fit with the environment at the organizational level and content dimensions at the domain level. Research on underemployment examining the overall fit between job demands and employee abilities (Bolino & Feldman, 2000; Johnson & Johnson, 1996) refers to demands–abilities fit with the environment at the job level and content dimensions at the global level. Research on need fulfillment comparing needs and supplies on specific dimensions from the perspective of the employee (Edwards & Harrison, 1993; Wanous & Lawler, 1972) signifies needs–supplies fit with the environment at the individual level and content dimensions at the facet

The Conceptual Domain of Person-Environment Fit

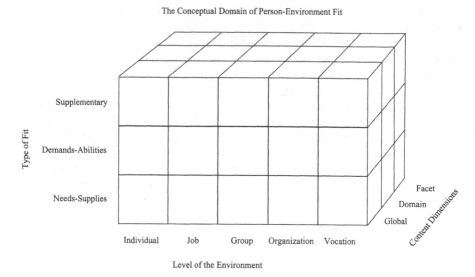

FIGURE 7–1. An integrative conceptualization of PE fit.

level. Other types of PE fit research can be organized within the framework to highlight their key similarities and differences.

The framework in Fig. 7–1 has several merits. First, it integrates and expands existing conceptualizations of PE fit, most of which have been limited to two (Edwards, 1991), three (Cable & DeRue, 2002; Kristof, 1996), or four (Bretz & Judge, 1994) types of fit. Our framework shows that integrating the distinctions in the PE fit literature considerably expands the types of fit open to inquiry. Second, the framework highlights types of PE fit that have been overlooked. For instance, person–job fit can refer not only to demands–abilities fit and needs–supplies fit (Edwards, 1991) but also to supplementary fit in which the environment involves other people in the same job as the focal person. Likewise, person–organization fit can involve supplementary fit (Cable & Judge, 1996) as well as demands–abilities fit and needs–supplies fit in which demands and supplies are conceptualized at the organization level (Kristof, 1996). Third, the framework increases the precision with which PE fit can be conceptualized and measured. For instance, the meaning and operationalization of value congruence differs, depending on whether the values dimensions are at the domain level (Adkins et al., 1996; Cable & Judge, 1996; Meglino et al., 1989; Saks & Ashforth, 1997) or facet level (Ashkanasy & O'Connor, 1997; Cable & Edwards, 2004; Finegan, 2000; Kalliath, Bluedorn, & Strube, 1999). Finally, the distinctions drawn in the framework have important implications for developing hypotheses regarding the effects of fit on outcomes, as discussed in the following section.

## OUTCOMES OF PERSON–ENVIRONMENT FIT

PE fit researchers have examined a wide range of outcomes (Assouline & Meir, 1987; Edwards, 1991; Kristof, 1996; Spokane et al., 2000; Verquer et al., 2003). We organize these outcomes into three broad categories. The first category comprises attitudes, as illustrated by studies relating PE fit to job satisfaction and organizational commitment (Dawis & Lofquist, 1984; Diener & Lucas, 2000; Locke, 1969; Rice, McFarlin, Hunt, & Near, 1985). The second category involves mental and physical health, as emphasized by research on the PE fit approach to stress (Edwards, Caplan, & Harrison, 1998; French et al., 1982). The third category consists of task and contextual performance, which signifies contributions of the person to his or her employer (Dawis & Lofquist, 1984; McGrath, 1976; Pervin, 1968). In this section, we draw from theories pertaining to these outcomes to explain how they relate to PE fit. We discuss PE fit in terms of supplementary fit, demands–abilities fit, and needs–supplies fit, which we consider the primary distinction in the framework in Fig. 7–1. We later explain how other distinctions in the framework help refine predictions about the effects of PE fit on outcomes. We should emphasize that each outcome we discuss has causes other than PE fit, and we do not intend or claim to give a complete account of all causes of each outcome. Rather, our goal is to show how theories pertaining to each outcome can be used to conceptualize the effects of PE fit.

### Attitudes

Numerous studies have examined the relationship between PE fit and attitudes (Assouline & Meir, 1987; Edwards, 1991; Kristof, 1996; Spokane et al., 2000; Tranberg et al., 1993). Here, we consider two widely studied attitudes, job satisfaction and organizational commitment, and examine the theoretical basis for their relationships with PE fit. We first consider how job satisfaction and organizational commitment have been defined and then draw from relevant theory to examine how these attitudes relate to PE fit.

#### Job Satisfaction

Although various definitions of job satisfaction have been proposed, most describe job satisfaction as an affective or emotional response that results from the cognitive comparison of actual and desired aspects of the job (Cranny, Smith, & Stone, 1992). For instance, Locke (1969) defined job satisfaction as a "pleasurable emotional state resulting from the appraisal of one's job as achieving or facilitating one's job values" (p. 317), where values refer to what the person consciously wants, desires, or seeks to attain. Likewise, Dawis and Lofquist (1984) defined job satisfaction as "a pleasurable affective condition resulting from one's appraisal of the way in which the experienced job situation meets one's needs, values, and expectations" (p. 72). Other researchers have similarly defined job satisfaction as an affective or emotional response to the comparison between actual and desired job characteristics (Katzell, 1964; Lawler, 1973; Locke, 1976; Smith, Kendall, & Hulin, 1969).

The foregoing definitions of job satisfaction combine two distinct features of attitudes, one that concerns affective reactions to the job and another that entails the evaluation of the job relative to desires of the person (Olson & Zanna, 1993). As such, these definitions confound job satisfaction as affect with cognitive evaluations that are theorized to cause job satisfaction (Brief, 1998). One way to avoid this confound is to define job satisfaction strictly in cognitive terms (Dawis & Lofquist, 1984; Motowidlo, 1996; Porter, 1961; Weiss, 2002). For instance, Weiss (2002) defined job satisfaction as "a positive (or negative) evaluative judgment one makes about one's job or job situation" (p. 175). Another way to circumvent the confound is to conceptualize job satisfaction in affective terms and treat cognitive evaluation as a separate and distinct cause of job satisfaction. This view is consistent with the bulk of job satisfaction research, in which perceptions and evaluations of the job are treated as causes of job satisfaction, not as job satisfaction itself (Lawler, 1973; Locke, 1969, 1976; Smith et al., 1969). This view is also consistent with research in which satisfaction is treated as a marker of the pleasantness dimension of affect and emotion (Russell, 1983; Watson & Tellegen, 1985). We adopt this perspective in the present discussion.

The effects of PE fit on job satisfaction can be deduced by drawing from theories of job satisfaction and emotion. As noted earlier, Locke (1969) indicated that job satisfaction results from the appraisal of the job relative to values, where values are what people desire, want, or seek to attain. Locke (1969) further argued that values can be distinguished according to desired amount and importance. *Desired amount* is the standard against which perceived amounts of job characteristics are compared to determine job satisfaction, whereas *importance* moderates the effect of this comparison. The perspective expressed by Locke (1969) is consistent with other theories of job satisfaction (Dawis & Lofquist, 1984; Lawler, 1973; Smith et al., 1969). This perspective is also reflected in discussions of the effects of cognitive appraisal on emotion. For instance, Lazarus (1991) indicated that emotions are influenced by goal congruence, which is "the extent to which a transaction is consistent or inconsistent with what the person wants" (p. 150). According to Lazarus (1991), goal congruence leads to positive emotions, whereas goal incongruence produces negative emotions. This notion is common in theories that address the effects of cognitive appraisal on emotion (Roseman, 1984; Scherer, 1988).

The causes of job satisfaction outlined in the preceding paragraphs have clear parallels with needs–supplies fit. These parallels are apparent in the theory of PE fit developed by French et al. (1982), who defined needs broadly to include biological and psychological requirements, values developed through learning and socialization, and goals and motives to achieve desired ends. Supplies are the extrinsic and intrinsic resources and rewards available to fulfill the needs of the person. French et al. (1982) indicated that needs and supplies can be either objective or subjective but emphasized that only subjective needs and supplies affect attitudinal and emotional outcomes. Subjective needs in PE fit theory correspond to valued or desired amounts of job characteristics in theories of job satisfaction (Lawler, 1973; Locke, 1976; Smith et al., 1969). PE fit theory also indicates that the effects of needs–supplies fit are moderated by the importance of the dimension to which needs and supplies refer (French et al., 1974; Harrison, 1985), which is consistent with the moderating effects of importance described by Locke (1969, 1976; Mobley & Locke, 1970). Hence, subjective needs–supplies fit parallels the comparison process underlying theories of job satisfaction, and therefore we expect needs–supplies fit to directly influence job satisfaction as an affective or emotional response.

In contrast to needs–supplies fit, demands–abilities fit is not expected to directly influence job satisfaction. Rather, the effects of demands–abilities fit on job satisfaction should depend on the implications of demands–abilities fit for fulfilling the desires of the person (Lawler, 1973; Locke, 1976; Smith et al., 1969). Stated in terms of PE fit, the effects of demands–abilities fit on job satisfaction are mediated by needs–supplies fit, which can be viewed a proximal cause of job satisfaction. Building on the work of Harrison (1978), we suggest three mechanisms by which demands–abilities fit can affect needs–supplies fit and thereby influence job satisfaction. First, demands–abilities fit can facilitate job performance, which brings intrinsic and extrinsic rewards that fulfill the needs of the person. This mechanism frames demands–abilities fit as instrumental to needs–supplies fit, which in turn enhances job satisfaction. Second, demands can become internalized as desires of the person, as when role expectations are accepted by the person as guidelines for his or her own behavior. The ability to meet these demands effectively yields supplies that fulfill the internalized desires. Thus, for demands that are internalized as desires, demands–abilities fit translates into needs–supplies fit, which should influence job satisfaction. Third, when the person is able to fulfill job demands, he or she is likely to experience a sense of competence that serves as a supply for the need for competence (Feather, 1991; White, 1959).

We also posit that the effects of supplementary fit on job satisfaction are indirect. We suggest three processes that can explain these effects. First, supplementary fit itself connotes similarity, which can serve as a supply for needs for affiliation and belonging (Baumeister & Leary, 1995; Feather, 1991; Koestner & McClelland, 1992), in that people who are similar are likely to develop strong social relationships (Byrne, 1971). Interacting with similar others can also enhance predictability and reduce ambiguity (Kluckhohn, 1951), thereby fulfilling needs for closure and clarity (Ivancevich & Donnelly, 1974; Lyons, 1971; Webster & Kruglanski, 1994). On the other hand, people also have needs to be different (Hornsey & Jetten, 2004), which can be inhibited when supplementary fit is high. On balance, we believe that the similarity associated with supplementary fit is more likely to enhance than to interfere with needs–supplies fit, with the caveat that the balance of these effects depends on the relative strength of the person's motives to be similar versus different. Second, the person and environment characteristics involved in supplementary fit can influence needs and supplies, respectively, involved in needs–supplies fit (Cable & Edwards, 2004). Consider value congruence, a widely studied form of supplementary fit (Cable & Judge, 1996; Chatman, 1989; Judge & Bretz, 1992; Meglino et al., 1989). Values considered important by the person should influence what the person wants from work (Hogan, 1991), and values viewed as important in an organization should affect the rewards it supplies to its members (Schein, 1992). For instance, an employee who considers autonomy important is likely to want high levels of autonomy at work, and an organization with values that emphasize autonomy is likely to promote autonomy in the workplace (Cable & Edwards, 2004). Through these effects, personal and organizational values can affect needs and supplies, respectively, with the fit between needs and supplies influencing satisfaction. Third, supplementary fit can foster communication and coordination (Adkins et al., 1996), which enable people to fulfill demands (Day & Bedeian, 1995; Motowidlo, 2003). This process enhances demands–abilities fit, which in turn influences needs–supplies fit and satisfaction through the mechanisms described earlier. The beneficial effects of similarity on performance can be diluted when tasks are nonroutine or require different perspectives (Adkins et al., 1996; Ancona & Caldwell, 1992; Schneider et al., 1997). For such tasks, supplementary fit could hinder the ability of the person to meet demands, thereby diminishing demands–abilities fit and its effects on needs–supplies fit and satisfaction. We elaborate these points in our discussion of the effects of PE fit on performance.

### Organizational Commitment

Another outcome frequently examined in PE fit research is organizational commitment. The meaning of organizational commitment has been discussed extensively (Cohen, 2003; Meyer & Allen, 1991; Morrow, 1983; Reichers, 1985; Wiener, 1982). Mowday, Porter, and Steers (1982) described organizational commitment as a person's identification with and involvement in an organization. O'Reilly and Chatman (1986) defined organizational commitment as the psychological attachment felt by the person for the organization, and Mathieu and Zajac (1990) viewed organizational commitment as a bond or link between the individual to the organization. These and other definitions of organizational commitment were reviewed and integrated by Meyer and Herscovitch (2001), who concluded that the essence of organizational commitment is a force that binds the person to a course of action with regard to the organization. Although various courses of action have been considered in organizational commitment research, the central course of action is continued membership in the organization (Meyer & Herscovitch, 2001).

Organizational commitment has been separated into dimensions that describe different forces that bind the person to the organization. The three dimensions proposed by Meyer and colleagues (Allen & Meyer, 1996; Meyer & Allen, 1991; Meyer, Allen, & Smith, 1993) have received considerable attention and integrate other dimensions in the literature (Meyer & Herscovitch, 2001). As articulated by Meyer and Allen (1991), *affective commitment* refers to the person's emotional attachment to, identification with, and involvement in the organization. Employees who are affectively committed stay with the organization because doing so fulfills their needs and desires. *Continuance commitment* is an awareness of the costs of leaving the organization. Employees who experience continuance commitment stay because leaving would mean forfeiting valued rewards or investments made in the organization, such as skills unique to a job or role. *Normative commitment* reflects a sense of obligation to remain in an organization. Employees who are normatively committed stay because they think they ought to do so, based on norms that dictate loyalty to the organization or generate a sense of reciprocity, such that staying with the organization compensates for rewards received from the organization.

Discussions of the antecedents of affective, continuance, and normative commitment (Meyer & Allen, 1991; Meyer & Herscovitch, 2001) suggested various linkages with PE fit. These linkages are apparent for needs–supplies fit. Meyer and Allen (1991) indicated that affective commitment results when work experiences fulfill the person's needs. Hence, when work experiences constitute supplies that create needs–supplies fit, affective commitment should result. Needs–supplies fit is also implied by continuance commitment, which is caused by the belief that rewards from the organization would be lost if the person left the organization. This notion implies that membership in the organization provides supplies that fulfill the person's needs, thereby creating needs–supplies fit, coupled with the belief that leaving the organization would reduce or eliminate these supplies. Normative commitment refers to norms of loyalty or reciprocity that are fulfilled by staying with the organization. When norms are internalized, they may be viewed as psychological needs or desires. By staying with the organization, these needs are fulfilled, creating needs–supplies fit. Thus, normative commitment can result from needs–supplies fit for which needs for loyalty or reciprocity are fulfilled by staying with the organization.

Affective, continuance, and normative commitment can be linked to demands–abilities fit through the mediating effects of need–supplies fit. Affective commitment should result from demands–abilities fit when the ability to meet demands provides rewards that are valued by the person (Harrison, 1978). Analogously, continuance commitment should occur when demands–abilities fit yields rewards that would be forfeited if the person left the organization (Mathieu & Zajac, 1990; Stevens, Beyer, & Trice, 1978). Demands–abilities fit can also lead to continuance commitment when, to fulfill demands, the person develops abilities that are specific to the organization. These idiosyncratic abilities can function as "side bets" (Becker, 1960), which are investments that would be lost if the person left the organization. Normative commitment can result from demands–abilities fit when norms of loyalty or reciprocity are perceived as role demands that the person would meet by staying (Wiener, 1982). Meeting these role demands can create needs–supplies fit by generating approval from role senders (Kahn & Quinn, 1970), which serves as a supply for approval needs (Crowne & Marlowe, 1964) or when role demands are internalized as needs that are fulfilled by remaining in the organization.

Supplementary fit can also influence affective, continuance, and normative commitment through its effects on needs–supplies fit. As noted earlier, supplementary fit provides supplies that can fulfill needs for affiliation, belonging, closure, and clarity. If these needs are stronger than the need to be different, then supplementary fit should enhance needs–supplies fit. Also, as previously explained, the person and environment constructs involved in supplementary fit can influence needs and supplies, respectively, thereby influencing needs–supplies fit. In addition, supplementary fit can enhance task performance, bringing intrinsic and extrinsic rewards that fulfill the needs of the person. Through these mechanisms, supplementary fit can affect need–supplies fit and thereby influence affective commitment. Supplementary fit should be positively related to continuance commitment when the person believes that the benefits of supplementary fit would be foregone by leaving the organization. Finally, supplementary fit may generate normative commitment when the person has values of loyalty and reciprocity similar to those of others. Being in the company of others who espouse these values makes them salient and creates social pressures that promote the internalization of values expressed by others as personal desires (Cable & Parsons, 2001), which can be fulfilled by remaining with the organization (Weiner, 1982).[2]

---

[2]Some researchers include supplementary fit, expressed as value congruence, in the operational definition of organizational commitment (Mowday et al., 1982; O'Reilly & Chatman, 1986). Doing so confounds organizational commitment with one of its causes (Edwards & Bagozzi, 2000). The approach we adopt treats supplementary fit and organizational commitment as distinct constructs, which is necessary to meaningfully examine their relationship with one another.

## Mental and Physical Well-Being

Another category of outcomes relevant to PE fit includes indicators of mental and physical well-being, such as anxiety, depression, tension, and somatic health. These outcomes have been studied extensively in research on stress (Baum & Posluszny, 1999; Danna & Griffin, 1999; Ganster & Schaubroeck, 1991; Kahn & Byosiere, 1992; Quick, Cooper, Nelson, Quick, & Gavin, 2003; Schneiderman, Ironson, & Siegel, 2005; Sonnentag & Frese, 2003; Taylor, Repetti, & Seeman, 1997). From a conceptual standpoint, stress has strong linkages to PE fit, given that many theories of stress implicitly or explicitly incorporate PE fit as a central concept (Edwards, 1992; French et al., 1982; Hobfoll, 1989; Lazarus & Folkman, 1984; McGrath, 1976; Schuler, 1980). Thus, we draw from the stress literature to examine the connections between PE fit and mental and physical well-being.

We begin by considering the definition of stress, which has generated considerable debate in the stress literature (Kahn & Byosiere, 1992; Lazarus, 1991; Parker & DeCotiis, 1983; Schuler, 1980). Several major approaches to defining stress can be distinguished. One approach treats stress as a stimulus in the environment that damages well-being (Beehr, 1998; Cooper & Marshall, 1976; Kahn & Quinn, 1970). Examples of such stimuli include role conflict, role ambiguity, work load, and responsibility for others (Beehr, 1998; Kahn & Byosiere, 1992). Stimulus definitions are problematic in that they overlook individual differences in the appraisal of the environment (Lazarus, 1966; McGrath, 1970) and are circular, given that a stimulus is defined as stressful only when it damages well-being (Edwards, 1992; Lazarus & Folkman, 1984). Another approach defines stress as a psychological or physiological response to demands, constraints, or opportunities faced by the person (Ivancevich & Matteson, 1980; Martin & Schermerhorn, 1983; Parker & DeCotiis, 1983; Selye, 1982). Response definitions are also circular, in that a response is classified as stress only when it results from its assumed causes (McGrath, 1970). In addition, response definitions fail to distinguish situations that are benign from those in which responses are ameliorated because of effective coping (Edwards, 1992; Lazarus & Folkman, 1984).

Problems with stimulus and response definitions are avoided by relational definitions, which identify stress in terms of the relationship between the person and situation (Eulberg, Weekley, & Bhagat, 1988; Lazarus & Folkman, 1984; Schuler, 1980). Relational definitions fall into two primary categories. One category defines stress in terms of situational demands that tax or exceed the abilities or resources of the person (Lazarus & Folkman, 1984; McGrath, 1976; Shirom, 1982). Another category indicates that stress exists when intrinsic or extrinsic rewards of the situation fall short of the needs, desires, or goals of the person (Cummings & Cooper, 1979; Edwards, 1992; Hobfoll, 2001; Schuler, 1980). Although these definitions appear inconsistent, Harrison (1978) contended that demands exceeding the abilities or resources of the person are stressful only if meeting demands yields valued outcomes or the person believes that meeting demands is inherently desirable (White, 1959). This reasoning is consistent with McGrath (1976) and Lazarus and Folkman (1984), who noted that excess demands are stressful only when failure to meet demands is considered costly by the person. Hence, relational definitions converge on the notion that stress arises when rewards fall short of the person's needs, desires, and goals (Cummings & Cooper, 1979; Edwards, 1992; Hobfoll, 1989; Schuler, 1980) where rewards may depend on whether the person is able to fulfill the demands of the situation (Edwards et al., 1998; Harrison, 1978; Lazarus & Folkman, 1984; McGrath, 1976).

Relational definitions of stress map onto needs–supplies fit, such that stress exists when supplies fall short of the person's needs. This correspondence is evident in the PE fit theory of stress (Edwards et al., 1998; French et al., 1982; Harrison, 1978), which defines stress as misfit between subjective needs and supplies. This theory also indicates that subjective needs–supplies misfit is the critical mechanism through which the person and environment jointly influence mental and physical well-being. Similarly, cybernetic theories of stress (Cummings & Cooper, 1979; Edwards, 1992) position the discrepancy between perceived and desired states as the proximal cause of well-being. Thus, needs–supplies misfit can be interpreted as stress when needs and supplies are both subjective and supplies fall short of needs. Theories that define stress in terms of needs–supplies misfit also indicate that the effects of stress on well-being are intensified when needs are important to the person (Cummings & Cooper, 1979; Edwards, 1992; French et al., 1982; Schuler, 1980), analogous to the moderating effects of importance on the relationship between needs–supplies fit and of job satisfaction (Locke, 1969, 1976; Mobley & Locke, 1970). Drawing from these theories, needs–supplies fit should directly affect mental and physical well-being, with greater effects for needs that are considered important by the person.

Based on the conceptualizations of stress reviewed in the preceding discussion, the effects of demands–abilities fit on well-being should be indirect, depending on the degree to which meeting demands yields supplies that fulfill the needs of the person. This notion is consistent with theories that treat stress as situational demands that exceed the abilities of the person, given that excess demands are considered stressful only if meeting demands yields intrinsic or extrinsic rewards that fulfill the needs of the person, thereby influencing needs–supplies fit (French et al., 1982; Lazarus & Folkman, 1984; McGrath, 1976). As noted earlier, demands–abilities fit can enhance needs–supplies fit when meeting demands facilitates performance and in turn generates rewards, when demands are internalized as personal desires, or when demands–abilities fit itself is perceived as a supply that fulfills the person's need for competence. Each of these mechanisms treats needs–supplies fit as a mediator of the effects of demands–abilities fit on well-being (Harrison, 1978).

We suggest two pathways by which supplementary fit influences well-being. First, as discussed earlier, supplementary fit can influence needs–supplies fit by serving as a supply for affiliation, belonging, closure, and clarity needs, by influencing needs and supplies involved in needs–supplies fit, and by influencing job performance and its attendant rewards. To the extent these mechanisms enhance needs–supplies fit, stress should be reduced and well-being should improve. Second, based on the similarity–attraction paradigm (Byrne, 1971), supplementary fit promotes the development of relationships that can provide social support, which ameliorates stress and improves well-being (Cohen & Wills, 1985; Coyne & Downey, 1991; House, 1981; Uchino, Cacioppo, & Kiecolt-Glaser, 1996). Two models that explain the effects of social support have been proposed, one indicating that social support directly influences well-being and another that casts social support as a buffer of the effects of stress on well-being (Cohen & Wills, 1985; House, 1981). In terms of PE fit, the direct effects of social support are consistent with the notion that support acts as a supply that fulfills affiliation needs. The buffering effects of social support suggest that support from others helps the person meet demands that generate stress, acquire supplies to fulfill needs, or reinterpret the subjective person or environment such that the effects of misfit are diminished (Cohen & McKay, 1984). Thus, social support research suggests a variety of mechanisms by which supplementary fit can ameliorate stress and improve well-being.

## Performance

The final category of outcomes we consider involves job performance. We adopt the definition of job performance advanced by Motowidlo (2003, p. 40) as the "total expected value to the organization of the discrete behavioral episodes that an individual carries out over a standard period of time." This definition focuses on individual behavior as distinct from its results, which can depend on situational factors beyond the control of the individual (Motowidlo, Borman, & Schmit, 1997). Conceptualizing performance in terms of individual behavior is also consistent with the psychological perspective that underlies much job performance research (Motowidlo, 2003).

In this discussion, we focus on task performance and contextual performance. *Task performance* refers to the recurring set of activities or expected behaviors of an individual that are typically described by formal job descriptions (Borman & Motowidlo, 1993; Katz & Kahn, 1978). These behaviors tend to be "highly elaborated, relatively stable, and defined to a considerable extent in explicit or even written terms" (March & Simon,

1958, p. 4). *Contextual performance* refers to behavior that contributes to organizational effectiveness through its effects on the psychological, social, and organizational work context (Borman & Motowidlo, 1993). Contextual performance overlaps with organizational citizenship behavior (OCB), which Organ (1988) defined as "individual behavior that is discretionary, not directly or explicitly recognized by the formal reward system, and that in the aggregate promotes the effective functioning of the organization" (p. 4). This definition excludes behaviors that are formally rewarded or perceived as nondiscretionary. Subsequent OCB research indicated that the boundaries defining formal rewards and discretionary behavior are often unclear (Morrison, 1994). In light of this research, Organ (1997) recently presented a revised definition of OCB that is synonymous with contextual performance. Discussions of contextual performance have separated it into several dimensions, such as following rules and policies, volunteering to carry out tasks, and helping others (Borman & Motowidlo, 1993). However, these dimensions are generally attributed to the same causes (Organ & Konovsky, 1989; Organ & Ryan, 1995). Therefore, we treat contextual performance as a summary concept, while recognizing that it comprises distinct performance behaviors.

Research points to different antecedents of task and contextual performance. Task performance is primarily a function of the abilities and motivation of the person. To successfully complete a task, an individual must have the appropriate abilities, knowledge, and skills and must also be motivated to complete the task (Hunter, 1983; Lawler, 1973; Motowidlo et al., 1997; Organ & Ryan, 1995; Vroom, 1964; Waldman & Spangler, 1989; Wanous, 1992). In contrast, contextual performance is primarily linked to attitudes (Organ, 1990; Organ & Ryan, 1995). For example, individuals are more likely to engage in contextual performance when they feel satisfied or are affectively committed to the organization (Organ & Ryan, 1995; Podsakoff, MacKenzie, Paine, & Bacharach, 2000). Although the primary causes of task and contextual performance have been treated as distinct, some researchers have pointed to causes that are common to both types of performance. For example, performing discretionary tasks should depend on the abilities of the person relevant to such tasks (Organ & Ryan, 1995). We examine the effects of PE fit on task and contextual performance by drawing from their primary causes and by selectively incorporating other causes that provide linkages to PE fit.

Demands–abilities fit should strongly predict task performance and, to a lesser extent, contextual performance. The performance literature points to ability as a key predictor of task performance (Hunter, 1983; Motowidlo et al., 1997; Vroom, 1964; Waldman & Spangler, 1989). Ability promotes the development of job knowledge and skills, which in turn facilitate task performance (Hunter, 1983; Schmidt, Hunter, & Outerbridge, 1986). Some researchers have further emphasized that performance depends upon the degree to which abilities match the requirements of the job (Motowidlo, 2003; Wanous, 1992). The match between abilities and job requirements corresponds to demands–abilities fit, which is linked to task performance in PE fit research (Dawis & Lofquist, 1984; Muchinsky & Monahan, 1987; Pervin, 1968). Demands–abilities fit may also influence contextual performance which, as noted previously, depends upon the ability to perform the intended behaviors (Motowidlo et al., 1997). Although the demands for such behavior may not be prescribed by the job, the person can gauge them from perceptions of the work role (Morrison, 1994) or infer them on the basis of personality or dispositional factors, such as conscientiousness (Motowidlo et al., 1997).

Needs–supplies fit should also relate to task and contextual performance. The effects of needs–supplies fit on task performance can be attributed to the motivating properties of supplies that are expected to fulfill needs. Motivation develops from the perception that effort will bring rewards that the person considers desirable (Lawler, 1973; Naylor, Pritchard, & Ilgen, 1980; Porter & Lawler, 1968; Vroom, 1964). Stated in terms of needs–supplies fit, a current unfulfilled need will motivate performance when anticipated supplies are expected to fulfill this need. This reasoning indicates that needs fulfilled by current supplies have no motivating potential. Rather, motivation results when the person experiences current needs–supplies misfit and expects that job performance will yield supplies that produce needs–supplies fit. As noted earlier, the effect of motivation on performance also requires that the person is able to meet task demands. Thus, we expect that current needs–supplies misfit will lead to task performance when anticipated supplies are expected to meet needs, provided the abilities of the person are sufficient to fulfill task demands.

Needs–supplies fit should affect contextual performance through job attitudes. Attitudes such as satisfaction and commitment are widely viewed as predictors of contextual performance (Morrison, 1994; Organ, 1990; Organ & Ryan, 1995; Podsakoff et al., 2000). When employees are satisfied, they are motivated to reciprocate as part of the exchange relationship with the employer (Organ, 1990). In addition, employees who are satisfied or committed tend to define their job responsibilities broadly, viewing contextual performance as part of their work role (Morrison, 1994). For these reasons, people who are satisfied or committed are likely to engage in contextual performance. As explained earlier, satisfaction and commitment result from the fit between needs and supplies. Therefore, needs–supplies fit can affect contextual performance indirectly, mediated by attitudes. Some researchers have suggested that contextual performance can result directly from the evaluation of job characteristics relative to needs, independent of job attitudes (Organ, 1990; Organ & Konovsky, 1989; Organ & Ryan, 1995). This logic implies a direct effect of needs–supplies fit on contextual performance. Based on this premise, needs–supplies fit influences contextual performance both directly and indirectly, mediated by attitudes such as satisfaction and commitment.

Finally, supplementary fit can influence task and contextual performance. For task performance, supplementary fit can facilitate communication and coordination with coworkers (Day & Bedeian, 1995; Neuman, Wagner, & Christiansen, 1999), which increase knowledge acquisition, role clarity, and predictability of behavior (Kluckhohn, 1951; Motowidlo, 2003). As a result, individuals may be better able to meet task demands, which in turn should increase task performance. On the other hand, supplementary fit can reduce variation in perspectives and approaches to problem solving, which can hinder the ability to meet the demands of tasks that are nonroutine or require different perspectives (Adkins et al., 1996; Ancona & Caldwell, 1992; Schneider et al., 1997). In such instances, supplementary fit would reduce demands–abilities fit and hamper task performance. The effects of supplementary fit on task performance should depend on the degree to which the person is interdependent with others in the environment (Ancona & Caldwell, 1992). If the person works independently, then the degree to which he or she is similar to others should have little effect on task performance. If the person is highly interdependent with others, then the effects of supplementary fit should be accentuated.

We suggest three mechanisms by which supplementary fit can influence contextual performance. First, supplementary fit can increase contextual performance because individuals prefer to help others who are similar to themselves (Graf & Riddell, 1972; Karylowski, 1976; Sole, Marton, & Hornstein, 1975), and helping is considered an important dimension of contextual performance (Podsakoff et al., 2000). Second, supplementary fit can affect contextual performance through needs–supplies fit. As described earlier, supplementary fit can increase needs–supplies fit when similarity provides supplies for needs for affiliation, belonging, closure, or clarity, when the person and environment constructs involved in supplementary fit influence needs and supplies, and when supplementary fit enhances job performance and brings rewards that fulfill needs. To the extent that needs are fulfilled, satisfaction increases and contextual performance is enhanced (Morrison, 1994; Organ, 1990; Organ & Ryan, 1995; Podsakoff et al., 2000). Finally, as described earlier, similarity can promote demands–abilities fit for routine tasks that involve interdependence. Demands–abilities fit in turn can influence task performance, bring desired rewards, and lead to satisfaction and contextual performance.

## Summary and Integration

Our discussion of the effects of PE fit on attitudes, well-being, and performance reveals several general themes. First, the effects of PE fit depend on the type of fit and outcome under consideration. For attitudes and well-being, needs–supplies fit is the primary cause, whereas demands–abilities fit and supplementary fit are expected to exert weaker effects. In contrast, task performance is linked to demands–abilities fit and the anticipation that needs–supplies fit will result from effective performance. The effects of supplementary fit on task performance depend on the nature of the task and the degree of interdependence between the person and others in the work environment. Unlike task performance, contextual performance should relate primarily to needs–supplies fit and, to a lesser extent, demands–abilities fit and supplementary fit. Hence, the distinctions between supplementary fit, demands–abilities fit, and needs–supplies fit are crucial for conceptualizing the effects of PE fit on the outcomes considered here.

Second, the effects of PE fit on outcomes involve combinations of different types of fit. For example, the conceptual logic relating demands–abilities fit to attitudes and well-being positions needs–supplies fit as a mediating mechanism, such that demands–abilities fit influences needs–supplies, which in turn affects attitudes and well-being. Similar logic applies to the effects of supplementary fit on attitudes and well-being, which are transmitted through needs–supplies fit and, in some instances, demands–abilities fit. For task performance, the effects of demands–abilities fit and needs–supplies fit are interactive, such that both types of fit are required for task performance to occur. These effects underscore the value of adopting an integrative view of PE fit and casting different types of fit as elements of a broader theoretical model.

Third, our discussion demonstrates that theories pertaining to outcomes provide a useful foundation for conceptualizing the effects of PE fit. For each outcome, we were able to derive reasoning from relevant theories pointing to person and environment constructs that fall within the domain of PE fit. Drawing from these theories helped explicate the process by which PE fit influences outcomes, which can enhance the theoretical rigor of PE fit research. The concept of PE fit can also enrich theories that explain outcomes. For instance, theories of performance emphasize ability as a key predictor of task performance, whereas the concept of demands–abilities fit underscores the point that task performance depends on how well abilities fit the demands of the task. Thus, integrating theories of PE fit with theories of outcomes can yield mutual benefits.

Our discussion of the effects of PE fit on outcomes focused on the distinction between supplementary fit, demands–abilities fit, and needs–supplies fit. However, other distinctions of the PE fit concept are relevant to the relationship between PE fit and outcomes. Referring to Fig. 7–1, the level of the environment has implications for the strength of the effects of PE fit. For instance, when the environment refers to the organization, as in studies of the congruence between personal and organizational values, the effects of fit should be strongest for outcomes that are also cast at the organizational level, such as organizational commitment (Rousseau, 1985). Value congruence with other individuals or social collectives, such as the supervisor or workgroup, should relate to commitment framed at the same environmental level, as represented by research that treats the supervisor and workgroup as the foci of commitment (Becker, 1992). The effects of PE fit on outcomes should also be strengthened when the person, the environment, and the outcome refer to the same content dimension. For example, we would expect needs–supplies fit regarding pay to have stronger effects on pay satisfaction than on satisfaction with other job facets or with the job as a whole (French et al., 1974). Thus, we expect the strongest effects of PE fit on outcomes when the outcome is commensurate with the person and environment and is at the same level as the environment.

## FUNCTIONAL FORMS RELATING PERSON–ENVIRONMENT FIT TO OUTCOMES

Thus far, our discussion of the effects of PE fit on outcomes has framed these effects in general terms. We now examine these effects in greater detail by considering their functional form. As noted earlier, much PE fit research is based on the assumption that fit is beneficial and that the effects of fit are the same regardless of the absolute levels of the person and environment or the direction of their difference. This assumption is reflected by the function in Fig. 7–2a, which depicts a two-dimensional relationship between PE fit and an outcome. The function shows that the outcome is maximized when the difference between the person and environment is zero and decreases symmetrically as the difference between the person and environment increases in either direction. By using the difference between the person and environment as a predictor, the function also implies that the absolute levels of the person and environment are irrelevant. For instance, the maximum value of the outcome in Fig. 7–2a is expected when the person and environment match, regardless of whether they are low, medium, or high in absolute terms.

The function in Fig. 7–2a oversimplifies the effects of PE fit in several respects. First, it reduces the inherently three-dimensional relationship between the person, the environment, and the outcome to two dimensions (Edwards, 1994). This point is illustrated by comparing Fig. 7–2a to Fig. 7–2b, which shows a three-dimensional surface relating the person and environment to the outcome. In Fig. 7–2b, the floor of the graph is bounded by the person and environment axes. The solid line running from the near corner to the far corner of the floor is the *fit line*, along which the person and environment are equal. The dashed line running from the left corner to the right corner is the *misfit line*, which captures varying degrees of deviation between the person and environment.[3] The

---

[3]Strictly speaking, any line running parallel to the misfit line reflects deviation between the person and environment. However, the misfit line in Fig. 7.2b encompasses more variation in misfit than any alternative line.

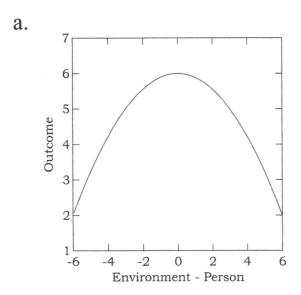

a.

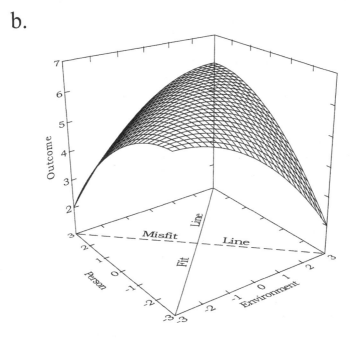

b.

FIGURE 7–2. Two-dimensional and three-dimensional conceptualizations of the effects of PE fit.

surface in Fig. 2b is algebraically equivalent to the function in Fig. 7–2a. However, the surface retains the person and environment as distinct constructs, which is a necessary precursor to conceptualizing the degree of fit between the person and environment. The three-dimensional conceptualization of PE fit in Fig. 7–2b can also capture a much wider range of hypotheses than the two-dimensional version in Fig. 7–2a, as we later demonstrate.

Second, the function in Fig. 7–2a represents one of many possible relationships between PE fit and the outcome. Consider the relationship between needs–supplies fit and satisfaction. When needs and supplies refer to dimensions such as pay, satisfaction is likely to increase not only as supplies increase toward needs but also as supplies exceed needs (Locke, 1976). This notion is reflected in conceptual discussions of PE fit (French et al., 1982; Naylor et al., 1980; Rice et al., 1985) and is consistent with research on need satisfaction (Porter & Lawler, 1968; Wanous & Lawler, 1972), which treats satisfaction as a function of the algebraic difference between needs and rewards. Other functions are conceptually plausible (French et al., 1982; Kulka, 1979; Naylor et al., 1980; Rice et al., 1985), but few have received attention in PE fit research.

Third, the function in Fig. 7–2a does not address variation in the outcome associated with the absolute levels of the person and environment. It stands to reason that the experience of PE fit should differ, depending on whether the person and environment constructs are high or low. To illustrate, for needs–supplies fit regarding job complexity, wanting and having a simple job is quite different from wanting and having a complex job. Likewise, the experience of demands–abilities fit is likely to differ, depending on whether demands and abilities correspond to a sixth-grade education or advanced graduate training. In similar fashion, congruence on the value of altruism between an employee and supervisor can have different implications, depending on whether both people consider altruism unimportant or highly important. By construction, the function in Fig. 7–2a is incapable of capturing variation in outcomes produced by the absolute levels of the person and environment.

In this section, we demonstrate an approach to developing hypotheses about the form of the relationship between the person, the environment, and the outcome. This approach focuses on the joint effects of the person and environment along the fit and misfit lines, as shown in Fig. 7–2b. Hypotheses along these lines can be combined to yield a predicted surface relating the person and environment to the outcome. We apply this approach to the effects of needs–supplies fit, demands–abilities fit, and supplementary fit, using outcomes that are prototypical for these forms of fit. As will be seen, the surfaces produced by this approach go far beyond the simplified surface corresponding to the function in Fig. 7–2a.

## Needs–Supplies Fit and Satisfaction

We first consider the effects of needs–supplies fit on satisfaction. For this illustration, we conceptualize the environment at the individual level and content dimensions at the facet level, as is common in needs–supplies fit research (Edwards, 1991). Along the misfit line, satisfaction should increase as supplies increase toward needs (Harrison, 1978). This argument draws from need fulfillment research, which indicates that, when supplies are insufficient to fulfill needs, people experience negative affect, which is manifested by decreased satisfaction (Dawis & Lofquist, 1984; Diener, 1984; Locke, 1969; Murray, 1938). This argument is consistent with the surfaces in Fig. 7–3, a, b, and c, each of which indicate that, along the misfit line, the outcome increases as the environment increases toward the person.

As supplies exceed needs, the effects on satisfaction are expected to vary, depending on the implications of excess supplies for other needs and for the same need at a later time. Satisfaction should decrease if excess supplies interfere with the fulfillment of needs on other dimensions, as when interaction with coworkers goes beyond the person's need for affiliation and interferes with his or her need for privacy (Eidelson, 1980; French et al., 1974; Harrison, 1978). Satisfaction should also decrease if excess amounts of a supply in the present reduce the availability of that supply in the future, as when an employee receives excess praise from a supervisor in the present and is later bypassed as the supervisor directs his or her approval to other subordinates. These two mechanisms have been labeled *interference* and *depletion*, respectively (Edwards, 1996), and result in a parabolic relationship along the misfit line, as indicated by the surface in Fig. 7–3a.

Two alternative mechanisms produce a positive relationship between excess supplies and satisfaction, corresponding to the surface in Fig. 7–3b. Specifically, excess supplies increase satisfaction when the excess can be used to fulfill other needs, as when autonomy supplies that exceed the person's need for control (Burger & Cooper, 1979) are used to initiate changes at work that fulfill needs on other dimensions. Excess supplies also increase satisfaction when supplies can be saved for later use, as when income that exceeds current economic needs is set aside for future economic needs. These mechanisms are labeled *carryover* and *conservation*, respectively (Edwards, 1996). If excess supplies are not subject to interference, depletion, carryover, or conservation, then an asymptotic relationship is expected along the misfit line, as depicted by the surface in Fig. 7–3c.

Along the fit line, we expect that satisfaction will generally be higher when needs and supplies are both high than when both are low. High needs represent ambitious standards held by the person, and high supplies

a.

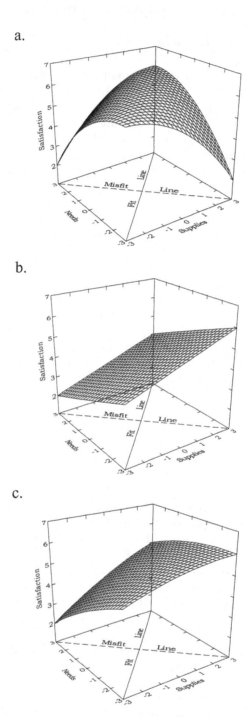

b.

c.

FIGURE 7–3.  Relationships between needs–supplies misfit and satisfaction.

signify that these standards have been met. Fulfilling high standards can itself serve as a supply for needs concerning growth and self-actualization (Alderfer, 1972; Maslow, 1954; Rokeach, 1973). In addition, high needs and supplies on a particular dimension can relate to high needs and supplies on other dimensions. For instance, jobs that are high in complexity often bring supplies such as pay, status, and recognition, and people who want complex jobs are likely to want high levels of pay, status, and recognition (Harrison, 1978). These relationships compound the benefits of high needs and supplies, further contributing to the fulfillment of needs for growth and self-actualization. If satisfaction is higher when needs and supplies are both high than when both are low, the surface relating needs and supplies to satisfaction will be positively sloped along the fit line, yielding the surfaces in Fig. 7–4a, b, and c.

## Demands–Abilities Fit and Performance

Next, we examine the effects of demands–abilities fit on performance. For illustration, we frame demands at the job level and content dimensions at the domain level, as represented by dimensions such as training, education, experience, and work load. In addition, we assume the person is motivated to perform, which is necessary for demands–abilities fit to influence performance (Porter & Lawler, 1968). Along the misfit line, we expect performance to increase as abilities increase toward demands, drawing from the premise that performance is hampered when abilities are insufficient for job requirements (Dawis & Lofquist, 1984; Muchinsky & Monahan, 1987; Waldman & Spangler, 1989; Wanous, 1992) and improves as this deficiency is resolved. This reasoning is depicted by the surfaces in Fig. 7–5a, b, and c, each of which shows that performance declines as abilities fall short of demands.

The effects of excess abilities on performance can be deduced using the principles of interference, depletion, carryover, and conservation. Interference occurs when excess abilities regarding one demand reduce abilities pertaining to other demands, as when developing a specific ability beyond the level required by the job leaves other abilities underdeveloped. Depletion results when excess ability in the present reduces the level of ability in the future, as when abilities that exceed demands are underutilized and atrophy, making it difficult to meet future demands (Baldwin & Ford, 1988). Interference and depletion produce a parabolic relationship along the misfit line, such that performance decreases as abilities deviate from demands in either direction. This relationship corresponds to the surface in Fig. 7–5a.

Carryover indicates that excess abilities can be applied to demands on other dimensions. For instance, developing technical skills beyond those required for a particular task could yield expertise that transfers to other tasks (Baldwin & Ford, 1988). Conservation applies to abilities that repre-

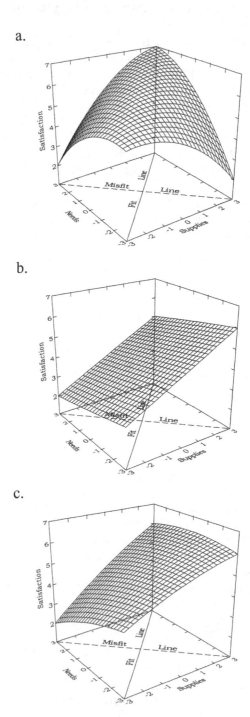

FIGURE 7–4. Relationships between needs–supplies misfit and satisfaction with positive slope along the fit line.

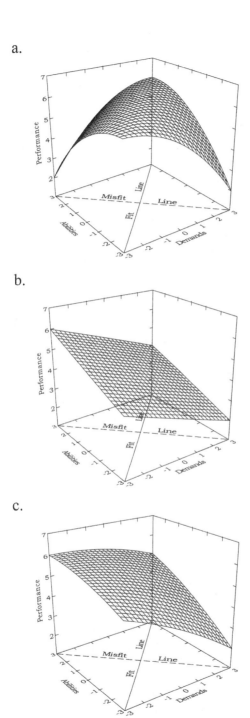

a.

b.

c.

FIGURE 7–5.   Relationships between demands–abilities misfit and performance.

sent personal resources, such as time and energy, for which excess levels in the present can be reserved for future demands. Carryover and conservation would result in a monotonic relationship along the misfit line, where performance increases as abilities increase toward demands and continues to increase as abilities exceed demands. This relationship is shown in Fig. 7–5b. If abilities are not prone to interference, depletion, carryover, or conservation, then performance would level off as abilities exceed demands and produce an asymptotic relationship along the misfit line, as in Fig. 7–5c.

Along the fit line, we expect that performance will be higher when demands and abilities are both high than when both are low, for two reasons. First, high demands coupled with high abilities means that the person is confronted with difficult performance requirements and is equipped to meet them. In contrast, low demands along with low abilities signify that the person faces easy performance requirements and can fulfill them. Assuming motivation is the same in both cases, performance would be higher in the former case than in the latter case, given that a higher performance standard is being met. Second, the combination of high demands and high abilities characterizes situations in which performance goals are difficult but attainable, which can intensify motivation and further enhance performance (Locke & Latham, 1991). These mechanisms lead to a positive relationship with performance along the demands–abilities fit line, as shown by the surfaces in Fig. 7–6 a, b, and c.

## Supplementary Fit and Affective Commitment

We now turn to the effects of supplementary fit on commitment. We discuss these effects in terms of value congruence and affective commitment, which are commonly studied in research on supplementary fit (Verquer et al., 2003). As noted earlier, affective commitment depends on the degree to which work experiences fulfill the needs of the person (Meyer & Herscovitch, 2001). Hence, affective commitment should be influenced by value congruence to the extent that value congruence leads to need fulfillment. We apply this principle as we consider the effects of value congruence on affective commitment along the fit and misfit lines.

In general, we expect a curvilinear relationship between affective commitment and value congruence along the misfit line, such that affective commitment is maximized when personal and organizational values are equal. Value congruence signifies interpersonal similarity on dimensions that describe the identity of the person and organization. Because value congruence signifies interpersonal similarity, it can fulfill needs for affiliation, belonging, closure, and clarity and can also promote coordination and communication that facilitate job performance and bring desired

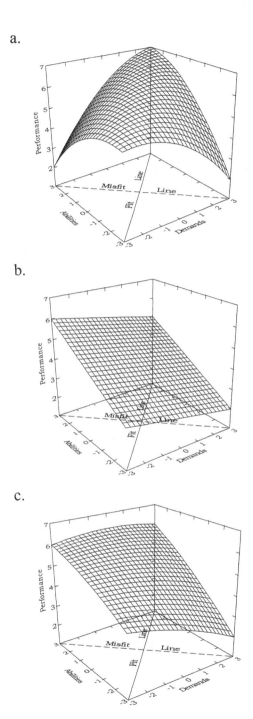

FIGURE 7–6.   Relationships between demands–abilities misfit and performance with positive slope along the fit line.

rewards. Given that interpersonal similarity decreases symmetrically as personal and organizational values deviate from one another in either direction, it follows that outcomes of value congruence that operate through interpersonal similarity will also decrease symmetrically. This reasoning leads to the surface in Fig. 7–7a.

The symmetric effects of value congruence on affective commitment shown in Fig. 7–7a can be altered to the extent that personal and organizational values influence the needs and supplies of the person and organization, respectively (Cable & Edwards, 2004). These effects follow from the premise that the values of the person should influence what the person wants (Hogan, 1991), and the values of the organization should affect the rewards supplied by the organization (Schein, 1992). The effects of personal and organizational values on needs and supplies should modify the shape of surface along the misfit line in the region where the values of the organization exceed those of the person. If organizational values are related to supplies that are prone to interference or depletion, then the decrease in affective commitment would be augmented, as in Fig. 7–7b. Alternately, if organizational values correspond to supplies that produce carryover or conservation, then the decrease in affective commitment would be dampened, as in Fig. 7–7c. These effects follow from the logic used to derive the effects of needs–supplies fit on satisfaction along the misfit line where supplies exceed needs.

The symmetric effects of value congruence can also be modified when personal and organizational values affect abilities and demands, respectively. These effects are based on the assumption that people develop abilities that enable them to pursue what they value (Noe & Wilk, 1993; Tharenou, 2003) and that organizations place demands on employees that reflect what the organization considers important (O'Reilly & Chatman, 1996; Schein, 1992). The fit between demands and abilities should influence performance, which in turn relates to intrinsic and extrinsic rewards that can fulfill the needs of the person, thereby enhancing affective commitment. However, as noted earlier, the effects of demands–abilities fit on performance along the misfit line depends on the consequences of excess abilities. If abilities are subject to interference or depletion, then excess abilities should reduce performance. If abilities such as these are linked to personal values, then performance would be hindered when personal values exceed organizational values, which in turn would reduce supplies that fulfill the person's needs, thereby decreasing affective commitment. This reasoning is reflected in Fig. 7–7d. Conversely, if abilities prone to carryover or conservation are linked to personal values, then performance would be enhanced when personal values are greater than organizational values. This would in turn lead to increased affective commitment, as shown in Fig. 7–7e. These effects draw from the reasoning associated with the effects of demands–abilities fit on performance along the misfit line when abilities exceed demands.

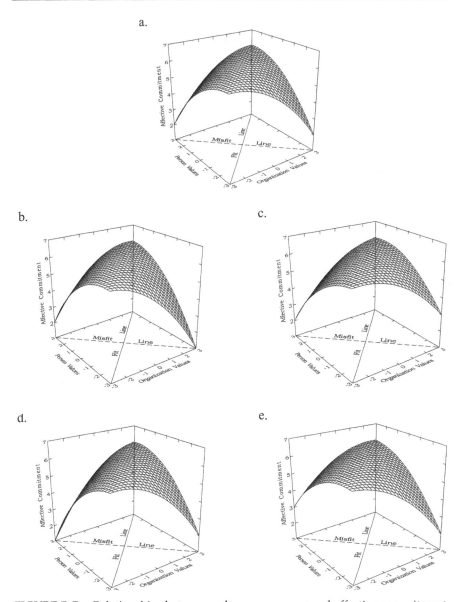

FIGURE 7–7. Relationships between values congruence and affective commitment.

Finally, along the fit line, we posit that affective commitment will be higher when personal and organizational values are both high than when both are low, for two reasons. First, if personal values are related to needs and abilities and, analogously, organizational values are related to supplies and demands, then high levels of personal and organizational values imply high levels of needs and supplies and high levels of demands and abilities. As argued earlier, high levels of needs and supplies enhance satisfaction, and high levels of demands and abilities increase performance, which in turn brings intrinsic and extrinsic rewards. Both of these mechanisms should strengthen affective commitment, for reasons explained earlier. Second, the effects of value congruence on affective commitment should be stronger when the person considers the value dimension important. For example, if a person highly values altruism, then congruence with an organization that values altruism will be important to the person, given that the strength of a value signifies its importance to the person (Rokeach, 1973). Importance should moderate the effects of value congruence on affective commitment, given that affective commitment is influenced by need fulfillment, the effects of which are moderated by need importance (French et al., 1982; Kristof, 1996; Locke, 1976; Mobley & Locke, 1970). These mechanisms indicate a positive slope along the fit line, transforming the surfaces in Fig. 7–7 into those in Fig. 7–8.

### Summary and Implications

The preceding discussion has demonstrated an approach to developing hypotheses along the fit and misfit lines that yield surfaces relating the person and environment to outcomes. This approach underscores the value of conceptualizing the effects of PE fit in three dimensions, which maintains the conceptual distinctions between person and environment constructs and captures the inherent complexity of their joint effects on outcomes. Some researchers have discussed relationships between PE fit and outcomes that go beyond the simplified function in Fig. 7–2a (French et al., 1982; Kulka, 1979; Locke, 1976; Naylor et al., 1980; Rice et al., 1985), but these relationships have been presented as possibilities to be explored. In contrast, the approach demonstrated here applies conceptual logic that leads to hypothesized surfaces to be formally tested. Moreover, in previous discussions of PE fit relationships, the effects of the absolute levels of person and environment constructs, as reflected by variation along the fit line, have rarely been considered. The approach demonstrated here can be extended to other person, environment, and outcome constructs, thereby enhancing the rigor and complexity of PE fit research.

### CONCLUSION

In this chapter, we have presented an integrative conceptualization of the PE fit concept, drawn from outcome theories to explain the effects of PE fit, and demonstrated an approach to conceptualizing the form of the joint effects of the person and environment on outcomes. Our goal was to provide a foundation for probing basic assumptions that underlie PE fit research, with the intent of advancing this important area of inquiry. Our discussion indicates that PE fit is not inherently beneficial and that the

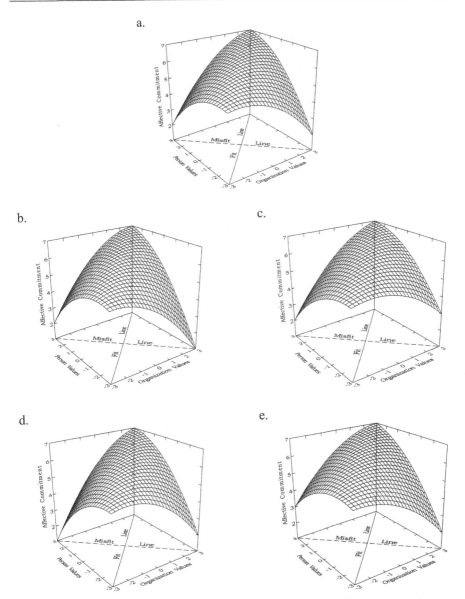

FIGURE 7–8. Relationships between values congruence and affective commitment with positive slope along the fit line.

effects of PE fit vary across person, environment, and outcome constructs. We also explained how the effects of PE fit depend on the absolute levels of the person and environment and the direction of their difference. We hope the conceptual issues we have raised will help PE fit researchers address the challenge of conceptualizing the effects of PE fit on outcomes.

At the same time, the literature relevant to the effects of PE fit is vast, and we have merely scratched the surface of conceptual issues that are deep and complex. Thus, rather than providing answers that are definitive and complete, we have raised questions and assumptions that merit scrutiny and demonstrated how they might be addressed, with the ultimate objective of enhancing the theoretical and conceptual rigor of PE fit research.

## ACKNOWLEDGMENT

We thank Daniel M. Cable for his helpful comments during the development of this chapter.

## REFERENCES

Adkins, C. L., Ravlin, E. C., & Meglino, B. M. (1996). Value congruence between co-workers and its relationship to work outcomes. *Group & Organization Management, 21,* 439–460.

Adkins, C. L., Russell, C. J., & Werbel, J. D. (1994). Judgments of fit in the selection process: The role of work value congruence. *Personnel Psychology, 47,* 605–623.

Alderfer, C. P. (1972). *Existence, relatedness, and growth: Human needs in organizational settings.* New York: Free Press.

Allen, N. J., & Meyer, J. P. (1996). Affective, continuance, and normative commitment to the organization: An examination of construct validity. *Journal of Vocational Behavior, 49,* 252–276.

Alutto, J. A., & Acito, F. (1974). Decisional participation and sources of job satisfaction: A study of manufacturing personnel. *Academy of Management Journal, 17,* 160–167.

Ancona, D. G., & Caldwell, D. F. (1992). Bridging the boundary: External activity and performance in organizational teams. *Administrative Science Quarterly, 37,* 634–665.

Antonioni, D., & Park, H. (2001). The effects of personality similarity on peer ratings of contextual work behaviors. *Personnel Psychology, 54,* 331–360.

Ashkanasy, N. M., & O'Connor, C. (1997). Value congruence in leader–member exchange. *Journal of Social Psychology, 137,* 647–662.

Assouline, M., & Meir, E. I. (1987). Meta-analysis of the relationship between congruence and well-being measures. *Journal of Vocational Behavior, 31,* 319–332.

Baldwin, T. T., & Ford, J. K. (1988). Transfer of training: A review and directions for future research. *Personnel Psychology, 41,* 63–105.

Barrett, R. S. (1995). Employee selection with the performance priority survey. *Personnel Psychology, 48,* 653–662.

Baum, A., & Posluszny, D. M. (1999). Health psychology: Mapping biobehavioral contributions to health and illness. *Annual Review of Psychology, 50,* 137–163.

Baumeister, R. F., & Leary, M. R. (1995). The need to belong: Desire for interpersonal attachments as a fundamental human motivation. *Psychological Bulletin, 117,* 497–529.

Becker, H. S. (1960). Notes on the concept of commitment. *American Journal of Sociology, 66,* 32–40.

Becker, T. E. (1992). Foci and bases of commitment: Are they distinctions worth making? *Academy of Management Journal, 35*, 232–244.

Beehr, T. A. (1998). An organizational psychology meta-model of occupational stress. In C. L. Cooper (Ed.), *Theories of organizational stress* (pp. 6–27). Oxford, England: Oxford University Press.

Beehr, T. A., Walsh, J. T., & Taber, T. D. (1976). Relationships of stress to individually and organizationally valued states: Higher-order needs as a moderator. *Journal of Applied Psychology, 61*, 41–47.

Betz, E. (1969). Need-reinforcer correspondence as a predictor of job satisfaction *Personnel and Guidance Journal, 47*, 878–883.

Blau, G. (1987). Using a person–environment fit model to predict job involvement and organizational commitment. *Journal of Vocational Behavior, 30*, 240–257.

Bolino, M. C., & Feldman, D. C. (2000). The antecedents and consequences of underemployment among expatriates. *Journal of Organizational Behavior, 21*, 889–911.

Borman, W. C., & Motowidlo, S. J. (1993). Expanding the criterion domain to include elements of contextual performance. In N. Schmitt & W. C. Borman (Eds.), *Personnel selection in organizations* (pp. 71–98). San Francisco: Jossey-Bass.

Bretz, R. D., & Judge, T. A. (1994). Person–organization fit and the theory of work adjustment: Implications for satisfaction, tenure, and career success. *Journal of Vocational Behavior, 44*, 32–54.

Brief, A. P. (1998). *Attitudes in and around organizations.* Thousand Oaks, CA: Sage.

Burch, G. S. J., & Anderson, N. (2004). Measuring person-team fit: Development and validation of the team selection inventory. *Journal of Managerial Psychology, 19*, 406–426.

Burger, J. M., & Cooper, H. M. (1979). The desirability of control. *Motivation and Emotion, 3*, 381–393.

Byrne, D. (1971). *The attraction paradigm.* New York: Academic Press.

Cable, D. M., & DeRue, D. S. (2002). The convergent and discriminant validity of subjective fit perceptions. *Journal of Applied Psychology, 87*, 875–884.

Cable, D. M., & Edwards, J. R. (2004). Complementary and supplementary fit: A theoretical and empirical integration. *Journal of Applied Psychology, 89*, 822–834.

Cable, D. M., & Judge, T. A. (1996). Person–organization fit, job choice decisions, and organizational entry. *Organizational Behavior & Human Decision Processes, 67*, 294–311.

Cable, D. M., & Parsons, C. K. (2001). Socialization tactics and person-organization fit. *Personnel Psychology, 54*, 1–24.

Caldwell, D. F., & O'Reilly, C. A. (1990). Measuring person–job fit with a profile comparison process. *Journal of Applied Psychology, 75*, 648–657.

Chan, D. (1996). Cognitive misfit of problem-solving style at work: A facet of person-organization fit. *Organizational Behavior and Human Decision Processes, 68*, 194–207.

Chatman, J. A. (1989). Improving interactional organizational research: A model of person-organization fit [Special Issue: Theory development forum.] *Academy of Management Review, 14*, 333–349.

Chatman, J. A. (1991). Matching people and organizations: Selection and socialization in public accounting firms. *Administrative Science Quarterly, 36*, 459–484.

Chatman, J. A., Caldwell, D. F., & O'Reilly, C. A. (1999). Managerial personality and performance: A semi-idiographic approach. *Journal of Research in Personality, 33,* 514–545.

Chatman, J. A., Polzer, J. T., Barsade, S. G., & Neale, M. A. (1998). Being different yet feeling similar: The influence of demographic composition and organizational culture on work processes and outcomes. *Administrative Science Quarterly, 43,* 749–780.

Chattopadhyay, P. (1999). Beyond direct and symmetrical effects: The influence of demographic dissimilarity on organizational citizenship behavior. *Academy of Management Journal, 42,* 273–287.

Cherrington, D. J., & England, J. L. (1980). The desire for an enriched job as a moderator of the enrichment-satisfaction relationship. *Organizational Behavior and Human Performance, 25,* 139–159.

Chisholm, R. F., Kasl, S. V., & Eskenazl, B. (1983). The nature and predictors of job related tension in a crisis situation: Reactions of nuclear workers to the Three Mile Island accident. *Academy of Management Journal, 26,* 385–405.

Choi, J. N. (2004). Person–environment fit and creative behavior: Differential impacts of supplies–values and demands–abilities versions of fit. *Human Relations, 57,* 531–552.

Christiansen, N., Villanova, P., & Mikulay, S. (1997). Political influence compatibility: Fitting the person to the climate. *Journal of Organizational Behavior, 18,* 709–730.

Coburn, D. (1975). Job-worker incongruence: Consequences for health. *Journal of Health and Social Behavior, 16,* 198–212.

Cohen, A. (2003). *Multiple commitments in the workplace: An integrative approach.* Mahwah, NJ: Lawrence Erlbaum Associates.

Cohen, S., & McKay, G. (1984). Social support, stress, and the buffering hypothesis: A theoretical analysis. In A. Baum, J. E. Singer, & S. E. Taylor (Eds.), *Handbook of psychology and health* (Vol. 4, pp. 253–267). Hillsdale, NJ: Lawrence Erlbaum Associates.

Cohen, S., & Wills, T. A. (1985). Stress, social support, and the buffering hypothesis. *Psychological Bulletin, 98,* 310–357.

Conway, T. L., Vickers, R. R., & French, J. R. (1992). An application of person–environment fit theory: Perceived versus desired control. *Journal of Social Issues, 48,* 95–107.

Cook, J., & Wall, T. (1980). New work attitude measures of trust, organizational commitment and personal need non-fulfillment. *Journal of Occupational Psychology, 53,* 39–52.

Cooper, C. L., & Marshall, J. (1976). Occupational sources of stress: a review of the literature relating to coronary heart disease and mental ill health. *Journal of Occupational Psychology, 49,* 11–28.

Costa, P. T., Jr., McCrae, R. R., & Kay, G. G. (1995). Persons, places and personality: Career assessment using the Revised NEO Personality Inventory. *Journal of Career Assessment, 3,* 123–139.

Coyne, J. C., & Downey, G. (1991). Social factors and psychopathology: Stress, social support, and coping processes. *Annual Review of Psychology, 42,* 401–425.

Cranny, C. J., Smith, P. C., & Stone, E. F. (1992). *Job satisfaction: How people feel about their jobs, and how it affects their performance.* New York: Lexington.

Crowne, D. P., & Marlowe, D. (1964). *The approval motive: Studies in evaluative dependence.* New York: Wiley.

Cummings, T. G., & Cooper, C. L. (1979). A cybernetic framework for studying occupational stress. *Human Relations, 32,* 395–418.

Danna, K., & Griffin, R. W. (1999). Health and well-being in the workplace: A review and synthesis of the literature. *Journal of Management, 25,* 357–384.

Dawis, R. V., & Lofquist, L. H. (1984). *A psychological theory of work adjustment.* Minneapolis, MN: University of Minnesota Press.

Day, D. V., & Bedeian, A. G. (1995). Personality similarity and work-related outcomes among African-American nursing personnel: A test of the supplementary model of person-environment congruence. *Journal of Vocational Behavior, 46,* 55–70.

Diener, E. (1984). Subjective well-being. *Psychological Bulletin, 95,* 542–575.

Diener, E., & Lucas, R. E. (2000). Explaining differences in societal levels of happiness: Relative standards, need fulfillment, culture and evaluation theory. *Journal of Happiness Studies, 1,* 41–78.

Edwards, J. R. (1991). Person–job fit: A conceptual integration, literature review, and methodological critique. In C. L. Cooper & I. T. Robertson (Eds.), *International review of industrial and organizational psychology* (Vol. 6, pp. 283–357). New York: Wiley.

Edwards, J. R. (1992). A cybernetic theory of stress, coping, and well-being in organizations. *Academy of Management Review, 17,* 238–274.

Edwards, J. R. (1996). An examination of competing versions of the person-environment fit approach to stress. *Academy of Management Journal, 39,* 292–339.

Edwards, J. R., & Bagozzi, R. P. (2000). On the nature and direction of the relationship between constructs and measures. *Psychological Methods, 5,* 155–174.

Edwards, J. R., Caplan, R. D., & Harrison, R. V. (1998). Person–environment fit theory: Conceptual foundations, empirical evidence, and directions for future research. In C. L. Cooper (Ed.), *Theories of organizational stress* (pp. 28–67). Oxford, England: Oxford University Press.

Edwards, J. R., & Harrison, R. V. (1993). Job demands and worker health: Three-dimensional reexamination of the relationship between person–environment fit and strain. *Journal of Applied Psychology, 78,* 628–648.

Edwards, J. R., & Rothbard, N. P. (1999). Work and family stress and well-being: An examination of person–environment fit in the work and family domains. *Organizational Behavior and Human Decision Processes, 77,* 85–129.

Eidelson, R. J. (1980). Interpersonal satisfaction and level of involvement: A curvilinear relationship. *Journal of Personality and Social Psychology, 39,* 460–470.

Elsass, P. M., & Veiga, J. F. (1997). Job control and job strain: A test of three models. *Journal of Occupational Health Psychology, 2,* 195–211.

Engle, E. M., & Lord, R. G. (1997). Implicit theories, self-schemas, and leader-member exchange. *Academy of Management Journal, 40,* 988–1010.

Enz, C. A. (1988). The role of value congruity in intraorganizational power. *Administrative Science Quarterly, 33,* 284–304.

Eulberg, J. R., Weekley, J. A., & Bhagat, R. S. (1988). Models of stress in organizational research: A metatheoretical perspective. *Human Relations, 41,* 331–350.

Feather, N. T. (1991). Human values, global self-esteem, and belief in a just world. *Journal of Personality, 59,* 83–107.

Feldman, D. C. (1976). A contingency theory of socialization. *Administrative Science Quarterly, 21,* 433–452.

Ferris, G. R., Youngblood, S. A., & Yates, V. L. (1985). Personality, training performance, and withdrawal: A test of the person–group fit hypothesis for organizational newcomers. *Journal of Vocational Behavior, 27,* 377–388.

Finegan, J. E. (2000). The impact of person and organizational values on organizational commitment. *Journal of Occupational and Organizational Psychology, 73,* 149–169.

French, J. R. P., Jr., Caplan, R. D., & Harrison, R. V. (1982). *The mechanisms of job stress and strain.* London: Wiley.

French, J. R. P., Jr., Rodgers, W., & Cobb, S. (1974). Adjustment as person–environment fit. In G. Coelho, D. Hamburg, & J. Adams (Eds.), *Coping and adaptation* (pp. 316–333). New York: Basic Books.

Ganster, D. C., & Schaubroeck, J. (1991). Work stress and employee health. *Journal of Management, 17,* 235–271.

Graf, R. G., & Riddell, J. C. (1972). Helping behavior as a function of interpersonal perception. *Journal of Social Psychology, 86,* 227–231.

Greenberg, J. (2002). Time urgency and job performance: Field evidence of an interactionist perspective. *Journal of Applied Social Psychology, 32,* 1964–1973.

Greenhaus, J. H., Seidel, C., & Marinis, M. (1983). The impact of expectations and values on job attitudes. *Organizational Behavior and Human Performance, 31,* 394–417.

Hall, D. T., Schneider, B., & Nygren, H. T. (1970). Personal factors in organizational identification. *Administrative Science Quarterly, 15,* 176–190.

Harrison, R. V. (1978). Person–environment fit and job stress. In C. L. Cooper & R. Payne (Eds.), *Stress at work* (pp. 175–205). New York: Wiley.

Harrison, R. V. (1985). The person–environment fit model and the study of job stress. In T. A. Beehr & R. S. Bhagat (Eds.), *Human stress and cognition in organizations* (pp. 23–55). New York: Wiley.

Higgins, C. A., & Judge, T. A. (2004). The effect of applicant influence tactics on recruiter perceptions of fit and hiring recommendations: A field study. *Journal of Applied Psychology, 89,* 622–632.

Hildebrand, J. O., & Walsh, W. B. (1988). Person–environment congruence and perceived work climate. *Journal of Career Development, 15,* 121–133.

Hobfoll, S. E. (1989). Conservation of resources: A new attempt at conceptualizing stress. *American Psychologist, 44,* 513–524..

Hoeglund, T. J., & Hansen, J. I. C. (1999). Holland-style measures of congruence: Are complex indices more effective predictors of satisfaction? *Journal of Vocational Behavior, 54,* 471–482.

Hogan, R. T. (1991). Personality and personality measurement. In L. M. Hough & M. D. Dunnette (Eds.), *Handbook of industrial and organizational psychology,* (2nd ed., Vol. 2, pp. 873–919). Palo Alto, CA: Consulting Psychologists Press.

Holland, J. L. (1979). *Professional manual for the self-directed search.* Palo Alto, CA: Consulting Psychologists Press.

Holland, J. L. (1997). *Making vocational choices: A theory of vocational personalities and work environments* (3rd. ed.). Lutz, FL: Psychological Assessment Resources.

Hollenbeck, J. R. (1989). Control theory and the perception of work environments: The effects of focus of attention on affective and behavioral reactions to work. *Organizational Behavior and Human Decision Process, 43,* 406–430.

Hollenbeck, J. R. (2000). A structural approach to external and internal person-team fit. *Applied Psychology: An International Review, 49,* 534–549.

Hollenbeck, J. R., Moon, H., Ellis, A. P. J., West, B. J., Ilgen, D. R., Sheppard, L., Porter, C. O. L. H., & Wagner, J. A. (2002). Structural contingency theory and individual differences: Examination of external and internal person-team fit. *Journal of Applied Psychology, 87,* 599–606.

Hornsey, M. J., & Jetten, J. (2004). The individual within the group: Balancing the need to belong with the need to be different. *Personality and Social Psychology Review, 8,* 248–264.

House, J. S. (1981). *Work, stress, and social support.* Reading, MA: Addison-Wesley.

Hunter, J. E. (1983). A causal analysis of cognitive ability, job knowledge, job performance, and supervisory ratings. In F. Landy, S. Zedeck, & J. Cleveland (Eds.), *Performance measurement and theory* (pp. 257–266). Hillsdale, NJ: Lawrence Erlbaum Associates.

Ivancevich, J. M., & Donnelly, J. H. (1974). A study of role clarity and need for clarity for three occupational groups. *Academy of Management Journal, 17,* 28–36.

Ivancevich, J. M., & Matteson, M. T. (1982). Occupational stress, satisfaction, physical well-being, and coping: A study of homemakers. *Psychological Reports, 50,* 995–1005.

Jamal, M. (1984). Job stress and job performance controversy: An empirical assessment. *Organizational Behavior and Human Performance, 33,* 1–21.

Jauch, L. R., Osborn, R. N., & Terpening, W. D. (1980). Goal congruence and employee orientation: The substitution effect. *Academy of Management Journal, 23,* 544–550.

Johnson, G. J., & Johnson W. R. (1996). Perceived overqualification and psychological well-being. *Journal of Social Psychology, 136,* 435–445.

Judge, T. A., & Bretz, R. D., Jr. (1992). Effects of work values on job choice decisions. *Journal of Applied Psychology, 77,* 261–271.

Judge, T. A., & Cable, D. M. (1997). Applicant personality, organizational culture, and organizational attraction. *Personnel Psychology, 50,* 359–394.

Kahn, R. L., & Byosiere, D. (1992). Stress in organizations. In M. D. Dunnette & L. M. Hough (Eds.), *Handbook of industrial and organizational psychology* (2nd ed., Vol. 3, pp. 571–650). Palo Alto, CA: Consulting Psychologists Press.

Kahn, R. L., & Quinn, R. P. (1970). Role stress: A framework for analysis. In A. McLean (Ed.), *Occupational mental health* (pp. 50–115). New York: Rand McNally.

Kalliath, T. J., Bluedorn, A. C., & Strube, M. J. (1999). A test of value congruence effects. *Journal of Organizational Behavior, 20,* 1175–1198.

Karylowski, J. (1976). Self-esteem, similarity, liking and helping. *Personality and Social Psychology Bulletin, 2,* 71–74.

Katz, D., & Kahn, R. (1978). *The social psychology of organizations* (2nd ed., pp. 18–68). New York: Wiley.

Katzell, R. A. (1964). Personal values, job satisfaction, and job behavior. In H. Borow (Ed.), *Man in a world at work* (pp. 341–363). Boston: Houghton Mifflin.

Kluckhohn, C. (1951). Values and value orientations in the theory of action. In T. Parsons & E. Shils (Eds.), *Toward a general theory of action* (pp. 388–433). Cambridge, MA: Harvard University Press.

Koestner, R., & McClelland, D. C. (1992). The affiliation motive. In J. W. Atkinson & C. P. Smith (Eds.), *Motivation and personality: Handbook of thematic content analysis* (pp. 205–210). New York: Cambridge University Press.

Kristof, A. L. (1996). Person–organization fit: An integrative review of its conceptualizations, measurement, and implications. *Personnel Psychology, 49,* 1–49.

Kristof-Brown, A. L. (2000). Perceived applicant fit: Distinguishing between recruiters' perceptions of person-job and person-organization fit. *Personnel Psychology, 53,* 643–671.

Kristof-Brown, A. L., Barrick, M. R., & Franke, M. (2002). Applicant impression management: Dispositional influences and consequences for recruiter perceptions of fit and similarity. *Journal of Management, 28,* 27–46.

Kristof-Brown, A. L., Jansen, K. J., & Colbert, A. E. (2002). A policy-capturing study of the simultaneous effects of fit with jobs, groups, and organizations. *Journal of Applied Psychology, 87,* 985–993.

Kristof-Brown, A. L., & Stevens, C. K. (2001). Goal congruence in project teams: Does the fit between members' personal mastery and performance goals matter? *Journal of Applied Psychology, 86,* 1083–1095.

Kuhn, T. S. (1996). *The structure of scientific revolutions* (3rd ed.). Chicago: University of Chicago Press.

Kulik, C. T., Oldham, G. R., & Hackman, J. R. (1987). Work design as an approach to person-environment fit. *Journal of Vocational Behavior, 31,* 278–296.

Kulka, R. A. (1979). Interaction as person-environment fit. In L. R. Kahle (Ed.), *New directions for methodology of behavioral science* (pp. 55–71). San Francisco: Jossey-Bass.

Lauver, K. J., & Kristof Brown, A. (2001). Distinguishing between employees' perceptions of person–job and person–organization fit. *Journal of Vocational Behavior, 59,* 454–470.

Lawler, E. E. (1973). *Motivation in work organizations.* Monterey, CA: Brooks/Cole.

Lawler, E. E., & Hall, D. T. (1970). Relationship of job characteristics to job involvement, satisfaction, and intrinsic motivation. *Journal of Applied Psychology, 54,* 305–312.

Lazarus, R. S. (1966). *Psychological stress and the coping process.* New York: McGraw-Hill.

Lazarus, R. S. (1991). *Emotion and adaptation.* New York: Oxford University Press.

Lazarus, R. S., & Folkman, S. (1984). *Stress, appraisal, and coping.* New York: Springer.

Livingstone, L. P., Nelson, D. L., & Barr, S. H. (1997). Person–environment fit and creativity: An examination of supply-value and demand-ability versions of fit. *Journal of Management, 23,* 119–146.

Locke, E. A. (1969). What is job satisfaction? *Organizational Behavior & Human Decision Processes, 4,* 309–336.

Locke, E. A. (1976). The nature and causes of job satisfaction. In M. Dunnette (Ed.), *Handbook of industrial and organizational psychology* (pp. 1297–1350). Chicago: Rand McNally.

Locke, E. A., & Latham, G. P. (1990). *A theory of goal setting and task performance.* Englewood Cliffs, NJ: Prentice Hall.

Lovelace, K., & Rosen, B. (1996). Differences in achieving person–organization fit among diverse groups of managers. *Journal of Management, 22,* 703–722.

Lyons, T. (1971). Role clarity, need for clarity, satisfaction, tension, and withdrawal. *Organizational Behavior and Human Performance, 6,* 99–110.

March, J. G., & Simon, H. A. (1958). *Organizations.* New York: Wiley.

Martin, T. N., & Schermerhorn, J. R., Jr. (1983). Work and nonwork influences on health: A research agenda using inability to leave as a critical variable. *Academy of Management Review, 8,* 650–659.

Maslow, A. H. (1954). *Motivation and personality*. New York: Harper.

Mathieu, J., & Zajac, D. (1990). A review and meta-analysis of the antecedents, correlates and consequences of organizational commitment. *Psychological Bulletin, 108*, 171–194.

McCain, B. E., O'Reilly, C. A., & Pfeffer, J. (1983). The effects of departmental demography on turnover: The case of a university. *Academy of Management Journal, 26*, 626–641.

McGrath, J. E. (1970). A conceptual formulation for research on stress. In J. E. McGrath (Ed.), *Social and psychological factors in stress* (pp. 10–21). New York: Holt, Rinehart, and Winston.

McGrath, J. E. (1976). Stress and behavior in organizations. In M. Dunnette (Ed.), *Handbook of industrial and organizational psychology.* (pp. 1351–1395). Chicago: Rand McNally.

Meglino, B. M., Ravlin, E. C., & Adkins, C. L. (1989). A work values approach to corporate culture: A field test of the value congruence process and its relationship to individual outcomes. *Journal of Applied Psychology, 74*, 424–432.

Meglino, B. M., Ravlin, E. C., & Adkins, C. L. (1992). The measurement of work value congruence: A field study comparison. *Journal of Management, 18*, 33–43

Meyer, J. P., & Allen, N. J. (1991). A three-component conceptualization of organizational commitment. *Human Resource Management Review, 1*, 61–89.

Meyer, J., Allen, N., & Smith, C. (1993). Commitment to organizations and occupations: extension and test of a three-component conceptualization. *Journal of Applied Psychology, 78*, 538–551.

Meyer, J. P., & Herscovitch, L. (2001). Commitment in the workplace: Toward a general model. *Human Resource Management Review, 11*, 299–326.

Mitchell, T. R., Holtom, B. C., Lee, T. W., Sablynski, C. J., & Erez, M. (2001). Why people stay: Using job embeddedness to predict voluntary turnover. *Academy of Management Journal, 44*, 1102–1121.

Mobley, W. H., & Locke, E. A. (1970). The relationship of value importance to satisfaction. *Organizational Behavior and Human Performance, 5*, 463–483.

Morrison, E. W. (1994). Role definitions and organizational citizenship behavior: The importance of the employee's perspective. *Academy of Management Journal, 37*, 1543–1567.

Morrow, P. C. (1993). *The theory and measurement of work commitment*. Greenwich, CT: JAI Press.

Motowidlo, S. J. (1996). Orientation toward the job and organization. In K. Murphy (Ed.), *Individual differences and behavior in organizations* (pp. 175–208). San Francisco: Jossey-Bass.

Motowidlo, S. J. (2003). Job performance. In W. C. Borman, D. R. Ilgen, & R. J. Klimoski (Eds.), *Handbook of psychology: Industrial and organizational psychology* (Vol. 12, pp. 39–53). New York: Wiley.

Motowidlo, S. J., Borman, W. C., & Schmit, M. J. (1997). A theory of individual differences in task and contextual performance. *Human Performance, 10*, 71–83.

Mowday, R. T., Porter, L. W., & Steers, R. (1982). *Organizational linkages: The psychology of commitment, absenteeism, and turnover*. San Diego, CA: Academic Press.

Muchinsky, P. M., & Monahan, C. J. (1987). What is person-environment congruence? Supplementary versus complementary models of fit. *Journal of Vocational Behavior, 31*, 268–277.

Murphy, S. E., & Ensher, E. A. (1999). The effects of leader and subordinate characteristics in the development of leader-member exchange quality. *Journal of Applied Social Psychology, 29*, 1371–1394.

Murray, H. A. (1938). *Explorations in personality; a clinical and experimental study of fifty men of college age.* New York: Oxford University Press.

Naylor, J. C., Pritchard, R. D., & Ilgen, D. R. (1980). *A theory of behavior in organizations.* New York: Academic Press.

Neuman, G. A., Wagner, S. H., & Christiansen, N. D. (1999). The relationship between work-team personality composition and the job performance of teams. *Group & Organization Management, 24*, 28–45.

Noe, R. A., & Wilk, S. L. (1993). Investigation of the factors that influence employees' participation in development activities. *Journal of Applied Psychology, 78*, 291–302.

O'Brien, G. E., & Dowling, P. (1980). The effects of congruency between perceived and desired job attributes upon job satisfaction. *Journal of Occupational Psychology, 53*, 121–130.

Olson, J. M., & Zanna, M. P. (1993). Attitudes and attitude change. *Annual Review of Psychology, 44*, 117–154.

O'Reilly, C. A., & Chatman, J. (1986). Organizational commitment and psychological attachment: The effects of compliance, identification, and internalization on prosocial behavior. *Journal of Applied Psychology, 71*, 492–499.

O'Reilly, C. A., & Chatman, J. A. (1996). Culture as social control: Corporations, cults, and commitment. In L. L. Cummings & B. M. Staw (Eds.), *Research in organizational behavior: An annual series of analytical essays and critical reviews* (Vol. 18, pp. 157–200). Greenwich, CT: Elsevier Science/JAI Press.

O'Reilly, C. A., Chatman, J., & Caldwell, D. F. (1991). People and organizational culture: A profile comparison approach to assessing person-organization fit. *Academy of Management Journal, 34*, 487–516.

Organ, D. W. (1988). *Organizational citizenship behavior: The good soldier syndrome*: Lexington, MA: Lexington Books/D.C. Heath.

Organ, D. W. (1990). The motivational basis of organizational citizenship behavior. In B. M. Staw & L. L. Cummings (Ed.), *Research in organizational behavior* (Vol. 12, pp. 43–72). Greenwich, CT: Elsevier Science/JAI Press.

Organ, D. W. (1997). Organizational citizenship behavior: Its construct clean-up time. *Human Performance, 10*, 85–97.

Organ, D. W., & Konovsky, M. (1989). Cognitive versus affective determinants of organizational citizenship behavior. *Journal of Applied Psychology, 74*, 157–164.

Organ, D. W., & Ryan, K. (1995). A meta-analytic review of attitudinal and dispositional predictors of organizational citizenship behavior. *Personnel Psychology, 48*, 775–802.

Parasuraman, S., & Purohit, Y. S. (2000). Distress and boredom among orchestra musicians: The two faces of stress. *Journal of Occupational Health Psychology, 5*, 74–83.

Parker, D. F., & DeCotiis, T. A. (1983). Organizational determinants of job stress. *Organizational Behavior and Human Performance, 32*, 160–177.

Pervin, L. A. (1968). Performance and satisfaction as a function of individual-environment fit. *Psychological Bulletin, 69*, 56–68.

Podsakoff, P. M., MacKenzie, S. B., Paine, J. B., & Bacharach, D. G. (2000). Organizational citizenship behaviors: A critical review of the theoretical and empirical literature and suggestions for future research. *Journal of Management, 26,* 513–563.

Porter, L. W. (1961). A study of perceived need satisfactions in bottom and middle management jobs. *Journal of Applied Psychology, 45,* 1–10.

Porter, L. W., & Lawler, E. E. (1968). *Managerial attitudes and performance.* Homewood, IL: Dorsey Press.

Pulakos, E. D., & Wexley, K. N. (1983). The relationship among perceptual similarity, sex, and performance ratings in manager-subordinate dyads. *Academy of Management Journal, 26,* 129–139.

Quick, J. C., Cooper, C. L., Nelson, D. L., Quick, J. D., & Gavin, J. H. (2003). Stress, health, and well-being at work. In J. Greenberg (Ed.), *Organizational behavior: The state of the science* (2nd. ed., pp. 53–89). Mahwah, NJ: Lawrence Erlbaum Associates.

Reichers, A. E. (1985). A review and reconceptualization of organizational commitment. *Academy of Management Review, 10,* 465–476.

Rice, R. W., McFarlin, D. B., & Bennett, D. E. (1989). Standards of comparison and job satisfaction. *Journal of Applied Psychology, 74,* 591–598.

Rice, R. W., McFarlin, D. B., Hunt, R. G., & Near, J. P. (1985). Organizational work and the perceived quality of life: Toward a conceptual model. *Academy of Management Review, 10,* 296–310.

Riordan, C. M., Weatherly, E. W., Vandenberg, R. J., & Self, R. M. (2001). The effects of pre-entry experiences and socialization tactics on newcomer attitudes and turnover. *Journal of Managerial Issues, 13,* 159–176.

Rokeach, M. (1973). *The nature of human values.* New York: Free Press.

Roseman, I. (1984). Cognitive determinants of emotions: A structural theory. In P. Shaver (Ed.), *Review of personality and social psychology: Vol. 5. Emotions, relationships, and health* (pp. 11–36). Beverly Hills, CA: Sage.

Rosman, P., & Burke, R. J. (1980). Job satisfaction, self-esteem, and the fit between perceived self and job on valued competencies. *Journal of Psychology, 105,* 259–269.

Rounds, J. B., Dawis, R. V., & Lofquist, L. H. (1987). Measurement of person-environment fit and prediction of satisfaction in the theory of work adjustment. *Journal of Vocational Behavior, 31,* 297–318.

Rousseau, D. M. (1985). Issues of level in organizational research: Multi-level and cross-level perspectives. In B. M. Staw & L. L. Cummings (Eds.), *Research in organizational behavior* (Vol. 7, pp. 1–37). Greenwich, CT: JAI Press.

Russell, J. A. (1980). A circumplex model of affect. *Journal of Personality & Social Psychology, 39,* 1161–1178.

Saks, A. M., & Ashforth, B. E. (1997). A longitudinal investigation of the relationships between job information sources, applicant perceptions of fit, and work outcomes. *Personnel Psychology, 50,* 395–426.

Scarpello, V., & Campbell, J. P. (1983). Job satisfaction and the fit between individual needs and organizational rewards. *Journal of Occupational Psychology, 56,* 315–328.

Schaubroeck, J., Cotton, J. L., & Jennings, K. R. (1989). Antecedents and consequences of role stress: A covariance structure analysis. *Journal of Organizational Behavior, 10,* 35–58.

Schaubroeck, J., & Lam, S. S. K. (2002). How similarity to peers and supervisor influences organizational advancement in different cultures. *Academy of Management Journal, 45,* 1120–1136.

Schein, E. H. (1992). *Organizational culture and leadership*. San Francisco: Jossey-Bass.

Scherer, K. R. (1988). Criteria for emotion-antecedent appraisal: A review. In V. Hamilton, G. H. Bower, & N. H. Frijda (Eds.), *Cognitive perspectives on emotion and motivation* (pp. 89–126). Dordrecht, the Netherlands: Nijhoff.

Schmidt, F. L., Hunter, J. E., & Outerbridge, A. N. (1986). Impact of job experience and ability on job knowledge, work sample performance, and supervisory ratings of job performance. *Journal of Applied Psychology, 71*, 432–439.

Schneider, B., Kristof, A. L., Goldstein, H. W., & Smith, D. B. (1997). What is this thing called fit? In N. R. Anderson & P. Herriott (Eds.), *Handbook of selection and appraisal* (2nd ed., pp. 393–412). London: Wiley.

Schneiderman, N., Ironson, G., & Siegel, S. D. (2005). Stress and health: Psychological, behavioral, and biological determinants. *Annual Review of Clinical Psychology, 1*, 19.1–19.22.

Schuler, R. S. (1980). Definition and conceptualization of stress in organizations. *Organizational Behavior and Human Performance, 25*, 184–215.

Selye, H. (1982). History and present status of the stress concept. In L. Goldberger & S. Breznitz (Eds.), *Handbook of stress: Theoretical and clinical aspects* (pp. 7–17). New York: Free Press.

Shaw, J. D., Duffy, M. K., & Stark, E. M. (2000). Interdependence and preference for group work: Main and congruence effects on the satisfaction and performance of group members. *Journal of Management, 26*, 259–280.

Shirom, A. (1982). What is organizational stress? A facet analytic conceptualization. *Journal of Occupational Behavior, 3*, 21–37.

Smith, P. C., Kendall, L., & Hulin, C. L. (1969). *The measurement of satisfaction in work and retirement*. Chicago: Rand McNally.

Sole, K., Marton, J., & Hornstein, H. A. (1975). Opinion similarity and helping: Three field experiments investigating the bases of promotive tension. *Journal of Experimental Social Psychology, 11*, 1–13.

Sonnentag, S., & Frese, M. (2003). Stress in organizations. In W. C. Borman & D. R. Ilgen (Eds.), *Handbook of psychology: Industrial and organizational psychology* (Vol. 12, pp. 453–491). New York: Wiley.

Spokane, A. R., Meir, E. I., & Catalano, M. (2000). Person–environment congruence and Holland's theory: A review and reconsideration. *Journal of Vocational Behavior, 57*, 137–187.

Stevens, J. M., Beyer, J. M., & Trice, H. M. (1978). Assessing personal, role, and organizational predictors of managerial commitment. *Academy of Management Journal, 21*, 380–396.

Strauss, J. P., Barrick, M. R., & Connerley, M. L. (2001). An investigation of personality similarity effects (relational and perceived) on peer and supervisor ratings and the role of familiarity and liking. *Journal of Occupational and Organizational Psychology, 74*, 637–657.

Taylor, S. E., Repetti, R. L., & Seeman, T. (1997). Health psychology: What is an unhealthy environment and how does it get under the skin? *Annual Review of Psychology, 48*, 411–447.

Taris, R., & Feij, J. A. (2001). Longitudinal examination of the relationship between supplies-values fit and work outcomes. *Applied Psychology: An International Review, 50*(1), 52–80.

Tharenou, P. (2003). The initial development of receptivity to working abroad: Self-initiated international work opportunities in young graduate employees. *Journal of Occupational and Organizational Psychology, 76*, 489–515.

Tranberg, M., Slane, S., & Ekeberg, S. E. (1993). The relation between interest congruence and satisfaction: A meta-analysis. *Journal of Vocational Behavior, 42*, 253–264.

Tsui, A. S., Egan, T. D., & O'Reilly, C. A., III (1992). Being different: Relational demography and organizational attachment. *Administrative Science Quarterly, 37*, 549–579.

Tsui, A. S., & O'Reilly, C. A., III (1989). Beyond simple demographic effects: The importance of relational demography in superior-subordinate dyads. *Academy of Management Journal, 32*, 402–423.

Tsui, A. S., Porter, L. W., & Egan, T. D. (2002). When both similarities and dissimilarities matter: Extending the concept of relational demography. *Human Relations, 55*, 899–929.

Turban, D. B., Dougherty, T. W., & Lee, F. K. (2002). Gender, race, and perceived similarity effects in developmental relationships: The moderating role of relationship duration. *Journal of Vocational Behavior, 61*, 240–262.

Turban, D. B., & Jones, A. P. (1988). Supervisor-subordinate similarity: Types, effects, and mechanisms. *Journal of Applied Psychology, 73*, 228–234.

Tziner, A., & Falbe, C. M. (1990). Actual and preferred climates of achievement orientation and their congruency: An investigation of their relationships to work attitudes and performance in two occupational strata. *Journal of Organizational Behavior, 11*, 159–168.

Uchino, B. N., Cacioppo, J. T., & Keicolt-Glaser, J. K. (1996). The relationship between social support and physiological processes: A review with emphasis on underlying mechanisms and implications for health. *Psychological Bulletin, 119*, 488–531.

Upperman, P. J., & Church, A. T. (1995). Investigating Holland's typological theory with Army occupational specialties. *Journal of Vocational Behavior, 47*, 61–75.

van Vianen, A. E. M. (2000). Person–organization fit: The match between newcomers' and recruiters' preferences for organizational cultures. *Personnel Psychology, 53*, 113–149.

Vancouver, J. B., Millsap, R. E., & Peters, P. A. (1994). Multilevel analysis of organizational goal congruence. *Journal of Applied Psychology, 79*, 666–679.

Vancouver, J. B., & Schmitt, N. W. (1991). An exploratory examination of person-organization fit: Organizational goal congruence. *Personnel Psychology, 44*, 333–352.

Vecchio, R. P., & Bullis, R. C. (2001). Moderators of the influence of supervisor–subordinate similarity on subordinate outcomes. *Journal of Applied Psychology, 86*, 884–896.

Verquer, M. L., Beehr, T. A., & Wagner, S. H. (2003). A meta-analysis of relations between person-organization fit and work attitudes. *Journal of Vocational Behavior, 63*, 473–489.

Vigoda, E., & Cohen, A. (2002). Influence tactics and perceptions of organizational politics: A longitudinal study. *Journal of Business Research, 55*, 311–324.

Vroom, V. H. (1964). *Work and motivation.* New York: Wiley.

Waldman, D. A., & Spangler, W. D. (1989). Putting together the pieces: A closer look at the determinants of job performance. *Human Performance, 2*, 29–59.

Wanous, J. P. (1992). *Organizational entry: Recruitment, selection, and socialization of newcomers* (2nd ed.). Reading, MA: Addison-Wesley.

Wanous, J. P., & Lawler, E. E., III (1972). Measurement and meaning of job satisfaction. *Journal of Applied Psychology, 56*, 95–105.

Watson, D., & Tellegen, A. (1985). Toward a consensual structure of mood. *Psychological Bulletin, 98*, 219–235.

Wayne, S. J., & Liden, R. C. (1995). Effects of impression management on performance ratings: A longitudinal study. *Academy of Management Journal, 38*, 232–260.

Webster, D. M., & Kruglanski, A. W. (1994). Individual differences in need for cognitive closure. *Journal of Personality and Social Psychology, 67*, 1049–1062.

Weick, K. E. (1995). What theory is *not*, theorizing *is*. *Administrative Science Quarterly, 40*, 385–390.

Weiss, H. M. (2002). Deconstructing job satisfaction: Separating evaluations, beliefs and affective experiences. *Human Resource Management Review, 12*, 173–194.

Werbel, J. D., & Gilliland, S. W. (1999). Person-environment fit in the selection process. In G. R. Ferris (Ed.), *Research in personnel and human resources management* (Vol. 17, pp. 209–243). Stamford, CT: JAI Press.

White, R. W. (1959). Motivation reconsidered: The concept of competence. *Psychological Review, 66*, 297–333.

Wiener, Y. (1982). Commitment in organizations: A normative view. *Academy of Management Review, 7*, 418–428.

Yukl, G., & Fu, P. P. (1999). Determinants of delegation and consultation by managers. *Journal of Organizational Behavior, 20*, 219–232.

Zalesny, M. D., & Highhouse, S. (1992). Accuracy in performance evaluations. *Organizational Behavior and Human Decision Process, 51*, 22–50.

# CHAPTER 8

# *The Search for Internal and External Fit in Teams*

## D. Scott DeRue and John R. Hollenbeck
### *Michigan State University*

In his essay commemorating the famous Hawthorne studies, Harold Leavitt (1975) suggested that people and organizations would be "better off" if groups, not individuals, were the basic building blocks of organizations (Hackman, 1987). Since his prophetic essay, the use of groups and teams in organizations has greatly expanded. As the focus of organizations shifted toward quality, innovation, and accountability, an emphasis on the use of work teams emerged (Kozlowski, Gully, Salas, & Cannon-Bowers, 1996). As a result, organizations have restructured and are continuing to restructure work around teams rather than individual jobs (Ilgen, 1994). In parallel, the need and demand for theoretical and empirical research on team functioning have intensified. Past reviews of the literature on small groups and teams indicated considerable growth in the volume of team research over this same time horizon (Cohen & Bailey, 1997; Ilgen, Hollenbeck, Johnson, & Jundt, 2005; Kozlowski & Bell, 2003; McGrath, Arrow, & Berdahl, 2000).[1]

The increased focus on team research has helped develop convergence on many conceptual developments in the team literature. A recent example is the consensus that has developed regarding teams as complex systems (McGrath et al., 2000). Teams perform over time and within context, creating an environment that introduces a level of complexity not accounted for within traditional cause and effect perspectives on team functioning. For

---

[1] Some research distinguishes work teams from work groups, but this chapter does not make this distinction and uses the term teams to refer to work teams and groups. Other scholars have chosen to follow this same path (e.g., Kozlowski & Bell, 2003).

instance, the theory of compilation proposed by Kozlowski, Gully, Nason, and Smith (1999) described team inputs, processes, and outputs that develop over time as teams interact in context. In a reciprocal nature, the team's external environment influences intrateam interactions, and intrateam interactions influence the external environment. Knowledge, attitudes, and behaviors are both inputs and processes that impact team performance in a developmental sequence. In return, team performance is recycled and serves as an input to team process. Similar theoretical conceptualizations that frame teams as complex systems have begun to emerge in the literature (Marks, Mathieu, & Zaccaro, 2001; McGrath et al., 2000). Although differences exist between the various perspectives put forth, all share a common underpinning in that teams are complex and exist in the context of people, tasks, technologies, and settings.

Despite these theoretical developments, the complexity inherent in work teams has not been adequately addressed in empirical research. Classic works of Steiner (1972) and Hackman (1987, 1990) expressed the nature of team performance using an I–P–O framework in which inputs lead to processes that in turn lead to outcomes. This framework has had significant influence on the direction of empirical research on work teams, much of which either explicitly or implicitly invokes the I–P–O framework. However, the utility of this framework as a guide to empirical research fails to reflect the emerging consensus of teams as complex systems. The I–P–O framework implies a linear progression of main effects proceeding from one category (I, P, or O) to the next. However, in an integrative review of the team literature, Ilgen et al., in the 2005 *Annual Review of Psychology,* document interactions between various inputs and processes (I X P), between various processes (P X P), between inputs and emergent states (I X ES), and between processes and emergent states (P X ES). Documentation of these various interactions and complexities suggests that an alternative to the traditional I–P–O framework is needed for guiding the evolution of team research.

Rather than implying a linear progression of main effects from one category of variables to another, the presence of interactions suggests contingent relationships both within and between categories of variables. These contingencies imply that the effects of any one given input or process in team effectiveness may depend upon the level of some other input or process. Thus, a variable that might be positively related to effectiveness under one set of conditions might be unrelated or negatively related to effectiveness under another set of conditions. For example, Beersma et al. (2003) found that competitive team reward structures (a classic input in I–P–O terms) were positively related to performance when operationalized in terms of speed but negatively related to performance when operationalized in terms of accuracy. Thus, a competitive reward structure is a good fit for situations that demand speed but a poor fit for situations that demand accuracy. Similarly, Stewart and Barrick (2000) found that the relationship between team structure and performance is contingent on the task environment. Teams with interdependent structures exhibit a U-shaped performance curve when engaged in conceptual tasks but experience an inverted U-shaped performance curve when performing behavioral tasks. Thus, conceptual tasks in a team context are a good fit when paired with very high or low levels of interdependence, and behavioral tasks are a good fit when the structure is designed with moderate interdependence.

Unlike what is implied by the traditional I–P–O model, these interactive and, in some cases, nonlinear relationships suggest that there is "no one best way" of creating team inputs or promoting team processes. Rather, there are different configurations of inputs and processes that need to be aligned, and a factor that might have positive effects in one context may not generalize when reproduced in a different context. Documenting these interactions has critical applied implications, as the unreflective adoption of a set of practices of one organization by another may result in unintended outcomes if the simple I–P–O model does not hold.

For example, many organizations that admired the management practices at the General Electric Company (GE) copied its use of forced ranking systems (FRS), in which a set percentage of low performers are terminated each year. However, unlike the results obtained at GE, many organizations (e.g., Ford) that simply imitated and adopted this FRS practice experienced disastrous results (Shirouzu, 2001). FRS reflects a competitive reward system (an input), and there is no simple and direct relationship between this practice and overall group performance as implied by I–P–O models.

Similarly, a new executive team at Home Depot, who were formerly with GE, tried to transport GE's relatively centralized structure for making purchasing decisions to Home Depot, again with disastrous results (Morse, 2003) The relationship between the group's decision-making structure (an input) and outcomes is again a complex function of a number of contingent factors that makes the kind of mimicry prompted by a belief in straightforward, I–P–O models a doomed venture from the start. Instead of searching for a single practice to copy, organizations need to recognize that certain sets of practices that fit in one type of task, or in one context, or with one group of people may not fit with a different type of task, a different context, or a different group of people.

To address these issues, in this chapter we develop a multilevel framework of team effectiveness that is conceptualized using individual and team-level dimensions of internal and external fit. This framework, in accord with past research, extends the general proposition that the relationship between individual differences and outcomes is contingent on the nature of the environment, task, and/or organization (Kristoff, 1996; Hollenbeck et al., 2002). Similar to other fit conceptualizations in their respective domains and levels of study, this framework shows that there is no one best way to organize at the team level. Also in accord with past research on fit, this framework applies the concept of fit in multiple directions. In other words, the fit among elements internal to the team as well as between the team and the external environment are important considerations.

Although use of the fit conceptualization at the team level is not unique to the framework developed here, it is essential for considering the complex nature of work teams. The notion of fit is often implicit in the patterns of congruence, interactions, and contingencies that are discussed throughout the team literature. However, the notion of fit is not necessarily synonymous with terms of contingency, and the fit perspective presented here offers a valuable extension beyond existing contingency perspectives on teams. Contingency implies moderation or an interaction between two or more constructs. Fit, as conceptualized here, extends the contingency perspective by more clearly specifying the form and nature of the interaction.

In other words, the framework offered here not only acknowledges the contingency-based relationship or interaction between two constructs but also specifies the level of each construct that produces an optimal alignment or match. As such, our focus is on the fit of people, tasks, and processes, where each of these is specified and assessed independently. In turn, we do not focus on summary perceptions of whether or not any one individual subjectively feels like he or she "fits" with the team on some unspecified dimension. Although this latter subjective perception of fit is often an outcome of creating an objectively good fit on a specific dimension of interest, it has limited diagnostic value as either a criterion or as a predictor because of its unspecified nature.

This chapter is organized into four sections. First, we introduce and describe the framework of internal and external fit in teams. The key dimensions of the framework and each element within the framework are thoroughly defined. Second, we review the existing theoretical and empirical research on teams using this framework as an organizing tool. In this in-depth, critical review of the team literature, we establish the theoretical and empirical foundation for the framework and outline what is currently understood regarding the role of internal and external fit in work teams. In conclusion, we identify and discuss a series of research questions that arise as a result of examining work team effectiveness through the lens of internal and external fit. These research questions establish the direction for future research on the role of fit in teams.

## INTERNAL AND EXTERNAL FIT IN TEAMS:
## A CONCEPTUAL FRAMEWORK

Traditional I–P–O frameworks (e.g., Hackman, 1987) of team effectiveness provide an insufficient and disjointed view of fit in teams by illustrating how select team inputs engender certain team processes and how select team processes generate specific team outputs. A key limitation of traditional I–P–O frameworks is determining how various team elements systematically "fit" together to generate their effects. The study and examination of fit in teams has recently emerged as a topic of interest (Hollenbeck et al., 2002; Kristoff-Brown & Stevens, 2001; Kristoff-Brown, Jansen, & Colbert, 2002; Werbel & Gilliland, 1999) and potential means of addressing these limitations in traditional frameworks. As researchers increasingly recognize the complex nature of work teams, the consideration of fit in teams will become even more critical.

To address this complexity, the framework considers two forms of fit in work teams (internal and external), identifies the team characteristics that have the most impact on the degree of fit in work teams, and illustrates how certain team variables serve as linking mechanisms between the internal and external dimensions of fit to engender team effectiveness. The choice of team elements considered in the framework is not exhaustive but does highlight those fit relationships which, based on existing empirical research, have the most impact on both individual and team-level outcomes. In this section of the chapter we present and define (a) each specific element within the framework and (b) the relationships between those elements.

Despite its recent application at the team level, use of the fit concept in organizational studies is deeply rooted. For instance, at the organization level, the structural contingency theory of organizations has "at its heart" the concept of fit (Donaldson, 2001). Structural contingency theory maintains that organizational performance is contingent on the fit between structure and the environment. At the individual level, Lewin's (1951) equation $B = f(P,E)$ spawned an entire stream of research on the fit between person and environment. Person–environment fit suggests that individuals will have positive experiences when work provides an environment that is compatible with their personal characteristics (Krisoff-Brown, Jansen, & Colbert, 2002). This framework extends those conceptualizations of fit to the team level.

When discussing fit at any level, it is vital that the term *fit* is defined precisely. Throughout the organizational literature, multiple ways of conceptualizing the notion of fit exist. Specific to internal and external fit in the context of teams, fit is best conceptualized as the congruence or alignment between a combined set of team elements that produces a relatively higher level of team effectiveness, including both individual (e.g., team member satisfaction) and team-level (e.g., team task performance) outcomes. In contrast, *misfit* is the incongruent combination of elements that results in relatively lower team effectiveness. This conceptualization is consistent with previous definitions of fit used in other individual and organization-level studies (e.g., Cable & DeRue, 2002; Donaldson, 2001; Pfeffer, 1997).

Fit, as conceptualized in this framework, is also multidimensional. First, fit can be internal (i.e., person-related) or external (i.e., task-related). Internal fit addresses the degree to which variables within the team (e.g., composition) are congruent with each other. As such, internal fit in teams can take on two forms. The first form of fit relates to within-team composition and refers to how team member characteristics (e.g., personalities and abilities) fit together. This form of internal fit connects individual-level characteristics with team-level composition. The second form of internal fit refers to the fit between team-level composition and the linking mechanisms (e.g., structure and rewards) that connect internal and external fit in teams. The distinction between the two forms of internal fit is important, as one can easily imagine a team having good within-team compositional fit (e.g., the right mix of personalities) but not having a good fit between team composition and a linking mechanism (e.g., the composition of personalities in the team does not match the reward structure). External fit refers to the alignment between certain team characteristics and the external environment. Within the context of this particular framework, the external environment is focused on task-related variables; however, other characteristics of the external environment (e.g., organizational context) could also be considered.

Second, within both the internal and external dimensions of fit, fit can be characterized as either supplementary or complementary. Supplementary fit occurs when elements share common qualities, and complementary fit occurs when elements have distinct qualities that have a supportive or reinforcing relationship (Muchinsky & Monahan, 1987). A team whose members have common values would represent supplementary fit, whereas a cross-functional work team whose members have distinct yet supportive areas of expertise would exhibit complementary fit. By considering the multiple dimensions of fit in teams, this framework illustrates how the congruence among team variables, both at the individual and team level, influences team effectiveness. Before we review the empirical research that establishes the foundation of this framework, each component of the model is defined.

## Individual-Level Elements

### Individual Profiles of Abilities and Traits

The collection of within-person characteristics that a particular team member possesses are referred to here as individual profiles. An individual's profile is composed of his or her skills, abilities, and psychological traits. In comparison with other conceptualizations of fit, the individual profile is similar to the *person* component of studies on person–environment and person–organization fit. Researchers of person–environment and person–organization fit often operationalize the person component as an individual's values, goals, personality, and attitudes (Cable & DeRue, 2002; Kristoff, 1996). Thus, individual profiles in this context point to the within-person characteristics, including knowledge, skills, and abilities, values, goals, and psychological traits (e.g., personality), that each team member brings to the team.

## Team-Level Elements

### Team Composition

Team composition is defined as the collective nature and attributes of all team members. The most appropriate form of measurement for team composition has historically been a key topic of interest. One common operationalization is to calculate a mean score for specific individual-level measures (Barrick, Stewart, Neubert, & Mount, 1998). Conversely, some have argued that conjunctive (the team's lowest scoring member) or disjunctive (the team's highest scoring member) measures may be theoretically more appropriate, depending upon the nature of the task and the trait (LePine, Hollenbeck, Ilgen, & Hedlund, 1997).

### Team Task Environment

Teams, by definition, are responsible for a collective task. The team task environment, or the nature of this collective task, has and continues to be an important consideration in the study of work teams. The key characteristics of the team task environment include the degree of uncertainty inherent in the task, the level of interdependence required among team members, and the timing associated with coordinating and orchestrating behavioral task sequences (Steiner, 1972; Wittenbaum, Vaughan, & Stasser, 1998).

## Linking Mechanisms

### Structure

Team structure addresses how team members are differentiated and how the independent actions of individuals are coordinated. One dimension of structure is departmentation, which refers to the basis on which labor is divided (Wagner, 2000). Departmentation is often conceptualized as functional (specialized roles) or divisional (broader, more independent roles). A second dimension of structure is the degree to which responsibility and decision-making are centralized or decentralized (Wagner, 2000) within the team.

## Technology

Recent literature offers two distinct definitions of technology. The first conceptualizes technology as workflow or coordination. In the context of this framework, this definition of technology overlaps with the team structure and team process variables and is thus not used. The second definition of technology, which is used in the context of this framework, refers to computers and other electronic devices used in the team context to perform a task. This definition of technology has garnered particular attention, given the recent emergence of virtual teams as an area of interest. With more than 50% of large companies using some form of virtual teams (De Lisser, 1999), the actual technology hardware used to facilitate team functioning and performance has become a critical element in the study of teams (Townsend, DeMarie, & Hendrickson, 1998). Examples of technology include fax and e-mail communication, electronic file transfer, Internet bulletin boards, and decision support systems (e.g., Dennis, Valacich, & Nunamaker, 1990; Qureshi, 1998).

## Rewards

Rewards refers to the system through which individual team members are paid and formally rewarded for their participation in the team. In general, reward systems in teams differ in the degree to which rewards in the team are cooperatively or competitively-based (Beersma et al., 2003; Deutsch, 1949; Miller & Hamblin, 1963; Stanne, Johnson, & Johnson, 1999). This dimension is particularly important when one considers the impact of rewards on internal and external team fit and thus team effectiveness.

## Team Process and Emergent States

Team process refers to team members' cognitive, behavioral, and verbal interpersonal acts that are directed toward organizing task work and achieving collective goals. Team process involves team members interacting with each other in context and does not include the actual task work (Marks et al., 2001). These interpersonal acts thus serve as mediators of the input to outcome relationship specified in traditional I–P–O models. In addition to formal team processes, team emergent states, which refer to the collective affective and emotional experiences of team members that develop over time, are also important mediators of the input to outcome process implied by I–P–O models. Ilgen et al., in the 2005

*Annual Review of Psychology*, identified six different mediational influences related to teams that encompassed both processes and emergent states: trusting, planning, structuring, bonding, adapting, and learning. All six of these mediators are important when one considers the degree of internal and external fit in teams and the subsequent implications for team effectiveness.

## INTERNAL AND EXTERNAL FIT IN TEAMS: A REVIEW OF THE LITERATURE

From a search of both the business and psychological literature indexes, we considered and reviewed several hundred articles for possible inclusion in this review. In our search, we used keywords such as *contingency, fit, congruence,* and *interaction,* preceded by the word *group* or *team.* Ultimately, we focused our review on 20 empirical studies (see Table 8–1) of teams in organizations, in all of which fit or contingency-based relationships in teams were examined . In the context of this review, we present a heuristic framework (see Fig. 8–1) for the role of internal and external fit in teams. This framework and the accompanying literature review illustrate (a) what we currently know about the role of fit in teams and (b) in which areas future researchers on teams need to focus. Table 8–1 outlines the empirical studies covered in this review, including which dimension(s) of fit is addressed (see Fig 8–1 for the corresponding framework), how the specific variables are conceptualized, and what the team outcome was.

The literature review is organized into two sections. We first focus on the domain of internal fit. Subsequently, we turn our attention to the domain of external fit. To the extent possible given existing empirical research, we discuss any evidence for differentiating between supplementary and complementary fit within each of these two sections.

### Dimensions of Internal Fit

The dimensions of internal fit, as seen in the upper region of Fig. 8–1, are anchored in the compositional elements of the team as well as the relationship between team composition and four team characteristics that we refer to as linking mechanisms: team structure, rewards, technology, and processes/emergent states. Person–team fit, one of these dimensions, spans across multiple levels (individual and team) of the model. Person–team fit, or the congruence between an individual team member's profile and the team's composition, is the team-level analog to person–organization fit (Adkins, Ravlin, & Meglino, 1996; Kristoff-Brown & Stevens, 2001). Research on person–organization fit suggests that congruence on psychological constructs such as goals (Vancouver & Schmitt, 1991), values (Boxx, Odom, & Dunn, 1991; Chatman, 1991), and person-

## TABLE 8–1.
### Review of Empirical Studies

| Dimension of Fit | Citation | Variables in the Fit Relationship | | Team Outcomes |
| --- | --- | --- | --- | --- |
| | | Variable A | Variable B | |
| 1a | Kristoff-Brown and Stevens (2001) | Member goals (performance, mastery) | Other team member goals (performance, mastery) | Team member satisfaction |
| 1a | Witt et al. (2001) | Member goals | Other team member goals | Team politics, satisfaction, and effectiveness |
| 1a | LePine et al. (1997) | Team cognitive ability, team conscientious-ness | Team leader cognitive ability, team leader conscientious-ness | Team task performance |
| 1a | Polzer et al. (2002) | Team diversity | Interpersonal congruence | Creativity, social integration, team identification |
| 1a | Barry and Stewart (1997) | Individual extraversion | Team-level extraversion | Team effectiveness, task focus |
| 1a | Barsade et al (2000) | Individual positive/ negative affect | Team-level positive/ negative affect | Task and emotional conflict, influence in team |
| 1b | Simons et al. (1999) | Job (tenure) and non-jobrelated (age, race) diversity sharing | Debate in team | Team effectiveness |
| 1c | Beersma et al. (2003) | Personality (extraversion, agreeableness) | Reward structure (cooperative/ competitive) | Team effectiveness |
| 1d | Hollenbeck et al. (2002) | Cognitive ability, emotional stability | Functional/ divisional team structure | Team effectiveness |
| 1d | LePine (2003) | Cognitive ability, achievement, openness, dependability | Constant/ changing role structure | Postchange team effectiveness |
| 1e | Colquitt et al. (2002) | Computer-assisted communication | Openness | Decision-making performance |
| 2a | Bonner et al. (2002) | Decision-making processes | Task complexity | Decision-making performance |

*(continued)*

TABLE 8–1.
(*Continued*)

| Dimension of Fit | Citation | Variables in the Fit Relationship | | Team Outcomes |
|---|---|---|---|---|
| | | Variable A | Variable B | |
| 2a | Jehn (1995) | Task/relationship conflict | Routine/non-routine task environment | Team effectiveness |
| 2a | De Dreu and Weingart (2003) | Task/relationship conflict | Task complexity | Team effectiveness |
| 2a | Alper et al. (1998) | Information sharing/ communication | Goal inter-dependence | Team effectiveness |
| 2b | Wageman and Baker (1997) | Reward inter-dependence | Task inter-dependence | Team effectiveness |
| 2b | Beersma et al. (2003) | Reward structure | Speed/accuracy task characteristics | Team effectiveness |
| 2c | Stewart and Barrick (2000) | Structural inter-dependence | Conceptual/ behavioral task environment | Team effectiveness |
| 2c | Hollenbeck et al. (2002) | Functional/ divisional team structure | Random/ predictable task environment | Team effectiveness |
| 2d | Sarter et al. (1997, 2000, 2001) | Autonomy, task complexity | Type of decision support system | Decision-making performance |

ality and attitudes (Bretz & Judge, 1994) can improve individuals' attitudes, participation, and performance in collective activities.

The concept of person–team fit extends this notion by leveraging similar psychological constructs at the team level. Recent research supports the notion that, when based on the congruence of member and team goals (Kristoff-Brown & Stevens, 2001; Witt, Hilton, & Hochwater, 2001), ability (LePine et al., 1997), and work style preferences (Polzer, Milton, & Swann, 2002), person–team fit can positively or negatively influence team effectiveness. In addition, although not based on empirical data and thus not part of our formal review, Werbel and colleagues (Werbel & Gilliland, 1999; Werbel & Johnson, 2001) suggested that person–team congruence on work values and norms will have a positive relationship

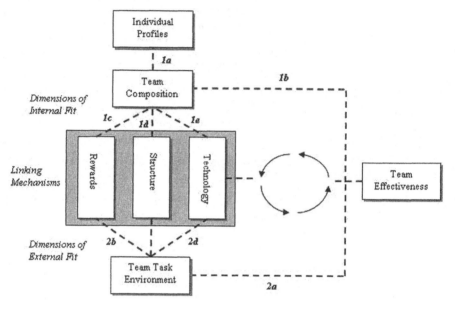

FIGURE 8–1. Heuristic framework for the role of internal and external fit in teams.

with team effectiveness. Effective study of person–team fit on work values and norms requires researchers to first identify and differentiate among work values and norms to determine which are most interesting with respect to fit in teams.

In a study of 23 matrix-structured teams, Witt et al. (2001) found that member–team goal congruence moderated the relationship between team-level politics and ratings of team effectiveness and member satisfaction. The negative influence of politics on team effectiveness and satisfaction is amplified in teams with low levels of person–team goal congruence, suggesting that one way to cope with team politics is to ensure person–team fit with respect to goals. Kristof-Brown and Stevens (2001), in a study of 64 project teams, not only found similar evidence supporting the need for congruence between personal and perceived team goals but also discovered that the effect on team- and individual-level outcomes depends on the type of goal. For instance, the highest levels of member satisfaction with the team occurred when person–team congruence was high on performance goals, but high congruence or fit on mastery goals did not have the same level of positive impact.

LePine et al. (1997) examined person–team fit using two distinct individual differences: cognitive ability and conscientiousness. This research found that team performance was highest when the team and the team leader both had high cognitive ability and levels of conscientiousness (high person–team fit). On the other hand, team task performance suffered if the relationship was incongruent (e.g., the team leader had low ability, but the team had high ability). Thus, a leader with low cognitive ability and/or conscientiousness could neutralize a good staff (and vice versa).

Exploring a different dimension of member personality, Barry and Stewart (1997) showed that the proportion of relatively extraverted members in the team has a curvilinear relationship with respect to task focus (an emergent state) and team performance. Thus, the effect of a single team member's level of extraversion on team outcomes is contingent on the current level of extraversion already in the team. For instance, if the team currently has a low level of extraversion, adding a highly extraverted member may enhance team effectiveness. However, if the team currently has a high level of extraversion, the addition of a highly extraverted member may negatively influence team effectiveness.

Barsade, Ward, Turner, and Sonnenfeld (2000), in a study of 62 U.S. top management teams, extended the person–team fit literature by considering the role of positive and negative affect. In this study, the influence of person–team fit (conceptualized as the fit between member affect and the affect of his or her team) on outcomes such as task and emotional conflict and influence in the team was examined. Findings suggested that greater affective fit is related to more positive individual attitudes in the team and perceptions of greater influence in the team. Member–team incongruence with respect to affective fit led to the chief executive officer, or team leader, using less participatory decision making and the team experiencing higher task and emotional conflict. Interestingly, fit or misfit with respect to negative affect in the team was not related to any individual- or team-level outcomes.

Polzer et al. (2002), in a study of 83 work teams, found that diversity in a team improved creativity task performance but only in teams with high interpersonal congruence. Team diversity was conceptualized along various demographic and experience dimensions, including gender, ethnicity, nationality, and previous job experience. Interpersonal congruence, in the context of this study, was defined as the degree to which team members saw others in the team as others saw themselves. In addition to the positive effects on creativity, interpersonal congruence also was found to positively affect social integration and team identification. Thus, team members can experience enhanced team processes and foster higher levels of team performance by expressing rather than suppressing the characteristics that make them unique.

In their conceptual model of person–team fit, Werbel and Johnson (2001) raised the issue that person–team fit is actually multidimensional. Applying person–team fit in a selection context, they suggested that a bias exists toward conceptualizing fit as supplementary, or development of similar qualities among team members. In contrast, however, all team members have some personal assets and deficiencies related to supporting team effectiveness. Thus, complementary person–team fit can often neutralize a single individual's weaknesses and, in turn, enhance overall team effectiveness.

Whereas Werbel and Johnson's (2001) work was purely conceptual and thus is not part of our formal review of empirical studies, LePine et al.'s (1997) study did show, as an example, how the interaction between characteristics of the team and those of the team's weakest member can offset the negative influence of the weakest member and thus positively influence team effectiveness. Future empirical researchers need to follow in this spirit and give more consideration to the differences between supplementary and complementary person–team fit. The effectiveness of complementary and supplementary fit in the context of teams is likely to depend on the variables in question, thus providing an interesting opportunity and challenge for future researchers.

The other dimensions of internal fit in teams, all operating at the team-level, are conceptualized as the fit between team composition and a series of linking mechanisms that then connect the composition-based dimensions of internal fit with the task-related dimensions of external fit. These linking mechanisms include team structure, technology, rewards, and processes/emergent states. The domain of team composition research has, at varying degrees of depth, explained the relationship between team composition and all four of these linking mechanisms.

It is important to note that many composition-focused studies are grounded at the individual level, and these studies examine the effects of individual attributes on team process. These studies do not represent a team-level dimension of internal fit. Rather, team-level composition is conceptualized as an attribute of the collective. Across the general team composition literature, both job- and nonjob-related compositional factors have been examined at the team-level, including positive and negative affect (Barsade et al., 2000), nationality (Earley & Mosakowski, 2000), age and race (Simons, Pelled, & Smith, 1999), gender (Rogelberg & Rumery, 1996), personality (Barrick et al., 1998; Barry & Stewart, 1997), ability (Barrick et al., 1998; Devine, 1999), and functional diversity (Bunderson & Sutcliffe, 2003). The degree to which congruence between team compositional factors and specific team processes influences team effectiveness is a fairly unexplored area of interest.

A recent study by Simons et al. (1999) illustrated just how this dimension of fit can influence team effectiveness. Data from this study suggested that debate in management teams increases the tendency for diversity to enhance team performance. Further, these positive effects are strongest when team diversity is based on job-related dimensions (e.g., functional background and company tenure) rather than on nonjob-related dimensions (e.g., age). By indicating that diversity must be in congruence with the appropriate debate processes for the team to benefit from diversity, this study established the rationale for exploring the role of interactions between team processes and emergent states and team composition.

In addition to studying the fit between team composition and team processes/emergent states, research has also been done to examine the fit between team composition and structure, technology, and rewards. All three of these dimensions of internal fit have recently emerged as important areas for empirical research. Although some have argued conceptually that rewards for individual performance should be eliminated from team contexts (Demming, 1986), only recently have empirical researchers begun to address such claims—and much of empirical evidence thus far has called into question such broad, undifferentiated claims. Most of the recent research suggests that, even in team contexts, the appropriate reward system depends on many other contingent factors, including team composition.

Despite numerous acknowledgements of its importance (Albanese & Van Fleet, 1985; DeMatteo, Eby, & Sundstrom, 1998; Gerhart & Milkovich, 1992), the congruency between team composition and team rewards has received little empirical attention. What evidence does exist, however, clearly shows that the fit between team composition and team rewards can significantly influence team effectiveness. Beersma et al. (2003) illustrated how the effects of personality on team performance are contingent on the type of reward structure used in the team. In general, teams composed of extraverted and agreeable members perform better within a cooperative reward structure (team-based reward system), whereas teams low on these dimensions of personality perform better within a competitive reward structure (individual-based reward system). Thus, not all teams should be rewarded as a team. Rather, the most appropriate reward system, individually or team-based, depends on the personality of the team.

With respect to team structure, clear empirical evidence exists to suggest that the fit between team composition and team structure is a critical determinant of team effectiveness. In other words, team composition interacts with team structure to affect team outcomes. Hollenbeck et al. (2002) examined, albeit at the individual level, the relationship between compositional factors and team structure. Results from their study indicated that general cognitive ability is positively related to performance but only in teams that use divisional structures that create broad roles. For teams structured functionally into narrow roles, this relationship does not hold.

Furthermore, when teams experienced poor external fit between structure and the task environment, emotional stability became the most critical personal attribute for predicting performance. Thus, high levels of emotional stability can attenuate the otherwise negative effects of a poor external fit between team structure and the team task environment.

Interestingly, results from this study suggested that functional team structures are not conducive to the manifestation of any type of individual difference effects. If true, the team composition–structure fit relationship is only meaningful if teams are structured divisionally.

LePine (2003) extended research on this dimension of internal fit to the team level by concentrating on the relationship between team–level cognitive ability, achievement, and openness with adaptations in role structure. Role structures, as defined by Katz and Kahn (1978), are the recurring task-focused actions of individuals interrelated with the recurring task-focused actions of others. LePine (2003) found that teams with higher levels of cognitive ability, achievement, and openness and lower levels of dependability performed superior to other teams after an unforeseen change in the team task. Thus, the performance of teams that experience unexpected changes in role structures is contingent on the level of cognitive ability, achievement, openness to experience, and dependability in the team.

The final linking mechanism with respect to the dimension of internal fit is technology, defined as the hardware or software technology used in team contexts to facilitate task performance. Interest in the role of technology in team-based work environments has increased in parallel with that of virtual teams. One particular area of interest is how technology interacts with team composition. Most studies on this topic focus on the congruence between individual-level attributes and the form or type of technology (e.g., Arthur, Young, Jordan, & Shebilske, 1996), thereby not representing a team-level dimension of fit. That said, a recent study by Colquitt, Hollenbeck, Ilgen, LePine, and Sheppard (2002) extended this notion to the team level by examining team-level openness and the role of computer-assisted communication in team decision making. Results from this study suggested that the positive effects of computer-assisted communication on team performance are contingent on the degree of openness in the team. Only those teams high in openness benefit from computer-assisted communication, supporting the notion that certain team compositions fit with technology in such a way that engenders superior team performance.

### Dimensions of External Fit

Since the beginnings of team research, the task has been an important consideration. Early distinctions between tasks focused on oversimplified dichotomies (e.g., simple versus complex). McGrath and Altman (1966) began a movement to conceptualize more systematically the characteristics of tasks in team contexts. This movement led to Steiner's (1972) typology of tasks, Hackman, Brousseau, and Weiss's (1976) task types, Laughlin's (1980) classification of group tasks, and then finally to McGrath's (1984) circumplex model of group tasks. Van de Ven, Delbecq, and Koenig (1976) defined task uncertainty as "the difficulty and variability of the work undertaken by an organizational unit." Wittenbaum et al. (1998), in discussing the coordination of tasks, incorporated the notion of task-related time pressure.

In recent years, a collection of empirical studies has been developed, documenting the importance of considering the team task environment when one examines team effectiveness. In these studies, the team task environment is typically framed as a critical boundary condition or as a moderator of effects (Kozlowski & Bell, 2003)—thus creating a situation for fit or misfit on the basis of the team task environment. Key task characteristics that are often considered include uncertainty (Van de Ven et al., 1976), degree of (cooperative and conflicting) interdependence (e.g., Steiner, 1972; McGrath, 1984), and task-related time pressure (e.g., Wittenbaum et al., 1998).

The multiple forms of external fit in teams, all operating at the team level, are conceptualized as the fit or congruence between the team task environment and the four linking mechanisms: team structure, rewards, technology, and processes/emergent states (see Fig. 8–1). Although each of these dimensions of external fit is supported in the literature, the fit relationship between team task environment and team processes/emergent states has been given the most empirical attention. Numerous empirical studies provide evidence for a contingency-based relationship between task environment and a variety of team processes/emergent states, including conflict (Jehn, 1995; De Dreu & Weingart, 2003), decision-making processes (Bonner, Baumann, & Dalal, 2002), and information sharing (Alper, Tjosvold, & Law, 1998). Although some of these studies only go as far as to identify the contingency or interaction between two variables, results from these studies should inform future research that specifies the level of each variable, which in turn creates a fit relationship.

Several distinct dimensions of the team task environment that moderate the effects of intrateam conflict on team effectiveness have been identified in empirical research. Jehn (1995), in a study of 105 work and management teams, showed that the effect of conflict on team effectiveness can be either positive or negative, depending on whether the task environment is novel or routine in nature. Specifically, task conflict in teams performing very routine tasks was found to be detrimental to team performance. On the other hand, task conflict in teams engaged in nonroutine tasks did not have a negative effect on team performance and in some cases was actually beneficial. Through interviews and observations, Jehn (1995) illustrated that effective teams in nonroutine task environments had high levels of task conflict and norms fostering open dialogue of team and task-related problems. This open debate about task conflict promoted critical evaluation and better problem solving within these teams, thus leading to superior team performance in this particular task environment.

De Dreu and Weingart (2003), in a meta-analysis of task and relationship conflict, also explored the contingent relationship between conflict and team task environment by focusing on the complexity of the task. In this study, relationship and task conflict were found to have strong and negative correlations with team performance and team member satisfaction. Interestingly, relationship and task-based conflict were found to have stronger negative relations with team performance in highly complex (e.g., decision-making) tasks than in less complex (production) tasks. In general, the emerging consensus is that task conflict is unhelpful for teams. As Ilgen et al. (2005) pointed out, the best context for team functioning is not one that is marked by conflict but rather one characterized by unemotional debate, trust among team members, openness to different ideas, and an ability to resist pressures to quickly compromise or reach premature consensus.

Similar to the contingent relationship between conflict and the team task environment, the decision-making processes within teams are also dependent on the nature of the task environment. Bonner et al. (2002) assessed the decision-making patterns of teams operating in both moderately difficult and simple task environments. Teams in moderately difficult task environments were found to adjust their decision-making processes to overweight the input of high-ability team members and underweight input from lower-ability team members. Teams working on simple tasks, however, did not adjust their decision-making routines according to differences in ability among team members. Interestingly, the form of decision making did not affect decision-making performance in this study. In other words, teams able to identify the relevant expert in the team did not perform better than other teams. Quite possibly, what teams gained by identifying the expert in the team was countered by reductions in teamwork, team effort, or team cohesiveness as a result of overweighting the input of the expert individual.

Beyond conflict and decision making, several researchers have examined the fit relationship between team task environment and information-sharing processes within teams. Alper et al. (1998), in a study of 60 self-managing teams, focused on the degree to which task-related goal interdependence was structured cooperatively or competitively and the subsequent interaction with information sharing in the team context. They found that the degree to which teams communicate and share information is contingent on the cooperative or competitive environment. Specifically, teams in a cooperative environment discussed opposing views openly and constructively in such a way that positively contributed to overall team effectiveness. Teams in a competitive environment, on the other hand, did not engage in this same constructive form of information sharing and, in turn, suffered from inferior team effectiveness.

Continuing with the dimensions of external fit, Deutsch (1949b) was one of the first researchers to declare that rewards enhance team performance only if the reward structure produces a win–win situation (i.e., cooperative) in which all team members benefit if the team is successful. Since then, others (e.g., Wageman, 1997) have also identified team-based rewards as a critical success factor for team performance. In contrast, several empirical studies have shown that actually (a) cooperative reward structures enhance performance only under certain conditions and (b) competitive reward structures can have a positive effect on team performance. Wageman and Baker (1997), for instance, demonstrated that high reward interdependence (i.e., team-based rewards) leads to superior team performance in extremely high or low task interdependence environments. When the task environment is moderately interdependent, however, a reward system with more moderate interdependence resulted in higher team performance.

Beersma et al. (2003), in their study of 75 four-person teams, found similar contingencies in their examination of differing impacts of reward structures on speed and accuracy dimensions of tasks. Beyond just classifying tasks based on degree of interdependence, a specific task can also be differentiated in terms of whether it demands speed, accuracy, or both speed and accuracy in its execution. For many tasks, the speed and accuracy dimensions represent a trade-off that must be made. In general, findings from this study suggested that competitive reward structures enhance the speed dimension of the task, but cooperative reward structures enhance the accuracy dimension of the task. Thus, the appropriate reward system depends on the nature of the team task environment, including the degree of interdependence and the relative importance placed on speed or accuracy when the task is executed.

Regarding team structure, several recent studies illustrate the impact fit or misfit between the team task environment and team structure can have on team effectiveness. Stewart and Barrick (2000) established that there is a distinction between conceptual and behavioral-oriented task environments. Accordingly, teams with an interdependent structure and engaged primarily in conceptual tasks exhibit a U-shaped performance curve. In contrast, teams with the same structure but engaged in primarily behavioral tasks experience an inverted U-shaped performance curve. Hollenbeck et al. (2002) examined the fit between team structure and task environment and concluded that divisional team structures are superior in unpredictable task environments and functional team structures are superior in predictable task environments.

Finally, as the need for teams to operate across partially or fully distributed locations (e.g., virtual teams) has intensified, interest in determining which forms of technology engender superior team performance within these environments has become an important area of inquiry. Several empirical researchers have begun to examine the fit or contingency-based relationship between team task environment and technology. For instance, a series of studies on flight crews by Sarter and colleagues (Sarter

& Schroeder, 2001; Sarter & Woods, 1997, 2000) examined (a) the challenges associated with automation in highly autonomous and complex task environments and (b) the role of decision support systems in high-risk task environments (e.g., flight and medicine). Findings from this research suggest that certain forms of technology may foster superior performance, given certain team task characteristics. For instance, in high-risk task environments, decision support systems that simply communicate monitoring or status-related information may be preferable to command systems that indicate a specific action to be taken, as the former are less vulnerable to automation biases such as using information without questioning its accuracy.

## TOWARD A THEORY OF FIT IN TEAMS: DIRECTIONS FOR FUTURE RESEARCH

As evidenced by the preceding literature review, empirical research exists to support the conceptual framework of internal and external fit in teams that is presented in this chapter. The framework is also helpful in identifying specific dimensions of fit that deserve or need greater attention in future empirical research. Where this framework falls short is in building a theory of internal and external fit in teams. Hempel (1965) pointed out that science has two basic functions: (a) to adequately describe the objects and events being investigated and (b) to establish theories by which events and objects can be explained and predicted. The framework presented here is not a theoretical statement but does provide a valuable description that should be the source for developing a theory of fit in teams.

As Bacharach (1989) indicated, a theory is a system of constructs and variables in which the constructs are related to each other by propositions and the variables are related to each other by hypotheses. Further, this theoretical system is bounded by a set of assumptions and conditions. To develop a theory of fit in teams, we must identify the boundaries of the theory and further explain which variables and constructs are relevant and how these variables and constructs relate to each other. In other words, we must identify which underlying values and spatial and temporal assumptions bound the theory. We must more clearly state the relationships among constructs, including but not limited to stating (a) how the linking mechanisms in the framework relate to each other and (b) if and how the linking mechanisms mediate the relationship between internal and external fit and team effectiveness. Not until we extend this framework to the development of a theory can the role of fit in teams be evaluated in terms of falsifiability and utility (Bacharach, 1989).

Despite its theoretical limitations, the framework of internal and external fit in teams serves as a valuable reference for establishing future research priorities. Upon examining Table 8–1, we can determine which dimensions of fit are adequately covered and best understood as well as those dimensions that are prime targets for future inquiry. Specific to the dimensions of internal fit, the contingency-based relationships between team composition and team rewards, structure, and technology need to be further explored. Specifically, those researching team rewards should explore the relationship between cooperative and competitive reward systems and elements of team composition other than personality, including but not limited to ability, affect, and experience. Future researchers on team structures should consider the contingencies associated with different structural forms within teams as well as compositional factors other than personality. Lastly, research should build on Simons et al.'s (1999) study and explore how different conceptualizations of team composition interact with various team processes/emergent states to influence team effectiveness.

With respect to the dimensions of external fit, the contingency-based relationships between the team task environment and the four linking mechanisms (team processes/emergent states, team rewards, structure, and technology) are beginning to emerge as important areas of study. These are areas for which additional conceptual development and empirical research are greatly needed. For instance, an understanding of how team reward structures fit or misfit with varying levels of task complexity or novelty and how that level of fit influences team effectiveness would be highly valuable. Also, determining which team processes work best within certain team task environments would be a considerable leap forward in our understanding of how best to manage work teams.

Beyond the specific dimensions of fit noted in the framework for internal and external fit in teams, there are several additional topics related to fit in teams that we feel are extremely important for future researchers to consider. These areas include the degree to which both internal and external fit are needed for engendering team effectiveness and the role of time in the study of fit in teams. First, a deep understanding of the differential importance of and potential interactions between dimensions of internal and external fit in teams is critical. Studies such as that by Hollenbeck et al. (2002) clearly showed that certain dimensions of fit, when in a state of fit, can neutralize states of misfit in other dimensions. This particular study raised a fundamental question about which dimensions of fit, both internal and external, can neutralize or potentially amplify the impact on team effectiveness.

Furthermore, under what conditions must teams achieve both internal and external fit to subsequently engender team effectiveness, or are there certain circumstances where only having internal or external fit is satisfactory? For those conditions that require both internal and external fit, which dimension of fit should be achieved first? One perspective is that external fit may need to come first because the team may have more control over compositional factors than it does over the nature of the task at hand. In this case, the team would achieve external fit first by aligning the team's processes, structures, rewards, and technologies with the team task environment and subsequently align the team's composition with the characteristics of the linking mechanisms. Alternatively, if a team has influence over what tasks it accepts but no influence over the composition of the team, then the team may need to achieve internal fit first and then only accept those tasks that fit with the existing team processes, structure, rewards, and technologies. Thus, achievement of both internal and external fit may demand a specific sequence, and the most appropriate sequence may be contingent on what dimensions the team can influence.

Secondly, teams operate over time and in context. The framework of internal and external fit in teams establishes the theoretical rationale for inquiry into the antecedents, contextual factors, and outcomes associated with teams moving in and out of internal or external fit. For instance, the composition of teams can change over time. As new members enter the team, the team may enter a state of misfit on the person–team fit dimension. Given the evidence suggesting that the effects of team composition and levels of diversity on team effectiveness can actually change over time (Earley & Mosakowski, 2000), this is an extremely important consideration. A similar case can be made for the external fit in teams when considering how team tasks can change over time. If misfit is the difference between actual and optimal, what are the implications associated with teams moving off of this optimal fit line, why and under what conditions do teams move off of the optimal line, and what team processes or interventions actually facilitate regaining optimal fit?

## CONCLUSION

The traditional I–P–O frameworks that have been used to organize research on team effectiveness do not adequately address the true complexity inherent in work teams and, thus, although valuable, are insufficient for explaining team effectiveness. Ever since Woodward's (1965) pioneering contingency study, in which he examined the fit between technology and organizational structure, congruence has been seen as the exemplar of fit–performance relationships. In this chapter, by building on these established congruence or contingency-based perspectives, we establish a framework that begins to explain the role of fit in teams. Extending the linearly focused I–P–O models of team effectiveness, this framework establishes a more integrative perspective using the internal and external fit relationships that are most important to team effectiveness.

## REFERENCES

Adkins, C. L., Ravlin, E. C., & Meglino, B. M. (1996). Value congruence between co-workers and its relationship to work outcomes. *Group & Organization Management, 21,* 439–460.

Albanese, R., & Van Fleet, D. D. (1985). Rational behavior in groups—The free-riding tendency. *Academy of Management Review, 10*, 244–255.

Alper, S., Tjosvold, D., & Law, K. S. (1998). Interdependence and controversy in group decision making: Antecedents to effective self-managing teams. *Organizational Behavior and Human Decision Processes, 74*, 33–52.

Arthur, W., Young, B., Jordan, J. A., & Shebilske, W. L. (1996). Effectiveness of individual and dyadic training protocols: The influence of trainee interaction anxiety. *Human Factors, 38*, 79–86.

Bacharach, S. B. (1989). Organizational theories—Some criteria for evaluation. *Academy of Management Review, 14*, 496–515.

Barrick, M. R., Stewart, G. L., Neubert, M. J., & Mount, M. K. (1998). Relating member ability and personality to work-team processes and team effectiveness. *Journal of Applied Psychology, 83*, 377–391.

Barry, B., & Stewart, G. L. (1997). Composition, process, and performance in self-managed groups: The role of personality. *Journal of Applied Psychology, 82*, 62–78.

Barsade, S. G., Ward, A. J., Turner, J. D. F., & Sonnenfeld, J. A. (2000). To your heart's content: A model of affective diversity in top management teams. *Administrative Science Quarterly, 45*, 802–836.

Beersma, B., Hollenbeck, J. R., Humphrey, S. E., Moon, H., Conlon, D. E., & Ilgen, D. R. (2003). Cooperation, competition, and team performance: Towards a contingency approach. *Academy of Management Journal, 46*, 572–590.

Bonner, B. L., Baumann, M. R., & Dalal, R. S. (2002). The effects of member expertise on group decision-making and performance. *Organizational Behavior and Human Decision Processes, 88*, 719–736.

Boxx, W. R., Odom, R. Y., & Dunn, M. G. (1991). Organizational values and value congruency and their impact on satisfaction, commitment, and cohesion—An empirical examination within the public sector. *Public Personnel Management, 20*, 195–205.

Bretz, R. D., & Judge, T. A. (1994). Person–organization fit and the theory of work adjustment—Implications for satisfaction, tenure, and career success. *Journal of Vocational Behavior, 44*, 32–54.

Bunderson, J. S., & Sutcliffe, K. A. (2003). Management team learning orientation and business unit performance. *Journal of Applied Psychology, 88*, 552–560.

Cable, D. M., & DeRue, D. S. (2002). The convergent and discriminant validity of subjective fit perceptions. *Journal of Applied Psychology, 87*, 875–884.

Chatman, J. A. (1991). Matching people and organizations—Selection and socialization in public accounting firms. *Administrative Science Quarterly, 36*, 459–484.

Cohen, S. G., & Bailey, D. E. (1997). What makes teams work: Group effectiveness research from the shop floor to the executive suite. *Journal of Management, 23*, 239–290.

Colquitt, J. A., Hollenbeck, J. R., Ilgen, D. R., LePine, J. A., & Sheppard, L. (2002). Computer-assisted communication and team decision-making performance: The moderating effect of openness to experience. *Journal of Applied Psychology, 87*, 402–410.

De Dreu, C. K. W., & Weingart, L. R. (2003). Task versus relationship conflict, team performance, and team member satisfaction: A meta-analysis. *Journal of Applied Psychology, 88*, 741–749.

De Lisser, E. (1999, October 5). Update on small business: Firms with virtual environments appeal to workers. *Wall Street Journal*, p. B2.

DeMatteo, J. S., Eby, L. T., & Sundstrom, E. (1998). Team-based rewards: Current empirical evidence and directions for future research, *Research in organizational behavior* (Vol. 20, pp. 141–183). JAI Press.

Demming, W. E. (1986). *Out of the crisis*. Cambridge, MA: MIT Press.

Dennis, A. R., Valacich, J. S., & Nunamaker, J. F. (1990). An experimental investigation of the effects of group size in an electronic meeting environment. *IEEE Transactions on Systems, Man, & Cybernetics, 20*, 1049–1057.

Deustch, M. (1949a). The effects of cooperation and competition upon group process. *Human Relations, 2*, 199–231.

Deutsch, M. (1949b). A theory of cooperation and competition. *Human Relations, 2*, 129–152.

Devine, D. J. (1999). Effects of cognitive ability, task knowledge, information sharing, and conflict on group decision-making effectiveness. *Small Group Research, 30*, 608–634.

Donaldson, L. (2001). *The contingency theory of organizations*. Thousand Oaks, CA: Sage.

Earley, P. C., & Mosakowski, E. (2000). Creating hybrid team cultures: An empirical test of transnational team functioning. *Academy of Management Journal, 43*, 26–49.

Gerhart, B., & Milkovich, G. T. (1992). Employee compensation: Research and practice. In M. D. Dunnette & L. M. Hough (Eds.), *Handbook of industrial and organizational psychology* (2nd ed., Vol. 2, pp. 481–569). Palo Alto, CA: Consulting Psychologists Press.

Hackman, J. R. (1987). The design of work teams. In J. Lorsch (Ed.), *Handbook of organizational behavior* (pp. 315–342). New York: Prentice Hall.

Hackman, J. R. (1990). *Groups that work (and those that don't)*. San Francisco: Jossey-Bass.

Hackman, J. R., Brousseau, K. R., & Weiss, J. A. (1976). Interaction of task design and group-performance strategies in determining group effectiveness. *Organizational Behavior and Human Performance, 16*, 350–365.

Hempel, C. (1965). *Aspects of scientific explanation*: New York Free Press.

Hollenbeck, J. R., Moon, H., Ellis, A. P. J., West, B. J., Ilgen, D. R., Sheppard, L., Porter, C., & Wagner, J. A. (2002). Structural contingency theory and individual differences: Examination of external and internal person-team fit. *Journal of Applied Psychology, 87*, 599–606.

Ilgen, D. R. (1994). Jobs and roles: Accepting and coping with the changing structure of organizations. In M. G. Rumsey, C. B. Walker, & J. H. Harris (Eds.), *Personnel selection and classification* (pp. 13–22). Hillsdale, NJ: Lawrence Erlbaum Associates.

Ilgen, D. R., Hollenbeck, J. R., Johnson, M., & Jundt, D. (2005). Teams in organizations: From input-process-output models to IMOI models. *Annual Review of Psychology, 56*, 517–543.

Jehn, K. A. (1995). A multimethod examination of the benefits and detriments of intragroup conflict. *Administrative Science Quarterly, 40*, 256–282.

Katz, D., & Kahn, J. (1978). *The social psychology of organizations*. New York: Wiley.

Kozlowski, S. W. J., & Bell, B. S. (2003). Work groups and teams in organizations. In W. C. Borman, D. R. Ilgen & R. Klimoski (Eds.), *Handbook of psychology: Industrial and organizational psychology* (Vol. 12, pp. 333–375). London: Wiley.

Kozlowski, S. W. J., Gully, S. M., Nason, E. R., & Smith, E. M. (1999). Developing adaptive teams: A theory of compilation and performance across levels and time. In D. R. Ilgen & E. D. Pulakos (Eds.), *The changing nature of performance: Implications for staffing, motivation, and development* (pp. 240–292). San Francisco: Jossey-Bass.

Kozlowski, S. W. J., Gully, S. M., Salas, E., & Cannon-Bowers, J. A. (1996). Team leadership and development: Theory, principles, and guidelines for training leaders and teams. In M. M. Beyerlein & D. A. Johnson (Eds.), *Advances in interdisciplinary studies of work teams: Team leadership* (Vol. 3, pp. 251–289). Greenwich, CT: JAI Press.

Kristof, A. L. (1996). Person-organization fit: An integrative review of its conceptualizations, measurement, and implications. *Personnel Psychology, 49,* 1–49.

Kristof-Brown, A. L., & Stevens, C. K. (2001). Goal congruence in project teams: Does the fit between members' personal mastery and performance goals matter? *Journal of Applied Psychology, 86,* 1083–1095.

Kristof-Brown, A. L., Jansen, K. J., & Colbert, A. E. (2002). A policy-capturing study of the simultaneous effects of fit with jobs, groups, and organizations. *Journal of Applied Psychology, 87,* 985–993.

Laughlin, P. R. (1980). Social combination processes of cooperative, problem-solving groups as verbal intellective tasks. In M. Fishbein (Ed.), *Progress in social psychology* (vol. 1, pp. 127–135). Hillsdale: Lawrence Erlbaum Associates.

Leavitt, H. J. (1975). "Suppose we took groups seriously. . . ." In E. L. Cass & F. G. Zimmer (Eds.), *Man and work in society* (pp. 67–77). New York: Van Nostrand Reinhold.

LePine, J. A. (2003). Team adaptation and postchange performance: Effects of team composition in terms of members' cognitive ability and personality. *Journal of Applied Psychology, 88,* 27–39.

LePine, J. A., Hollenbeck, J. R., Ilgen, D. R., & Hedlund, J. (1997). Effects of individual differences on the performance of hierarchical decision-making teams: Much more than g. *Journal of Applied Psychology, 82,* 803–811.

Lewin, K. (1951). *Field theory in social science: Selected theoretical papers.* Westport, CT: Greenwood Press.

Marks, M. A., Mathieu, J. E., & Zaccaro, S. J. (2001). A temporally based framework and taxonomy of team processes. *Academy of Management Review, 26,* 356–376.

McGrath, J. E. (1984). *Groups: Interaction and performance.* Englewood Cliffs, NJ: Prentice Hall.

McGrath, J. E., & Altman, I. (1966). *Small group research: A synthesis and critique of the field.* New York: Holt, Rinehart, & Winston.

McGrath, J. E., Arrow, H., & Berdahl, J. L. (2000). The study of groups: Past, present, and future. *Personality and Social Psychology Review, 4,* 95–105.

Miller, L. K., & Hamblin, R. L. (1963). Interdependence, differential rewarding, and productivity. *American Sociological Review, 27,* 768–778.

Morse, D. (2003, January 17). Home Depot is struggling to adjust to new blueprint. *The Wall Street Journal Online,* pp. 1–5.

Muchinsky, P. M., & Monahan, C. J. (1987). What is person-environment congruence? Supplementary versus complementary models of fit. *Journal of Vocational Behavior, 31,* 268–277.

Pfeffer, J. (1997). *New directions for organizational theory: Problems and prospects.* New York: Oxford University Press.

Polzer, J. T., Milton, L. P., & Swann, W. B. J. R. (2002). Capitalizing on diversity: Interpersonal congruence in small work groups. *Administrative Science Quarterly, 47,* 296–324.

Qureshi, S. (1998). Supporting a network way of working in an electronic social space. *Group Decision and Negotiation, 7,* 399–416.

Rogelberg, S. G., & Rumery, S. M. (1996). Gender diversity, team decision quality, time on task, and interpersonal cohesion. *Small Group Research, 27,* 79–90.

Sarter, N. B., & Schroeder, B. (2001). Supporting decision making and action selection under time pressure and uncertainty: The case of in-flight icing. *Human Factors, 43,* 573–583.

Sarter, N. B., & Woods, D. D. (1997). Team play with a powerful and independent agent: Operational experiences and automation surprises on the Airbus A-320. *Human Factors, 39,* 553–569.

Sarter, N. B., & Woods, D. D. (2000). Team play with a powerful and independent agent: A full-mission simulation study. *Human Factors, 42,* 390–402.

Shirouzu, N. (2001, July 11). Ford stops using letter rankings to rate workers. *The Wall Street Journal,* p. B1.

Simons, T. L., & Peterson, R. S. (2000). Task conflict and relationship conflict in top management teams: The pivotal role of intragroup trust. *Journal of Applied Psychology, 85,* 102–111.

Simons, T., Pelled, L. H., & Smith, K. A. (1999). Making use of difference: Diversity, debate, and decision comprehensiveness in top management teams. *Academy of Management Journal, 42,* 662–673.

Stanne, M. B., Johnson, D. W., & Johnson, R. T. (1999). Does competition enhance or inhibit motor performance: A meta-analysis. *Psychological Bulletin, 125,* 133–154.

Steiner, I. D. (1972). *Group process and productivity.* New York: Academic Press.

Stewart, G. L., & Barrick, M. R. (2000). Team structure and performance: Assessing the mediating role of intrateam process and the moderating role of task type. *Academy of Management Journal, 43,* 135–148.

Townsend, A. M., DeMarie, S. M., & Hendrickson, A. R. (1998). Virtual teams: Technology and the workplace of the future. *The Academy of Management Executive, 12,* 17–29.

Van de Ven, A. H., Delbecq, A. L., & Koenig, R., Jr. (1976). Determinants of coordination modes within organizations. *American Sociological Review, 41,* 322–338.

Vancouver, J. B., & Schmitt, N. W. (1991). An exploratory examination of person–organization fit—Organizational goal congruence. *Personnel Psychology, 44,* 333–352.

Wageman, R. (1997). Critical success factors for creating superb self-managing teams. *Organizational Dynamics, 26,* 49–61.

Wageman, R., & Baker, G. (1997). Incentives and cooperation: The joint effects of task and reward interdependence on group performance. *Journal of Organizational Behavior, 18,* 139–158.

Wagner, J. A. (2000). Organizations. In A. E. Kazkin (Ed.), *Encyclopedia of Psychology* (Vol. 6, pp. 14–20). New York: Oxford University Press.

Werbel, J. D., & Gilliland, S. W. (1999). The use of person–environment fit in the selection process. In G. R. Ferris (Ed.), *Research in personnel and human resource management* (Vol. 17, pp. 209–243). Greenwich, CT: JAI Press.

Werbel, J. D., & Johnson, D. J. (2001). The use of person–group fit for employment selection: A missing link in person–environment fit. *Human Resource Management, 40,* 227–240.

Witt, L. A., Hilton, T. F., & Hockwarter, W. A. (2001). Addressing politics in matrix teams. *Group & Organization Management, 26,* 230–247.

Wittenbaum, G. M., Vaughan, S. I., & Stasser, G. (1998). Coordination in task-performing groups. In R. S. Tindale (Ed.), *Social psychological applications to social issues: Theory and research on small groups* (pp. 177–204). New York: Plenum Press.

Woodward, J. (1965). *Industrial organization: Theory and practice.* Oxford, England: Oxford University Press.

# CHAPTER 9

# *Survival of the Fittest or the Least Fit? When Psychology Meets Ecology in Organizational Demography*

## Aimee D. Ellis and Anne S. Tsui
*Arizona State University*

Psychological theories explain the tendency toward homogeneity in organizations and groups with research showing that homogeneity produces a positive outcome at the affective level but negative outcomes at the cognitive and behavioral levels with the ultimate danger of extinction. Yet, homogeneous groups and organizations abound and some even prosper. In the United States labor force, Whites comprise 70% of employees but occupy 84.8% of managerial positions (Equal Employment Opportunity Commission, 2004). In contrast, Blacks represent 13.9% of the workforce but only 6.6% of the managers and officials; Hispanics, 10.9% of the workforce, hold only 4.8% of managerial positions. Women, 47.5% of the workforce, occupy only 34.7% of managerial positions. How has homogeneity prevailed? Why have homogeneous groups or organizations avoided extinction? Using ideas from conservation biology, we argue that social systems have a natural instinct for survival and thus import or create a requisite level of diversity. In this chapter, we explain how homogeneous groups persist despite their homogeneity through a variety of adaptation responses.

Demographic homogeneity is the extent to which individuals have similar observable demographic attributes such as age, gender, race, ethnicity, and national origin as well as deeper or less observable characteristics such as shared beliefs, attitudes, personalities, religion, functional background, and so on. However, these characteristics are more revealing when considered in the context of the composition of the group. Do the individuals in a dyad, group, or organization as a whole have similar or disparate characteristics? For example, the gender of an individual produces different experiences, depending on the gender composition of his or her group (Tsui, Egan, & O'Reilly, 1992). A man will have different experiences depending on whether he is the lone man in a group, one of several men in a group with only one woman, or a man in a group evenly divided between men and women.

Demographic homogeneity represents a type of fit, with fit being harmony, a state of agreement or accord, or the degree of closeness between surfaces in an assembly of parts. Alternatively, demographic heterogeneity represents a misfit or misalignment. Demographic fit or misfit can occur at many different levels: person–supervisor fit, person–group fit, person–organization fit, group–organization fit, and organization–environment fit. A detailed discussion of these various types of fit can be found in the introductory chapter (see Ostroff & Schulte, chap. 1, this volume). Here, we offer a very brief definition for the purpose of the current discussion. At the dyad level, person–supervisor fit occurs when a supervisor and subordinate share common characteristics. Within groups, person–group fit occurs when a member of a team shares common qualities with other members of the team. Within organizations, person–organization fit occurs when a person shares common characteristics with the organization as a whole. Group–organization fit takes place when the workgroup and the entire organization share common qualities. Finally, organization–environment fit represents an alignment of the organization within its larger environment, including other organizations in its field (i.e., the industry and the geopolitical system surrounding it). Fit is a desired state being strived for by all social entities, individuals, groups, and organizations alike; thus, fit produces a pervasive and powerful homogenizing tendency.

Before introducing our framework, we should first clarify that there are two general approaches in the study of demographic fit of the types described earlier. They are the compositional and the relational approaches (Tsui & Gutek, 1999). Composition demography refers to demographic fit or distribution among all the elements within a unit, such as a workgroup or an organization. The analysis is at the unit level, focusing on outcomes for the unit. Relational demography refers to the fit between an element (e.g., the lower level that makes up the unit) within the unit and all other elements in that unit. The analysis is at the lower or element level, focusing on outcomes at the lower or element level. Our analysis in this chapter focuses on possible outcomes for both the elements within the unit (i.e., the lower level) and the unit itself (i.e., the higher level). Therefore, the ideas offered in this chapter accommodate both the relational demography and the compositional demography approaches.

## THE HOMOGENIZING TENDENCY AND ITS OUTCOMES

Individuals consistently seek out similar others, thereby forming dyads or groups with homogeneous memberships. With demographic homogeneity or demographic fit, shared understandings are assumed, uncertainty is reduced, and self-esteem is enhanced. The psychological drive for companionship with like others can be explained by several theories, including Byrne's (1971) similarity–attraction paradigm, Tajfel's (1982) social identity theory, Turner's (1985) social categorization theory, and Schnieder's (1987) attraction–selection–attrition framework and institutional theory at the firm level (Meyer & Rowan, 1977).

Byrne's (1971) similarity–attraction paradigm provided an explanation particularly relevant for person–supervisor or person–group fit. According to this paradigm, individuals display interpersonal attraction toward those who share similar attitudes, backgrounds, or any number of other characteristics. Blau (1977), for example, theorized that individuals associate disproportionately with members of their own group than with others in different groups. Newcomb (1956, 1961) asserted that mutual attraction was most likely to be observed among individuals with similar attitudes on basic issues. Gibbons and Olk (2003) found that ethnic identification was strongly associated with friendship development among students in an executive MBA program. Association with an individual sharing the same beliefs provides social validation, reduces uncertainty, and offers positive reinforcement (Berscheid & Walster, 1978). Because demographic characteristics provide an easily accessible proxy for deeper, unknown attitudes, diversity researchers assert that individuals of like demographic qualities—individuals with demographic fit—will have greater attraction to each other and will prefer the company of similar demographic others to that of dissimilar others (Chatman & O'Reilly, 2004; McPherson, Smith-Lovin, & Cook, 2001). Such claims have been widely demonstrated in empirical studies. For example, Glaman, Jones, and Rozelle (1996) found, in a study of 190 dyadic pairs, that initial social liking and coworker preference were predicted by demographic similarity. Likewise, Marsden (1988) found that individuals were more likely to engage in confiding relationships with individuals of similar race/ethnicity or religion. At work, friendships are based primarily on race or gender rather than proximity (Lincoln & Miller, 1979; Mollica, Gray, & Trevino, 2003). Additional studies have shown that the similarity–attraction hypothesis holds for economic status, race, and gender (Hinds, Carley, Krackhardt, & Wholey, 2000; Shaw, 1971).

Although social identity theory is also based on easily accessible information such as demographic attributes, it extends the similarity–attraction hypothesis by contending that people will categorize others—and themselves—into social groups, using either observed or assumed similarities. This process of categorization and self-categorization leads to a social identity through which individuals can understand themselves (Ashforth & Mael, 1989; Tajfel & Turner, 1986). Because this social identity serves as a source of self-esteem, individuals tend to accentuate the differences between their own group and other groups by emphasizing the positive features of the group to which they belong and the negative features of the group to which they do not belong.

Explaining individual–organization fit, Schneider's (1987) attraction–selection–attrition framework posited that people with similar personalities are attracted to particular careers and organizations. Organizations, in turn, select individuals with desired competencies (e.g., marketing skills) whose personalities corresponds with that of the organization. Individuals who do not "fit" the organization leave through voluntary or involuntary turnover. As such, "the range of variance in individual differences in a setting is much less than would be expected by chance—or by the random assignment of people to settings" (Schneider, 1987, p. 442). A study of almost 13,000 managers from 142 firms showed, indeed, that the personality attributes of managers in the same firm were relatively homogeneous (Schneider, Smith, Taylor, & Fleenor, 1998).

Institutional theory best explains the underlying dynamics of workgroup–organization and organization–industry fit. Meyer and Rowan (1977) described the importance of institutional myths that give organizations legitimacy, whereas DiMaggio and Powell (1983) outlined three processes—coercive, mimetic, and normative—by which organizations become similar or homogeneous in their operating procedures or even demographic makeup. Institutional practices give firms legitimacy in maintaining the status quo on demographic homogeneity. These isomorphic processes force "one unit in a population to resemble other units that face the same set of environmental conditions" (DiMaggio & Powell, 1983, p. 149). Staw and Epstein (2000) showed how the adoption of total quality management programs proliferated and gave companies favorable reputations, although the programs did nothing to improve corporate performance. The proliferation of total quality management programs resulted from mimetic isomorphism, in which organizations model themselves on each other. Coercive isomorphism can also create homogeneity in organizations, as Tolbert and Zucker (1983) showed in their study on the diffusion of civil service procedures through city governments after legislation by the state. In this case, legislation mandated that all the organizations in their study adopt the same procedures. As a result of these isomorphic forces, organizations become similar over time.

Because intraorganization groups face the same institutional environment (e.g., internal structures, processes, and culture), the need for legitimacy and the pressure of evaluation may propel groups to become more alike within the same organization than between organizations. In other words, groups, possibly a new project team and a quality control team, within Company A will tend to resemble each other more than they will resemble comparable groups in Company B.

Together, these theories help explain the overwhelming tendency to "drive out diversity" (Milliken & Martins, 1996, p. 420). Individuals favor like others; organizations require their teams to resemble one another; industries reward homogeneous firms. As a result of these psychological impulses and institutional processes, dyads, groups, and organizations become homogeneous with respect to age, gender, race, attitudes, personality, and even structural characteristics. This tendency toward homogenization, dubbed "homosocial reproduction" by Kanter (1977), engenders positive affective outcomes in individuals and teams and acceptance among organizations. The numerous theories explaining why individuals seek out similar others are applicable and relevant to homogenization based on both surface and deep-level diversity; however, in our model linking demography, fit, and outcomes, we focus primarily on demographic homogeneity.

## MODEL OVERVIEW

The model of demographic fit presented in this chapter explains the effects of homogeneity (heterogeneity) in groups and organizations over time; in so doing, it provides an overarching framework for understanding previous research on diversity, such as why heterogeneity is related to higher productivity and effectiveness (as well as the reverse, why homogeneity is associated with reduced productivity and effectiveness). This model also begins to shed light on some of the conflicting results arising from empirical studies. It further provides clarity to the mediating process from demographic fit or misfit to eventual performance or survival outcomes.

In the first stage of our model, psychological forces and organizational and institutional contexts drive individuals, groups, and organizations to associate with and prefer the company of similar others. The concentration of demographically similar individuals, from the process of homosocial reproduction, begets numerous positive affective states, including social integration, attachment, satisfaction, harmony, empowerment, and positive identity reinforcement. At the group or organizational level, affective outcomes include legitimacy and harmony with the others in the institutional environment. Stage II or cognitive outcomes result over time as homogeneous dyads, groups, and firms interact with each other in the process of performing tasks. The cognitive results of demographic fit include inertia, commitment to the status quo, groupthink, and low knowledge diversity. As these cognitive outcomes manifest themselves, Stage III, or behavioral outcomes become apparent. These include low learning, creativity, and innovation, low flexibility, defective decision making, low turnover, reduced access to resources, isolation, and, ultimately, sub par performance. The culmination of demographic homogeneity is extinction (Stage IV). This demographic fit four-stage process model is illustrated in Fig. 9–1.

As we will discuss in detail, Stage III outcomes can trigger negative feedback or a state of disequilibrium, which can lead to adaptive or nonadaptive responses. As a result of these responses, extinction can be avoided by importing a requisite level of heterogeneity into the system.

## Affective (Stage I) Outcomes

Simply put, being around like others feels good; empirical research has demonstrated the wide range of positive affective outcomes initially arising from homogeneity or demographic fit at all levels. "People who are similar in backgrounds may have similar values, share common life experiences, and, therefore, find the experience of interacting with each other positively reinforcing" (Milliken & Martins, 1996, p. 415). In groups with demographic fit, men and women showed more positive affect when they were part of groups dominated by their own sex (Chatman & O'Reilly, 2004). Interactions within diverse groups can create stress and anxiety for some individuals (Richeson & Shelton, 2003). Diversity, too, can decrease attachment to one's workgroup. Tsui et al. (1992) found that Whites in racially diverse groups and men in mixed gender groups had lower attachment to their organizations.

Superior–subordinate dyads with demographic fit not only enjoy increased cohesion and social integration; demographic similarity between supervisors and subordinates also relates to higher-quality relationships than those experienced by dissimilar dyads. For example, both Tsui and O'Reilly (1989) and Varma and Stroh (2001) stated that supervisors reported liking same-sex subordinates more than dissimilar-sex subordinates and that their affective response led to higher performance ratings for the subordinate in demographically similar dyads. Conversely, dissimilarity in gender leads to lower supervisor–subordinate exchange quality, as was found by Green, Anderson, and Shivers (1996).

At the group level, affective outcomes take the form of cohesion or social integration. As defined by O'Reilly, Caldwell, and Barnett (1989), social integration is a complex phenomenon reflecting attraction to a group, satisfaction with other group members, and positive social interaction among group members. This positive social cohesive group state was predicted by similarity in age and tenure within groups (O'Reilly et al., 1989). In his investigation of new product and applied research development groups, Keller (2001) found functional diversity to be negatively related to group cohesion. Increasing workgroup diversity is also associated with increased emotional and relationship conflict. In contrast,

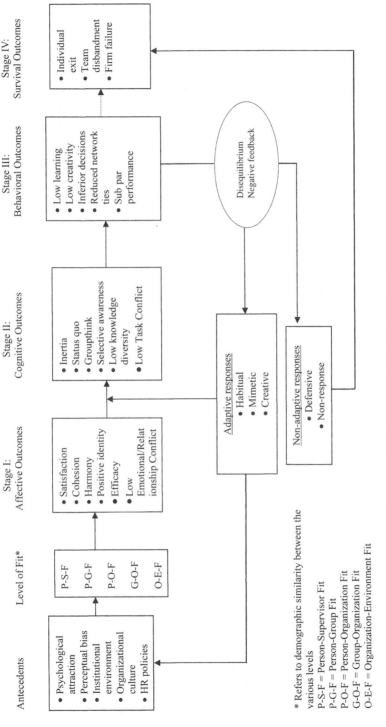

FIGURE 9-1. Demography, fit, and multistage outcomes.

Stage IV:
Survival Outcomes

- Individual exit
- Team disbandment
- Firm failure

Stage III:
Behavioral Outcomes

- Low learning
- Low creativity
- Inferior decisions
- Reduced network ties
- Sub par performance

Disequilibrium
Negative feedback

Stage II:
Cognitive Outcomes

- Inertia
- Status quo
- Groupthink
- Selective awareness
- Low knowledge diversity
- Low Task Conflict

Stage I:
Affective Outcomes

- Satisfaction
- Cohesion
- Harmony
- Positive identity
- Efficacy
- Low Emotional/Relationship Conflict

Adaptive responses
- Habitual
- Mimetic
- Creative

Non-adaptive responses
- Defensive
- Non-response

Level of Fit*

P-S-F
P-G-F
P-O-F
G-O-F
O-E-F

Antecedents

- Psychological attraction
- Perceptual bias
- Institutional environment
- Organizational culture
- HR policies

* Refers to demographic similarity between the various levels

P-S-F = Person-Supervisor Fit
P-G-F = Person-Group Fit
P-O-F = Person-Organization Fit
G-O-F = Group-Organization Fit
O-E-F = Organization-Environment Fit

members of racially homogeneous teams felt greater team empowerment as defined by meaningfulness, autonomy, potency, and impact (Kirkman, Tesluk, & Rosen, 2004).

Fit between employees and organizations also generates positive affectivity and relates to higher levels of job satisfaction and organizational commitment (Chatman, 1991; O'Reilly, Chatman, & Caldwell, 1991; Verquer, Beehr, & Wagner, 2003). These positive emotional responses to homogeneity fuel the homosocial reproduction cycle. With like others, individuals feel a boost in their self-esteem (Tajfel & Turner, 1986), as well as reduced uncertainty, greater loyalty, and increased trust (Kanter, 1977). Similarity leads to comfort and contentment. However, homophily also produces complacency and restricted cognitive capability. Over time, demographic fit leads to dysfunctional cognitive outcomes, a topic we visit next.

## Cognitive (Stage II) Outcomes

Despite the evidence demonstrating the positive emotional effects of demographic fit, cognitive outcomes suffer from homogeneity. The ease of communication among demographically similar individuals or within homogenous groups and organizations, while initially an affective boom for participants, can lead to impaired cognitive ability. When members share opinions and hold the same point of view, they feel reassured that their shared views are correct. Enhanced self-esteem combined with affirmation of the group's fundamental "rightness" leads to hubris. The entity, then, is unable to step outside the bounds of its own experience and self-reflect or question its experience because doing so would threaten the pleasure derived from cohesion, efficacy, and satisfaction. Consequently, the entity's overconfidence creates a negative cognitive capability.

Ethnocentrism, "an attitude or outlook in which values derived from ones' own cultural background are applied to other cultural contexts where different values are operative" (LeVine & Campbell, 1972, p. 1) is endemic to homogeneous groups. Levine and Resnick (1993) suggested that increased in-group affinity is associated with greater suspicion and antagonism toward out-group members. This refusal to acknowledge or listen to out-group members' perspectives damages the potential for creative problem solving.

The susceptibility to in-group influences and resistance to alternative perspectives makes individuals susceptible to groupthink, a way of thinking in which people, deeply involved in an in-group, strive for unanimity and fail to realistically evaluate alternative ideas or courses of action that deviate from the dominant view (Janis, 1972). A related phenomenon is group polarization, the tendency for initial preferences of a group to become exaggerated or stronger (Moscovici & Zavalloni, 1969;

Myers & Lamm, 1976) in groups with demographic fit. Because similar group members share opinions and beliefs, they are likely to amplify initial thoughts and decisions with support and agreement to enhance group standing and provide a boost to self-esteem (McGarty, Turner, Hogg, David, & Wetherell, 1992).

Therefore, demographically fit groups possess low levels of knowledge diversity in the form of dominant logics; alternatively, they have a high level of attentional homogeneity, or shared schemas. Dominant logic refers to how managers conceptualize "the business and the administrative tools to accomplish goals and make decisions" (Prahalad & Bettis, 1986, p. 491) whereas attentional homogeneity captures "the degree of similarity in the foci of attention of top managers across organizations" (Abrahamson & Hambrick, 1997, p. 514). A form of shared schemas or similar dominant logic, low cognitive diversity limits the variety of information available to the group for problem solving or decision making. In a study of 315 individuals comprising 41 different teams, Rentsch and Klimoski (2001) found that demographic similarity significantly related to team member schema agreement. As explained by Ely and Thomas (2001), the knowledge and experiences of diverse employees "are potentially valuable resources that the work group can use to rethink its primary tasks and redefine its markets, products, strategies, and business practices in ways that will advance its mission" (p. 240). Evidence is clear that groups with demographic fit have a more limited range of knowledge resources than groups that are demographically diverse (Milliken & Martins, 1996; Williams & O'Reilly, 1998).

At the organizational level, the effect of cognitive limitation has been found in top management teams. For example, demographic homogeneity has been related to inertia and commitment to the status quo (Hambrick, Geletkanycz, & Fredrickson, 1993; Miller & Chen, 1994). Hambrick, Cho, and Chen (1996) found demographic heterogeneity in top management teams to be associated with not only a longer response time to the competitive actions of other firms but also the propensity to not respond at all. Although commitment to a chosen course of action is not necessarily negative, these tendencies can impede organizations attempting to develop new products or solve vexing problems.

## Behavioral (Stage III) Outcomes

Whereas the initial emotional responses to homogeneity, especially at the individual and group levels, are positive, over time, the cognitive outcomes of demographic fit include low access to knowledge resources, inertia, and polarization. These conditions set in motion behaviors that damage groups and organizations. Without a strong and wide-ranging knowledge base, homogeneous entities face stagnation as they are unable to advance or develop new ideas, creative solutions, and innovative perspectives. Homogeneous groups or organizations may suffer from lower creativity, less task conflict, groupthink, lower turnover, and poor quality decisions, all of which are potentially damaging to the entity's functioning and performance.

Research evidence on the negative behavioral consequences of demographic fit is abundant. Groups with demographic fit exhibit low levels of creativity (Jackson, May, & Whitney, 1995; Levin & Moreland, 1998; McLeod, Lobel, & Cox, 1996; Paulus, 2000), and demographic homogeneity (at the top management level) is associated with lower levels of organizational innovation (Bantel & Jackson, 1989; Campbell, 1965). "Because greater demographic diversity entails relationships among people with different sets of contacts, skills, information, and experiences, heterogeneous teams enjoy an enhanced capacity for creative problem solving" (Reagans & Zuckerman, 2001, p. 502). Homogeneous groups in contrast are less flexible (Paulus, 2000; Pfeffer, 1985). With rigidity, tasks are completed in strict fashion, according to well-established rules, eliminating doubt, ambivalence, and complication. When that happens, organizations lose the ability to adapt because they are unable to act outside the prescribed rules (Weick, 1979) or, to use a favorite popular term, to "think outside the box."

Decision making, too, can be impaired by homogeneity. One reason demographically fit groups make poor decisions is over-reliance on shared schemas, pointing "to the negative consequences of too much intersubjectivity, which can prevent groups from fully exploiting the cognitive resources of their members (cf. Levin, & Moreland, 1991)" (Levine & Resnick, 1993, p. 601). Demographically fit groups overestimate their collective efficacy, escalating commitment to incorrect actions or policies (Lee & Farh, 2004; Whyte, 1998; Whyte, Saks, & Hook, 1997). At the organizational level, Finkelstein and Hambrick (1997) proposed that heterogeneous top management teams could generate higher-quality strategic decisions than could homogeneous teams because heterogeneous teams develop more innovative alternatives and subject those choices to greater scrutiny. Decisions regarding product–market innovation strategies made by heterogeneous management teams lead to increased market share relative to decisions made by homogeneous groups (Lyon & Ferrier, 2002).

Disagreements focusing on the scope, content, and implementation of particular assignments, or task conflict, can benefit groups by injecting new ideas, forcing consideration of alternatives, and disrupting the status quo. This type of beneficial conflict is rare in homogeneous groups. Jehn, Chadwick, and Thatcher (1997) found that teams in which members held similar values experienced less task conflict. Conversely, heterogeneity in terms of educational and functional background and type of position has been related to higher levels of task conflict (Jehn, Northcraft, & Neale, 1999).

In some instances, turnover is a positive outcome for the organization (Staw, 1980), especially when turnover weeds out low performers and brings in new blood. In homogeneous dyads, groups, or organizations, turnover rates decrease. For example, groups heterogeneous with respect to age have greater turnover than those with members around the same age (O'Reilly et al., 1989; Wagner, Pfeffer, & O'Reilly, 1984), whereas employees who work with racially similar others were less likely to quit (Zatzick, Elvira, & Cohen, 2003). Individuals sharing the same values as an organization will also be less likely to leave. "The degree to which individual preferences matched organizational realities was predictive of turnover two years later" (O'Reilly et al., 1991, p. 510). In a study of accounting recruits, new employees whose values best matched those of the firm had the lowest intention to leave and were the least likely to quit one year later (Chatman, 1991).

Demographically fit groups may have more reduced network ties, dampening the flow of new information into and contacts for the group. Stable group membership (homogeneity in tenure) may lead to isolation from other groups. Katz (1982) showed that high-longevity teams have fewer interactions with external teams. Conversely, diversity in functional background increases communication with individuals outside the team (Ancona & Caldwell, 1992).

Given the numerous detriments associated with homogeneous groups, it is not surprising that they experience sub par performance. Research has show that demographically fit groups are less likely to succeed. Rogelberg and Rumery (1996) observed that groups with mixed gender performed better than all-male groups. In another study, all-male groups were found to make overaggressive decisions and perform poorly in group tasks (LePine, Hollenbeck, Ilgen, Colquitt, & Ellis, 2002). Katz (1982) found that long-tenured groups demonstrated lower performance in three areas of research and development—in research, in development, and in technical service. Robust evidence showing the advantage of demographic heterogeneity in the organization for above-average firm performance has been accumulated (Frink et al., 2003; Richard, 2000; Richard, Barnett, Dwyer, & Chadwick, 2004; Wilbert, 2004). For example, a higher percentage of racial minorities in an organization was related to higher financial return for the company (Richard, 2000). Return on equity and return to shareholders percentages were better for firms with higher percentages of women executives than those with homogeneous executive ranks (Sellers, 2004), and announcements of Department of Labor awards for affirmative action programs improved the firms' stock returns (Wright, Ferris, Hiller, & Kroll, 1995).

## Survival (Stage IV) Outcomes

Given the negative behavioral and performance outcomes associated with demographic fit, individuals, groups, or firms with homogeneity should have a low survival capability. Individuals will find a low-performing, stagnant group to be dissatisfying, thereby reducing self-image and promoting departure. Stagnant groups are more likely to be selected out by the firm, leading to disbandment. Sub par performance of homogeneous firms would eventually lead to failures. Yet, homogeneity prevails in many effective groups and successful firms. How do we explain the inconsistency between the logical outcome of demographic misfit and the empirical observation of the persistence of homogeneity? We propose that groups and firms possess a survival instinct, much like biological systems, which enables them to import sufficient diversity to maintain survival or enact a variety of adaptive responses to curb the aforementioned negative cognitive outcomes. We use ecological theory, conservation biology, and genetics to explain how homogeneous groups are likely to become extinct in the long term. Conservation biology, a multidisciplinary science, not only explains how the mass extinction of species on earth results from a loss of biological diversity (Primack, 1998) but also offers insight into how and why survival is better for the genetically, or demographically in our case, least fit.

In reproduction, a manifestation of the survival instinct, the man and woman each contribute genetic material for a heritable trait. Each individual has two alleles, the name designated for the specific form of the inherited trait (Caughley & Gunn, 1996). These two alleles can be identical or they can be different, depending on the contribution from the parents. When the parents are very similar, the offspring is more likely to inherit two like alleles. Consider the example of the thalassemias, a group of inherited blood diseases:

> When two carriers [of thalassemia] become parents, there is a one-in-four chance that any child they have will inherit a thalassemia gene from each parent and have a severe form of the disease. There is a two-in-four chance that the child will inherit one of each kind of gene and become a carrier like its parents; and a one-in-four chance that the child will inherit two normal genes from its parents and be completely free of the disease or carrier state. These odds are the same for each pregnancy when both parents are carriers. (*Quick Reference and Fact Sheets: Thalassemia*, 2004)

In contrast, when the parents are dissimilar, and only one parent carriers the allele, the child's chance of contracting the disease is eliminated, and the child has only a 25% chance of becoming a carrier. The more similar the genetic code of the parents, the more likely a child will inherit the disease. Thus, genetic similarity or fit reduces an individual's survival chances.

Heterozygous (having the two alleles at corresponding loci on homologous chromosomes different for one or more loci) individuals enjoy increased survivability because, if they inherit a single defective gene, they are not debilitated by its effects. In addition, when competing for resources, heterozygous offspring often do better than the less robust homozygous progeny. When homozygous individuals with the same or very similar genetic backgrounds mate, they have a greater chance of producing offspring with genetic abnormalities, with a low chance for survival, a result called inbreeding depression (Senner, 1980). Inbreeding depression is characterized by high mortality of progeny, fewer children, or offspring who are weak, infertile, or unable to mate. In addition, as more and more offspring inherit homogeneous genetic material, the genetic pool shrinks, and genetic diversity is lost among groups and populations.

According to conservation biology, diversity among gene pools, species, and ecosystems is necessary for adaptation to shifting environmental conditions; species with little genetic diversity are vulnerable to extinction when the environment changes. The loss of genetic variation impedes a population's ability to adapt to changing environments or environmental stressors (Heschel & Paige, 1995). "The eventual fate of a small, closed population of animals is nearly always extinction" (Senner, 1980, p. 209).

Inbreeding, or the mating of two very similar individuals, is analogous to the homosocial reproduction generated by the psychological drive to associate with similar others. The joining of similar others in dyads, groups, or organizations engenders negative outcomes comparable to those produced via physical reproduction. The union of similar parents creates offspring who are weak, unable to reproduce, or incapable of adapting to changing environmental conditions. Likewise, the dyads, groups, and organizations created from homosocial reproduction suffer impaired cognitive and behavior outcomes resulting from the concentration of similar individuals. As described earlier, these outcomes include decreased cognitive resources, low learning, low levels of knowledge, lack of creativity and innovation, low turnover, impaired decision making, and sub par performance.

Firms can fail, tantamount to species extinction, as the result of inbreeding depression. Given finite resources in the environment, firms will compete for common employees, customers, and other inputs (Baum & Singh, 1994). Demographically fit firms, feeble and rigid owing to homosocial reproduction and homogeneity in its ranks, will be less fit to compete with more robust organizations. The homogeneous firms will be selected out by the environment (Baum & Singh, 1994). Such a case was observed by Picher and Smith (2001) during an 8-year study of a large financial services organization. These authors traced the declining heterogeneity of the top management team between 1983 and 1991, attributing market-to-book values much lower than that of its competitors to the top management team's demographic fit. In 1994, the firm became extinct via a takeover. The environment can support more firms that are diverse and that, therefore, use complimentary resources than it can homogeneous firms competing for the same resources (Aldrich, 1979; Baum & Singh,

1994; Gimeno, Folta, Cooper, & Woo, 1997; Hannan & Freeman, 1977). One method by which firms survive is to specialize in fine grain, or stable, environments and generalize in coarse grain, or uncertain, environments. Generalist firms have diverse capabilities that allow them to respond to changes in the environment, much like genetic diversity allows species to adapt to environmental alterations. This specialization versus generalization is a natural and logical response to environmental conditions for ensuring survival. In the next section we will discuss adaptation responses in more detail.

## The Adaptation Responses

Recall the stages of our model of demographic fit: Psychological processes, perceptual biases, organizational culture, and institutional environments push organisms, be they individuals, groups, or organizations, to achieve fit, which can occur at the level of person–supervisor, person–group, person–organization, group–organization, or organization–environment. Fit at these levels leads to Stage I, affective outcomes, which include satisfaction, cohesion, positive identity, efficacy, and low emotional conflict. These positive affective states engender Stage II, cognitive outcomes: inertia, commitment to the status quo, groupthink, selective awareness, low knowledge diversity, and low task conflict. Stage III, behavioral outcomes, such as low learning, low creativity, poor decisions, reduced network ties, and sub par performance, result. Finally, Stage IV, survival outcomes, represents survival or extinction: individual exit, group disbandment, or, ultimately, firm failure. This process represented in our model of demographic fit may appear counterintuitive. If homogeneity initially leads to desired affective outcomes, but ultimately impairs an individual's, a group's, or an organization's survival chances, how can so many homogenous dyads, teams, and firms exist? If the model we have presented holds true, certainly we would see *less* demographic fitness at all levels. Only the heterogeneous groups or firms should survive the selection forces. What explains the abundance of homogeneity at all levels?

To explain this apparent contradiction, we turn to cybernetics, or control theory. Here again is a contradiction—How might cybernetics, a postmodern, even futuristic approach, associated with cyborgs and artificial intelligence on the one hand and ecology and biology, fields firmly grounded in the building blocks of natural life on the other, be integrated into a common model? Indeed, such a combination is not too far-fetched. In their book, *Attention and Self-Regulation: A Control-Theory Approach to Human Behavior*, Carver and Scheier (1981) outlined several natural systems that correspond to control theory. Their thesis rests on the ability to apply control theory to the behavior of individuals or social systems.

In control theory, when a standard is made salient, a person (or group or firm) will compare that standard to his or her current state or behavior.

When faced with discrepancies, individuals will alter their behavior so that their current state or behavior more closely conforms to the standard (Carver & Scheier, 1981). The negative feedback loop represents a test–operate–test–exit (T–O–T–E) process, the *test* being the comparison between existing state and standard and the *operate* conforming to alteration. Entities in the operate phase may adapt, a natural, unconscious response to restore balance, or they will adjust, or intentionally modify behavior or standards, to stabilize inconsistency. The test–operate loop continues until the current state corresponds with the standard; at that point, *exit* ends the cycle (Carver & Scheier, 1981).

Using this framework, individuals in demographically fit groups detect a discrepancy between their ideal state and their current state. Here, we assume that the ideal state goes beyond simply affective outcomes and includes behavioral outcomes, such as high performance, learning, and creativity as well. This gap between an ideal state and current state is captured in the "disequilibrium" circle in Fig. 9–1. At Stage I, the entity has little incentive to change because individuals or groups experience positive affective outcomes. If the affirming emotions of Stage I have not yet morphed into dysfunctional cognitive or behavioral outcomes, the entity will not be driven to alter its current state. However, in Stage II or Stage III, the positive affective states arising from demographic similarity dissipate when the unit is faced with lack of innovation and creativity, reduced access to resources, isolation, or sub par performance. Individuals or units in Stage II or Stage III desire enhanced self-esteem but receive negative feedback in terms of new product development, research dollars, or sales. Such negative feedback signals a discrepancy between ideal and actual conditions, and the incongruity between these two states will initiate the T–O–T–E loop. The individual, group, or organization will make adjustments or adaptations until the incongruity is diminished to the point of imperceptibility.

Adaptations are not necessarily conscious; nor are they of necessity causally linked to the discrepancy. In other words, although the negative outcomes result from homogeneity, the process triggered by discrepancies between actual and desired states does not necessarily examine *why* the incongruity exists. These adjustments are attempts of the organism to return to homeostasis or balance. Innumerable factors, such as the legal and ethical environment, status hierarchies, extent of deliberation regarding the source of negative feedback, and individual differences of entity members, will determine which response or combination of responses the entity selects. Because the T–O–T–E process does not necessarily include an evaluation of alternatives, adaptations may be dysfunctional as well as productive.

The number of adaptations and adjustments available to organisms are potentially infinite; however, we will examine five representative responses, three adaptive and two nonadaptive, adopting the categories

of responses by individuals who experience dissatisfaction or disequilibrium between their ideal and current state in general (Hom & Griffeth,
1994; Rossé & Hulin, 1985; Rossé & Kraut, 1983) or on performance in
particular (Tsui, Ashforth, St. Claire, & Xin, 1995). Hom and Griffeth
(1994) discussed four categories of responses by individuals experiencing dissatisfaction. (a) Past reinforcement history guides response selection. People who previously performed certain responses learn about
their relative utility and later choose those responses having the maximum utility. (b) Individuals may observe role models and emulate actions
that successfully resolved past dissatisfaction. (c) Social norms prohibit-
ing or proscribing certain actions in a given context may dictate adaptive
choices. (d) Perceived constraints on behaviors (both personal and environmental barriers) influence adaptive responses (p. 194). For the current
purpose, we refer to the first types as *habitual* or *routine responses*. The
entity reflects on past success and engages in extra effort or simply requests more resources (e.g., personnel or time). We combine imitation of
role models and adoption of social norms in one category because they
both represent *mimetic responses*, that is, imitating other's actions or
behavior. We add two new categories, one involving new or *creative
responses* that the entity has not used before and the other involving managing impressions or changing expectations held by outsiders (Tsui et al.,
1995). The latter may be considered a form of *defensive responses*. A final
action is doing nothing (*nonresponse*), avoiding or ignoring the negative
feedback or disequilibrium, which is a nonadaptive response because it
maintains the status quo. Forming a basic typology of responses to disequilibrium, these five categories are summarized in Table 9–1, with examples at the levels of the individual, the group, and the organization. They
are also represented in Fig. 9–1 as outcomes of disequilibrium/negative
feedback.

In natural ecosystems, extinction is avoided through biodiversity, which
allows species to thrive despite environmental changes or catastrophes.
Why discuss the range of active or adaptive responses? Would not
entities within an organization or industrial environment engaged in the
T–O–T–E process automatically increase demographic heterogeneity to
avoid their own extinctions? Such an adjustment, however, may not
occur naturally or willingly because increasing misfit will remove or
reduce the affective state that members enjoy in Stage I. Therefore, the
challenge is to find the optimal adjustment that maintains positive affective outcomes while minimizing the negative cognitive and behavioral
results of later stages of the demographic fit process. The genetic diversity necessary for the survival of biological systems has its analog in the
knowledge diversity embedded in the demographic diversity, heterogeneity, or misfit of social systems. Adaptive responses that increase
knowledge diversity are essential for ensuring individual, group, or organizational survival in the long term. Each of the five adaptive responses

**TABLE 9–1.**

**Typology of Adaptations to Performance Decline Due to Demographic Homogeneity**

| Type of Adaptation Responses | Sample Responses | | |
| --- | --- | --- | --- |
| | *Individual* | *Group* | *Organization* |
| Habitual responses (duplicate own behaviors rewarded in the past) | Exert higher levels of effort; Request more resources from the organization | Focus on style instead of substance; Increase visibility within business unit(s) | Introduce new product; Divest underperforming or unrelated unit(s); Restructure |
| Mimetic responses (imitate adaptive responses of others) | Copy the observable actions of others in similar situations; Copy the actions of highly adaptive individuals | Change group leadership; Job rotation among members | Develop diversity training program; External hire of CEO; Increase diversity of top management team; Alter diversity of board membership |
| Creative responses (develop new approaches) | Seek outside counsel; Seek new perspective; Research problem area; Complete additional training; Join professional association | Provide cross-training; Require continuing education; Stimulate task conflict | Acquire firm with complementary skills; Specialize in niche market; Join alliance or joint venture; Change organizational culture; Introduce new human resource policies |
| Defensive responses (manage impressions or change expectations) | Recast standard for performance; Focus attention on positive results; Modify relationship with supervisor; Rationalize low performance by blaming others' incompetence; Shift ambitions | Promote group goals within organization; Undermine other groups' performances; Encourage organization to use different measurement standards; Explain low performance by claiming organization did not provide adequate resources | Create public relations campaign to change organization's image; Establish foundation to fund charitable activities; Lobby for tariffs on imported products; Blame sub par performance on economic conditions |
| Nonresponse (refuse to act) | Rationalization | Ignore the discrepancy | Strategic persistence |

outlined in Table 9–1 implies a different degree of success in increasing knowledge diversity. Knowledge diversity is our focus because a range of knowledge diversity protects against other negative cognitive outcomes—inertia, commitment to the status quo, groupthink, selective awareness, and reduced task conflict.

### Adaptive Responses at the Individual Level

Individuals will experience negative feedback when they perceive ineffectual decision making in the group, impaired problem-solving capability, or reduced status of the group relative to others in the organization. When confronted with a discrepancy between actual and desired states, individuals may engage in habitual responses; in other words, they will duplicate behaviors rewarded in the past, such as exerting a higher level of effort or asking for additional resources. These responses do not disrupt the individuals' affect toward the group but also do not increase the knowledge diversity of the individual or of the group. Alternatively, individuals may invoke mimetic responses by attempting to reduce discrepancies through emulating role models or following social norms. Individuals may look to other individuals who are in similar discrepant situations and imitate their responses. They may also observe and copy the behavior of effective individuals or units. These mimetic responses may increase the adaptive capability but would not increase survival chances because their knowledge diversity would not surpass that of the others being imitated.

Creative responses may take the form of seeking outside counsel, soliciting new perspectives, completing additional training or education, or joining a professional association to increase the opportunity for new knowledge. These behaviors are more likely to improve the knowledge base of the individuals and contribute to knowledge diversity of the group or the organization to which the individuals belong.

Less constructive are the defensive responses, including managing impressions by focusing attention on positive results and dismissing negative feedback. Individuals may also try to change how a supervisor or coworker perceives them by increasing communication or through networking. Instead of responding to negative feedback by working to restore balance, individuals may try to change their perception, so that the imagined state more closely aligns with the actual state. In some cases, individuals may shift ambitions, telling themselves that they did not really want a promotion because of the increased time demands accompanying the position. Tsui et al. (1995) referred to this as lowering one's standards of effectiveness. Lastly, when refusing to act, individuals ignore the negative feedback through withdrawal behaviors that ultimately lead to an individual's exit from the organization.

*Adaptive Responses at the Group Level*

Although group responses fall into the same five categories as do individual responses, they take different forms. In the category of habitual response, a group, following past actions, in addition to exerting more effort or requesting more resources such as time, also may focus on style instead of substance. They might produce impressively designed reports that hide the lack of content contained therein. They may attempt to increase their visibility within the organization by encouraging members to serve on high-profile committees. These activities do not increase knowledge diversity and hence are unlikely to restore homeostasis to the group, although the individuals within the groups may still enjoy satisfaction, harmony, and cohesion. Similar to individuals, groups may enact mimetic responses by scanning the environment for other groups facing similar discrepant conditions and imitate their responses. Responses most visible to outsiders are changes in leadership (appointing a different leader) or rotation of members' roles. Such imitation may marginally elevate adaptive capability but not substantively change the knowledge diversity of the group.

Some groups may engage in creative responses that include activities such as cross-training, requiring continuing education, or appointing a devil's advocate to stimulate task conflict. For example, job rotation or cross-training has been linked to higher levels of organizational learning (de Weerd-Nederhof, Pacitti, da Silva Gomes, & Pearson, 2002), whereas appointing a devil's advocate can lead to higher quality and more numerous alternatives (Stone, Sivitanides, & Magro, 1994). Harrison, Price, Gavin, and Florey (2002) found that high levels of collaboration decreased negative effects of demographic diversity, such that team social integration increased. All these activities may increase knowledge diversity within the group without damaging the positive emotions from demographic fit within the group. By using creative responses that are not commonly adopted by all groups, survival chances are enhanced. In essence, such responses modify the genetic (knowledge) pool through internal mutation rather than introduce new variants from the external environment by importing diverse individuals.

Of course, increasing the actual heterogeneity of the demographic composition would be the most adaptive response if the group conscientiously introduces this approach with an eye toward smoothing out the temporary disharmony created by the inclusion of new and different members in the group. Because most groups have a natural preference to keep the status quo, especially in terms of demography, this activity although not creative, may have the most promise of enhancing positive outcomes for the group.

The dysfunctional defensive responses by groups include promoting group goals within the organization, undermining the performance of other teams by withholding information or resources, or denigrating the achievements of other groups. Groups may lobby the organization to use different performance standards to evaluate group performance or rationalize sub par performance by claiming that the organization did not provide the necessary resources, arguing that had they been available, the group would have been successful. Again, without actually changing the knowledge diversity, the group does not change the course of its progression toward extinction according to the demographic fit and outcome process model.

### Adaptive Responses at the Organizational Level

Using habitual responses, organizations may respond as they have in the past by restructuring, introducing a new product, divesting underperforming units, or changing top management personnel. A homogeneous organization may change niches, where the environmental variety is low, or specialize, so that it is better able to meet demands. Such a strategy was used by Heidelberger Druckmaschinen AG of Germany, when, faced with decreasing profits, they sold their digital imaging interests to Kodak and their web and newspaper presses to Goss International to better focus on their core sheet-fed offset press business ("Heidelberg transfers," 2004). These activities will not be likely to inject knowledge diversity into the firm, but neither will they dampen the positive affective state of demographic fit. Through imitation, some firms may institute diversity-training programs or work–life balance initiatives. Such behaviors may offer some marginal increase in knowledge diversity, but they do not involve introducing actual diversity into the firm and thus positive emotions will not be threatened. Organizations also may attempt to reverse their performance problems by replacing their chief executive officers (CEOs) with outsiders, an approach perceived favorably by the stock market. Huson, Malatesta, and Parrino (2004) found that, for poorly performing firms, abnormal stock returns followed turnover announcements; the improvement is more pronounced for firms appointing outside CEOs. Favorable market reaction to the appointment of outsider CEOs has also been demonstrated both for bankrupt firms (Davidson, Worrell, & Dutia, 1993) and high-performing firms (Chung, Rogers, Lubatkin, & Owers, 1987). Increasing racial and gender diversity on company boards of directors, a practice that is becoming more and more prevalent, offers firms access to stakeholder groups, resources, and legitimacy, ostensibly leading to more effective firm performance (Hillman, Cannella, & Harris, 2002; Hillman, Keim, & Luce, 2001). Although increasing diversity has the potential to increase the requisite variety for survival, it is easily imitable by other firms. Thus, such a response may not give the firm an unusual competitive advantage. The more competitive and creative responses are those that involve changing the intangible aspects of the organization, such as the "diversity culture" (Ely & Thomas, 2001) or a strong organizational culture that replaces demographic factors as the basis for members' social identity (Tsui & Gutek, 1999). The organization becomes the primary group for self and social categorization. Demographic diversity (and hence cognitive diversity) can be increased without jeopardizing positive self-image and cohesion. Another creative response is the creation of alliances or joint ventures to address the firm's negative performance. Ironically, when two organizations that differ widely on operating norms and cultures merge, the integration process may be very difficult, but the potential for long-term survival may be great because of the boost in knowledge diversity created by the fusion of two vastly different entities. Such a scenario is supported by the work of Park and Ungson (1997), who found that despite cultural differences, joint ventures founded by U.S. and Japanese firms are less likely to dissolve than joint ventures established by two firms from the United States.

However, the similarity–attraction force is pervasive and persistent. Although CEOs of poorly-performing firms are likely to rely on the advice of executives from other firms, they tend to seek the counsel of those with whom they share functional backgrounds, industry of employment, and friendship ties (McDonald & Westphal, 2003). These similar others provide reinforcement of the CEOs' current beliefs and perceptual biases, leading to strategic inertia.

In general, organizations engage in defensive, nonadaptive responses such as impression management, rationalization, or denial as do individuals and groups. When the organization does not want to change its processes, it may attempt to manage external impressions by establishing a foundation to fund charitable activities or creating a public relations campaign to promote a positive image of the firm. Alternatively, it might try to lobby the government for restrictions on competitors, such as tariffs on imported products. Facing sub par performance, organizations engage in external attribution by blaming failure on environmental conditions (Bettman & Weitz, 1983). An organization may deny the threat to its survival altogether by persisting in the status quo even in the fact of dramatic environmental changes as was observed in a study of the airline and trucking industries (Audia, Locke, & Smith, 2000). After deregulation, organizations that were successful in the past persisted with their current strategies, and such strategic persistence led to performance declines. Crises such as poor performance also invoke defense mechanisms, such as reliance primarily on familiar rules and procedures, which reduce "uncertainty as they yield rapid reaction to similar situations and stimuli" (Marcus, 1988, p. 389). This initiates a "'vicious cycle' in which poorly performing organizations respond with rule-bound behavior, a response which only perpetuates their poor performance" (Marcus, 1988, p. 387).

In summary, among the multitude of responses available, the challenge is to create optimal heterogeneity within the social system so that knowledge diversity is enhanced, whereas positive affective states are maintained. Such responses fall into the creative response category. These behaviors allow for a combination of fitting and misfitting attributes among entity members, be they individual, groups, or organizations. Table 9–1 provides some illustrative examples of adaptive and nonadaptive responses or adjustments by individuals, groups, and organizations.

The adaptive responses serve to change the initial conditions that affect the nature and level of fit at the various levels, as will be discussed in the following section. They also modify the link between the affective outcomes in Stage I and the cognitive outcomes in Stage II such that the positive emotions will not degenerate into narrow cognitive capabilities. Nonadaptive responses, on the other hand, do not change the status quo, leading to perpetuation of the negative behavioral outcomes. These outcomes generate more defensive or nonadaptive responses, leading to eventual extinction of the unit in the form of exit by members, disbandment of the groups, or dissolution of the organization as a whole.

## Antecedents or Initial Conditions

The various types of adjustments or adaptation responses made by individuals, groups, and organizations will change the initial conditions or antecedents of the homogenizing tendency, creating a new understanding of fit and altering the entire model such that survival chances are enhanced. Individuals may become more aware of their perceptual biases and the negative consequences of falling victim to attraction toward similar others. Organizations may embrace new cultures that appreciate the potential value of knowledge diversity embedded in people with different backgrounds and perspectives. New human resources policies to reward innovation and creativity may be introduced. Yet, despite concerted efforts, the initial conditions dangerous to survival may be marginally and minimally changed because of resistance and inertia stemming from defensive or nonresponsive adaptations. In such cases, the primary antecedents of homogeneity—psychological attraction, perceptual biases, institutional environments, organizational cultures, and human resource policies—operate to create comfortable and familiar routines that are deeply embedded in psychological processes. In effect, the model of demographic fitness represents a continuous feedback loop in which the potentially productive habitual, mimetic, and creative adaptive responses generate conditions in which survival outcomes are more likely; conversely, nonadaptive responses lead to extinction.

## CONCLUSION

Empirical evidence consistently shows positive consequences of demographic homogeneity to individuals. Data further illustrate that groups and organizations suffer from impaired cognitive capability along with consequential negative behavioral outcomes. Using the fit analogy and ideas from conservation biology, we show that the deeper and long-term impact of homogeneity on groups or organizations is diminished survival potential. However, the survival instinct triggers adaptation, which could include an optimal level of heterogeneity or increasing resources or adaptive capacity without changing the demographic heterogeneity of the group or the firm. This analysis solves the puzzle of why the fittest in terms of demographic composition in groups or organizations have survived and how the survival chances are even better for the least fit.

Future demography researchers can benefit from incorporation of this model into their theoretical and empirical analyses. In current research the link of demographic fit to survival outcomes has not been observed, and even less attention has been given to adaptive and nonadaptive responses and how they impact the very notion of fit and eventual survival of the unit. Researchers can focus on affective, cognitive, and behavioral outcomes as simultaneous or sequential consequences of demographic fit, therefore testing the validity of the proposed mediating process. Further, future researchers could examine the specific mechanisms by which individuals and groups become aware of disequilibrium conditions and how each type of adaptive response—habitual, mimetic, and creative—affects antecedent conditions, and, ultimately the entire cycle.

The idea of time is central in the proposed process model of demographic fit. Although longitudinal observation is always a desirable approach when time is a key element of a theoretical framework, aspects of this model could be examined using cross-sectional data through careful sampling to include the presence of units that are at different stages of the process. Finally, the model spans multiple levels of analysis, and, thus, we hope that there is something for every researcher whether he or she is interested at the individual, dyad, group, organizational, or environmental level. We hope that the model we proposed has sufficient "variety" in it to sustain the test of time, interest, and scholarly selection.

## REFERENCES

Abrahamson, E., & Hambrick, D. C. (1997). Attentional homogeneity in industries: The effect of discretion. *Journal of Organizational Behavior, 18,* 513–532.

Aldrich, H. (1979). *Organizations and environments.* Englewood Cliffs, NJ: Prentice-Hall.

Ancona, D. G., & Caldwell, D. F. (1992). Demography and design: Predictors of new product team performance. *Organization Science, 3,* 321–341.

Ashforth, B. E., & Mael, F. (1989). Social identity theory and the organization. *Academy of Management Review, 14,* 20–39.

Audia, P. G., Locke, E. A., & Smith, K. G. (2000). The paradox of success: An archival and a laboratory study of strategic persistence following radical environmental change. *Academy of Management Journal, 43,* 837–853.

Bantel, K. A., & Jackson, S. E. (1989). Top management innovations in banking: Does the composition of the top team make a difference? *Strategic Management Journal, 10,* 107–124.

Baum, J. A. C., & Singh, J. V. (1994). Organizational niches and the dynamics of organizational mortality. *American Journal of Sociology, 100,* 346–380.

Berscheid, E., & Walster, E. H. (1978). *Interpersonal attraction* (2nd ed.). Reading, MA: Addison-Wesley.

Bettman, J. R., & Weitz, B. A. (1983). Attributions in the board room: Causal reasoning in corporate annual reports. *Administrative Science Quarterly, 28,* 165–183.

Blau, P. M. (1977). *Inequality and heterogeneity: A primitive theory of social structure.* New York: Free Press.

Byrne, D. (1971). *The attraction paradigm.* New York: Academic Press.

Campbell, D. J. (1965). Variation and selective retention in socio-cultural evolution. In H. R. Barringer, G. I. Blanksten, & R. W. Mack (Eds.), *Social change in developing areas: A reinterpretation of evolutionary theory* (pp. 19–49). Cambridge, MA: Schenkman.

Carver, C. S., & Scheier, M. F. (1981). *Attention and self-regulation: A control-theory approach to human behavior.* New York: Springer-Verlag.

Caughley, G., & Gunn, A. (1996). *Conservation biology in theory and practice.* Cambridge, MA: Blackwell Science.

Chatman, J. A. (1991). Matching people and organizations: Selection and socialization in public accounting firms. *Administrative Science Quarterly, 36,* 459–484.

Chatman, J. A., & O'Reilly, C. A. (2004). Asymmetric reactions to work group sex diversity among men and women. *Academy of Management Journal, 47,* 193–208.

Chung, K. H., Rogers, R. C., Lubatkin, M., & Owers, J. E. (1987). Do insiders make better CEOs than outsiders? *The Academy of Management Executive, 1,* 325–331.

Davidson, W. N., III., Worrell, D. L., & Dutia, D. (1993). The stock market effects of CEO succession in bankrupt firms. *Journal of Management, 19,* 517–533.

de Weerd-Nederhof, P. C., Pacitti, B. J., da Silva Gomes, J. F., & Pearson, A. W. (2002). Tools for the improvement of organizational learning processes in innovation. *Journal of Workplace Learning, 14,* 320–331.

DiMaggio, P. J., & Powell, W. W. (1983). The iron cage revisited: Institutional isomorphism and collective rationality in organizational fields. *American Sociological Review, 48,* 147–160.

Ely, R. J., & Thomas, D. A. (2001). Cultural diversity at work: The effects of diversity perspectives on work group processes and outcomes. *Administrative Science Quarterly, 46,* 229–273.

Equal Employment Opportunity Commission. (2004). *Occupational employment in private industry by race/ethnic group/sex, and by industry, United States, 2002.* Retrieved July 15, 2004, from http://www.eeoc.gov/stats/jobpat/2002/us.html.

Finkelstein, S., & Hambrick, D. C. (1997). Top management teams: Group bases of executive action. In *Strategic leadership: Top executives and their effects on organizations* (pp. 115–161). New York: West.

Frink, D. D., Robinson, R. K., Reithel, B., Arthur, M. M., Ammeter, A. P., Ferris, G. R., Kaplan, D. M., & Morrisette, H. S. (2003). Gender demography and organization performance: A two-study investigation with convergence. *Group and Organization Management, 28,* 127–147.

Gibbons, D., & Olk, P. M. (2003). Individual and structural origins of friendship and social position among professionals. *Journal of Personality and Social Psychology, 84,* 340–351.

Gimeno, J., Folta, T. B., Cooper, A. C., & Woo, C. Y. (1997). Survival of the fittest? Entrepreneurial human capital and the persistence of underperforming firms. *Administrative Science Quarterly, 42,* 750–783.

Glaman, J. M., Jones, A. P., & Rozelle, R. M. (1996). The effects of co-worker similarity on the emergence of affect in work teams. *Group & Organization Management, 21,* 192–215.

Green, S. G., Anderson, S. E., & Shivers, S. L. (1996). Demographic and organizational influences on leader–member exchange and related work attitudes. *Organizational Behavior and Human Decision Processes, 66,* 203–214.

Hambrick, D. C., Cho, T. S., & Chen, M. J. (1996). The influence of top management team heterogeneity on firms' competitive moves. *Administrative Science Quarterly, 41,* 659–684.

Hambrick, D. C., Geletkanycz, M. A., & Fredrickson, J. W. (1993). Top executive commitment to the status-quo—Some tests of its determinants. *Strategic Management Journal, 14,* 401–418.

Hannan, M. T., & Freeman, J. (1977). The population ecology of organizations. *American Journal of Sociology, 82,* 929–964.

Harrison, D. A., Price, K. H., Gavin, J. H., & Florey, A. T. (2002). Time, teams, and task performance: Changing effects of surface- and deep-level diversity on group functioning. *Academy of Management Journal, 45,* 1029–1045.

Heidelberg transfers digital division to Eastman Kodak, web offset business to Goss. (2004, April 1). Retrieved July 12, 2004, from http://americanprinter .com/mag/printing_heidelberg_transfers_digital/index.html.

Heschel, M.-S., & Paige, K.-N. (1995). Inbreeding depression, environmental stress, and population size variation in scarlet gilia (*Ipomopsis aggregata*). *Conservation Biology, 9,* 126–133.

Hillman, A. J., Cannella, A. A., Jr., & Harris, I. C. (2002). Women and racial minorities in the boardroom: How do directors differ? *Journal of Management, 28,* 747–763.

Hillman, A. J., Keim, G. D., & Luce, R. A. (2001). Board composition and stakeholder performance: Do stakeholder directors make a difference? *Business and Society, 40,* 295–314.

Hinds, P. J., Carley, K. M., Krackhardt, D., & Wholey, D. (2000). Choosing work group members: Balancing similarity, competence, and familiarity. *Organizational Behavior and Human Decision Processes, 81,* 226–251.

Hom, P. W., & Griffeth, R. W. (1994). *Employee turnover.* Cincinnati, OH: South-Western.

Huson, M. R., Malatesta, P. H., & Parrino, R. (2004). Managerial succession and firm performance. *Journal of Financial Economics, 74,* 237–275.

Jackson, S. E., May, K. E., & Whitney, K. (1995). Understanding the dynamics of diversity in decision-making teams. In R. A. Guzzo, E. Salas, & Associates (Eds.), *Team effectiveness and decision-making in organizations* (pp. 204–261). San Francisco: Jossey-Bass.

Janis, I. L. (1972). *Victims of groupthink: A psychological study of foreign-policy decisions and fiascoes.* Boston: Houghton.

Jehn, K. A., Chadwick, C., & Thatcher, S. M. B. (1997). To agree or not to agree: The effects of value congruence, individual demographic dissimilarity, and conflict on workgroup outcomes. *International Journal of Conflict Management, 8,* 287–305.

Jehn, K. A., Northcraft, G. B., & Neale, M. A. (1999). Why differences make a difference: A field study of diversity, conflict, and performance in workgroups. *Administrative Science Quarterly, 44,* 741–763.

Kanter, R. M. (1977). *Men and women of the corporation.* New York: Basic Books.

Katz, R. (1982). The effects of group longevity on project communication and performance. *Administrative Science Quarterly, 27,* 81–104.

Keller, R. T. (2001). Cross-functional project groups in research and new product development: Diversity, communications, job stress, and outcomes. *Academy of Management Journal, 44,* 547–555.

Kirkman, B. L., Tesluk, P. E., & Rosen, B. (2004). The impact of demographic heterogeneity and team leader-team member demographic fit on team empowerment and effectiveness. *Group & Organization Management, 29,* 334–368.

Lee, C., & Farh, J. L. (2004). Joint effects of group efficacy and gender diversity on group cohesion and performance. *Psychologie Appliquee—Revue Internationale [Applied Psychology—an International Review], 53,* 136–154.

LePine, J. A., Hollenbeck, J. R., Ilgen, D. R., Colquitt, J. A., & Ellis, A. (2002). Gender composition, situational strength, and team decision-making accuracy: A criterion decomposition approach. *Organizational Behavior and Human Decision Processes, 88,* 445–475.

Levin, J. M., & Moreland, R. L. (1998). Small groups. In D. T. Gilbert, S. T. Fiske, & G. Lindzey (Eds.), *The handbook of social psychology* (4th ed., Vol. 2, pp. 415–469). New York: McGraw-Hill.

Levine, J. M., & Resnick, L. B. (1993). Social foundations of cognition. *Annual Review of Psychology, 44,* 585–612.

LeVine, R. A., & Campbell, D. T. (1972). *Ethnocentrism: Theories of conflict, ethnic attitudes, and group behavior.* New York: Wiley.

Lincoln, J. R., & Miller, J. (1979). Work and friendship ties in organizations: A comparative analysis of relational networks. *Administrative Science Quarterly, 24,* 181–199.

Lyon, D. W., & Ferrier, W. J. (2002). Enhancing performance with product–market innovation: The influence of the top management team. *Journal of Managerial Issues, 14*(4), 452–469.

Marcus, A. A. (1988). Responses to externally induced innovation: Their effects on organizational performance. *Strategic Management Journal, 9,* 387–402.

Marsden, P. V. (1988). Homogeneity in confiding relations. *Social Networks, 10,* 57–76.

McDonald, M. L., & Westphal, J. D. (2003). Getting by with the advice of their friends: CEOs' advice networks and firms' strategic responses to poor performance. *Administrative Science Quarterly, 48,* 1–32.

McGarty, C., Turner, J. C., Hogg, M. A., David, B., & Wetherell, M. S. (1992). Group polarization as conformity to the prototypical group member. *British Journal of Social Psychology, 31*, 1–20.

McLeod, P. L., Lobel, S. A., & Cox, J. T. H. (1996). Ethnic diversity and creativity in small groups. *Small Group Research, 27*, 248–264.

McPherson, M., Smith-Lovin, L., & Cook, J. M. (2001). Birds of a feather: Homophily in social networks. *Annual Review of Sociology, 27*, 415–444.

Meyer, J. W., & Rowan, B. (1977). Institutionalized organizations: Formal structure as myth and ceremony. *The American Journal of Sociology, 83*, 340–363.

Miller, D., & Chen, M. J. (1994). Sources and consequences of competitive inertia—a study of the United States airline industry. *Administrative Science Quarterly, 39*, 1–23.

Milliken, F. J., & Martins, L. L. (1996). Searching for common threads: Understanding the multiple effects of diversity in organizational groups. *Academy of Management Review, 21*, 402–433.

Mollica, K. A., Gray, B., & Trevino, L. K. (2003). Racial homophily and its persistence in newcomers' social networks. *Organization Science, 14*, 123–136.

Moscovici, S., & Zavalloni, M. (1969). Group as a polarizer of attitudes. *Journal of Personality and Social Psychology, 12*, 125–135.

Myers, D. G., & Lamm, H. (1976). Group polarization phenomenon. *Psychological Bulletin, 83*, 602–627.

Newcomb, T. (1956). The prediction of interpersonal attraction. *American Psychologist, 11*, 575–586.

Newcomb, T. (1961). *The acquaintance process.* New York: Holt.

O'Reilly, C. A., Caldwell, D. F., & Barnett, W. P. (1989). Work group demography, social integration, and turnover. *Administrative Science Quarterly, 34*, 21–37.

O'Reilly, C. A., Chatman, J., & Caldwell, D. F. (1991). People and organizational culture: A profile comparison approach to assessing person-organization fit. *Academy of Management Journal, 34*, 487–516.

Park, S. H., & Ungson, G. R. (1997). The effect of national culture, organizational complementarity, and economic motivation on joint venture dissolution. *Academy of Management Journal, 40*, 279–307.

Paulus, P. B. (2000). Groups, teams, and creativity: The creative potential of idea-generating groups. *Psychologie Appliquee—Revue Internationale [Applied Psychology—An International Review], 49*, 237–262.

Pfeffer, J. (1985). Organizational demography: Implications for management. *California Management Review, 28*, 67–81.

Pitcher, P., & Smith, A. D. (2001). Top management team heterogeneity: Personality, power, and proxies. *Organization Science, 12*, 1–18.

Prahalad, C. K., & Bettis, R. A. (1986). The dominant logic: A new linkage between diversity and performance. *Strategic Management Journal, 7*, 485–501.

Primack, R. B. (1998). *Essentials of conservation biology* (2nd ed.). Sunderland, MA: Sinauer Associates.

*Quick reference and fact sheets: Thalassemia.* (2004). Retrieved July 8, 2004, from http://www.marchofdimes.com/professionals/681_1229.asp.

Reagans, R., & Zuckerman, E. W. (2001). Networks, diversity, and productivity: The social capital of corporate R&D teams. *Organization Science, 12*, 502–517.

Rentsch, J. R., & Klimoski, R. J. (2001). Why do 'great minds' think alike?: Antecedents of team member schema agreement. *Journal of Organizational Behavior, 22,* 107–120.

Richard, O. C. (2000). Racial diversity, business strategy, and firm performance: A resource-based view. *Academy of Management Journal, 43,* 164–177.

Richard, O., Barnett, T., Dwyer, S., & Chadwick, K. (2004). Cultural diversity in management, firm performance, and the moderating role of entrepreneurial orientation dimensions. *Academy of Management Journal, 47,* 255–266.

Richeson, J. A., & Shelton, J. N. (2003). When prejudice does not pay: Effects of interracial contact on executive function. *Psychological Science, 14,* 287–290.

Rogelberg, S. G., & Rumery, S. M. (1996). Gender diversity, team decision quality, time on task, and interpersonal cohesion. *Small Group Research, 27,* 79–90.

Rossé, J. G., & Hulin, C. L. (1985). Adaptation to work: An analysis of employee health, withdrawal, and change. *Organizational Behavior and Human Decision Processes, 36,* 324–347.

Rossé, J. G., & Kraut, A. I. (1983). Reconsidering the vertical dyad linkage model of leadership. *Journal of Occupational Psychology, 56,* 63–71.

Schneider, B. (1987). The people make the place. *Personnel Psychology, 40,* 437–453.

Schneider, B., Smith, D. B., Taylor, S., & Fleenor, J. (1998). Personality and organizations: A test of the homogeneity of personality hypothesis. *Journal of Applied Psychology, 83,* 462–470.

Sellers, P. (2004, February 9). Women and profits: Return on equity improves with gender diversity. *Fortune, 149,* 22.

Senner, J. W. (1980). Inbreeding depression and the survival of zoo populations. In M. E. Soulé & B. A. Wilcox (Eds.), *Conservation biology: An evolutionary-ecological perspective* (pp. 209–224). Sunderland, MA: Sinauer Associates.

Shaw, M. E. (1971), *Group dynamics: The psychology of small group behavior.* New York: McGraw-Hill.

Staw, B. (1980). The consequences of turnover. *Journal of Occupational Behavior, 1,* 253–273.

Staw, B. M., & Epstein, L. D. (2000). What bandwagons bring: Effects of popular management techniques on corporate performance, reputation, and CEO pay. *Administrative Science Quarterly, 45,* 523–556.

Stone, D. N., Sivitanides, M. P., & Magro, A. P. (1994). Formalized dissent and cognitive complexity in group processes and performance. *Decision Sciences, 25,* 243–261.

Tajfel, H. (1982). *Social identity and intergroup relations.* Cambridge, England: Cambridge University Press.

Tajfel, H., & Turner, J. C. (1986). The social identity theory of intergroup behavior. In S. Worchel & W. G. Austin (Eds.), *Psychology of intergroup relations* (pp. 7–24). Chicago: Nelson-Hall.

Tolbert, P. S., & Zucker, L. G. (1983). Institutional sources of change in the formal structure of organizations: The diffusion of civil service reform, 1880–1935. *Administrative Science Quarterly, 28,* 22–39.

Tsui, A. S., Ashford, S. A., St. Claire, L., & Xin, K. R. (1995). Dealing with discrepant expectations: Response strategies and managerial effectiveness. *Academy of Management Journal, 38,* 1515–1543.

Tsui, A. S., Egan, T. D., & O'Reilly, C. A. (1992). Being different: Relational demography and organizational attachment. *Administrative Science Quarterly, 37,* 549–579.

Tsui, A. S., & Gutek, B. A. (1999). *Demographic differences in organizations: Current research and future directions.* Lanham, MD: Lexington Books.

Tsui, A. S., & O'Reilly, C. A. (1989). Beyond simple demographic effects: The importance of relational demography in superior-subordinate dyads. *Academy of Management Journal, 32,* 402–423.

Turner, J. C. (1985). Social categorization and the self-concept: A self-cognitive theory of group behavior. In H. Tajfel (Ed.), *Social identity and intergroup relations* (pp. 15–40). Cambridge, England: Cambridge University Press.

Varma, A., & Stroh, L. K. (2001). The impact of same-sex LMX dyads on performance evaluations. *Human Resource Management, 40,* 309–320.

Verquer, M. L., Beehr, T. A., & Wagner, S. H. (2003). A meta-analysis of relations between person-organization fit and work attitudes. *Journal of Vocational Behavior, 63,* 473–489.

Wagner, W. G., Pfeffer, J., & O'Reilly, C. A. (1984). Organizational demography and turnover in top-management groups. *Administrative Science Quarterly, 29,* 74–92.

Weick, K. E. (1979). *The social psychology of organizing* (2nd ed.). Reading, MA: Addison-Wesley.

Whyte, G. (1998). Recasting Janis's groupthink model: The key role of collective efficacy in decision fiascoes. *Organizational Behavior and Human Decision Processes, 73,* 185–209.

Whyte, G., Saks, A. M., & Hook, S. (1997). When success breeds failure: The role of self-efficacy in escalating commitment to a losing course of action. *Journal of Organizational Behavior, 18,* 415–432.

Wilbert, T. (2004, February 1). Diversity pays at Home Depot. *The Atlanta Journal Constitution,* p. 1Q.

Williams, K. Y., & O'Reilly, C. A. (1998). Demography and diversity in organizations: A review of 40 years of research. In *Research in Organizational Behavior* (Vol. 20, pp. 77–140). Stanford, CT: JAI Press.

Wright, P., Ferris, S. P., Hiller, J. S., & Kroll, M. (1995). Competitiveness through management of diversity: Effects on stock-price valuation. *Academy of Management Journal, 38,* 272–287.

Zatzick, C. D., Elvira, M. M., & Cohen, L. E. (2003). When is more better? The effects of racial composition on voluntary turnover. *Organization Science, 14,* 483–496.

# CHAPTER 10

# *Horizontal and Vertical Fit in Human Resource Systems*

## Barry Gerhart
### *University of Wisconsin–Madison*

Human resource (HR) management has traditionally focused on how employment-related policy decisions, such as selection, development, training, compensation, and work design, influence organizational effectiveness. Until the last decade or so, effectiveness was almost exclusively studied at the individual level of analysis (e.g., using individual performance ratings as the dependent variable). However, the field of HR has evolved such that significant emphasis is now placed on also understanding linkages between HR practices and effectiveness at the aggregate level (Becker & Gerhart, 1996), including facility level outcomes such as cost, productivity, and quality, as well as firm level outcomes such as total shareholder return, profitability, and survival.

The term, *HR system,* refers to the fact that different combinations of individual HR practices are possible, and a key question is whether the effects are additive or, as hypothesized by several perspectives, is the effect of any one HR practice dependent on the nature of other HR practices? A second key question is whether the specific effect of any particular HR practice or HR system depends on contextual factors, such as organizational strategy. These two questions have to do with the issues of horizontal (or internal) fit and vertical (or external) fit, respectively.

Although my focus is primarily on the business performance dependent variable, I recognize that effectiveness can be defined more broadly, for example, using a stakeholder perspective where, at a minimum, shareholder, customer, and employee outcomes are considered. Clearly, HR systems can differ in how favorable their consequences are for different stakeholders. Some HR systems may be of the mutual gains nature

(Kochan & Osterman, 1994), whereas others may create more of a zero-sum situation. I operate under the assumption that some minimally competitive level of business performance is typically good for everyone. Without it, there will not only be less money to be made by investors and less satisfied customers, but also fewer jobs to be had by workers. For a discussion of how HR systems may affect worker outcomes, see Godard and Delaney (2000) and the following comment by Kochan (2000). Several recent empirical studies are now available also (Godard, 2001; Handel & Gittleman, 2004; Hunter & Lafkas, 2003; Parker, 2003).

My goals in this chapter are to (a) review the conceptual basis and measurement of HR systems in the literature and their evolution, (b) consider evidence on the consequences for effectiveness of horizontal and vertical fit of HR systems, and (c) provide suggestions for future research on these issues, as well as a model of HR systems and business performance. I begin with a survey of models and measurement of HR systems and the conceptual basis.

## HR SYSTEMS

### Conceptual Basis

As noted, HR systems have been most often defined in terms of policies (e.g., staffing, job design, and so forth), and system refers to the particular array or combination of HR practices in an organization. Typically, an HR system is seen as most directly influencing what might be termed intermediate employment effectiveness outcomes, such as ability, motivation, attitudes, and performance. (Outcomes such as attraction and retention could also be added.) These intermediate employment outcomes, in turn, are expected to influence business performance outcomes. This mediation model, although fundamental to the HR systems literature, is also largely untested.

#### AMO Framework

A general framework for conceptualizing and studying HR systems has emerged in the recent literature on high performance work systems (HPWSs). Although Boxall and Purcell (2003) observe that "the definition of components of HPWSs is confusingly varied" (see also Becker & Gerhart, 1996, Table 2), they find an increasingly common "very basic theory of performance" being used, which they refer to as "AMO theory." Boxall and Purcell summarize it as

$$P = f(A, M, O)$$

where $P$ is performance, $A$ is ability, $M$ is motivation, and $O$ is opportunity. In other words, HR systems will be most effective when they foster ability, motivation, and opportunity to contribute to effectiveness.

The AMO logic was most clearly spelled out in Appelbaum, Bailey, Berg, and Kalleberg (2000) and Bailey (1993) and earlier by Katz, Kochan, and Weber (1985) ("many theoretical arguments have suggested that individual worker ability, motivation, and participation in job-related decision making affect both organizational effectiveness and individual worker satisfaction," p. 513). Recent empirical studies (e.g., Appelbaum et al. (2000); Batt, 2002; Huselid, 1995; MacDuffie, 1995) use this conceptual framework or something akin to it.

Boxall and Purcell (2003) noted that the AMO model is actually an "an old rubric." This is certainly correct in that each of the components has been studied extensively (see later), albeit with different degrees of emphasis, depending on the discipline/field. However, the clarity and parsimony of the AMO model is helpful, and the equal importance it assigns to the $A$, $M$, and $O$ components in its holistic approach is fairly novel. (Previous literatures from several disciplines had been typically focused on one or two of the components.) Given the multidisciplinary (and thus somewhat dispersed) basis for the AMO framework, a brief review of the basis for each component is in order.

The $A$ component can be traced most directly to the industrial/organizational (I/O) psychology and economics of human capital literatures. The former provides extensive evidence that individual abilities strongly predict individual job performance (Heneman & Judge, 2003; Schmidt & Hunter, 1998). The HR system policy implication is that employee selection practices will be most effective when valid predictors such as ability are used and when employers are selective (Brogden, 1949). Human capital theory (Becker, 1964) and research (e.g., Mincer, 1974) hold that investments in people (e.g., education and training) make them more productive and that the choice by individuals and employers to invest depends on their expected rate of return. The I/O psychology literature also gives significant attention to training and development (e.g., Noe, 1999).

The $M$ component is addressed in the literatures of many disciplines (Gerhart & Rynes, 2003). Williamson, Wachter, and Harris (1975) refer to the managerial goal of obtaining behavioral "consummate cooperation." As Simon (1951; see also Barnard, 1951) pointed out, this depends on workers' view of their exchange relationship with the employer: Employees provide contributions based on their view of inducements, monetary and otherwise, provided by the employer. In recent work on different forms of the psychological contract (Rousseau & Parks, 1992) and of the employment relationship (Lepak & Snell, 1999; Tsui, Pearce, Porter, & Tripoli, 1997) a similar logic was used.

The I/O psychology literature on motivation includes models such as goal-setting (Locke & Latham, 1990), expectancy (Campbell & Pritchard, 1976; Lawler, 1971; Vroom, 1964), and equity theories (Adams, 1965), which focus primarily on the individual level and on the psychological mechanisms that explain motivation (Gerhart & Rynes, 2003). Much of empirical work was conducted in laboratory settings. Theories that are more grounded in the economics literature such as efficiency wage (Yellen, 1984), transaction costs (Williamson, 1975), and agency (Fama & Jensen, 1983) typically exclude psychological mechanisms (in empirical work at least) and are focused more on compensation policies in work organizations.

One of the more explicit discussions of the $A$ and $M$ components is found in Vroom (1964, p. 203), who stated that "the effects of motivation on performance are dependent on the level of ability of the worker, and the relationship of ability to performance is dependent on the motivation of the worker." In other words, "the effects of ability and motivation on performance are not additive but interactive" (p. 203). Thus, Vroom proposed the following formula:

Performance $= f$(Ability $\times$ Motivation) or $P = f(A, M)$.

Vroom observed that establishing the validity of this formula had "considerable implications for managerial practice" (p. 203) because "It would suggest that managerial efforts to obtain and develop persons with skill and ability and to motivate these persons must proceed concurrently" (p. 203). This is the same logic that characterizes recent HR systems models that propose the importance of horizontal/internal fit or bundling.

The similarity of the Vroom formula of $P = f(A, M)$ to the AMO formula of $P = f(A, M, O)$ is obvious as is the lone difference: the lack of an O component in Vroom's formula. Like Vroom, Campbell's (1990) chapter in the *Handbook of Industrial and Organizational Psychology* focused on the A and M components as determinants of job performance (e.g., his Fig. 3, p. 707), and he used the simplifying assumption that situational effects are "held constant" (p. 707). This line of work on performance prediction (e.g., as summarized by Campbell, 1990) led Peters and O'Connor (1980, p. 391) to observe that situational constraints on performance was "a frequently overlooked construct." Even here, the situation was seen more as a constraint on M and A and less as an important contributing factor to effectiveness in its own right. Although I/O psychology (mostly the "O" part of the I/O field) has given substantial attention to job design (Hackman & Lawler, 1971; Hackman & Oldham, 1976; McGregor, 1960; Turner & Lawrence, 1965), this literature does not seem to have been strongly linked to that part of the I/O literature (mostly the "I" part) focused on performance as the dependent variable.

The *O* component has also received substantial attention in the industrial relations literature. Typically, the premise here is that workers should have a say in decisions that affect their terms and conditions of employment. In the United States, labor law seeks to allow workers to decide whether to engage in concerted action and collectively bargain these terms and conditions. In much of Europe, worker representation in decisions is mandated (Brewster, 1999). Not surprisingly then, the primary contribution by the industrial relations literature has been on the *O* dimension by emphasizing that business performance may be significantly affected by taking advantage of the ideas or workers and contributions they are capable of making, if given the opportunity.

Initially, much of the focus of the industrial relations literature was on the level of conflict between employers and labor unions (over terms and conditions of employment) as well as on how effectively the conflict was institutionalized and resolved (Katz et al., 1985; Cutcher-Gershenfeld, 1991). Gradually, however, this literature also began to show the incorporation of "new" or "cooperative" labor relations practices such as the use of suggestion systems and work teams, designed to give workers more opportunity to influence business performance (e.g., Arthur, 1994; MacDuffie, 1995) and to do so through a less adversarial (and perhaps more effective) process. Notable by its absence in the earlier studies (and more recent ones for that matter) is much attention to employee characteristics such as ability (i.e., the A component).

I have argued that the AMO components, although mostly familiar individually, had not been dealt with in a concise and holistic fashion, at least in the more academic literature. However, the AMO framework is, in essence, the one that has been used for many years by HR textbooks, from Heneman, Schwab, Fossum, and Dyer in 1980 to Noe, Hollenbeck, Gerhart, and Wright more recently in 2005. Heneman et al., for example, focused on the fit between the job attributes of rewards and ability requirements (similar to opportunity to contribute) and the person attributes of values and abilities. Thus, each of the components of the AMO model is incorporated. Heneman et al. further made clear the fact that different HR practices and policies have their main effects on ability, motivation, and, to some degree, ability requirements/opportunity. As one example, selection, training, and development policies are expected to have their primary effect on ability (and related expectancy motivation perceptions). Job design and job analysis primarily determine ability requirements/opportunity and, to some degree (intrinsic), rewards offered. Compensation has its primary effect on rewards offered and instrumentality perceptions (motivation). Motivation needs/values were primarily influenced by employee selection.

Economists too, although later, developed a framework of three employment-related factors that are hypothesized to influence effectiveness. Brickley, Smith, and Lease (1997) spoke of "organizational architecture," which includes decision rights, performance controls, and reward controls. Decision rights are defined as level of empowerment, thus corresponding to the *O* factor in AMO. Reward and performance controls, although separate, tended to be discussed together by Brickley et al. (1997) and correspond to the *M* component under AMO.

What Brickley et al. (1997) left out entirely, however, was any discussion of individual characteristics (Gerhart & Rynes, 2003), the *A* component. Their logic was that "Managers are typically interested in structuring an organizational architecture that . . . does not depend on specific people" because people "come and go" (pp. 27–28). This implication, that workers are interchangeable, is of course, inconsistent with evidence from the I/O psychology and human capital literatures, which emphasize worker heterogeneity and the fact that different workers may be differentially productive under different HR systems.

Although the AMO model is based largely on individual-level theories, its application to HR systems is often used to explain aggregate-level outcomes. This application has the risk of committing the fallacy of the wrong level (Ostroff, 1993; Robinson, 1950) by assuming that HR policy and effectiveness relationships at the individual level hold up conceptually and empirically at higher levels of analysis and are similarly mediated by AMO mechanisms. Whether this assumption is correct remains to be seen (Kozlowski & Klein, 2000; Ostroff & Bowen, 2000).

In summary, a model of HR systems has evolved from the literatures of several disciplines, each of which provides at least some important part of the story. The AMO framework provides a straightforward summary and gives a larger role to the *O* factor in HR systems as a path to business performance. However, level of analysis issues remain to be addressed.

## HR Systems: Content and Effectiveness

Early efforts to link HR practices to business performance demonstrated that business performance was positively related to industrial relations climate (e.g., lower levels of grievances and conflict and better employee attitudes) and the use of labor–management cooperation programs (Cutcher-Gershenfeld, 1991; Katz, Kochan, & Gobeille, 1983; Katz, Kochan, & Weber, 1985). This work, typically done in unionized settings, did not include employment practices related to (compensation-based) motivation or ability but was an important basis for future work on HR systems.

Another set of early studies was focused on single HR practices pertaining to motivation and ability, demonstrating, for example, a positive association with business performance of pay for performance in managerial compensation (Gerhart & Milkovich, 1990) and with the use of valid employee selection procedures (Terpstra & Rozell, 1993). Thus, by the early 1990s, business performance had been linked to single HR practices having to do with ability, motivation, and opportunity to contribute and to specific industrial relations climate variables (e.g., conflict level and resolution). However, the linkage between business performance and HR systems containing practices in all three AMO areas had not yet been studied.

The HR system approach, as we know it today, was initiated (on the empirical front) at the facility level by Arthur (1994), MacDuffie (1995), and Ichniowski, Shaw, and Prennushi (1993, 1997) in manufacturing and in the service sector by Batt (2001, 2002). At the firm level, an early study was conducted by Huselid (1995).

Almost uniformly, these and subsequent studies have demonstrated that the choice of HR systems relates to business performance, often strongly. (See Cappelli & Neumark, 2001, for an exception.) For example, Gerhart's (1999) review found that a 1 SD increase in HR system practices (relative to the mean) was associated with roughly 20% better business performance. The observed relationships are not only large, but also robust (Guest, Michie, Conway, & Sheehan, 2003):

> a large majority of published studies find an association between HR practices and firm performance, regardless of whether they are cross-sectional or longitudinal, whether conducted at establishment or company level, whether based on strong performance data or subjective estimates, whatever sector they are based on, whatever operational definition of HR is used and wherever they are conducted. (p. 294)

An examination of the specific HR system measures used in nine key studies (Appelbaum et al., 2000; Arthur, 1994; Batt, 2002; Cutcher-Gershenfeld, 1991; Delery & Doty, 1996; Guest et al., 2003; Huselid, 1995; Ichniowski et al., 1993, 1997; MacDuffie, 1995) suggests the following.[1] First, the O component seems to be thoroughly addressed in each study (e.g., using items pertaining to teams, influence, and autonomy/discretion in decisions). Second, the M component is also regularly addressed, but typically using only items that pertain to group- and organization-based (rather than individual) pay for performance or incentives. (Some studies also include items pertaining to employment security, which is treated as part of the M component.). Finally, although the A component (e.g., hours of training) appears in each study, rarely are items pertaining to employee selection or employee characteristics included, a serious omission given what we know from the I/O psychology literature.

In 1996, Becker and Gerhart pointed out that there was a great deal of inconsistency across studies in the types of practices included in empirical work to that point, and Boxall and Purcell (2003) echoed this concern. Our

---

[1]A table summarizing the HR systems measures used in each of the eight studies is available from the author.

reading of the nine studies (see the list in the preceding paragraph), however, suggests to us that some greater degree of consistency is evolving.

## HR SYSTEMS AND FIT

Fit refers to the notion that the effects of individual HR practices depend on the nature of (a) other HR practices in the HR system or (b) contextual factors (e.g., business strategy). The former is known as internal fit and the latter is known as external fit (Baird & Meshoulam, 1988), or what I prefer to call horizontal and vertical fit, respectively. The definitions of fit used in the HR literature (see later) suggest that statistical interaction is what is usually intended and authors such as Huselid (1995) and MacDuffie (1995) have included tests of statistical interactions in their attempts to evaluate fit hypotheses.

### Horizontal Fit

Horizontal fit is the idea that the effects of individual HR practices on effectiveness are not additive and that looking at individual human resource practices alone may give misleading results (Gerhart, Trevor, & Graham, 1996). According to Milgrom and Roberts (1992; see also Holmstrom & Milgrom, 1994): "Several activities are mutually complementary if doing more of any activity increases (or at least does not decrease) the marginal profitability of any other activity in the group" (p. 108). They then propose a more stringent definition: "a group of activities is *strongly complementary* when raising the levels of a subset of activities in the group greatly increases the returns to raising the levels of the other activities" (p. 109).

Based on this definition, Ichniowski et al. (1997), for example, stated that "firms realize the largest gains in productivity by adopting clusters of complementary practices, and benefit little from making 'marginal' changes in any one HR practice" (p. 295). These "interaction effects among HR policies" are "important determinants of productivity" (p. 295). Likewise, MacDuffie (1995) argued that "Innovative HR practices are often studied in a vacuum, with more attention paid to isolating the effect of individual practices than to understanding how different HR practices interact to reinforce one another, or how they are linked to business functions and strategy" (pp. 197–198). Therefore, he emphasized the importance of studying "bundles" of practices because of the "overlapping and mutually reinforcing effect of multiple practices" (p. 204).

In a similar vein, Appelbaum et al. (2000) spoke of "synergy" (see also Gerhart et al., 1996), and, in their opinion, "the argument that firms adopting a coherent set of workplace practices designed to maximize horizontal fit should have superior performance is compelling" (p. 34). They note that although "there are still few studies of this relationship," these studies "suggest that bundles, systems, or configurations of internally coherent practices . . . do a better job of explaining establishment performance than the individual practices do" (p. 34).

Brickley et al. (1997, pp. 182–183) likewise argued that "the components of organizational architecture are highly interdependent. The appropriate control system depends on the allocation of decision rights, and vice versa." As one example, they note that "if decision rights are decentralized, it is important to have a control system that provides incentives for employees to make value-enhancing decisions. Reward and performance-evaluation systems have to be developed that compensate the worker based on performance outcomes." They conclude that "the components of organizational architecture are like *three legs of a stool*" and "Changing one leg without careful consideration of the other two is typically a mistake."

### Empirical Evidence

We have seen that the hypothesis regarding horizontal fit (synergy, bundles, complementarity) is pervasive. What does the empirical evidence say?[2] Cooke (1994) examined the relationship between productivity (value added per employee) and the use of group-based incentives (profit sharing or gain sharing) and employee participation programs (work teams) in a sample of union and nonunion manufacturing firms. He hypothesized, consistent with the AMO framework and work by Levine and Tyson (1990), that employees need to have both motivation to put their knowledge to use and opportunity in the form of work organization structures (e.g., work teams) that enable them to do so. His results, however, did not provide much support for the hypothesized interaction in either the union or nonunion firms. Indeed, in the union firms, incentives and work teams had larger positive effects when used alone then when used together—a sort of negative synergy.

Kruse (1993) compared the productivity of 112 organizations using profit sharing (for employees other than top management) with productivity of 163 organizations that did not. He found that productivity growth was higher in profit-sharing organizations but that there was only "weak" (p. 87) evidence of an interaction with information sharing and "very little support" (p. 89) for interactions between profit sharing and the other human resource variables (e.g., job enrichment, work teams, and suggestion systems) he studied.

Arthur (1994) examined the impact of a control HR system versus a commitment HR system on labor hours and scrap rates in steel minimills.

---

[2]Much of this literature was previously reviewed by Gerhart et al. (1996). We draw here on that review and add a discussion of studies that were conducted subsequent to that.

The use of a commitment HR system was associated with lower labor hours and lower scrap rates. He also found an interaction such that turnover was unrelated to labor hours and scrap rates in a control HR setting, whereas more turnover was associated with higher labor hours and scrap rates under an HR commitment system. Consequently, turnover, which might be seen as a proxy for ability here, was more disruptive under the commitment system.

MacDuffie (1995) studied the link between "human resource management policies" and "work systems" and productivity and quality in 62 auto assembly plants from around the world. The HR policies included items measuring hiring practices, training, status barriers, and the degree to which pay was contingent on various measures of performance. The work systems scale contained items pertaining to the use of teams, employee involvement, suggestions systems, and job rotation.

To test for bundles (i.e., horizontal fit), MacDuffie (1995) examined statistical interactions between his HR policies and work systems scales and a third scale that measured the use of production buffers (e.g., inventory size) to guard against disruptions of production. Support was mixed, with somewhat stronger support being found in the productivity equations than in the quality equations. In the productivity analyses, two of the three two-way interactions were statistically significant as was the three-way interaction. In the quality analyses, two of the three two-way interactions were statistically significant, but one in the opposite of the direction hypothesized. The three-way interaction was not statistically significant.

Huselid (1995) studied the link between financial performance and two dimensions of what he referred to as high performance work practices (HPWPs), labeling them employee skills/organizational structures and employee motivation. Both dimensions included a variety of human resource practices. Huselid found that firms scoring higher on the two HPWP dimensions had higher levels of financial performance. To test a key internal fit hypothesis, he entered the cross product of the two HPWP dimensions into a regression equation in one analysis and entered the difference between the scores on the two HPWP dimensions in another analysis. Little support was found. Huselid concluded that these results "on the whole . . . did not support . . . fit" (p. 663).

Ichniowski et al. (1993, 1997) used monthly observations on 30 steel finishing lines. Their dependent variable was line uptime and their independent variables were HR practices, either alone or combined via cluster analysis into HR systems. Their key conclusion was that "Systems of HR policies determine productivity. Marginal changes in individual policies have little or no effect on productivity. Improving productivity requires substantial changes in a set of HR policies" (p. 37).

Gerhart et al. (1996), however, questioned whether their results really supported this conclusion. For each HR individual practice, Ichniowski et al. (1993, 1997) estimated a separate equation. The coefficient of each HR practice was then compared, with and without HR system dummy variables in the equation. The individual HR practice coefficients were smaller when the HR system dummy variables were in the model. This formed the basis for Ichniowski et al.'s conclusion that changes in sets of HR policies are necessary. However, as Gerhart et al. noted, the fact that the HR system variables (see their p. 28) were derived on the basis of the individual HR practices using a clustering algorithm probably meant that the HR system variables were collinear with the individual practices. As such, the fact that the coefficients on individual HR practices are diminished when the HR system variables are in the model could just show collinearity. It is not clear why such evidence indicates fit or complementarities between individual HR practices. Ichniowski et al. do not report the $R^2$ for the equations using (a) separate HR practices and (b) HR practices combined into clusters/systems. Thus, there is no means of comparing the fit of (a) versus (b) on the basis of their article.

Unfortunately, the Ichniowski et al. (1993, 1997) method of testing fit continues to be used. Like that of Ichniowski et al., the research reported by Appelbaum et al. (2000) is well done and interesting. However, their approach to testing for fit has similar problems. They concluded that "The synergies created by bundling these [HR and work] practices together have a stronger effect on performance than do the individual practices" (p. 142). My reexamination of their results, however, turns up nothing that really supports this claim. When I simply add the linear effects of the individual HR and work practices variables, I obtain predicted values of their uptime dependent variable that are quite similar to those obtained using the system variables (derived using cluster analysis). In addition, the adjusted $R^2$ for the performance equation containing the separate HR practices is larger (.81 in their Table 8.7) than the $R^2$ in the corresponding performance equation containing the HR clusters/systems (.75 in their Table 8.8). This provides no support for a statistical interaction, which is the basis for the fit or "synergy" hypothesis.

The same problem is also found in a study by Laursen and Foss (2003) of Danish business firms. I see no evidence of internal fit in their study. Further, an examination of their Table 3, Model iii, suggests to us that there is a diminishing return to the use of multiple HR practices, just the opposite of the complementarity hypothesis.

So, although in some empirical studies researchers claimed to find support for horizontal fit (specifically, complementarity), upon closer inspection, the empirical results do not always seem to support the hypothesis. This is a very important conclusion to get right because, from a policy point of view, we do not want to tell companies that they have to "buy the whole package" of HR system practices to obtain improvement if, in fact, that is not necessary. This general issue is one that very much needs to be addressed more carefully.

To say that previous research testing complementarity among multiple HR practices may have problems is not to say that research should focus exclusively on individual HR practices. Indeed, to the degree that individual HR practices are collinear, their standard errors will increase and their individual regression coefficients may not be very informative. An alternative, the configural approach (e.g., Delery & Doty, 1996), would suggest that alternative combinations and levels of HR practices can be equally effective. This then would suggest the potential value of identifying different sets or configurations of HR practices (rather than just one hypothesized best configuration) and studying how these different sets of practices relate to effectiveness, rather than trying to parse out the effects of individual HR practices and rather than assuming more of everything is necessarily better. (See "Challenges in Studying Fit.")

**Vertical Fit**

The AMO framework is a good place to start in any analysis of HR systems. It identifies key intermediate employment outcomes (i.e., AMO), as well as HR and employment policies likely to influence each. It also gives due consideration to the horizontal fit of these HR policies. What the AMO framework and research do not provide is much guidance on the possibility that different HR systems may be differentially effective, depending on contextual factors such as the organization's strategy (i.e., vertical fit) or the environment (e.g., uncertainty and change) that influence strategy.

Appelbaum et al. (2000) handled this issue by arguing that "conditions are changing to increasingly favor HPWSs because they are more effective . . . for emerging markets using recent technologies" and that this "is much more likely to be an indication of a long-term trend than yet another cycle" (p. 39). In other words, HPWSs are, as a general rule, increasingly in vertical alignment with the evolving business strategies of most firms. This is essentially a universalistic (i.e., "one best way") argument.

Vertical fit models in HR have been developed for staffing strategy (e.g., Olian & Rynes, 1984; Sonnenfeld & Peiperl, 1988), compensation strategy (Gomez-Mejia & Balkin, 1992), and the broader HR strategy spectrum of practices (e.g., Baird & Meshoulam, 1988; Cappelli & Singh, 1992; Dyer & Holder, 1988; Lengnick-Hall & Lengnick-Hall, 1988; Miles & Snow, 1984; Schuler & Jackson, 1987). Generally speaking, these models tend to begin with the Porter competitive strategy model (i.e., cost leadership versus differentiation) or the similar Miles–Snow model (i.e., defenders vs. prospectors), which both distinguish between high value–added (differentiation/prospector) and low value–added (cost leadership/defender) strategies. To greatly simplify, high value added strategies are seen as being more successful with HR systems that are higher on the three AMO areas.

*Empirical Work on HR Systems and Business/Corporate Strategy*

Despite the prevailing wisdom that vertical fit matters, the evidence is mixed at best (Delery, 1998; Dyer & Reeves, 1994; Gerhart et al., 1996). Indeed, the title of a 1999 review by Wright and Sherman began with the words "Failing to Find Fit."

In a study described earlier, Huselid (1995) entered the cross-product of business unit strategy (based on Porter) with each of the two HPWP dimensions into a regression equation and did a parallel analysis using the difference scores based on business unit strategy and the two HPWP dimensions. As noted earlier, Huselid's general conclusion was that his results "on the whole . . . did not support . . . fit" (p. 663). Of the studies on HR systems appearing in a 1996 special research forum, Becker and Gerhart (1996) termed the support for vertical fit as "weak" in two (Delaney & Huselid, 1996; Delery & Doty, 1996) and as "mixed" in the other (Youndt, Snell, Dean, & Lepak, 1996).

As with horizontal fit, even when support is claimed for vertical fit, under close scrutiny, the claim may be less strongly supported. For example, Hitt, Bierman, Shimizu, and Kochhar (2001) concluded that "human capital moderates the relationship between strategy and firm performance, thereby supporting a resource–strategy–contingency fit" (p. 13). However, the statistical interaction they most emphasized, among human capital, service diversification (number and importance of legal services), and geographic diversification (of legal services), although statistically significant, had a sign opposite that hypothesized.

Finally, we can briefly examine the pay strategy literature for related evidence, although it should be understood that the focus here is often on executives, and, of course, on a single HR practice area. Evidence for vertical fit is more supportive than it is in the HR systems literature. A better fit between pay strategy and business strategy (e.g., cost leadership and differentiations) and corporate strategy (e.g., growth stage and diversification) has both been found to enhance firm performance (for reviews, see Gerhart, 2000; Gerhart & Rynes, 2003; Gomez-Mejia & Balkin, 1992). These relationships, of course, are not deterministic and there are many examples of successful companies that do not use the pay strategies that are hypothesized to fit their business/corporate strategies (Gerhart & Rynes, 2003).

*Cost and "Low-Road" versus "High-Road" HR Systems*

The AMO approach focuses on high-road policies that increase worker responsibility and autonomy, which may require a higher-quality workforce and more offline time (e.g., time spent in meetings instead of getting product out the door). As a consequence, a firm may find that its costs are higher because it may need to have a higher pay level and because of lost production time at work. To the extent that the high-road HR system is costly, it may not align as well with a cost leadership business strategy as would a less costly, low-road strategy. Historically, this is perhaps most readily seen in the way that firms often move low-skill work offshore to locations where it can be done much more cheaply. More recently, there has been a great deal of attention given to the movement of skilled work (e.g., writing computer code or tax preparation) offshore to less expensive locations.

Cost is an outcome that has been explicitly recognized and quantified in models such as utility analysis (Boudreau, 1991; Brogden, 1949) and in literatures in fields having to do with compensation (Gerhart & Rynes, 2003; Sturman, Trevor, Boudreau, & Gerhart, 2003) and program evaluation (e.g., Cain & Watts, 1970). However, in discussions of HR systems sometimes less attention seems to be paid to cost, except insofar as it is implicitly recognized by using dependent variables that incorporate cost or investment (e.g., return on assets or total shareholder return). Other dependent variables, however, such as quality and productivity, do not incorporate cost at all. For example, in the automobile industry, both academic (e.g., MacDuffie, 1995) and benchmarking work (see the Harbour Report and J. D. Power and Associates survey results mentioned later) focused on quality measures such as defects per vehicle and productivity measures such as hours to assemble a vehicle.

Cappelli and Neumark (2001) explicitly separate the effect of HR systems on outcomes that consider costs and those that do not. They are cautious in their conclusions, saying that one interpretation of their findings is that high-road HR systems "raise employee compensation without necessarily harming the overall profitability and competitiveness of the firms that implement them." However, they say that "an even more careful conclusion would be that [high road HR systems] raise labor costs . . . but the net effect on overall profitability is unclear" (p. 766).

The key work in the recognition that firms differ in their choice of low-road versus high-road HR systems, even within narrow industries, has been conducted by Hunter (2000) in health care and Batt (2001) in telecommunications. Batt, for example, reported that firms having a focus on large-business customers paid 68% higher wages than firms with no dominant customer focus and that most of this higher pay was due to hiring workers with higher levels of human capital.

Boxall and Purcell (2003) provided a nice summary, which only needs to be amended with the observation that, as we have just seen, value-added may differ within sectors:

> Overall, research suggests that the sort of HR practices that foster high commitment from talented employees are most popular in those sectors where quality is a major competitive factor and where firms need to exploit advanced technology (as in complex manufacturing) or engage in a highly skilled interaction with clients (as in professional services). In these sorts of higher value-added sectors,

firms need more competence and loyalty from their employees and are more able to pay for them. In sectors where these conditions are not met—where output per employee is not high—employers adopt more modest employment policies. (p. 68)

## Challenges in Studying Fit

We have seen that despite an apparent widespread belief that horizontal and vertical fit matter, the evidence seems to be weak or, at best, mixed. Why is this the case? To begin first with vertical fit, several possible explanations have been mentioned. First, it is well known that generation of sufficient statistical power to test interactions is difficult, and this problem is probably exacerbated in the HR systems literature by the use of relatively small samples, which to some degree, is an occupational hazard of conducting research at the establishment and firm levels of analysis and using unreliable measures (Gerhart et al., 1996).[3]

Second, it is possible that the consequences of truly poor fit (vertical and/or horizontal) are serious enough in some cases that firms or establishments do not survive to be observed (Hannan & Freeman, 1977; Welbourne & Andrews, 1996). If so, alignment may be so important that it is almost impossible to observe substantial departures from alignment.

Third, our theoretical models of fit may be too simple, relying as they do on correspondingly simple generic business strategy logic (Chadwick & Cappelli, 1999). Fourth, in addition to sharing concerns regarding the adequacy of theory, Wright and Sherman (1999) attributed some of the difficulty to poorly thought out and inconsistent measures of HR (Becker & Gerhart, 1996) and confusion of levels of analysis.

Finally, Becker and Gerhart (1996) noted that fit may depend on the level of analysis. At a sufficiently abstract level (the "architectural" level), there may be best practice principles (e.g., rewarding performance) that all firms would do well to follow. However, at the implementation level of analysis, this principle may best be implemented differently (e.g., emphasis on individual merit pay versus emphasis on say, team incentives), depending on the context. (See Becker & Gerhart, 1996, Table 3.)

Turning to internal fit, many of the same general problems exist. On the theory side, however, Boxall and Purcell (2003) noted that a happy medium between two goals must be found for horizontal fit. One goal is to have practices that are consistent with and supportive of one another (as

---

[3]Two key multiplicative functional forms (i.e., statistical interactions) specified by Vroom (1964) have failed to receive consistent empirical support: the Expectancy × Instrumentality × Valence Motivation hypothesis (Van Eerde & Thierry, 1996) and the Ability × Motivation hypothesis (Sackett, Gruys, & Ellingson, 1998), although the latter used personality characteristics as a proxy for motivation. In any case, these difficulties suggest that finding support for an $A \times M \times O$ interaction was probably not very likely, particularly without large sample sizes.

emphasized earlier). For example, recouping investments in selective hiring practices and training/development could be difficult without practices (e.g., pay, promotion, and benefits) that help ensure employee retention. Likewise, it would perhaps not make sense to hire highly individualistic employees and then expect them to take on roles and be covered by pay systems that are heavily team based. Delery (1998) referred to these situations as "deadly combinations" and Gerhart et al. (1996) earlier depicted these situations as creating "negative synergies."

At the same time, there is also a second goal of avoiding diminishing returns due to unnecessary redundancies in HR system practices. In the aforementioned example, it may be that above-market benefits are sufficient to enhance retention enough to make the selective hiring and training/development investments worthwhile. Although an above-market pay level would also be consistent with enhancing retention, it may be unnecessary. The idea here is similar to the focus of the utility literature on the incremental utility of an additional investment in new or additional HR practices (Boudreau, 1991).

Practices in the three AMO areas can surely be complementary without all being at their highest levels, but previous empirical tests, because of inadequate theory or translation of theory into method, may not allow that possibility to be found. The logic of previous tests is probably even more of an issue when one looks within the three AMO practice areas. For example, if a study includes questions in the ability area regarding training for new hires, training for experienced employees, selectivity in hiring, and so forth, how many of these alternative means of achieving a high-ability workforce need to be high? Consider the following single company and how the conclusion regarding its emphasis on ability would change as a function of the survey items. Assume scores are 1 = low, 2 = average, and 3 = high.

| Company A (four-item survey) | | Company A (one-item survey) | |
| --- | --- | --- | --- |
| Extensive use of tests in hiring | 3 | Extensive use of tests in hiring | 3 |
| Education level of workforce | 2 | | |
| Training of new hires | 2 | | |
| Training of all employees | 2 | | |
| Average score | 2.25 | Average score | 3 |

In the survey with four items pertaining to ability, Company A's scale score average would be 2.25, whereas in a survey having a single item it would be 3. What sense does it make to score Company A lower as a result of including more survey items? Also, perhaps Company A has decided there would be diminishing returns and duplication if it were to invest at the maximum level in every HR practice having to do with ability. I question whether empirical studies have been designed to allow for this fact.

## Fit and Flexibility

Although fit is typically seen as an important goal, its importance should perhaps be tempered by the possibility that fit can be a double-edged sword when it comes to HR systems. Gerhart et al. (1996) drew on work regarding tight and loose coupling (Orton & Weick, 1990; Perrow, 1984; Weick, 1976) and Schneider's (1987) work on how HR systems can result in a homogeneous work force. Gerhart et al. pointed out that the HR system (and resulting workforce) that fits the current business strategy may quickly become a poor fit if the business strategy changes. A less tightly aligned set of HR practices, where bets were hedged, might make a successful adaptation more likely. As Boxall and Purcell (2003) put it: "Aiming to meet current competitive needs . . . is important but so too are goals for supporting organization flexibility over time. In a changing environment, there is always a strategic tension between performing in the present context and preparing for the future" (p. 56).

Perhaps in recognition of the limitations of static vertical fit, some recent work on HR systems emphasized the importance of agility in HR systems and strategy (Dyer & Shafer, 1999) and, relatedly, of flexibility (Wright & Snell, 1998), or what might be seen as a capability for achieving dynamic fit. In this vein, Wright and Snell stated that "Flexibility, however, is not a temporary state but an actual characteristic (e.g., a trait) of an organization" (p. 757).

Wright and Snell (1998) quoted Sanchez (1995, p. 138) and defined flexibility as "a firm's abilities to respond to various demands from dynamic competitive environments." They distinguish between fit and flexibility as follows:

> In contrast to fit's focus on an interface of two variables—one internal and one external—flexibility is purely internal, made possible via such firm characteristics as broad, heterogeneous skills and competencies of the workforce, organic administrative systems, and so on that enable a firm to adapt to some change in the environment. (p. 757)

Although I am not certain that flexibility is purely internal, the emphasis on heterogeneous skills seems important and consistent with earlier work (Gerhart et al., 1996; Schneider, 1987). Wright and Snell (1998) argued that "fit and flexibility are complementary" (p. 757), but do not develop this argument. I am inclined to believe that they are somewhat complementary: Fit does not preclude flexibility. However, I also believe that they may be competing objectives at some point because too much fit to the current environment may constrain the internal heterogeneity needed to adapt. Thus, I am inclined to agree with Boxall and Purcell's (2003) description of this as a "strategic tension."

## THE RESOURCE-BASED VIEW OF THE FIRM

As we have seen, the dominant vertical fit focus in the HR systems literature has been on the fit between HR systems and *generic* (competitive) business strategies. Although this fit or contingency approach is strategic in the sense that different firms are thought to benefit from different strategies, it also has elements of a best practice approach because similarly situated firms (e.g., in the same narrow industry) are expected to benefit from using similar strategies (Becker & Gerhart, 1996).

By contrast, the resource-based view (RBV) of the firm emphasizes how firms "look inside" for resources that not only add value but are also rare and difficult to imitate and that can be leveraged to build sustained competitive advantage. Industry characteristics and business strategy place limits on managerial discretion, but a significant amount remains. Generic business strategy models are seen as leading to parity with the competition because, if generic prescriptions are followed, competing firms will develop similar HR systems. Competitive advantage, however, requires that firms be unique by developing and deploying resources in unique ways that add value and are difficult to imitate (Barney, 1991; Rumelt, 1984; Wernerfelt, 1984).

The RBV distinguishes between competitive parity and (sustained) competitive advantage. A company having an HR system that creates value but is not unique because competing firms use similar HR systems can achieve competitive parity but not competitive advantage. The latter requires, in addition, that the HR system be rare and difficult to imitate. This situation then requires an important new assumption—that given the same contextual factors, different HR systems may be effective (equifinality). In other words, there is no one best way. This idea is also found in configurational approaches (e.g., Delery & Doty, 1996). Applications of the RBV approach to HR systems include the works of Lado and Wilson (1994), Barney and Wright (1998), Gerhart et al. (1996), and Wright, Dunford, and Snell, 2001).

According to Pfeffer (1994), the success generated by HR systems "is often not visible or transparent as to its source," which evokes Barney's (1991) concept of inimitability through causal ambiguity. Pfeffer goes on to say that issues such as culture, HR management, and the consequences they have for employee behavior are often underestimated because they are seen as soft issues. Moreover, even when their importance is given more weight, the social complexity and causal ambiguity of the RBV seem to prohibit imitation:

> it is often hard to comprehend the dynamics of a particular company and how it operates because the way people are managed often fits together in a system. It is easy to copy one thing but much more difficult to copy numerous things. This is because the change needs to be more comprehensive and also because the ability to understand the system of management practices is hindered by its very extensiveness. (Pfeffer, 1994, p. 15)

Although HR systems are now seen as providing an important avenue toward sustained competitive advantage (Barney & Wright, 1998; Becker & Gerhart, 1996; Fulmer, Gerhart, & Scott, 2003; Gerhart et al., 1996), to our knowledge, there has been little or no pertinent empirical research. One partial exception is the study by Fulmer et al., who explicitly incorporated the RBV framework and showed that employee relations, mostly defined in terms of how positive mean employee attitude was at a firm, was stable over time, was rare (at the highest levels of mean employee attitude), and added value, as indicated by subsequent business performance being higher for companies having the most favorable employee relations. Related research has documented a positive relationship between attitudes and performance at the individual level (see the meta-analysis of Judge, Thoresen, Bono, & Patton, 2001), between attitudes and financial performance at the facility level (Harter, Schmidt, & Hayes, 2002; Ryan, Schmit, & Johnson, 1996), and, at the organization level, between attitudes and nonfinancial performance (Ostroff, 1992) and between attitudes and financial performance (Fulmer et al., 2003, as discussed earlier; Schneider, Hanges, Smith, & Salvaggio, 2003).

AMO and related frameworks emphasize the fact that business performance will be higher with better horizontal fit of HR system components. Horizontal fit, however, can also be a major factor from the RBV point of view, not just because of its potential to create greater value, but also because an HR system with optimal horizontal fit is presumably rarer and more difficult to imitate than HR systems lacking these attributes (Gerhart et al., 1996). As such, taking the RBV and AMO perspectives together further emphasizes the importance of horizontal fit. However, as I have noted, the AMO framework seems to offer a universalistic set of prescriptions, whereas RBV emphasizes the payoff to being unique.

## Can Competitive Advantage Be "Sustained"?

Boxall and Purcell (2003) acknowledge the importance of the focus of the RBV on being unique, but feel there is "the tendency of authors to focus only on sources of idiosyncrasy, thus exaggerating differences between firms in the same sector" (p. 81). They argue that any distinctive capability "tends to be emulated by others [and] then becomes part of the 'table stakes' in the industry and firms that seek superior performance must search for other ways to differentiate themselves" (p. 82). March and Sutton (1997) make a similar argument. Likewise, one must acknowledge that there are also institutional (in addition to market) pressures for conformity and similarity to the degree that firms face similar environments.[4] Nevertheless, one can question whether competitive advantage is so short-lived.

Boxall and Purcell (2003) cite Hamel and Prahalad's (1994) example of the auto industry in which they argue that quality, measured as defects per vehicle, was once a "genuine differentiator for Japanese car producers . . . [but] has become a prerequisite for every car maker" (p. 232). Perhaps it has. But, has every car maker met this prerequisite to the same degree? An examination of reports from J. D. Power and Associates and Harbour Consulting suggests that the answer is "no." In the *Machine That Changed the World*, a major study of the automobile industry published in 1990 and using data from the late 1980s, Womack, Jones, and Roos reported a major advantage of Japanese-owned car assembly plants over American-owned (and European-owned) plants in terms of quality and productivity. The 2004 J. D. Power and Associates press release for its Vehicle Dependability Study[SM] (of 3-year-old vehicles) reported that "while the Domestics continue to outpace the Europeans in long-term quality, the Japanese continue to dominate" and that Toyota and Honda have the highest quality vehicles. The 2004 J. D. Power and Associates Initial Quality Study[SM] (vehicles in their first 90 days of ownership) likewise reported that Toyota and Honda have the highest quality vehicles and that the average improvement in initial quality between 1998 and 2004 was identical (32%) for Japanese-branded vehicles and domestic-branded vehicles. This, of course, means that there was no narrowing of the Japanese vehicle initial quality advantage.

On the productivity front, the Harbour Report (*Washington Post*, June 11, 2004) found that Nissan had the most efficient automobile assembly plants, followed by Honda and Toyota. GM ranked fourth and was the only U. S. company to do better than the industry average. The estimated profit per vehicle was also higher for Japanese companies (Nissan, $2,402; Toyota, $1,742; and Honda, $1,488) with GM being the only domestic company to have a profit ($178 per vehicle). Estimated loss per vehicle was $48 for Ford and $496 for Chrysler.

---

[4]Conceptual treatments and comparisons of institutional and RBV theoretical implications for HR systems can be found in Gerhart et al. (1996), Paauwe (2004), and Paauwe and Boselie (2003). A very interesting empirical study integrating institutional and RBV perspectives on HR and the diffusion of innovative employment practices in the U. S. legal industry can be found in Sherer and Lee (2002).

In summary, in the automobile industry, one can argue that competitive advantage on the part of the major Japanese producers has been sustained for a significant time period. Of course, this one example is not sufficient to evaluate the general argument regarding the sustainability of competitive advantage. In my view, the main point to emphasize is that although no competitive advantage is indefinitely sustainable, neither is it fleeting nor does it mean that superior business performance for a decade or two is unimportant. Shareholders, employees, and other stakeholders can benefit greatly from competitive advantage that is sustained (even if not indefinite).

A different way to approach the sustainability issue is to look not at business performance but at the diffusion of HR practices. If competitive advantage that has its basis in HR strategy is fleeting, we would expect this to be the case when "best practices" rapidly diffuse to competitors, who, upon adopting these practices, close the competitive advantage gap. But, is this what the literature on HR practice diffusion shows?

Osterman's (2000) reported a survey of four "innovative work systems" practices from 1992 and 1997. These results are summarized in the table for the 457 establishments that responded to both surveys. Note that Osterman instructed establishments to report that they used a practice only if it covered at least 50% of its core employees.

| Practice | 1992 | 1997 |
| --- | --- | --- |
| Quality circles | 29% | 58% |
| Job rotation | 24% | 47% |
| Teams | 40% | 41% |
| Total quality management | 24% | 51% |

One can read these results in different ways. On the one hand, there clearly were significant increases in three of the four practices. On the other hand, these practices have been around for quite some time and yet as of 1997, only about one-half of the establishments used the practices in each case.

Other sources also call into question the degree of diffusion. For example, Guest et al. (2003) observed that "the number and range of HR practices applied across the organizations in [our] sample is relatively low" (pp. 303–304). Vallas (2003) described "a disturbing gap between theoretical models of new work practices and the empirical evidence concerning their actual implementation" (p. 223). (Further work on understanding diffusion can be found in a number of recent interesting studies: Erickson & Jacoby, 2003; Hunter, MacDuffie, & Doucet, 2002; Pil & MacDuffie, 1996, 1999; Sherer & Lee, 2002.)

Another challenge to the notion of ready diffusion arises from data on the share of establishments implementing multiple such practices.

Again, based on establishments reporting in both 1992 and 1997 and imposing the restriction that the practice cover at least 50% of core employees, the results are summarized in the table (Osterman, 2000)

| No. of Practices | 1992 | 1997 |
|:---:|:---:|:---:|
| 0 | 35% | 15% |
| 1 | 27% | 14% |
| 2 | 25% | 32% |
| 3 | 9% | 24% |
| 4 | 4 | 16 |

A minority (40%) of establishments used three or more of the four practices. Gittelman, Horrigan, and Joyce (1998), using 1993 survey data on six similar practices, reported even weaker evidence for diffusion of systems of practices. Osterman (2000) reported that a substantial portion of establishments having these practices in 1992 did not have them in 1997, as well as a substantial portion that did not have the practices in 1992 but implemented them later. Thus, although an establishment may report having a practice in place, it may or may not have been in place for long and it may or may not stay in place for long (Gerhart et al., 1996). In our view, this situation conveys something less than widespread diffusion and sustainability of practices when they have diffused, consistent with the evidence and interpretation of Kochan and Osterman (1994). One hypothesis is that it is more difficult (more socially complex) to design and implement effective bundles of practices than it is for a single practice. So, although the value of multiple, horizontally aligned practices has a high potential payoff, it is also more difficult and perhaps more risky (Gerhart et al., 1996).

## HR SYSTEMS AND COMPETITIVE ADVANTAGE: A MODEL

Drawing on the AMO/industrial relations, I/O psychology, and economic models of HR systems, as well as the frameworks found in many HR textbooks (e.g., Heneman et al., 1980), I formulated the model shown in Fig. 10–1. It shows an HR diamond, meant to identify the (a) core HR system content areas of roles (job design and worker influence), rewards (intrinsic and extrinsic incentives/motivators), and people (staffing, training, and development), and the importance of their (b) horizontal fit (lines HF1–HF3) and (c) vertical fit (lines VF1–VF3). Roles, rewards, and people HR system policy decisions have consequences for opportunity, motivation, and ability, as well as cost. These consequences are also a function of contextual factors of the sort found in a number of models (Boxall & Purcell, 2003; Heneman et al., 1980; Noe et al., 2005; Paauwee, 2004).

To the degree that ability, motivation, and opportunity objectives are achieved via decisions about people, rewards, and roles, while managing

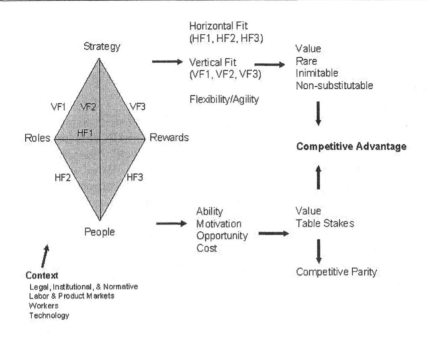

Horizontal Fit
HF1   Roles with Rewards
HF2   Roles with People
HF3   People with Rewards

Vertical Fit
VF1   Strategy with Roles
VF2   Strategy with People
VF3   Strategy with Rewards

FIGURE 10–1.    HR strategy diamond and outcomes.

cost, the HR system creates value and competitive parity (i.e., business performance comparable to that of key competitors), which gives the firm a chance ("table stakes") to go beyond parity. This, however, depends on creating fit (horizontal and vertical), which can not only create greater value, but may also do so in a way that is difficult to imitate or substitute for, thus facilitating sustained competitive advantage. Strategies geared toward achieving (sustained) competitive advantage in this way may also carry greater risk of failure (Gerhart et al., 1996). Flexibility/agility is also important (Dyer & Shafer, 1999; Wright & Snell, 1998), especially to the degree that context is rapidly changing for a firm.

The model I have presented still remains to be validated. Among the challenges that have been recognized for some time now (e.g., Becker & Gerhart, 1996) are the need to better understand and empirically test mediating hypotheses and the need to develop better theories of fit. Additional challenges concern methodology, which I have discussed, in part, and to which I now return.

## Methodology

Whereas, as noted earlier, in their summary, Guest et al.'s (2003) concluded that a robust relationship existed between HR and business performance, they nevertheless raised cautions as well: "Despite the positive thrust of most published empirical findings, Wood (1999) among others has noted that the quality of the research base supporting the relationship between HR and performance is relatively weak . . . questions remain about the measurement of both HR and performance, and about the weight and relevance of tests of association and causation" (p. 295). Beyond covariation between HR and performance, causal inference, of course (e.g., Cook & Campbell, 1979), also depends on time precedence (facilitated by longitudinal data) and ruling out alternative causal explanations (e.g., omitted variables, selection bias, or simultaneity).

As we also saw earlier, one key issue is how to test for fit, especially horizontal fit. Other standard issues are causal inference (simultaneity, omitted variables, and especially the potential selection bias introduced by ignoring the survival probabilities of different HR systems). Another ongoing challenge is to include data from different sources and levels of analysis (Bowen & Ostroff, 2004), given that HR system policies (often measured by asking HR executives) are typically theorized to operate through individual-level employee reactions such as motivation, ability, and opportunity (Ichniowski, Kochan, Levine, Olson, & Strauss, 1996). Yet, these multilevel/multisource data are largely absent from the HR systems literature (Becker & Gerhart, 1996). This absence makes it difficult to understand how consistent and strong the "message" that the HR system transmits to employees is (Bowen & Ostroff, 2004).

Studying an HR system, which is composed of individual HR practices, also requires measurement decisions, such as who provides the HR data, whether data on different employee groups and different business units or establishments should be pooled or analyzed separately, whether and how items should be combined into scales, and whether data should be in the form of stated policies or rather experienced practices. (Two firms may both report that they have a particular policy in place, but the actual intensity and pervasiveness of that policy in how they conduct business may differ dramatically.) Many of these issues have been discussed in a give and take series of articles in *Personnel Psychology* (Gerhart, Wright, & McMahan, 2000; Gerhart, Wright, McMahan, & Snell, 2000; Huselid & Becker, 2000).

Reliability is one of the issues for which empirical evidence is available. Consistent with other literatures in applied psychology, evidence shows that single-rater measures of HR systems (the norm) may be no better than .20 (Gerhart et al., 2000a). This fact can be interpreted in two ways. First, because low reliability generally attenuates relationships, the observed relationships between HR and business performance underestimate the true relationship. Thus, HR system decisions are even more important than empirical findings indicate. Second, and alternatively, there may be a concern that correcting the already substantial HR and business performance relationship yields a "corrected" estimate that is so large as to be implausible (Gerhart, 1999; Gerhart et al., 2000a).

Finally, as we have noted, levels of analysis issues are central to work on HR systems. Conceptual models must not only map out intervening and moderator variables, but also explain how these variables, which are sometimes most grounded in individual level models (e.g., AMO), operate across levels.

## CONCLUSION

I have reviewed the conceptual foundation for work on HR systems, approaches to HR system measurement, and theory and research on how content of HR systems (including their horizontal and vertical fit) can influence business performance (or competitive advantage). I have also presented a model intended to capture these issues.

There has been a great deal of interesting work conducted, and the relationship between HR systems and effectiveness has been established using a variety of measures and at different levels of analysis. Challenges remain in better establishing that the relationship is causal (e.g., through using longitudinal data, mediating variables, and better controls) and in better understanding the degree to which HR systems must include a comprehensive set of consistent policies and finally, the degree to which the choice of an HR system should depend on the strategy and context. Meaningful policy recommendations depend on having valid answers to these questions.

## ACKNOWLEDGMENTS

I thank Charlie Trevor and Cheri Ostroff for their helpful comments.

## REFERENCES

Adams, J. S. (1965). Inequity in social exchange. In L. Berkowitz (Ed.), *Advances in experimental social psychology*. New York: Academic Press.

Appelbaum, E., Bailey, T., Berg, P., & Kalleberg, A. (2000) *Manufacturing advantage*: *Why high performance work systems pay off*. Ithaca, NY: Cornell University Press.

Arthur, J. B. (1994). Effects of human resource systems on manufacturing performance and turnover. *Academy of Management Journal, 37,* 670–687.

Bailey, T. (1993). *Discretionary effort and the organization of work: Employee participation and work reform since Hawthorne.* Unpublished manuscript, Teachers College, Columbia University, New York.

Baird, L., & Meshoulam, I. (1988). Managing two fits of strategic human resource management. *Academy of Management Review, 13,* 116–128.

Barnard, C. I. (1951). *The functions of the executive.* Cambridge, MA: Harvard University Press.

Barney, J. B. (1991). Firm resources and sustained competitive advantage. *Journal of Management, 17,* 99–120.

Barney, J. B., & Wright, P. M. (1998). On becoming a strategic partner: The role of human resources in gaining competitive advantage. *Human Resource Management, 37,* 31–46.

Batt, R. (2001). Explaining intra-occupational wage inequality in telecommunications services: Customer segmentation, human resource practices, and union decline. *Industrial & Labor Relations Review, 54,* 425–449.

Batt, R. (2002). Managing customer services: Human resource practices, quit rates, and sales growth. *Academy of Management Journal, 45,* 587–597.

Becker, G. S. (1964). *Human capital.* New York: Columbia.

Becker, B., & Gerhart, B. (1996). The impact of human resource management on organizational performance: Progress and prospects. *Academy of Management Journal, 39,* 779–801.

Boudreau, J. W. (1991). Utility analysis for decisions in human resource management. In M. D. Dunnette & L. M. Hough (Eds.), *Handbook of industrial and organizational psychology* (2nd ed., Vol. 2, pp. 621–745). Palo Alto, CA: Consulting Psychologists Press.

Bowen, D. E., & Ostroff, C. (2004). Understanding HRM-firm performance linkages: The role of the 'strength' of the HRM system. *Academy of Management Review, 29,* 203–221.

Boxall, P., & Purcell, J. (2003). *Strategy and human resource management.* Hampshire, England: PalgraveMacmillan.

Brewster, C. (1999). Different paradigms in strategic HRM: Questions raised by comparative research. In P. M. Wright, L. Dyer, J. W. Boudreau, & G. T. Milkovich (Eds.), *Strategic human resources management in the twenty-first century.* Supplement to G. R. Ferris (Ed.), *Research in personnel and human resources management* (pp. 213–238). Stanford, CT: JAI Press.

Brickley, J. A., Smith, C., & Lease, S. C. (1997). *Managerial economics and organizational architecture.* Chicago: Irwin.

Brogden, H. E. (1949). When testing pays off. *Personnel Psychology, 2,* 171–185.

Cain, G. G., & Watts, H. W. (1970). Problems in making policy inferences from the Coleman report. *American Sociological Review, 35,* 228–252.

Campbell, J. P. (1990). Modeling the performance prediction problem in industrial and organizational psychology. In M. D. Dunnette & L. M. Hough (Eds.), *Handbook of industrial and organizational psychology* (2nd ed., Vol. 1, pp. 687–732). Palo Alto, CA: Consulting Psychologists Press.

Campbell, J. P., & Pritchard, R. D. (1976). Motivation theory in industrial and organizational psychology. In M. Dunnette (Ed.), *Handbook of industrial and organizational psychology* (pp. 63–130). Chicago: Rand McNally.

Cappelli, P., & Neumark, D. (2001). Do "high-performance" work practices improve establishment-level outcomes? *Industrial & Labor Relations Review, 54,* 737–775.

Cappelli, P., & Singh, H. (1992). Integrating strategic human resources and strategic management. In D. Lewin, O. S. Mitchell, & P. D. Sherer (Eds.), *Research frontiers in industrial relations and human resources* (pp. 165–192). Madison, WI: Industrial Relations Research Association.

Chadwick, C., & Cappelli, P. (1999). Alternatives to generic strategy typologies in strategic human resources management. In P. M. Wright, L. Dyer, J. W. Boudreau, & G. T. Milkovich (Eds.), *Strategic human resources management in the twenty-first century.* Supplement to G. R. Ferris (Ed.), *Research in personnel and human resources management* (pp. 1–29). Stanford, CT: JAI Press.

Cook, T. D., & Campbell, D. T. (1979). *Quasi-experimentation.* Chicago: Rand McNally.

Cooke, W. N. (1994). Employee participation programs, group-based incentives, and company performance: A union-nonunion comparison. *Industrial & Labor Relations Review, 47,* 594–609.

Cutcher-Gershenfeld, J. (1991). The impact on economic performance of a transformation in workplace relations. *Industrial & Labor Relations Review, 44,* 241–260.

Delaney, J. T., & Huselid, M. A. (1996). The impact of human resource management practices on perceptions of organizational performance. *Academy of Management Journal, 39,* 949–969.

Delery, J. E. (1998). Issues of fit in strategic human resource management research: Implications for research. *Human Resource Management Review, 8,* 289–309.

Delery, J. E., & Doty, D. H. (1996). Modes of theorizing in strategic human resource management: Tests of universalistic, contingency, and configurational performance predictions. *Academy of Management Journal, 39,* 802–835.

Dyer, L., & Holder, G. W. (1988). Toward a strategic perspective of human resource management. In L. Dyer (Ed.), *Human resource management: Evolving roles and responsibilities* (pp. 1–46). Washington, DC: Bureau of National Affairs.

Dyer, L., & Reeves, T. (1994). *HR strategies and firm performance: What do we know and where do we go from here?* (Working Paper 94–29). Ithaca, NY: Center for Advanced Human Resource Studies, Cornell University.

Dyer, L., & Shafer, R. A. (1999). From human resource strategy to organizational effectiveness: Lessons from research on organizational agility. In P. M. Wright, L. Dyer, J. W. Boudreau, & G. T. Milkovich (Eds.), *Strategic human resources management in the twenty-first century.* Supplement to G. R. Ferris (Ed.), *Research in personnel and human resources management* (pp. 145–174). Stanford, CT: JAI Press.

Erickson, C. L., & Jacoby, S. M. (2003). The effect of employer networks on workplace innovation and training. *Industrial & Labor Relations Review, 56,* 203–223.

Fama, E. F., & Jensen, M. C. (1983). Separation of ownership and control. *Journal of Law and Economics, 26,* 301–325.

Fulmer, I. S., Gerhart, B., & Scott, K. S. (2003). Are the 100 best better? An empirical investigation of the relationship between being a "great place to work" and firm performance. *Personnel Psychology, 56,* 965–993.

Gerhart, B. (1999). Human resource management and firm performance: Measurement issues and their effect on causal and policy inferences. In P. M. Wright, L. Dyer, J. W. Boudreau, & G. T. Milkovich (Eds.), *Strategic human resources management in the twenty-first century.* Supplement to G. R. Ferris (Ed.), *Research in personnel and human resources management* (pp. 31–51). Stanford, CT: JAI Press.

Gerhart, B. (2000). Compensation strategy and organizational performance. In S. L. Rynes & B. Gerhart (Eds.), *Compensation in organizations.* San Francicso: Jossey-Bass.

Gerhart, B., & Milkovich, G. T. (1990). Organizational differences in managerial compensation and financial performance. *Academy of Management Journal, 33,* 663–691.

Gerhart, B., & Rynes, S. L. (2003). *Compensation: Theory, evidence, and strategic implications.* Thousand Oaks, CA: Sage.

Gerhart, B., Trevor, C., & Graham, M. (1996). New directions in employee compensation research. In G. R. Ferris (Ed.), *Research in personnel and human resources management* (pp. 143–203). Stanford, CT: JAI Press.

Gerhart, B., Wright, P. M., & McMahan, G. C. (2000a). Measurement error in research on the human resources and firm performance relationship: Further evidence and analysis. *Personnel Psychology, 53,* 855–872.

Gerhart, B., Wright, P. M., McMahan, G. C., & Snell, S. A. (2000b). Measurement error in research on human resources and firm performance: How much error is there and how does it influence effect size estimates? *Personnel Psychology, 5,* 803–834.

Gittleman, M., Horrigan, M., & Joyce, M. (1998). Flexible workplace practices: Evidence from a nationally representative survey. *Industrial & Labor Relations Review, 52,* 99–115.

Godard, J. (2001). High performance and the transformation of work? The implications of alternative work practices for the experience and outcomes of work. *Industrial & Labor Relations Review, 54,* 776–805.

Godard, J., & Delaney, J. T. (2000). Reflections on the "high-performance" paradigm's implications for industrial relations as a field. *Industrial & Labor Relations Review, 53,* 482–502.

Gomez-Mejia, L. R., & Balkin, D. B. (1992). *Compensation, organizational strategy, and firm performance.* Cincinnati, OH: South-Western.

Guest, D., Michie, J., Conway, N., & Sheehan, M. (2003). Human resource management and corporate performance in the UK. *British Journal of Industrial Relations, 41,* 291–314.

Hackman, J. R., & Lawler, E. E. (1971). Employee reactions to job characteristics. *Journal of Applied Psychology Monograph, 55,* 259–286.

Hackman, J. R., & Oldham, G. R. (1976). Motivation through the design of work: Test of a theory. *Organizational Behavior and Human Performance, 16,* 250–279.

Hamel, G., & Prahalad, C. K. (1994). *Competing for the future.* Boston: Harvard Business School Press.

Handel, M., & Gittleman, M. (2004). Is there a wage payoff to innovative work practices? *Industrial Relations, 43,* 67–97.

Hannan, M. T., & Freeman, J. (1984). Structural inertia and organizational change. *American Sociological Review, 49,* 149–164.

Harter, J. K., Schmidt, F. L., & Hayes, T. L. (2002). Business-unit-level relationship between employee satisfaction, employee engagement, and business outcomes: A meta-analysis. *Journal of Applied Psychology, 87,* 268–279.

Heneman, H. G., III, & Judge, T. A. (2003). *Staffing organizations* (3rd ed.). Boston: McGraw-Hill/Irwin.

Heneman, H. G., III, Schwab, D. P., Fossum, J. A., & Dyer, L. (1980). *Personnel/ human resource management.* Homewood, IL: Irwin.

Hitt, M. A., Bierman, L., Shimizu, K., & Kochhar, R. (2001). Direct and moderating effects of human capital on strategy and performance in professional service firms: A resource-based perspective. *Academy of Management Journal, 44,* 13–28.

Holmstrom, B., & Milgrom, P. (1994). The firm as an incentive system. *American Economic Review, 94,* 972–991.

Hunter, L. W. (2000).What determines job quality in nursing homes? *Industrial & Labor Relations Review, 53,* 463–481.

Hunter, L. W., & Lafkas, J. J. (2003). Opening the box: Information technology, work practices, and wages. *Industrial & Labor Relations Review, 56,* 224–243.

Hunter, L. W., MacDuffie, J. P., & Doucet, L. (2002). What makes teams take? Employee reactions to work reforms. *Industrial & Labor Relations Review, 55,* 448–472.

Huselid, M. A. (1995). The impact of human resource management practices on turnover, productivity, and corporate financial performance. *Academy of Management Journal, 38,* 635–672.

Huselid, M. A., & Becker, B. E. (2000). Comment on "Measurement Error in Research on Human Resources and Firm Performance: How Much Error is There and How Does it Influence Effect Size Estimates?" by Gerhart, Wright, McMahan, and Snell. *Personnel Psychology, 53,* 835–854.

Ichniowski, C., Kochan, T. A., Levine, D., Olson, C. A., & Strauss, G. (1996). What works at work: Overview and assessment. *Industrial Relations, 35,* 299–333.

Ichniowski, C., Shaw, K., & Prennushi, G. (1993, September). *The effects of human resource management practices on productivity: A study of steel finishing lines.* Cornell/ILR Labor Economics Workshop, Ithaca, NY.

Ichniowski, C., Shaw, K., & Prennushi, G. (1997). The effects of human resource management practices on productivity: A study of steel finishing lines. *American Economic Review, 87,* 291–313.

Judge, T. A., Thoresen, C. J., Bono, J. E., & Patton, G. K. (2001). The job satisfaction–job performance relationship: A qualitative and quantitative review. *Psychological Bulletin, 127,* 376–407.

Katz, H. C., Kochan, T. A., & Gobeille, K. R. (1983). Industrial relations performance, economic performance, and QWL programs: An interplant analysis. *Industrial & Labor Relations Review, 37,* 3-17.

Katz, H. C., Kochan, T. A., & Weber, M. R. (1985). Assessing the effects of industrial relations systems and efforts to improve the quality of working life on organizational effectiveness. *Academy of Management Journal, 28,* 509–526.

Kochan, T. A. (2000). On the paradigm guiding industrial relations theory and research: Comment on John Godard and John T. Delaney, "Reflections on the 'High-Performance' Paradigm's Implications for Industrial Relations as a Field." *Industrial and Labor Relations Review, 53,* 704–711.

Kochan, T. A., & Osterman, P. (1994). *The mutual gains enterprise: Forging a winning partnership among labor, management, and government.* Boston: Harvard Business School Press.

Kozlowski, S. W. J., & Klein, K. J. (2000). A multilevel approach to theory and research in organizations: Contextual, temporal, and emergent processes. In K. J. Klein & S. W. J. Kozlowski (Eds.), *Multilevel theory, research, and methods in organizations: Foundations, extensions, and new directions* (pp. 3–90). SIOP Frontiers Series. San Francisco: Jossey-Bass.

Kruse, D. L. (1993). *Profit sharing: Does it make a difference?* Kalamazoo, MI: Upjohn Institute for Employment Research.

Lado, A. A., & Wilson, M. C. (1994). Human resource systems and sustained competitive advantage: A competency-based perspective. *Academy of Management Review, 19*, 699–728.

Laursen, K., & Foss, N. J. (2003). New human resource management practices, complementarities, and impact on innovation performance. *Cambridge Journal of Economics, 27*, 243–263.

Lawler, E. E., III (1971). *Pay and organizational effectiveness: A psychological view.* New York: McGraw-Hill.

Lepak, D. P., & Snell, S. A. (1999). The human resource architecture. *Academy of Management Review, 24*, 31–49.

Lengnick-Hall, C. A., and Lengnick-Hall, M. L. (1988). Strategic human resources management: A review of the literature and a proposed typology. *Academy of Management Review, 13*, 454–470.

Levine, D. I., & Tyson, L. D. (1990). Participation, productivity, and the firm's environment. In A. S. Blinder (Ed.), *Paying for productivity* (pp. 183–237). Washington, DC: Brookings Institute.

Locke, F. A., & Latham, G. P. (1990). *A theory of goal-setting and performance.* Englewood Cliffs, NJ: Prentice-Hall.

Macduffie, J. P. (1995). Human resource bundles and manufacturing performance: Organizational logic and flexible production systems in the world auto industry. *Industrial & Labor Relations Review, 47*, 197–221.

March, J. G., & Sutton, R. I. (1997). Organizational performance as a dependent variable. *Organization Science, 8*, 698–706.

McGregor, D. (1960). *The human side of enterprise.* New York: McGraw-Hill.

Miles, R. E., & Snow, C. C. (1984). Designing strategic human resource systems. *Organizational Dynamics, 13*(1), 36–52.

Milgrom, P., & Roberts, J. (1992). *Economics, organization & management.* Englewood Cliffs, NJ: Prentice-Hall.

Mincer, J. (1974). *Schooling, experience, and earnings.* New York: National Bureau of Economic Research.

Noe, R. A. (1999). *Employee training and development.* Boston: Irwin/McGraw-Hill.

Noe, R. A., Hollenbeck, J. R., Gerhart, B., & Wright, P. M. (2005). *Human resource management: Gaining a competitive advantage* (5th ed.). Boston: Irwin/McGraw-Hill.

Olian, J. D., & Rynes, S. L. (1984). Organizational staffing: Integrating practice and strategy. *Industrial Relations, 23*, 170–183.

Orton, J. D., & Weick, K. E. (1990). Loosely coupled systems: A reconceptualization. *Academy of Management Review, 15*, 203–223.

Osterman, P. (2000). Work reorganization in an era of restructuring: Trends in diffusion and effects on employee welfare. *Industrial & Labor Relations Review, 53*, 179–196.

Ostroff, C. (1992). The relationship between satisfaction, attitudes, and performance: An organizational level analysis. *Journal of Applied Psychology, 77*, 963–974.

Ostroff, C. (1993). Comparing correlations based on individual-level and aggregated data. *Journal of Applied Psychology, 78*, 569–582.

Ostroff, C., & Bowen, D. E. (2000). Moving HR to a higher level: HR practices and organizational effectiveness. In K. J. Klein & S. W. J. Kozlowski (Eds.), *Multilevel theory research, and methods in organizations: Foundations, extensions, and new directions* (pp. 211–266). SIOP Frontiers Series. San Francisco: Jossey-Bass.

Parker, S. K. (2003). Longitudinal effects of lean production on employee outcomes and the mediating role of work characteristics. *Journal of Applied Psychology, 88*, 620–634.

Paauwee, J. (2004). *HRM and performance: Achieving long term viability.* New York: Oxford University Press.

Paauwe, J., & Boselie, J. P. (2003). Challenging 'strategic HRM' and the relevance of institutional setting. *Human Resource Management Journal, 13*, 56–70.

Perrow, C. (1984). *Normal accidents: Living with high-risk technologies.* New York: Basic Books.

Peters, L. H., & O'Connor, E. J. (1980). Situational constraints and work outcomes: The influences of a frequently overlooked construct. *Academy of Management Review, 5*, 391–397.

Pfeffer, J. (1994). *Competitive advantage through people.* Boston: Harvard Business School Press.

Pil, F. K., & MacDuffie, J. P. (1996). The adoption of high-involvement work practices. *Industrial Relations, 35*, 423–455.

Pil, F. K., & MacDuffie, J. P. (1999). What makes transplants thrive: Managing the transfer of "best practice" at Japanese auto plants in North America. *Journal of Worl Business, 34*(4), 372–391.

Robinson, W. S. (1950). Ecological correlations and the behavior of individuals. *American Sociological Review, 15*, 351–357.

Rousseau, D. M., & Parks, J. M. (1992). The contracts of individuals and organizations. In L. L. Cummings & B. M. Staw (Eds.), *Research in organizational behavior* (Vol. 15, pp. 1–43). Greenwich, CT: JAI Press.

Rumelt, R. P. (1984). Toward a strategic theory of the firm. In R. Lamb (Ed.), *Competitive strategic management* (pp. 556–570). Englewood Cliffs: NJ: Prentice-Hall.

Ryan, A. M., Schmit, M., J., & Johnson, R. (1996). Attitudes and effectiveness: Examining relations at an organizational level. *Personnel Psychology, 49*, 853–882.

Sanchez, R. (1995). Strategic flexibility in product competition. *Strategic Management Journal, 16*, 135–159.

Schmidt, F. L., & Hunter, J. E. (1998). The validity of selection methods in personnel psychology: Practical and theoretical implications of 85 years of research findings. *Psychological Bulletin, 124*, 262–274.

Schneider, B. (1987). The people make the place. *Personnel Psychology, 40*, 437–453.

Schneider, B., Hanges, P. J., Smith, B., & Salvaggio, A. N. (2003). Which comes first: employee attitudes or organizational financial and market performance. *Journal of Applied Psychology, 88*, 836–851.

Schuler, R. S., & Jackson, S. E. (1987). Linking competitive strategies with human resource management practices. *Academy of Management Executive, 1*, 207–219.

Sherer, P., & Lee, K. (2002). Institutional change in law firms: A resource dependency and institutional perspective. *Academy of Management Journal, 45*, 102–119.

Simon, H. A. (1951). Formal theory of the employment relationship. *Econometrica, 19*, 293–305.

Sonnenfeld, J. A., & Peiperl, M. A. (1988). Staffing policy as a strategic response: A typology of career systems. *Academy of Management Review, 13*, 588–600.

Sturman, M. C., Trevor, C. O., Boudreau, J. W., & Gerhart, B. (2003). Is it worth it to win the talent war? Evaluating the utility of performance-based pay. *Personnel Psychology, 56*, 997–1035.

Terpstra, D. E., & Rozell, E. J. (1993). The relationship of staffing practices to organizational level measures of performance. *Personnel Psychology, 46*, 27–48.

Tsui, A., Pearce, J. L., Porter, L., & Tripoli, A. M. (1997). Alternative approaches to the employee–organization relationship: Does investment in employees pay off? *Academy of Management Journal, 40*, 1089–1121.

Turner, A. N., & Lawrence, P. R. (1965). *Industrial jobs and the worker.* Cambridge, MA: Harvard University, Graduate School of Business Administration.

Vallas, S. P. (2003). Why teamwork fails: Obstacles to workplace change in four manufacturing plants. *American Sociological Review, 68*, 223–250.

Van Eerde, W., & Thierry, H. (1996). Vroom's expectancy models and work-related criteria: A meta-analysis. *Journal of Applied Psychology, 81*, 575–586.

Vroom, V. H. (1964). *Work and motivation.* New York: Wiley.

Weick, K. E. (1976). Educational organizations as loosely coupled systems. *Administrative Science Quarterly, 21*, 1–19.

Welbourne, T. M., & Andrews, A. O. (1996). Predicting the performance of initial public offerings: Should human resource management be in the equation? *Academy of Management Journal, 39*, 891–919.

Wernerfelt, B. (1984). A resource-based view of the firm. *Strategic Management Journal, 5*, 171–180.

Williamson, O. (1975). *Markets and hierarchies.* New York: Free Press.

Williamson, O., Wachter, M. L., & Harris, J. E. (1975). Understanding the employment relation: The analysis of idiosyncratic exchange. *Bell Journal of Economics, 6*, 250–278.

Womack, J. P., Jones, D. T., & Roos, D. (1990). *The machine that changed the world.* New York: MacMillan.

Wood, S. (1999). Human resource management and performance. *International Journal of Management Reviews, 1*, 397–413.

Wright, P. M., Dunford, B. B., & Snell, S. A. (2001). Human resources and the resource-based view of the firm. *Journal of Management, 27*, 701–721.

Wright, P. M., & Sherman, W. S. (1999). Failing to find fit in strategic human resource management: Theoretical and empirical problems. In P. M. Wright, L. Dyer, J. W. Boudreau, & G. T. Milkovich (Eds.), *Strategic human resources management in the twenty-first century.* Supplement to G. R. Ferris (Ed.), *Research in personnel and human resources management* (pp. 53–74). Stanford, CT: JAI Press.

Wright, P. M., & Snell, S. A. (1998). Toward a unifying framework for exploring fit and flexibility in strategic human resource management. *Academy of Management Review, 23*, 756–773.

Yellen, J. L. (1984). Efficiency wage models of unemployment. *American Economic Review, 74*, 200–205.

Youndt, M. A., Snell, S. A., Dean, J. W., Jr., & Lepak, D. P. (1996). Human resource management, manufacturing strategy, and firm performance. *Academy of Management Journal, 39*, 836–865.

# PART II

## Linking Theory and Analysis

The chapters in this volume clearly demonstrate that fit has been examined across a variety of different topic areas, from a number of different theoretical perspectives and at different organizational levels of analysis. Despite the almost ubiquitous use of fit across content domains in organizational research, different techniques and methodologies for assessing fit have been developed within domains. Further, even within a particular content area (e.g., cultural values or relational demography), some controversy exists over appropriate methodologies and statistical indices of fit.

The methodological problems and controversies stem in part from a lack of conceptual clarity about the type and form of fit being hypothesized. In addition, a variety of issues have surfaced over the years and across domains, including questions about the most appropriate indices to capture fit (e.g., difference scores, distance measures, and polynomial regression), how to capture overall fit across multiple dimensions as opposed to fit on independent dimensions, the appropriateness of using perceptual versus objective measures, and questions about using the same respondents to capture both person ($P$) and environment ($E$) as opposed to independent assessments of $P$ and $E$. Fit research at higher organizational levels (e.g., group or organization) has raised concerns about the appropriateness of different approaches, such as interactions, profiles, configurations, factor analysis, and cluster analysis.

Chapter 11 provides an overview of some of the different methodological strategies and analytical techniques that have been used in fit research. Chapter 12 builds upon this foundation by explicating linkages between the theoretical question being addressed and the advantages and limitations of various methodologies and techniques.

# CHAPTER 11

# *Methodological and Analytical Techniques in Fit Research*

In this chapter, an overview of some of the more common methodological and statistical approaches that have been used in studies of fit is provided. A variety of statistical indices and methodological approaches are available for fit research. From a methodological design standpoint, these issues include the sources from which measures are derived, direct and indirect assessment of fit, subjective, and actual fit, and general study design procedures. The most commonly used statistical indices used to analyze fit data include polynomial regression, profile comparison measures, heterogeneity indices, and cluster analysis.

There is no "one" methodology or analytical procedure that is appropriate for all fit studies. Indeed, there is some debate about which techniques are more or less appropriate. In what follows, experts in each of these areas have provided an overview about a particular technique or set of techniques so that readers may gain an appreciation of each procedure in isolation and see the commonalities and differences among the various analytical procedures. The goal here is not to evaluate or advocate a particular procedure, nor is it to resolve differences among the procedures. Rather, the goal is to provide a snapshot of different procedures, presented side-by-side, so that readers can begin to make some informed choices about which procedures may be appropriate for their research study.

## 11.1   GENERAL METHODOLOGICAL AND DESIGN ISSUES

*Cherri Ostroff*

As explained in Ostroff and Schulte (chap, 1, this volume), fit can be approached from a number of different perspectives. One distinction in fit research concerns the extent to which a composition (supplementary) or a compilation (complementary) perspective is of interest. A second issue pertains to how the environment is conceptualized in a study of person ($P$) and environment ($E$) fit. $E$ can be conceptualized through people and personal attributes or through situational context elements. As such, when individual level outcomes are of interest in a study of PE fit, distinctions can be made between person–person fit (fit between an individual's attributes and the attributes of others in the setting) and person-situation fit (fit between an individual's attributes and the elements of the situational context). Third, at higher levels of analysis, three perspectives can be taken: (a) both $P$ and $E$ factors may be of interest in a study of PE fit collectively, (b) only $P$ factors are of interest to study fit or complementarities among people in the group or organization as a whole, or (c) only $E$ factors are of interest to examine fit or complementarities among situational elements.

Because of these different distinctions and perspectives, a number of different methodological approaches and study design features have been used. The primary choices for a researcher concern the questions of whether $P$ factors should be measured independently of $E$ factors and the sources for assessing the $P$ and $E$ factors, sampling issues, time, and aggregation.

### Direct and Indirect Measurement in PE Fit

Two primary approaches—indirect and direct—have been taken in assessing the extent of fit in PE fit research (Kristof, 1996). In the direct approach, $P$ and $E$ factors are not assessed independently. Rather, individuals are asked to report on the extent to which they believe a good fit exists in their job, group, or organization. In essence, direct fit is a person's subjective judgment or feeling about how well he or she fits in the environment (Cable & Judge, 1997). As such, this conceptualization of fit is in some ways analogous to other measures of affective responses to the organizational situation (e.g., job satisfaction) in that it captures an overall subjective or affective reaction to the contextual environment. Direct measures do not allow for examining whether an individual actually fits the environment but focuses on the extent to which an individual perceives or has a feeling of fit.

In contrast, indirect measurement focuses on separate assessments of the $P$ and $E$ factors. Measures of $P$ factors are obtained separately from measures of $E$ factors and then the two are compared or combined, through some analytical procedure, to derive an index that captures the extent of fit. In a number of studies both $P$ and $E$ factors were collected from the same individuals. The underlying assumption in such research is similar to that of Endler and Magnusson (1976), namely, that it is an individual's own attributes in combination with an individual's own perception of the environment (not the objective environment per se) that is the critical determinant for behaviors and responses. It should be noted here that when both $P$ and $E$ factors are derived from the same individuals, the focus is on two subjective or perceptual measures—that is, individuals report on their own personal attributes and individuals report on their own perceptions of the environment. Other researchers, following Roberts, Hulin, and Rousseau (1978) have argued that $E$ should be assessed independently of responding people or units under investigation to minimize subjective biases as well as response bias problems. Here, $P$ is typically assessed from focal individuals under investigation, whereas $E$ is often based on the aggregated responses of others or on some objective measure. This approach conceptualizes fit as the extent to which individuals' characteristics match or fit to some environmental or contextual attribute that is separate from the individuals' cognitions and perceptions.

## Sources of Measurement and Aggregation

As alluded to previously, the sources from which the measures of the $P$ and $E$ factors are derived may vary. Obviously, in direct assessments of fit, the source of measurement is the individual. Likewise, when the focus is on fit between an individual's own characteristics and an individual's own perceptions of the environment, the appropriate source for both $P$ and $E$ measures is the individual.

However, when a cross-level view (e.g., when an individual's characteristic is compared to some group level or organizational level environmental attribute) or higher level view (e.g., when fit is viewed as a match between the collective attributes of group members and the contextual attributes of the group) is taken, the sources for measures of the $P$ and $E$ factors will often need to shift. That is, the appropriate source for the $P$ factor is likely to be the individual, whereas some single index is needed to represent the $E$ such that all individuals within the same $E$ have the same score on that environmental attribute. This $E$ factor can be assessed globally or objectively (e.g., on the basis of a supervisor's assessment or from objective or archival data) or, when a global index is not available, $E$ is often based on aggregated data from individuals. Aggregating data to represent an $E$ construct (or even aggregating to represent a collective $P$ in higher level studies) raises additional issues.

To illustrate, consider a cross-level study of fit between an individual's personality (*P*) and the climate of the organization (*E*) assessed with commensurate dimensions (cf. Ostroff, 1993). The appropriate source of measurement for both constructs is the individual level of analysis. That is, both the construct of personality and the construct of climate (defined as shared perceptions) reside within individuals and hence deriving measures from individuals is theoretically appropriate. However, the definition of unit level or organizational level climate rests on shared perceptions. Agreement among individuals within the same context must be demonstrated before aggregating individual perceptions of climate to represent organizational climate. Once demonstrated, the aggregate score can then taken to represent the higher level climate (*E*) and can be compared to individual personality (*P*) to derive indices of fit. The point is that when *E* is taken to be a higher level construct and is based on aggregated data from individuals, researchers must carefully consider the appropriateness of aggregation (see Klein et al., 2000, for a review of aggregation issues). A similar issue arises in a higher level study (e.g., group or organizational level) of fit. In such a case, *P* factors may need to be aggregated in addition to *E* factors.

A final point here is that when *P* and *E* are both based on measures collected from individuals, response bias is likely to exacerbate relationships between them. At the individual level of analysis, separating measures in time can help ameliorate this problem. Alternatively, when cross-level or higher level studies are of interest, a split sample approach whereby half the respondents provide measures for P and half provide measures for E can help to minimize response bias problems (see Ostroff, Kinicki, & Clark, 2002, for details).

## Commensurate Measures and Interactionism

In the last 20 years, a strong emphasis has been placed on assessing both the *P* and *E* components with the same or commensurate dimensions (e.g., Caplan, 1987; Edwards, 1991; Schneider, Kristof-Brown, Goldstein, & Smith, 1997). From a theoretical standpoint, commensurate measures ensure that the P and E factors are directly and conceptually relevant to one another so that the degree of fit between them can be assessed (Edwards, 1991). From an analytical standpoint, commensurate dimensions can also simplify the determination of the index of fit between the two.

In recent years, the use of noncommensurate dimensions to assess PE fit has been virtually dismissed. Yet, there is still some argument that noncommensurate dimensions in PE fit studies may be appropriate for some research questions and for some content domains (Kristof, 1996). As an example, Judge and Cable (1997) predicted that certain personality types would be differentially attracted to organizational cultural values (e.g., extroverted individuals prefer and seek out team-oriented cultures). The underlying rationale for their predictions was based on the notion that individuals prefer and seek out situations that fit or are congruent with their personality. Others indicated that a fit or match can be achieved across two noncommensurate dimensions, provided that the degree and type of match are clearly specified (e.g., Hollenbeck et al., 2002). To illustrate, Aronoff and Wilson (1985) provided a comprehensive typology of individual and group characteristics based on congruence models. They proposed, for example, that the various personality types achieve congruence with various situational aspects such as the group structure, reward basis in the group and the task difficulty. They did not rely solely on the notion that the $P$ and $E$ elements interact but specified the form of the interaction as one of congruence. That is, they specifically addressed the level of the personality variable (e.g., high, medium, or low) that is congruent with a certain level of the task variable (e.g., high, medium, or low task complexity). For example, affiliation should be moderate when the task is highly complex, achievement should be high when the task is highly important and highly complex, rewards should be based on time (not ability) to fit with a dependent personality, and so forth. When specific levels of noncommensurate dimensions are conceptualized in such a way so that the point of congruence or match is theorized (e.g., high values of $P$ when linked to moderate values of $E$ define the match), then some scholars argue that noncommensurate dimensions may be appropriate in fit models. When the point of congruence or match is not specifically addressed, but the general notion is that the relationship between $P$ and outcomes depends on some level of $E$, an interactionist model, not a fit model, is relevant.

Despite the debate over the necessity of commensurate dimensions in PE fit studies, when a broader perspective of fit is taken, particularly when fit is examined at higher levels of analysis, noncommensurate dimensions are relevant. This is clearly the case in systems fit (see Ostroff and Schulte, chap. 1, this volume), where the focus is on the fit, compatibility, or compilation among different contextual elements (e.g., structure, goals, work structure, and collective human capital). Similar issues arise in considerations of compilation among individuals' personal characteristics within a unit. The combination of different team members' different types of abilities or personalities, for example, can be configured or patterned in such a way as to provide a "whole" for the unit. Thus, the use of noncommensurate dimensions is often theoretically and methodologically necessary in complementary or compilation views of fit at higher levels of analysis.

## Sampling Issues

Studies of PE fit can be complicated by the fact that the individuals within the same unit or organization are exposed to the same environmental conditions; hence, variability on $E$ is of concern. For example, in a single study whereby variability exists on $P$ but $E$ is the same or relatively similar for all individuals, the study will be reduced to an individual difference study, not a true fit study, because $E$ is a constant across those under investigation. Similarly, based on the attraction–selection–attrition process, individuals within a unit are likely to be relatively homogeneous (e.g., Schneider et al., 1997), making variability on $P$ a potential concern. Taken together, PE fit studies conducted within a single unit or organization are likely to exhibit severe restrictions on the variability of both $P$ and $E$ factors. This often necessitates collection of data across units and/or across organizations to provide the necessary variability on both factors.

## Timing of Data Collection

As with any study, when all measures ($P$ and $E$ factors, antecedents, and outcomes) are collected at the same time, from the same sources, response bias is likely to be a problem. These problems can be ameliorated to some degree by careful attention to the design of the measures as well by providing time lags between collection of measures (e.g., Harrison, McLaughlin, & Coalter, 1996). Equally important is the consideration of fit as a dynamic process that occurs over time (Tinsley, 2000). The notion that individuals can change the $E$ and that $E$ can change individuals' attributes over time requires longitudinal and panel type of designs as opposed to concurrent measurement strategies.

In this section of the chapter, some basic measurement and design issues were highlighted. In the remaining subsections of this chapter, each author summarizes a specific statistical or analytical technique that can be used to assess fit and test fit hypotheses.

## 11.2 PROFILE COMPARISON METHODS FOR ASSESSING PERSON–SITUATION FIT

*David F. Caldwell, Jennifer A. Chatman and Charles A. O'Reilly*

Characterizing people and situations and comparing them in meaningful ways remain key challenges for person–environment (PE) fit researchers. One common approach is to identify a specific individual characteristic, such as a personality trait, and a specific situational characteristic, such as a job attribute, and to directly investigate the joint effects or interactions between the two variables on some outcome. Such an approach is effective for testing specific predictions, such as whether sales people who are more extraverted fit the customer-oriented demands of the jobs and therefore sell more than those who are less extraverted. This type of approach is appropriate when strong theoretical links between the specific $P$ and $E$ variables exist, and the variables are considered centrally relevant to describing both the person and situation. For example, compared with introverted people, extraverted people should be more comfortable with the high level of interpersonal interaction required to be successful in sales jobs (Volard & McCarthy, 1979).

This approach is not appropriate, however, for answering questions that require information about a person's overall fit to a situation and how that fit influences behavioral outcomes. Overall fit is important because neither people nor situations are unidimensional. Thus, one attribute of an individual could fit well with a particular situational attribute, but the person might also have other characteristics that are incompatible with important attributes also present in that situation. This becomes important even if a person or situation is characterized by two dimensions rather than by one. To extend the aforementioned example of extraversion and interpersonal abilities, for example, it is possible that only extraverted people who are also conscientious are effective as sales representatives because success in sales involves both getting along with others as well as gathering information, being prepared to answer questions, and following up with customer requests (e.g., Barrick, Mount, & Strauss, 1993). Using techniques that only assess the fit between a single person and situation attribute to predict an outcome may result in ambiguous and, potentially, misleading findings. For example, the relationship between extraversion and sales performance would be completely obscured if half of the extraverted people were highly conscientious and half were not conscientious at all. Thus, the primary threat to conducting valid person–situation fit research involves omitting important attributes that characterize persons and situations in appropriately comprehensive and relevant terms (e.g., Chatman, 1989).

Because people and situations are multidimensional, meaningful and valid tests of fit hypotheses require comprehensive descriptions of both persons and situations. One advantage of profile methods is that a profile can describe both the person and situation across a large number of dimensions. Further, a single index that captures the overall degree of fit across dimensions is created. Profiles, therefore, have the potential to be more comprehensive than, for example, approaches that are based on experimental designs examining the interaction between a person and situation variable (e.g., Chatman & Barsade, 1995) or approaches that use statistical interactions (e.g., Edwards, 1995) to study person situation fit.

A second important difference between profile techniques and other ways of assessing fit is that profiles allow for a semi-idiographic assessment of fit, yielding the benefits of both idiographic and nomothetic approaches. Most methods for assessing fit are essentially nomothetic in that they focus on between-person comparisons and assess individual differences by comparing the target person to others, usually on a single dimension. While nomothetic methods enable comparisons across people or across time (e.g., Luthans & Davis, 1982), they do not allow researchers to assess important within-person comparisons that also influence an individual's behavior or affect.

As Pelham (1993) has noted, assessing the relative importance of traits to that individual may yield very different results than when those same traits are assessed by comparing that person to other people. And, the extent to which a trait is part of an individual's self-concept influences how he or she processes information relevant to that trait (Markus, 1977). Theoretical conceptualizations of fit often assume that either the personal traits or situational characteristics being assessed are equally relevant to all individuals. This assumption is inappropriate for certain research questions such as how various traits relate to other traits within a person, how well a person's knowledge, skills, and abilities fit with an array of requisite job attributes (e.g., Caldwell & O'Reilly, 1990), or how well a person's values fit with an organization's overall culture (e.g., Chatman, 1991; O'Reilly, Chatman, & Caldwell, 1991). Thus, an advantage of profiling techniques is that they can be used semi-idiographically to understand a person's uniquely configured characteristics while still allowing for meaningful comparisons between people.

## Profiles as Assessment Tools

The profile comparison process is derived from Q-methodology and, specifically, from its application in personality assessment (e.g., Block, 1978). In a Q-sort procedure, the respondent is presented with a large number of attributes or statements (typically between 50 and 100) and asked to sort those statements into a set of predetermined categories according to some criterion, usually the extent to which the statement is characteristic of the individual. Typically, the respondent is asked to sort the items into nine categories ranging from *most characteristic* to *most uncharacteristic*. The number of items to be placed in each category is specified by a 9-point unimodal, symmetrical distribution so that the largest numbers of items are placed in the middle categories and the smallest numbers in the extreme categories. For example, if a respondent was sorting 70 items, he or she might be asked to designate 3 items as *most characteristic* (Category 9) and 3 items as *most uncharacteristic* (Category 1). The middle categories would have substantially more items. In this case the middle category, *neither characteristic nor uncharacteristic* (Category 5), might contain 18 items.

The forced shape of the distribution offers a number of advantages over free rating schemes. In free rating schemes, respondents are permitted to place any number of items in any category and are not required to place all items in categories, thereby making this method purely idiographic because it results in a unique configuration for each focal individual; however, the unequal numbers of attributes per category precludes comparisons across individuals (Block, 1978). In particular, the items assigned to the middle categories are relatively less important in describing an individual than are those assigned to the extreme categories, yet raters find discriminating among the items in the middle categories to be relatively difficult. Increasing the number of items that must be placed in the middle categories (as in a forced distribution method) minimizes these difficult, yet relatively unimportant, discriminations and better fits with people's cognitive capabilities to discriminate reliability among attributes.

Profile techniques are also robust in that the concourse of items individuals are asked to sort can vary, as can the definition of the categories into which the items are sorted. Although for most of the early uses of the technique individuals were asked to sort personality descriptors, we have used competencies (Caldwell & O'Reilly, 1990) and values (Chatman, 1991; O'Reilly, Chatman, & Caldwell, 1991) in addition to personality descriptors (Chatman, Caldwell, & O'Reilly, 1999). Researchers can also use standard sets of items [e.g., California Adult Q-Sort (Block, 1978) or Organization Culture Profile (O'Reilly et al., 1991) or a unique set of items constructed for specific research contexts.

Respondents are frequently asked to sort items in terms of how characteristic of them they are; however, they can also be asked to sort the items on another dimension. In a personality–situation fit study, for example, items might be sorted to create both "real" and "ideal" personality profiles (e.g., Chatman et al., 1999). To test fit hypotheses, job experts might sort competencies on the extent to which they are required in a particular job and job incumbents might sort the same items in terms of how self-descriptive they are (e.g., Caldwell & O'Reilly, 1990).

## Analyzing Profile Data

The statistical techniques for analyzing profile data are straightforward. The value of each item sorted is based on the category to which it is assigned. For example, with nine categories, an item placed in the *most characteristic* category would receive a value of 9, whereas an item described as *neither characteristic or uncharacteristic* would receive a value of 5. In a typical person–situation fit study, one set of raters might array a set of situational attributes in terms of the traits that are required to be successful in a job. A set of job incumbents would be asked to sort the same set of traits in terms of how self-descriptive they are. Fit would be measured by simply correlating the vectors of values assigned to the items (e.g., for each individual, an individual's self-profile is correlated with the situational profile derived from expert raters). Fit is, thus, operationalized as a correlation coefficient.

In many cases, multiple raters might provide profiles of either the individual or the situational variables. When multiple raters act as informants, the vector of scores can be calculated by averaging across their responses. The consistency of raters' responses can be assessed by a variation of the Spearman–Brown general prophecy formula (e.g., Chatman, 1989). In the case of profile data, this coefficient is interpreted as evidence of agreement among raters rather than evidence of the underlying construct and specifically reflects the stability of the profile. An intraclass correlation coefficient, calculated as the median correlation coefficient among all pairs of raters, can also be used to assess agreement among raters on the focal individual or situation (e.g., Block, 1978; Kenny, Albright, Malloy, & Kashy, 1994).

## Using Profile Data

The semi-idiographic nature of profiles allows comparison between individuals yet also provides a fine-grained picture of both people and situations. People's relative fit to a situation can be assessed by comparing the magnitude of the correlation coefficients between each individual's profile and a common profile of the situation. In this sense, correlation coefficients reflect the overall fit of an individual to a situation, relative to other individuals, across a wide range of dimensions.

The idiographic nature of the profile can provide a rich, clinical picture of the individual or the situation. In a typical profile study, individuals who are familiar with the situation, either through their tenure, experience, or expertise, would sort items about the situation. Similarly, raters who were familiar with the focal individual (either him or herself or observers) would sort the same items to describe the person. This eliminates common-response bias, and it also allows the use of true "experts" who are likely to be distinctly familiar with either the person or the situation, but not both. In addition, inspecting the rankings of the items and clustering of related items can provide an interpretative portrait of the both the person and situation. Differences between the person and situation across these clusters of items can provide insights into why a person might fit or not fit a particular situation.

Although the semi-idiographic nature of profile data offers advantages in studying fit, there is no guarantee that profile methodology will provide a more accurate test of a specific hypothesis than a completely nomothetic approach. The ipsative nature of profile data limits the use of some statistical techniques. Further, the correlation-based fit score provides an overall measure of fit, but no statistical test of the nature and significance of mismatches between individual variables and situational variables exists and researchers have relied on judgment to determine what constitutes relative fit or misfit. For example, two individuals could have the same overall fit score yet in one case it was because the individual was higher on some individual variables than called for in the situation and the other individual was lower on those same items. Although inspecting the profiles could provide insights regarding those differences, the ipsative nature of the data make some statistical tests problematic.

The use of difference scores to interpret profile data has been criticized because of their potential unreliability (e.g., Edwards, 1995). Johns (1981), however, listed a number of ways in which difference scores can be reliably developed and assessed including using commensurate terms, which we strongly advocate, and using different raters to create the situational and person profiles. Further, although Edwards' (1995) critique raised a number of valid points, profile comparison approaches remain valuable tools for fit research because they allow researchers to answer important and different types of research questions that take into account the multidimensional nature of people and situations. Profile approaches enable researchers to derive a single index that simultaneously captures fit across multiple dimensions, thereby making it possible to test notions regarding the importance of overall fit, as well as relationships between overall fit and various behavioral and attitudinal responses in organizations.

## 11.3 POLYNOMIAL REGRESSION AND RESPONSE SURFACE METHODOLOGY

*Jeffrey R. Edwards*

Person–environment (PE) fit research often relies on methods that collapse $P$ and $E$ measures into a single score intended to represent PE fit. Typically, these methods involve computing the difference between person and environment measures or the similarity between profiles of measures that describe person and environment on multiple dimensions. These methods suffer from numerous methodological problems, as documented elsewhere (Cronbach, 1958, 1992; Edwards, 1994; Johns, 1981). Problems with difference scores and profile similarity indices are avoided by polynomial regression (Edwards, 1994, 2002; Edwards & Parry, 1993), which uses separate measures of $P$ and $E$ and examines their joint relationships with causes and consequences of PE fit. Polynomial regression is based on the premise that $P$ and $E$ measures represent distinct constructs and the assumptions embedded in difference scores and profile similarity indices represent hypotheses that should be tested empirically.

In this section polynomial regression and its relevance to P-E fit research are discussed. The section has three objectives: (a) to show how polynomial regression can be viewed as a generalization of difference scores and profile similarity indices; (b) to explain how results from polynomial regression analyses can be understood using response surface methodology; and (c) to emphasize that polynomial regression and response surface methodology can facilitate theory development in PE fit research. This overview focuses on fit as a cause of outcomes, and procedures for treating fit as an outcome are briefly discussed at the end of the summary.

## Polynomial Regression as a Generalization of Difference Scores and Profile Similarity Indices

The basics of polynomial regression can be understood by contrasting it with difference scores and profile similarity indices. To illustrate, consider Fig. 11–1a, which depicts a positive relationship between an algebraic difference score and an outcome. This relationship can be represented by the following regression equation:

$$Z = b_0 + b_1(X - Y) + e, \tag{1}$$

where $X$ is the environment, $Y$ is the person, $Z$ is the outcome, and $e$ is a random disturbance term. The positive relationship in Fig. 11–1a corresponds to a positive value for $b_1$ in Equation 1. The connection between Equation 1 and polynomial regression can be seen by expanding Equation 1, which yields

$$Z = b_0 + b_1X - b_1Y + e. \tag{2}$$

Equation 2 shows that using an algebraic difference as a predictor is equivalent to using the components of the difference as predictors and constraining their coefficients to be equal in magnitude and opposite in sign. The relationship of $X$ and $Y$ with $Z$ indicated by Equation 2 is illustrated by the three-dimensional surface in Fig. 11–2a. The constraint imposed by Equation 2 can be empirically tested using the following equation:

$$Z = b_0 + b_1X + b_2Y + e. \tag{3}$$

Equation 3 is a linear polynomial regression equation in which the relationships of $X$ and $Y$ with $Z$ can differ in sign and magnitude. Results from Equation 3 can be used to determine whether $b_1 = -b_2$, as indicated by Equation 2, and whether $b_1$ is positive and $b_2$ is negative, as implied by Fig. 11–2a.

## a. Two-Dimensional Algebraic Difference Function

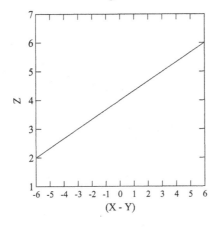

## b. Two-Dimensional Absolute Difference Function

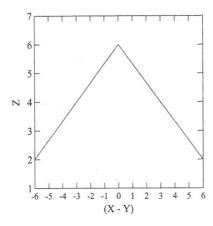

## c. Two-Dimensional Squared Difference Function

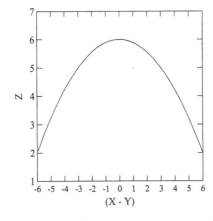

FIGURE 11–1. Two-dimensional difference score functions.

a. Three-Dimensional Algebraic Difference Function

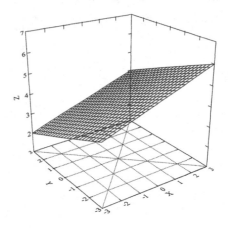

b. Three-Dimensional Absolute Difference Function

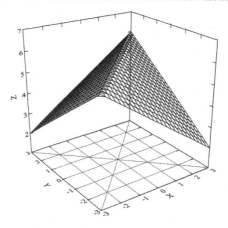

c. Three-Dimensional Squared Difference Function

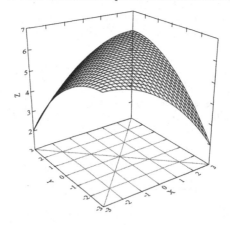

FIGURE 11–2.   Three-dimensional difference score surfaces.

Figure 11–1b shows an inverted-V relationship, such that the outcome is maximized when $X$ and $Y$ are equal. The relationship in Fig. 11–1b is captured by the following regression equation:

$$Z = b_0 + b_1|X - Y| + e. \tag{4}$$

Equation 4 uses the absolute value of the difference between $X$ and $Y$ as a predictor of $Z$. A negative value for $b_1$ would correspond to the inverted-V relationship in Fig. 11–1b. As written, Equation 4 cannot be algebraically expanded, because an absolute difference is a logical rather than an algebraic transformation. This dilemma is overcome by replacing Equation 4 with the following equation (Edwards, 1994):

$$Z = b_0 + b_1(1 - 2W)(X - Y) + e. \tag{5}$$

In Equation 5, $W$ is a dummy variable that equals 0 when $X - Y$ is positive, equals 1 when $X - Y$ is negative, and is randomly set to 0 or 1 when $X = Y$. As a result, when $X - Y$ is positive, $1 - 2W$ equals 1, and the compound term $(1 - 2W)(X - Y)$ reduces to $(X - Y)$. In contrast, when $X - Y$ is negative, $1 - 2W$ equals $-1$, and the term $(1 - 2W)(X - Y)$ becomes $-(X - Y)$. Hence, when $X - Y$ is positive, its sign is unaltered, and when $X - Y$ is negative, its sign is reversed, producing the same result as the absolute value transformation. When $X = Y$, $(1 - 2W)(X - Y)$ equals 0 regardless of the value of $W$. Expanding Equation 5 yields

$$Z = b_0 + b_1X - b_1Y - 2b_1WX + 2b_1WY + e. \tag{6}$$

Equation 6 shows that using an absolute difference as a predictor effectively constrains the coefficients on $X$ and $Y$ to be equal in magnitude but opposite in sign, constrains the coefficients on $WX$ and $WY$ to be equal in magnitude but opposite in sign, and constrains the coefficient on $WY$ to be twice as large as the coefficient on $X$. Equation 6 also indicates that the coefficient on $W$ is constrained to 0, given that it is excluded from the equation. Fig. 11–2b shows a three-dimensional surface that corresponds to Equation 6. The constraints imposed by Equation 6 can be tested with the following equation:

$$Z = b_0 + b_1X + b_2Y + b_3W + b_4WX + b_5WY + e. \tag{7}$$

Equation 7 is a piecewise polynomial regression equation. Coefficient estimates from this equation can be used to assess the constraints imposed by Equation 6 by testing whether (a) $b_1 = -b_2$, (b) $b_4 = -b_5$, (c) $b_5 = 2b_1$, and (d) $b_3 = 0$. The direction of the inverted-V relationship in Fig. 11–2b further stipulates that $b_1$ and $b_5$ are positive and that $b_2$ and $b_4$ are negative.

Figure 11–1c shows an inverted-U relationship. Like Fig. 11–1b, Fig. 11–1c indicates that the outcome is maximized when $X$ and $Y$ are equal. However, as the difference between $X$ and $Y$ increases, the outcome decreases linearly in Fig. 11–1b, as opposed to the curvilinear decrease in Fig. 11–1c. The relationships shown in Fig. 11–1b and c are usually treated the same in PE fit research. This relationship in Fig. 11–1c corresponds to the following regression equation:

$$Z = b_0 + b_1(X - Y)^2 + e. \tag{8}$$

Equation 8 uses the squared difference between $X$ and $Y$ as a predictor of $Z$. For the relationship in Fig. 11–1c, the sign of $b_1$ in Equation 8 would be negative. Expanding Equation 8 yields:

$$Z = b_0 + b_1X^2 - 2b_1XY + b_1Y^2 + e. \tag{9}$$

Equation 9 indicates that using a squared difference as a predictor constrains the coefficients on $X^2$ and $Y^2$ to be equal and the coefficient on $XY$ to be twice as large in magnitude and opposite in sign of the coefficient on $X^2$ or $Y^2$. Equation 9 also implicitly constrains the coefficients on $X$ and $Y$ to be 0, given that both of these variables are excluded from Equation 9. A three-dimensional surface corresponding to Equation 9 is shown in Fig. 11–2c, and the four constraints imposed by Equation 9 can be tested with the following equation:

$$Z = b_0 + b_1X + b_2Y + b_3X^2 + b_4XY + b_5Y^2 + e. \tag{10}$$

Equation 10 is a quadratic polynomial regression equation. Coefficient estimates from Equation 10 can be used to evaluate the constraints imposed by Equation 9 by testing whether (a) $b_1 = 0$; (b) $b_2 = 0$; (c) $b_3 = b_5$; and (d) $b_4 = -2b_3$. The direction of the inverted-U relationship in Fig. 11–2b further indicates that $b_3$ and $b_5$ are negative and $b_4$ is positive.

The logic used to translate difference scores into polynomial regression equations can be applied to profile similarity indices (Cronbach & Gleser, 1953; Edwards, 1993, 1994). For example, profile similarity indices that represent sums of algebraic, absolute, or squared differences can be written by extending Equations 2, 6, and 9, respectively, to include multiple pairs of $X$ and $Y$ measures in which each pair represents a dimension on which the profiles are compared. The constraints imposed by these indices can be tested using extended versions of Equations 3, 7, and 10. Euclidean distance and profile correlation indices, which are commonly used in PE fit research, cannot be algebraically expanded, but the conceptual principles they are intended to capture can be examined using unconstrained regression equations for the sums of absolute or squared differences (Edwards, 1993).

## Applying Response Surface Methodology to Polynomial Regression Analysis

When polynomial regression yields coefficients that satisfy the constraints associated with Equations 2, 6, and 9, results are easily interpreted because they conform to the idealized surfaces shown in Fig. 11–2. However, these constraints are usually rejected, which complicates the interpretation of results. Furthermore, the surfaces in Fig. 11–2 comprise a narrow subset of hypotheses that could be developed regarding the joint effects of the person and environment on outcomes. For example, outcomes produced by PE misfit may differ depending on whether the environment is greater than or less than the person (Edwards, Caplan, & Harrison, 1998; Naylor, Pritchard, & Ilgen, 1980; Rice, McFarlin, Hunt, & Near, 1985). In addition, the effects of PE fit may depend on whether the person and environment are both low or high in an absolute sense (Edwards & Rothbard, 1999). Complexities such as these are important from a theoretical standpoint but are not captured by the surfaces in Fig. 11–2.

The foregoing issues can be addressed using response surface methodology (Edwards & Parry, 1993), which allows researchers to rigorously analyze three-dimensional surfaces relating the person and environment to outcomes. Response surface methodology facilitates substantive interpretation when constraints imposed by difference scores are rejected, as is usually the case. Perhaps more importantly, response surface methodology allows PE fit researchers to develop and test hypotheses that go far beyond the simplified surfaces shown in Fig. 11–2.

Response surface methodology involves analyzing features of surfaces that correspond to polynomial regression equations. The quadratic equation in Equation 10 captures a wide range of hypotheses relevant to PE fit research and is therefore the focus of the present discussion. A quadratic equation reflects one of three types of surfaces: (a) *concave*, which is dome-shaped; (b) *convex*, which is bowl-shaped; and (c) *saddle*, which is shaped like a saddle. For each surface, response surface methodology involves the analysis of three basic features.

The first feature is the stationary point, which is the point at which the surface is flat. For a concave surface, the stationary point is the overall maximum of the surface. For a convex surface, the stationary point is the overall minimum of the surface. For a saddle surface, the stationary point is the intersection of the lines along which the upward and downward curvatures of the surface are greatest. The location of the stationary point can be computed by inserting the estimated coefficient values from a quadratic regression equation into the following formulas:

$$X_0 = \frac{b_2 b_4 - 2b_1 b_5}{4b_3 b_5 - b_4^2} \tag{11}$$

$$Y_0 = \frac{b_1 b_4 - 2 b_2 b_3}{4 b_3 b_5 - b_4^2} \tag{12}$$

where $X_0$ and $Y_0$ are the coordinates of the stationary points in the $X, Y$ plane.

The second feature involves the *principal axes,* which describe the orientation of the surface in the $X, Y$ plane. The principal axes run perpendicular to one another and intersect at the stationary point. For a concave surface, the first principal axis is the line of minimum downward curvature, and the second principal axis is the line of maximum downward curvature. For a convex surface, the first principal axis is the line of maximum upward curvature, and the second principal axis is the line of minimum upward curvature. Finally, for a saddle surface, the first principal axis is the line of maximum upward curvature, and the second principal axis is the line of maximum downward curvature.

The principal axes can be written as equations that describe lines in the $X, Y$ plane. An equation for the first principal axis is

$$Y = p_{10} + p_{11} X. \tag{13}$$

The slope of the first principal axis (i.e., $p_{11}$) is computed as follows:

$$p_{11} = \frac{b_5 - b_3 + \sqrt{(b_3 - b_5)^2 + b_4^2}}{b_4} \tag{14}$$

The intercept of the first principal axis (i.e., $p_{10}$) is computed as follows:

$$p_{10} = Y_0 - p_{11} X_0. \tag{15}$$

Likewise, an equation for the second principal axis is

$$Y = p_{20} + p_{21} X. \tag{16}$$

The slope of the second principal axis (i.e., $p_{21}$) is computed using the following formula:

$$p_{21} = \frac{b_5 - b_3 - \sqrt{(b_3 - b_5)^2 + b_4^2}}{b_4} \tag{17}$$

The intercept of the second principal axis (i.e., $p_{20}$) is computed as follows:

$$p_{20} = Y_0 - p_{21} X_0. \tag{18}$$

The third feature entails the shape of the surface along relevant lines in the $X,Y$ plane, which can be computed by substituting the equation for the line into Equation 10. To illustrate, the $Y = X$ line is meaningful to PE fit research because it represents values for which the person and environment are equal. For the surface in Fig. 11–2c, this line runs diagonally across the floor of the graph from the near corner to the far corner. Substituting $Y = X$ into Equation 10 yields

$$Z = b_0 + b_1X + b_2X + b_3X^2 + b_4X^2 + b_5X^2 + e$$
$$= b_0 + (b_1 + b_2)X + (b_3 + b_4 + b_5)X^2 + e. \tag{19}$$

As Equation 19 shows, the curvature of the surface along the $Y = X$ line is represented by the sum $b_3 + b_4 + b_5$, and the slope of the surface at the point $X = 0$ (and $Y = 0$, given that $Y = X$) is $b_1 + b_2$. If these sums equal zero, then the surface is flat along the $Y = X$ line, consistent with the surface in Fig. 11–2c.

Another line of interest in PE fit research is the $Y = -X$ line. When $X$ and $Y$ measures are centered at the midpoint of their scales, as recommended for polynomial regression analysis (Edwards, 1994; Edwards & Parry, 1993), the $Y = -X$ line runs diagonally across the $X,Y$ plane and represents varying degrees of PE misfit. In Fig. 11–2c, the $Y = -X$ line extends from the left corner to the right corner of the floor of the graph. The shape of the surface along this line represents the effect of PE misfit. Substituting $Y = -X$ into Equation 10 yields

$$Z = b_0 + b_1X - b_2X + b_3X^2 - b_4X^2 + b_5X^2 + e$$
$$= b_0 + (b_1 - b_2)X + (b_3 - b_4 + b_5)X^2 + e. \tag{20}$$

The curvature of the surface along the $Y = -X$ line equals $b_3 - b_4 + b_5$, and the slope of the surface when $X = 0$ (and $Y = 0$, given than $Y = -X$) equals $b_1 - b_2$. For the surface in Fig. 11–2c, $b_3 - b_4 + b_5$ is negative and $b_1 - b_2$ equals 0, meaning that the surface has a downward curvature along the $Y = -X$ line and is flat at $X = 0$, $Y = 0$.

The shape of the surface along other lines can be determined in a similar manner. For instance, the shape of the surface along the first principal axis is found by substituting Equation 13 into Equation 10, which yields

$$Z = b_0 + b_1X + b_2(p_{10} + p_{11}X) + b_3X^2$$
$$+ b_4X(p_{10} + p_{11}X) + b_5(p_{10} + p_{11}X)^2 + e$$
$$= b_0 + b_2p_{10} + b_5p_{10}^2 + (b_1 + b_2p_{11} + b_4p_{10}$$
$$+ 2b_5p_{10}p_{11})X + (b_3 + b_4p_{11} + b_5p_{11}^2)X^2 + e. \tag{21}$$

Likewise, the shape of the surface along the second principal axis is

$$
\begin{aligned}
Z &= b_0 + b_1 X + b_2(p_{20} + p_{21}X) + b_3 X^2 \\
&\quad + b_4 X(p_{20} + p_{21}X) + b_5(p_{10} + p_{11}X)^2 + e \\
&= b_0 + b_2 p_{20} + b_5 p_{20}^2 + (b_1 + b_2 p_{21} + b_4 p_{20} \\
&\quad + 2b_5 p_{20}p_{21})X + (b_3 + b_4 p_{21} + b_5 p_{21}^2)X^2 + e.
\end{aligned}
\tag{22}
$$

This procedure can be extended to other lines of theoretical interest.

## Empirical Example

Figure 11–3 depicts a response surface based on data from 358 job seekers who reported the actual variety, desired variety, and satisfaction associated with jobs for which they had recently interviewed. The estimated polynomial regression was

$$
Z = 5.628 + 0.314X - 0.118Y - 0.145X^2 + 0.299XY - 0.102Y^2 + e. \tag{23}
$$

The $R^2$ for the equation was .162, and coefficients for all variables except $Y$ and $Y^2$ were statistically significant at $p < .05$. The corresponding surface is shown in Fig. 11–3. The stationary point was located at $X = -0.951$, $Y = -1.973$. The first principal axis had an intercept and slope of $-0.875$ and $1.154$, respectively, and is represented by the solid line crossing the $X,Y$ plane. The second principal axis had an intercept and slope of $-2.797$ and $-0.866$, respectively, and is depicted by the heavy dashed line in the $X,Y$ plane. Along the $Y = X$ line, the surface had a curvature of $0.052$ and a slope of $0.196$ at the point $X = 0$, $Y = 0$, indicating that satisfaction increased at an increasing rate. Along the $Y = -X$ line, the surface had a curvature of $-0.546$ and a slope of $0.432$ at the point $X = 0$, $Y = 0$. These results indicate that satisfaction increased as actual variety increased toward desired variety, continued to increase at the point where actual and desired variety were equal (i.e., $X = 0$, $Y = 0$), and began to decrease when actual variety exceeded desired variety by about 0.5 units, as indicated by the point where the $Y = -X$ line crossed the first principal axis.

Comparing the surface in Fig. 11–3 to Fig. 11–2c highlights two key findings revealed by polynomial regression and response surface methodology that would have been missed by using a squared difference score. First, Fig. 11–3 shows that, along the line of PE fit, satisfaction is higher when actual and desired variety are both high rather than low, whereas in Fig. 11–2c, satisfaction is forced to remain constant along the PE fit line. The increase in satisfaction as actual and desired variety increase makes sense from a conceptual standpoint, given that jobs with higher variety

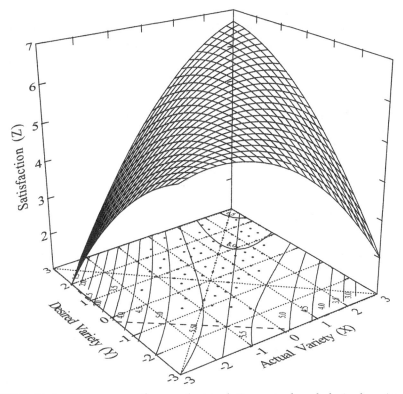

FIGURE 11–3. Response surface analysis relating actual and desired variety to satisfaction.

often bring additional rewards such as autonomy and challenge, and people who value variety are also likely to value these rewards. Second, Fig. 11–3 shows that, along the line of PE misfit, satisfaction is greatest when actual variety exceeds desired variety, whereas in Fig. 11–2c, satisfaction is constrained to reach its maximum when actual and desired variety are equal. Again, the fact that satisfaction is greatest when actual variety exceeds desired variety makes sense, because a moderate excess of variety brings opportunities for challenge and self-development, which can increase overall satisfaction with the job.

## The Theoretical Value of Polynomial Regression and Response Surface Methodology

The incremental insights yielded by polynomial regression and response surface methodology are important for interpreting results as well as for developing theory. By conceptualizing the effects of PE fit as a three-dimensional surface rather than a two-dimensional function, an enormous range of hypotheses can be pursued. These hypotheses can address asymmetries in the effects of PE misfit, variation in outcomes along the line of PE fit, surface rotations indicating that the optimal combination of P and E depends on whether both are high or low, and so forth (Edwards, 1996; Edwards & Rothbard, 1999). Traces of hypotheses such as these are evident in the PE fit literature (Edwards et al., 1998; Rice et al., 1985), but efforts to develop and test them have been hampered by the use of difference scores. Polynomial regression and response surface methodology encourage PE fit researchers to adopt an expanded conceptualization of PE fit that opens new avenues for theory and research.

## 11.4  HETEROGENEITY AS MISFIT

### David A. Harrison and Hock-Peng Sin

Just as similarity to the salient features of a person's job (person–job [PJ] fit) or organization (person–organization [PO] fit) can be regarded as supplementary fit, so can similarity to the salient features of others in a person's workgroup (person–group (PG) fit) or dyad (person–person (PP) fit). Many theories predict that fit, interpersonal similarity, or homogeneity, has positive attitudinal and behavioral consequences (Byrne, 1971; Newcomb, 1961; Schneider, 1987). In the obverse, interpersonal differences or heterogeneity can be construed as a form of misfit, which is expected to have negative outcomes for teams (Harrison, Price, Gavin, & Florey, 2002) or for a focal person, P, within them (Chatman, 1991). To the extent that team members are dissimilar from one another, they may feel less psychologically connected or attached to a collective. Thus, heterogeneity as misfit is an unipolar construct, in that it ranges from zero (perfect fit or perfect similarity—P is a clone of another P, or of the rest of the workgroup G) to some large amount (strong PP or PG differences). As such, misfit can be conceptualized and operationalized at both the team level (aggregation of all possible PP pairs of misfit within a team) and at the individual level (a measure of PG fit).

### Misfit at the Team Level

Investigations of misfit at the team level are best represented in the burgeoning domain of research on workgroup diversity, although the diversity terminology tends not to overlap with fit research. In the diversity paradigm, researchers first assess the individual-level attribute in question and then compute one of several indices of the *dispersion* of those individual attributes within the group (see Table 11–1 and Harrison & Sin, 2006, for a detailed review). Investigators of demographic diversity often assess members' attributes such as sex, race, age, tenure, and so on, and then compute a team level diversity value depending on the scale of

**TABLE 11-1.**
**Common Diversity Indices Useful for Operationalizing Interpersonal Misfit**

| Index | Formula | Theoretical Min/Max | Operational Min/Max | Assumed Scale Level of X |
|---|---|---|---|---|
| Blau[a] | $-\Sigma[\text{prop}_k]2$ | 0 to 1 | 0 to $(k-1)/k$ | Categorical/ordinal |
| Teachman[a] | $-\Sigma[\text{prop}_k] \times \ln[\text{prop}_k]$ | 0 to $+\infty$ | 0 to $-1 \times \ln(1/k)$ | Categorical/ordinal |
| Coefficient of variation[a] | $\text{sqrt}[\Sigma(X_i - X_{\text{mean}})^2/n]/X_{\text{mean}}$ | 0 to $+\infty$ | 0 to $\text{sqrt}(n-1)$ | Ratio |
| Gini[a] | $(\Sigma\lvert X_i - X_j\rvert)/2 \times n^2 \times X_{\text{mean}}$ | 0 to $+1$ | 0 to $1-(1/n)$ | Ratio |
| Standard deviation[a] | $\text{sqrt}[\Sigma(X_i - X_{\text{mean}})^2/n]$ | 0 to $+\infty$ | 0 to $[(U-L)/2]$ | Interval |
| Euclidean distance[b] | $\text{sqrt}[\Sigma_j(X_i - X_j)^2/n]$ | 0 to $+1$ | 0 to $\text{sqrt}[(n-1)/n]$ | Categorical/ordinal |
| | | 0 to $+\infty$ | 0 to $\text{sqrt}[(n-1)(U-L)^2/n]$ | Interval |

*Note.* $n$ is the number of members in group or team; $k$ is the number of categories in a categorical variable, or ranks in an ordinal variable; $\text{prop}_k$ is the proportion of team members in the $k$th category; $i$ and $j$ are the $i$th and $j$th persons in a team; $U$ is the upper endpoint of a finite measurement scale; and $L$ is the lower endpoint (e.g., $U = 5$ and $L = 1$ for a Likert-type scale).

[a]Team level.
[b]Individual level.

measurement for the attribute in question. For categorical attributes such as sex or ethnicity, Blau's and Teachman's indices are commonly used (e.g., Bunderson & Sutcliffe, 2002). For interval or ratio variables, the standard deviation (SD), Gini index, or coefficient of variation (CV) is more appropriate (e.g., Klein, Conn, Smith, & Sorra, 2001). Those who study psychological diversity derive team-level measures based on members' attitudes (e.g., Harrison, Price, & Bell, 1998), personality dimensions (e.g., Barrick, Stewart, Neubert, & Mount, 1998), or values (Barsade, Ward, Turner, & Sonnenfeld, 2000), following the same match of measurement scale to diversity (misfit) index. All such indices, whether for PP or PG fit, are minimized at zero, the point at which everyone in the group is identical on the attribute in question.

Maximum values are a different story. For categorical variables, values of diversity or heterogeneity indices (e.g., Blau's and Teachman's) are maximized when equal portions of a team make up each of the $k$ possible classifications in the category system. A little-recognized property of the categorical indices is that they reach different maxima under different values of $k$, and hence, cannot be compared when different attributes have different numbers of categories. For instance, Blau's index for a team with maximum sex diversity (two categories and 50% male, 50% female) is .50. If members are instead, evenly spread across five possible ethnic categories, Blau's index is maximized at .80. If homogeneity is fit and heterogeneity is misfit, then the maximum value for misfit among team members does not approach the same number with different categorical variables.

In a similar vein, diversity or misfit indices for interval and ratio attributes take maximum values under quite different within-team distribution shapes. A sharply positively skewed distribution within a team will yield a larger value of CV and the Gini index. Indeed, both of these indices, when used as measures of misfit, are maximized when a single person in a team is at the highest point, and everyone else shares the lowest point (Allison, 1978). For example, if one team member had 10 years of tenure, and her three teammates were brand new, CV would be maximized at 1.73). On the other hand, indices such as SD will yield values that are increasingly large as the positions of team members approach a bimodal distribution (Harrison & Sin, 2006; note that here and elsewhere, researchers are not estimating a population parameter and therefore should use $n$ the total number of team members in the denominator of the SD formula, rather than the conventional $n - 1$). In the aforementioned skewed example, SD is 4.33. But, if two team members had 10 years of tenure each and the other two members were brand new, SD would be 5.00. Note that in this latter case, CV is only 1.00, less than the original, positively skewed distribution. Hence, CV (and its variations) versus SD tell us substantially different stories about misfit at the team level.

CV and the Gini index also have other somewhat unusual properties. Their maximum values depend on (the square root of) team size and, hence, are not comparable across teams with different $n$s. If, in the aforementioned example, the team had seven brand new members and one member with 10 years of tenure, the CV would be 2.65 (SD = 3.31). In the bimodal case for an eight-person team, however, the CV remains at 1.00 (and the SD remains at 5.00), identical to the values for the four-person team. Reversing the scores within the team will produce substantially different CV and Gini values. With seven veteran team members and only one new member, the CV is 0.38. On the other hand, SD is symmetric; it remains at 3.31 in the reversed case. In our estimation, these latter properties work against the use of Gini or CV as misfit indices, unless a theory of fit clearly specifies that maximum interpersonal misfit occurs when one member has an excess of an attribute relative to all other members in a group.

## Misfit at the Individual Level

Misfit can also be assessed at the individual level, by examining how different a person is relative to one (e.g., a supervisor) or all of the other persons within a team, and treating that difference as a distance. A typical operationalization is the Euclidean distance formula between $P$ and another person (PP, dyadic distance) or the average Euclidean distance between P and his or her counterparts (mean PG distance; see Tsui, Egan, & O'Reilly, 1992; Tsui & O'Reilly, 1989). This index can be used for both categorical and continuous variables. For categorical variables, (a) the Euclidean distance between any two different categories is considered to be 1, (b) the distance between those who share a category is 0, and (c) the values of the index can theoretically range from 0 to +1, although the upper bound depends operationally on team size (see Table 11–1). Its maximum value occurs when the individual is different from everyone else, as would be the case if someone was the only female in a four-person team. Her Euclidean distance would be the square root of $[(1 - 0)^2 + (1 - 0)^2 + (1 - 0)^2]/n$ or sqrt(.75) = .87. For continuous variables, the values of a Euclidean distance index can theoretically range from 0 to $+\infty$, although the upper bound depends operationally on both team size and the endpoints of the instrument used to measure the attribute (Harrison & Sin, 2006). Using the aforementioned example, if the female member was the 10-year veteran in the group, her Euclidean distance from the other members on tenure would be $[(10 - 0)^2 + (10 - 0)^2 + (10 - 0)^2]/n$ or sqrt(300/4) = 8.67. On the other hand, each of the rookies is identical to all of the other rookies, but different from her. Each rookie's Euclidean distance would be $[(0 - 0)^2 + (0 - 0)^2 + (10 - 0)^2]/n$ or sqrt(100/4) = 5.00.

An interesting feature of Tsui et al.'s (1992) formula, as shown in Table 11–1, is that their computation of Euclidean distance depends on team size. To gauge one's distance or misfit from others, Tsui et al. (1992) recommend dividing by $n$ (all team members) instead of $n - 1$ (all other team members) to "derive a metric that captures both the size and the compositional effects" (p. 562). For example, being the only female in a three-, five-, seven-, or nine-person team will yield Euclidean distances or PG misfit indices of .82, .89, .93, and .94, respectively. The rationale behind this computational subtlety, that the psychological impact of misfit/dissimilarity varies nonlinearly as a function of team size, is an empirical question that may warrant investigation in itself. That is, to address the assumption embedded in the individual-level misfit index, one only needs to include team size as a statistical control variable or moderator.

## Signed versus Unsigned Distances in Person–Team Misfit

Note also that Euclidean distances are symmetric. This would be appropriate for variables that are "lateral," "horizontal," or status-free, such as attitudes or personality. If there is psychological meaning in person $P$ having higher or lower levels of resources or status than the other team members, then misfit is directional. For example, a team member who is *superior* (has excess relative to others) in cognitive ability might receive a greater amount of recognition and reward, whereas a team member who is *inferior* (is deficient relative to others) might be ignored. A similar degree of absolute PG misfit could lead to very different outcomes. Fit researchers can construct a per-individual mean of the signed Euclidean distances to capture such a phenomenon.

## Cautionary Note on Dimensionality

A final caveat deals with the multidimensional nature of fit. Can a single number reflect a team's or person's *overall* misfit? We believe that it would be at best imprudent and at worst misleading. The logic underlying such aggregation assumes either a latent or emergent construct based on positive correlations among the constituent elements of fit (Harrison, 2002). For instance, if one wanted to create a "total demographic misfit" index, measurement logic would require that diversity in ethnicity, age, sex, and so on would be positively related to one another. The composite would then represent the shared or overlapping components of the diversity variables. However, this is rarely the case. More importantly, there is often no conceptual basis for expecting different dimensions of interpersonal misfit to be associated with each other (especially for demographic attributes). Perhaps a better approach would be to treat them as a multivariate set rather than adding them together to reach a less meaningful total score (Lau & Murnighan, 1998, treat them interactively). We contend that interpersonal misfit is most meaningful when it is more narrowly defined or dimensionalized.

## Conclusion

Overall, the empirical treatment of misfit can appropriate some of the ideas from research in the area of workgroup diversity to operationalize (collective) PP and PG misfit. Likewise, some of the commonly used indices in those areas, relational demography, and supervisor–subordinate differences can be adopted for the study of misfit. Specifically, we recommend Blau's and Teachman's indices for team-level misfit on categorical variables, SD for team-level misfit on continuous variables, and Euclidean distances for PP and PG misfit at the individual level. When the direction of misfit is important (when interpersonal superiority or inferiority on an attribute is meaningful), signed distances are reasonable. Finally, we note that the team indices discussed here could also be used at higher levels of analysis (e.g., division or organizational level) to capture the extent of homogeneity (fit) or heterogeneity (misfit) on demographic and psychological variables at these higher levels.

## 11.5  CLUSTER ANALYSIS

*Michael D. Mumford and Jazmine Espejo*

The term *cluster analysis* refers to a set of statistical techniques, really decision rules, whereby entities, people, objects, or environments are grouped into a smaller set of "types." In cluster analytic studies, inferences about fit are made with respect to the group the individual is similar to, or a member of, on the basis of cross-group differences in relation to performance on measures held to reflect fit effects. This approach has proven attractive in studies of person (*P*)–environment (*E*) fit for two reasons (Mumford, Stokes, & Owens, 1990; Owens & Schoenfeldt, 1979). First, it permits a wide range of different types of variables to be considered simultaneously in fit assessments. Second, clustering procedures allow for qualitative differences and nonlinear effects.

Cluster analysis has been used in studies of PE fit for almost half a century (cf., Owens, 1968). In essence, cluster analysis captures the particular profile or pattern across attributes. For example, individuals could be "typed" or grouped into categories based on their patterns or profiles across measures of their ability and desires (e.g., one profile might reflect high ability, a strong desire for autonomy, and a weak desire for job variety, whereas another pattern could reflect high ability, strong autonomy, and strong job variety desires). Cluster analysis has been used to classify persons based on the pattern of their different *P* attributes or the work context based on different *E* characteristics, and the different types derived from the cluster analysis have been linked to various outcomes. In other studies (e.g., Gustafson & Mumford, 1995), independent *P* and *E* patterns have been derived and then have been considered simultaneously in relation to outcomes.

One-way cluster analysis is used in studies of PE fit is to identify types, or subsets, of people who display similarity on measures of personality, life history, or values and interests and then to examine cross-type differences with respect to performance in a given work environment. For example, Mumford, Zaccaro, Johnson, Diana, and Threlfall (2000) identified seven types of leaders commonly found on army jobs with only three of these types advancing to and performing well in more senior leadership positions. Another way cluster analysis has been applied in studies of PE fit is to identify the major kinds of psychosocial environments to which people must adapt. One example of this application may be found in Hofstede (1998), who used climate inventory scores to identify the major types of work environments operating within a particular firm. Still another way cluster analysis is used in studies of PE fit is to assess how different types of people differ in their reactions to, or performance in, different types of work environments. In one study along these lines, Gustafson and Mumford (1995) found that some types of people performed well in multiple types of work environments, whereas other types of people performed well in just one type of work environment.

## Cluster Analysis Methods

Clustering techniques have not been widely applied in PE fit due to the complexity of the methods involved and certain vagaries surrounding requisite methodological operations—an issue we hope to help resolve in the present section. To begin, cluster analysis is not a single method but rather a family of methodological techniques subsuming single linkage analysis, centroid analysis, and multidimensional scaling among other techniques (see Anderberg, 1973; Everitt, 1979, for a more complete description of basic methods).

Despite these procedural differences, all cluster analysis techniques apply a similar general strategy to grouping entities into types. Essentially, entities (people, environments, and others) are measured on a set of variables and the profile of variable scores is obtained. Then, the similarity of each entities' profile to all other profiles is assessed using a similarity metric—typically a distance metric or correlation coefficient. Once similarity has been assessed, decision rules are applied to metric scores to determine the entities, or entity clusters, that can be merged together at any given point in an iterative sequence. Entities with similar profiles are merged together into a type that can be distinguished from other types. Single linkage methods cluster entities based on the distance between the nearest neighbors in relevant clusters, whereas centroid methods, such as the Ward and Hook (1963) procedure, cluster entities to minimize within-group variation around the cluster centroid or mean profile.

In hierarchical methods, the most common kind of cluster analysis, the sequence of combinations begins by treating each entity as a cluster in and of itself and continues until all entities have been merged into a single cluster. The number of clusters to be retained is determined by identifying the point in this iterative sequence at which further combinations result in sharp increases in within-cluster differences. Hierarchical procedures are used to identify the number and nature of the clusters to be retained in a population when no prior knowledge exists about likely subpopulations.

Nonhierarchical procedures, such as k-means, begin with a priori seed points. As a result, the accuracy of nonhierarchical analyses depends on initial specification of these seed points. Frequently in clustering studies, a nonhierarchical analysis follows a hierarchical analysis in which the results of the hierarchical analysis provide the seed points used in the nonhierarchical analysis. The stability of entity assignments across these two procedures is used to assess replicability in assignments and control for drift due to the retention of early sequence assignees within clusters. Additionally, nonhierarchical procedures allow fit to be assessed to idealized type profiles, permitting theory-based clustering or appraisals of entity fit to standards (e.g., fit of an individual's climate perception to the climate perceptions of different groups).

This thumbnail sketch of the basic procedures applied in cluster analysis not only describes the general method but also points to the key methodological considerations likely to appear in any cluster analytic study of PE fit. In the ensuing discussion, we will address these six major methodological issues: (a) sampling, (b) measurement, (c) similarity assessment, (d) choice of clustering procedure, (e) evaluation of cluster solutions, and (f) applications of clusters in PE fit studies.

## Sampling

Traditionally, it has been assumed that cluster analytic investigations require rather large samples. A Monte Carlo study by Overall and Magee (1992), however, indicated that clustering procedures can adequately capture a true underlying subpopulation structure if as few as 8–10 entities from the relevant subpopulations are represented in the sample. Thus, if only 5 clusters are expected, a sample size of 50 may be adequate. Hence, cluster analysis can be applied in small samples if the number of groups under consideration is not large—conditions that often apply in environmental studies or studies of groups.

In this regard, however, it is important to bear in mind the conditions calling for larger samples. Typically, larger samples will be required when: (a) the number of expected clusters is large, (b) clusters are not well separated from each other, (c) a number of small outlier clusters might emerge, and (d) the reliability of measures is low. Additionally, a larger sample will be required if an attempt is to be made to cross-validate cluster solutions.

## Measures

Of course, the success of any cluster analysis depends on the quality of the measures used to describe the similarities and differences among entities. As a result, use of more reliable measures (e.g., scales as opposed to items) improves the accuracy of clustering. Clustering, moreover, does not have the linear restraint problem characteristic of other multivariate analyses. As a result, the addition of more measures, particularly measures providing more independent information, is desirable. In fact, cluster analysis results can improve with the inclusion of measures drawn from different domains, for example, both people and environmental measures, if this is substantively appropriate (Scott, Leritz, & Mumford, in press).

The proviso here, however, is that the measures under consideration must capture differences between likely subpopulations. Breckenridge (2000), in another Monte Carlo study, found that specification error, the inclusion of variables not relevant to subpopulation discrimination, led to noteworthy decrements in the performance of most major clustering procedures with respect to identification of the true number of underlying clusters. This finding is consistent with the observations of Gati, Garty, and Fassa (1996) indicating that fit effects on satisfaction are stronger when fit is appraised with respect to core occupational characteristics. Taken together, these studies suggest that substantial attention should be given to the selection and development of the measures to be applied in clustering with either theory or prior empirical work being used to identify measures likely to capture critical differences.

## Similarity Assessment

A complete assessment of profile similarity takes into account the pattern, elevation, and scatter of scores on the measures under consideration. Full similarity assessments can be obtained through distance metrics—either Euclidian (independent variables) or mahalanobis (correlated variables). Correlations (or $\kappa$ statistics for nonparametric data) describing similarity in score patterns are also commonly used to assess similarity in cluster analysis (Milligan, 1981). What is of note here is that these correlational indices ignore elevation and scatter resulting in a clustering based solely on pattern. Along similar lines, standardization of variable scores by setting means to 0 and standard deviations to 1 will result in a cluster analysis that considers only pattern.

These points are of some importance in studies of PE fit because there is a need to specify the elements of profile similarity that will be considered in cluster definition. For example, in studies of values in which centrality and differentiation are of concern, substantive considerations will lead to the use of distance metrics. In other studies in which the concern is identifying relative differences between people (Blashfield & Morey, 1980), a focus on pattern differences is more appropriate, thereby recommending correlational indices or the use of distance metrics based on standard scores. In this regard, however, it should be noted that if unstandardized metrics are applied, greater weight will be given to more variable measures and arbitrary cross-scale differences in range may distort cluster identification.

## Choice of Clustering Procedure

Although a number of methods, really decision algorithms, have been devised to group entities together on the basis of similarity metrics. The four most commonly applied methods are (a) single linkage, (b) complete linkage, (c) average linkage, and (d) centroid (see Gnanadesikan et al., 1989, for details of these types). Single linkage clustering proceeds by joining clusters with the smallest distance between the two closest cluster members. Complete linkage proceeds by joining clusters where the two most distant members of the clusters under consideration are less distant than all other alternatives. Average linkage proceeds by joining those clusters with the smallest average distance between all pairwise linkages of cluster members. The centroid method proceeds by combining the two clusters that minimize within-group variation around the centroid, or average profile, of cluster members. The effectiveness of these alternative methods depends to some extent on the underlying structure of the relationships among subpopulations (Gnanadesikan et al., 1989). Monte Carlo studies examining how clustering procedures perform under different conditions (Breckenridge, 2000; Milligan, 1981) indicate that the centroid and average linkage methods are more accurate than other available techniques in identifying the true number of clusters and assigning entities to their true clusters—findings that recommend the use of centroid and average linkage procedures in studies of PE fit.

## Evaluation of Cluster Solutions

The first question that arises in evaluating the results of a cluster analysis is how many clusters should be retained? Although some statistical procedures have been developed to answer this question (Everitt, 1979), the difficulty in formulating adequate null models has led investigators to continue to rely on scree tests. In a scree test, the plot of within-group differences, or within-group variation, is obtained at each step in the iteration. The number of clusters to be retained is determined by finding that point at which further cluster combinations result in a sharp increase in within-cluster differences. The problems that arise in applying this approach are that (a) clustering procedures are biased toward retaining too many groups and (b) scree tests typically are ambiguous, indicating two or three potential solutions. Given these problems, the common strategy used to select a solution is to obtain, for each of the available alternatives, the distances between clusters, the number of entities assigned to each cluster, and the cluster members' average score profiles. The solution retained is the one for which clusters are well separated, relatively few unduly small clusters are identified, and the clusters evidence substantively meaningful score profiles.

After identification of a plausible solution, a more formal evaluation of the candidate solution occurs that typically involves some combination of the following analyses: (a) assessment of the stability of the cluster solution by replicating the clustering in the cross-validation samples, (b) assessment of assignment replication using a nonhierarchical procedure applied to entities in the validation and cross-validation samples, (c) assessment of simple structure in the assignment of entities to clusters, (d) assessment of the number of variables used in clustering evidencing significant differences across clusters, (e) assessment of the substantive coherence of the observed differences, (f) assessment of the results obtained in a discriminant analysis in which relevant measures serve as predictors of cluster membership to obtain canonical correlations, chi-square values, and an understanding of the underlying variables that distinguish clusters, and (g) assessment of the differences observed among clusters on a set of reference measures, measures not applied in the initial clustering, to provide evidence for the convergent and divergent validity of the solution with respect to observed group differences.

### Application of Clusters

After identification of a cluster solution and provision of some evidence for its validity, it becomes possible to apply the cluster solution in studies of PE fit. What should be recognized here, however, is that clusters per se have no direct implications for PE fit. Instead, it is the pattern of differences evidenced by cluster members on criteria indicative of fit, such as satisfaction (Bretz & Judge, 1994), more rapid skill development (De Fruyt, 2002), or higher creativity (Livingstone, Nelson, & Barr, 1997), that permits inferences about the effects of fit. Thus, the application of clusters in PE fit studies requires careful development of criteria, ideally process as well as performance criteria, and demonstration of differences on these criteria across clusters.

In analyses along these lines, however, it should be borne in mind that because individual and environmental characteristics exert main effects, differences across clusters in criterion scores speak to PE effects only under two conditions. First, when the environment is "fixed," differences in process or performance measures across clusters can be attributed to persons', or types', differential reactions to a common environment. Second, when interactions between certain person types and environmental types emerge, under conditions where people are not exposed to a common environment, differences in criterion scores point to PE effects.

These boundary conditions on PE fit inferences should be evaluated in light of the advantageous characteristics of the cluster analysis approach. First, the clustering strategy allows fit effects to be examined across a wide range of measures, potentially allowing the development of more comprehensive models of the processes and outcomes of PE fit. Second, these processes and outcomes need not be constant across all clusters. As a result, it becomes possible to develop both person-specific and/or environment-specific models of fit processes and outcomes (Mumford, Snell, & Hein, 1993).

## Conclusions

The promise of applying cluster analysis in studies of PE fit is that it may allow us to develop more sophisticated models of fit processes and outcomes tailored to the unique characteristics of certain types of people and the demands of certain types of environments. It is particularly relevant for assessing complementary fit. Models of this sort will permit us to move beyond superficial statements about general fit effects that ignore the unique ways different people adapt to different environmental demands. It is hoped that the present effort, by clarifying the methodological requirements for cluster analytic studies of PE fit, will provide an impetus for a new wave of research along these lines.

## ACKNOWLEDGMENTS

The major sections of this chapter were authored as follows: General Methodological and Design Issues was authored by Cheri Ostroff; Profile Comparison Methods for Assessing Person–Situation Fit was authored by David F. Caldwell, Jennifer A. Chatman, and Charles A. O'Reilly; Polynomial Regression and Response Surface Methodology was authored by Jeffrey R. Edwards; Heterogeneity as Misfit was authored by David A. Harrison and Hock-Peng Sin; and Cluster Analysis was authored by Michael D. Mumford and Jasmine Espejo.

## REFERENCES

Allison, P. D. (1978). Measures of inequality. *American Sociological Review, 43,* 865–880.

Anderberg, M. R. (1973). *Cluster analysis for applications.* New York: Academic Press.

Aronoff, J., & Wilson, J. P. (1985). *Personality in the social process.* Hillsdale, NJ: Lawrence Erlbaum Associates.

Barrick, M. R., Mount, M. K., & Strauss, J. P. (1993). Conscientiousness and performance of sales representatives. *Journal of Applied Psychology, 78,* 715–723.

Barrick, M. R., Stewart, G. L., Neubert, M. J., & Mount, M. K. (1998). Relating member ability and personality to work-team processes and team effectiveness. *Journal of Applied Psychology, 83,* 377–391.

Barsade, S. G., Ward, A. J., Turner, J. D. F., & Sonnenfeld, J. (2000). To your heart's content: A model of affective diversity in top management teams. *Administrative Science Quarterly, 45,* 802–836.

Blashfield, R., & Morey, J. (1980). A comparison of four clustering methods using MMPI Monte Carlo data. *Applied Psychological Measurement, 4,* 57–64.

Block, J. H. (1978). *The Q-sort method in personality assessment and psychiatric research.* Palo Alto, CA: Consulting Psychologist Press.

Breckenridge, J. N. (2000). Validating cluster analysis: Consistent replication and symmetry. *Multivariate Behavioral Research, 35,* 261–285.

Bretz, R. D., & Judge, T. A. (1994). Person-organization fit and the theory of work adjustment: Implications for satisfaction, tenure, and career success. *Journal of Vocational Behavior, 44,* 32–54.

Bunderson, J. S., & Sutcliffe, K. M. (2002). Comparing alternative conceptualizations of functional diversity in management teams: Process and performance effects. *Academy of Management Journal, 45,* 875–893.

Byrne, D. (1971). *The attraction paradigm.* New York: Academic Press.

Cable, D. M., & Judge T. A. (1997). Person-organization fit, job choice decisions, and organizational entry. *Organization Behavior and Human Decision Processes, 67,* 294–311.

Caldwell, D. F., & O'Reilly, C. A. (1990). Measuring person-job fit using a profile comparison process. *Journal of Applied Psychology, 75,* 648–657.

Caplan, R. D. (1987). Person-environment fit theory and organizations: Commensurate dimensions, time perspectives, and mechanisms. *Journal of Vocational Behavior, 31,* 248–267.

Chatman, J. A. (1989). Improving interactional organizational research: A model of person-organization fit. *Academy of Management Review, 14,* 333–349.

Chatman, J. A. (1991). Matching people and organizations: Selection and socialization in public accounting firms. *Administrative Science Quarterly, 36,* 459–484.

Chatman, J. A., & Barsade, S. G. (1995). Personality, organizational culture, and cooperation: Evidence from a business simulation. *Administrative Science Quarterly, 40,* 423–443.

Chatman, J. A., Caldwell, D. F., & O'Reilly, C. A. (1999). Managerial personality and performance: A semi-idiographic approach. *Journal of Research in Personality, 33,* 514–545.

Cronbach, L. J. (1958). Proposals leading to analytic treatment of social perception scores. In R. Tagiuri & L. Petrullo (Eds.), *Person perception and interpersonal behavior* (pp. 353–379). Stanford, CA: Stanford University Press.

Cronbach, L. J. (1992). Four *Psychological Bulletin* articles in perspective. *Psychological Bulletin, 112,* 389–392.

Cronbach, L. J., & Gleser, G. C. (1953). Assessing the similarity between profiles. *Psychological Bulletin, 50,* 456–473.

De Fruyt, F. (2002). A person-centered approach to P-E fit questions using a multiple-trait model. *Journal of Vocational Behavior, 60,* 73–90.

Edwards, J. R. (1991). Person-job fit: A conceptual integration, literature review, and methodological critique. *International Review of Organizational Psychology, 6,* 283–357.

Edwards, J. R. (1993). Problems with the use of profile similarity indices in the study of congruence in organizational research. *Personnel Psychology, 46*, 641–665.

Edwards, J. R. (1994). The study of congruence in organizational behavior research: Critique and a proposed alternative. *Organizational Behavior and Human Decision Processes, 58*, 51–100 [Erratum, *58*, 323–325].

Edwards, J. R. (1995). Alternatives to difference scores as dependent variables in the study of congruence in organizational research. *Organizational Behavior and Human Decision Processes, 64*, 307–324.

Edwards J. R. (1996). An examination of competing versions of the person-environment fit approach to stress. Academy of Management Journal, 39, 292–339,

Edwards, J. R. (2002). Alternatives to difference scores: Polynomial regression analysis and response surface methodology. In F. Drasgow & N. W. Schmitt (Eds.), *Advances in measurement and data analysis* (pp. 350–400). San Francisco: Jossey-Bass.

Edwards, J. R., Caplan, R. D., & Harrison, R. V. (1998). Person-environment fit theory: Conceptual foundations, empirical evidence, and directions for future research. In C. L. Cooper (Ed.), *Theories of organizational stress* (pp. 28–67). Oxford, England: Oxford University Press.

Edwards, J. R., Klein, K. J., Shipp, A. J., & Lim, B. C. (2003, April). *The study of dispersion in organizational behavior research: An analytical framework using distributional moments.* Paper presented at the 18th annual meeting of the Society for Industrial and Organizational Psychology, Orlando, FL.

Edwards, J. R., & Parry, M. E. (1993). On the use of polynomial regression equations as an alternative to difference scores in organizational research. *Academy of Management Journal, 36*, 1577–1613.

Edwards, J. R., & Rothbard, N. P. (1999). Work and family stress and well-being: An examination of person–environment fit in the work and family domains. *Organizational Behavior and Human Decision Processes, 77*, 85–129.

Endler, N. S., & Magnusson, D. (1976). *Interactional psychology and personality.* Washington DC: Hemisphere.

Everitt, B. S. (1979). Unresolved problems in cluster analysis. *Biometrics, 35*, 169–181.

Gati, I., Garty, Y., & Fassa, N. (1996). Using career-related aspects to assess person–environment fit. *Journal of Counseling Psychology, 43*, 196–206.

Gnanadesikan, R., Blashfield, R. K., Breiman, L., Dunn, O. J., Friedman, J. H., Fu, K., Hartigan, J. A., Kettenring, J. R., Lachenbruch, P. A., Olshen, R. A., & Rohlf, F. J. (1989). Discriminant analysis and clustering. *Statistical Science, 4*, 34–69.

Gustafson, S. B., & Mumford, M. D. (1995). Personal style and person-environment fit: A pattern approach. *Journal of Vocational Behavior, 46*, 163–188.

Harrison, D. A. (2002). Meaning and measurement of work role withdrawal: Current controversies and future fallout under changing technology. In M. Koslowsky & M. Krausz (Eds.), *Voluntary employee withdrawal and inattendance: A current perspective* (pp. 95–132). London: Plenum.

Harrison, D. A., McLaughlin, M. E., & Coalter, T. M. (1996). Context, cognition, and common method variance: Psychometric and verbal protocol evidence. *Organizational Behavior and Human Decision Processes, 68*, 246–261.

Harrison, D. A., Price, K. H., & Bell, M. P. (1998). Beyond relational demography: Time and the effects of surface- and deep-level diversity on work group cohesion. *Academy of Management Journal, 41*, 96–107.

Harrison, D. A., Price, K. H., Gavin, J. H., & Florey, A. T. (2002). Time, teams, and task performance: Changing effects of surface- and deep-level diversity on group functioning. *Academy of Management Journal, 45*, 1029–1045.

Harrison, D. A., & Sin, H. P. (2006). What is diversity and how should it be measured? In A. Konrad, P. Prasad, and J. Pringle (Eds.), *Handbook of workplace diversity* (pp. 191–216). Thousand Oaks, CA: Sage.

Hollenbeck, J. R., Moon, H., Ellis, A. P. J., West, B. J., Ilgen, R. R., Sheppard, L., Porter, C. O. L. H., & Wagner, J. A., III. (2002). Structural contingency theory and individual differences: Examination of external and internal person-team fit. *Journal of Applied Psychology, 87*, 599–606.

Hofstede, G. (1998). Identifying organizational subcultures: An empirical approach. *Journal of Management Studies, 35*, 1–12.

Johns, G. (1981) Difference score measures of organizational behavior variables: A critique. *Organizational Behavior and Human Performance, 27*, 443–464.

Judge, T. A., & Cable, D. M. (1997). Applicant personality, organizational culture, and organizational attraction. *Personnel Psychology, 50*, 359–394.

Kenny, D. A., Albright, L., Malloy, T. E., & Kashy, D. A. (1994). Consensus in interpersonal perception: Acquaintance and the big five. *Psychological Bulletin, 116*, 245–258.

Klein, K. J., Bliese, P. D., Kozlowski, S. W. J., Dansereau, F., Gavin, M. B., Griffin, M. A., Hofmann, D. A., James, L. R., Yammarino, F. J., & Bligh, M. C. (2000). Multilevel analytical techniques: Commonalities, differences and continuing questions. In K. J. Klein and S. W. J. Kozlowski (Eds.), *Multilevel theory, research and methods in organizations* (pp. 512–553). San Francisco: Jossey-Bass.

Klein, K. J., Conn, A. B., Smith, D. B., & Sorra, J. S. (2001). Is everyone in agreement? An exploration of within-group agreement in employee perceptions of the work environment. *Journal of Applied Psychology, 86*, 3–16.

Kristof, A. L. (1996). Person-organization fit: an integrative review of its conceptualizations, measurement, and implications. *Personnel Psychology, 49*, 1–49.

Lau, D. C., & Murnighan, J. K. (1998). Demographic diversity and faultlines: The compositional dynamics of organizational groups. *Academy of Management Review, 23*, 325–340.

Livingstone, L. P., Nelson, D. L., & Barr, S. H. (1997). Person-environment fit and creativity: An examination of supply-value and demand-ability versions of fit. *Journal of Management, 23*, 119–146.

Luthans, F., & Davis, T. (1982). An idiographic approach to organizational behavior research: The use of single case experimental designs and direct measures. *Academy of Management Review, 7*, 380–391.

Markus, H. R. (1977). Self-schemata and process information about the self. *Journal of Personality and Social Psychology, 34*, 63–78.

Milligan, G. W. (1981). A review of Monte Carlo tests of cluster analysis. *Multivariate Behavioral Research, 16*, 379–407.

Mumford, M. D., Snell, A. F., & Hein, M. B. (1993). Varieties of religious experience: Continuity and change in religious involvement. *Journal of Personality, 61*, 69–88.

Mumford, M. D., Stokes, G. S., & Owens, N. A. (1990). *Patterns of life adaptation: The ecology of human individuality.* Hillsdale, NJ: Lawrence Erlbaum Associates.

Mumford, M. D., Zaccaro, S. J., Johnson, J. R., Diana, M., & Threlfall, K. V. (2000). Patterns of leader characteristics: Implications for performance and development. *The Leadership Quarterly, 11,* 115–133.

Naylor, J. C., Pritchard, R. D., & Ilgen, D. R. (1980). *A theory of behavior in organizations.* New York: Academic Press.

Newcomb, T. M. (1961). *The acquaintance process.* New York: Holt, Rinehart, and Winston.

O'Reilly, C. A., Chatman, J. A., & Caldwell, D. F. (1991). People and organizational culture: A profile comparison approach to assessing person-organization fit. *Academy of Management Journal, 34,* 487–516.

Ostroff, C. (1993). The effects of climate and personal influences on individual behavior and attitudes in organizations. *Organizational Behavior and Human Decision Processes, 56,* 56–90.

Ostroff, C., Kinicki, A. J., & Clark, M. A. (2002). Substantive and operational issues of response bias across levels of analysis: An example of climate-satisfaction relationships. *Journal of Applied Psychology, 87,* 355–368.

Overall, J. E., & Magee, K. N. (1992). Replication as a rule for determining the number of clusters in hierarchical cluster analysis. *Applied Psychological Measurement, 16,* 119–128.

Owens, W. A., (1968). Toward one discipline of scientific psychology. *American Psychologist, 26,* 947–997.

Owens, W. A., & Schoenfeldt, L. F., (1979). Toward a classification of persons. *Journal of Applied Psychology, 64,* 596–607.

Pelham, B. W. (1993). On the highly positive thoughts of the highly depressed. In R. F. Baumeister (Ed.), *Self-esteem: The puzzle of low self-regard* (pp. 183–199). Plenum Series in Social/Clinical Psychology. New York: Plenum.

Rice, R. W., McFarlin, D. B., Hunt, R. G., & Near, J. P. (1985). Organizational work and the perceived quality of life: Toward a conceptual model. *Academy of Management Review, 10,* 296–310.

Roberts, K. H., Hulin, C. L., & Rousseau, D. M. (1978). *Developing an interdisciplinary science of organization.* San Francisco: Jossey-Bass.

Schneider, B. (1987). The people make the place. *Personnel Psychology, 41,* 437–453.

Schneider, B., Kristof-Brown, A., Goldstein, H. W., & Smith D. B. (1997). What is this thing called fit? In. N. Anderson and P. Herriot (Eds.), *International Handbook of Selection and Assessment* (pp. 393–412). Chichester, England: Wiley.

Scott, G. M., Leritz, L. E., & Mumford, M. D. (in press). Types of creativity training: Approaches and their effectiveness. *Journal of Creative Behavior.*

Tinsley, H. E. A. (2000). The congruence myth: An analysis of the efficacy of the person-environment fit model. *Journal of Vocational Behavior, 56,* 147–179.

Tsui, A. S., Egan, T. D., & O'Reilly, C. (1992). Being different: Relational demography and organizational attachment. *Administrative Science Quarterly, 37,* 549–579.

Tsui, A. S., & O'Reilly, C. (1989). Beyond simple demographic effects: The importance of relational demography in supervisor-subordinate dyads. *Academy of Management Journal, 32,* 402–423.

Volard, S. V., & McCarthy, P. J. (1979). Do extraverted people make better sales representatives? *Management Decision, 17,* 467–486.

Ward, J. H., & Hook, M. E. (1963). Application of an hierarchical grouping procedure to a problem of grouping profiles. *Educational and Psychological Measurement, 1,* 69–81.

# CHAPTER 12

# *Pitching Fits in Applied Psychological Research: Making Fit Methods Fit Theory*

## David A. Harrison
*The Pennsylvania State University*

As an outsider peering through the store window of this book on fit theory and research, I get the sense that if fit doesn't encompass the entirety of creation, it comes awfully close. The merchandise racks have titles for *micro, meso, macro,* and *multilevel* conceptualizations. There is *direct* and *indirect* assessment of *perceived* and *actual* fit. Fit comes in *supplementary* or *complementary* flavors (*sedimentary* anybody? maybe not). In one display corner there is a tool for fit by profile comparison, and in another there is fit by response-surface methodology. A case by the checkout stand holds a box of gooey *fit clusters.* Fit can be *similarity, congruence, alignment, agreement, composition, compilation, configuration, matching,* and *interactionist.* There are *needs–supplies* barrels of fit fruit and *demands–abilities* bins of fit grain. On one shelf, there is PJ fit. Another holds PG fit. Across the way, there are barcodes for PO, PV, PP, PS, SV, NS, and SS fit.

I'm lost in the supermarket of fit research, and I haven't yet stepped inside!

My original charge in this chapter was to summarize the state of fit between fit theory and fit methods and put forward some recommendations. After wandering through my reading of the widespread fit literature (including the contributions to this book), I am going to start by reconsidering what is and is not, can and cannot, be *fit.* Then, I will try to organize and evaluate some of the methods for studying it.

## DEFINING AND CONCEPTUALIZING FIT

### (Re-)Considering the Core Meaning
### of Person (P)–Environment (E) Fit

To be sure, strong efforts have been are being made to organize this vast warehouse of fit ideas and approaches (see Cable & Edwards, 2004; Drazin & Van de Ven, 1986; Venkatraman, 1989; Ostroff & Schulte, chapter 1, this volume). Empirical summaries of a multitude of fit effects have already been assembled (Kristof-Brown, Zimmerman, & Johnson, 2005). Yet, as an outsider who wants to learn about and arrange fit research alongside other realms of study in the organizational sciences, my first inclination is to place fit ideas into a crucible, burn off the excess, and see what fit *is*. It is vital to uncover the unassailable kernel of its meaning, to find a touchpoint or home base of agreement for researchers. If that is possible, the philosophical core of PE fit research might become more discernible from its periphery (Lakatos, 1970). And, for the purposes of the present chapter, some assessment might then be made of the fit between theories and methods . . . for fit.

With all the disparate notions listed above, no wonder Ben Schneider had fits about fit, even though his fits were self-reportedly healthy (2001, p. 141). His contention has been that PE fit might be the dominant, although implicit, conceptualization of all phenomena studied in applied psychology (Schneider, 2001; Schneider, Kristof-Brown, Goldstein, & Smith, 1997). His creative energy has stoked the engine of fit investigations for decades (e.g., Schneider, 1987; Schneider, Goldstein, & Smith, 1995). In his original treatments, the individual difference or *I-side*, and Lewinian or *O-side*, traditions of the field merely treat Ps and Es as focal variables versus moderators, with the investigator's own tradition prescribing which (P or E) variable serves in which role. Fit could therefore be regarded as *any P * E interaction* we study or as any joint consideration of *P* and *E* variables. Moreover, if this conceptualization is pervasive, and the current volume reinforces such a perception, perhaps we are all doing fit research.

Perhaps not. Fit can't be everything. If fit is everything, then it is nothing—at least nothing with scientific utility. For fit to be meaningful, for fit to be a valuable and vibrant conception for understanding the organizational world, it needs to have recognizable borders and a coherent definition that distinguishes it from other conceptions. And, if those borders are so vast and so porous as to cover any simultaneous combination of *P* and *E* variables, then fit would come close to spanning most of the known universe of organizational research. The cozy fit emporium would swell into a daunting megastore.

Of course, these are provocative, even extreme, statements. The provocation is intentional, because I believe a re-thinking of the label and conventional definition of fit is in order. Acting as a proxy for interested but not necessarily fit-savvy researchers, who are likewise squinting to see through the glass of the fit supermarket, I am undertaking this as a sense-making exercise for the barely initiated. At best, I hope to stimulate greater convergence within and clearer divergence between the aisles. At least, I'll have swabbed some of the foggiest store windows.

## A(nother) Definition of PE Fit

As with other galvanizing terms in organizational scholarship (e.g., *diversity*; Harrison & Sin, 2006), there does not appear to be a consensual, stipulated meaning for fit that gives it tenable boundaries. A stipulated meaning or constitutive definition of such boundaries about the substance of a construct (Schwab, 1980) is necessary to collect, compare, and contrast the many methods and findings about fit that currently populate the literature (Harrison, 2002). As I rummage through and settle on such a meaning, it is important to note here that I am distinguishing fit as a construct from fit as a theoretical paradigm. The latter might be closer to what Schneider (1997, 2001) and colleagues have discussed, but the former might be closer to what Kristof-Brown et al. (2005) and others (Ostroff, Shin, & Kinicki, 2005) treat as fit.

Invoking a window-shopper's hubris and risking further indignation from those who have been doing wonderfully intriguing and engaging fit research for decades, I offer such a construct definition and meaning. *Fit* is a state of the compatibility of *joint* values of one or more attributes, $a, b, c, \ldots j$, of a focal entity ($P$), and a *commensurate* set of attribute values, $a, b, c, \ldots j$ of the entity's environment ($E$). In algebraic terms, fit is about $[(P_a, P_b, P_c, \ldots P_j) \cap (E_a, E_b, E_c, \ldots E_j)]$, which is similar to prior formulations (e.g., Edwards, 1991; Kristof-Brown et al., 2005) but not identical. This stipulation contains elements of, but is not the same as, the (nearly universally) positive notion of fit that seems to underlie other definitions in the literature. That is, this definition makes no assumptions about or distinctions between what yields positive or negative outcomes for the entity $P$ or its environment $E$. In much fit research, or in a broader fit paradigm, this complex construct appears to serve more often as an independent variable rather than a dependent one. The methods described in this volume tend to follow that trend.

## What PE Fit Is

Obviously, the above definition demarcates a PE treatment, but the abstract nature of the definition means it can apply to any level of analysis. That is, $P$ and $E$ are mainly placeholders in this definition rather than mandates about the necessary foci or content domains of fit researchers. The entity or $P$ side of fit will most likely be attributes of an individual, dyad, or group for applied psychologists, but the entity could just as well be a system, organization, network, or even community for an investigator (e.g., Doty & Glick, 1993). Just as the $P$ side does not have to be an individual person, the E side does not have to refer to a particular form of the environment. It is simply a convenient label for a broad category of all things logically defined as fit partners or context outside the P entity. The E side could be a job ($J$), vocation ($V$), supervisor or partner (another $P$), team or group ($G$), organization ($O$), system ($S$), or community or culture ($C$). The E side might be an aggregate of other $P$ entities outside the focal $P$ (Ostroff et al., 2005; Schneider, 1987; Van Vianen, 2000). Finally, although it is stated most generally as a multiattribute or multidimensional configuration, the aforementioned definition works just as well for uniattribute or unidimensional ideas about fit: $[(P_a) \cap (E_a)]$.

### Fit Is Affinity: Supplementary Fit

The term *compatibility* in the above definition might be a harbinger for eventual trouble. It possibly (over)emphasizes the similarity of values of $P_a$ and $E_a$ (the magnitudes of $P_a$ and $E_a$, if $a$ is a continuous attribute) or of the vectors $(P_a, P_b, P_c, \ldots P_j)$ and $(E_a, E_b, E_c, \ldots E_j)$. The greater the similarity of the values of the P ($P_a, P_b, P_c, \ldots P_j$) and E ($E_a, E_b, E_c, \ldots E_j$) vectors, the more compatibility—the more fit—there is. Such a definition might also be expanded to accommodate multi-entity notions of fit, with several $P$ (entity) vectors and/or more several $E$ (environment) vectors. Similarity in magnitudes is perhaps the most routinely summoned notion of fit, referred to as *supplementary fit* (Muchinsky & Monahan, 1987) in current work. At a dyadic level, when $a$, $b$, $c$, and so on are features of an ego ($P$) as well as an alter ($E$), this kind of fit is proposed to spark interpersonal attraction and strong interpersonal ties (Byrne, 1971). If one is still grappling with terms as an outsider to this research area, however, "supplementary" fit seems to be a phrase that generates confusion rather than a tacit or immediate understanding. Connotatively, it suggests either $P$ or $E$ is being "added on." Despite the lilting rhyme with another popular term (see later), this kind of fit is neither an additive function nor a statement about something being annexed or appended. Instead, this is a compatibility borne of greater PE likeness. It represents *affinity*.

### Fit Is Interlock: Complementary Fit

On the other hand, *compatibility* in the above definition could be a kind of intermeshing, in which the $P$ and $E$ sides follow each other's contours, like the trim of a dovetail joint or the edges of adjacent jigsaw pieces. Some authors include needs–supplies and demands–abilities formulations of this form of fit, such as an amount of a particular attribute that an individual desires that can be provided by the organization (Caplan, 1987;

Kristof, 1996). Others more narrowly define this kind of fit based on *compilation*, in that a focal attribute must occupy a prior void to make the system whole (Ostroff & Shulte, chapter 1, this volume). The essential idea is that *P* (or *E*) is some glove to be filled on attribute *a*, say *a–*. The other side of the equation is the hand that does the filling. Although it is tempting to say this fit as *interlock* is "opposites attract" and fit as affinity is "birds of a feather," it is not clear that the former captures the missingness character original proposed for what has become known as *complementary fit* (Muchinsky & Monahan, 1987). It is also tempting to carry this physical metaphor further and to predict what carpenters and stonemasons have known for millennia: fit as interlock is stronger and longer lasting than fit as affinity. Although both might coexist (see Cable & Edwards, 2004, for one interpretation about how it is possible), fit as affinity appears to rule the psychological day (e.g., Schneider et al., 1995).

A psychological place wherein complementary fit might seem to operate is a group context. For example, a complex task might demand skills *d, e, f,* and *g,* but the existing team members are knowledgeable only in *d, e,* and *f*. As far as fitting their working environment (*E*), they have a state of missingness on *g*: given a notation here of *g–*. If a person (*P*) being evaluated for selection to the team has a high level of *g*, he or she complements the rest of the members by possessing and delivering the missing and demanded attribute in the environment. Such a formulation would also appear to follow the strictures of Muchinsky and Monahan's (1987) original use of complementarity. The idea can also be reoriented to a team (rather than member-within-a-team) level of analysis and be considered fit as affinity. The environment demands a high level of variable *h*, which is *variety* of team member skills (Harrison & Klein, in press); a team can (mis)fit the environment by (not) delivering the requisite level of variety $[(P_h) \cap (E_h)]$. This idea is inherent in one of the most well-known principles of engineering control systems: Ashby's (1956) principle of requisite variety as a match between *P* and *E* in cybernetics.

Despite my guardedly optimistic tone, I must state that I am not convinced that fit as interlock or complementarity is viable under the proposed definition or that it is *fit* under broader definitions. The reason that some of the examples above appear to work is that when *P* fills in the missingness of an attribute on *E*, or vice versa, some positive consequence ensues. When one says that a task "demands" skill *g*, they mean that *g* is necessary for the task's *effective* completion. Later (under "Fit Is Not a Theory"), I beat a slow but not complete retreat from this asynchronous department of the sprawling fit store.

### Fit Is a Property of Commensurate Attributes

One might reasonably argue that fit is really a bidimensional construction, even when talking about a single *a* attribute, because there is a *P* and an *E* value for it. However, the word *commensurate* in the definition means that attribute *a* (or *b* or *c* or . . .) is defined in terms of the same content. The substance of *a* is the same, but it is delivered from or housed in different *P* and *E* domains (French, Rogers, & Cobb, 1974). For example, *a* might be the value (importance) of risk-taking for the person *P*, and the organization *E*, to which she or he belongs. In using this characterization, I admit to being fully stricken with Schneider's (2001) "affliction" in pushing for commensurate *a*, *b*, *c*, . . . *j* attributes (along with other authors, e.g., Caplan, 1987; Harrison, 1978; Kristof-Brown et al., 2005), although I see no need to anthropomorphize the attributes to make them so.

Refraining from stipulating that fit involves commensurate attributes would seem to let fit research drift back into the megamall of all possible *P* * *E* interactions. If so, fit is simply interactional psychology. Not that there's anything wrong with interactional psychology. Indeed, constitutive definitions of constructs cannot be inherently wrong or right, despite some protestations (Locke, 2003), because they are stipulated and conceptual rather than investigated and empirical. Construct definitions cannot be disproved by data (one could stipulate a formative rather than reflective construct if operationalizations did not covary; Jarvis, MacKenzie, & Podsakoff, 2003). Still, constructs can be more or less consensual among those investigating a particular domain, and they can be more or less serviceable in terms of their logical connection to a research enterprise—including how easy they are to operationalize. I believe workplace researchers get more usefulness from *fit* if it is both less, in terms of the span of its construct space, and more, in terms of the depth of its construct meaning, than interactional psychology in general (Dawis & Lofquist, 1984; Endler & Magnusson, 1976).

To bring these ideas closer to an organizational psychology home, the definition and boundaries I am proposing would mean that Job Satisfaction = Growth Need Strength * Task Identity is not a fit equation (Hackman & Oldham, 1976). Note that those highly regarded authors also did not present it in that way, and that I am continuing to discuss fit as a construct rather than as a paradigm. Neither is Individual Performance = Job Complexity * Cognitive Ability to be regarded as a fit equation under the proposed definition. Each of these theoretical constructions involves a joint consideration of *P* and *E* terms. The former equation might be thought to be a kind of needs–supplies fit and the latter equation might be demands–abilities fit. Yet, casting the same net around each of these and other elemental propositions in our field that have comparable structures and then calling them "fit," does not appear to give them additional explanatory power or generate new substantive insights.

Counterarguments abound for this approach that I am foisting on fit. The logic and stipulations might be said to be largely semantic. However, our research machinery (theories, surveys, interviews, data, and articles) is also largely semantic, built on a linguistic foundation that is difficult to shake. More exacting precision in language use should have advantages in clarifying what we are studying, and then, what we have found. Critics of the aforementioned narrow definition provided above and, hence, of more precisely targeted research strategies, might also say it is akin to looking for an elephant (fit) under a rock (the proposed definition), and, failing to find one, claiming that elephants do not exist. Instead, I am saying that we seem to be currently studying an entire continent and calling every animal we find in it an elephant. Some are wildebeests and wart hogs.

## What PE Fit Is Not

### Fit Is Not Merely Coherence

With verbal and algebraic stakes sunk into the ground to help define clearer conceptual boundaries, it should be easier to see what is included versus excluded as fit. Fit is defined here as the state of compatibility of two (vectors of) commensurate attributes. If the attributes on $P$ and $E$ are clearly not commensurate—say $P_a \cap E_b$—then my proposed definition would hold that an investigator is no longer studying a fit construct per se. But, do the $P$ and $E$ attributes have to be identical rather than coherent (Murphy & Medin, 1985; Rehder & Hastie, 2004)? Is commensurateness not in the eye of the researcher, and does strict content equivalence not drum much of the cleverness out of fit research? Perhaps there is a middle ground involving "sort of" commensurate attributes: $P_a$ and $E_{a'}$, where $a$ and $a'$ have a large proportion of overlapping content or shared abstraction. Just as likely is the within-entity case, in which $P_a$ and $P_{a'}$ (and $P_{a''}$ and so on) are featured together, such as with *regulatory fit* (Higgins, 2000) or internal fit among human resources practices (Gerhart, chap. 10, this volume).

For example, suppose a job candidate, Pria ($P$), was applying to work as an accountant at Enron. As purveyor of one of the greatest financial frauds in history as well as artificially inflating the price of electric power when it was desperately needed, the Enron organization ($E$) has become the poster child of sordid business practices. One might suggest that Enron anchors the lowest endpoint on the dimension of organizational-level ethical reputation: $E_{a'}$. Suppose further that Enron administers accounting integrity tests to incoming employees, and, therefore, Pria has a score on such a test, $P_a$. Should researchers talk about or investigate the fit of those two values? The answer I am advancing is *no* (if, on the other hand, we had a mean of the same test score for all of the other members of Pria's work unit, the answer is *yes*).

A further, within-entity example might be illustrative. Suppose that the behavioral history of each prospective Enron employee was also measured, by checking $P_b$, the number of warnings or reprimands accrued on previous jobs, and $P_c$, public records of traffic tickets, misdemeanor arrests, indictments, or convictions. Should researchers in this area refer to the *fit* of $P_a$, $P_b$, and $P_c$ as well? Again, I believe that such covariation, although possibly indicative of a broader psychological construct, is not useful to describe as fit, much as it would not be useful to jointly consider this broad construct and the more specific (un)ethical task environment for Enron employees such as Pria to be fit.

Fearful of losing my fit shoppers' card, but sheepishly bucking the jargon further, I propose instead that these latter cases and examples be given a different label. Rather than stretching system *fit* (see the discussion by Ostroff & Shulte, Chapter 1, this volume) into something that has a high potential to be misshapen, such an idea might be more clearly conveyed as something else. I suggest that the notion might better be described as the (internal, or internal jointly with external) coordination or *coherence* of a set of positively correlated but noncommensurate features of *P*, of *E*, or of *P* and *E*. Coherent features tend to go together, but are not identical. Research in marketing uses the coherence label to describe concordant configurations of brand or product attributes (e.g., Kayende, Roberts, Lilien, & Fong, 2006; Meyers-Levy & Tybout, 1989). Within persons, an arguably similar theoretical approach has been vetted for years as cognitive dissonance theory (Festinger, 1957) or as the concordance of mental categories (Murphy & Medin, 1985; Rehder & Hastie, 2004). At the organizational level, such a grouping of attributes is often referred to as *strategic alignment* (Henderson & Venkatraman, 1989).

The primary point here is that the definition of PE fit necessitates a consideration of compatibility between commensurate *P* and *E* elements, but that other, noncommensurate alignments may be related to but are not part of the definition of PE fit. At the least, a parsing of *fit* from *coherence* paradigms would make it easier for new research customers to head down the correct aisle and more readily find helpful ideas and evidence on the shelves.

### Fit Is Not a Lay Construct

The notion of fit gets slipperier if (a) the commensurate features of *P* and *E* are not specified a priori, (b) compatibility is not explicitly pinned down as affinity versus interlock beforehand, and (c) the nexus of fit changes for every criterion to which it might be linked in a theory. In that regard of making explicit, a priori statements, fit is stipulated to be what it is by researchers—as is true for all scientific constructs (Hulin, Drasgow, & Parsons, 1983). It is not defined as a construct by polling research participants about what they see as fit. That is, as I discuss below, fit is not constitutively defined by the entities we study telling us "what goes together," unless the focus of study is an entity's implicit theory or phenomenology of fit (Cable & Edwards, 2004). Perceived fit is not equivalent to fit.

*Fit Is Not a Warm Glow*

As alluded to earlier, the proposed definition does not and should not specify the range or nature of the *outcomes* of fit. This definition and most methods that assess fit as a construct under this definition should therefore be "criterion-free" (Venkatraman, 1989, p. 425; note that the definition also fits Venkatraman's notion of "fit as matching"). That is, despite the positive connotation of the word, in the present definition fit is not a good thing or a bad thing. It is merely a thing. Sometimes a state of fit might lead to stasis or stagnation. When *P* fits *E* remarkably well, it could mean that the entity *P* becomes complacent and does not build a reservoir of adaptive behaviors to respond when there is a change in *E*. Fit can create unproductive oysters. Misfit can create pearls.

In other words, fit under this stipulation is not a state of comfort or happiness or success on a dependent construct. It is not desired state on $Y$ equals $f[(P_a, P_b, P_c, \ldots P_j) \cap (E_a, E_b, E_c, \ldots E_j)]$. To define the range or nature of its outcomes as part of the construct of fit and then to study those outcomes empirically is to affirm a tautology. Consequences are not part of the definition of a construct; they are instead part of the falsifiable hypotheses that contain predicted relationships with the construct (Popper, 1963). This is perhaps most apparent if a researcher wants to study fit as a dependent rather than an independent construct.

Herein lies another nettlesome problem in studying fit. The verbal probe or cue for the word *fit* is almost universally considered to be positive. That positive connotation reaches past the holistic perceptions of our (participant) data sources, and it seeps into many of the scholarly incarnations of fit. Therefore, I am going to belabor this lack-of-criterion-in-the-definition point a bit further and try to make it support an important distinction.

*Fit Is Not a Theory*

Part of the confusion that I believe others share with me regarding the scattered conceptions that are pitched as fit is that those conceptions seem to start, at least implicitly, with a dependent variable that a researcher wants to be optimized. For instance, in the human resources arena, much of selection is cast as a search for fit between a candidate and his or her job specification or work role. If the job involves selling mattresses at a furniture store, one would argue that such a position demands that a job holder be outgoing and chatty and excited about dealing with customers. Hence, extroverted people *fit* the position, because they meet its demands for what it takes to do well. The selection process is designed with a goal of maximizing (anticipated) performance (see my earlier caveats on fit as interlock). The performance criterion defines fit. Under such a meaning, fit is anything about *P* that works with *E* for facilitating *Y*. Fit is always beneficial. As I alluded to earlier, fit becomes the effectiveness of a *P* ∩ *E* combination for creating higher levels of a valued criterion *Y*.

This problem of defining fit only as combinations of *P* and *E* independent variables that promote more desirable levels of dependent variables brings up nontrivial problems of considering fit as a mode of theorizing versus fit as a construct. Under the fit-as-theorizing approach, fit is the function, the mathematical apparatus, or the response surface, *f*, that relates the joint *P* and *E* variables to *Y*. It is the *effect on* or *relation of* the *P* ∩ *E* combination to *Y*: the steeper or tighter that *f* relation, which is operationalized as increasingly large amounts of variance explained in *Y* by *P* ∩ *E*, the greater the fit. When fit is used as this overarching kind of theorizing, it is a broad perspective that refers to any underlying combination through which (sets of) *P* and *E* factors might jointly promote a desired outcome. Fit is what happens when you put together a cold Sam Adams beer, warm huevos rancheros with tomatillo salsa, a Robert Mitchum movie, and me (on second thought, perhaps I am being too critical of this approach). Fit becomes a heuristic for describing any straight or twisty road for consolidating various *P* and *E* attributes to get to felicity. This, in turn, favors "cast a broad net" types of measurement methodologies and "kitchen sink" statistical models.

If research walks down this pathway of fit as a form of theorizing, then fit simultaneously cannot be proposed as an independent construct. The upshot would be that *Y* exhibits fit with . . . er . . . well . . . fit. Moreover, there is a vanishingly small empirical risk of this kind of fit-as-effect being unimportant. The only way that fit could fail is if the *f* function is null, which is the same as saying that the particular *P* and *E* attributes, whatever they are and in whatever configurations they are arranged, are completely inconsequential for *Y*. Failing to find fit is possible. But, all of the mixes of *P* and *E* variables that would constitute such an expansive version of fit would also seem to dilute its usefulness as a scientific idea.

### Fit Is Not Exploring Oblique Terrain

This last contention leads to a transitional observation about fit theory and fit methods, and one that I hope will sharpen the hypotheses and tighten the investigations that are currently nestled under the capacious billboard at the fit store. Organizational scientists differentiate themselves from other agents by sticking their necks out publicly—making a priori predictions about the world and gathering data to refute them. In contrast, a large portion of the current thinking and technology for doing research in this area seems to be geared toward being as generic and exploratory as possible, finding some relationship between configurations of $(P_a, P_b, P_c, \ldots P_j)$, $(E_a, E_b, E_c, \ldots E_j)$, and *Y* (or $[Y_q, Y_r, Y_s, \ldots Y_w]$) and calling that a fit function. And, what seems to be found is evidence instead for the unique impacts of forms of misfit on $Y$ (e.g., Jansen & Kristof-Brown, 2005), a nomenclature I will adopt in later sections (see "Choosing . . .").

For the techniques discussed in the following sections to have their greatest power, another change in research orientation seems warranted. Hypotheses about fit need to start with broad theoretical questions that name the $a$ (and the $b$ and the $c$ . . .) attribute on which fit is specified, and explain how and why fit ($P_a \cap E_a$) on that attribute leads to more or less of some outcome. Or, just as importantly under this broad paradigm, hypotheses must explain how and why misfit leads to less or more of that outcome (see Edwards & Rothbard, 1999, for an example). As Edwards and his colleagues have pointed out (e.g., Edwards & Harrison, 1993), the definition I am promoting tends to lead to sharp hypotheses, because if no rationale is given for relating the fit construct to some outcome $Y$, it would predict a peaked or hill-shaped surface of $P_a$, $E_a$, and $Y$. However, if that function does not match the data, it is not enough merely to show that excess ($P_a > E_a$) or deficiency ($P_a < E_a$) or some more complex connection contorts the fit mountain range to maximize explained variance in $Y$. If the ridge line of fit does not provide a proper explanation (Edwards & Shipp, chapter 7, this volume), another explanation needs to be generated, and a new hypothesis about misfit needs to be stated and tested with new evidence, using something that approximates the precision of the original prediction about fit. That is, for research in this domain to move forward, fewer post hoc configurations of P and E variables should be generically labeled as supportive of a broad paradigm of fit—after the terrain has already been mapped.

## OPERATIONALIZING FIT AND TESTING FIT THEORIES

If the definition I proposed above gains a customer base in the burgeoning fit community and at least some of the arguments supporting it make sense, then deliberate steps in undertaking fit research are highlighted or perhaps even mandated. Although those steps are described in the following as discrete choices of fit methods by investigators, they are clearly bound up in one another. That is, rather than being offered a la carte in the fit cafeteria, they are often part of ready-to-serve meals, at least as they have been laid out in other chapters in this volume. Understanding the choices available, and then choosing well, should provide more rigorous tests of fit theories.

### Choosing the Number of Attributes (*j*)

Starting the choice sequence with the decision to follow a multi- versus uniattribute approach to fit might seem out of place. Yet, choosing from generally molar versus molecular fit paradigms, as well as choosing the content of the attribute(s) within them based on a priori theory (see below), is fundamental. It is also the point at which fit tools already begin to diverge, following long-standing dilemmas about breadth versus depth in methodology (McGrath, 1982).

The Caldwell, Chatman, and O'Reilly (chapter 11.2, this volume) technique is a gumbo; their approach is steadfastly multiattribute. An individual ($P$) has a *configuration* or set of $j$ personal values: ($P_a$, $P_b$, $P_c$, ... $P_j$). Researchers compare it to the configuration or set of an organization's ($E$) $j$ cultural values: ($E_a$, $E_b$, $E_c$, ... $E_j$). A particular mechanism of comparison (in this case, correlation of values on the two sets) determines the level of fit (Caldwell & O'Reilly, 1990; O'Reilly, Chatman, & Caldwell, 1991). Theory dictates that persons and their environments should be treated holistically in such a paradigm; this method is best fit to theories describing persons and environments as wholes (Chatman, 1989, 1991). What results from this holistic combination of attributes is a single, molar number that serves as an index of overall fit, which can be used as an independent, dependent, or even moderating variable. As such, even though the Caldwell et al. methods can be argued to be idiographic, they emphasize breadth in the breadth–depth trade-off. This technique is limited in its more specific theoretical and practical application because it cannot ascertain which attributes of (mis)fit are most important for particular outcomes and in what direction. As a molar approach, it assumes that the direction and relative degree of fit across attributes is not of substantive interest.

Mumford and Espejo's (chapter 11.5, this volume) clustering methods are also explicitly multiattribute and molar, likewise trading increased breadth for reduced depth. Their proposed means for identifying situational archetypes is similar to Venkatraman's (1989) notion of "fit as gestalts." Discriminating among types of situations requires measurement of many environmental features, $j$, and seeing which environmental ingredients clump together the most tightly under various distance-based clustering algorithms: ($E_a$, $E_b$, $E_c$, ... $E_j$). Although they are described primarily as tools for creating taxonomies of $E$s, they might also be used to group $P$s as well. In either case, the breadth of sampling of those attributes is crucial (see Schneider, 2001, for entreaties to build extensive amounts of variance into the $E$ side of fit). Clustering allows differential weights on attributes $a$, $b$, $c$ ... $j$, with solutions gravitating toward those attributes that have the greatest systematic variance. The main goal of such clustering techniques is theory building about the lumpy, multivariate porridge of those $j$ attributes distributed among organizations. Examining fit of persons across these environmental clusters can be accomplished with other techniques (see later).

The response-surface methods (RSM) espoused by Edwards and Shipp (chapter 7, this volume) are more of a uniattribute puree (I use RSM as an acronym here because polynomial regression is a more general technique that subsumes the special case of RSM). Even if a fit researcher measured multiple attributes $a, b, c \ldots j$, they would be sealed in separate mason jars: $[P_a \cap E_a], [P_b \cap E_b], [P_c \cap E_c], \ldots [P_j \cap E_j]$. That is, each attribute requires its own, in-depth RSM analysis; this approach is best matched to PE fit theories interested in *parts* of $P$ and $E$ rather than *wholes*. And, each one gets a three-dimensional picture. Who doesn't like pictures? Fit is described for one attribute at a time as a 45-degree line in RSM, where $P_a = E_a$. Such a description makes it clear that fit is assumed (or stipulated, in the case of my definition) to be the same joint state despite of varying magnitudes of $a$. Although I think it is fair to describe the RSM paradigm as molecular, saying so does not mean it is more reductionist than the others. It actually creates more flexible and nuanced empirical structures. It ends with five parameter estimates per attribute $a$ ($P_a, E_a, P_a^2, E_a^2$, and $P_a E_a$) that are eventually used to create functions that may or may not straddle the fit line.

As a point of contrast, rather than the $j * 5$ parameter estimates per attribute for each possible fit-to-outcome ($Y$) function that are part of Edward and Shipp's (chapter 7, this volume) RSM, the profile comparison method of Caldwell et al. (chapter 11.2, this volume) yields a single number collapsed across all $j$ attributes, regardless of the proposed outcomes of fit. The RSM techniques are unique in this way. They do not provide an index of fit so much as they provide an in-depth view of how particular regions of stipulated fit and misfit on each attribute are connected in different ways to different psychological consequences. With such data-driven forms, they seem especially useful for exploring and theory building, although they can and are used in conjunction with strong a priori predictions about the slopes and shapes of $Y = f(P_a, E_a, P_a^2, E_a^2$, and $P_a E_a)$.

Obviously, these techniques anchor another extreme in fit methodology. Rather than learning a little about a lot, which is a reasonable criticism of the bigger-picture, molar approaches, with RSM methods one learns a lot about a little, doing so in a one-spot-at-a-time fashion, and not allowing for a simultaneous look at the whole. Moreover, despite their rigor, they also require large sample sizes to bootstrap adequate standard error estimates, an issue that often vexes applied research.

Fit techniques borrowed from the diversity literature and outlined as heterogeneity measures by Harrison and Sin (chapter 11.4, this volume) share properties of all of these paradigms. But, they are best characterized as uniattribute and molecular. They deal with forms of PE fit wherein the $E$ side is constituted by other persons (mainly person-group [PG] fit, but some of the methods would apply to person-person [PP] fit as well). Still, such fit is indexed separately for each $a, b, c \ldots j$ under investigation. The same authors (Harrison & Sin, 2006) and others (Lau & Murnighan, 1998) spoke forcefully against aggregating attributes $a, b, c \ldots j$ either before or after computing the attribute-at-time indices (Chatman & Flynn, 2001).

One of their reasons is that the demographic features often used to theorize about and study interpersonal (mis)fit are measured variously on nominal, ordinal, interval, and ratio scales. Such scales have little meaning when they are summed across types.

On the other hand, there is another kind of combination going on behind the scenes. An assumption buried in their suggestions about PG fit is that commonly used indices (Blau's, Teachman's, Euclidean distance, and standard deviation) equally weight all of the $k-1$ "other" members of the group (multiple elements of $E$) that are outside the focal $P$. The same process is implicit in forming an average of (other) group members when operationalizing a unit- or organization-level measure for attribute $a$ ($E_a$) and that average can be part of the profile comparison or RSM techniques as well (Jansen & Kristof-Brown, 2005; O'Reilly et al., 1991).

## Choosing the Content of Fit Attributes

Obviously, fit theory should dictate the choice of attribute $a$ (and $b, c, \ldots j$; French et al., 1974). Several other chapters in this volume describe such theories of values, attitudes, orientations, abilities, personalities, goals, norms, and strategies (Ellis & Tsui, chap. 9, this volume; Gerhart, chap. 10, this volume), but it is a more subtle choice than might appear at first blush. Beyond being part of a uni- or multiattribute paradigm, $a, b, c, \ldots j$ should have commensurate content for the $P$ and $E$ domains. More specifically, the attributes need to have the same constitutive definition within each domain.

For example, if $P$ and $E$ are a subordinate's and supervisor's "value for innovation," then the researcher's verbal stipulation of the meaning for the construct must be the same for both parties. This is not to say that the supervisors and subordinates themselves will ascribe exactly the same lay meaning to the construct. Such a difference would be a source of misfit and could be captured empirically. Indeed, this example illustrates that PE research under the proposed definition would be the simplest and most straightforward to carry out when the same types of entities (e.g., individuals) are responding to the same types of instrumentation on both $P$ and $E$ sides of the fit equation.

Response-surface methodology (Edwards & Shipp, chapter 7, this volume) makes such simplicity explicit, but RSM would also appear to implicitly assume parallel measurement for $P$ and $E$. If measures were only t-equivalent across $P$ and $E$, a shift of the response surface into an "excess" or "deficiency" region might reflect a measurement artifact rather than a substantive finding. Similar arguments would come up about RSM slopes if measures were only congeneric across $P$ and $E$. Other, less elaborate regression technologies are not as restrictive or as sensitive in their conclusions to differences in operationalization.

Additional subtleties come up when $P$ and $E$ hold different levels of analysis. If a fit researcher were doing PG or person–organization (PO) comparisons—Ostroff and Shulte's (chapter 1, this volume) compositional fit—choices would be required about how the G or O level of attribute $a$ must be assessed to maintain commensurateness or isomorphism of meaning between the two sides of fit. One possibility with the value for innovation example above is to use the same instrumentation for everyone, but when comparing $P$ with $E$, average $k - 1$ (other person's) scores for $E$ and set it against the $k$th score for $P$. When doing so, evidence has to be mustered for using such a compositional model on the $E$ side (Chan, 1998). Another possibility is to have different referents in the two different instruments, one that refers to ego ($P$) and the other that refers to the alters ($E$) in the group or organization A referent–shift compositional model needs to be summoned under these circumstances (Klein, Conn, Smith, & Sorra, 2001). A third option would be to have the individual respond about himself or herself for the $P$ side but have the group or organization respond as a team, deciding each commensurate answer on the $E$ side in unison (an in vivo consensus model).

It is important to note here once more that rich variance on the $E$ side of all such enterprises is imperative. The larger a group or organization ($E$) from which multiple Ps are sampled, the more the $E_a$ value will approach a constant $K$ and the more that the discrepancy of the Ps discrepancy from that value will simply be a linear transformation: $P_a - E_a = P_a - K$. Any seeming effect of fit would really be an effect of $P$. However, having each $P$ sampled from each of a set of widely varying Es mitigates the problem (see also Ostroff & Harrison, 1999).

Guidelines for having commensurate PE attribute content might follow the prescriptions in attitude theory regarding target, action, context, and time (Ajzen & Fishbein, 1980). If different sources provide data on the $P$ and $E$ sides of the fit definition (see later), then attribute $a$ should be assessed at the same level of generality or specificity across those sides (Harrison, Newman, & Roth, 2006). When the attribute in question is a general attitude, value, or belief, then the target or stimulus of the $P$ and $E$ instruments should be identical. If the attribute is a(n expected) behavior pattern, then the specific activity, physical context, and time frame must be stated in equivalent ways, or used to design observational or archival measures for $a$.

All of these prescriptions should make sense when fit is cast as affinity or similarity between the levels of $P_a$ and $E_a$. However, further difficulties arise when fit is cast as interlock or complementarity between $P_a$ and $E_{a-}$, $P_{a-}$ and $E_a$, or compilational fit (Ostroff & Shulte, chap. 1, this volume) between vectors of missing and "filling" attributes. Defining a state of (amount of) missingness is not part of conventional research methods in applied psychology, except perhaps in job or task analysis. To do so requires knowledge of the normal or homeostatic condition of a PE system and then observing deviations from it, which in turn means having very deep knowledge of the entities and contexts under investigation. On the other hand, interlock-based measures might be as simple as asking sources from either the $E$ or $P$ side of the definition how much of attribute $a$ they are "missing" or that they "need," and then measuring how much the opposing $P$ or $E$ side carries attribute $a$. Because such probes of missingness or need beg an unspoken question of "for what?" and the likely answer to that question represents an unspoken theory of the effective functioning of the PE combination rather than of the fit construct per se, I am even more apprehensive about researchers pursuing this approach to fit.

## Choosing Sources of Data

If fit researchers are serious about a joint consideration of persons and environments, I believe it is vital that data come from separate observers or different occupants of these two different realms. At least a few other theorists and investigators share this belief (e.g., Roberts, Hulin, & Rousseau, 1978; Ostroff & Shulte, chapter 1, this volume). That is, from my outsider's viewpoint, fit methodology would seem to be optimal when researchers study what has been referred to as *objective fit* ($P$ and $E$ data on attributes $a, b, c \ldots j$ come from separate sources; French et al., 1974), rather than *subjective fit* ($P$ and $E$ data come from the same source, almost always $P$'s perceptions of $E$; see Kristof-Brown et al, 2005, for a similar discussion). Given well-known perceptual biases and self-report tendencies, subjective fit is likely to be a poor stand-in for objective fit (Cable & Judge, 1996; Harrison, McLaughlin, & Coalter, 1996), although it might be studied in its own right as an individual's phenomenology or implicit theory of fit (Cable & DeRue, 2002; Cable & Edwards, 2004; Edwards & Shipp, chapter 7, this volume).

To add to the confusion, other pairs of terms are sometimes used interchangeably with subjective (and objective) fit, but they have distinct meanings regarding data sources and processes under study. One of these pairs contrasts *direct* versus *indirect* assessments of fit (Kristof, 1996). Direct assessment follows the tenets of classical measurement theory, positing a latent construct of fit, cuing a source (again, virtually always the focal entity, $P$) to repeatedly provide to the researcher some noticed level of it. The researcher averages those responses to produce a numerical value for fit. Despite its positive-sounding label, *direct* assessment of fit is directly at odds with the definition staked out in this chapter and found with mild variations in the literature. The construct of fit is not direct or simple. It is combinatorial and complex. Therefore, fit itself is not subject to true-score architecture, although $P_a$, $E_a$, $P_b$, and $E_b$ could be. It would seem that the best measures of fit—those that provide (separate) estimates of $P_a$ and $E_a$, $P_b$ and $E_b$, and so forth—constitute what is currently referred to as an indirect assessment.

In other words, in typical methodological usage, direct measurement is generally regarded as unfettered and higher in construct validity. Indirect measurement is generally regarded as taking place at arm's length and probably ceding lower construct validity (Webb, Campbell, Schwartz, Sechrest, & Grove, 1981). The opposite seems to be true here, at least relative to fit's constitutive definition. Rather than forcing new entrants or existing customers in the fit store to puzzle over the incongruity of these terms while they fill their shopping carts with fit methods, I would ask that we discontinue these items and take their labels off the shelves. Direct and indirect assessment should go the way of Betamax and Pintos.

The last pair of terms reflecting data sources is *perceived* versus *actual* fit. Perceived fit is equivalent to a direct assessment. Actual fit is an indirect assessment, but it can measured via objective or subjective means (see earlier; French et al., 1974; Kristof-Brown et al., 2005; Ostroff & Shulte, chapter 1, this volume). Wuh? Not only am I lost in the fit supermarket, but I have a whanging headache.

It is not clear that a full factorial combination of these terms and their associated methodologies has appeared across the fit literature. Instead, there seem to be two basic approaches in use. The study of perceived fit seems to rely on many of the servings in the RSM meal described above. The same focal person tends to provide assessments of perceived levels of supplied or demanded levels of attributes in the environment (perceived $E$), as well as commensurate—needed or delivered—personal levels of that same attribute (e.g., Cable & Edwards, 2004; Edwards, 1996; Edwards & Harrison, 1993; Edwards & Rothbard, 1999). The dependent variables for fit also come from the same personal source. Authors in this stream are careful within their papers to mark their work as being about perceived fit (which is coupled with subjective estimates of fit components), the mental structure of, or the phenomenology of fit. Cognitive mechanisms appraising the *consonance, concordance,* or *correspondence* between perceived $E$ and felt $P$ are of primary interest. If that nomenclature is consistently used as a signal in article titles and abstracts, then some of the confusion about fit methods might be mitigated.

The second basic approach is the study of actual fit. The central construct is defined in terms of the compatible levels of commensurate attributes in $P$ and $E$, not in terms of their perceived (by $P$) compatibility by research participants. Those are the levels that need to be measured, ideally through means involving separate data sources within $P$ and $E$. *Objective fit* is an ostentatious term for such a measurement approach, but it meshes well with the aspirational tone of the term *actual fit*. If those purporting to study actual PE fit are hamstrung to use same-source, subjective measures of both sides, then personal phenomenologies of "what goes together" are likely to obscure findings. That is, researchers investigating actual fit might instead be tapping into implicit theories of how a favorable criterion $Y$, is maximized when $P_a$ and $E_a$ are matched. If $P_a$, $E_a$, and $Y$ were all measured at same time from same person, it might translate into spurious support for a fit theory regarding $P_a$, $E_a$, and $Y$ (or for fit theories that involve multiple attributes), as one might construe the comparative effect sizes in the Kristof-Brown et al. (2005) meta-analysis.

To counter potential pseudo-findings, time lags and palate-cleansing or *cognitive rebooting* techniques could be used to intervene between the individual-level measures of $P$ and $E$ attributes, as well as between those fit components and their hypothesized criterion, $Y$ (Harrison et al., 1996). If a researcher is studying fit at the team level and the team size is $k \geq 6$, he or she could nearly eliminate the same problem with a random, within-group split. A third of the members would report on $P$, another third on $E$, and the final third on $Y$ (Brown, Treviño, & Harrison, 2005; Ostroff, Kinicki, & Clark, 2002).

## Choosing Perfect Fit

If fit is a complex combination, what constitutes more or less of it? To answer that question, one must first define what constitutes the *most* fit. In one sense, the answer is trivial. Perfect or maximum fit is when $P_a = E_a$ for a single attribute or when $P_a = E1_a = E2_a = \ldots Ek_a$, which is perfect homogeneity or a 0 standard deviation for PG fit or heterogeneity measures (Harrison & Sin, chap. 11.4, this volume). Each of these might also be regarded as perfect fit in a molecular paradigm. For multiple attributes, it is the combinatorial state of $[(P_a, P_b, P_c, \ldots P_j) \cap (E_a, E_b, E_c, \ldots E_j)]$ where there are zero differences across commensurate $P$ and $E$ attributes: $P_a = E_a$, $P_b = E_b$, $\ldots$ and $P_j = E_j$. It occurs mathematically when there is an identical vector of $P_{abc\ldots j}$ and $E_{abc\ldots j}$ in $j$ dimensional space.

There is a small wrinkle in the fabric of this space, and it occurs in molar paradigms. When absolute or squared distances between multiattribute $P_{abc\ldots j}$ and $E_{abc\ldots j}$ vectors (it is helpful to mentally pictures them as arrows) are calculated as the operator $\cap$ of (mis)fit, the stipulation of perfect fit is tied very tightly with its operationalization. Zero distance equals perfect fit. However, when a correlation is calculated between $P_{abc\ldots j}$ and $E_{abc\ldots j}$, it could indicate perfect fit ($r = 1.0$) when scores are not identical (technically, one might argue that $r = 1.0$ is perfect supplementary/affinity fit and $r = -1.0$ is perfect complementary/interlock fit, but I am not aware of such a treatment in the literature).

A correlation is the cosine of an angle between two vectors. If the vectors point in exactly the same direction, the correlation between them is unity; it does not reflect sizes of difference or distances between the vectors. The vectors could lie on top of one another, but one could be shorter or longer ($P_{abc\ldots j}$ and $E_{abc\ldots j}$ are a constant multiple of one another), and the correlation of $r = 1.0$ would still indicate perfect fit. Similarly, the origin of the $P_{abc...j}$ or $E_{abc...j}$ vector could be displaced ($P_{abc...j}$ or $E_{abc...j}$ is "shifted" over from the other, yet still be parallel in space; $P$ and $E$ are an additive constant away from one another), but the correlation would be $r = 1.0$ as well. In sum, even when $E$ is consistently higher or lower than $P$ across attributes, a correlation can indicate seemingly perfect fit.

The general form of the profile comparison techniques of Caldwell et al. (chapter 11.2, this volume) is susceptible to this wrinkle, but they iron it out by using ranks of attributes, creating an ipsative measure of each attribute's importance that is bounded by 1 and $j$ on both the $P$ and $E$ side of the fit aisle. Other researchers who might use ratings instead of ranks for fitting $a, b, c \ldots j$ profiles of $P$ and $E$ attributes would need to perform within-$P$ and within-$E$ standardization of those ratings—for every entity and environment sampled—to avoid the $r = 1.0$ indeterminacy. Yet, by doing so, differences between $P$ and $E$ on the attributes would already have been reduced (recalling a similar problem in the area of interrater agreement versus interrater reliability; Kozlowski & Hattrup, 1992). Or, the usually meager variance on the $E$ side of the fit equation would be "stretched" to look as though it were just as large as the $P$ side, absolving researchers of the task of doing broad environmental sampling (something Mumford and Espejo, chapter 11.5, this volume, hope researchers would counter with their methods). In any case, if absolute magnitudes of $a, b, c \ldots j$ matter, investigators should knowingly stipulate whether the more accommodating latter definition or the more stringent former definition constitutes perfect fit for them.

One final word of caution about the state of fit nirvana has been repeatedly noted by Edwards and colleagues (e.g., Edwards, 1995). Geometrically, perfect fit is a line and not a point for any attribute $a$. It is a hyperplane for $a, b, c \ldots j$. This does not change the definition of maximum fit per se. It does, however, have implications for the outcomes of fit. An entity ($P$) needing $100 and receiving $100 from the environment ($E$) might go through substantially different psychological reactions than an entity needing $10,000 and receiving $10,000. That is, outcomes might be higher (or lower) when the level of the attribute is higher (or lower). Molar approaches to fit cannot discriminate among those reactions, because they occur under what is treated as a constant independent variable. An even more elaborate argument applies to different ranges of misfit that are given the same numerical value. I turn to those next.

## Choosing a Metric for Misfit

The basic question that fit researchers need to answer at this stage of their design is, What operations should I perform and what metric should I use in ascribing numbers to misfit? The above discussion implies that under the molecular paradigms, perfect fit tends be given the value 0 and for the molar paradigms it is given a 1. When one is talking about misfit, it tends to be easier to adopt the first standard. Zero is perfect fit and minimum misfit. On the other hand, it is not so easy to define maximum misfit (minimum fit).

Logically, misfit occurs when any attribute $a$ is different for $P$ and $E$, and the largest amount of misfit on that attribute should occur when $P_a$ and $E_a$ are as different as possible. Theoretically, if $a$ is on an unbounded, psychological continuum, then the largest difference might be positive infinity. Empirically, the largest such difference occurs when $E$ and $P$ are at opposite ends of $a$'s range of operationalization (or the largest possible difference in the scale range). Under such circumstances, choices of (mis)fit metrics include absolute distances ($|P_a - E_a|$), signed distances ($P_a - E_a$), and squared distances ($P_a - E_a)^2$ (see also Venkatraman, 1989) Each of these metrics involves algebraic assumptions that have been fully vetted in the methodological work on difference scores (e.g., Edwards, 1991). Squared (Euclidean) distances are the metric underlying the molar approaches of Caldwell et al. (chapter 11.2, this volume) and Mumford and Espejo (chapter 11.5, this volume) and some of the of heterogeneity indices outlined by Harrison and Sin (chapter 11.4, this volume).

As the latter authors note, even these distances are not necessarily comparable across attributes $a, b, c \ldots j$, unless the attributes are all measured on the same metric. That is, if $a$ is the personality dimension of agreeableness, measured on Goldberg's (2006) International Personality Item Pool scales, but $j$ is perceived justice of organizational procedures (Colquitt, 2001), the endpoints for $a$ and $j$ are quite different and the misfit numbers for those attributes would not be commensurate, because the scales themselves differ. In a related way, when studying PG fit, a person's misfit from the rest of his or her unit members can be affected by team size. If an investigator stays with a molar approach, standardization to a common distance would once again be called for, cautiously, across attributes and team sizes. Rather than converting all $P$ and $E$ to within-entity $z$-scores (forcing every person or every environment to have an across-attribute standard deviation of 1.0) a meeker form of standardization might be possible. A linear transformation of each attribute to have the same scale endpoints (the same hypothetical maximum and minimum on $a, b, c \ldots j$), and therefore, the same range, would roughly equate distances without cutting each $P$ and each $E$ into the same cookie of equal observed variance.

Even with such standardization, however, there is still consternation about what a single, molar estimate of misfit means across several PE attributes. The problem is one of equifinality. Typically, if a researcher aggregates across attributes, as in the profile comparison approach, signs of PE differences are lost. If so, and even with just two attributes, maximum misfit can occur in four different ways. Consider $a$ (low) and $a$ (high) to be the lower bound and upper bound, respectively, of attribute $a$. Similar notation can apply to attribute $j$. Now consider four possibilities:

1. $[P_a(low), P_j(low)] \cap [E_a(high), E_j(high)]$
2. $[P_a(low), P_j(high)] \cap [E_a(high), E_j(low)]$
3. $[P_a(high), P_j(low)] \cap [E_a(low), E_j(high)]$
4. $[P_a(high), P_j(high)] \cap [E_a(low), E_j(low)]$.

If absolute or squared distance is used as a misfit metric across attributes (e.g. Venkatraman, 1989), all four of these possibilities reveal maximum misfit, even though a casual observer might argue that argue that all of these conditions are whoppingly different. Complex combinations of perhaps asymmetric misfit across attributes yield a single, simple, symmetric index.

Researchers sold on the molecular, RSM approach might be tempted to add "deceivingly" to the adjectives describing that simple molar index. Person 1 is in a doubly excess situation (Edwards & Shipp, chapter 7, this volume); the environment is providing much more than what he or she wants, needs, or has on $a$ and $j$. Person 4 is in a doubly deficient situation. The environment is providing much less than he or she wants, needs, or has. Any psychological theory built to address circumstances related to these (e.g., Adams, 1963; Kahneman & Tversky, 1979) would predict starkly different psychological frames of mind for Persons 1 and 4, despite both being ascribed the same overall value of misfit. Yet, it must also be stated that several of those theories and the RSM approach in general would also not provide unique a priori predictions for Person 2 versus Person 3, because they do not handle simultaneous, cross-cutting forms of such differences.

A final caveat applies to both molar and molecular approaches. The choice of an overall distance or response surface presupposes at least an interval level of measurement for $a$. However, for categorical (usually demographic) attributes of $P$ and $E$, there is no distance metric beyond same (0) versus different (1). Little has been done to explore these types of discontinuous differences. Larger or smaller values of individual-level categorical indices merely reflect the relative proportion of alters that differ from the ego, masking what might be markedly distinct psychological states of misfit. For example, if race or ethnicity is the fit attribute in question, an African American ($P$) would show the same number of differences from a group ($E$) of four other White members, as he or she would from a group that also contains one White, one Hispanic, one Asian, and one Native American member. At some point, a more sophisticated, multivariate form of accounting for these different patterns is necessary (see Riordan & Shore, 1997, for the first steps under the rubric of demographic diversity rather than fit).

## Choosing Outcomes

As with the choice of attribute content, the choice of dependent constructs for fit investigations relies obviously and primarily on theory. Yet, some of the same threads running through the prior choices can be found here as well. Molar approaches tend to make the single index of fit predict larger, broader, and more distal patterns of entity ($P$) attitudes and behavior when there are high amounts of fit. Some of the main predictions are well known, such as individuals being happier with their jobs, more socially integrated with their peers, and more committed to their organizations when they have high PE fit (in this case, person–organization fit: Chatman, 1989). They are also less likely to quit (Caldwell & O'Reilly, 1990).

Those researchers following molecular approaches tend to make more focused predictions about more proximal criteria. When $E$ supplies $P$'s needed amount of $a$, $P$ tends to perceive more PE fit on $a$ and is more satisfied with $a$ as a dimension of work life (French, Caplan, & Harrison, 1982). More recent studies have extended the outcome variables to somewhat broader outcomes (Cable & Edwards, 2004; Edwards & Rothbard, 1993). Again, however, prediction of each outcome involves a different response surface for fit and another 5 (* $j$) parameter estimates, making steep demands on sample size.

The normal exhortations for rigorous research are just as important for PE fit studies as for all studies. I will not dwell on them, although my vague impression is that such studies sometimes get a pass on the dependent side of the ledger for being so elaborate in their treatment of the independent (fit) side. Still, *dependent constructs* should be operationalized at a time and contact definition that is far enough removed from the fit measures to minimize cognitive carryover (Podsakoff, MacKenzie, Lee, & Podsakoff, 2003) but near enough for the causal forces to still be active (Harrison & Hulin, 1989). Predictions about behavioral outcomes of PE fit are riskier and seen as more valuable than predictions about perceptual or affective outcomes. Large samples of $P$ entities who have experienced the formative stimuli ($E$) in their environments are good—necessary even, if one is moving through the supermarket queue toward the register of the molecular approach. Longitudinal studies with multiple data sources are preferred to cross-sectional studies with single data sources. Single-item measures of $Y$ are bad. So are cigarettes.

## CONCLUSION AND FURTHER INSTIGATION

### Summary

I have tried to argue (perhaps unsuccessfully) that, when pitching fit, it is at its most logically defensible and empirically researchable, when defined as a complex, PE construct rather than as an overarching theory. I have suggested a tightening of the definition of fit to be the compatibility of joint values of one or more attributes, $a$, $b$, $c$, ... $j$, of a focal entity ($P$) and a commensurate set of attribute values, $a$, $b$, $c$, ... $j$, of the entity's environment ($E$): $[(P_a, P_b, P_c, \ldots P_j) \cap (E_a, E_b, E_c, \ldots E_j)]$. That state of compatibility most likely refers to similarity or affinity in the pairs of $P \cap E$ values. A steady stream of work operates under the premise that compatibility can be interlock (complementarity) of missingness on one side that is filled in by the other, although its operationalization gets trickier under the latter notion. Commensurateness or equivalent content definitions of $a$ (and $b$ and $c$ .... and $j$) across the $P$ and $E$ domains is vital for restricting fit research to refer to a particular class of constructs rather than all $P \times E$ interactions.

Fit is not the internal consistency or coherence of several content attributes within $P$ or $E$. It is not a lay perception, although perceived fit (I prefer an entirely different term such as *consonance*) is a construct in its own. Instead, it is a stipulated (by scholars), elaborate configuration of the levels of parallel variables in two domains. Most importantly, although there are theories of what leads to fit and what fit leads to, fit itself is not a model of how $P$ and $E$ jointly produce higher levels of a desired criterion, $Y$. Fit is not good or bad, but it can cause good or bad consequences. It is instead a combinatorial (and often multivariate) state of $P$ and $E$ that could produce higher or lower levels of $Y$, or be completely unrelated to $Y$. That is, fit is not a paradigm that equates greater fit with greater explained variance in $Y$ by $P$ and $E$.

To be sure, there are multiple paradigms for studying fit. They fall under two basic approaches, which I have termed molar or molecular bundles of fit methods. When one is following such approaches, six choices must be made explicit. They reflect assumptions about the meaning of fit, and they underscore some paradoxes of simplicity and complexity. The first choice already tends to bifurcate the paradigms, with multiattribute ($j$ at a time) approaches taking the broad, molar path, and uniattribute (1 at a time) approaches taking the deep, molecular path. The second choice is about the content of attributes, and it should follow directly from one's theory about fit. That content specification needs to include tight, commensurate statements of what $a$ ($b$, $c$, ... $j$) constitute in the $P$ and $E$ domains. The third choice is currently obscured by a number of confusing terms, but it should boil down to whether a researcher is interested in the cognitive representation or phenomenology of subjective and perceived fit versus the operation of objective and actual fit. Studies of the latter are improved by getting estimates of attribute levels from separate sources in the $P$ and $E$ domains. The fourth choice, which I think could and should be routinely stated by researchers in their papers, deals with how maximum or perfect fit is specifically defined. The fifth choice is linked firmly to the fourth, as it involves a decision about how to define maximum *mis*fit, and thereby the range and metric of the (mis)fit continuum being used in a particular study. Those first five choices are likely to lead to sharply different sets of designs and analyses, each of which might follow the contours of profile-comparison versus response-surface methods. The sixth choice—of criterion constructs—is less prepackaged with methodology and is more a reflection of the substantive theory that is driving the investigation at hand. Not working through these choices can have serious and negative consequences for a fit investigation, because the construct is so complex and the paradigms are so multifaceted.

## So What Is Left That's Interesting About Fit?

That may seem like a silly question, especially if it is addressed to those who have picked up this volume. But, I'm afraid that my chapter has taken a fair amount of the wind out of the sails of fit studies and replaced it with my own hot air. Confusion about the boundaries of a research area often comes with intrigue, and a vast space in which to maneuver as a scholar. The proposed definition and my recipe of choices are meant to allay confusion, but they might just as well drum much of the intrigue out and remove many of the joyful degrees for freedom from fit scholarship. I have tried to reduce the size and reorganize much of the layout of the fit store.

Therefore, let me highlight a handful of the many interesting questions that might still be addressed within those somewhat narrower confines. Fit as interlock is, in some ways, non- or even counterintuitive. Environments and persons are always missing some attributes, but we tend not to study them if they are not requisite for task performance. Adding members to teams with different or new knowledge might sometimes fill a void that the team did not know existed. Does the attribute for which there is missingness need to be salient (to $P$ or $E$) for it to be part of complementary fit? Being in tune to what is *not* there in a person or environment requires novel thinking and less intrusive research methods.

That thought leads to other questions. What attribute realms—$l, m \ldots p$—are legitimate sources of (mis)fit (see Higgins, 2000, for a clever, relatively new example)? Do theories propose forms of fit that we have been reticent to pursue as investigators? One such form that psychologists tend to rue deals with physical features. Beyond the effects of race, gender, or ethnicity, does being short, obese, or disabled in a work team that is populated by like (fit) versus unlike (misfit) others have an impact on cohesiveness and task performance? Presuming reasonable measures can be constructed, how about fit on a general dimension of physical attractiveness? What about fit on the extravagance or simplicity of organizational dress?

I have stipulated above that fit need not be good. Theories that predict negative consequences of fit would attract a great deal of attention because they not only deny but also contradict the existing assumption base. Do negative consequences of fit exist as Schneider, Smith and Goldstein (2000) suggested? Do they differ among job, team, or organization types? Likewise, fit might be so constraining that it engenders a needs for specialization, highlighting of unique characteristics, or an urge to move to a level of *optimal distinctiveness* from one's peers (Brewer, 1991).

Contexts in which creative or innovative products are developed friction of misfit to spark new ideas. That is, less fit could be predicted to have some positive consequences under particular conditions. Such a prediction might be tested with archival data from jazz, pop, or rock bands, and compared with data from sports teams (e.g., basketball) for whom a high level of task interdependence and synchronization characterizes their work.

See? Shopping for fit theories and methods can still be fun. Following my recommendations might mean the effort-prices have risen. I hope the mark-up is worth it in knowledge value.

## REFERENCES

Adams, J. S. (1963). Toward an understanding of inequity. *Journal of Abnormal and Social Psychology, 67,* 422–436.

Ajzen, I., & Fishbein, M. (1980). *Understanding attitudes and predicting social behavior.* Englewood Cliffs, NJ: Prentice-Hall.

Ashby, W. R. (1956). *Introduction to cybernetics.* London; Wiley.

Brewer, M. B. (1991). The social self: On being the same and different at the same time. *Personality and Social Psychology Bulletin, 17,* 475–482.

Brown, M. E., Treviño, L. K., & Harrison, D. A. (2005). Ethical leadership: A social learning theory perspective for construct development. *Organizational Behavior and Human Decision Processes, 97,* 117–134.

Byrne, D. (1971). *The attraction paradigm.* New York: Academic Press.

Cable, D. M., & DeRue, S. (2002). The construct convergent and discriminant validity of subjective fit perceptions. *Journal of Applied Psychology, 87,* 875–884.

Cable, D. M., & Edwards, J. R. (2004). Complementary and supplementary fit: A theoretical and empirical investigation. *Journal of Applied Psychology, 89,* 822–834.

Cable, D. M., & Judge, T. A. (1996). Person-organizational fit, job choice, decisions, and organizational entry. *Organizational Behavioral Human Decision Processes, 67,* 294–311.

Caplan, R. D. (1987). Person-environment fit theory: Commensurate dimensions, time perspectives, and mechanisms. *Journal of Vocational Behavior, 31,* 248–267.

Caldwell, D. F., & O'Reilly, C. A. (1990). Measuring person–job fit using a profile comparison process. *Journal of Applied Psychology, 75,* 648–657.

Chan, D. (1998). Functional relations among constructs in the same content domain at different levels of analysis: A typology of composition models. *Journal of Applied Psychology, 83,* 234–246.

Chatman, J. A. (1989). Improving interactional organizational research: A model of person-organization fit. *Academy of Management Review, 14,* 333–349.

Chatman, J. A. (1991). Matching people and organizations: Selection and socialization in public accounting firms. *Administrative Science Quarterly, 36,* 459–484.

Chatman, J. A., & Flynn, F. J. (2001). The influence of demographic heterogeneity on the emergence and consequences of cooperative norms in work teams. *Academy of Management Journal, 44,* 956–974.

Colquitt, J. A. (2001). On the dimensionality of organizational justice: A construct validation of a measure. *Journal of Applied Psychology, 86,* 386–400.

Dawis, R. V., & Lofquist, L. H. (1984). *A psychological theory of work adjustment.* Minneapolis, MN: University of Minnesota Press.

Doty, D. H., & Glick, W. H. (1993). Fit, equifinality, and organizational effectiveness: A test of two configurational theories. *Academy of Management Journal, 36,* 1196–1251.

Drazin, R., & Van de Ven, A. H. (1986). Alternative forms of fit in contingency theory. *Administrative Science Quarterly, 30,* 514–539.

Edwards, J. R. (1991). Person–job fit: A conceptual integration, literature review, and methodological critique. *International Review of Industrial/Organizational Psychology, 6,* 283–357.

Edwards, J. R. (1995). Alternatives to difference scores as dependent variables in the study of congruence in organizational research. *Organizational Behavior and Human Decision Processes, 64,* 307–324.

Edwards, J. R. (1996). An examination of competing versions of the person-environment fit approach to stress. *Academy of Management Journal, 39,* 292–339.

Edwards, J. R., & Harrison, R. V. (1993). Job demands and worker health: Three-dimensional reexamination of the relationship between person–environment fit and strain. *Journal of Applied Psychology, 78,* 628–648.

Edwards, J. R., & Rothbard, N. P. (1999). Work and family stress and well-being: An examination of person–environment fit in the work and family domains. *Organizational Behavior and Human Decision Processes, 77,* 85–129.

Endler, N. S., & Magnusson, D. (1976). *Interactional psychology and personality.* New York: Wiley.

Festinger, L. (1957). *A theory of cognitive dissonance.* Stanford, CA: Stanford University Press.

French J. R. P. Jr., & Caplan, R., D., & Harrison, R. V. (1982). *The mechanisms of job stress and strain.* New York: Wiley.

French, J. R. P., Jr., Rogers, W., & Cobb, S. (1974). Adjustment as person–environment fit. In D. A. H. G. V. Coelho & J. E. Adams (Eds), *Coping and adaptation* (pp. 316–333). New York: Basic Books.

Goldberg, L. R. (2006). *International personality item pool: A scientific collaboratory for the development of advanced measures of personality and other individual differences.* Retrieved April 2006, from http://ipip.ori.org/ipip/.

Hackman, J. R., & Oldham, G. R. (1976). Motivation through the design of work: Test of a theory. *Organizational Behavior and Human Performance, 16,* 250–279.

Harrison, D. A. (2002). Meaning and measurement of work role withdrawal: Current controversies and future fallout under changing technology. In M. Koslowsky & M. Krausz (Eds.), *Voluntary employee withdrawal and inattendance: A current perspective* (pp. 95–132). London: Plenum Publishing.

Harrison, D. A., & Hulin, C. L. (1989). Investigations of absenteeism: Using event history models to study the absence-taking process. *Journal of Applied Psychology, 74,* 300–316.

Harrison, D. A., & Klein, K. J. (in press). What's the difference? Diversity constructs as separation, variety, or disparity in organizations. *Academy of Management Review.*

Harrison, D. A., McLaughlin, M. E., & Coalter, T. M. (1996). Context, cognition, and common method variance: Psychometric and verbal protocol evidence. *Organizational Behavior and Human Decision Processes, 68,* 246–261.

Harrison, D. A., Newman, D. A., & Roth, P. L. (2006). How important are job attitudes?: Meta-analytic comparisons for integrative behavioral outcomes and time sequences. *Academy of Management Journal, 49,* 305–326.

Harrison, D. A., & Sin, H.-S. (2006). What is diversity and how should it be measured? In A. M. Konrad, P. Prasad, & J. K. Pringle (Eds.), *Handbook of workplace diversity* (pp. 191–216).Newbury Park, CA: Sage.

Harrison, R. V. (1978). Person–environment fit and job stress. In C. L. Cooper & R. Payne (Eds.), *Stress at work* (pp. 175–205). New York: Wiley.

Henderson, J. C., & Verkatraman, N. (1989). *Strategic alignment: A framework for strategic information technology management.* Cambridge, MA: Center for Information Systems Research, Sloan School of Management, Massachusetts Institute of Technology.

Higgins, E. T. (2000). Making a good decision: Value from fit. *American Psychologist, 55,* 12–17–1230.

Hulin, C. L., Drasgow, F., & Parsons, C. K. (1983). *Item response theory: Application to psychological measurement.* Homewood, IL: Dow Jones-Irwin.

Jansen, K. J., & Kristof-Brown, A. L. (2005). Marching to the beat of a different drummer: Examining the impact of pacing congruence. *Organizational Behavior and Human Decision Processes, 97,* 93–102.

Jarvis, C. B., MacKenzie, S. B., & Podsakoff, P. M. (2003). A critical review of construct indicators and measurement model misspecification in marketing and consumer research. *Journal of Consumer Research, 30,* 199–218.

Kahneman, D., & Tversky, A. (1979). Prospect theory: An analysis of decision under risk. *Econometrica, 47,* 263–291.

Kayende, U., Roberts, J. H., Lilien, G. L., & Fong, K. H. (in press). Mapping the bounds of incoherence: How far can you go and how does it affect your brand? *Marketing Science.*

Klein, K. J., Conn, A. B., Smith, D. B., & Sorra, J. S. (2001). Is everyone in agreement? An exploration of within-group agreement in employee perceptions of the work environment. *Journal of Applied Psychology, 86,* 3–16.

Kristof, A. L. (1996). Person-organization fit: An integrative review of its conceptualizations, measurement, and implications. *Personnel Psychology, 49,* 1–49.

Kristof-Brown, A. L., Zimmerman, R. D., & Johnson, E. C. (2005). Consequences of individuals' fit at work: A meta-analysis of person–job, person–organization, person–group, and person–supervisor fit. *Personnel Psychology, 58,* 281–343.

Kozlowski, S. W. J., & Hattrup, K. (1992). A disagreement about within-group agreement: Disentangling issues of consistency versus consensus. *Journal of Applied Psychology, 77,* 161–167.

Lakatos, I. (1970). Falsification and the methodology of scientific research programs. In I. Lakatos and A. Musgrave (Eds.), *Criticism and the growth of knowledge* (pp. 91–196). Cambridge: Cambridge University Press.

Lau, D. C., & Murnighan, J. K. (1998). Demographic diversity and faultlines: The compositional dynamics of organizational groups. *Academy of Management Review, 23,* 325–340.

Locke, E. A. (2003). Good definitions: The epistemological foundation of scientific progress. In J. Greenberg (Ed.), *Organizational behavior: The state of the science* (pp. 415–444). Mahwah, NJ: Lawrence Erlbaum Associates.

McGrath, J. E. (1982). Dilemmatics: The study of research choices and dilemmas. In J. E. McGrath, J. Martin, & R. A. Kulka (Eds.), *Judgment calls in research* (pp. 69–102). Beverly Hills, CA: Sage.

Meyers-Levy, J., & Tybout, A. (1989). Schema congruity as a basis for product evaluation. *Journal of Consumer Research, 16,* 39–54.

Muchinsky, P. M., & Monahan, C. J. (1987). What is person-environment congruence? Supplementary versus complimentary models of fit. *Journal of Vocational Behavior, 31,* 268–277.

Murphy, G. L., & Medin, D. L. (1985). The role of theories in conceptual coherence. *Psychological Review, 92,* 289–316.

O'Reilly, C. A., Chatman, J. A., & Caldwell, D. F. (1991). People and organizational culture: A profile comparison approach to assessing person-organization fit. *Academy of Management Journal, 34,* 487–516.

Ostroff, C., & Harrison, D. A. (1999). Meta-analysis, level of analysis, and best estimates of population correlations: Cautions for interpreting meta-analytic results in organizational behavior. *Journal of Applied Psychology, 84,* 260–270.

Ostroff, C., Kinicki, A. J., & Clark, M. A. (2002). Substantive and operational issues of response bias across levels of analysis: An example of climate-satisfaction relationships. *Journal of Applied Psychology, 87,* 355–368.

Ostroff, C., Shin, Y., & Kinicki, A. J. (2005). Multiple perspectives of congruence: Relationships between value congruence and employee attitudes. *Journal of Organizational Behavior, 26,* 591–623.

Podsakoff, P. M., MacKenzie, S. M., Lee, J., & Podsakoff, N. P. (2003). Common method variance in behavioral research: A critical review of the literature and recommended remedies. *Journal of Applied Psychology, 88,* 879–903.

Popper, K. R. (1963). *Conjectures and refutations.* London: Routledge.

Rehder, B., & Hastie, R. (2004). Category coherence and category based property induction, *Cognition, 91,* 113–153.

Riordan, C. M., & Shore, L. M. (1997). Demographic diversity an employee attitudes: An empirical examination of relational demography within work units. *Journal of Applied Psychology, 82,* 342–358.

Roberts, K. H., Hulin, C. L., & Rousseau, D. M. (1978). *Developing an interdisciplinary science of organizations.* San Francisco: Jossey-Bass.

Schwab, D. P. (1980). Construct validity in organizational behavior. In L. L. Cummings & B. M. Staw (Eds.), *Research in organizational behavior* (Vol. 2, pp. 3–43). Greenwich, CT: JAI Press.

Schneider, B. (1987). The people make the place. *Personnel Psychology, 40,* 437–453.

Schneider, B. (2001). Fits about fit. *Applied Psychology: An International Review, 50,* 141–152.

Schneider, B., Goldstein, H. W., & Smith, D. B. (1995). The ASA framework: An update. *Personnel Psychology, 48,* 747–773.

Schneider, B., Kristof,-Brown, A. L., Goldstein, H. W., & Smith, D. B. (1997). What is this thing called fit? In N. R. Anderson & P. Herriott (Eds.), *International handbook of selection and appraisal* (pp. 393–412). London: Wiley.

Schneider, B., Smith, D. B., & Goldstein, H. W. (2000). Attraction–selection attrition: Toward a person–environment psychology of organizations. In. W. B. Walsh, K. H. Craik, & R. H. Price (Eds.), *Person–environment psychology* (pp. 25–60). Mahwah, NJ: Lawrence Erlbaum Associates.

Van Vianen, A. E. M. (2000). Person–organization fit: The match between newcomers' and recruiters' preferences for organizational cultures. *Personnel Psychology, 53,* 113–150.

Venkatraman, N. (1989). The concept of fit in strategy research: Toward verbal and statistical correspondence. *Academy of Management Review, 14,* 423–444.

Webb, E. J., Campbell, D. T., Schwartz, R. D., Sechrest, L. J., & Grove, J. B. (1981) *Nonreactive measures in the social sciences.* (2nd ed.). New York: Houghton Mifflin.

# PART III

# *Concluding Remarks*

The final chapter in this volume provides a commentary on each chapter. In addition, new insights to guide fit research in the upcoming years are offered.

# CHAPTER 13

# The Future of Person–
# Organization Fit Research:
# Comments, Observations,
# and a Few Suggestions

Timothy A. Judge
*University of Florida*

This is both an exciting—and somewhat troubling—time to be doing fit research. It is exciting because one sees a body of literature that has established a solid base in organizational psychology and is both deepening its roots and branching out into new directions. It is troubling because some of the contributions in the past decade or so have suggested a certain *methodological stalemate* (Larson & Csikszentmihalyi, 1983) in fit research. Both of these elements, the notes of optimism and of pessimism, I believe, are suggested by the chapters in this volume. In this concluding chapter, I offer a few thoughts on each chapter and end by noting some issues, quandaries, questions, and future directions that I believe deserve attention by fit researchers.

Before digging in, however, I want to express two notes of thanks. First, I want to thank Cheri Ostroff for being a wonderful collaborator. Cheri was the genesis of this book, and throughout she has displayed a remarkable mix of initiative, diligence, patience, and enthusiasm. In my experience, this constellation of qualities is unusual, and I am glad to have had the chance to work with her. Second, as Cheri and I noted in the preface, we are grateful to the contributors to this volume. As even a causal reader of the fit literature knows, this set of authors is a real *tour de force* of contributors. It has been a joy to read their work.

# COMMENTARY ON CHAPTERS

## Ostroff and Schulte: Levels of Analysis and Fit

The first chapter, by Ostroff and Schulte, takes a levels of analysis approach to fit. Ostroff was ahead of her time in thinking about levels of analysis issues in the fit literature (Ostroff, 1992; Ostroff & Schmitt, 1993), so there is no better person to tackle this complex area. As Ostroff and Schulte note, most research on fit has bifurcated into micro and macro areas, with the former being more voluminous than the latter. In one sense, this is surprising because perhaps the dominant perspective on person–organization fit is Schneider's (1987) attraction–selection–attrition (ASA) model, which incorporates both micro and macro perspectives (see Schneider, Smith, Taylor, & Fleenor, 1998). On the other hand, the micro–macro divide is a deep one in social science (Bar-Tal, 2006; Goldspink & Kay, 2004), and in this sense it is no surprise that fit research has experienced a similar chasm. One has to be excited by the authors' effort to bridge this gap.

Ostroff and Schulte do an excellent job of providing a brief review of the history of person–environment and person–organization fit research. Then they move to their real mission—to provide some much needed integration of the micro and macro perspectives to bridge this aforementioned gp. To do so, they introduce some terms, some old (person–job fit) and some new (person–person compilation and person–individual fit). These terms vary by target or level (depending on whether the person is fitting to a job, to a work group, etc.), by mode (person–person, person–situation, and situation–situation), and by type (supplementary and complimentary). This is challenging stuff, and I give Ostroff and Schulte credit for their effort to integrate the extant terms and concepts of fit. I must confess some amount of confusion about the interrelationships among the categories and terms, and one might arrange or conceptualize the concepts differently. However, as in the case of a recent integrative work (Edwards, Cable, Williamson, Lambert, & Shipp, 2006), one sees great value in attempting to draw some boundaries around fit concepts and then trying to establish links among them. There are many important insights to be gained from a careful reading of the chapter. Although (given their efforts at integration) the authors might disagree, given the complexity of the model and the alternative conceptualizations possible, I think research that tests their concepts by tearing off bites at a time might prove most useful. I hope that researchers will draw inspiration from their integrative efforts and test these concepts: a few efforts would advance the fit literature further.

## Higgins and Freitas: Regulatory Fit

Although the general premise of person–environment interactionism—that individuals and their environment exist in mutual interaction—is hardly a new concept in psychology, there have been surprisingly few theoretical statements that specify exactly how this interaction takes place. Higgins' (2000, 2005) regulatory focus theory is thus an important addition to psychology, as evidenced by its application to many areas of psychological science in just the past few years, such as romantic relationships (Roese et al., 2006), test-taking performance (Keller & Bless, 2006), interracial interactions (Trawalter & Richeson, 2006), reactions to antismoking advertisements (Kim, 2006), consumer preferences (Yeo & Park, 2006), affect and decision-making (Leone, Perugini, & Bagozzi, 2005), negotiation (Galinsky, Leonardelli, & Okhuysen, 2005), and cross-cultural differences in motivation (Lockwood, Marshall, & Sadler, 2005). This is a theory that is being applied to myriad psychological and social–psychological processes, and the link to the person–organization fit literature is an obvious but relatively unexplored one.

Indeed, although one might see regulatory focus theory fitting under the umbrella of approach–avoidance motivation, which is attracting renewed interest (e,g., Centerbar & Clore, 2006; Elliot, Gable, & Mapes, 2006; Updegraff, Gable, & Taylor, 2004), what is unique about Higgins' work is that it places motivation in a fit context. Specifically, according to regulatory focus theory, promotion-focus striving (working toward a goal with a sense of hope and eagerness—from a sense of "feeling right") is oriented toward bringing the actual self in line with the *ideal* self, whereas prevention focus striving (working toward a goal from a sense of duty and vigilance—from a sense of "feeling wrong") seeks to bring the actual self in line with the *ought* self. What is intriguing about regulatory focus theory is that it is not merely whether a goal is attained; how it is attained matters (in this way it is similar to the self-concordance model [Sheldon & Elliot, 1999]). In a real sense, this is a radical shift in thinking. As Higgins and Freitas noted, since the "cognitive revolution" in the 1960s, there has been considerable attention paid toward goal strivings. The implicit assumption of these various literatures is that the objective is goal attainment. Although regulatory focus theory does not deny the potential relevance of goal attainment, it indeed shifts focus from outcome (goal attainment) to process (reasons underlying goal striving).

Another exciting aspect of regulatory focus theory is the diverse way in which its effects have been tested, beyond the array of topical areas noted earlier: There have been both within-individual and between-individual designs, both direct and indirect measures, laboratory studies and field studies, experimental and correlational designs, and regulatory focus measured as experienced (i.e., self-reported) and regulatory focus induced (e.g., manipulated similar to framing effects in prospect theory). Although the results are not always fully consistent, in general, the results support the view that promotion focus is associated with more positive thoughts and feelings and prevention focus with more negative thoughts and feelings.

What is somewhat surprising, though, is the limited degree to which any of this work is associated with the person–environment or person–organization fit literature. There is a reason for this. As we saw in the Ostroff and Schulte's chapter, the vast majority of fit research is oriented toward fit with organizations, vocations, jobs, and workgroups. Much less is known about how well people fit with the goals they pursue (Judge & Kristof-Brown, 2004). Because both the ideal and ought selves are probably prominent identities for most individuals at work, one can see all sorts of questions relevant to fit research. For example:

- What sort of workplace moods and emotions are regulatory fit discrepancies associated with? Do people who experience discrepancies between their actual and ought identities experience guilt?
- Because work–family conflict, by definition, means a conflict in roles, how is regulatory focus relevant in the work and family domains? Do promotion and prevention strivings differ in the work and the family domains?
- Are promotion-focused people more likely to experience actual/objective/indirect fit and perceived/subjective/direct fit? Are they better at perceiving actual fit (have a closer correspondence between actual and perceived fit)?

## Kammeyer-Mueller: Newcomer Fitting In

As Kammeyer-Mueller notes, there has been somewhat of a divide between those who study newcomer socialization/mentoring, which tends to take a dynamic or change-oriented perspective, and those who study person–organization fit, who generally take a more static view of individuals (by focusing on personality and values, which are generally seen as stable). Thus, one might argue that most person–organization fit researchers take the perspective that the person "reads" the organization (makes an assessment of his or her values or personality and determines how well this matches the organization, the workgroup, or the job) and makes a choice of whether to join or remain in the organization (or job or group) based on this reading, and the organization does the same (reads the values and personality of the applicant or employee and makes personnel decisions about the person accordingly). This perspective assumes that people "are who they are" and that fit is dynamic only so far as misfits exit and those who fit enter (and thrive). To be sure, there are some who have brought these perspectives together (e.g., Cable & Parsons, 2001; Caldwell, Herold, & Fedor, 2004; Cooper-Thomas, van Vianen, & Anderson, 2004), but such undertakings are the exception rather than the rule.

Having learned a fair degree from the "reading" approach, as noted by Kammeyer-Mueller, an exciting avenue to pursue is whether values and personality might actually change. When this change represents a movement toward the organization (or job or workgroup), then fit increases, even if the people are the same (no one exits or enters). I have long felt that we in organizational psychology have assumed, to an inordinate degree, that personality is fixed—that because it has genetic origins (true), it is immutable (false, only the genetic part is fixed, and even that can interact with the environment). There is clear evidence that personalities do change and as Caspi, Roberts, and colleagues (Caspi & Roberts, 2001; Caspi, Roberts, & Shiner, 2005; Roberts, Walton, & Viechtbauer, 2006) have noted, one can find evidence to support the stability and the change perspectives. Given the centrality of work to people's identities (Hulin, 2002), if the situation can lead to a change in personality, the work environment (or construals thereof) certainly might be a place where that might happen. It is exciting to see Kammeyer-Mueller take a dynamic perspective on *fixed* individual differences (personality and values). I await eagerly some data to test this concept and approach.

### Kristof-Brown and Jansen: Person–Organization Fit

Relative to the other chapters in this volume, Kristof-Brown and Jansen offer a narrower and more discrete perspective. Specifically, the authors review past evidence on whether person–organization fit is relevant to the most commonly studied criterion in organizational behavior (OB), and discuss how fit should be assessed. In the second half of their chapter, they turn their attention to future issues in fit research. With its focus on person–organization fit and the literature directly in that area, the scope may be somewhat more bounded than that of other chapters, but it is no less important because most fit research in OB has focused on person–organization fit. Their review of past research on person–organization fit provides an excellent summary of where we are.

Perhaps the highlight of the chapter, however, is when the authors turn their attention to future research and focus specifically on temporal dynamics. As I have noted in reviewing Kammeyer-Mueller's chapter, most investigations of fit have been relatively static in nature. As Kristof-Brown and Jansen note, "Some individuals who don't fit don't always leave." What do organizations do with employees who do not fit their culture or intended goals? What do individuals do when they are embedded in a job or organization that misfits them? The ASA model discusses selecting in and selecting out strategies, but it does not consider the question of what happens when these forces are blocked (for whatever reason). Although neither I nor the authors can answer these questions, I do think a particularly promising place to look for inspiration is the attitude literature. In reading Eagley and Chaiken's (1992) seminal book on attitudes, I have always been surprised by how much of it focuses on attitude change and related topics such as persuasion. If person–organization fit (at least direct judgments of it) can be likened to an attitude, then perhaps some of the concepts and approaches can be adapted from the attitude literature to study changes in fit perceptions over time.

## Cable and Yu: Recruitment, Selection and Fit Perceptions

A social psychologist once wrote: Of all the things we have learned about social psychology, perhaps none is more pervasive than the similarity–attraction paradigm. By the same token, we have learned from person–organization fit research that nothing attracts an individual to an organization or an organizational member to an individual as the belief that they are similar. Consistent with this viewpoint, in their chapter, Ellis and Tsui comment: "Fit is a desired state of being strived for by all social entitites." The power of this statement is tempered, however, upon deeper consideration of its meaning—it may be important for people to perceive fit, but what does that really mean? What does it really mean when a job seeker thinks that "a job is a good fit for him," or when an interviewer chooses an applicant because "she is a good fit?" If fit perceptions were easily broken down into discrete elements, then such statements would be simple enough in their meaning and implications. However, as Edwards et al. (2006) recently noted in their excellent article, it appears that different approaches and measurements of fit are not interchangeable and that "the approaches apparently tap into different subjective experiences" (p. 818). So I return to the question: What does it really mean when someone perceives fit?

Cable and Yu address this question by focusing on the role of recruitment and selection practices in shaping perceptions of fit. The authors draw on a blend of theory and research from "outside" disciplines (communication, attitudes, and persuasion) in arguing that individuals' beliefs regarding fit are shaped by the credibility of the source and the richness of the information: the more credible the source, and the richer the information (such as face-to-face interactions), the more likely that perceptions of fit will be shaped by messages given by the organization. By applying these concepts to recruitment and selection methods, the authors are able to analyze the possible effects of different recruitment and selection methods (web pages vs. interviews, for example) as potential sources of fit perceptions. In research that would test their model, or pieces of it, further elaboration would be required (e.g., are we talking only about molar fit perceptions here?), but such tests would have the unusual potential to blend basic theory in social psychology with practical issues germane to the recruitment literature (which recruitment methods work best?).

### Atwater and Dionne: Leader–Follower Fit

As Atwater and Dionne note, although fit research has focused on how individuals fit in different contexts (to the vocation, to the organization, and to the job), there is a paucity of research linking fit between leaders and followers. To be sure, there are leadership concepts (most notable, as the authors state, is leader–member exchange theory) that consider fit in a broad sense. However, such leadership theories have not been integrated with research in person–organization fit, despite some compelling parallels. Toward this end, Atwater and Dionne develop a process model that attempts to build on past leader–follower research.

Indeed, I think their model has the potential to contribute to both leadership and person–organization fit research. In terms of fit research, most research is based on the premise that fit perceptions flow from inherent congruities (or incongruities) between values (or some other characteristic). Atwater and Dionne turn this hypothesis around and posit that early leader–follower similarity will induce attempts to align values, attitudes, and personality. This is a great insight. As robust as the similarity-attraction model is—Bryne and Nelson (1965) went so far as to label it the *"law* [italics added] of attraction"—one can easily conjure up situations in which an individual who likes someone else strives to find points of similarity with that person and to find areas of divergence from people they do not like. I do not think Atwater and Dionne mean to deny the merits of the similarity–attraction paradigm, nor do I, but I do think their point is that the causality can run the other way, and sometimes constructions of similarity follow from early attraction. As I will note later, I think alternative causal sequences in the person–organization fit literature are needed, and Atwater and Dionne provide one here.

In terms of the leadership literature, I think the Atwater and Dionne's chapter (and their model) is a real step forward in that it focuses on (a) dynamic (time-variant) processes and (b) the role of congruence as a linking mechanism, either in bringing the leader and follower closer together or in driving them farther apart. Leadership research continues to lack process explanations (although that situation has improved in the past decade), and I think leader–follower similarity is a particularly interesting and promising area for future research. As is no surprise given my praise of the dynamic models in Kammeyer-Mueller's and Kristof-Brown and Jansen's chapters, I think the change- or state-like nature of their model is a particularly exciting avenue for future person–organization fit research and for leadership research too.

## Edwards and Shipp: How Fit Matters

Edwards and Shipp's chapter, like the Ostroff and Schulte's, illustrates the complexity of fit. Edwards and Shipp distinguish fit by three dimensions, two of which have three levels and the other has five levels. This is a lot to ponder, especially when one considers that 45 distinct fit configurations are suggested by the model. It is somewhat difficult to distinguish proximal categories, although the authors do note that their model is mainly for heuristic purposes.

I think the real heart of the chapter is when Edwards and Shipp begin to apply their conceptualization of fit to outcomes. Few in the fit literature (I most certainly include myself in this criticism) do as careful a job linking their conceptualization of fit to the theoretical nature of the outcome/criterion variable. Because their approach is extraordinarily well grounded, it is unusually easy to find points of convergence and divergence.

One area of divergence lies in how Edwards and Shipp often label broad concepts as confounded. For example, they argue that some definitions of job satisfaction confound affect and cognition. Although to some extent this is true, I think it is true of any broad concept. As the British empiricist David Hume noted, an idea is an abstraction from specific impressions, but that does not mean that ideas are inherently problematic as might be implied by the term *confounded*. The point of clear thinking, in Hume's philosophy, is to be able to separate ideas from impressions, but this is not meant to deny the importance of ideas.

Similarly, we can investigate affects and cognitions as distinct influences on job satisfaction, but (a) that is difficult to do (few important cognitions are affect-free) and (b) that does not mean there is anything contaminated or otherwise wrong about general measures of broad concepts (like a measure of overall or general job satisfaction). Broad and specific concepts have their mutual purposes. But we make a mistake in arguing that a broad concept is confounded. To be fair, Edwards and Shipp do not directly argue that job satisfaction or other broad measures are flawed. However, I am afraid that their arguments about confounding could be misconstrued and thus misused.

In terms of convergence, the argument that needs–supplies fit is more directly related to job satisfaction than demands–abilities fit strikes me as right. I like the way that Edwards and Shipp translate Locke's value–percept theory into needs–supplies (although I have always felt that *need* is a concept that is practically impossible to meaningfully define). What I particularly like about the chapter is that Edwards and Shipp move from a discussion of conceptual linkages between their forms of fit and attitudes toward specifying the functional forms of those linkages. For example, they note that a typical discrepancy model (their Fig. 7.2a) is insufficient (an oversimplification of fit) because it ignores the levels of the variables. As they note, "wanting and having a simple job is very different from wanting and having a complex job," even though the degree of absolute misfit in these two cases could be exactly the same. Of course, Edwards has made this point before, but here the point is useful in specifying the expected relations between different forms of fit and various, important outcomes. I do not doubt that empirical data would show that some of their hypothesized forms are supported and that some are not, but the key is that this is the right way to look at the relationships, both conceptually and statistically.

## DeRue and Hollenbeck: Fit in Teams

I remember when I first learned about John Hollenbeck's foray into the teams literature. It was 1994, I was an assistant professor at Cornell, and we were trying to convince John to join us at Cornell (our efforts failed). John presented his ideas about the increasing importance of work teams in organizations and discussed his ideas about personality and team composition. I was convinced that John was the right person for the job; I was less convinced that team research was going to pan out. Scores of publications later, John is perhaps even better known for his teams research than for the research I admired him for then (and still do: his research on motivation and applied research methods). How could a sage prognosticator be wrong? Certainly, I underestimated the processes that could be manipulated and measured in a laboratory setting. Also, I underestimated the complexity of team composition, the interesting processes, interactions, and outcomes that could be studied from a team vantage point.

It is on this issue—the complexity of teams—that DeRue and Hollenbeck focus their attention. Their premise is that past teams research has not fully captured the complexity of how teams work and what interactions might make them work better. The model that they derive from that premise, with its focus on internal and external fit, is a masterstroke. What leads me to such a strong conclusion? First, their model effectively summarizes the Hollenbeck–Ilgen team laboratory (HITL) research, which has predominantly focused on team composition issues, under the rubric of internal fit. As DeRue and Hollenbeck note, team composition is about fit; for example, if it is valuable to have a highly conscientious team member, what about two highly conscientious team members, or having all team members being highly conscientious? Or, how might personality differences, or trait constellations, fit with one another? These are all what DeRue and Hollenbeck term *internal fit* issues, and the HITL research provides answers to these team composition questions.

Increasingly, the HITL folks have turned their attention to process, systems, and outcomes and that is reflected in the guts of the model DeRue and Hollenbeck present, as well as in what they label *external fit*. Having provided a wealth of interesting findings concerning team composition and aspects of internal fit, I had thought that HITL researchers were probably winding down. As their section on external fit shows, however, there are myriad interesting and important questions yet to be answered. And this is where, as the authors recognize, the fit literature can be especially helpful. Because team composition research is, in Ostroff and Schulte's lexicon, person–person oriented, the environment has a somewhat limited role. However, because by definition external fit concerns the match between teams or team members and their environment, this is where person–environment fit concepts and research are especially apropos.

In sum, if this chapter is any illustration of things to come, it appears that I have underestimated Hollenbeck and the HITL yet again. They show no signs of exhausting the array of interesting ideas and tests of those ideas anytime soon. I look forward to reading their research and hope they do more, as is evidenced here, to link their work to the fit literature.

## Ellis and Tsui: Fitting and Surviving

Ellis and Tsui make the compelling case, supported by mounds of research from various literatures (including the similarity–attraction paradigm, whose centrality to social psychology I discussed earlier), that organizations and the individuals in them strive to achieve homogeneity on salient characteristics, including demography. The authors take the position that homogeneity produces positive affective outcomes at Stage 1 (positive feelings and psychological states such as satisfaction, cohesion, and efficacy), but negative outcomes at Stage 2 (negative cognitive outcomes such as inertia, groupthink, and low conflict), Stage 3 (negative behavioral outcomes such as low learning and creativity, impaired decision-making, and poor performance), and Stage 4 (negative survival outcomes such as individual exit and firm failure). I think this multistage process model is unusually clear and provocative. For one who likes academic disagreement, here I make a few points. But do not infer that I find the work of Ellis and Tsui troubling—quite the contrary, I think it is very thought-provoking and here are three counterthoughts I had in reading their work.

First, on the link between demographic homogeneity and affective outcomes, does demographic similarity always lead to positive feelings? Would that not depend on the person? Do men always prefer to work with other men (or women with women)? Might not those who are dispositionally open value diversity (believing that encountering people from different backgrounds makes life more interesting)? Or, would organizational climate (whether leaders support diversity) make a difference?

Second, the model assumes that positive affective outcomes generally lead to negative cognitive outcomes. Although clearly one can think of situations in which this might be the case, one can think of many (arguably more) examples for which that would not be the case. For example, would satisfaction and efficacy generally lead to low conflict or groupthink? It may or may not. My point is not to "hammer" the model for its failure to include moderating influences. After all, any model at some level omits moderating (and mediating) mechanisms. Rather, these are questions that are relevant for future research testing this part of the model.

Third, I can think of many situations in which the negative cognitive outcomes (such as inertia and low conflict) are adaptive. For example, the idea that low task conflict is associated with low group performance has been recently questioned (De Dreu & Weingart, 2003). To reiterate, I raise these questions not to criticize Ellis and Tsui. A model that raises so many questions on an important topic is exactly what one would want in a book chapter. Imagine if researchers committed themselves to testing the aforementioned questions? To quote that great philosopher Martha Stewart: "That's a good thing."

I should note that the authors do not argue that diversity is unequivocally negative for their Stage 2–4 outcomes. They do a good job of reviewing evidence suggesting, in some cases and with some studies, negative effects of demographic diversity. However, their general orientation toward demographic homogeneity is, in their words, "the deeper and long-term impact of homogeneity on groups or organizations is diminished survival potential." There is a difference between valuing demographic diversity in an intrinsic sense and valuing it in a social scientific sense. It behooves us to separate these two, not favoring one over the other, but recognizing that the former is an individual or societal value choice and thus is inherently subjective, whereas the latter depends on a cold, hard look at the evidence (at least to the degree that researchers are capable of doing that).

Overall, I think the authors have done a laudable job of leading the reader to think about the long-term outcomes of homogeneity. Of course, scholars in organizational psychology (Schneider, Smith, & Goldstein, 2000), social psychology (Tajfel & Turner, 1986), organizational behavior (Ibarra, 1992), and organization theory (Hannan & Freeman, 1984; Powell & DiMaggio, 1991) have written about the dangers of homogeneity. However, the authors' perspective here, even in some of the linkages that I question, represents a good review of what we have learned about demographic diversity and where future research might profitably head.

## Gerhart: Human Resource Management and Fit

As Gerhart notes and as I commented previously, the vast majority of fit research is at the individual level of analysis. In this chapter, Gerhart applies fit to a topic—human resource (HR) systems—at the organizational level of analysis. In so doing, he makes use of the concepts of internal and external fit, but in a way different from that of DeRue and Hollenbeck. In Gerhart's model, internal fit is horizontal fit, or how well HR practices fit with one another (e.g., it hardly makes sense to hire on the basis of factors presumed to indicate motivation and then fail to reward motivation once these highly motivated employees are hired), and external fit is vertical fit, or the match between HR systems and contextual factors such as business conditions (e.g., investing a great deal in a sophisticated selection system would not appear to make much sense if business or industry conditions required hiring of nearly every available applicant).

As someone who still has the cobwebs of memories from my economics, strategy, and organization theory training from Illinois, it was enlightening to see Gerhart review these concepts, with some new thinking from the industrial relations literature with which I was unfamiliar. Although I hardly qualify as an expert, it seems to me that Gerhart does an excellent job of reviewing this new way of thinking of fit in terms of HR systems, while also grounding this work in the literature with which industrial/organizational psychologists are more familiar.

In terms of internal fit, judging from Gerhart's review, there seems to be a prevailing view that "bundling" complementary HR systems or practices leads to higher organizational effectiveness. As Gerhart notes, testing whether such bundles or horizontal fit is indeed associated with higher performance is a complicated issue, and the results appear, at least to Gerhart's keen eye, to be inconsistent. What to do about this inconsistency is not an easy question to answer. However, as I will note later, this is a question that fit researchers at the individual level should be asking themselves as well. In terms of vertical (external) fit, judging from Gerhart's review, the situation appears much the same as with horizontal (internal) fit: ample claims of its importance, but few strong tests with consistent results.

I think the most intriguing part of Gerhart's paper and the one that should be of interest to any fit researcher (micro, macro, or otherwise), is his section "Challenges in Studying Fit." He, naturally, focuses his attention here on the HR systems literature, yet any of the difficulties that he notes can be generalized to the person–organization fit literature. For example, Gerhart discusses statistical power issues and selectivity problems (variation in poor fit may be restricted because firms with poorly aligned systems go out of business), and indeed I will have more to say on both of these issues later. In sum, I urge you to read Gerhart's chapter. Although it surely has value for researchers who study macro/HR systems–oriented fit, it is highly accessible and a source of many relevant insights into the micro/person–organization fit literature.

## The Methods Chapter: Methods/Statistical Issues in Fit Research

One evening a few years ago, one of my best friends and I were enjoying dinner at a local restaurant. Each of us ordered fish: I ordered grouper and my friend ordered tilapia. When the plates arrived, we did what diners do—we first glanced at our own plate, and then looked at the other's plate. Rarely had two presentations been so different; my plate had a large, firm, fresh-looking piece of fish, surrounded by an attractive set of accompaniments. My friend's plate had a somewhat limp, tired-looking piece of fish (it was dead after all), on top of an unimaginative clump of rice, surrounded by limp, overcooked vegetables. As we looked again at our plates, my friend pointed at my plate and said, "Uhm, I think they mixed up our orders; you have my fish." We promptly exchanged plates, and I am sorry to tell you that "my" plate of fish tasted as stale as it looked. After our waiter noticed that we switched plates, he informed us that we, in fact, had been served the right plates. My friend (unwittingly) thought that my fish was his because my plate turned out so well. (We have enjoyed many a laugh about this episode since.)

Following this story line, the idea for this chapter was mine. No, in all seriousness, the idea for this chapter was Cheri's. When Cheri asked me about it, I immediately thought: "What a great idea; rather than having one researcher's perspective on methodological issues, readers can enjoy multiple perspectives." Assuming that you have read chapter 11, I think you will agree that it works. It is gratifying to know my idea turned out so well (just kidding, Cheri).

Ostroff's section is the first one in the chapter, and in it she discusses several important methodological issues in fit research, including measurement of fit (direct or indirect measures), levels of analysis, and possible sources of bias. This is good material. I particularly liked her treatment of commensurability (questioning the "virtual dismissal" of it in the fit literature) and restriction of range (under the heading "Sampling Issues").

Next, Caldwell, Chatman, and O'Reilly discuss profile comparison methods for assessing fit. When Dan Cable first introduced me to the Organizational Culture Profile, I remember feeling excited. As the authors note, one advantage of a profile comparison approach is that the person and the environment are matched on the same basis. Another advantage is that a correlation can be computed for each person, reflecting his or her degree of correspondence with the environment. The problem with profile comparison approaches, as Edwards aptly notes in his section, is in analyzing the data. There are better and worse ways to analyze fit data, including ipsative data. However, no matter how data are analyzed, various statistical problems are introduced when we analyze ipsative data using standard statistical techniques. Thus, in a technical sense, I do not disagree with a single word that Edwards writes. I will stop here, though, as I have more to write on this issue later.

In the fourth section of the chapter, Harrison and Sin provide a review of measures of misfit—measures that reflect dispersion or diversity. As the authors note, fit researchers generally have used measures of fit (higher scores indicate a higher degree of fit), so a review of measures with the opposite objective and interpretation (higher scores indicate a lesser degree of fit) is worthwhile. They do an unusually good job of clearly and concisely reviewing the various measures of misfit, such as variability (standard deviation or variance), coefficient of variation (which controls for the fact that variability is correlated with the mean), and Euclidean distance (such as $D$ or $D^2$). In reflecting on their recommendations, I could not help wondering how Edwards would react to some of their recommendations. For example, Harrison and Sin recommend $D$ or $D^2$ for measuring misfit at the individual level. Edwards has criticized such measures, which makes me wonder how Harrison and Sin react to the criticisms (for example, although $D$ loses less information than $D^2$, used by itself it still ignores differences underlying two equal $D$ scores (e.g., $D = 3$ [5 – 2] and $D = 3$ [9 – 6]). Again, this is an issue to which I will return shortly.

Finally, Mumford and Espejo discuss cluster analysis. Although I have used cluster analysis in the past, I must admit to be chastened somewhat by criticisms of the method. The choice of the clustering algorithm is subjective, yet important; using the nearest neighbor method will often produce very different results from using Ward's method. Interpretation of the results is also subjective (it is often a very subjective decision about how many clusters are derived. A three-cluster solution often will look very different from a four- or two-cluster solution. In fairness, one might argue that unless we allow ourselves to be yoked to the ox of statistical significance or null hypothesis significance testing, interpretation of effect sizes is inherently subjective and in that sense cluster analysis is no better or no worse than other statistical methods. However, because the metrics underlying cluster analysis are not meaningful (similar in that way to sum of squares in analysis of variance), we do not have meaningful effect sizes to interpret nor confidence intervals around estimates. Now, it is true that the clusters derived from the analysis can be tested (perhaps even validated) against other criteria, but often the tests involve statistical procedures with problems of their own (analysis of variance, discriminant analysis, and others). Despite limitations, as Mumford and Espejo note, there are questions for which cluster analysis is uniquely situated to answer. Whether the gain is worth the price is something for the reader to decide.

### Harrison: Testing the Construct of Fit

In opening this chapter, I argued that one could find reasons for hope and despair in pondering the fit literature. Harrison's thought-provoking chapter, to this reader at least, exposes some of the reasons for despair. Although he does not use this terminology, I think Harrison makes a persuasive case that the literature on fit is an exemplar of weak paradigm development. In Kuhn's (1996) way of thinking, stronger paradigms have fewer debates "over legitimate methods, problems, and standards of solution" (p. 48). To Kuhn, the consequences of a weak paradigm are high rejection rates, heavy emphasis placed on particularism versus universalism (in short, favoring pedigree, status, and networks over the meritocracy of ideas) and, ultimately, stunted scientific progress. Although one may well disagree with Kuhn's causes and consequences of paradigm development, surely most would agree that fit as a field is so weakly developed that we see disagreements even as to the scope of the field. Moreover, the area has been dominated by methodological debates, a plethora of labels, various levels of analysis, fuzzy boundaries, and so on. It is true that, to some degree, these arguments could be made about most any OB topic. However, as Harrison notes in specific cases, questions of "what is fit" loom large over the area. As Schneider (2001) concluded, "There is considerable ambiguity over what is appropriate research from a person–environment fit perspective" (p. 150).

One might argue that if fit research is to advance, we should do more than celebrate the diversity of ideas and approaches. Intellectual debate is interesting and undoubtedly at some level healthy. However, I also think we are fooling ourselves if we think a field so wracked with dissensus does not circumscribe the contributions of the field to intellectual thought in organizational behavior. I am not arguing for a forced consensus, nor am I really suggesting any "solution." However, we must try to see things as they are rather than how we might wish them to be. Harrison's chapter reminds us that the fit literature has problems. To some intrepid researcher, problems become opportunities, but, today, problems are problems.

To his credit, Harrison proposes the beginnings of one path to stronger paradigm development. He seeks to delineate what is, and as importantly, what is not, fit. It is possible that his effort does not clarify but rather shifts ambiguity in a different direction. For example, he argues that commensurability is critical to a useful definition of fit. From this assumption, he then rejects alternative conceptions of fit that do not, in his view, meet the commensurability test. The problem, I think, then lies in what one defines as commensurate. If one were to conduct a study showing that individuals high in need for achievement were attracted to organizations that based pay on performance (see Turban & Keon, 1993), this would appear to fail Harrison's test of commensurability. Would this, then, not be a study of person–organization fit? I wonder whether researchers will see fit (excuse the pun) to follow Harrison's lead. I do believe, though, that to engage his argument is critical if the field is to develop a stronger paradigm and realize the consequent advantages as suggested by Kuhn (1996).

## FUTURE FIT RESEARCH

Having reviewed the chapters and made note of their many contributions, I conclude my review by noting some areas for future fit research. Of course, there are many such areas suggested in the chapters themselves, which I do not repeat here. Some of the topics below pick up on some of the points made in the chapters, and some are ideas that arose from or were reinforced by reading the chapters.

## Terminology Confusion

As the astute reader will have noted, there is inconsistency in labels to describe fit—person–environment fit, person–organization fit, person–job fit, person–group fit, person–individual fit, dyadic fit, and so forth. Some use the broad term person–environment fit, others use person–organization fit as an umbrella term, and still others distinguish person–organization from other foci such as person–job, person–group, person–person, and so on. Alternatively, one could argue that person–organization fit is a more specific instantiation of the more general person–environment fit. Fifteen years ago Jerry Ferris and I complained that the literature on fit was confusing and plagued by conceptual ambiguities (Judge & Ferris, 1992). I am not sure that the situation has improved. We are swimming in terms and concepts and, in some ways, this book has only added water to an already overflowing pond. I think, rather obviously, that the key is not stop to conceptualizing but to emphasize works that will integrate the terms/concepts and to encourage "ideational consolidation" (Felps, 2006). Although some of chapters make progress toward integration, I think the field awaits more integrative work. The recent Edwards et al. (2006) article, I believe, is one step in the right direction. We need more, lest we act out the Chinese proverb, "One step forward, two steps back."

## The Problems of Endogeneity and Selectivity Biases

In my doctoral education at Illinois, labor economists were abundant. At times I felt that if I heard the terms *endogeneity bias* and *selectivity bias* one more time I was going to scream. Still, such biases pose a perverse problem in the fit literature because the very concept we are studying is itself manifested in selectivity bias (both employee self-selection and employer selection), as shown by Schneider (1987, 2001) and supported by Schneider et al. (1998). As Schneider (2001) aptly noted, "I think the point cannot be overemphasized: When either the person variable or the environmental variable (or both) is restricted in range, finding a significant effect for fit (or a significant effect for an algebraic interaction) will be constrained" (p. 146).

To review, selectivity (or selection) bias occurs when the dependent variable is measured for only a select portion of the sample. In a classic example from labor economics, if we use a dummy variable (union vs. nonunion) to predict wages for the pooled sample of workers and conclude that the coefficient on this variable represents the union–nonunion wage differential, we have a selectivity bias because we observe an individual's union wage only if he or she belongs to a union. This problem becomes magnified if we consider the endogeneity bias—individuals who join unions may be different for unobserved reasons that are correlated with earnings and thus the coefficient estimate does not accurately represent the causal impact of unionization on wages. For example, if lower-ability individuals are more likely to join a union, then the coefficient on the union dummy variable will be downwardly biased because it is confounding two effects (the effects of joining a union on earnings and the effects of ability on earnings).

As this example suggests, such processes may wreak havoc with the fit literature. If we link a measure of person–organization fit to an employment outcome (e.g., a direct measure of perceived fit on job performance), we very likely do so without regard to possibility selectivity and endogeneity biases. For example, because individuals may self-select and be selected into organizations or jobs based on perceived similarity, we have a selectivity problem in that poorly fitting people never joined the organization. Moreover, we also have possible endogeneity effects because personality (Judge & Cable, 1997) or ability (Kristof-Brown, 2000) may influence direct or indirect measures of fit.

As is often the case, it is easier to identify the problem than to delineate simple solutions. However, drawing from our friends in labor economics, we can address endogeneity biases by, as much as possible, including the distal characteristics that may predict variation in measures of fit. For example, if we are linking the degree to which organizational members fit to an outcome variable, then to eliminate the endogeneity bias, we can include in our regression those variables (such as personality, abilities, and values) that may be antecedents to the fit measure. A variation of this technique is to use a two-stage regression approach (the same thing can be accomplished in structural equation modeling) that explicitly models the effect of the distal variables on fit the measure. Results from properly specific models will then inform us about the causes of fit and also provide more accurate estimates of the effect of fit on outcomes.

## Changes in Fit

Fit is, by implication, a state that may vary over time. It is true that, depending on how one defines fit (e.g., values or traits), both the person and situation component may be relatively stable. However, even in these cases, neither the person nor the situation variable is wholly stable, which means that fit can be expected to vary over time. When dealing with direct perceptions of fit, one might even expect to see day-to-day fluctuations, as has been shown with respect to other attitudes (e.g., Fisher, 2000; Fuller et al., 2003). There are good longitudinal studies in the fit literature. However, there are not many researchers who have looked at changes in fit over time nor who have attempted to decompose variance into between-individual (individual differences in fit) and within-individual (intraindividual variation in fit over time) sources. Studying fit in such a multilevel context would seem to be a particularly promising area for future research.

## Is Fit More Illusory Than Real?

In one of his more interesting (and certainly controversial) points, Harrison argues that direct measures of fit (meaning overall perceptions of fit) are so meaningless as to deserve abolishment from the literature. Although most, me included, disagree with such a strong recommendation, he has a point in this sense: If direct measures of fit are relatively poorly related to indirect measures and there is reason to believe that this is the case (Edwards et al., 2006), then what does that tell us about the ontological meaning of direct measures of fit? It could tell us that indirect measures are so fraught with measurement problems as to be meaningless.

However, it also could mean that perceived or direct measures of fit are more illusory than real. By illusory, I mean: Is person–organization fit mostly a general impression that may say as much about a person's general attitude toward his or her organization? Recently, in another article, Harrison, Newman, and Roth (2006) found that specific job attitudes (job satisfaction or organizational commitment) are indicated by a common factor and that the common factor was better suited to predict broad organizational criteria. It may be that one could use other attitudes, such as direct perceptions of fit, as additional indicators of this broad job attitude factor and that, when considered in this light, there is little unique variance attributable to direct perceptions of fit beyond this general factor. In short, although direct measures of fit may be correlated with organizational criteria (Kristof-Brown, Zimmerman, & Johnson, 2005), this does not mean that direct perceptions of fit have any unique meaning beyond their indication of a broad job attitude factor. As Ostroff notes in her section in chapter 11, direct measures of fit are ". . . in some ways analogous to other measures of affective responses to the organizational situation (e.g., job satisfaction) in that it captures an overall subjective or affective reaction to the contextual environment." If we show that direct or molar perceptions of fit are "important" in terms of their relationship to certain outcomes, are these molar perceptions merely indicators of some more general orientation toward the job or organization, as suggested by Harrison's study?

## Statistical Issues

Edwards and Harrison each make persuasive cases for the problems with indirect (*D*-scores, profile similarity indices) and direct (global fit perceptions) assessments of person–organization fit. By and large, I agree with their criticisms. I worry, however, that the remedy may kill the patient as quickly as the disease. The previous comment may be a bit of hyperbole, but the correct way of measuring and analyzing fit—using polynomial regression/surface modeling—has limitations of its own. Allow me to elaborate.

Moderated regression, a simpler form of polynomial regression, relies on rarely tested assumptions, such as homogeneity of error variances and freedom from range restriction (Aguinis & Stone-Romero, 1997; Alexander & DeShon, 1994). Moreover, A × B interaction terms have high power requirements (i.e., require very large sample sizes to have a reasonable probability of detecting a true interaction). As Alexander and DeShon (1994) noted: "A major problem in reliably detecting interaction effects is that even in the best of circumstances, such tests have very low power" (p. 312). There is a common refrain one hears in response to this issue, which is, "Yes, but since our interaction term (terms) was (were) significant, this is a nonissue." That may be true enough if a pure null hypothesis significant testing approach were followed (I hesitate in using *pure* and *null hypothesis significant testing* in the same sentence, but bear with me), but this approach is not always followed. In some situations, I think the authors "peek" at their results before writing their introduction, and it would be naïve to assume that such peeks have no implications for what is developed and tested in the their articles. Because such results may capitalize on chance, then the acid test is whether the interaction is replicated independently. With simple A × B interactions, there is reason enough to be dubious about replicability. With polynomial regression, both the statistical power and the ability to replicate the specific response surfaces seem to me to be quite low. What I am asking is this: Given the power problems with moderated regression (McClelland & Judd, 1993), much less with polynomial regression (which includes interactions, quadratics, and interactions with quadratics), and the fact that some of the surface plots may have been inductively derived (at least in part), what is the probability that each significant coefficient (which is critical to the nuanced interpretation of polynomial regression) would be replicated in a future study? Unfortunately, few such efforts are visible in the literature, which makes the question all the more salient.

## How People Make the Place

Since Schneider's ASA model (Schneider, 1987, 2001; Schneider et al., 2000), fit researchers have implicitly accepted the notion that the environment may be "made" by the people. There is evidence to support the model at the individual and the organizational level. At the individual level, people whose values match the dominant organizational culture appear to be more likely to be selected, and to self-select, into the organization compared with people whose values do not match (Chapman, Uggerslev, Carroll, Piasentin, & Jones, 2005). Similarly, individuals who are mismatched appear to be more likely to exit the organization (Arthur, Bell, Villado, & Doverspike, 2006). At the organizational level, there is significantly greater homogeneity in personality within organizations than between organizations (Schneider et al., 1998). However, we have relatively little data on the subject of what makes the environment. To be sure, at a somewhat obvious level, an organization's culture might be substantially defined by the personalities and values of the people in it (particularly in the upper echelons). However, if this does happen, how does it happen? And, as Schneider (2001) noted, we have relatively little understanding about the environment in fit research.

I wonder if greater utilization of Mead's (1934) and Blumer's (1969) concept of symbolic interactionism might be of use here. Symbolic interactionism assumes that "reality" is a subjective concept that is construed or even created by the actor, and these construals are based on pragmatism—people base their knowledge on what has proven to be useful and adaptive for them. Under this view, there is no actual or objective fit. Fit is a perceptual process, based on individuals' interactions with others and based on the utility of their perceptions. Thus, in contrast to Harrison's view, symbolic interactionism might suggest that perceptions of fit do have an important meaning. However, to be meaningful, symbolic interactionism would require that such perceptions be studied in a radically different way. It would require giving up the idea of veridicality of perceptions and focus on the causes—and consequences—of such perceptions in their own right. One of the key tenets of symbolic interactionism is that we see ourselves as we believe others see us. As noted by Jussim, Soffin, Brown, Ley, and Kohlhepp (1992), "Others' evaluations influence targets' self-concept indirectly, as mediated by targets' perceptions of those evaluations" (p. 403). If people do internalize such reflected appraisals, then it becomes interesting to try to understand how people arrive at judgments that they fit into an organization (or occupation or group). To use Myers-Briggs Type Indicator acronyms, if someone learns that he or she is an INFP and his or her supervisor is an ESTJ, how does such feedback influence appraisals of fit? Feedback from others is a powerful source of beliefs about our selves, and fit should be no exception. As Stryker (1987) noted, symbolic interactionism has garnered more than its share of criticism, some of which is justified, but it continues to be of interest to social psychologists. It may have a role in fit research as well.

## Fit and Personnel Selection

If this concept of fit is so pervasive, why has it really not proven itself in personnel selection research? Although there is recent support for Trait ×

Trait interactions in the selection literature (Witt, Burke, Barrick, & Mount, 2002), as well as moderators based on job or organizational characteristics (Rothstein & Goffin, 2006), by and large, the validities of the best predictors of job performance appear to be quite robust for general mental ability (Schmidt & Hunter, 2004), conscientiousness (Barrick & Mount, 2005), integrity (Ones & Viswesvaran, 2001), work samples (Roth, Bobko, & McFarland, 2005), and interviews (Huffcutt, Roth, & McDaniel, 1996). Generalizing from these results, one has to wonder whether fit is all that is relevant to job performance, at least as far as the research literature has been able to demonstrate.

To be sure, cognitive ability is more predictive of performance in complex than in relatively simple jobs, but it is still has significant validity for relatively simple jobs (Bertua, Anderson, & Salgado, 2005). I think fit probably is a relevant concept for many jobs and explains why the interview continues to be used (Judge & Ferris, 1992). However, if one believes this, one cannot help but be disappointed by the relative failure of the selection literature to support the view. Perhaps, as Edwards and Shipp's chapter implies, we have not conceptualized or investigated the relationship in the right way. By and large, the personnel selection literature has been focused on abilities but, again, at least as far as individual differences are concerned, the assumption has been the more ability, the better. And the evidence does not seem to contradict this view. So, is demands–abilities fit irrelevant for personnel selection? Why is it that selection researchers have been relatively uninterested in this type of fit? Are other types of fit (e.g., needs–supplies), or other fit concepts (e.g., molar fit) properly outside the realm of personnel selection? In industrial–organizational psychology, we have selection researchers and fit researchers, but there seems to be very little integration of the two fields. Such collaboration might contribute to each area.

### Is Homogenizing Around Fit Ethical?

*An employer has no business with a man's [sic] personality. Employment is a specific construct calling for specific performance, and for nothing else. Any attempt of an employer to go beyond this is usurpation. It is immoral as well illegal intrusion of privacy. It is abuse of power. An employee owes no "loyalty," he owes no "love," and no "attitudes"—he owes performance and nothing else.*

—Drucker (1973, pp. 424–425)

I find this quote fascinating, in no small part because it raises interesting ethical questions for those of us interested in personalities, emotions, and attitudes at work. It seems clear that research has shown that these concepts are relevant to workplace attitudes and behaviors. Ellis and Tsui argue that fit is socially desirable, and Kammeyer-Mueller notes that fit is an implicit outcome in socialization processes. Clearly, though, if one tries to reconcile Drucker's comment with the beliefs that (a) fit is desirable from the vantage point of an organization (Ellis & Tsui) and (b) organizations attempt to increase fit through selection and socialization processes (Kammeyer-Mueller), further questions arise. If fit is desirable, is it viewed only in terms of work outcomes (those that might be derived from work demands)? Do socialization efforts concern themselves only with specific performance outcomes? If one answers these questions in the negative, then Drucker's comment suggests ethical concerns. I do not suggest answers to these questions, but in the fit literature one sees little effort to grapple with them. One can certainly envision an organization ensuring attitudinal homogeneity along the lines of Oceania's Ministry of Truth or The World State's "Community, Identity, Stability." When do efforts to achieve fit cross a moral boundary?

### Fit in Terms of What?

With few exceptions (Kristof-Brown, 2000), little research has been done to compare different operationalizations of fit. Is fit around values more important in driving fit perceptions and outcomes than fit around personality or goals? And, if personality and values are important, which aspects are most important? Even if one is concerned only with values, there are different types of values. Rokeach (1973) defined values as "desired end states" or "ways of being." Locke (1976) defined values more narrowly, as "that which one acts to gain and/or keep" (p. 1304).

As noted by Edwards and Schipp and Harrison, omnibus measures of fit collapse across all values of traits, obscuring important practical and conceptual information on whether fit on some values or traits is more important than fit on others. In the relationship literature, research has suggested that fit in terms of the Big Five traits operates quite differently by trait. For extraversion, there is evidence to support complementarity, such that dominant interaction partners prefer submissive partners and submissive partners prefer dominant ones (Tiedens & Fragale, 2003). For other traits, similarity appears to rule the day for which, of the Big Five traits, similarity in conscientiousness may be most important to marital (Nemechek & Olson, 1999) and roommate (Kurtz & Sherker, 2003) satisfaction. And, finally, there are traits for which fit seems unimportant. For example, the main effect of the agreeableness of one's spouse seems to be more important to marital satisfaction than how similar one is to one's spouse in agreeableness (Kurtz & Sherker, 2003). The point is that if we are going to learn more about what really drives fit, we need more comparative studies of personality, values, and goals and finer-grained analyses of fit by each specific trait, value, or goal.

## CONCLUSION

It is an exciting time to be doing fit research. As I have noted in my comments, I do believe there are some problems that are seemingly intractable. However, it is at times like this that the greatest innovations are made. Very recently, a reclusive Russian mathematician, Grigory Perelman, won (and refused to accept) the Fields Medal, the highest honor in mathematics, for introducing the solution to Poincaré's conjecture, a hypothesis involving the (very complex) structure of three-dimensional objects (Johnson, 2006). Many mathematicians had considered the conjecture insoluble. In the admittedly more prosaic fit area, in the future someone is going to figure out solutions for some of these formidable problems. Will it not be exciting to see what that future holds?

## REFERENCES

Aguinis, H., & Stone-Romero, E. F. (1997). Methodological artifacts in moderated multiple regression and their effects on statistical power. *Journal of Applied Psychology, 82*, 192–206.

Alexander, R. A., & DeShon, R. P. (1994). Effect of error variance heterogeneity on the power of tests for regression slope differences. *Psychological Bulletin, 115*, 308–314.

Arthur, W., Jr., Bell, S. T., Villado, A. J., & Doverspike, D. (2006). The use of person–organization fit in employment decision making: An assessment of its criterion-related validity. *Journal of Applied Psychology, 91*, 786–801.

Barrick, M. R., & Mount, M. K. (2005). Yes, personality matters: Moving on to more important matters. *Human Performance, 18*, 359–372.

Bar-Tal, D. (2006). Bridging between micro and macro perspectives in social psychology. In P. A. M. Van Lange (Ed.), *Bridging social psychology: Benefits of transdisciplinary approaches* (pp. 341–346). Mahwah, NJ: Lawrence Erlbaum Associates.

Bertua, C., Anderson, N., & Salgado, J. F. (2005). The predictive validity of cognitive ability tests: A UK meta-analysis. *Journal of Occupational and Organizational Psychology, 78*, 387–409.

Blumer, H. (1969). *Symbolic interactionism: Perspective and method.* Berkeley, CA: University of California Press.

Byrne, D., & Nelson, D. (1965). Attraction as a linear function of proportion of positive reinforcements. *Journal of Personality and Social Psychology, 1*, 659–663.

Cable, D. M., & Parsons, C. K. (2001). Socialization tactics and person–organization fit. *Personnel Psychology, 54*, 1–23.

Caldwell, S. D., Herold, D. M., & Fedor, D. B. (2004). Toward an understanding of the relationships among organizational change, individual differences, and changes in person-environment fit: A cross-level study. *Journal of Applied Psychology, 89*, 868–882.

Caspi, A., & Roberts, B. W. (2001). Target article: Personality development across the life course: The argument for change and continuity. *Psychological Inquiry, 12*, 49–66.

Caspi, A., Roberts, B. W., & Shiner, R. L. (2005). Personality development: Stability and change. *Annual Review of Psychology, 56,* 453–484.

Centerbar, D. B., & Clore, G. L. (2006). Do approach-avoidance actions create attitudes? *Psychological Science, 17,* 22–29.

Chapman, D. S., Uggerslev, K. L., Carroll, S. A., Piasentin, K. A., & Jones, D. A. (2005). Applicant attraction to organizations and job choice: A meta-analytic review of the correlates of recruiting outcomes. *Journal of Applied Psychology, 90,* 928–944.

Cooper-Thomas, H. D., van Vianen, A., & Anderson, N. (2004). Changes in person–organization fit: The impact of socialization tactics on perceived and actual P–O fit. *European Journal of Work and Organizational Psychology, 13,* 52–78.

De Dreu, C. K. W., & Weingart, L. R. (2003). Task versus relationship conflict, team performance, and team member satisfaction: A meta-analysis. *Journal of Applied Psychology, 88,* 741–749.

Drucker, P. F. (1973). *Management: tasks, responsibilities, practices.* New York: Harper & Row.

Eagley, A. H., & Chaiken, S. (1992). *The psychology of attitudes.* San Diego, CA: Harcourt Brace Jovanovich.

Edwards, J. R., Cable, D. M., Williamson, I. O., Lambert, L. S., & Shipp, A. J. (2006). The phenomenology of fit: Linking the person and environment to the subjective experience of person-environment fit. *Journal of Applied Psychology, 91,* 802–827.

Elliot, A. J., Gable, S. L., & Mapes, R. R. (2006). Approach and avoidance motivation in the social domain. *Personality and Social Psychology Bulletin, 32,* 378–391.

Felps, W. (2006, August). *The problem of old wine in new bottles: Moving towards ideational consolidation.* Symposium presentation at the Annual Meeting of the Academy of Management, Atlanta, GA.

Fisher, C. D. (2000). Mood and emotions while working: Missing pieces of job satisfaction? *Journal of Organizational Behavior, 21,* 185–202.

Fuller, J. A., Stanton, J. M., Fisher, G. G., Spitzmüller, C., Russell, S. S., & Smith, P. C. (2003). A lengthy look at the daily grind: Time series analysis of events, mood, stress, and satisfaction. *Journal of Applied Psychology, 88,* 1019–1033.

Galinsky, A. D., Leonardelli, G. J., & Okhuysen, G. A. (2005). Regulatory focus at the bargaining table: Promoting distributive and integrative success. *Personality and Social Psychology Bulletin, 31,* 1087–1098.

Goldspink, C., & Kay, R. (2004). Bridging the micro-macro divide: A new basis for social science. *Human Relations, 57,* 597–618.

Hannan, M. T., & Freeman, J. H. (1984). Structural inertia and organizational change. *American Sociological Review, 49,* 149–64.

Harrison, D. A., Newman, D. A., & Roth, P. L. (2006). How important are job attitudes? Meta-analytic comparisons of integrative behavioral outcomes and time sequences. *Academy of Management Journal, 49,* 305–325.

Higgins, E. T. (2000). Making a good decision: Value from fit. *American Psychologist, 55,* 1217–1230.

Higgins, E. T. (2005). Value from regulatory fit. *Current Directions in Psychological Science, 14,* 209–213.

Huffcutt, A. I., Roth, P. L., & McDaniel, M. A. (1996). A meta-analytic investigation of cognitive ability in employment interview evaluations: Moderating characteristics and implications for incremental validity. *Journal of Applied Psychology, 81*, 459–473.

Hulin, C. L. (2002). Lessons from industrial and organizational psychology. In J. M. Brett & F. Drasgow (Eds.), *The psychology of work: Theoretically based empirical research* (pp. 3–22). Mahwah, NJ: Lawrence Erlbaum Associates.

Ibarra, H. (1992). Homophily and differential returns: Sex differences in network structure and access in an advertising firm. *Administrative Science Quarterly, 37*, 422–447.

Johnson, G. (2006, August 27). The math was complex, the intentions, strikingly simple. *New York Times*. Retrieved August 31, 2006, from http://www.ny times.com

Judge, T. A., & Cable, D. M. (1997). Applicant personality, organizational culture, and organization attraction. *Personnel Psychology, 50*, 359–394.

Judge, T. A., & Ferris, G. R. (1992). The elusive criterion of fit in human resources staffing decisions. *Human Resource Planning, 15*, 47–68.

Judge, T. A., & Kristof-Brown, A. (2004). Personality, interactional psychology, and person-organization fit. In B. Schneider & D. B. Smith (Eds.), *Personality and organizations* (pp. 87–109). Mahwah, NJ: Lawrence Erlbaum Associates.

Jussim, L., Soffin, S., Brown, R., Ley, J., & Kohlhepp, K. (1992). Understanding reactions to feedback by integrating ideas from symbolic interactionism and cognitive evaluation theory. *Journal of Personality and Social Psychology, 62*, 402–421.

Keller, J., & Bless, H. (2006). Regulatory fit and cognitive performance: The interactive effect of chronic and situationally induced self-regulatory mechanisms on test performance. *European Journal of Social Psychology, 36*, 393–405.

Kim, Y. (2006). The role of regulatory focus in message framing in antismoking advertisements for adolescents. *Journal of Advertising, 35*, 143–151.

Kristof-Brown, A. L. (2000). Perceived applicant fit: Distinguishing between recruiters' perceptions of person–job and person–organization fit. *Personnel Psychology, 53*, 643–671.

Kristof-Brown, A. L., Zimmerman, R. D., & Johnson, E. C. (2005). Consequences of individual's fit at work: A meta-analysis of person–job, person–organization, person–group, and person–supervisor fit. *Personnel Psychology, 58*, 281–342.

Kuhn, T. S. (1996). *The structure of scientific revolutions* (3rd ed.). Chicago: University of Chicago Press.

Kurtz, J. E., & Sherker, J. L. (2003). Relationship quality, trait similarity, and self-other agreement on personality ratings in college roommates. *Journal of Personality, 71*, 21–48.

Larson, R., & Csikszentmihalyi, M. (1983). The experience sampling method. In H. T. Reis (Ed.), *Naturalistic approaches to studying social interaction* (Vol. 15, pp. 41–56). San Francisco: Jossey-Bass.

Leone, L., Perugini, M., & Bagozzi, R. P. (2005). Emotions and decision making: Regulatory focus moderates the influence of anticipated emotions on action evaluations. *Cognition & Emotion, 19*, 1175–1198.

Locke, E. A. (1976). The nature and causes of job satisfaction. In M. D. Dunnette (Ed.), *Handbook of industrial and organizational psychology* (pp. 1297–1349). Chicago: Rand McNally.

Lockwood, P., Marshall, T. C., & Sadler, P. (2005). Promoting success or preventing failure: Cultural differences in motivation by positive and negative role models. *Personality and Social Psychology Bulletin, 31,* 379–392.

McClelland, G. H., & Judd, C. M. (1993). Statistical difficulties of detecting interactions and moderator effects. *Psychological Bulletin, 114,* 376–390.

Mead, G. H. (1934). *Mind, self and society.* Chicago: University of Chicago Press.

Nemechek, S., & Olson, K. R. (1999). Five-factor personality similarity and marital adjustment. *Social Behavior and Personality, 27,* 309–318.

Ones, D. S., & Viswesvaran, C. (2001). Integrity tests and other criterion-focused occupational personality scales (COPS) used in personnel selection. *International Journal of Selection and Assessment, 9,* 31–39.

Ostroff, C. (1992). The relationship between satisfaction, attitudes, and performance: An organizational level analysis. *Journal of Applied Psychology, 77,* 963–974.

Ostroff, C., & Schmitt, N. (1993). Configurations of organizational effectiveness and efficiency. *Academy of Management Journal, 36,* 1345–1361.

Powell, P. J., & DiMaggio, W. W. (1991). Introduction. In P. J. Powell & W. W. DiMaggio (Eds.), *The new institutionalism in organizational analysis* (pp. 1–38). Chicago: University of Chicago Press.

Roberts, B. W., Walton, K. E., & Viechtbauer, W. (2006). Patterns of mean-level change in personality traits across the life course: A meta-analysis of longitudinal studies. *Psychological Bulletin, 132,* 1–25.

Roese, N. J., Pennington, G. L., Coleman, J., Janicki, M., Li, N. P., & Kenrick, D. T. (2006). Sex differences in regret: All for love or some for lust? *Personality and Social Psychology Bulletin, 32,* 770–780.

Rokeach, M. (1973). *The nature of human values.* New York: The Free Press.

Roth, P. L., Bobko, P., & McFarland, L. A. (2005). A meta-analysis of work sample test validity: Updating and integrating some classic literature. *Personnel Psychology, 58,* 1009–1037.

Rothstein, M. G., & Goffin, R. D. (2006). The use of personality measures in personnel selection: What does current research support? *Human Resource Management Review, 16,* 155–180.

Schmidt, F. L., & Hunter, J. (2004). General mental ability in the world of work: Occupational attainment and job performance. *Journal of Personality and Social Psychology, 86,* 162–173.

Schneider, B. (1987). The people make the place. *Personnel Psychology, 40,* 437–453.

Schneider, B. (2001). Fits about fit. *International Review of Applied Psychology, 50,* 141–152.

Schneider, B., Smith, D. B., & Goldstein, H. W. (2000). Attraction–selection–attrition: Toward a person-environment psychology of organizations. In W. B. Walsh, K. H. Craik, & R. H. Price (Eds.), *Person–environment psychology: New directions and perspectives* (2nd ed., pp. 61–85). Mahwah, NJ: Lawrence Erlbaum Associates.

Schneider, B., Smith, D. B., Taylor, S., & Fleenor, J. (1998). Personality and organizations: A test of the homogeneity of personality hypothesis. *Journal of Applied Psychology, 83,* 462–470.

Sheldon, K. M., & Elliot, A. J. (1999). Goal striving, need satisfaction, and longitudinal well-being: The Self-Concordance Model. *Journal of Personality and Social Psychology, 76,* 546–557.

Stryker, S. (1987). The vitalization of symbolic interactionism. *Social Psychology Quarterly, 50,* 83–94.

Tajfel, H., & Turner, J. C. (1986). The social identity theory of inter-group behavior. In S. Worchel & L. W. Austin (Eds.), *Psychology of intergroup relations* (pp. 7–24). Chicago: Nelson-Hall.

Tiedens, L. Z., & Fragale, A. R. (2003). Power moves: Complementarity in dominant and submissive nonverbal behavior. *Journal of Personality and Social Psychology, 84,* 558–568.

Trawalter, S., & Richeson, J. A. (2006). Regulatory focus and executive function after interracial interactions. *Journal of Experimental Social Psychology, 42,* 406–412.

Turban, D. B., & Keon, T. L., (1993). Organizational attractiveness: An interactionist perspective. *Journal of Applied Psychology, 78,* 184–193.

Updegraff, J. A., Gable, S. L., & Taylor, S. E. (2004). What makes experiences satisfying? The interaction of approach–avoidance motivations and emotions in well-being. *Journal of Personality and Social Psychology, 86,* 496–504.

Witt, L. A., Burke, L. A., Barrick, M. A., & Mount, M. K. (2002). The interactive effects of conscientiousness and agreeableness on job performance. *Journal of Applied Psychology, 87,* 164–169.

Yeo, J., & Park, J. (2006). Effects of parent-extension similarity and self regulatory focus on evaluations of brand extensions. *Journal of Consumer Psychology, 16,* 272–282.

# Author Index

Page numbers in *italics* refer to the reference lists at the end of each chapter.
Page numbers in roman refer to citations in text.

# Subject Index

Printed in the United States
by Baker & Taylor Publisher Services